THIRTEENTH EDITION

SUBJECT & STRATEGY

A WRITER'S READER

PAUL ESCHHOLZ

University of Vermont

ALFRED ROSA

University of Vermont

Bedford/St. Martin's

Boston • New York

For Bedford/St. Martin's

Publisher for Composition: Leasa Burton
Developmental Editor: Alyssa Demirjian
Senior Production Editor: Lori Chong Roncka
Senior Production Supervisor: Jennifer L. Peterson
Marketing Manager: Emily Rowin
Associate Editor: Regina Tavani
Editorial Assistant: Amanda Legee
Production Assistant: Erica Zhang
Copy Editor: Susan Moore
Indexer: Laura Dewey
Photo Researcher: Julie Tesser
Permissions Manager: Kalina K. Ingham
Senior Art Director: Anna Palchik
Text Design: Meryl Levavi
Cover Design: Marine Miller
Cover Photo: Landing Jetty on Lake Coniston, Cumbria. © Travelpix Ltd./Getty Images
Composition: Jouve
Printing and Binding: RR Donnelley and Sons

President, Bedford/St. Martin's: Denise B. Wydra
Editorial Director, English and Music: Karen S. Henry
Director of Marketing: Karen R. Soeltz
Production Director: Susan W. Brown
Director of Rights and Permissions: Hilary Newman

Manufactured in the United States of America.

9 8 7 6 5 4
f e d c b a

For information, write: Bedford/St. Martin's, 75 Arlington Street, Boston, MA 02116
(617-399-4000)

ISBN 978-1-4576-3691-2 (Student Edition)
ISBN 978-1-4576-5395-7 (Instructor's Edition)

Acknowledgments

Preface for Instructors

SUBJECT & STRATEGY IS A READER FOR COLLEGE WRITERS. THE NINETY-six selections in this edition were chosen to entertain students, to inform them, and to contribute to their self-awareness and their understanding of the world around them. Above all, however, we've brought together readings, integrated media, and thought-provoking apparatus to help students become better writers.

As its title suggests, *Subject & Strategy* places equal emphasis on the content and form of good writing. While all readers pay attention to content, far fewer notice the strategies — narration, description, illustration, process analysis, comparison and contrast, division and classification, definition, cause and effect analysis, and argumentation — that writers, artists, film-makers, journalists, and storytellers use to organize their work and to make their subjects understandable and effective for a given audience. Because these strategies are such an essential element of the writer's craft, we have designed *Subject & Strategy* to help students understand what they are and how they work. Each print and media selection skillfully models the use of the strategies, while questions, writing prompts, visuals, and other pedagogy further support students in writing well-constructed essays of their own.

FAVORITE FEATURES OF *SUBJECT & STRATEGY*

We continue to include the key features — developed and refined over twelve previous editions — that have made *Subject & Strategy* a classic introductory text.

Timely, Teachable, and Diverse Readings

Ninety-six selections — sixty-nine professional selections, twelve student essays, and fifteen media e-Pages selections — offer a broad spectrum of subjects, styles, and cultural points of view. The work of well-known writers — including Malcolm X, Maya Angelou, Steven Pinker, and Martin Luther

King Jr.—as well as emerging voices—including Joel Stein, Nicholas D. Kristof, Sheryl WuDunn, Firoozeh Dumas, and Andrew Sullivan—demonstrates for students the versatility and strengths of the different rhetorical strategies.

Thorough Coverage of the Reading and Writing Processes

Chapter 1, "Reading," discusses effective reading habits and illustrates attentive, analytical reading of essays and visuals using Cherokee Paul McDonald's "A View from the Bridge," Thomas L. Friedman's "My Favorite Teacher," a photograph of a street scene, and charts from the *Wall Street Journal* about college admissions.

Chapter 2, "Writing," offers writing advice and provides a case study of a student paper in progress, which illustrates one student's writing process and shows what can be accomplished with careful, thoughtful revision.

Chapter 3, "Writers on Writing," showcases inspiration, insight, and advice on writing well from professional writers Russell Baker, Anne Lamott, Linda S. Flower, William Zinsser, Susan Orlean, and Stephen King. In the e-Pages, an engaging, narrated animation by Jonathan Beer offers students concrete suggestions for improving their own writing practice.

Detailed Introductions to Each Rhetorical Strategy

The introduction to each rhetorical chapter opens with an example of the strategy at work in everyday life and then examines its use in written texts, discusses the various purposes for which writers use the strategy, and offers advice on how to use it in various college disciplines. This discussion is followed by detailed advice on how to write an essay using the strategy, including guidelines on selecting topics, developing thesis statements, considering audiences, gathering evidence, and using other rhetorical strategies in support of the dominant strategy.

Annotated Student Essays

An annotated student essay appears in each rhetorical chapter, offering students realistic models for successfully incorporating a particular strategy into their own writing. Discussion questions follow each student essay, encouraging students to analyze and evaluate the overall effectiveness of the rhetorical strategies employed in the example.

Extensive Rhetorical Apparatus

Numerous questions and prompts for thought, discussion, in-class activities, and writing accompany each professional essay:

- **Preparing to Read** prompts ask students to write about their own knowledge and/or experiences with the subject of each selection before they read.

- **Thinking Critically about the Text** prompts ask students to analyze, elaborate on, or take issue with a key aspect of each selection. From time to time, discussion questions and writing assignments ask students to revisit their responses to these prompts and reflect on them before moving ahead with more formal writing tasks.

- **Questions on Subject** focus students' attention on the content of each selection as well as on the author's purpose. These questions help students check their comprehension and provide a basis for classroom discussion.

- **Questions on Strategy** direct students to the various rhetorical strategies and writing techniques the writer has used. These questions encourage students to put themselves in the writer's place and to consider how they might employ the strategies in their own writing. In addition, questions in this section ask students to identify and analyze places where the author has used one or more rhetorical strategies to enhance or develop the essay's dominant strategy.

- **Questions on Diction and Vocabulary** emphasize the importance of diction, word choice, and verbal context.

- **Classroom Activities** accompanying each essay — usually requiring no more than ten to fifteen minutes of class time and designed for students to complete individually, in small groups, or as a class — allow students to apply their understanding of the strategies at work in a given selection.

- **Writing Suggestions** focus on the particular rhetorical strategy under discussion and/or explore the subject of the essay or a related topic.

End-of-Chapter Writing Suggestions

Writing suggestions at the end of each rhetorical chapter (Chapters 4 through 14) provide additional topics suitable to the strategy covered in each chapter. Select questions include **Writing with Sources** and brand-new **Writing in the Workplace** headings to emphasize these skills. Many of the suggestions refer back to particular selections or to multiple selections in the chapter. Instructors can use these writing suggestions as complements to or substitutes for the more focused writing topics that accompany individual selections.

Advice for Writing Researched Essays

Chapter 14, "Writing with Sources," helps students master this essential academic skill by offering sound, detailed advice on avoiding plagiarism and on effectively integrating sources through quotation, summary, and paraphrase. The chapter also features four essays that integrate outside sources. Questions and prompts direct students' attention to how they can use sources in their own writing.

Chapter 15, "A Brief Guide to Researching and Documenting Essays," provides an overview of the research process, with a focus on finding, evaluating, and analyzing sources; taking notes; and documenting sources. Up-to-date model MLA citations are provided for the most widely used types of sources, along with a sample documented student essay.

Editing Advice

Chapter 16, "Editing for Grammar, Punctuation, and Sentence Style," provides a concise guide to twelve of the most common writing challenges, from sentence run-ons and fragments to wordiness and lack of sentence variety.

Thematic Contents

Immediately after the main table of contents, a second table of contents groups the reading selections into general thematic categories, providing further opportunities for discussion and writing based on the content of individual selections. New to this edition, an appendix of thematic writing assignments further supports cross-chapter connections.

Glossary of Rhetorical Terms

The glossary at the end of *Subject & Strategy* provides concise definitions of terms italicized in the text and called out in the questions that follow each reading selection.

NEW TO THIS EDITION OF *SUBJECT & STRATEGY*

Substantially updated for its thirteenth edition, *Subject & Strategy* combines the currency of a brand-new text with the effectiveness of a thoroughly class-tested one. Guided by comments and advice from instructors and students across the country who have used previous editions, we have made a number of significant changes to the text.

Engaging New Readings, Compelling Perspectives

Forty-two readings—about 50 percent of this edition's selections—are new, including

- **Human rights advocates Nicholas D. Kristof and Sheryl WuDunn's** provocative praise of sweatshops
- **Former *TIME* managing editor Walter Isaacson** on defining the iconic Steve Jobs
- **Best-selling writer Jeannette Walls's** poignant acceptance of her mother's homelessness
- ***New Yorker* staff-writer Susan Orlean** on "voice" and the way personalities guide writers to the right words
- **Renowned journalist Robert Krulwich** on our evolving understanding of how caterpillars become butterflies
- **Essayist Firoozeh Dumas** on hilarious moments in her Iranian-American childhood
- **Law professors Kal Raustiala and Chris Sprigman's** surprising "pro-copycat" view of culture
- **Three new, annotated student essays** on types of "textspeak," celebrity obsession, and cyberbullying at college

A Fresh Take on Argument

To reflect the multiplicity of possible perspectives on any complex topic and to discourage students from thinking of argument as winner-take-all conflict, we have the following new argument clusters:

- ***Sports and Doping: Is There a Solution?*** Technology journalist Ian Steadman, sportswriter Reid Forgrave, former professional cyclist Jonathan Vaughters, and philosopher Peter Singer debate the ethics and policy implications of drug use in professional sports.
- ***Technology and Privacy: Are You Worried?*** Journalists Joel Stein and Massimo Calabresi, security consultant Rafi Ron, and information policy expert Jim Harper examine the trade-offs between surveillance and security in the Information Age.
- ***The Value of College: Is It Worth the Cost?*** Economists Michael Greenstone and Adam Looney, university president Teresa Sullivan, *Jezebel* co-founder Maureen "Moe" Tkacik, and Senator Lamar Alexander explore the long-term effects of a college education.

e New Bedford Integrated Media

Fifteen brand-new, carefully curated selections in e-Pages take advantage of what the Web can do. Readings go beyond the print page, with support for analyzing texts, such as video, images, and audio. Clear cross-references at the end of chapters and throughout the argument clusters direct students to the e-Pages for that strategy or topic. You and your students can access the e-Pages at **bedfordstmartins.com/subjectandstrategy**. Students receive access automatically with the purchase of a new print book. If students rent a book or buy a used book, they can purchase access at that site. Instructors receive access information in a separate e-mail. You can also log in or request access information at **bedfordstmartins.com/subjectandstrategy**. A comprehensive list of all e-Pages can be found at the back of the book. Selections include

- **Videos** that explore a soldier's experience during "Don't Ask, Don't Tell," life in a Venezuelan skyscraper-turned-slum, the latest anthropological research on human and chimpanzee fossils, convergence in the modern media landscape, and a humorous take on "texting while walking"
- **High-resolution infographics** that delve into the changing nature of the American dream, how to sustainably compost food waste, and trends in social media demographics
- **Animations** that break down tips for the writing process, ask students to think critically about global work conditions, and demystify concepts like why the sky is blue
- **Text articles** that expand the argument clusters and showcase *Brain Pickings* founder Maria Popova's Curator's Code, a system for online source attribution

Stronger Support for Thematic Connections

A new appendix of thematic writing assignments extends the traditional thematic table of contents and provides support for cross-chapter connections. Key readings, chapter-opening images, and e-Pages selections are organized into small groups and accompanied by writing prompts on such topics as the immigration experience, education, gender, nature, industrial food, inequality, innovation, crime and ethics, the power of language, privacy, and more.

New Assignments Emphasize Professional Writing

Ten new Writing in the Workplace assignments, found in the end-of-chapter writing suggestions in every modal chapter, prompt students to think about how each strategy might be applied in a professional document and setting.

Renewed Focus on Visuals

Acknowledging both the increasing prominence of visuals in our culture and the many predominantly visual learners among us, we have made every attempt to add visuals to this edition where they could serve a clear pedagogical purpose:

- **Every chapter now has opening images,** underlining the importance and ubiquity of the strategies, topics, and themes, using real-world examples from artist portfolios, ads, graphic novels, magazines, cartoons, and more. A brief discussion of the image opens the chapter, and a writing prompt related to the image appears among the end-of-chapter writing assignments.
- **Reading visuals is discussed in greater depth** in Chapter 1 in order to help students read visuals actively and critically. In addition to the traditional photograph, we've included charts to prompt discussion about analyzing graphic presentations of data.
- **A new, simple design for the whole book** supports the accessible, patterned organization of each chapter; offers more space for note taking; and showcases more visuals to stimulate discussion and aid student focus.

THE INSTRUCTOR'S EDITION OF *SUBJECT & STRATEGY*

We have designed *Subject & Strategy* to be as accessible as possible to all teachers of composition, including new graduate students, full-time faculty, and very busy adjuncts. Toward that end, we provide an Instructor's Manual (ISBN 978-1-4576-6602-5), bound together with the student text in a special Instructor's Edition and available separately online, which suggests responses to the questions and prompts that accompany each selection in *Subject & Strategy*, including the questions in the e-Pages.

YOU GET MORE CHOICES

Bedford/St. Martin's offers resources and format choices that help you and your students get even more out of the book and your course. To learn more about or order any of the following products, contact your Bedford/St. Martin's sales representative, e-mail sales support (**sales_support@bfwpub.com**), or visit the Web site at **bedfordstmartins.com/subjectandstrategy/catalog**.

Choose the Flexible *Bedford e-Portfolio*

Students can collect, select, and reflect on their coursework and personalize and share their e-portfolio for any audience. Instructors can provide as much or as little structure as they see fit. Rubrics and learning outcomes can be aligned to student work, so instructors and programs can gather reliable and useful assessment data. Every *Bedford e-Portfolio* comes pre-loaded with *Portfolio Keeping* and *Portfolio Teaching*, by Nedra Reynolds and Elizabeth Davis. *Bedford e-Portfolio* can be purchased separately or packaged with the book at a significant discount. An activation code is required. To order *Bedford e-Portfolio* with the print book, use ISBN 978-1-4576-8131-8. Visit **bedfordstmartins.com/eportfolio**.

Watch Peer Review Work

Eli Review lets instructors scaffold their assignments in a clearer, more effective way for students—making peer review more visible and teachable. *Eli Review* can be purchased separately or packaged with the book at a significant discount. An activation code is required. To order *Eli Review* with the print book, use ISBN 978-1-4576-8132-5. Visit **bedfordstmartins.com/eli**.

Select Value Packages

Add value to your course by packaging one of the following resources with *Subject & Strategy* at a significant discount. To learn more about package options, contact your Bedford/St. Martin's sales representative or visit **bedfordstmartins.com/subjectandstrategy/catalog**.

- *EasyWriter,* **Fifth Edition, by Andrea Lunsford,** distills Andrea Lunsford's teaching and research into the essentials that today's writers need to make good choices in any rhetorical situation. To order *EasyWriter* packaged with *Subject & Strategy*, use ISBN 978-1-4576-8679-5.
- **A Pocket Style Manual, Sixth Edition, by Diana Hacker and Nancy Sommers,** is a straightforward, inexpensive quick reference, with content flexible enough to suit the needs of writers in the humanities, social sciences, sciences, health professions, business, fine arts, education, and beyond. To order *A Pocket Style Manual* with *Subject & Strategy*, use ISBN 978-1-4576-8680-1.
- *LearningCurve for Readers and Writers,* Bedford/St. Martin's adaptive quizzing program, quickly learns what students already know and helps them practice what they don't yet understand. Game-like quizzing motivates students to engage with their course, and reporting tools help teachers discern their students' needs. An activation code is required. To order LearningCurve packaged with the print book, use ISBN 978-1-4576-8135-6. For details, visit **bedfordstmartins.com/englishlearningcurve**.

- *Portfolio Keeping,* **Third Edition, by Nedra Reynolds and Elizabeth Davis,** provides all the information students need to use the portfolio method successfully in a writing course. *Portfolio Teaching,* a companion guide for instructors, provides the practical information instructors and writing program administrators need to use the portfolio method successfully in a writing course. To order *Portfolio Keeping* packaged with the print book, use ISBN 978-1-4576-8138-7.

Try *Re:Writing 2* for Fun

What's the fun of teaching writing if you can't try something new? The best collection of free writing resources on the Web, *Re:Writing 2* gives you and your students even more ways to think, watch, practice, and learn about writing concepts. Listen to Nancy Sommers on using a teacher's comments to revise. Try a logic puzzle. Consult our resources for writing centers. All free for the fun of trying it. Visit **bedfordstmartins.com/rewriting**.

Instructor Resources

You have a lot to do in your course. Bedford/St. Martin's wants to make it easy for you to find the support you need—and to get it quickly.

- **TeachingCentral (bedfordstmartins.com/teachingcentral)** offers the entire list of Bedford/St. Martin's print and online professional resources in one place. You'll find landmark reference works, sourcebooks on pedagogical issues, award-winning collections, and practical advice for the classroom—all free for instructors.
- *Bedford Bits* **(bedfordbits.com)** collects creative ideas for teaching a range of composition topics in an easily searchable blog format. A community of teachers—leading scholars, authors, and editors—discuss revision, research, grammar and style, technology, peer review, and much more.
- **Bedford Coursepacks (bedfordstmartins.com/coursepacks)** allow you to easily download digital materials from Bedford/St. Martin's for your course for the most common course management systems—Blackboard, Angel, Desire2Learn, Canvas, Moodle, or Sakai.

ACKNOWLEDGMENTS

We are gratified by the reception and use of the twelve previous editions of *Subject & Strategy.* Composition teachers in hundreds of community colleges, liberal arts colleges, and universities have used the book. Many teachers responded to our detailed review questionnaire, thus helping tremendously in conceptualizing the improvements to this edition. We thank Rosalie Avin, Brookdale Community College; James Boswell, Harrisburg Area Community College; Arnold Bradford, Northern Virginia Community College; Christopher Bullmer, Kalamazoo Central High School; Jane Cable, Saint John Vianney High School; Christine Peters Cucciarre, University of Delaware; Michelle Dalrymple, Palomar College; William Donohue, Lincoln University; Helen Duclos, Arkansas State University; Charlene Engleking, Lindenwood University; Sharynn Owens Etheridge-Logan, Claflin University; Andrea Hart, Delaware County Community College; Florence Johnson, North Dakota State College of Science; Lewis Kahler, Mohawk Valley Community College; Jamie Kelly-DiMeglio, Delaware County Community College; Ruth Laker, Delaware County Community College; Jaime Sanchez, Volunteer State Community College; Judy Schmidt, Harrisburg Area Community College; Christina Short, Riverside City College; Carlos Smith, Tougaloo College; Anne Taylor, North Dakota State College of Science; Patricia Teel, Victor Valley College; Katherine Turner, Mary Baldwin College; Victor Uszerowicz, Miami-Dade College; Linda Weeks, Dyersburg State Community College; and Kim Zabel, Rochester Community and Technical College.

At Bedford/St. Martin's, we thank our talented and enthusiastic developmental editor, Alyssa Demirjian, for her commitment to *Subject & Strategy*. Together we have charted some new territories for this enduring text, and the process has been truly exciting. Thanks go also to the rest of the Bedford/ St. Martin's team: Joan Feinberg, Co-President of Macmillan Higher Education; Denise Wydra, President of Bedford/St. Martin's; Leasa Burton, Publisher for Composition and Business and Technical Writing; and Karen Henry, Editorial Director for English and Music. We would also like to acknowledge Jennifer Peterson, Lori Roncka, Molly Parke, Emily Rowin, Donna Dennison, Marine Miller, Regina Tavani, and Amanda Legee. Special thanks go to Sarah Federman, Courtney Novosat, Shannon Walsh, and Kate Mayhew for their assistance with developing the Instructor's Manual, additional apparatus, and sample documents. We are also happy to recognize those students whose work appears in *Subject & Strategy* for their willingness to contribute their time and effort in writing and rewriting their essays: Barbara Bowman, Gerald Cleary, Kevin Cunningham, Gerald Dromos, Keith Eldred, Mark Jackson, Jake Jamieson, Paula Kersch, Tara E. Ketch, Laura LaPierre, Shoshanna Lew, Christine Olson, Howard Solomon Jr., Kate Suarez, Courtney Sypher, and Jim Tassé. We are grateful to all of our writing students at the University of Vermont for their enthusiasm for writing and for their invaluable responses to materials included in this book.

And we also thank our families for sharing in our commitment to quality teaching and textbook writing.

Finally, we thank each other. Beginning in 1971 we have collaborated on many textbooks on language and writing, all of which have gone into multiple editions. With this thirteenth edition of *Subject & Strategy*, we enter more than forty years of working together. Ours must be one of the longest-running and most mutually satisfying writing partnerships in college textbook publishing. The journey has been invigorating and challenging as we have come to understand the complexities and joys of good writing and have sought new ways to help students become better writers.

PAUL ESCHHOLZ

ALFRED ROSA

Contents

e For readings that go beyond the printed page,
see bedfordstmartins.com/subjectandstrategy.

2 Writing 23

3 Writers on Writing 49

4 Narration 79

5 Description 127

"I fretted about them, but I was embarassed by them, too, and ashamed of myself for wearing pearls and living on Park Avenue while my parents were busy keeping warm and finding something to eat."

"We called her *Lobo*. The word means 'wolf' in Spanish, an odd name for a generous and loving aunt."

"Members of the barrio describe their entire area as their home. It is a home, but it is more than this. The barrio is a refuge from the harshness and the coldness of the Anglo world."

"This seemed an utterly enchanted sea, this lake you could leave to its own devices for a few hours and come back to, and find that it had not stirred."

"She acted just as refined as whitefolks in the movies and books and she was more beautiful, for none of them could have come near that warm color without looking gray by comparison."

8 Comparison and Contrast 281

12 Argumentation   489

"We hold these truths to be self-evident, that all men are created equal, that they are endowed by their Creator with certain unalienable Rights, that among these are Life, Liberty and the pursuit of Happiness."

"A lot of small words, more than you might think, can meet your needs with a strength, grace, and charm that large words do not have."

"I have a dream that my four little children will one day live in a nation where they will not be judged by the color of their skin but by the content of their character."

"Dangerous ideas are likely to confront us at an increasing rate, and we are ill-equipped to deal with them."

"The campaign against sweatshops risks harming the very people it is intended to help."

Thematic Contents

Discover more thematic connections as well as writing assignments in the appendix on pages 754–60.

CONTEMPORARY SOCIAL ISSUES

DISCOVERIES AND EPIPHANIES

EDUCATION

THE NATURAL WORLD

PEER PRESSURE

WOMEN AND MEN

THE WORLD OF WORK

WRITING ABOUT WRITING

SUBJECT & STRATEGY

A WRITER'S READER

CHAPTER 1

Reading

SUBJECT & STRATEGY PLACES EQUAL EMPHASIS ON CONTENT AND form—that is, on the *subject* of an essay and on the *strategies* an author uses to write it. All readers pay attention to content. Far fewer, however, notice form—the strategies authors use to organize their writing and the means they use to make it clear, logical, and effective.

When you learn to read actively and analytically, you come to appreciate the craftsmanship involved in writing—a writer's choice of an appropriate organizational strategy or strategies and his or her use of descriptive details, representative and persuasive examples, sentence variety, and clear, appropriate, vivid diction.

The image opposite—one of a series of surreal scenes conceived by photographer Joel Robison—seems quite whimsical for the way the man has collected or encountered many books along a remote riverbank. Yet it also underscores the very real importance of selecting just one book or essay at a time for attentive study and then carefully reflecting upon what we've encountered.

DEVELOPING AN EFFECTIVE READING PROCESS

Active, analytical reading requires, first of all, that you commit time and effort to it. Second, it requires that you try to take a positive interest in what you are reading, even if the subject matter is not immediately appealing. To help you get the most out of your reading, this chapter provides guidelines for an effective reading process.

Step 1: Prepare Yourself to Read the Selection

Instead of diving right into any given selection in *Subject & Strategy*, you need first to establish a context for what you will be reading. What's the essay about? What do you know about the author's background and reputation? Where was the essay first published? Who was the intended audience? And, finally, how much do you already know about the subject of the selection?

The materials that precede each selection in this book—the title, headnote, and Preparing to Read prompt—are intended to help you establish this context. From the *title* you often discover the writer's position on an issue or attitude toward the topic. The title can also give clues about the writer's intended audience and reasons for composing the piece.

Each *headnote* contains four essential elements:

1. A *photo* of the author lets you put a face to a name.
2. The *biographical note* provides information about the writer's life and work, as well as his or her reputation and authority to write on the subject.
3 The *publication information* for the selection that appears in the book tells you when the essay was published and where it first appeared. This information can also give you insight into the intended audience.
4. The *content and rhetorical highlights* of the selection preview the subject and point out key aspects of the writing strategies used by the author.

Finally, the Preparing to Read *journal prompt* encourages you to reflect and record your thoughts and opinions on the topic before you begin reading.

Carefully review the context-building materials on page 5 that accompany Cherokee Paul McDonald's "A View from the Bridge" to see how they can help you establish a context for the reading. The essay itself appears on pages 8–10.

A View from the Bridge

Title

CHEROKEE PAUL MCDONALD

Author

Headnote

Biographical note

A fiction writer and journalist, Cherokee Paul McDonald was raised and schooled in Fort Lauderdale, Florida. In 1970, he returned home from a tour of duty in Vietnam and joined the Fort Lauderdale Police Department, where he remained until 1980, resigning with the rank of sergeant. During this time, McDonald received a degree in criminal science from Broward Community College. He left the police department to become a writer and worked a number of odd jobs before publishing his first book, *The Patch*, in 1986. McDonald has said that almost all of his writing comes from his police work, and his common themes of justice, balance, and fairness reflect his life as part of the "thin blue line" (the police department). In 1991, he published *Blue Truth*, a memoir. His first novel, *Summer's Reason*, was released in 1994. His most recent book, *Into the Green: A Reconnaissance by Fire* (2001), is a memoir of his three years as an artillery forward observer in Vietnam.

Publication information

Content and rhetorical highlights

"A View from the Bridge" was originally published in *Sunshine*, a monthly magazine filled with uplifting short articles and stories, in 1990. The essay shows McDonald's usual expert handling of fish and fishermen, both in and out of water, and reminds us that things are not always as they seem. Notice his selective use of details to describe the young fisherman and the fish he has hooked on his line.

Preparing to Read

Journal prompt

The great American philosopher and naturalist Henry David Thoreau has written: "The question is not what you look at, but what you see." We've all had the experience of becoming numb to sights or experiences that once struck us with wonderment; but sometimes, with luck, something happens to renew our appreciation. Think of an example from your own experience. What are some ways we can retain or recover our appreciation of the remarkable things we have come to take for granted?

From reading these preliminary materials, what expectations do you have for "A View from the Bridge"? While McDonald's *title* does not give any specific indication of his topic, it does suggest that he will be writing about the view from a particular bridge and that what he sees is worth sharing with his readers. The *biographical note* reveals that McDonald, a Vietnam veteran and former policeman, is a fiction writer and journalist. The titles of his books suggest that much of his writing comes from his military and police work, where he developed important observational skills and sensitivity to people and the environment. From the *publication information* for the selection, you learn that the essay first appeared in 1990 in *Sunshine*, a monthly magazine with short, uplifting human-interest articles for a general readership. The *content and rhetorical highlights* advise you to look at how McDonald's knowledge about fish and fishing and his use of descriptive details help him paint a verbal picture of the young fisherman and the battle he has with the fish on his line. Finally, the *journal prompt* asks for your thoughts on why we become numb to experiences that once awed us. What, for you, is the difference between to "look at" and to "see," and how can we preserve our appreciation for the awesome things that we sometimes take for granted? After reading McDonald's essay, you can compare your reflections on "seeing" with what McDonald learned from his own experience with the boy who fished by the bridge.

Step 2: Read the Selection

Always read the selection at least twice, no matter how long it is. The first reading lets you get acquainted with the essay and get an overall sense of what the writer is saying, and why. As you read, you may find yourself modifying the sense of the writer's message and purpose that you derived from the title, headnote, and your response to the writing prompt. Circle words you do not recognize so that you can look them up in a dictionary. Put a question mark alongside any passages that are not immediately clear. However, you will probably want to delay most of your annotating until a second reading so that your first reading can be fast, enabling you to concentrate on the larger issues of message and purpose.

Step 3: Reread the Selection

Your second reading should be quite different from your first. You will know what the essay is about, where it is going, and how it gets there; now you can relate the individual parts of the essay more accurately to the whole. Use your second reading to test your first impressions, developing and deepening your sense of how (and how well) the essay is written. Because you now have a general understanding of the essay, you can pay special attention to the author's purpose and means of achieving it. You can look for strategies of organization (see pages 31–32) and style and adapt them to your own work.

Step 4: Annotate the Selection

When you annotate a selection you should do more than simply underline what you think are important points. It is easy to underline so much that the notations become almost meaningless, and it's common to forget why you underlined passages in the first place, if that's all you do. Instead, as you read, write down your thoughts in the margins or on a separate piece of paper. Mark the selection's main point when you find it stated directly. Look for the strategy or strategies the author uses to explore and support that point, and jot this information down. If you disagree with a statement or conclusion, object in the margin: "No!" If you feel skeptical, write "Why?" or "Explain." If you are impressed by an argument or turn of phrase, write "Good point!" Place vertical lines or a star in the margin to indicate especially important points.

What to Annotate in a Text

Here are some examples of what you may want to mark in a selection as you read:

- Memorable statements or important points
- Key terms or concepts
- Central issues or themes
- Examples that support a major point
- Unfamiliar words
- Questions you have about a point or passage
- Your responses to a specific point or passage

Remember that there are no hard-and-fast rules for annotating elements. Choose a method of annotation that will make sense to you when you go back to recollect your thoughts and responses to the essay. Jot down whatever marginal notes come naturally to you. Most readers combine brief written responses with underlining, circling, highlighting, stars, or question marks.

Above all, don't let annotating become burdensome. A word or phrase is usually as good as a sentence. One helpful way to focus your annotations is to ask yourself questions such as those on page 11 while reading the selection a second time.

▶ An Example: Annotating Cherokee Paul McDonald's "A View from the Bridge"

Sets the scene

I was coming up on the little bridge in the Rio Vista neighborhood of Fort Lauderdale, deepening my stride and my breathing to negotiate the slight incline without altering my pace. And then, as I neared the crest, I saw the kid. **1**

Nice description

He was a lumpy little guy with baggy shorts, a faded T-shirt and heavy sweat socks falling down over old sneakers. **2**

Partially covering his shaggy blond hair was one of those blue baseball caps with gold braid on the bill and a sailfish patch sewn onto the peak. Covering his eyes and part of his face was a pair of those stupid-looking '50s-style wrap-around sunglasses. **3**

Why "fumbling"?

He was fumbling with a beat-up rod and reel, and he had a little bait bucket by his feet. I puffed on by, glancing down into the empty bucket as I passed. **4**

"Hey, mister! Would you help me, please?" **5**

The shrill voice penetrated my jogger's concentration, and I was determined to ignore it. But for some reason, I stopped. **6**

Jogger sounds irritated

With my hands on my hips and the sweat dripping from my nose I asked, "What do you want, kid?" **7**

"Would you please help me find my shrimp? It's my last one and I've been getting bites and I know I can catch a fish if I can just find that shrimp. He jumped outta my hand as I was getting him from the bucket." **8**

Shrimp is clearly visible, so why does kid ask for help?

Exasperated, I walked slowly back to the kid, and pointed. **9**

"There's the damn shrimp by your left foot. You stopped me for *that?*" **10**

Kid's polite

As I said it, the kid reached down and trapped the shrimp. **11**

"Thanks a lot, mister," he said. **12**

I watched as the kid dropped the baited hook down into the canal. Then I turned to start back down the bridge. **13**

That's when the kid let out a "Hey! Hey!" and the prettiest tarpon I'd ever seen came almost six feet out of the water, twisting and turning as he fell through the air. **14**

Dialogue enhances drama

"I got one!" the kid yelled as the fish hit the water with a loud splash and took off down the canal. **15**

I watched the line being burned off the reel at an alarming rate. The kid's left hand held the crank while the extended fingers felt for the drag setting. **16**

Jogger gets
involved once
kid hooks fish

"No, kid!" I shouted. "Leave the drag alone . . . just keep 17
that damn rod tip up!"

Then I glanced at the reel and saw there were just a few 18
loops of line left on the spool.

"Why don't you get yourself some decent equipment?" I 19
said, but before the kid could answer I saw the line go slack.

"Ohhh, I lost him," the kid said. I saw the flash of silver as 20
the fish turned.

Starts
coaching kid

"Crank, kid, crank! You didn't lose him. He's coming 21
back toward you. Bring in the slack!"

The kid cranked like mad, and a beautiful grin spread 22
across his face.

"He's heading in for the pilings," I said. "Keep him out of 23
those pilings!"

The kid played it perfectly. When the fish made its play for 24
the pilings, he kept just enough pressure on to force the fish
out. When the water exploded and the silver missile hurled
into the air, the kid kept the rod tip up and the line tight.

Impressive fish

As the fish came to the surface and began a slow circle in 25
the middle of the canal, I said, "Whooee, is that a nice fish or
what?"

The kid didn't say anything, so I said, "Okay, move to the 26
edge of the bridge and I'll climb down to the seawall and pull
him out."

When I reached the seawall I pulled in the leader, leaving 27
the fish lying on its side in the water.

"How's that?" I said. 28

Kid makes
strange
request

"Hey, mister, tell me what it looks like." 29

"Look down here and check him out," I said, "He's 30
beautiful."

Wow!

But then I looked up into those stupid-looking sunglasses 31
and it hit me. The kid was blind.

"Could you tell me what he looks like, mister?" he said 32
again.

Jogger's new
awareness
makes him
self-conscious

"Well, he's just under three, uh, he's about as long as one 33
of your arms," I said. "I'd guess he goes about 15, 20 pounds.
He's mostly silver, but the silver is somehow made up of *all* the
colors, if you know what I mean." I stopped. "Do you know
what I mean by colors?"

The kid nodded. 34

Drawing verbal
picture

"Okay. He has all these big scales, like armor all over his 35
body. They're silver too, and when he moves they sparkle. He

has a strong body and a large powerful tail. He has big round eyes, bigger than a quarter, and a lower jaw that sticks out past the upper one and is very tough. His belly is almost white and his back is a gunmetal gray. When he jumped he came out of the water about six feet, and his scales caught the sun and flashed it all over the place."

By now the fish had righted itself, and I could see the 36 bright-red gills as the gill plates opened and closed. I explained this to the kid, and then said, more to myself, "He's a beauty."

What a kid!

"Can you get him off the hook?" the kid asked. "I don't 37 want to kill him."

I watched as the tarpon began to slowly swim away, tired 38 but still alive.

By the time I got back up to the top of the bridge the kid 39 had his line secured and his bait bucket in one hand.

He grinned and said, "Just in time. My mom drops me off 40 here, and she'll be back to pick me up any minute."

He used the back of one hand to wipe his nose. 41

"Thanks for helping me catch that tarpon," he said, "and 42 for helping me to see it."

Point of story — jogger's insight

I looked at him, shook my head, and said, "No, my friend, 43 thank you for letting *me* see that fish."

I took off, but before I got far the kid yelled again. 44

"Hey, mister!" 45

I stopped. 46

Like his attitude!

"Someday I'm gonna catch a sailfish and a blue marlin and 47 a giant tuna and *all* those big sportfish!"

As I looked into those sunglasses I knew he probably 48 would. I wished I could be there when it happened.

Now that you have learned what you should do to prepare yourself to read a selection, what you should look for during a first reading and during a second reading, and what you should annotate, it is time to move on to the next step: analyzing a text by asking yourself questions as you reread it.

Step 5: Analyze and Evaluate the Selection

As you continue to study the selection, analyze it for a deeper understanding and appreciation of the author's craft and try to evaluate its overall effectiveness as a piece of writing. Here are some questions you may find helpful as you start the process:

Questions for Analysis and Evaluation

1. What is the writer's topic?

2. What is the writer's main point or thesis?

3. What is the writer's purpose in writing?

4. What strategy or strategies does the writer use? *Where* and *how* does the writer use them?

5. Do the writer's strategies suit his or her subject and purpose? Why, or why not?

6. How effective is the essay? Does the writer make his or her points clear and persuade the reader to accept them?

Each essay in *Subject & Strategy* is followed by study questions similar to these but specific to the essay. Some of the questions help you analyze the content of an essay, while others help you analyze the writer's use of the rhetorical strategies. In addition, there are questions about the writer's diction and style. As you read the essay a second time, look for details related to these questions, and then answer the questions as fully as you can.

THE READING PROCESS IN ACTION: THOMAS L. FRIEDMAN'S "MY FAVORITE TEACHER"

To give you practice using the five-step reading process that we have just explored, we present an essay by Thomas L. Friedman, including the headnote material and the Preparing to Read prompt. Before you read Friedman's essay, think about the title, the biographical and rhetorical information in the headnote, and the Preparing to Read prompt. Make some notes of your expectations about the essay and write out a response to the prompt. Next, continue following the five-step process outlined in this chapter. As you read the essay for the first time, try not to stop; take it all in as if in one breath. The second time through, pause to annotate the text. Finally, using the questions listed above, analyze and evaluate the essay.

My Favorite Teacher

THOMAS L. FRIEDMAN

New York Times foreign affairs columnist Thomas L. Friedman was born in Minneapolis, Minnesota, in 1953. He graduated from Brandeis University in 1975 and received a Marshall Scholarship to pursue modern Middle East studies at St. Anthony's College, Oxford University, where he earned a master's degree. He has worked for the *New York Times* since 1981— first in Lebanon, then in Israel, and since 1989 in Washington, D.C. He was awarded the Pulitzer Prize in 1983 and 1988 for his reporting and again in 2002 for his commentary. Friedman's 1989 best-seller, *From Beirut to Jerusalem*, received the National Book Award for nonfiction. His most recent books are *The Lexus and the Olive Tree: Understanding Globalization* (2000), *Longitudes and Attitudes: Exploring the World after September 11* (2002), *The World Is Flat: A Brief History of the Twenty-First Century* (2005), *Hot, Flat, and Crowded: Why We Need a Green Revolution—And How It Can Renew America* (2008), and *That Used to Be Us: How America Fell Behind in the World It Invented and How We Can Come Back* (2011), with Michael Mandelbaum.

In the following essay, which first appeared in the *New York Times* on January 9, 2001, Friedman pays tribute to his tenth-grade journalism teacher. As you read Friedman's profile of Hattie M. Steinberg, note the descriptive detail he selects to create the dominant impression of "a woman of clarity in an age of uncertainty."

Preparing to Read

If you had to name your three favorite teachers of all time, who would they be? Why do you consider each one a favorite? Which one, if any, are you likely to remember twenty-five years from now? Why?

L ast Sunday's *New York Times Magazine* published its annual 1 review of people who died last year who left a particular mark on the world. I am sure all readers have their own such list. I certainly do. Indeed, someone who made the most important difference in my life died last year—my high school journalism teacher, Hattie M. Steinberg.

I grew up in a small suburb of Minneapolis, and Hattie was the legend- 2 ary journalism teacher at St. Louis Park High School, Room 313. I took her intro to journalism course in 10th grade, back in 1969, and have never needed, or taken, another course in journalism since. She was that good.

Hattie was a woman who believed that the secret for success in life was 3 getting the fundamentals right. And boy, she pounded the fundamentals of journalism into her students—not simply how to write a lead or accurately transcribe a quote, but, more important, how to comport yourself in a professional way and to always do quality work. To this day, when I forget to wear a tie on assignment, I think of Hattie scolding me. I once interviewed an ad exec for our high school paper who used a four-letter word. We debated whether to run it. Hattie ruled yes. That ad man almost lost his job when it appeared. She wanted to teach us about consequences.

Hattie was the toughest teacher I ever had. After you took her journalism course in 10th grade, you tried out for the paper, *The Echo*, which she supervised. Competition was fierce. In 11th grade, I didn't quite come up to her writing standards, so she made me business manager, selling ads to the local pizza parlors. That year, though, she let me write one story. It was about an Israeli general who had been a hero in the Six-Day War, who was giving a lecture at the University of Minnesota. I covered his lecture and interviewed him briefly. His name was Ariel Sharon. First story I ever got published.

The Internet can make you smarter, but it can't make you smart.

Those of us on the paper, and the yearbook that she also supervised, lived in Hattie's classroom. We hung out there before and after school. Now, you have to understand, Hattie was a single woman, nearing sixty at the time, and this was the 1960s. She was the polar opposite of "cool," but we hung around her classroom like it was a malt shop and she was Wolfman Jack. None of us could have articulated it then, but it was because we enjoyed being harangued by her, disciplined by her, and taught by her. She was a woman of clarity in an age of uncertainty.

We remained friends for thirty years, and she followed, bragged about, and critiqued every twist in my career. After she died, her friends sent me a pile of my stories that she had saved over the years. Indeed, her students were her family—only closer. Judy Harrington, one of Hattie's former students, remarked about other friends who were on Hattie's newspapers and yearbooks: "We all graduated forty-one years ago; and yet nearly each day in our lives something comes up—some mental image, some admonition that makes us think of Hattie."

Judy also told the story of one of Hattie's last birthday parties, when one man said he had to leave early to take his daughter somewhere. "Sit down," said Hattie. "You're not leaving yet. She can just be a little late."

That was my teacher! I sit up straight just thinkin' about her.

Among the fundamentals Hattie introduced me to was the *New York Times*. Every morning it was delivered to Room 313. I had never seen it before then. Real journalists, she taught us, start their day by reading the *Times* and columnists like Anthony Lewis and James Reston.

I have been thinking about Hattie a lot this year, not just because she died on July 31, but because the lessons she imparted seem so relevant now. We've just gone through this huge dot-com-Internet-globalization bubble—during which a lot of smart people got carried away and forgot the fundamentals of how you build a profitable company, a lasting portfolio, a nation state, or a thriving student. It turns out that the real secret of success in the information age is what it always was: fundamentals—reading, writing, and arithmetic; church, synagogue, and mosque; the rule of law and good governance.

The Internet can make you smarter, but it can't make you smart. It can   11
extend your reach, but it will never tell you what to say at a P.T.A. meeting. These fundamentals cannot be downloaded. You can only upload them, the old-fashioned way, one by one, in places like Room 313 at St. Louis Park High. I only regret that I didn't write this column when the woman who taught me all that was still alive.

Once you have read and reread Friedman's essay, write your own answers to the six basic questions listed on page 11. Then compare your answers with those that follow.

1. **What is the writer's *topic*?**

   Friedman's topic is his high school journalism teacher, Hattie M. Steinberg; more broadly, his topic is the "secret for success in life," as taught to him by Steinberg.

2. **What is the writer's *main point* or *thesis*?**

   Friedman writes about Steinberg because she was "someone who made the most important difference in my life" (paragraph 1). His main point seems to be that "Hattie was a woman who believed that the secret for success in life was getting the fundamentals right" (3). Friedman learned this from Hattie and applied it to his own life. He firmly believes that "the real secret of success in the information age is what it always was: fundamentals" (10).

3. **What is the writer's *purpose* in writing?**

   Friedman's purpose is to memorialize Steinberg and to explain the importance of the fundamentals that she taught him more than forty years ago. He wants his readers to realize that there are no shortcuts or quick fixes on the road to success. Without the fundamentals, success often eludes people.

4. **What *strategy* or *strategies* does the writer use? *Where* and *how* does the writer use them?**

   Overall, Friedman uses the strategy of illustration, fleshing out his profile of Steinberg with specific examples of the fundamentals she instilled in her students (paragraphs 3 and 9). Friedman uses description as well to develop his profile of Steinberg. We learn that she was Friedman's "toughest teacher" (4), that she was "a single woman, nearing sixty at the time," that she was "the polar opposite of 'cool,'" and that she was "a woman of clarity in an age of uncertainty" (5). Finally, Friedman's brief narratives about an advertising executive, Ariel Sharon, Steinberg's classroom hangout, and one of the teacher's last birthday parties give readers insight into her personality by showing us what she was like instead of simply telling us.

5. **Do the writer's *strategies* suit his *subject* and *purpose*? Why, or why not?**

Friedman uses exemplification as a strategy to show why Steinberg had such a great impact on his life. Friedman knew that he was not telling Steinberg's story, or writing narration, so much as he was showing what a great teacher she was. Using examples of how Steinberg affected his life and molded his journalistic skills allows Friedman to introduce his teacher as well as to demonstrate her importance.

In developing his portrait of Steinberg in this way, Friedman relies on the fundamentals of good journalism. When taken collectively, his examples create a poignant picture of this teacher. Steinberg would likely have been proud to see her former student demonstrating his journalistic skills in paying tribute to her.

6. **How effective is the essay? Does the writer make his points clear and persuade the reader to accept them?**

Friedman's essay serves his purpose extremely well. He helps his readers visualize Steinberg and understand what she gave to each of her journalism students. In his concluding two paragraphs, Friedman shows us that Steinberg's message is as relevant today as it was more than forty years ago in St. Louis Park High School, Room 313.

ABOUT THE PHOTOGRAPHS AND VISUAL TEXTS IN THIS BOOK

Subject & Strategy has a visual dimension to complement the many verbal texts. Each chapter opens with a visual text that provides insight into the chapter's writing strategy. In addition, we have illustrated at least one essay in each chapter with a photograph that captures one or more themes in the essay. Finally, we have included an assortment of visual texts in the Classroom Activities that accompany each essay in *Subject & Strategy*. It is our hope that, by adding this visual medium to the mix of written essays and text-based analytical activities and assignments, we can demonstrate not only another approach to themes and strategies but also how a different medium portrays these themes and strategies.

There's nothing unnatural or wrong about looking at a photograph and naming its subject or giving it a label. For example, summarizing the content of the photograph on page 17 is easy enough. We'd simply say, *"Here's a photograph of a man sitting in front of a store."*

The problem comes when we mistake *looking* for *seeing*. If we think we are seeing and truly perceiving but are only looking, we miss a lot. Our visual sense can become uncritical and nonchalant, perhaps even numbed to what's going on in a photograph.

To reap the larger rewards, we need to move in more closely on an image. If we take a closer look, we will see all kinds of important details that we perhaps missed the first time around. We see elements in harmony as well as conflict. We see comparisons and contrasts. We see storytelling. We see process and change. We see highlights and shadows, foreground and background, light and dark, and a myriad of shades in between. There is movement—even in still photographs. There is tension and energy, peace and harmony, and line and texture. We see all this because we are seeing and not merely looking.

If we examine the photograph of the man again and truly *see* it, we might observe the following:

1. A man sits on a ledge that is low to the ground. He is likely traveling since he has two bags, one of which is so heavy that a wheeled cart is useful. Behind him is a store-window display with mannequins posed in various positions.

2. A casual observer might think the scene is in a mall, but closer observation reveals that the ledge is alongside an outdoor sidewalk. The glass of the store window reflects the activity of a busy urban street. We see the side of a bus and a set of handlebars reflected there. The man holds a cigarette in his right hand, evidence that he is outside.

3. The light square tiles of the sidewalk contrast with the round-edged, glossy dark ledge.

4. The man is not particularly meticulous about his appearance, unbothered by the street potentially dirtying his clothes. His white shirt is unbuttoned and rumpled. His athletic sneakers, loose-fitting camouflage jacket, and baseball cap suggest that he prioritizes comfort over style. The shadow on his cap indicates flexible, broken-in fabric. He may wear the hat often.

5. The man stares blankly ahead, uninterested in the goings-on outside the photograph. If he tried to observe the area in front of him, the cart's handle would obscure his view. His posture is rounded, and his arms rest on his knees. He seems tired. Perhaps it's late in the day or, if he has been traveling, it's been a complicated journey.

6. In contrast to the man's appearance and manner, the front-window display is formal and fashionable. We see decorative plant fronds in an ornate holder. Luxurious, fringed blankets and jacquard pillows rest on

the right side of a squared, modern white bench. The headless, seated mannequin is styled with great care, dressed in skinny high heels, a short dress, and a three-buttoned jacket with a fur collar. The sharp angles of the mannequin's elbows strike a self-assured, confident pose.

7. It's clear that the store carries upscale women's clothes and home furnishings. The clean, litter-free street suggests that the store may be in a well-kept area, perhaps catering to upscale shoppers.

8. The fact that both the mannequin and the man wear light, open jackets suggests a temperate, cool time of year. If we were to zoom on the window's text placard, we would see Chinese characters, suggesting that this takes place in a Chinese city.

9. The most striking thing about the photograph is the juxtaposition of the weary, casually dressed man with the formal and upscale mannequins in the store window. The man seems content to sit and smoke his cigarette, showing little interest in his surroundings. One wonders why he selected that particular spot.

Based on these detailed observations, we can begin to identify a number of themes at work in the photo: class and lifestyle differences, cultural contradictions, and the clash between concepts like work and leisure. Likewise, we can see that several rhetorical strategies are at work: comparison and contrast predominantly, but also description and illustration.

Photographs are not the only visual texts that we encounter in our daily lives. Both in print and on the Internet, governments, organizations, and individuals present us with visual information in graphs, diagrams, flow charts, and ads. Consider the following graphic, which appeared in the *Wall Street Journal* in October 2012. Between July and September 2012, Kaplan Test Prep surveyed admissions officers from 350 of the top 500 colleges as ranked by U.S. News & World Report's *Ultimate College Guide* and Barron's *Profiles of American Colleges*. Admissions officers were asked whether or not they had searched online for information about an applicant and whether results had ever negatively affected an applicant's chance at admission.

Before looking at their responses, ask yourself if you ever considered that college admissions officers might check you out online during the application process. Now study the graphic.

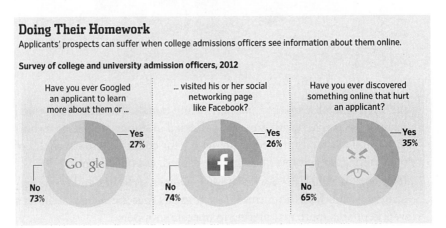

Doing Their Homework
Applicants' prospects can suffer when college admissions officers see information about them online.

Survey of college and university admission officers, 2012

Have you ever Googled an applicant to learn more about them or ...	... visited his or her social networking page like Facebook?	Have you ever discovered something online that hurt an applicant?
Yes 27%	Yes 26%	Yes 35%
No 73%	No 74%	No 65%

What were you able to see communicated in this graphic? Here is what we observed:

1. The answers to the questions are presented in the form of three doughnut charts, which show the relationship of parts to the whole, much like a pie chart.

2. Each doughnut is divided between two possible response options: "yes" and "no."

3. The shaded portion of each doughnut represents the percentage of respondents who answered "yes."

4. In each case, more than half of the respondents replied "no," suggesting that although a significant number of admissions officers have searched for information about applicants online, it's not yet a majority practice.

5. The difference between searching on Google or on social media is a mere one-percentage point, so an observer might generalize that each is "roughly a quarter of admissions officers."

6. From the answers to the first two options, it's not clear how many of the admissions officers used both Google and social media, and how many used just one or the other.

7. Because 35 percent of admissions officers reported that they have uncovered information that negatively affected an applicant, we can conclude the total number of admissions officers who have ever checked an applicant's online presence is, in fact, higher than a quarter after all.

A similar close analysis of the other visuals in this book will enhance your understanding of how themes and strategies work in these visual texts. Practice in visual analysis will, in turn, add to your understanding of the reading selections. In reading, too, we need to train ourselves to pay close attention to catch all nuances and to be attuned to what is *not* expressed as well as to what is. By sharpening our observational skills, we penetrate to another level of meaning—a level not apparent to a casual reader. Finally, strengthening your ability to see and read deeply will also strengthen your ability to write. We need to see first, clearly and in detail, before we attempt, as writers, to find the appropriate words to help others see.

THE READING-WRITING CONNECTION

Reading and writing are two sides of the same coin. Active reading is one of the best ways to learn to write and to improve writing skills. By reading we can see how others have communicated their experiences, ideas, thoughts, and feelings in their writing. We can study how they have effectively used the various elements of the essay—thesis, organizational strategies, beginnings and endings, paragraphs, transitions, effective sentences, word choice, tone, and figurative language—to say what they wanted to say. By studying the style, technique, and rhetorical strategies of other writers—by reading, in effect, *as* writers—we learn how to write more effectively ourselves.

▶ Reading as a Writer

What does it mean to read as a writer? Most of us have not been taught to read with a writer's eye, to ask why we like one piece of writing and not another. Likewise, most of us do not ask ourselves why one piece of writing is more believable or convincing than another. When you learn to read with a writer's eye, you begin to answer these important questions and, in the process, come to appreciate what is involved in selecting a subject.

At one level, reading stimulates your imagination by providing you with ideas on what to write about. After reading Thomas L. Friedman's "My Favorite Teacher," Malcolm X's "Coming to an Awareness of Language," David P. Bardeen's "Not Close Enough for Comfort," or Jeannette Walls's "A Woman on the Street," you might decide to write about a turning point in your life. Or, after reading Pat Mora's "Remembering Lobo," Maya Angelou's "Sister Flowers," or Robert Ramírez's "The Barrio," you might be inspired to write about a person or place of similar personal significance to you.

Reading also provides you with information, ideas, and perspectives that can serve as jumping-off points for your own essays. For example, after reading Rosalind Wiseman's "The Queen Bee and Her Court," you might want to elaborate on what she has written, agreeing with her examples or generating better ones; qualify her argument or take issue with it; or use a variation of her classification scheme to discuss male relationships (i.e., "The King and His Court"). Similarly, if you wanted to write an essay in which you take a stand on an issue, you would find the essays on various controversies in the "Argumentation" chapter an invaluable resource.

Reading actively and analytically will also help you recognize effective writing and learn to emulate it. When you see, for example, how Deborah Tannen uses a strong thesis statement about the value of directness and indirectness in human communication to control the parts of her essay ("How to Give Orders Like a Man"), you can better appreciate the importance of having a clear thesis statement in your writing. When you see the way Andrew Sullivan ("iPod World: The End of Society?") uses transitions to link key phrases and important ideas so that readers can recognize how the parts of his essay are meant to flow together, you have a better idea of how to achieve such coherence in your writing. And when you see how Suzanne Britt ("Neat People vs. Sloppy People") uses a point-by-point organizational pattern to show the differences between neat and sloppy people, you see a powerful way in which you can organize an essay using the strategy of comparison and contrast.

Perhaps the most important reason to master the skill of reading like a writer is that, for everything you write, you will be your own first reader. How well you scrutinize your own drafts will affect how well you revise them, and revising well is crucial to writing well.

CHAPTER 2

Writing

NOTHING IS MORE IMPORTANT TO YOUR SUCCESS IN SCHOOL AND IN the workplace than learning to write well. You've heard it so often you've probably become numb to the advice. Let's ask the big question, however: Why is writing well so important? The simple answer is that no activity develops your ability to think better than writing does. Writing allows you to develop your thoughts and to "see" and reflect critically on what you think: In that sense, writing also involves its twin sister, reading. Small wonder, then, that employers in all fields are constantly looking for people who can read and write well. Simply put, employers want to hire and retain the best minds they can to further their business objectives, and the ability to read and write well is a strong indication of a good mind.

Moreover, in today's technology-driven economy, there is virtually no field of work that doesn't require clear, accurate, and direct expression in writing, whether it be writing cover letters and résumés, internal e-mails, self-appraisals, laboratory reports, contract bids, proposals, loan or grant applications, sales reports, market analyses, or any other document. Perhaps more than any other factor, your ability to organize your thoughts and clearly present them will affect your overall success on the job and in life.

College is a practical training ground for learning to write. In college, with the help of instructors, you will write essays, analyses, term papers, reports, reviews of research, critiques, and summaries. Take advantage of the opportunity college provides to develop your skills as a writer: What you learn now will be fundamental, not only to your education, but also to your later success.

DEVELOPING AN EFFECTIVE WRITING PROCESS

Writers cannot rely on inspiration alone to produce effective writing. Good writers follow a writing *process*: They analyze their assignment, gather ideas, draft, revise, edit, and proofread. Remember, however, that the writing process is rarely as simple and straightforward as this. Often the process is recursive, moving back and forth among different stages. Moreover, writing is personal—

no two people go about it the same way. Consider this chapter's opening image, Alison Bechdel's depiction of her creative process, a mix of brainstorming, research, planning, writing, drawing, breaks, printing, distractions, and successes. As she would surely attest, writing well takes *time*. Still, it is nonetheless possible to describe basic guidelines for developing a writing process, thereby allowing you to devise your own reliable method for undertaking a writing task.

Step 1: Understand Your Assignment

A great deal of the writing you do in college will be in response to very specific assignments. Your American history professor, for example, may ask you to write a paper in which you explain the causes of the Spanish-American War; your environmental studies professor may ask you to report both the pro and con arguments for regulating industrial carbon emissions; or your English professor may ask you to compare and contrast the text and film versions of H. G. Wells's *The War of the Worlds*. It is important, therefore, that you understand exactly what your instructor is asking you to do. The best way to understand assignments such as these (or exam questions, for that matter) is to identify *subject* words (words that indicate the content of the assignment) and *direction* words (words that indicate your purpose or the writing strategy you should use). In the first example given above, the subject words are *Spanish-American War* and the direction word is *explain*. In the second example, the subject words are *industrial carbon emissions* and the direction word is *report*. Finally, the subject words in the third example are *text and film versions of H. G. Wells's* The War of the Worlds, while the direction words are *compare and contrast*.

Most direction words are familiar to us, but we are not always sure how they differ from one another or exactly what they are asking us to do. The following list of direction words, along with explanations of what they call for, will help you analyze paper and exam assignments.

Direction Words

Analyze: take apart and examine closely

Argue: make a case for a particular position

Categorize: place into meaningful groups

Compare: look for differences; stress similarities

Contrast: look for similarities; stress differences

Critique: point out positive and negative features

Define: provide the meaning for a term or concept

Evaluate: judge according to some standard

Explain: make plain or comprehensible

Illustrate: show through examples

Interpret: explain the meaning of something

List: catalog or enumerate steps in a process

Outline: provide abbreviated structure for key elements

Prove: demonstrate truth through logic, fact, or example

Review: summarize key points

Synthesize: bring together or make connections among elements

Trace: delineate a sequence of events

FINDING A SUBJECT AREA AND FOCUSING ON A TOPIC.   Although you will often be given specific assignments in your writing course, you may sometimes be given the freedom to choose your subject matter and topic. In this case, begin by determining a broad subject that you like to think about and might enjoy writing about—a general subject like the Internet, popular culture, or foreign travel. Something you've recently read—one of the essays in *Subject & Strategy*, for example—may help bring particular subjects to mind. You might consider a subject related to your career ambitions—perhaps business, journalism, teaching, law, medicine, architecture, or computer programming. Another option is to list some subjects you enjoy discussing with friends: food, sports, television programs, or politics. Select several likely subjects, and explore their potential. Your goal is to arrive at an appropriately narrowed topic.

Suppose, for example, you select as possible subject areas "farming" and "advertising." You could develop each according to the following chart.

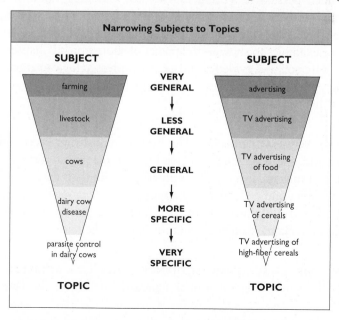

DETERMINING YOUR PURPOSE. All effective writing springs from a clear purpose. Most good writing seeks specifically to accomplish any one of the following three purposes:

- To express thoughts and feelings about life experiences
- To inform readers by explaining something about the world around them
- To persuade readers to adopt some belief or take some action

In *expressive writing*, or writing from experience, you put your thoughts and feelings before all other concerns. When Cherokee Paul McDonald reacts to watching a young boy fishing (Chapter 1), when Malcolm X shows his frustration at not having appropriate language to express himself (Chapter 4), and when Jeannette Walls describes seeing her homeless mother (Chapter 5), each one is writing from experience. In each case, the writer has clarified an important life experience and has conveyed what he or she learned from it.

Informative writing focuses on telling the reader something about the outside world. In informative writing, you report, explain, analyze, define, classify, compare, describe a process, or examine causes and effects. When Michael Pollan explains how the beef we eat travels from factory farms to our tables (Chapter 7) and when Deborah Tannen discusses examples of orders given and received in the workplace (Chapter 6), each one is writing to inform.

Argumentative writing seeks to influence readers' thinking and attitudes toward a subject and, in some cases, to move them to a particular course of action. Such persuasive writing uses logical reasoning, authoritative evidence, and testimony, and it sometimes includes emotionally charged language and examples. In writing their arguments, Richard Lederer uses numerous examples to show us the power of short words (Chapter 12) and Thomas Jefferson uses evidence and clearly expressed logic to argue that the fledgling American colonies are within their rights to break away from Britain (Chapter 12).

KNOWING YOUR AUDIENCE. The best writers always keep their audience in mind. Once they have decided on a topic and a purpose, writers present their material in a way that empathizes with their readers, addresses their difficulties and concerns, and appeals to their rational and emotional faculties. Based on knowledge of their audience, writers make conscious decisions on content, sentence structure, and word choice.

WRITING FOR AN ACADEMIC AUDIENCE. Academic writing most often employs the conventions of formal standard English, or the language of

Formal versus Informal Writing

Formal Writing	Informal Writing
Uses standard English, the language of public discourse typical of newspapers, magazines, books, and speeches	Uses nonstandard English, slang, colloquial expressions (*anyways, dude, freaked out*), and shorthand (*OMG, IMHO, GR8*)
Uses mostly third person	Uses first and second person most often
Avoids most abbreviations (*Professor, brothers, miles per gallon, Internet, digital video recorder*)	Uses abbreviations and acronyms (*Prof., bros., mpg, Net, DVR*)
Uses an impersonal tone (*The speaker took questions from the audience at the end of her lecture.*)	Uses an informal tone (*It was great the way she answered questions at the end of her talk.*)
Uses longer, more complex sentences	Uses shorter, simpler sentences
Adheres to the rules and conventions of proper grammar	Takes a casual approach to the rules and conventions of proper grammar

educated professionals. Rather than being heavy or stuffy, good academic writing is lively and engaging and holds the reader's attention by presenting interesting ideas supported with relevant facts, statistics, and detailed information. Informal writing, usually freer and simpler in form, is typically used in notes, journal entries, e-mail, text messages, instant messaging, and the like.

In order not to lessen the importance of your ideas and your credibility, be sure that informal writing does not carry over into your academic writing. Always keeping your audience and purpose in mind will help you achieve an appropriate style.

When you write, your audience might be an individual (your instructor), a group (the students in your class), a specialized group (art history majors), or a general readership (readers of your student newspaper). To help identify your audience, ask yourself the questions posed in the box that begins below.

Questions about Audience

- Who are my readers? Are they a specialized or a general group?
- What do I know about my audience's age, gender, education, religious affiliation, economic status, and political views?

(continued on next page)

(continued from previous page)

- What does my audience know about my subject? Are they experts or novices?
- What does my audience need to know about my topic in order to understand my discussion of it?
- Will my audience be interested, open-minded, resistant, or hostile to what I have to say?
- Do I need to explain any specialized language so that my audience can understand my subject? Is there any language that I should avoid?
- What do I want my audience to do as a result of reading my essay?

Step 2: Gather Ideas and Formulate a Thesis

Ideas and information (facts and details) lie at the heart of good prose. Ideas grow out of information; information supports ideas. Before you begin to draft, gather as many ideas as possible and as much information as you can about your topic in order to inform and stimulate your readers intellectually.

BRAINSTORMING.   A good way to generate ideas and information about your topic is to *brainstorm*: Simply list everything you know about your topic, freely associating one idea with another. At this point, order is not important. Write quickly, but if you get stalled, reread what you have written; doing so will jog your mind in new directions. Keep your list handy so that you can add to it over the course of several days.

Here, for example, is a student's brainstorming list on why Martin Luther King Jr.'s "I Have a Dream" speech (Chapter 12) is enduring:

WHY "I HAVE A DREAM" IS MEMORABLE

- Delivered on steps of Lincoln Memorial during civil rights demonstration in Washington, D.C.; crowd of more than 200,000 people
- Repetition of "I have a dream"
- Allusions to the Bible, spirituals
- "Bad check" metaphor and other memorable figures of speech
- Echoes other great American writings — Declaration of Independence and Gettysburg Address
- Refers to various parts of the country and embraces all races and religions
- Sermon format
- Displays energy and passion

CLUSTERING.   Clustering allows you to generate material and to sort it into meaningful groupings. Put your topic, or a key word or phrase about your topic, in the center of a sheet of paper and draw a circle around it. Draw four or five (or more) lines radiating out from this circle, and jot down main ideas about your topic; draw circles around them as well. Repeat the process by drawing lines from the secondary circles and adding examples, details, and any questions you have.

Here is a student's cluster on television news programs:

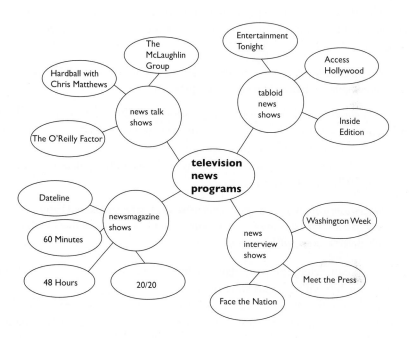

RESEARCHING.   You may want to supplement what you know about your topic with research. This does not necessarily mean formal library work or even online research. Firsthand observations and interviews with people knowledgeable about your topic are also forms of research. Whatever your form of research, take careful notes, so you can accurately paraphrase an author or quote an interviewee.

REHEARSING IDEAS.   Consider rehearsing what you are going to write by taking ten or fifteen minutes to talk your way through your paper with a roommate, friend, or family member. Rehearsing in this way may suit your personality and the way you think. Moreover, rehearsing may help you generate new ideas.

FORMULATING A THESIS. The thesis of an essay is its main idea, the major point the writer is trying to make.

A thesis should be

- The most important point you make about your topic
- More general than the ideas and facts used to support it
- Focused enough to be covered in the space allotted for the essay

The thesis is often expressed in one or two sentences called a *thesis statement*. Here is an example of a thesis statement about television news programs:

> The so-called serious news programs are becoming too like tabloid news shows in both their content and their presentation.

A thesis statement should not be a question but rather an assertion. If you find yourself writing a question for a thesis statement, answer the question first—this answer will be your thesis statement.

An effective strategy for developing a thesis statement is to begin by writing, "What I want to say is that . . .":

> *What I want to say is that* unless language barriers between patients and health care providers are bridged, many patients' lives in our most culturally diverse cities will be endangered.

Later you can delete the formulaic opening, *What I want to say is that*, and you will be left with a thesis statement.

To determine whether your thesis is too general or too specific, think hard about how easy it will be to present data—that is, facts, statistics, names, examples or illustrations, and opinions of authorities—to support it. If you stray too far in either direction, your task will become much more difficult. A thesis statement that is too general will leave you overwhelmed by the number of issues you must address. For example, the statement "Malls have ruined the fabric of American life" would lead to the question "How?" To answer it, you would probably have to include information about traffic patterns, urban decay, environmental damage, economic studies, and so on. To cover all of this in the time and space you have for a typical college paper would mean taking shortcuts, and your paper would be ineffective. On the other hand, too specific a thesis statement will leave you with too little information to present. "The Big City Mall should not have been built because it reduced retail sales at existing Big City stores by 21.4 percent" does not leave you with any opportunity to develop an argument.

The thesis statement is usually presented near the beginning of the essay. One common practice in shorter college papers is to position the thesis statement as the final sentence of the first paragraph.

Will Your Thesis Hold Up to Scrutiny?

Once you have a possible thesis statement in mind for an essay, ask yourself the following questions:

- Does my thesis statement take a clear position on an issue? If so, what is that position?
- Is my thesis the most important point I make about my topic?
- Is my thesis neither too general nor too specific? Will I be able to argue it in the time and space allotted?

Step 3: Organize and Write Your First Draft

There is nothing mysterious or difficult about the nine organizational strategies discussed in this book. In fact, you're familiar with most of them already. Whenever you tell a story, for example, you use the strategy of *narration*. When you need to make a decision, you *compare and contrast* the things you must choose between. When you want to describe how to make a pizza, you use the strategy of *process analysis* to figure out how to explain it. What might make these strategies seem unfamiliar, especially in writing,

---

Organizational* Strategies

Narration	Telling a story or giving an account of an event
Description	Presenting a picture in words
Illustration	Using examples to explain a point or an idea
Process Analysis	Explaining how something is done or happens
Comparison and Contrast	Demonstrating likenesses and differences
Division and Classification	Breaking down a subject into its parts and placing them in appropriate categories
Definition	Explaining what something is
Cause and Effect Analysis	Explaining the causes of an event or the effects of an action
Argumentation	Using reason and logic to persuade

*Also known as *rhetorical* or *writing* strategies.

is that most people use them more or less intuitively. Sophisticated thinking and writing, however, do not come from simply using these strategies, but rather from using them consciously and purposefully.

Writing strategies are not like blueprints or plaster molds that determine in advance exactly how the final product will be shaped. Rather, these strategies are flexible and versatile, with only a few fundamental rules or directions to define their shape—like the rules for basketball, chess, or other strategic games. Such directions leave plenty of room for imagination and variety. In addition, because these strategies are fundamental ways of thinking, they will help you in all stages of the writing process—from prewriting and writing a first draft through revising and editing your composition.

DETERMINING A STRATEGY FOR DEVELOPING YOUR ESSAY.   Good essays often employ components of more than one strategy. In determining which strategies to use, the language of the writing assignment is very important. If a description is called for, or you need to examine causes and effects, or, as is often the case, you are asked to argue for a position on an important issue, the language of the assignment will include key direction words and

Determining What Strategies to Use with a Specific Assignment

Key Direction Words and Phrases	Suggested Writing Strategy
Give an account of; tell the story of; relate the events of	Narration
Describe; present a picture; discuss the details of	Description
Show; demonstrate; enumerate; discuss; give examples of	Illustration
Explain how something is done; explain how something works; explain what happens; analyze the steps	Process Analysis
Compare; contrast; explain differences; explain similarities; evaluate	Comparison and Contrast
Divide and classify; explain what the components are; analyze the parts of	Division and Classification
Explain; define a person, place, or thing; give the meaning of	Definition
Explain causes; explain effects; give the reasons for; explain the consequences of	Cause and Effect Analysis
Argue for or against; make a case for or against; state your views on; persuade; convince; justify	Argumentation

phrases that will indicate the primary strategy or strategies you should use in developing your essay.

In the chart on page 32, the first column lists some key direction words and phrases you may encounter in your writing assignments. The second column lists the strategy that is most likely called for by the use of those words.

Often in academic writing your instructor may not give you a specific assignment; instead, he or she may ask only that you write a paper of a specific length. In such cases you are left to determine for yourself what strategy or strategies might best accomplish your purpose. If you are not given a specific assignment and are uncertain as to what strategy or strategies you should use in developing your essay, you might try the following four-step method:

Determining What Strategies to Use with an Open Assignment

1. State the main idea of your essay in a single phrase or sentence.
2. Restate the main idea as a question — in effect, the question your essay will answer.
3. Look closely at both the main idea and the question for key words or concepts that go with a particular strategy, just as you would when working with an assignment that specifies a topic.
4. Consider other strategies that would support your primary strategy.

CHOOSING STRATEGIES ACROSS THE DISCIPLINES. The following examples show how a student writing in different disciplines might decide what strategies to use.

American Literature

1. **MAIN IDEA:** John Updike relies on religion as a major theme in his fiction.

2. **QUESTION:** In what instances does John Updike use religion as a major theme?

3. **STRATEGY:** Illustration. The phrase "in what instances" suggests that it is necessary to show examples of where Updike uses the theme of religion to further his narrative purposes.

4. **SUPPORTING STRATEGIES:** Definition. What is meant by *religion* needs to be clear.

Biology

1. **MAIN IDEA:** Mitosis is the process by which cells divide.

2. **QUESTION:** How does the process of mitosis work?

3. **STRATEGY:** Process analysis. The words *how*, *process*, and *work* suggest a process analysis essay.

4. **SUPPORTING STRATEGIES:** Illustration. A good process analysis includes examples of each step in the process.

Political Science

1. **MAIN IDEA:** The threat of terrorism has changed the way people think about air travel.

2. **QUESTION:** What effects does terrorism have on air travel?

3. **STRATEGY:** Cause and effect. The phrase "what effects" asks for a listing of the effects.

4. **SUPPORTING STRATEGIES:** Illustration. The best presentation of effects is through vivid examples.

These are just a few examples of how to decide on a writing strategy and supporting strategies that are suitable for your topic. In every case, your reading can guide you in recognizing the best plan to follow. In Chapter 13, you will learn more about combining strategies.

WRITING YOUR FIRST DRAFT. First drafts are exploratory and sometimes unpredictable. While writing your first draft, you may find yourself getting away from your original plan. What started as a definition essay may develop into a process analysis or an effort at argumentation. For example, a definition of *school spirit* could turn into a process analysis of how a pep rally is organized or an argument about why school spirit is important (or detrimental). A definition of *manners* could become an instructive process analysis on how to be a good host, or it could turn into an argument that respect is based on the ways people treat one another. A definition of *democracy* could evolve into a process analysis of how democracy works in the United States or into an argument for democratic forms of government.

If your draft is leaning toward a different strategy from the one you first envisioned, don't force yourself to revert to your original plan. Allow your inspiration to take you where it will. When you finish your draft, you can see whether the new strategy works better than the old one or whether it would be best to go back to your initial strategy. Use your first draft to explore your ideas; you will always have a chance to revise later.

It may also happen that, while writing your first draft, you run into a difficulty that prevents you from moving forward. For example, suppose you want to tell about something that happened to you, but you aren't certain whether you should be using the pronoun *I* so often. If you turn to the essays in Chapter 4 to see how authors of narrative essays handle this problem, you will find that it isn't necessarily a problem at all. For an account of a personal experience, it's perfectly acceptable to write *I* as often as you need to. Or suppose that after writing several pages describing someone you think is quite a character, you find that your draft seems flat and doesn't express how lively and funny the person really is. If you read the introduction to Chapter 5, you will learn that descriptions need lots of factual, concrete detail; the chapter selections give further proof of this. You suddenly realize that just such detail is what's missing from your draft.

If you do run into difficulties writing your first draft, don't worry or get upset. Even experienced writers run into problems at the beginning. Just try to keep going. Think about your topic, and consider your details and what you want to say. You might even want to go back and look over your original brainstorming work or the information you've gathered.

Step 4: Revise Your Essay

Once you have completed your first draft, set it aside awhile and do something else. When you are refreshed and again ready to give it your full attention, you are ready to revise.

Revision is a vital part of the writing process. It is not to be confused with editing or "cleaning up" a draft but should be regarded as a set of activities wherein a rough draft may be transformed into a polished essay that powerfully expresses your ideas. In fact, many writers believe that all writing is essentially *re*writing. When you revise, you give yourself a chance to re-see how well you have captured your subject, to see what has worked and what still needs to be done.

In revising, you might need to reorganize your paragraphs or the sentences within some paragraphs, generate more information because you have too few examples, revise your thesis statement so that it better fits your argument, or find better transitions to bind your sentences and thoughts together. Rather than an arduous task, many writers find revision a very satisfying process because they are able to bring their work into sharper focus and give themselves a better chance of connecting with their audience.

Tips for Revising Your Draft

- Triple-space your draft so that you can make changes more easily.
- Make revisions on a hard copy of your paper.
- Read your paper aloud, listening for parts that do not make sense.
- Have a fellow student read your essay and critique it.

The following sections offer proven techniques for initiating and carrying out one or more revisions of your developing essays.

TAKING ADVANTAGE OF PEER CRITIQUES.   Peer critiquing is one of the best ways to encourage revision and improve your drafts. Peer critiquing is based on two ideas. The first is that by reading your writing aloud, by objectifying it, you can determine for yourself where you need to make changes. Often writers will say that when they read their work aloud they themselves were bored or unclear about what they were trying to say. Revisions can follow very easily from such realizations. The second point is that peer critiquing requires an audience, one or more people who are listening to you read what you have written. By asking some simple but important questions your listeners can verify that what you have meant to say is what they have heard. If some discrepancies occur, it's usually because you have not

A Brief Guide to Peer Critiquing

When critiquing someone else's work:

- Read the essay carefully. Read it to yourself first and, if possible, have the writer read it to you at the beginning of the session. Some flaws only become obvious when read aloud.

- Ask the writer to state his or her purpose for writing and to identify the thesis statement within the paper itself.

- Be positive, but be honest. Never denigrate the paper's content or the writer's effort, but do your best to identify how the writer can improve the paper through revision.

- Try to address the most important issues first. Think about the thesis and the organization of the paper before moving on to more specific topics like word choice.

- Do not be dismissive, and do not dictate changes. Ask questions that encourage the writer to reconsider parts of the paper that you find confusing or ineffective.

When someone critiques your work:

- Give your reviewer a copy of your essay before your meeting, if possible.

- Listen carefully to your reviewer, and try not to argue each issue. Record comments, and evaluate them later.

- Do not get defensive or explain what you wanted to say if the reviewer misunderstands what you meant. Try to understand the reviewer's point of view, and learn what you need to revise to clear up the misunderstanding.

- Consider every suggestion, but only use the ones that make sense to you in your revision.

- Be sure to thank your reviewer for his or her effort on your behalf.

expressed yourself as well as you thought and you need to revise. Typical problems are with the purpose for writing and the articulation of a thesis, with lesser problems concerning organization, evidence, and paragraphs and sentences coming afterward.

When you critique work with other students—yours or theirs—it is important to maximize the effectiveness and efficiency of the exercise. The tips outlined in the box on page 36 will help you get the most out of peer critiques.

REVISING THE LARGER ELEMENTS OF YOUR ESSAY. During revision, you should focus first on the larger issues of thesis, purpose, content, organization, and paragraph structure to make sure that your writing says what you want it to say. One way to begin is to make an informal outline of your first draft—not as you planned it, but as it actually came out. What does your outline tell you about the strategy you used? Does this strategy suit your purpose? Perhaps you meant to compare your two grandmothers, but you have not clearly shown their similarities and differences. Consequently, your draft is not one unified comparison and contrast essay but two descriptive essays spliced together.

Even if you are satisfied with the overall strategy of your draft, an outline can still help you make improvements. Perhaps your classification essay on types of college students is confusing because you create overlapping categories: computer science majors, athletes, and foreign students (a computer science major could, of course, also be an athlete, a foreign student, or both). You may uncover a flaw in your organization, such as a lack of logic in an argument or faulty parallelism in a comparison and contrast. Now is the time to discover these problems and to fix them.

The following list of questions addresses the larger elements of your essay: thesis, purpose, organization, paragraphs, and evidence. Use it as a guide when reviewing your work as well as when reviewing the work of others during peer critique sessions.

Questions for Revising the Larger Elements of Your Essay

- Have I focused my **topic**?
- Does my **thesis statement** clearly identify my topic and make an assertion about it?
- Is the **writing strategy** I have chosen the best one for my purpose?
- Are my **paragraphs** adequately developed, and does each support my thesis?
- Is my **beginning** effective in capturing my reader's interest and introducing my topic?

(continued on next page)

(continued from previous page)

- Is my **conclusion** effective? Does it grow naturally from what I've said in the rest of my essay?
- Have I accomplished my **purpose**?

WRITING BEGINNINGS AND ENDINGS. Beginnings and endings are very important to the effectiveness of an essay, but they can be daunting to write. Inexperienced writers often feel they must write their essays sequentially when, in fact, it is usually better to write both the beginning and the ending after you have completed most or all of the rest of your essay. Once you see how your essay develops, you will know better how to capture your reader's attention and introduce the rest of the essay. As you work through the revision process, ask yourself the questions in the box below.

Questions for Writing Beginnings and Endings

- Does my introduction grab the reader's attention?
- Is my introduction confusing in any way? How well does it relate to the rest of the essay?
- If I state my thesis in the introduction, how effectively is it presented?
- Does my essay come to a logical conclusion or does it seem to just stop?
- Does the conclusion relate well to the rest of the essay? Am I careful not to introduce topics or issues that I did not address in the essay?
- Does my conclusion underscore important aspects of the essay, or is it merely a mechanical rehashing of what I wrote earlier?

REVISING THE SMALLER ELEMENTS OF YOUR ESSAY. Once you have addressed the larger elements of your essay, you should turn your attention to the finer elements of sentence structure, word choice, and usage. The following questions focus on these concerns.

If, after serious efforts at revision, you still find yourself dissatisfied with specific elements of your draft, look at some of the essays in *Subject & Strategy* to see how other writers have dealt with similar situations. For example, if you don't like the way the essay starts, find some beginnings you think are particularly effective. What characterizes those beginnings? If your paragraphs don't seem to flow into one another, examine how various writers use transitions. If you have lapsed into informal language, take a look at how other writers express themselves. If an example seems unconvincing, examine the way other writers include details, anecdotes, facts, and statistics to strengthen their illustrations.

Remember that the readings in this text are a resource for you as you write, as are the strategy chapter introductions, which outline the basic features of each strategy. In addition, the readings in Chapter 3, "Writers on Writing," will provide you with inspiration and advice to help you through the writing process.

Questions for Revising Sentences

- Do my sentences convey my thoughts clearly, and do they emphasize the most important parts of my thinking?
- Are all my sentences complete sentences?
- Are my sentences stylistically varied? Do I alter their pattern and rhythm for emphasis? Do I use some short sentences for dramatic effect?
- Are all my sentences written in the active voice?
- Do I use strong action verbs and concrete nouns?
- Is my diction fresh and forceful? Do I avoid wordiness?
- Have I achieved an appropriate degree of formality in my writing?
- Have I committed any errors in usage?

Step 5: Edit and Proofread Your Essay

During the *editing* stage, you check your writing for errors in grammar, punctuation, capitalization, spelling, and manuscript format. Chapter 16 of this book provides help for common problems with grammar, punctuation, and sentence style. A dictionary and a grammar handbook may be necessary for less common or more specific editing questions.

After editing, proofread your work carefully before turning it in. Though you may have used your computer's spell-checker, you might find that you have typed *their* instead of *there* or *form* instead of *from*. (A computer won't know the difference, as long as you've spelled *some* word correctly.)

Questions to Ask during Editing and Proofreading

- Do I have any sentence fragments, comma splices, or run-on sentences?
- Have I used commas properly in all instances?
- Do my verbs agree in number with their antecedents?
- Do my pronouns clearly and correctly refer to their antecedents?
- Do any dangling or misplaced modifiers make my meaning unclear?
- Do I use parallel grammatical structures correctly in my sentences?

(continued on next page)

(continued from previous page)

- Have I used specific nouns and strong verbs wherever possible?
- Have I made any unnecessary shifts in person, tense, or number?
- Have I eliminated unnecessary words?
- Are my sentences appropriately varied and interesting?
- Have I checked for misspellings, mistakes in capitalization, commonly confused words like *its* and *it's*, and typos?
- Have I followed the prescribed guidelines for formatting my manuscript?

A STUDENT ESSAY IN PROGRESS

When he was a first-year student at the University of Vermont, Keith Eldred enrolled in Written Expression, an introductory writing course.

Step 1: Keith's Assignment

Near the middle of the semester, Keith's assignment was to write a three-to-five-page definition essay. After reading the introduction to Chapter 10 in *Subject & Strategy* (pages 387–90) and the essays his instructor assigned from that chapter, Keith was ready to get to work.

Step 2: Keith's Ideas

Keith had already been introduced to the Hindu concept of the *mantra*, and he decided that he would like to explore this concept, narrowing his focus to the topic of mantras as they operate in the secular world. To get started, he decided to brainstorm. His brainstorming provided him with several examples of what he intended to call *secular mantras*; a dictionary definition of the word *mantra*; and the idea that a good starting point for his rough draft might be the story of "The Little Engine That Could." Here are the notes he jotted down:

Mantra: "a mystical formula of invocation or incantation" (Webster's)

Counting to ten when angry

"Little Engine That Could" (possible beginning)

"Let's Go Bulls" — action because crowd wants players to say it to themselves

Swearing (not always a mantra)

Tennis star — "Get serious!"

"Come on, come on" (at traffic light)

"Geronimo" "Ouch!"

Hindu mythology

Step 3: Keith's First Draft

After mulling over his list, Keith began to organize his ideas with the following scratch outline:

1. Begin with story of "Little Engine That Could"
2. Talk about the magic of secular mantras
3. Dictionary definition and Hindu connections
4. Examples of individuals using mantras
5. Crowd chants as mantras — Bulls
6. Conclusion — talk about how you can't get through the day without using mantras

Based on this outline as well as what he learned from *Subject & Strategy* about definition as a writing strategy, Keith came up with the following first draft of his essay:

Secular Mantras: Magic Words

Keith Eldred

Do you remember "The Little Engine That Could"? If you recall, it's the story about the tiny locomotive that hauled the train over the mountain when the big, rugged locomotives wouldn't. Do you remember how the Little Engine strained and heaved and chugged "I think I can—I think I can—I think I can" until she reached the top of the mountain? That's a perfect example of a secular mantra in action.

A secular mantra (pronounced man-truh) is any word or group of words that helps a person use his or her energy. The key word here is "helps"—repeating a secular mantra doesn't *create* energy; it just makes it easier to channel a given amount. The Little Engine, for instance, obviously had the strength to pull the train up the mountain; apparently, she could have done it without saying a word. But we all know she wouldn't have been able to, any more than any one of us would be able to skydive the first time without yelling "Geronimo" or not exclaim "Ouch" if we touched a hot stove. Some words and phrases simply have a certain magic that makes a job easier or that makes us feel better when we repeat them. These are secular mantras.

It is because of their magical quality that these expressions are called "secular mantras" in the first place. A mantra (Sanskrit for "sacred counsel") is "a mystical formula of invocation or incantation" used in Hinduism (*Webster's*). According to Hindu mythology, Manu, lawgiver and

1

2

3

progenitor of humankind, created the first language by teaching people the thought-forms of objects and substances. "VAM," for example, is the thought-form of what we call "water." Mantras, groups of these ancient words, can summon any object or deity if they are miraculously revealed to a seer and properly repeated silently or vocally. Hindus use divine mantras to communicate with gods, acquire superhuman powers, cure diseases, and for many other purposes. Hence, everyday words that people concentrate on to help themselves accomplish tasks or cope with stress act as secular mantras.

All sorts of people use all sorts of secular mantras for all sorts of reasons. A father counts to 10 before saying anything when his son brings the car home dented. A tennis player faults and chides himself, "Get serious!" A frustrated mother pacing with her wailing baby mutters, "You'll have your own kids someday." A college student writhing before an exam instructs himself not to panic. A freshly spanked child glares at his mother's back and repeatedly promises never to speak to her again. Secular mantras are everywhere.

4

Usually, we use secular mantras to make ourselves walk faster or keep silent or do some other act. But we can also use them to influence the actions of other persons. Say, for instance, the Chicago Bulls are behind in the final minutes of a game. Ten thousand fans who want them to win scream, "Let's go, Bulls!" The Bulls are roused and win by 20 points. Chalk up the victory to the fans' secular mantra, which transferred their energy to the players on the court.

5

If you're not convinced of the power of secular mantras, try to complete a day without using any. Don't mutter anything to force yourself out of bed. Don't utter a sound when the water in the shower is cold. Don't grumble when the traffic lights are long. Don't speak to the computer when it's slow to boot up. And don't be surprised if you have an unusually long, painful, frustrating day.

6

Step 4: Keith's Revised Essay

Keith read his paper in a peer critique session with two of his fellow students who had the opportunity afterward to ask him questions about secular mantras, in particular. His classmates wrote what he gave as answers to their questions and presented him with their worksheets with those answers:

- Do a better job of defining *secular mantra* — expand it and be more specific — maybe tell what secular mantras are not.

- Get more examples, especially from everyday experience and TV.

- Don't eliminate background information about mantras.

- Thought Chicago Bulls example didn't work — keep or delete?

- Keep "The Little Engine That Could" example at the beginning of the draft.

- Write new conclusion — present conclusion doesn't follow from what you have written.

In subsequent drafts, Keith worked on each of the areas the students had suggested. While revising, he found it helpful to reread portions of the selections in Chapter 10. His reading led him to new insights about how to strengthen his essay. As he revised further, he found that he needed to make yet other unanticipated changes.

Keith revised his definitions of *mantra* and *secular mantra* to include the following meanings for the related *terms:*

Revised historical definition of mantra

Mantra means "sacred counsel" in Sanskrit and refers to a "mystical formula of invocation or incantation" used in Hinduism (*Webster's*). According to Hindu mythology, the god Manu created the first language by teaching humans the thought-form of every object and substance. "VAM," for example, was what he told them to call the stuff we call "water." But people altered or forgot most of Manu's thought-forms. Followers of Hinduism believe mantras, groups of these ancient words revealed anew by gods to seers, can summon specific objects or deities if they are properly repeated, silently or vocally. Hindus repeat mantras to gain superhuman powers, cure diseases, and for many other purposes. Sideshow fakirs chant "AUM" ("I agree" or "I accept") to become immune to pain when lying on beds of nails.

Expanded definition of secular mantra

Our "mantras" are "secular" because, unlike Hindus, we do not attribute them to gods. Instead, we borrow them from tradition or invent them to fit a situation, as the Little Engine did. They work not by divine power but because they help us, in a way, to govern transmissions along our central nervous systems.

Added explanation of how secular mantras work

Secular mantras give our brains a sort of dual signal-boosting and signal-damping capacity. The act of repeating them pushes messages, or impulses, with extra force along our nerves or interferes with incoming messages we would rather ignore. We can then perform actions more easily or cope with stress that might keep us from functioning the way we want to. We may even accomplish both tasks at once. A skydiver might yell "Geronimo," for example, both to amplify the signals telling his legs to jump and to drown out the ones warning him he's dizzy or scared.

He also rewrote the conclusion, adding yet more examples of secular mantras, this time drawn largely from television advertising. Finally, he made his conclusion more of a natural outgrowth of his thesis and purpose and thus a more fitting conclusion for his essay.

Sentence of examples moved from paragraph 4

Final sentence, which links to thesis and purpose, added

You probably have favorite secular mantras already. Think about it. How many of us haven't uttered the following at least once: "Just do it"; "I'm lovin' it"; "Got milk?"; "Can you hear me now?"; or "Have it your way"? How about the phrases you mumble to yourself from your warm bed on chilly mornings? And those words you chant to ease your impatience when the traffic lights are endless? And the reminders you mutter so that you'll remember to buy bread at the store? If you're like most people, you'll agree that your life is much less painful and frustrating because of those magic words and phrases.

Step 5: Keith's Edited Essay

After expanding his definitions and strengthening his conclusion, as well as making other necessary revisions, Keith was now ready to edit his essay. His instructor told him to avoid the use of first- or second-person address in his essay, and to correct sentences starting with coordinating conjunctions like *and* or *but*. In addition, he had to correct smaller but equally important errors in word choice, spelling, punctuation, and mechanics. He had put aside these errors to make sure his essay had the appropriate content. Now he needed to make sure it was grammatically correct. For example, here is how he edited the first paragraph of his essay:

R
~~Do you~~ remember "The Little Engine That Could"? ~~If you recall, it's~~
That's
the story about the tiny loc^omotive that hauled the train over the mountain
when the big, rugged loc^omotives wouldn't. ~~Do you~~ R remember how the
Little Engine strained and heaved and chugged, "I think I can—I think I
can—I think I can" until she reached the top of the mountain? That's a
perfect example of a secular mantra in action.

By the deadline, Keith had written his essay, revised and edited it, printed it, proofread it one last time, and turned it in. Here is the final draft of his essay:

Secular Mantras
Keith Eldred

"The Little Engine That Could" is a story about a tiny locomotive that 1
hauls a train over a mountain when the big, rugged locomotives refuse:
The Little Engine strains and heaves and chugs, repeating "I think I
can—I think I can—I think I can" until she reaches the top of the mountain. This refrain—"I think I can—I think I can"—is a perfect example
of a secular mantra in action.

A secular mantra (pronounced "man-truh") is any word or group of 2
words that focuses energy when consciously repeated. Most readers of
this essay have already used a secular mantra today without realizing it.
Some additional explanation is necessary, however, in order to understand what distinguishes a secular mantra from any other kind of
phrase.

To be a secular mantra, a phrase must help the speaker focus and 3
use energy. Thus, "I wish I were at home" is not a secular mantra if it's
simply a passing thought. The same sentence becomes a secular mantra
if, walking home on a cold day, a person repeats the sentence each time
she takes a step, willing her feet to move in a steady, accelerated rhythm
and take her quickly someplace warm. By the same token, every curse

word a person mutters in order to bear down on a job is a secular mantra, while every curse word that same person unthinkingly repeats is simple profanity.

It is important to understand, however, that secular mantras only help people use energy: They don't create it. The Little Engine, for instance, obviously had enough power to pull the train up the mountainside—she could have done it without a peep. Still, puffing "I think I can" clearly made her job easier, just as, say, chanting "left-right-left" makes marching in step easier for soldiers. Any such word or phrase that, purposefully uttered, helps a person perform something difficult qualifies as a secular mantra.

Why, though, use the term *secular mantra* to describe these phrases, rather than something else? *Mantra* means "sacred counsel" in Sanskrit and refers to a "mystical formula of invocation or incantation" used in Hinduism (*Webster's*). According to Hindu mythology, the god Manu created the first language by teaching humans the thought-form of every object and substance. VAM, for example, was what Manu taught humans to call "water." People unfortunately forgot or altered most of Manu's thought-forms, however. Followers of Hinduism believe that mantras, groups of these ancient words revealed anew by gods to seers, can summon specific objects or deities if they are properly repeated, silently or aloud. Hindus repeat mantras to gain superhuman powers, cure diseases, and for many other purposes. Sideshow fakirs chant AUM ("I agree" or "I accept") to become immune to pain when lying on a bed of nails.

The mantras that are the topic of this paper are called *secular* because Western culture does not claim that they are divine in origin; instead, they derive from tradition or are invented to fit a situation, as in the case of the Little Engine. In addition, most Westerners assume that they work not by divine power but through the mind-body connection, by helping govern transmissions along the central nervous system.

The Western, scientific explanation for the power of secular mantras runs something like this: Secular mantras give people's brains a sort of dual signal-boosting and signal-damping capacity. The act of repeating them pushes messages, or impulses, with extra force along the nerves or blocks incoming messages that would interfere with the task at hand. People repeating mantras are thus enabled to perform actions more easily or cope with stress that might keep them from functioning optimally. Mantras may even convey both benefits at once: A skydiver might yell "Geronimo!," for example, both to amplify the signals telling his legs to jump and to drown out the signals warning him he's dizzy or afraid.

Anyone can use words in this way to help accomplish a task. A father might count to ten to keep from bellowing when Junior returns the family car with a huge dent. A tennis player who tends to fault may shout "Get serious!" as he serves, to concentrate harder on controlling the ball. An exhausted new mother with her wailing baby can make her chore less painful by muttering, "Someday you'll do chores for me." Chanting "Grease cartridge" always cools this writer's temper because doing so once headed off a major confrontation with a friend while working on a cantankerous old Buick.

Most readers of this essay probably have favorite secular mantras already. Most people—at least those exposed in any way to contemporary popular culture—have at one point uttered one of the following: "Just do it"; "No worries"; "It's all good"; "I'm king of the world!!"; "We are the champions!"; or something similar. Many people have ritual phrases they mutter to get themselves to leave their warm beds on chilly mornings; others blurt out habitual phrases to help them get over impatience when traffic lights don't change or to help them endure a courtesy call to a neighbor they've never really liked. Most people, if they really think about it, will admit that the seeming magic of secular mantras has made their lives much less painful, less frustrating, and perhaps even a little more fun.

While it's not perfect, "Secular Mantras" is a fine essay of definition. Keith provides a clear explanation of the concept, offers numerous examples to illustrate it, and suggests how mantras work and how we use them. Keith's notes, rough draft, samples of revised and edited paragraphs, and final draft demonstrate how such effective writing is accomplished. By reading analytically—both his own writing and that of experienced writers—Keith came to understand the requirements of the strategy of definition. An honest and thorough appraisal of his rough draft led to thoughtful revisions, resulting in a strong and effective piece of writing.

CHAPTER 3

Writers on Writing

LIKE ANY OTHER CRAFT, WRITING INVOLVES LEARNING BASIC SKILLS AS well as more sophisticated techniques that can be refined and then shared among practitioners. Some of the most important lessons a student writer encounters may come from the experiences of other writers: suggestions, advice, cautions, corrections, encouragement. This chapter contains essays in which writers discuss their habits, difficulties, and judgments while they express both the joy of writing and the hard work it can entail. These writers deal with the full range of the writing process—from freeing the imagination in journal entries to correcting punctuation errors for the final draft. The advice they offer is pertinent and sound.

Sometimes, simply getting started can be its own challenge, but the more carefully you pay attention to your reading, surroundings, and reactions to your experiences, the easier it will be to transform your thoughts into written words. The photo opposite was taken in New York City's Zuccotti Park during the protests for Occupy Wall Street, a 2011 movement that criticized systemic economic inequality. It's not clear whether the man is typing an essay, an article, or even a letter, but there can be no doubt that he's using the charged political climate around him to stimulate his thinking. Of course, good writing can spring from any subject. We often have an abundance of ideas before we even realize it. As Fyodor Dostoyevsky wrote, "But how could you live and have no story to tell?"

Discovering the Power of My Words

RUSSELL BAKER

Russell Baker has had a long and distinguished career as a newspaper reporter and columnist. He was born in Morrisonville, Virginia, in 1925 and enlisted in the navy in 1943 after graduating from Johns Hopkins University. In 1947, he secured his first newspaper job, as a reporter for the *Baltimore Sun*, then moved to the *New York Times* in 1954, where he wrote the "Observer" column from 1962 to 1998. His incisive wit, by turns melancholic and sharp-edged, is well represented in such quips as these: "Children rarely want to know who their parents were before they were parents, and when age finally stirs their curiosity, there is no parent left to tell them" and "Is fuel efficiency really what we need most desperately? I say that what we really need is a car that can be shot when it breaks down."

Baker's columns have been collected in numerous books over the years. In 1979, he was awarded the Pulitzer Prize, journalism's highest award, as well as the George Polk Award for Commentary. Baker's memoir, *Growing Up* (1983), also received a Pulitzer. His autobiographical follow-up, *The Good Times*, was published in 1989. His other works include *Russell Baker's Book of American Humor* (1993); *Inventing the Truth: The Art and Craft of Memoir*, with William Zinsser and Jill Ker Conway (revised 1998); and *Looking Back* (2002), a collection of Baker's essays for the *New York Review of Books*. From 1993 to 2004 he hosted the distinguished PBS series *Exxon Mobil Masterpiece Theatre*.

The following selection is from *Growing Up*. As you read Baker's account of how he discovered the power of his own words, note particularly the joy he felt hearing his writing read aloud.

Preparing to Read

What has been your experience with writing teachers in school? Have any of them helped you become a better writer? What kind of writer do you consider yourself now — excellent, above average, good, below average? Why?

The notion of becoming a writer had flickered off and on in my 1 head . . . but it wasn't until my third year in high school that the possibility took hold. Until then I'd been bored by everything associated with English courses. I found English grammar dull and baffling. I hated the assignments to turn out "compositions," and went at them like heavy labor, turning out leaden, lackluster paragraphs that were agonies for teachers to read and for me to write. The classics thrust on me to read seemed as deadening as chloroform.

When our class was assigned to Mr. Fleagle for third-year English I anticipated another grim year in that dreariest of subjects. Mr. Fleagle was notorious among City students for dullness and inability to inspire. He was said to be stuffy, dull, and hopelessly out of date. To me he looked to be sixty or seventy and prim to a fault. He wore primly severe eyeglasses, his wavy hair was primly cut and primly combed. He wore prim vested suits with neckties blocked primly against the collar buttons of his primly starched white shirts. He had a primly pointed jaw, a primly straight nose, and a prim manner of speaking that was so correct, so gentlemanly, that he seemed a comic antique.

I anticipated a listless, unfruitful year with Mr. Fleagle and for a long time was not disappointed. We read *Macbeth*. Mr. Fleagle loved *Macbeth* and wanted us to love it, too, but he lacked the gift of infecting others with his own passion. He tried to convey the murderous ferocity of Lady Macbeth one day by reading aloud the passage that concludes

> . . . I have given suck, and know
> How tender 'tis to love the babe that milks me.
> I would, while it was smiling in my face,
> Have plucked my nipple from his boneless gums . . .

The idea of prim Mr. Fleagle plucking his nipple from boneless gums was too much for the class. We burst into gasps of irrepressible snickering. Mr. Fleagle stopped.

"There is nothing funny, boys, about giving suck to a babe. It is the — the very essence of motherhood, don't you see."

He constantly sprinkled his sentences with "don't you see." It wasn't a question but an exclamation of mild surprise at our ignorance. "Your pronoun needs an antecedent, don't you see," he would say, very primly. "The purpose of the Porter's scene, boys, is to provide comic relief from the horror, don't you see."

Late in the year we tackled the informal essay. "The essay, don't you see, is the . . ." My mind went numb. Of all forms of writing, none seemed so boring as the essay. Naturally we would have to write informal essays. Mr. Fleagle distributed a homework sheet offering us a choice of topics. None was quite so simpleminded as "What I Did on My Summer Vacation," but most seemed to be almost as dull. I took the list home and dawdled until the night before the essay was due. Sprawled on the sofa, I finally faced up to the grim task, took the list out of my notebook, and scanned it. The topic on which my eye stopped was "The Art of Eating Spaghetti."

This title produced an extraordinary sequence of mental images. 7
Surging up from the depths of memory came a vivid recollection of a night
in Belleville when all of us were seated around the supper table—Uncle
Allen, my mother, Uncle Charlie, Doris, Uncle Hal—and Aunt Pat served
spaghetti for supper. Spaghetti was an exotic treat in those days. Neither
Doris nor I had ever eaten spaghetti, and none of the adults had enough
experience to be good at it. All the good humor of Uncle Allen's house
reawoke in my mind as I recalled the laughing arguments we had that night
about the socially respectable method for moving spaghetti from plate to
mouth.

Suddenly I wanted to write about that, about the warmth and good 8
feeling of it, but I wanted to put it down simply for my own joy, not for Mr.
Fleagle. It was a moment I wanted to recapture and hold for myself. I
wanted to relive the pleasure of an evening at New Street. To write it as
I wanted, however, would violate all the rules of formal composition I'd
learned in school, and Mr. Fleagle would surely give it a failing grade.
Never mind. I would write something else for Mr. Fleagle after I had written this thing for myself.

When I finished it the night was half gone and there was no time left 9
to compose a proper, respectable essay for Mr. Fleagle. There was no
choice next morning but to turn in my private reminiscence of Belleville.
Two days passed before Mr. Fleagle returned the graded papers, and he
returned everyone's but mine. I was bracing myself for a command to
report to Mr. Fleagle immediately after school for discipline when I saw
him lift my paper from his desk and rap for the class's attention.

"Now, boys," he said, "I want to read 10
you an essay. This is titled 'The Art of Eating
Spaghetti.'"

And he started to read. My words! He 11
was reading *my words* out loud to the entire
class. What's more, the entire class was listening. Listening attentively. Then somebody laughed, then the entire class was
laughing, and not in contempt and ridicule,
but with open-hearted enjoyment. Even Mr.
Fleagle stopped two or three times to
repress a small prim smile.

> And he started to read.
>
> My words! He was
>
> reading *my words* out
>
> loud to the entire class.
>
> What's more, the entire
>
> class was listening.

I did my best to avoid showing pleasure, but what I was feeling was 12
pure ecstasy at this startling demonstration that my words had the power
to make people laugh. In the eleventh grade, at the eleventh hour as it
were, I had discovered a calling. It was the happiest moment of my entire
school career. When Mr. Fleagle finished he put the final seal on my

happiness by saying, "Now that, boys, is an essay, don't you see. It's — don't you see — it's of the very essence of the essay, don't you see. Congratulations, Mr. Baker."

For the first time, light shone on a possibility. It wasn't a very heartening possibility, to be sure. Writing couldn't lead to a job after high school, and it was hardly honest work, but Mr. Fleagle had opened a door for me. After that I ranked Mr. Fleagle among the finest teachers in the school.   13

Thinking Critically about the Text

In his opening paragraph, Baker states, "I hated the assignments to turn out 'compositions,' and went at them like heavy labor, turning out leaden, lackluster paragraphs that were agonies for teachers to read and for me to write." Have you ever had any assignments like these? How are such assignments different from Mr. Fleagle's assignment to write an informal essay about "The Art of Eating Spaghetti"? How do you think Baker would respond to the following cartoon about writing assignments?

"When writing your essays, I encourage you to think for yourselves while you express what I'd most agree with."

Discussing the Craft of Writing

1. How does Baker describe his teacher, Mr. Fleagle, in the second paragraph? What dominant impression does Baker create of this man? (Glossary: *Dominant Impression*)

2. Mr. Fleagle's homework assignment offered Baker and his classmates "a choice of topics." Is it important to have a "choice" of what you write about? Explain.

3. Once Baker's eye hits the topic of "The Art of Eating Spaghetti" on Mr. Fleagle's list, what happens? What triggers Baker's urge to write about the night his Aunt Pat served spaghetti for supper?

4. Why is Baker reluctant to submit his finished essay?

5. In paragraph 11, Baker states, "And he started to read. My words! He was reading *my words* out loud to the entire class. What's more, the entire class was listening. Listening attentively." Why do you suppose this episode was so memorable to Baker? What surprised him most about it?

6. What insights into the nature of writing does Baker's narrative offer? Explain.

Shitty First Drafts

ANNE LAMOTT

Born in San Francisco in 1954, Anne Lamott graduated from Goucher College in Baltimore and is the author of six novels, including *Rose* (1983), *All the New People* (1989), *Crooked Little Heart* (1997), and *Blue Shoes* (2002). She has also been a food reviewer for *California* magazine, a book reviewer for *Mademoiselle*, and a columnist for *Salon*. Her nonfiction books include *Operating Instructions: A Journal of My Son's First Year* (1993), in which she describes life as a single parent; *Traveling Mercies: Some Thoughts on Faith* (1999), in which she charts her journey toward faith in God; *Plan B: Further Thoughts on Faith* (2005); *Grace (Eventually): Thoughts on Faith* (2007); *Some Assembly Required: A Journal of My Son's First Son* (2012), and *Help, Thanks, Wow: The Three Essential Prayers* (2012). Lamott has taught at the University of California–Davis, as well as at writing conferences around the country. Reflecting on the importance of writing and reading, Lamott has written, "Writing and reading decrease our sense of isolation. They deepen and widen and expand our sense of life: They feed the soul."

In the following selection, taken from Lamott's popular book about writing, *Bird by Bird: Some Instructions on Writing and Life* (1994), she argues for the need to let go and write those "shitty first drafts" that lead to clarity and sometimes brilliance in subsequent drafts.

Preparing to Read

Many professional writers view first drafts as something they have to do before they can begin the real work of writing — revision. How do you view the writing of your first drafts? What patterns, if any, do you see in your writing behavior when working on them? Is the work liberating or restricting? Pleasant or unpleasant?

Now, practically even better news than that of short assignments 1 is the idea of shitty first drafts. All good writers write them. This is how they end up with good second drafts and terrific third drafts. People tend to look at successful writers, writers who are getting their books published and maybe even doing well financially, and think that they sit down at their desks every morning feeling like a million dollars, feeling great about who they are and how much talent they have and what a great story they have to tell; that they take in a few deep breaths, push back their sleeves, roll their necks a few times to get all the cricks out, and dive in, typing fully formed passages as fast as a court reporter. But this is just the fantasy of the uninitiated. I know some very great writers, writers you love who write beautifully and have made a great deal of money, and not *one* of them sits down routinely feeling wildly enthusiastic and confident. Not one of them writes elegant first drafts. All right, one of them does, but we do not like her very much. We do not think that she has a rich inner life or that God likes her or can even stand her. (Although when I mentioned this to my priest friend Tom, he said you can safely assume you've created God in your own image when it turns out that God hates all the same people you do.)

> All good writers write them. This is how they end up with good second drafts and terrific third drafts.

Very few writers really know what they are doing until they've done it. 2 Nor do they go about their business feeling dewy and thrilled. They do not type a few stiff warm-up sentences and then find themselves bounding along like huskies across the snow. One writer I know tells me that he sits down every morning and says to himself nicely, "It's not like you don't have a choice, because you do—you can either type or kill yourself." We all often feel like we are pulling teeth, even those writers whose prose ends up being the most natural and fluid. The right words and sentences just do not come pouring out like ticker tape most of the time. Now, Muriel Spark is said to have felt that she was taking dictation from God every morning—sitting there, one supposes, plugged into a Dictaphone, typing away, humming. But this is a very hostile and aggressive position. One might hope for bad things to rain down on a person like this.

For me and most of the other writers I know, writing is not rapturous. 3 In fact, the only way I can get anything written at all is to write really, really shitty first drafts.

The first draft is the child's draft, where you let it all pour out and then 4 let it romp all over the place, knowing that no one is going to see it and that you can shape it later. You just let this childlike part of you channel whatever voices and visions come through and onto the page. If one of the characters wants to say, "Well, so what, Mr. Poopy Pants?," you let her. No one is going to see it. If the kid wants to get into really sentimental, weepy, emotional territory, you let him. Just get it all down on paper, because there may be something great in those six crazy pages that you would never have gotten to by more rational, grown-up means. There may be something in the very last line of the very last paragraph on page six that you just love, that is so beautiful or wild that you now know what you're supposed to be writing about, more or less, or in what direction you might go—but there was no way to get to this without first getting through the first five and a half pages.

I used to write food reviews for *California* magazine before it folded. 5 (My writing food reviews had nothing to do with the magazine folding, although every single review did cause a couple of canceled subscriptions. Some readers took umbrage at my comparing mounds of vegetable puree with various ex-presidents' brains.) These reviews always took two days to write. First I'd go to a restaurant several times with a few opinionated, articulate friends in tow. I'd sit there writing down everything anyone said that was at all interesting or funny. Then on the following Monday I'd sit down at my desk with my notes, and try to write the review. Even after I'd been doing this for years, panic would set in. I'd try to write a lead, but instead I'd write a couple of dreadful sentences, xx them out, try again, xx everything out, and then feel despair and worry settle on my chest like an X-ray apron. It's over, I'd think, calmly. I'm not going to be able to get the magic to work this time. I'm ruined. I'm through. I'm toast. Maybe, I'd think, I can get my old job back as a clerk-typist. But probably not. I'd get up and study my teeth in the mirror for a while. Then I'd stop, remember to breathe, make a few phone calls, hit the kitchen and chow down. Eventually I'd go back and sit down at my desk, and sigh for the next ten minutes. Finally I would pick up my one-inch picture frame, stare into it as if for the answer, and every time the answer would come: All I had to do was to write a really shitty first draft of, say, the opening paragraph. And no one was going to see it.

So I'd start writing without reining myself in. It was almost just typing, 6 just making my fingers move. And the writing would be *terrible*. I'd write a lead paragraph that was a whole page, even though the entire review could only be three pages long, and then I'd start writing up descriptions of the food, one dish at a time, bird by bird, and the critics would be sitting on my shoulders, commenting like cartoon characters. They'd be pretending to snore, or rolling their eyes at my overwrought descriptions, no matter how hard I tried to tone those descriptions down, no matter how conscious I was of what a friend said to me gently in my early days of restaurant reviewing. "Annie," she said, "it is just a piece of *chicken*. It is just a bit of *cake*."

But because by then I had been writing for so long, I would eventually 7 let myself trust the process—sort of, more or less. I'd write a first draft that was maybe twice as long as it should be, with a self-indulgent and boring beginning, stupefying descriptions of the meal, lots of quotes from my black-humored friends that made them sound more like the Manson girls than food lovers, and no ending to speak of. The whole thing would be so long and incoherent and hideous that for the rest of the day I'd obsess about getting creamed by a car before I could write a decent second draft.

I'd worry that people would read what I'd written and believe that the accident had really been a suicide, that I had panicked because my talent was waning and my mind was shot.

The next day, though, I'd sit down, go through it all with a colored   8
pen, take out everything I possibly could, find a new lead somewhere on the second page, figure out a kicky place to end it, and then write a second draft. It always turned out fine, sometimes even funny and weird and helpful. I'd go over it one more time and mail it in.

Then, a month later, when it was time for another review, the whole   9
process would start again, complete with the fears that people would find my first draft before I could rewrite it.

Almost all good writing begins with terrible first efforts. You need to   10
start somewhere. Start by getting something — anything — down on paper. A friend of mine says that the first draft is the down draft — you just get it down. The second draft is the up draft — you fix it up. You try to say what you have to say more accurately. And the third draft is the dental draft, where you check every tooth, to see if it's loose or cramped or decayed, or even, God help us, healthy.

What I've learned to do when I sit down to work on a shitty first draft   11
is to quiet the voices in my head. First there's the vinegar-lipped Reader Lady, who says primly, "Well, *that's* not very interesting, is it?" And there's the emaciated German male who writes these Orwellian memos detailing your thought crimes. And there are your parents, agonizing over your lack of loyalty and discretion; and there's William Burroughs, dozing off or shooting up because he finds you as bold and articulate as a houseplant; and so on. And there are also the dogs: let's not forget the dogs, the dogs in their pen who will surely hurtle and snarl their way out if you ever *stop* writing, because writing is, for some of us, the latch that keeps the door of the pen closed, keeps those crazy ravenous dogs contained.

Quieting these voices is at least half the battle I fight daily. But this is   12
better than it used to be. It used to be 87 percent. Left to its own devices, my mind spends much of its time having conversations with people who aren't there. I walk along defending myself to people, or exchanging repartee with them, or rationalizing my behavior, or seducing them with gossip, or pretending I'm on their TV talk show or whatever. I speed or run an aging yellow light or don't come to a full stop, and one nanosecond later am explaining to imaginary cops exactly why I had to do what I did, or insisting that I did not in fact do it.

I happened to mention this to a hypnotist I saw many years ago, and   13
he looked at me very nicely. At first I thought he was feeling around on the floor for the silent alarm button, but then he gave me the following exercise, which I still use to this day.

Close your eyes and get quiet for a minute, until the chatter starts up. 14
Then isolate one of the voices and imagine the person speaking as a mouse.
Pick it up by the tail and drop it into a mason jar. Then isolate another
voice, pick it up by the tail, drop it in the jar. And so on. Drop in any high-
maintenance parental units, drop in any contractors, lawyers, colleagues,
children, anyone who is whining in your head. Then put the lid on, and
watch all these mouse people clawing at the glass, jabbering away, trying to
make you feel like shit because you won't do what they want—won't give
them more money, won't be more successful, won't see them more often.
Then imagine that there is a volume-control button on the bottle. Turn it
all the way up for a minute, and listen to the stream of angry, neglected,
guilt-mongering voices. Then turn it all the way down and watch the frantic mice lunge at the glass, trying to get to you. Leave it down, and get back
to your shitty first draft.

A writer friend of mine suggests opening the jar and shooting them all 15
in the head. But I think he's a little angry, and I'm sure nothing like this
would ever occur to you.

Thinking Critically about the Text

What do you think of Lamott's use of the word *shitty* in her title and in the essay
itself? Is it in keeping with her tone? (Glossary: *Tone*) Are you offended by the
word? Explain. What would be lost or gained if she used a different word?

Discussing the Craft of Writing

1. Lamott says that the perception most people have of how writers work is different from the reality. She refers to this in paragraph 1 as the "fantasy of the
   uninitiated." What does she mean?

2. In paragraph 7, Lamott refers to a time when, through experience, she "eventually let [herself] trust the process — sort of, more or less." She is referring to
   the writing process, of course, but why "more or less"? Do you think her wari-
   ness is personal, or is she speaking for all writers? Explain.

3. From what Lamott has to say, is writing a first draft more about content or
   psychology? Do you agree when it comes to your own first drafts? Explain.

4. What is Lamott's thesis? (Glossary: *Thesis*)

5. Lamott adds humor to her argument for "shitty first drafts." Give some examples. Does her humor add to or detract from the points she makes? Explain.

6. In paragraph 5, Lamott narrates her experiences in writing a food review, during which she refers to an almost ritualistic set of behaviors. What is her purpose in telling her readers this story about her difficulties? (Glossary: *Purpose*)
   Is this information helpful? Explain.

Writing for an Audience

LINDA S. FLOWER

Linda S. Flower is a professor of English at Carnegie Mellon University, where she directed the Business Communication program for a number of years and is currently the director of the Center for the Study of Writing and Literacy. She has been a leading researcher on the composing process, and the results of her investigations shaped and informed her influential writing text *Problem-Solving Strategies for Writing in College and Community* (1997). She has also written *The Construction of Negotiated Meaning: A Social Cognitive Theory of Writing* (1994).

In this selection, which is taken from *Problem-Solving Strategies,* Flower's focus is on audience — the people for whom we write. She believes that writers must establish a "common ground" between themselves and their readers that lessens their differences in knowledge, attitudes, and needs. Although we can never be certain who might read what we write, it is nevertheless important for us to have a target audience in mind. Many of the decisions that we make as writers are influenced by that real or imagined reader.

Preparing to Read

Imagine for a moment that you just received a speeding ticket for going sixty-five miles per hour in a thirty-mile-per-hour zone. How would you describe the episode to your best friend? To your parents? To the judge in court? Sketch out the three versions. What differences, if any, do you find in the three versions? Explain.

T he goal of the writer is to create a momentary common ground between the reader and the writer. You want the reader to share your knowledge and your attitude toward that knowledge. Even if the reader eventually disagrees, you want him or her to be able for the moment to *see things as you see them.* A good piece of writing closes the gap between you and the reader.

ANALYZE YOUR AUDIENCE

The first step in closing that gap is to gauge the distance between the two of you. Imagine, for example, that you are a student writing your parents, who have always lived in New York City, about a wilderness survival expedition you want to go on over spring break. Sometimes obvious differences such as age or background will be important, but the critical differences for writers usually fall into three areas: the reader's *knowledge* about the topic; his or her *attitude* toward it; and his or her personal or professional *needs*. Because these differences often exist, good writers do more than simply express their meaning; they pinpoint the critical differences between themselves and their reader and design their writing to reduce those differences. Let us look at these areas in more detail.

Knowledge

This is usually the easiest difference to handle. What does your reader 3
need to know? What are the main ideas you hope to teach? Does your reader have enough background knowledge to really understand you? If not, what would he or she have to learn?

Attitudes

When we say a person has knowledge, we usually refer to his conscious 4
awareness of explicit facts and clearly defined concepts. This kind of knowledge can be easily written down or told to someone else. However, much of what we "know" is not held in this formal, explicit way. Instead it is held as an attitude or image—as a loose cluster of associations. For instance, my image of lakes includes associations many people would have, including fishing, water skiing, stalled outboards, and lots of kids catching night crawlers with flashlights. However, the most salient or powerful parts of my image, which strongly color my whole attitude toward lakes, are thoughts of cloudy skies, long rainy days, and feeling generally cold and damp. By contrast, one of my best friends has a very different cluster of associations: to him a lake means sun, swimming, sailing, and happily sitting on the end of a dock. Needless to say, our differing images cause us to react quite differently to a proposal that we visit a lake. Likewise, one reason people often find it difficult to discuss religion and politics is that terms such as "capitalism" conjure up radically different images.

> A good piece of writing closes the gap between you and the reader.

As you can see, a reader's image of a subject is often the source of 5
attitudes and feelings that are unexpected and, at times, impervious to mere facts. A simple statement that seems quite persuasive to you, such as "Lake Wampago would be a great place to locate the new music camp," could have little impact on your reader if he or she simply doesn't visualize a lake as a "great place." In fact, many people accept uncritically any statement that fits in with their own attitudes—and reject, just as uncritically, anything that does not.

Whether your purpose is to persuade or simply to present your per- 6
spective, it helps to know the image and attitudes that your reader already
holds. The more these differ from your own, the more you will have to do
to make him or her *see* what you mean.

Needs

When writers discover a large gap between their own knowledge and atti- 7
tudes and those of the reader, they usually try to change the reader in some
way. Needs, however, are different. When you analyze a reader's needs, it
is so that you, the writer, can adapt to him. If you ask a friend majoring in
biology how to keep your fish tank from clouding, you don't want to hear
a textbook recitation on the life processes of algae. You expect a friend
to adapt his or her knowledge and tell you exactly how to solve your
problem.

The ability to adapt your knowledge to the needs of the reader is often 8
crucial to your success as a writer. This is especially true in writing done on
a job. For example, as producer of a public affairs program for a television
station, 80 percent of your time may be taken up planning the details of
new shows, contacting guests, and scheduling the taping sessions. But
when you write a program proposal to the station director, your job is to
show how the program will fit into the cost guidelines, the FCC requirements for relevance, and the overall programming plan for the station.
When you write that report, your role in the organization changes from
producer to proposal writer. Why? Because your reader needs that information in order to make a decision. He may be *interested* in your scheduling problems and the specific content of the shows, but he *reads* your
report because of his own needs as station director of the organization. He
has to act.

In college, where the reader is also a teacher, the reader's needs are a 9
little less concrete but just as important. Most papers are assigned as a
way to teach something. So the real purpose of a paper may be for you to
make connections between two historical periods, to discover for yourself
the principle behind a laboratory experiment, or to develop and support
your own interpretation of a novel. A good college paper doesn't just
rehash the facts; it demonstrates what your reader, as a teacher, needs to
know — that you are learning the thinking skills his or her course is trying
to teach.

Effective writers are not simply expressing what they know, like a stu- 10
dent madly filling up an examination bluebook. Instead they are *using*
their knowledge: reorganizing, maybe even rethinking their ideas to meet
the demands of an assignment or the needs of their reader.

Thinking Critically about the Text

What does Flower believe constitutes a "good college paper" (paragraph 9)? Do you agree? Why, or why not?

Discussing the Craft of Writing

1. How, according to Flower, does a competent writer achieve the goal of closing the gap between himself or herself and the reader? How does a writer determine what a reader's "personal or professional needs" (paragraph 2) are?

2. What, for Flower, is the difference between knowledge and attitude? Why is it important for writers to understand this difference?

3. In paragraph 4, Flower discusses the fact that many words have both positive and negative associations. How do you think words come to have associations? (Glossary: *Connotation/Denotation*) Consider, for example, such words as *home*, *anger*, *royalty*, *welfare*, *politician*, and *strawberry shortcake*.

4. Flower wrote this selection for college students. How well did she assess your needs as a member of this audience? Does Flower's use of language and examples show a sensitivity to her audience? Provide specific examples to support your view.

5. When using technical language in a paper on a subject you are familiar with, why is it important for you to know your audience? Explain. How could your classmates, friends, or parents help you?

Simplicity

WILLIAM ZINSSER

Born in New York City in 1922, William Zinsser was educated at Princeton University. After serving in the army
in World War II, he worked at the *New York Herald Tribune* as an editor, writer, and critic. During the 1970s he
taught a popular course in nonfiction at Yale University,
and from 1979 to 1987 he was general editor of the
Book-of-the-Month Club. Zinsser has written more than
a dozen books, including *The City Dwellers* (1962), *Pop
Goes America* (1966), *Spring Training* (1989), and six
widely used books on writing: *On Writing Well, 30th
Anniversary Edition: The Classic Guide to Writing Non-
fiction* (2006); *Writing with a Word Processor* (1983); *Writing to Learn* (1988); *Writing
About Your Life: A Journey into the Past* (2005); *Writing Places: The Life Journey of
a Writer and Teacher* (2010); and *The Writer Who Stayed* (2012). Currently, he
teaches journalism at Columbia University, and his freelance writing regularly appears in leading magazines.

The following selection is taken from *On Writing Well.* This book grew out of
Zinsser's many years of experience as a professional writer and teacher. In this essay,
Zinsser exposes what he believes is the writer's number one problem — "clutter." He
sees Americans "strangling in unnecessary words, circular constructions, pompous
frills, and meaningless jargon." His solution is simple: Writers must know what they
want to say and must be thinking clearly as they start to compose. Then self-disci-
pline and hard work are necessary to achieve clear, simple prose. No matter what
your experience as a writer has been, you will find Zinsser's observations sound and
his advice practical.

Preparing to Read

Some people view writing as "thinking on paper." They believe that by seeing something written on a page they are better able to "see what they think." Write about the
relationship, for you, between writing and thinking. Are you one of those people who
likes to see ideas on paper while trying to work things out? Or do you like to think
through ideas before writing about them?

C lutter is the disease of American writing. We are a society   1
strangling in unnecessary words, circular constructions,
pompous frills, and meaningless jargon.

Who can understand the clotted language of everyday   2
American commerce: the memo, the corporation report, the business letter, the notice from the bank explaining its latest "simplified" statement?

What member of an insurance or medical plan can decipher the brochure explaining his costs and benefits? What father or mother can put together a child's toy from the instructions on the box? Our national tendency is to inflate and thereby sound important. The airline pilot who announces that he is presently anticipating experiencing considerable precipitation wouldn't think of saying it may rain. The sentence is too simple—there must be something wrong with it.

But the secret of good writing is to strip every sentence to its cleanest 3 components. Every word that serves no function, every long word that could be a short word, every adverb that carries the same meaning that's already in the verb, every passive construction that leaves the reader unsure of who is doing what—these are the thousand and one adulterants that weaken the strength of a sentence. And they usually occur in proportion to education and rank.

We are a society strangling in unnecessary words, circular constructions, pompous frills, and meaningless jargon.

During the 1960s the president of 4 my university wrote a letter to mollify the alumni after a spell of campus unrest. "You are probably aware," he began, "that we have been experiencing very considerable potentially explosive expressions of dissatisfaction on issues only partially related." He meant that the students had been hassling them about different things. I was far more upset by the president's English than by the students' potentially explosive expressions of dissatisfaction. I would have preferred the presidential approach taken by Franklin D. Roosevelt when he tried to convert into English his own government's memos, such as this blackout order of 1942:

> Such preparations shall be made as will completely obscure all Federal buildings and non-Federal buildings occupied by the Federal government during an air raid for any period of time from visibility by reason of internal or external illumination.

"Tell them," Roosevelt said, "that in buildings where they have to keep 5 the work going to put something across the windows."

Simplify, simplify. Thoreau said it, as we are so often reminded, and no 6 American writer more consistently practiced what he preached. Open *Walden* to any page and you will find a man saying in a plain and orderly way what is on his mind:

> I went to the woods because I wished to live deliberately, to front only the essential facts of life, and see if I could not learn what it had to teach, and not, when I came to die, discover that I had not lived.

How can the rest of us achieve such enviable freedom from clutter? 7
The answer is to clear our heads of clutter. Clear thinking becomes clear writing; one can't exist without the other. It's impossible for a muddy thinker to write good English. He may get away with it for a paragraph or two, but soon the reader will be lost, and there's no sin so grave, for the reader will not easily be lured back.

Who is this elusive creature, the reader? The reader is someone with 8
an attention span of about 30 seconds—a person assailed by many forces competing for attention. At one time these forces were relatively few: newspapers, magazines, radio, spouse, children, pets. Today they also include a galaxy of electronic devices for receiving entertainment and information—television, VCRs, DVDs, CDs, video games, the Internet, e-mail, cell phones, BlackBerries, iPods—as well as a fitness program, a pool, a lawn, and that most potent of competitors, sleep. The man or woman snoozing in a chair with a magazine or a book is a person who was being given too much unnecessary trouble by the writer.

It won't do to say that the reader is too dumb or too lazy to keep pace 9
with the train of thought. If the reader is lost, it's usually because the writer hasn't been careful enough. The carelessness can take any number of forms. Perhaps a sentence is so excessively cluttered that the reader, hacking through the verbiage, simply doesn't know what it means. Perhaps a sentence has been so shoddily constructed that the reader could read it in several ways. Perhaps the writer has switched pronouns in mid-sentence, or has switched tenses, so the reader loses track of who is talking or when the action took place. Perhaps Sentence B is not a logical sequel to Sentence A; the writer, in whose head the connection is clear, hasn't bothered to provide the missing link. Perhaps the writer has used a word incorrectly by not taking the trouble to look it up.

Faced with such obstacles, readers are at first tenacious. They blame 10
themselves—they obviously missed something, and they go back over the mystifying sentence, or over the whole paragraph, piecing it out like an ancient rune, making guesses and moving on. But they won't do that for long. The writer is making them work too hard, and they will look for one who is better at the craft.

Writers must therefore constantly ask: What am I trying to say? 11
Surprisingly often they don't know. Then they must look at what they have written and ask: Have I said it? Is it clear to someone encountering the subject for the first time? If it's not, some fuzz has worked its way into the machinery. The clear writer is someone clearheaded enough to see this stuff for what it is: fuzz.

I don't mean that some people are born clearheaded and are therefore 12
natural writers, whereas others are naturally fuzzy and will never write

well. Thinking clearly is a conscious act that writers must force on themselves, as if they were working on any other project that requires logic: making a shopping list or doing an algebra problem. Good writing doesn't come naturally, though most people seem to think it does. Professional writers are constantly bearded by people who say they'd like to "try a little writing sometime" — meaning when they retire from their real profession, like insurance or real estate, which is hard. Or they say, "I could write a book about that." I doubt it.

Writing is hard work. A clear sentence is no accident. Very few sentences come out right the first time, or even the third time. Remember this in moments of despair. If you find that writing is hard, it's because it *is* hard. 13

Thinking Critically about the Text

What assumptions does Zinsser make about readers? According to Zinsser, what responsibilities do writers have to readers? How do these responsibilities manifest themselves in Zinsser's writing?

Discussing the Craft of Writing

1. What exactly is clutter? When do words qualify as clutter, and when do they not?

2. In paragraph 2, Zinsser states that "Our national tendency is to inflate and thereby sound important." What do you think he means by *inflate*? Provide several examples to illustrate how people use language to inflate.

3. One would hope that education would help in the battle against clutter, but, as Zinsser notes, wordiness "usually occur[s] in proportion to education and rank" (paragraph 3). Do your own experiences or observations support Zinsser's claim? Explain.

4. Zinsser believes that writers need to ask themselves two questions — "What am I trying to say?" and "Have I said it?" — constantly as they write. How would these questions help you eliminate clutter from your own writing? Give some examples from one of your essays.

5. In order "to strip every sentence to its cleanest components," we need to be sensitive to the words we use and know how they function within our sentences. For each of the "adulterants that weaken the strength of a sentence," which Zinsser identifies in paragraph 3, provide an example from your own writing.

6. Zinsser knows that sentence variety is an important feature of good writing. Locate several examples of the short sentences (seven or fewer words) he uses in this essay, and explain how each relates in length, meaning, and impact to the sentences around it.

7. Having read Zinsser's article, how do you react to the following cartoon? Do you find it humorous? Why, or why not? How do you think Zinsser would react?

© Mark Parisi. Permission required for use.

On Voice

SUSAN ORLEAN

Susan Orlean writes the following about herself: "I'm an author, a staff writer for the *New Yorker*, a dog owner, a gardener, a parent, a frequent lecturer/speaker, an occasional teacher, a very occasional guest editor, a once-in-a-blue-moon movie inspiration, and doodler." She was born in Cleveland, Ohio, in 1955 and graduated from the University of Michigan before working on several newspapers and writing stories for the *New York Times*, *Esquire*, *Vogue*, *Spy*, and *Rolling Stone*. Her books include *The Orchid Thief* (made into the film *Adaptation*) (1998), *The Bullfighter Checks Her Makeup: My Encounters with Extraordinary People* (2001), and *Rin Tin Tin: The Life and the Legend* (2011). She has also edited such collections as *My Kind of Place: Travel Stories from a Woman Who's Been Everywhere* (2004) and *Best American Travel Writing 2007* (2007). In 2004, Orlean was chosen as a Neiman Fellow at Harvard University.

In "On Voice," taken from *Telling True Stories* (2007), an anthology of writings adapted from authors' presentations at the Neiman Conference on Narrative Nonfiction, Orleans tells us what voice is and explains how voice is created in writing.

Preparing to Read

Whenever you read aloud what you have written, you are better able to hear your writer's voice. If you have had that experience, what did you notice about your particular voice? Was it humorous, dark, witty, curt, drawn out, sarcastic, faint, bold, or did it reveal some other quality? What in your writing style do you think accounts for the impression it creates?

D eveloping a writer's voice is almost a process of unlearning, one analogous to children's painting. Young children often create fabulous paintings, only to be told after they start school that real houses don't look that way. At that point, most people lose their ability to be visually creative. Truly great painting retains some element of a child's emotional authenticity. Great writing does, too.

Self-analysis is crucial to developing a strong voice. *Who am I? Why do I write?* Your identity and your self-understanding become subliminal parts of your writer's voice—especially in long-form narrative writing. Imagine yourself telling friends about a story that excites you. Your friends follow the story even though it's not linear but circles back as you tell it. The way you tell a story over dinner is true to who you are, whether that is deeply analytical or extremely witty. At such moments you aren't self-conscious, and you aren't thinking about your editor.

You can't invent a voice. And you can't imitate someone else's voice, 3 though trying to can be a good exercise. It can lead you to begin to understand the *mechanisms* that convey the voice. Read your stories out loud so you can *hear* how you tell stories. As you read, ask yourself: *Does it sound real? Would I have said it that way?* If the answer to either question is no, you have done something wrong. I find that sometimes when I give readings of my published work, I skip parts that seem boring to me. Then I wonder, would it have been better to edit that out in the first place? When you read aloud, extraneous material falls away. Voice is — as the word itself tells us — the way a writer *talks*. You are *speaking* to your readers. Sometimes we think we have to come up with something clever, but cleverness for its own sake is rarely powerful.

> The way you tell a story over dinner is true to who you are, whether that is deeply analytical or extremely witty.

Pace, the sense of timing in a piece, is linked to voice. Pace determines 4 whether attempts at humor will succeed. Change your story's pace to change the mood. Long sentences can slow down the reader. Short sentences race the reader through a scene. As you read your piece aloud, you hear how your readers will make their way through it. Then you can control that movement.

Word choice is another element of voice. When you make an analogy, 5 it's not just to give the reader an image but to advance a larger idea or theme. Once I had a fight with an editor because I wanted to describe a basketball player's feet as "banana-shaped." My editor argued that feet can't really be banana-shaped. And, further, thinking about bananas takes the reader away from the subject: a person playing basketball. "You're giving the reader a ticket to the tropics," he said. I spent hours trying to find the right image to replace *banana*. Suddenly, it came to me: *pontoon*. His feet were pontoon-shaped; he floated over the basketball court. Analogies like these don't usually come as I am reporting. I have to sit at my desk and really work at finding the strongest image possible.

Another aspect of voice is taking on your characters' voices. Sometimes, 6 immersed in my reporting, I find myself thinking in the same rhythm as someone I'm writing about. This is part of my temperament; I tend to become caught up in other worlds. As long as I don't slide into mimicry, it can help a piece of writing. You don't want to hijack someone's voice but draw inspiration from it. It is often a sign that you have submerged yourself deeply in a story, inhabiting it. I wrote half of "The American Man at Age

Ten" in the voice of a boy. I stepped in and out of that persona throughout the story.

Soon after I started writing, I realized that I was crafty and could come   1
up with gimmicks to make my work look jazzy. As I matured as a writer and gained more confidence, I began losing what I had mistakenly understood to be my style. I returned to something simpler. One watershed moment was the realization that my writing voice had circled back to something natural, intuitive, and instinctive.

Thinking Critically about the Text

In paragraph 1, Orlean writes, "Developing a writer's voice is almost a process of unlearning, one analogous to children's painting." How does she explain the analogy? Later in paragraph 5, she writes, "When you make an analogy, it's not just to give the reader an image but to advance a larger idea or theme." How successful, in your opinion, has Orlean been in following her own advice about analogies?

Discussing the Craft of Writing

1. What, in your own words, is voice? Why is it important?

2. Why does Orlean say "self-analysis" is so important in developing one's voice? Can you illustrate this point from your own experience?

3. Why does reading aloud to a reader or an audience seem to reveal voice? Why do you think that reading to oneself does not accomplish the same goal?

4. Why is pacing so important in writing? Illustrate some instances in your own writing where pace makes a difference. How does a writer control pace?

5. What does Orlean's editor mean in paragraph 5 when he says to her, "'You're giving the reader a ticket to the tropics'"?

6. Is voice a different word for style? Explain.

7. Why do you think Orlean finds it important to define herself as she does in the headnote to this selection?

Reading to Write

STEPHEN KING

Born in 1947, Stephen King is a 1970 graduate of the University of Maine. He worked as a janitor in a knitting mill, a laundry worker, and a high school English teacher before he struck it big with his writing. Today, many people consider King's name synonymous with the macabre; he is, beyond dispute, the most successful writer of horror fiction today. He has written dozens of novels and hundreds of short stories, novellas, and screenplays, among other works. His books have sold well over 300 million copies worldwide, and many of his novels have been made into popular motion pictures, including *Stand by Me*, *Misery*, *The Green Mile*, and *Dreamcatcher*. His fiction, starting with *Carrie* in 1974, includes *Salem's Lot* (1975), *The Shining* (1977), *The Dead Zone* (1979), *Christine* (1983), *Pet Sematary* (1983), *The Dark Half* (1989), *The Girl Who Loved Tom Gordon* (1999), *From a Buick 8* (2002), *Everything's Eventual: Five Dark Tales* (2002), *The Colorado Kid* (2005), *Cell* (2006), *Lisey's Story* (2006), *Duma Key* (2008), *Under the Dome* (2009), *11/22/63: A Novel* (2012), and *The Wind Through the Keyhole: A Dark Tower Novel* (2012). Other works include *Danse Macabre* (1980), a nonfiction look at horror in the media, and *On Writing: A Memoir of the Craft* (2000).

In the following selection taken from *On Writing*, King discusses the importance of reading in learning to write. Reading, in his words, "offers you a constantly growing knowledge of what has been done and what hasn't, what is trite and what is fresh, what works and what just lies there dying (or dead) on the page."

Preparing to Read

In your opinion, are reading and writing connected in some way? If the two activities are related, what is the nature of that relationship? Do you have to be a reader to be a good writer, or is writing an activity that can be learned quite apart from reading?

I f you want to be a writer, you must do two things above all others: Read 1 a lot and write a lot. There's no way around these two things that I'm aware of, no shortcut.

I'm a slow reader, but I usually get through seventy or eighty books 2 a year, mostly fiction. I don't read in order to study the craft; I read because I like to read. It's what I do at night, kicked back in my blue chair. Similarly, I don't read fiction to study the art of fiction, but simply because I like stories. Yet there is a learning process going on. Every book you pick up has its own lesson or lessons, and quite often the bad books have more to teach than the good ones.

When I was in the eighth grade, I happened upon a paperback novel   3
by Murray Leinster, a science fiction pulp writer who did most of his work
during the forties and fifties, when magazines like *Amazing Stories* paid a
penny a word. I had read other books by Mr. Leinster, enough to know
that the quality of his writing was uneven. This particular tale, which was
about mining in the asteroid belt, was one of his less successful efforts.

Only that's too kind. It was terrible, actually, a story populated by paper-thin characters and driven by outlandish plot
developments. Worst of all (or so it seemed
to me at the time), Leinster had fallen in
love with the word *zestful*. Characters
watched the approach of ore-bearing as-
teroids with *zestful smiles*. Characters sat
down to supper aboard their mining ship
with *zestful anticipation*. Near the end of the book, the hero swept the
large-breasted, blonde heroine into a *zestful embrace*. For me, it was the
literary equivalent of a smallpox vaccination: I have never, so far as I know,
used the word *zestful* in a novel or a story. God willing, I never will.

> If you want to be a writer, you must do two things above all others: Read a lot and write a lot.

Asteroid Miners (which wasn't the title, but that's close enough) was an   4
important book in my life as a reader. Almost everyone can remember losing his or her virginity, and most writers can remember the first book he/
she put down thinking: *I can do better than this, Hell, I am doing better
than this!* What could be more encouraging to the struggling writer than to
realize his/her work is unquestionably better than that of someone who
actually got paid for his/her stuff?

One learns most clearly what not to do by reading bad prose—one   5
novel like *Asteroid Miners* (or *Valley of the Dolls, Flowers in the Attic*, and
The Bridges of Madison County, to name just a few) is worth a semester at
a good writing school, even with the superstar guest lecturers thrown in.

Good writing, on the other hand, teaches the learning writer about   6
style, graceful narration, plot development, the creation of believable characters, and truth-telling. A novel like *The Grapes of Wrath* may fill a new
writer with feelings of despair and good old-fashioned jealousy—"I'll
never be able to write anything that good, not if I live to be a thousand"—but such feelings can also serve as a spur, goading the writer to
work harder and aim higher. Being swept away by a combination of great
story and great writing—of being flattened, in fact—is part of every writer's necessary formation. You cannot hope to sweep someone else away by
the force of your writing until it has been done to you.

So we read to experience the mediocre and the outright rotten; such   7
experience helps us to recognize those things when they begin to creep

into our own work, and to steer clear of them. We also read in order to measure ourselves against the good and the great, to get a sense of all that can be done. And we read in order to experience different styles.

You may find yourself adopting a style you find particularly exciting, 8 and there's nothing wrong with that. When I read Ray Bradbury as a kid, I wrote like Ray Bradbury—everything green and wondrous and seen through a lens smeared with the grease of nostalgia. When I read James M. Cain, everything I wrote came out clipped and stripped and hard-boiled. When I read Lovecraft, my prose became luxurious and Byzantine. I wrote stories in my teenage years where all these styles merged, creating a kind of hilarious stew. This sort of stylistic blending is a necessary part of developing one's own style, but it doesn't occur in a vacuum. You have to read widely, constantly refining (and redefining) your own work as you do so. It's hard for me to believe that people who read very little (or not at all in some cases) should presume to write and expect people to like what they have written, but I know it's true. If I had a nickel for every person who ever told me he/she wanted to become a writer but "didn't have time to read," I could buy myself a pretty good steak dinner. Can I be blunt on this subject? If you don't have time to read, you don't have the time (or the tools) to write. Simple as that.

Reading is the creative center of a writer's life. I take a book with me 9 everywhere I go, and find there are all sorts of opportunities to dip in. The trick is to teach yourself to read in small sips as well as in long swallows. Waiting rooms were made for books—of course! But so are theater lobbies before the show, long and boring checkout lines, and everyone's favorite, the john. You can even read while you're driving, thanks to the audiobook revolution. Of the books I read each year, anywhere from six to a dozen are on tape. As for all the wonderful radio you will be missing, come on — how many times can you listen to Deep Purple sing "Highway Star"?

Reading at meals is considered rude in polite society, but if you expect 10 to succeed as a writer, rudeness should be the second-to-least of your concerns. The least of all should be polite society and what it expects. If you intend to write as truthfully as you can, your days as a member of polite society are numbered, anyway.

Where else can you read? There's always the treadmill, or whatever 11 you use down at the local health club to get aerobic. I try to spend an hour doing that every day, and I think I'd go mad without a good novel to keep me company. Most exercise facilities (at home as well as outside it) are now equipped with TVs, but TV—while working out or anywhere else—really is about the last thing an aspiring writer needs. If you feel you must have the news analyst blowhards on CNN while you exercise, or the stock market blowhards on MSNBC, or the sports blowhards on ESPN, it's time for you to question how serious you really are about becoming a writer. You must be prepared to do some serious turning inward toward the life of the imagination, and that means, I'm afraid, that Geraldo, Keith Olbermann, and Jay Leno must go. Reading takes time, and the glass teat takes too much of it.

Once weaned from the ephemeral craving for TV, most people will   12
find they enjoy the time they spend reading. I'd like to suggest that turning off that endlessly quacking box is apt to improve the quality of your life as well as the quality of your writing. And how much of a sacrifice are we talking about here? How many *Frasier* and *ER* reruns does it take to make one American life complete? How many Richard Simmons infomercials? How many whiteboy/fatboy Beltway insiders on CNN? Oh man, don't get me started. Jerry-Springer-Dr.-Dre-Judge-Judy-Jerry-Falwell-Donny-and-Marie, I rest my case.

When my son Owen was seven or so, he fell in love with Bruce   13
Springsteen's E Street Band, particularly with Clarence Clemons, the band's burly sax player. Owen decided he wanted to learn to play like Clarence. My wife and I were amused and delighted by this ambition. We were also hopeful, as any parent would be, that our kid would turn out to be talented, perhaps even some sort of prodigy. We got Owen a tenor saxophone for Christmas and lessons with Gordon Bowie, one of the local music men. Then we crossed our fingers and hoped for the best.

Seven months later I suggested to my wife that it was time to discon-   14
tinue the sax lessons, if Owen concurred. Owen did, and with palpable relief—he hadn't wanted to say it himself, especially not after asking for the sax in the first place, but seven months had been long enough for him to realize that, while he might love Clarence Clemons's big sound, the saxophone was simply not for him—God had not given him that particular talent.

I knew, not because Owen stopped practicing, but because he was   15
practicing only during the periods Mr. Bowie had set for him: half an hour after school four days a week, plus an hour on the weekends. Owen mastered the scales and the notes—nothing wrong with his memory, his lungs, or his eye-hand coordination—but we never heard him taking off, surprising himself with something new, blissing himself out. And as soon as his practice time was over, it was back into the case with the horn, and there it stayed until the next lesson or practice time. What this suggested to me was that when it came to the sax and my son, there was never going to be any real playtime; it was all going to be rehearsal. That's no good. If there's no joy in it, it's just no good. It's best to go on to some other area, where the deposits of talent may be richer and the fun quotient higher.

Talent renders the whole idea of rehearsal meaningless; when you find   16
something at which you are talented, you do it (whatever *it* is) until your

fingers bleed or your eyes are ready to fall out of your head. Even when no one is listening (or reading, or watching), every outing is a bravura performance, because you as the creator are happy. Perhaps even ecstatic. That goes for reading and writing as well as for playing a musical instrument, hitting a baseball, or running the four-forty. The sort of strenuous reading and writing program I advocate—four to six hours a day, every day—will not seem strenuous if you really enjoy doing these things and have an aptitude for them; in fact, you may be following such a program already. If you feel you need permission to do all the reading and writing your little heart desires, however, consider it hereby granted by yours truly.

The real importance of reading is that it creates an ease and intimacy   17 with the process of writing; one comes to the country of the writer with one's papers and identification pretty much in order. Constant reading will pull you into a place (a mind-set, if you like the phrase) where you can write eagerly and without self-consciousness. It also offers you a constantly growing knowledge of what has been done and what hasn't, what is trite and what is fresh, what works and what just lies there dying (or dead) on the page. The more you read, the less apt you are to make a fool of yourself with your pen or word processor.

Thinking Critically about the Text

What does King mean when he writes that reading a bad novel is "worth a semester at a good writing school, even with the superstar guest lecturers thrown in" (paragraph 5)? Do you take his observation seriously? In your own words, what can one learn about writing by reading a bad novel? What can one learn by reading a good novel?

Discussing the Craft of Writing

1. In paragraph 3, King berates the author Murray Leinster for his repeated use of the word *zestful*. He says he himself has, as far as he knows, never used the word. Why do you suppose he doesn't like the word? Have you ever used it in your own writing? Explain. (Glossary: *Diction*)

2. In paragraph 7, King says that "we read in order to experience different styles." What examples does he use to support this statement? If you have learned from someone else's style, what exactly was it that you learned? (Glossary: *Evidence*)

3. Authors, especially those as famous as King, are very much sought after as guests on television shows, at writing conferences, and at celebrity and charity events. Why does King believe that it is incompatible for one to be both a member of polite society and an author? Do you agree with him? Why, or why not?

4. King does not like TV. What does he find wrong with it, especially for writers?

5. Admittedly, not everyone who wants to write well also aspires to be a great novelist. What value, if any, does King's advice about reading and writing have for you as a college student? Explain.

6. How do you react to the following cartoon? What is a Klout score? Do you find the cartoon humorous? Why, or why not? Do you think Stephen King would find it humorous?

"I'm sorry, Paige, but grades are based on the quality
of the writing, not on your Klout score."

---

 e-Pages

Writing Process Animation

JONATHAN BEER

Watch writing advice come alive on the Web. Go to bedfordstmartins.com/
subjectandstrategy for a narrated animation and study questions about writing,
revising, and improving your writing process.

LIFE IN THE WOODS

I WENT TO THE WOODS BECAUSE I WISHED TO LIVE DELIBERATELY.

I BROUGHT ALONG A FEW THINGS IN CASE I GOT BORED.

THERE I EXPERIENCED THE PROFOUND JOY OF SOLITUDE...

AND MADE SURE EVERYONE ELSE KNEW ABOUT IT.

#majestic

I MARCHED TO THE RHYTHMS OF NATURE, THE SOUNDS OF THE FOREST...

AND THE BEAT OF MY KILLER WILDERNESS PLAYLIST.

THE WOODS WERE FILLED WITH MANY WONDROUS CREATURES.

I TURNED THEM INTO MEMES.

CONDESCENDING OWL
IS WISER THAN YOU

DEVIL SQUIRREL
WANTS YOUR SOUL

CONFUSED GOOSE
FLIES NORTH FOR WINTER

ALONE IN THE DARKNESS, I FOUND TRUE ILLUMINATION...

BY THE LIGHT OF MY EVER-GLOWING SCREENS.

CHAPTER 4

Narration

WHAT IS NARRATION?

Whenever you recount an event or tell a story or an anecdote to illustrate an idea, you are using narration. In its broadest sense, narration includes any account of an event, or a series of events, presented in a logical sequence. As the tremendous popularity in our culture of narrative forms like action movies, television dramas, celebrity gossip, graphic novels, and even the Facebook status update attests, nearly everyone loves a good story. Given a decent character and a good beginning, we all want to find out what happens next.

For one example of narration in popular culture, take a look at Grant Snider's "Life in the Woods" reproduced on the opposite page. Snider constructs his narrative with a series of pictures that provide snapshots of the narrator's experience in the woods. As we "read" the images and the accompanying text, we mentally fill in the gaps between panels to form a continuous progression of events, a story of the narrator's infatuation with the great outdoors. Starting with a purpose that echoes Thoreau's purpose in going to the woods in *Walden*, this totally contemporary narrator breaks with tradition and brings "along a few things in case [he gets] bored." Ironically, these electronic devices trivialize the narrator's appreciation for the solitude, the rhythms of nature, and the wondrous creatures he experienced.

NARRATION IN WRITTEN TEXTS

In the area of written texts, most of us associate narration with novels and short fiction. Narration is also useful and effective, however, in nonfiction writing, such as biography, autobiography, history, and news reporting. A good narrative essay provides a meaningful account of some significant event—anything from an account of recent U.S. involvement in the Middle East to a personal experience that gave you new insight about yourself or others. A narrative may present a straightforward message or moral, or it may make a more subtle point about us and the world we live in.

Consider, for example, the following narrative by E. J. Kahn Jr. about the invention of Coca-Cola, as both a medicine and a soft drink, from his book *The Big Drink: The Story of Coca-Cola.*

Establishes context for narrative Uses third-person point of view Organizes narrative chronologically, using time markers Focuses on the discovery that led to Coca-Cola's popularity as a soft drink	In 1886—a year in which, as contemporary Coca-Cola officials like to point out, Conan Doyle unveiled Sherlock Holmes and France unveiled the Statue of Liberty—[John Styth] Pemberton unveiled a syrup that he called Coca-Cola. He had taken out the wine and added a pinch of caffeine, and, when the end product tasted awful, had thrown in some extract of cola (or kola) nut and a few other oils, blending the mixture in a three-legged iron pot in his back yard and swishing it around with an oar. He distributed it to soda fountains in used beer bottles, and [his bookkeeper Frank M.] Robinson, with his flowing bookkeeper's script, presently devised a label on which "Coca-Cola" was written in the fashion that is still employed. Pemberton looked upon his concoction less as a refreshment than as a headache cure, especially for people whose throbbing temples could be traced to overindulgence. On a morning late in 1886, one such victim of the night before dragged himself into an Atlanta drugstore and asked for a dollop of Coca-Cola. Druggists customarily stirred a teaspoonful of syrup into a glass of water, but in this instance the factotum on duty was too lazy to walk to the fresh-water tap, a couple of feet off. Instead, he mixed the syrup with some charged water, which was closer at hand. The suffering customer perked up almost at once, and word quickly spread that the best Coca-Cola was a fizzy one.

A good narrative essay, like the paragraph above, has four essential features. The first is *context*: The writer makes clear when the action happened, where it happened, and to whom. The second is *point of view*: The writer establishes and maintains a consistent relationship to the action, either as a participant or as a reporter looking on. The third is *selection of detail*: The writer carefully chooses what to include, focusing on those actions and details that are most important to the story while playing down or even eliminating others. The fourth is *organization*: The writer arranges the events of the narrative in an appropriate sequence, often a strict chronology with a clear beginning, middle, and end.

As you read the selections in this chapter, watch for these features and for how each writer uses them to tell his or her story. Think about how each writer's choices affect the way you react to the selections.

USING NARRATION AS A WRITING STRATEGY

The most basic and most important purpose of narration is to share a meaningful experience with readers. Another important purpose of narration is to report and instruct—to give the facts, to tell what happened. Journalists and historians, in reporting events of the near and more distant past, provide us with information that we can use to form opinions about a current issue or to better understand the world around us. A biographer gives us another person's life as a document of an individual's past but also, perhaps, as a portrait of more general human potential. And naturalists recount the drama of encounters between predators and prey in the wild. We expect writers to make these narratives as objective as possible and to distinguish between facts and opinions.

Narration is often used in combination with one or more of the other rhetorical strategies. In an essay that is written primarily to explain a process—reading a book, for example—a writer might find it useful to tell a brief story or anecdote demonstrating an instance when the process worked especially well (Mortimer Adler, "How to Mark a Book," Chapter 7). In the same way, a writer attempting to define the term *poverty* might tell several stories to illustrate clearly the many facets of poverty (Jo Goodwin Parker, "What Is Poverty?," Chapter 10). Finally, a writer could use narrative examples to persuade—for example, to argue for the positive contributions of Asian sweatshops (Nicholas D. Kristof and Sheryl WuDunn, "Two Cheers for Sweatshops," Chapter 12) or to demonstrate for readers the power and clarity of monosyllabic words (Richard Lederer, "The Case for Short Words," Chapter 12).

USING NARRATION ACROSS THE DISCIPLINES

When writing essays in the academic disciplines, you will have many opportunities to use the strategy of narration to both organize and strengthen the presentation of your ideas. To determine whether or not narration is the right strategy for you in a particular paper, use the guidelines described in Chapter 2 (Determining a Strategy for Developing Your Essay, pages 32–33). Consider the following examples, which illustrate how these guidelines work for typical college papers.

American History

1. **MAIN IDEA:** Although Abraham Lincoln was not the chief speaker at Gettysburg on November 19, 1863, the few remarks he made that day shaped the thinking of our nation as perhaps few other speeches have.

2. **QUESTION:** What happened at Gettysburg on November 19, 1863, that made Abraham Lincoln's speech so memorable and influential?

3. **STRATEGY:** Narration. The thrust of the main idea as well as the direction words *what happened* say "tell me the story," and what better way to tell what happened than to narrate the day's events?

4. **SUPPORTING STRATEGY:** Cause and Effect Analysis. The story and how it is narrated can be used to explain the impact of this speech on our nation's thinking.

Anthropology

1. **MAIN IDEA:** Food-gathering and religious activities account for a large portion of the daily lives of native peoples in rural Thailand.

2. **QUESTION:** What happens during a typical day or week in rural Thailand?

3. **STRATEGY:** Narration. The direction words in both the statement of the main idea (*account* and *daily*) and the question (*what happens*) cry out for a narration of what happens during any given day.

4. **SUPPORTING STRATEGY:** Illustration. The paper might benefit from specific examples of the various chores related to food gathering as well as examples of typical religious activities.

Life Science

1. **MAIN IDEA:** British bacteriologist Sir Alexander Fleming discovered penicillin quite by accident in 1928, and that discovery changed the world.

2. **QUESTION:** How did Fleming happen to discover penicillin, and why was this discovery so important?

3. **STRATEGY:** Narration. The direction words *how* and *did happen* call for the story of Fleming's accidental discovery of penicillin.

4. **SUPPORTING STRATEGY:** Argument. The claims that Fleming's discovery was *important* and *changed the world* suggest that the story needs to be both compelling and persuasive.

SAMPLE STUDENT ESSAY USING NARRATION AS A WRITING STRATEGY

After reading several personal narratives — Elisa Mala's "Crime Family" and Malcolm X's "Coming to an Awareness of Language" in particular — Laura LaPierre decided to write a narrative of her own. Only weeks prior to writing this essay Laura had received some very bad news. It was the experience of living with this news that she decided to write about. The writing was painful, and not everyone would feel comfortable with a similar task. Laura, however, welcomed the opportunity because she came to a more intimate understanding of her own fears and feelings as she moved from one draft to the next. What follows is the final draft of Laura's essay.

Why Are You Here?

Laura LaPierre

Title: asks central question

Beginning: engages reader and establishes context — when, where, who

Balancing between a crutch on one side and an IV pole with wheels on the other, I dragged my stiff leg along the smooth, sterile floor of the hospital hall. All around me nurses, orderlies, and doctors bustled about, dodging well-meaning visitors laden with flowers and candy. The fluorescent lights glared down with a brightness so sharp that I squinted and thought that sunglasses might be in order. Sticking close to the wall, I rounded the corner and paused to rest for a moment. I breathed in the hot, antiseptic-smelling air which I had grown accustomed to and sighed angrily.

Details create image of harsh, unfriendly environment

Point of view: first person

Tears of hurt and frustration pricked at the corner of my eyes as the now familiar pain seared my leg. I tugged my bathrobe closer around my shoulder and, hauling my IV pole with me, I continued down the hall. One, two — second door on the left, she had said. I opened the heavy metal door, entered, and realized that I must be a little early because no one else was there yet. After glancing at my watch, I sat down and looked around the room, noting with disgust the prevalence of beige: beige walls, beige ceiling, shiny beige floor tiles. A small cot stood in one corner with a beige bedspread, and in the opposite corner there was a sink, mirror, and beige waste basket. The only relief from the monotony was the circle of six or seven chairs where I sat. They were a vivid rust color and

Organization: straight-forward and chronological

Time reference maintains flow

Descriptive details create dominant impression of an uninviting room

1

2

helped to brighten the dull room. The shades were drawn, and the lights were much dimmer than they had been in the hall. My eyes gradually relaxed as I waited.

People began to drift in until five of the seats were filled. A nurse was the head of the odd-looking group. Three of us were attached by long tubes to IV poles, and then there was a social worker. The man to my left wore a slightly faded, royal blue robe. He had a shock of unruly gray hair above an angular face with deeply sunken cheeks. His eyes were sunken, too, and glassy with pain. Yet he smiled and appeared untroubled by his IV pole.

Wearing a crisp white uniform and a pretty sweater, the nurse, a pleasant-looking woman in her late twenties, appeared friendly and sympathetic, though not to the point of being sappy. My impressions were confirmed as she began to speak.

"Okay. I guess we can begin. Welcome to our group, we meet every Monday at . . . ." She went on, but I wasn't paying attention anymore. I looked around the group and my eyes came to rest on the man sitting next to the nurse. In contrast to the other man's shriveled appearance, this man was robust. He was tall, with a protruding belly and a ruddy complexion. Unlike the other man, he seemed at war with his IV pole. He constantly fiddled with the tube and with the tape that held the needle in his arm. Eyes darting around the room, he nervously watched everyone.

I heard the nurse continue, "So, let's all introduce ourselves and tell why we are here." We went around the circle clockwise, starting with the nurse, and when we got to the social worker, I looked up and surveyed her while she talked. Aside from contributing to the beige monotony with her pants, she was agreeable both in appearance and disposition.

When it was my turn, I took a deep breath and with my voice quavering began, "My name is Laura and—"

"Hi, Laura!" interrupted the cheerful man on my left. I turned and smiled weakly at him.

Fighting back the tears, I continued, "And I have bone cancer."

Details show that people in group are obviously ill, but specifics not revealed

Dialogue adds life to narrative

Comparison and contrast: describes other patients

Central question of title introduced

Description shows writer's fear

Cheerful man momentarily relieves tension

Laura faces her fear — her moment of truth

3

4

5

6

7

8

9

Analyzing Laura LaPierre's Narration Essay:
Questions for Discussion

1. What context does Laura provide for her narrative? What else, if anything, would you have liked to know about the situation? What would have been lost had she told you more?

2. Laura tells her story in the first person. How would the narrative have changed had she used a third-person point of view?

3. For you, what details conveyed Laura's fear at being in the hospital? Are there places where she could have done more "showing" and less "telling"? Explain.

4. Laura uses a straightforward chronological organization for her narrative. Can you see any places where she might have used a flashback? What would have been the effect?

5. What meaning or importance do you think this experience holds for Laura?

SUGGESTIONS FOR USING NARRATION AS A WRITING STRATEGY

As you plan, write, and revise your narrative essay, be mindful of the writing process guidelines described in Chapter 2. Also, pay particular attention to the basic requirements and essential ingredients for this writing strategy.

❯ Planning Your Narration Essay

Planning is an essential part of writing a good narrative essay. You can save yourself a great deal of inconvenience by taking the time to think about the key components of your essay before you actually begin to write.

SELECT A TOPIC THAT HAS MEANING FOR YOU. In your writing course, you may have the freedom to choose the story you want to narrate, or your instructor may give you a list of topics from which to choose. Instead of jumping at the first topic that looks good, however, brainstorm a list of events that have had an impact on your life and that you could write about. Such a list might include your first blind date, catching frogs as a child, making a team or a club, the death of a loved one, a graduation celebration, a trip to the Grand Canyon, the loss of a pet, learning to drive a car, or the breakup of a relationship.

As you narrow your options, look for an event or an incident that is particularly memorable. Memorable experiences are memorable for a reason; they offer us important insights into our lives. Such experiences are worth narrating because people want to read about them.

DETERMINE YOUR POINT AND PURPOSE.   Before you begin writing, ask yourself why the experience you have chosen is meaningful. What did you learn from it? How are you different as a result of the experience? What has changed? Your narrative point (the meaning of your narrative) and purpose in writing will influence which events and details you include and which you leave out. Suppose, for example, you choose to write about how you learned to ride a bicycle. If you mean mainly to entertain, you will probably include a number of unusual incidents unique to your experience. If your purpose is mainly to report or inform, it will make more sense to concentrate on the kinds of details that are common to most people's experience. However, if your purpose is to tell your readers step-by-step how to ride a bicycle, you should use process analysis, a strategy used by writers whose purpose is to give directions for how something is done or to explain how something works (see Chapter 7).

The most successful narrative essays, however, do more than entertain or inform. While narratives do not ordinarily have a formal thesis statement, readers will more than likely expect your story to make a statement or to arrive at some meaningful conclusion—implied or explicit—about your experience. The student essay by Laura LaPierre, for example, shows how important it was for her to confront the reality of her bone cancer. In addressing her fears, she gains a measure of control over her life.

As you prepare to write, look for the significance in the story you want to tell—some broader, more instructive points it could make about the ways of the world. Learning to ride a bicycle may not suggest such points to you, and it may therefore not be a very good subject for your narrative essay. However, the subject does have possibilities. Here's one: Learning to master a difficult, even dangerous, but definitely useful skill like riding a bicycle is an important experience to have in life. Here's another: Learning to ride a bicycle is an opportunity for you to acquire and use some basic physics, such as the laws of gravity and the behavior of a gyroscope. Perhaps you can think of others. If, however, you do not know why you are telling the story and it seems pointless even to you, your readers will pick up on the ambivalence in your writing, and you should probably find another, more meaningful story to tell.

ESTABLISH A CONTEXT.   Early in your essay, perhaps in the opening paragraphs, establish the context, or setting, of your story—the world within which the action took place:

> *When it happened*—morning; afternoon; 11:37 on the dot; 1997; winter
>
> *Where it happened*—in the street; at Wendy's; in Pocatello, Idaho
>
> *To whom it happened*—to me; to my father; to the assistant; to Teri Hopper

Without a clear context, your readers can easily get confused or even completely lost. And remember, readers respond well to specific contextual information because such details make them feel as if they are present, ready to witness the narrative.

CHOOSE THE MOST APPROPRIATE POINT OF VIEW.   Consider what point of view to take in your narrative. Did you take part in the action? If so, it will seem most natural for you to use the first-person (*I, we*) point of view. On the other hand, if you weren't there at all and must rely on other sources for your information, you will probably choose the third-person (*he, she, it, they*) point of view, as did the author writing about the invention of Coca-Cola earlier in this chapter. However, if you were a witness to part or all of what happened but not a participant, then you will need to choose between the more immediate and subjective quality of the first person and the more distanced, objective effect of the third person. Whichever you choose, you should maintain the same point of view throughout your narrative.

GATHER DETAILS THAT "SHOW, DON'T TELL."   When writing your essay, you will need enough detail about the action, the people involved, and the context to let your readers understand what is going on. Start collecting details by asking yourself the traditional reporter's questions:

* Who was involved?
* What happened?
* Where did it happen?
* When did it happen?
* Why did it happen?
* How did it happen?

Generate as many details as you can because you never know which ones will ensure that your essay *shows* and doesn't *tell* too much. For example, instead of telling readers that she dislikes being in the hospital, Laura LaPierre shows us what she sees, feels, hears, and smells and lets us draw our own conclusion about her state of mind.

As you write, you will want to select and emphasize details that support your point, serve your purpose, and show the reader what is happening. You should not, however, get so carried away with details that your readers become confused or bored by excess information: In good storytelling, deciding what to leave out can be as important as deciding what to include.

▶ Organizing Your Narration Essay

IDENTIFY THE SEQUENCE OF EVENTS IN YOUR NARRATIVE. Storytellers tend to follow an old rule: Begin at the beginning, and go on till you come to the end; then stop. Chronological organization is natural in narration because it is a retelling of the original order of events; it is also easiest for the writer to manage and the reader to understand.

Some narratives, however, are organized using a technique called *flash-back*: The writer may begin midway through the story, or even at the end, with an important or exciting event, then use flashbacks to fill in what happened earlier to lead up to that event. Some authors begin in the present and then use flashbacks to shift to the past to tell the story. Whatever organizational pattern you choose, words and phrases like "for a month," "afterward," and "three days earlier" will help you and your reader keep the sequence of events straight.

It may help you in organizing to jot down a quick outline before tackling the first draft of your narrative. Here's the outline that Laura LaPierre used to order the events in her narrative chronologically:

> Narration about my first group meeting at the hospital
>
> Point: At some point I had to confront the reality of my illness.
>
> Context: Hospital setting
>
> 1. Start slow walk down hospital hall attached to IV pole.
>
> 2. Sights, sounds, and smells of hospital hallway set scene.
>
> 3. Locate destination — first one to arrive for group meeting.
>
> 4. Describe "beige" meeting room.
>
> 5. Other patients arrive.
>
> 6. Young nurse leads our group meeting.
>
> 7. We start by introducing ourselves.
>
> 8. My turn — my moment of truth.

Such an outline can remind you of your point, your organization, and the emphasis you want when you write your first draft.

▶ Writing Your Narration Essay

KEEP YOUR VERB TENSE CONSISTENT. Most narratives are in the past tense, and this is logical: They recount events that have already happened, even if very recently. But writers sometimes use the present tense to create an effect of immediacy, as if the events were happening as you read about them. The important thing to remember is to be consistent. If you are re-counting an event that has already occurred, use the past tense throughout. For an event in the present, use the present tense consistently. If you find yourself jumping from a present event to a past event, as in the case of a flashback, you will need to switch verb tenses to signal the change in time.

USE NARRATIVE TIME FOR EMPHASIS.   The number of words or pages you devote to an event does not usually correspond to the number of min-utes or hours the event took to happen. You may require several pages to recount an important or complex quarter of an hour, but then pass over several hours or days in a sentence or two. Length has less to do with chron-ological time than with the amount of detail you include, and that's a func-tion of the amount of emphasis you want to give to a particular incident.

USE TRANSITIONAL WORDS TO CLARIFY NARRATIVE SEQUENCE. Transitional words like *after, next, then, earlier, immediately*, and *finally* are useful, as they help your readers smoothly connect and understand the sequence of events that make up your narrative. Likewise, a specific time mark like "on April 20," "two weeks earlier," and "in 2004" can indicate time shifts and can signal to readers how much time has elapsed between events.

Inexperienced writers sometimes overuse these words; this makes their writing style wordy and tiresome. Use these conventional transitions when you really need them, but when you don't — when your readers can follow your story without them — leave them out.

USE DIALOGUE TO BRING YOUR NARRATIVE TO LIFE.   Having people in a narrative speak is a very effective way of showing rather than telling or summarizing what happened. Snippets of actual dialogue make a story come alive and feel immediate to the reader.

Consider this passage from an early draft of a student narrative:

> I hated having to call a garage, but I knew I couldn't do the work myself and I knew they'd rip me off. Besides, I had to get the car off the street before the police had it towed. I felt trapped without any choices.

Now compare this early draft with the revised draft below, in which the situ-ation is revealed through dialogue.

> "University Gulf, Glen speaking. What can I do for ya?"
> "Yeah, my car broke down. I think it's the timing belt, and I was wondering if you could give me an estimate."
> "What kind of car is it?" asked Glen.
> "A Nissan Sentra."

"What year?"

"2008," I said, emphasizing the 8.

"Oh, those are a bitch to work on. Can ya hold on for a second?"

I knew what was coming before Glen came back on the line.

With dialogue, readers can hear the direct exchange between the car owner and the mechanic. You can use dialogue in your own writing to deliver a sense of immediacy to the reader.

❱ Revising and Editing Your Narration Essay

SHARE YOUR DRAFT WITH OTHERS.   Try sharing the draft of your essay with other students in your writing class to make sure that your narrative makes sense. Ask them if there are any parts that they do not understand. Have them tell you what they think is the point of your narrative. If their answers differ from what you intended, have them indicate the passages that led them to their interpretations so that you can change your text accordingly. To maximize the effectiveness of conferences with your peers, utilize the guidelines presented on page 36. Feedback from these conferences often provides one or more places where you can start revising.

QUESTION YOUR OWN WORK WHILE REVISING AND EDITING.   Revision is best done by asking yourself key questions about what you have written. Begin by reading, preferably aloud, what you have written. Reading aloud forces you to pay attention to every single word, and you are more likely to catch lapses in the logical flow of thought.

For help with twelve common writing problems, see Chapter 16, "Editing for Grammar, Punctuation, and Sentence Style." After you have read your paper through, answer the following questions for revising and editing, and make the necessary changes.

Questions for Revising and Editing: Narration

1. Is my narrative well focused, or do I try to cover too long a period of time?

2. What is my reason for telling this story? Is that reason clearly stated or implied for readers?

3. Have I established a clear context for my readers? Is it clear when the action happened, where it happened, and to whom?

4. Have I used the most effective point of view to tell my story? How would my story be different had I used a different one?

5. Have I selected details that help readers understand what is going on in my narrative, or have I included unnecessary details that get in the way of what I'm trying to say? Do I give enough examples of the important events in my narrative?

6. Is the chronology of events in my narrative clear? Have I taken advantage of opportunities to add emphasis, drama, or suspense with flashbacks or other complications of the chronological organization?

7. Have I used transitional expressions or time markers to help readers follow the sequence of events in my narrative?

8. Have I employed dialogue in my narrative to reveal a situation, or have I told about or summarized the situation too much?

9. Have I avoided run-on sentences and comma splices? Have I used sentence fragments only deliberately to convey mood or tone?

10. Have I avoided other errors in grammar, punctuation, and mechanics? Is my sentence style as clear, smooth, and persuasive as possible?

11. Is the meaning of my narrative clear, or have I left my readers thinking, "So what?"

Coming to an Awareness of Language

MALCOLM X

Born Malcolm Little in Omaha, Nebraska, in 1925, Malcolm X rose from a world of street crime to become one of the most powerful and articulate African American leaders in the United States during the 1960s. On February 21, 1965, his life was cut short at age thirty-nine; he was shot and killed as he addressed an afternoon rally in Harlem. Malcolm X told his life story in *The Autobiography of Malcolm X* (1964), written with the assistance of *Roots* author Alex Haley. The book, a moving account of his life and his struggle for fulfillment, is still read by hundreds of thousands each year. In 1992, the life of this influential African American leader was reexamined in Spike Lee's film *Malcolm X*.

The following selection from *The Autobiography* refers to a period Malcolm X spent in federal prison. In the selection, Malcolm X explains how he was frustrated by his inability to express his ideas and how this frustration led him to a goal: acquiring the skills of reading and writing. Later he would say, "As I see it, the ability to read awoke inside me some long dormant craving to be mentally alive."

Preparing to Read

Our educational system places a great emphasis on our having a large and varied working vocabulary. Has anyone ever stressed to you the importance of developing a good vocabulary? What did you think when you heard this advice? In what ways can words be used as powerful tools? How would you judge your own vocabulary?

I've never been one for inaction. Everything I've ever felt strongly about, 1
I've done something about. I guess that's why, unable to do anything else, I soon began writing to people I had known in the hustling world, such as Sammy the Pimp, John Hughes, the gambling house owner, the thief Jumpsteady, and several dope peddlers. I wrote them all about Allah and Islam and Mr. Elijah Muhammad. I had no idea where most of them lived. I addressed their letters in care of the Harlem or Roxbury bars and clubs where I'd known them.

I never got a single reply. The average hustler and criminal was too 2
uneducated to write a letter. I have known many slick, sharp-looking hustlers, who would have you think they had an interest in Wall Street; privately, they would get someone else to read a letter if they received one. Besides, neither would I have replied to anyone writing me something as wild as "the white man is the devil."

What certainly went on the Harlem and Roxbury wires was that 3
Detroit Red was going crazy in stir, or else he was trying some hype to
shake up the warden's office.

During the years that I stayed in the Norfolk Prison Colony, never did 4
any official directly say anything to me about those letters, although, of
course, they all passed through the prison censorship. I'm sure, however,
they monitored what I wrote to add to the files
which every state and federal prison keeps on
the conversion of Negro inmates by the teachings of Mr. Elijah Muhammad.

> I saw that the best
> thing I could do
> was get hold of a
> dictionary—to study,
> to learn some words.

But at that time, I felt that the real reason 5
was that the white man knew that he was the
devil.

Later on, I even wrote to the Mayor of 6
Boston, to the Governor of Massachusetts,
and to Harry S. Truman. They never answered;
they probably never even saw my letters. I handscratched to them how the
white man's society was responsible for the black man's condition in this
wilderness of North America.

It was because of my letters that I happened to stumble upon starting 7
to acquire some kind of a homemade education.

I became increasingly frustrated at not being able to express what I 8
wanted to convey in letters that I wrote, especially those to Mr. Elijah
Muhammad. In the street, I had been the most articulate hustler out
there—I had commanded attention when I said something. But now, trying to write simple English, I not only wasn't articulate, I wasn't even functional. How would I sound writing in slang, the way I would *say* it, something such as, "Look, daddy, let me pull your coat about a cat. Elijah
Muhammad—"

Many who today hear me somewhere in person, or on television, or 9
those who read something I've said, will think I went to school far beyond
the eighth grade. This impression is due entirely to my prison studies.

It had really begun back in the Charlestown Prison, when Bimbi first 10
made me feel envy of his stock of knowledge. Bimbi had always taken
charge of any conversation he was in, and I had tried to emulate him.
But every book I picked up had few sentences which didn't contain anywhere from one to nearly all of the words that might as well have been in
Chinese. When I just skipped those words, of course, I really ended up
with little idea of what the book said. So I had come to the Norfolk Prison
Colony still going through only book-reading motions. Pretty soon, I
would have quit even these motions, unless I had received the motivation
that I did.

I saw that the best thing I could do was get hold of a dictionary—to   11
study, to learn some words. I was lucky enough to reason also that I should
try to improve my penmanship. It was sad. I couldn't even write in a
straight line. It was both ideas together that moved me to request a dictionary along with some tablets and pencils from the Norfolk Prison Colony
school.

I spent two days just riffling uncertainly through the dictionary's pages.   12
I'd never realized so many words existed! I didn't know *which* words I needed
to learn. Finally, just to start some kind of action, I began copying.

In my slow, painstaking, ragged handwriting, I copied into my tablet   13
everything printed on that first page, down to the punctuation marks.

I believe it took me a day. Then, aloud, I read back, to myself, every-   14
thing I'd written on the tablet. Over and over, aloud, to myself, I read my
own handwriting.

I woke up the next morning, thinking about those words—immensely   15
proud to realize that not only had I written so much at one time, but I'd
written words that I never knew were in the world. Moreover, with a little
effort, I also could remember what many of these words meant. I reviewed
the words whose meanings I didn't remember. Funny thing, from the dictionary first page right now, that "aardvark" springs to my mind. The dictionary had a picture of it, a long-tailed, long-eared, burrowing African
mammal, which lives off termites caught by sticking out its tongue as an
anteater does for ants.

I was so fascinated that I went on—I copied the dictionary's next   16
page. And the same experience came when I studied that. With every
succeeding page, I also learned of people and places and events from history. Actually the dictionary is like a miniature encyclopedia. Finally the
dictionary's A section had filled a whole tablet—and I went on into the
B's. That was the way I started copying what eventually became the entire
dictionary. It went a lot faster after so much practice helped me to pick up
handwriting speed. Between what I wrote in my tablet, and writing letters,
during the rest of my time in prison I would guess I wrote a million words.

I suppose it was inevitable that as my word-base broadened, I could   17
for the first time pick up a book and read and now begin to understand
what the book was saying. Anyone who has read a great deal can imagine
the new world that opened. Let me tell you something: from then until I
left that prison, in every free moment I had, if I was not reading in the
library, I was reading on my bunk. You couldn't have gotten me out of
books with a wedge. Between Mr. Muhammad's teachings, my correspondence, my visitors . . . and my reading of books, months passed without my
even thinking about being imprisoned. In fact, up to then, I never had
been so truly free in my life.

Thinking Critically about the Text

We are all to one degree or another prisoners of our own language. Sometimes we lack the ability to communicate as effectively as we would like. Why do you think this happens, and what do you think can be done to remedy it? How can improved language skills also improve a person's life?

Questions on Subject

1. In paragraph 8, Malcolm X refers to the difference between being "articulate" and being "functional" in his speaking and writing. What is the distinction he makes? In your opinion, is it a valid one?

2. Malcolm X offers two possible reasons for the warden's keeping track of African American inmates' conversion to the teachings of Elijah Muhammad. What are those two assertions, and what is their effect on the reader?

3. What is the nature of the freedom that Malcolm X refers to in the final sentence? In what sense can language be said to be liberating?

Questions on Strategy

1. Malcolm X narrates his experiences as a prisoner using the first-person *I*. Why is the first person particularly appropriate? What would be lost or gained had he narrated his story using the third-person pronoun *he*?

2. In the opening paragraph, Malcolm X refers to himself as a man of action and conviction. What details does he include to support this assertion?

3. Many people think of "vocabulary building" as learning strange, multisyllabic, difficult-to-spell words. But acquiring an effective vocabulary does not have to be so intimidating. How would you characterize Malcolm X's vocabulary in this narrative? Did you find his word choice suited to what he was trying to accomplish in this selection?

4. What is Malcolm X's narrative point in this selection? How do you know? What does he learn about himself as a result of this experience?

5. In reflecting on his years in prison, Malcolm X comes to an understanding of the events that caused him to reassess his life and take charge of his own education. Identify those events, and discuss the changes that resulted from Malcolm X's actions. How does his inclusion of these causal links enhance the overall narrative? (Glossary: *Cause and Effect Analysis*)

Questions on Diction and Vocabulary

1. Although Malcolm X taught himself to be articulate in writing, we can still hear a street-savvy voice in his writing. Cite examples of his diction that convey a streetwise sound. (Glossary: *Diction*)

2. What do you do when you encounter new words in your reading? Do you skip those words as Malcolm X once did, do you take the time to look them up, or do you try to figure out their meanings from the context? Explain the strategies you use to determine the meaning of a word from its context. Can you think of other strategies?

3. Refer to your dictionary to determine the meanings of the following words as Malcolm X uses them in this selection: *hustler* (paragraph 2), *slick* (2), *hype* (3), *frustrated* (8), *emulate* (10), *riffling* (12), *inevitable* (17).

Classroom Activity Using Narration

Good narrative depends on a sense of continuity or flow, a logical ordering of events and ideas. The following sentences, which make up the first paragraph of E. B. White's essay "Once More to the Lake," have been rearranged. Place the sentences in what seems to be a coherent sequence based on such language signals as transitions, repeated words, pronouns, and temporal references. Be prepared to explain your reason for the placement of each sentence.

1. I have since become a salt-water man, but sometimes in summer there are days when the restlessness of the tides and the fearful cold of the sea water and the incessant wind that blows across the afternoon and into the evening make me wish for the placidity of a lake in the woods.

2. We all got ringworm from some kittens and had to rub Pond's Extract on our arms and legs night and morning, and my father rolled over in a canoe with all his clothes on; but outside of that the vacation was a success and from then on none of us ever thought there was any place in the world like that lake in Maine.

3. A few weeks ago this feeling got so strong I bought myself a couple of bass hooks and a spinner and returned to the lake where we used to go, for a week's fishing and to revisit old haunts.

4. One summer, along about 1904, my father rented a camp on a lake in Maine and took us all there for the month of August.

5. We returned summer after summer — always on August 1st for one month.

Writing Suggestions

1. Using Malcolm X's essay as a model, write a narrative about some goal you have set and achieved in which you were motivated by a strong inner conflict. What was the nature of your conflict? What feeling did it arouse in you, and how did the conflict help you to accomplish your goal?

2. **Writing with Sources.** Malcolm X solved the problems of his own near-illiteracy by carefully studying the dictionary. Would this be a practical solution

to the national problem of illiteracy? In your experience, what does it mean to be literate? After investigating contemporary illiteracy in your college library or on the Internet, write a proposal on what can be done to promote literacy in this country. You might also consider what is being done now in your community. For models of and advice on integrating sources into your essay, see Chapters 14 and 15.

Crime Family

ELISA MALA

Freelance journalist Elisa Mala was born in New York City in 1987 and has lived there all but one year of her life. A graduate of Queens College, Mala is fluent in five languages. She has been a regular contributor to the *New York Times, Newsweek, ESPN The Magazine, Psychology Today,* and the *New York Post.* In recognition of her potential as one of tomorrow's brightest foreign correspondents, she was named an Overseas Press Club Foundation Scholar in 2012. Currently Mala is in graduate school at Columbia University where she holds the Flora Lewis Internship.

In the following selection, which first appeared in the *New York Times Magazine* on November 11, 2012, Mala recalls two women who just might be friends or even family of the three men who mugged her and reflects on what she learned from sharing space and conversation with them. Pay attention to the narrative details that Mala selected in order to show readers what's happening, instead of having to tell them.

Preparing to Read

Have you ever been mugged or witnessed such a crime? How did you react to the situation? If you were the victim yourself, did you ever get to confront your attackers? If you witnessed the crime, did you come forward and testify, or did you choose not to get involved? Looking back now, how do you feel about your behavior?

So I'm nineteen and climbing into the back seat of a cop car in the middle of the night. Despite the absence of handcuffs around my wrists, I am crying and asking myself, over and over again, what I could have done differently. If I had crossed the street as those three men were approaching, would that have stopped them from mugging me? Or would pseudo-profiling have set in motion a more violent turn of events? For a moment, after being shoved to the ground, I even imagined getting up and giving chase until I was reunited with my prized possessions: $70 from baby-sitting gigs, an underused PalmPilot from my first corporate boss, most of my teeny-bopper CD collection, and, irreplaceably, a college semester's worth of notes. At least the ordeal was over.

But the N.Y.P.D. had other plans. I sat in the back of the squad car as it canvassed the area. A crackling radio voice announced a suspicious group of guys lurking near the subway station four blocks away. Shielded from view by the car's tinted windows, I had a front-row seat to the arrest:

authoritative voices booming over the loudspeaker; the perps squinting in the beams of spotlights. A teenage girl stood in the sidelines of the mayhem, shivering in her puffy coat and jeans, her moon-shaped face looking as bewildered as I felt.

Transported to the precinct in separate cars, the suspects and I entered through alternate doors before being routed to different floors. Then, the report filed, I was moved to a general waiting area. The idea was that the cops would collect me after discussing the case. But when midnight brought a changing of the guard, I remained forgotten on the bench, with an elderly woman and a teenage girl as seatmates.

> I am crying and asking myself, over and over again, what I could have done differently. If I had crossed the street as those three men were approaching, would that have stopped them from mugging me?

Boredom got the best of me. "What brings you here?" I asked.

"We're waiting for . . . a friend," the woman responded, her voice catching.

When the teenage girl refused to meet my eye, my curiosity was piqued further. I noticed the moon-shaped face and the puffy jacket and took in the large hoop earrings and hairspray-heavy ponytail. Here, inches away, sat the girl from the subway station. Whoever else they were, these women were the friends or family of the three guys the cops said jumped me. The little curiosity I had was immediately replaced by dread.

When the older woman inquired what I was doing there, I didn't have the presence of mind to respond with anything other than the truth. "There was an earlier incident," I fumbled.

"I have a math test tomorrow," the teenager volunteered, eyes glued to the ceiling.

In our unusual trio, the grandmotherly type seemed most out of place in the precinct, clad in a white oxford shirt, duty-length tweed skirt, thin-rimmed glasses, and silver hair tucked away in a ballerina's bun. Her unaccented, highbrow English would have gone over the heads of my Thai immigrant parents. The possibilities of her life story seemed endless (paralegal, librarian, government employee?), but it was far easier to determine what she was not: belligerent, drunk, violent, or visibly dysfunctional.

As the sole adult among teenagers, she took it upon herself to feed us with the only option on hand. She bought barbecue-flavored chips—my favorite flavor—from the vending machine. Before taking one for herself, she tilted the bag toward me, the way my mother might have. Her eyes were generous, beseeching. I stared for a moment too long. "No, thanks,"

I said, though I was famished. I could share a space, a conversations, and even empathy with the family of those I believed had mugged me. But breaking bread was more than I could bear. In silence, we occupied the small space, biding our time until release.

The police later told me they had always been sure that they had the right guys, but a lack of physical evidence made it impossible to hold anyone in custody. Without warning, the suspects bounded down the stairs and out the door, followed wordlessly by the two women. I did what New Yorkers do best and avoided eye contact.

11

For two weeks, a patrol car was stationed around the corner from my apartment. But for all that the men and I seemed to share—a neighborhood address, possibly streets apart; at least one mannerly, educated, and stable guardian; foul-weather friends—I had the feeling that our first encounter would be our last.

12

Thinking Critically about the Text

Why do you think Mala took the time to tell us about the time she was mugged? What, if anything, do you think she learned from this experience? Why do you think that she "had the feeling that our first encounter would be our last" (paragraph 12)?

Questions on Subject

1. What did the muggers steal from Mala? What does the inclusion of these details add to Mala's story?

2. What discovery did the narrator make while sitting next to the elderly woman and teenage girl in the police station?

3. Why wasn't the narrator able to accept a barbecue-flavored chip when offered even though she was hungry?

4. Why were the police unable to hold the three suspects?

5. Why do you think the two women followed the three suspects out the jail door "wordlessly"? In what ways is this an example of a "show, don't tell" detail? Explain.

Questions on Strategy

1. What context for her narrative does Mala establish in her opening paragraph?

2. Mala tells her story from the first-person point of view. What would have been lost or gained had she decided to tell it from the third-person point of view?

3. The narrator provides a description of the elderly woman and the teenage girl. Why do you suppose she never tells us much about the three suspects? In

what ways does Mala's use of description enhance her narrative? (Glossary: *Description*)

4. How does the one-sentence paragraph — "Boredom got the best of me" (4) — function in the context of Mala's essay? Explain.

5. What transitional devices does Mala use to help her readers move from one paragraph to the next smoothly? (Glossary: *Transitions*)

Questions on Diction and Vocabulary

1. Would you describe Mala's diction in this essay as being formal or informal? Identify five or six words or phrases that led you to your conclusion. (Glossary: *Colloquial Expressions*) Did you find her diction appropriate for the story she is telling? Explain.

2. Refer to a dictionary to determine the meanings of the following words as Mala uses them in this selection: *pseudo-profiling* (paragraph 1), *canvassed* (2), *piqued* (6), *belligerent* (9), *beseeching* (10), *famished* (10).

Classroom Activity Using Narration

Dialogue is an effective way to bring life to your narrative, to let the people in your story speak for themselves. It is important, however, that you create dialogue that flows logically from one speaker to another. The following sentences, which include dialogue, have been scrambled. Using language cues in each of the sentences, rearrange them in chronological order.

1. The sky was gray and gloomy for as far as she could see, and sleet hissed off the glass.

2. "Oh, hi, Sarah, I'm glad you called," she said happily, but her smile dimmed when she looked outside.

3. As Betsy crossed the room, the phone rang, startling her.

4. "No, the weather's awful, so I don't think I want to leave the house today — I'm still nursing that cold, you know," she sighed.

5. "Hello?" she said, and she wandered over to the window, dragging the phone cord behind her.

6. "Thought you'd like to get a coffee on a day like today," Sarah urged.

Writing Suggestions

1. Using Mala's narrative as a model, write an essay about a traumatic event that you or someone close to you experienced. Be sure to select a meaningful event, to establish a context for this event, to choose an appropriate point of view, and to determine how you wish to organize or sequence the narrative details before you begin writing.

2. Have you ever witnessed a crime or a terrible accident? How did you react at the time? Did you rush to the assistance of the victim(s)? Did you call the police or the 911 emergency line? Did you cooperate with police who asked witnesses to come forward? Or, did you choose to do nothing, to walk away? How do you account for the choice you made? Do you think that other people would behave similarly? Why, or why not? Write a narrative essay that demonstrates either public involvement or public apathy.

Not Close Enough for Comfort

DAVID P. BARDEEN

David P. Bardeen was born in 1974 in New Haven, Connecticut, and grew up in Seattle, Washington. He graduated cum laude from Harvard University in 1996 and then worked for J. P. Morgan & Co. as an investment banking analyst. In 2002, he received his J.D. from the New York University School of Law, where he was the managing editor of the school's *Law Review*. After graduation, he joined the law firm of Cleary, Gottlieb, Steen & Hamilton and became a member of the New York Bar. Bardeen is proficient in Spanish, and his practice focuses on international business transactions involving clients in Latin America. A freelance writer on a variety of topics, he is also active with Immigration Equality, a national organization fighting for equality for lesbian, gay, bisexual, transgender, and HIV-positive immigrants.

In the following article, which appeared in the *New York Times Magazine* on February 29, 2004, Bardeen tells the story of a lunch meeting at which he reveals a secret to his twin brother, a secret that had derailed their relationship for almost fifteen years.

Preparing to Read

Recall a time when a parent, sibling, friend, teacher, or some other person close to you kept a secret from you. How did the secret affect your relationship? How did you feel once the secret was revealed? How has the relationship fared since?

I had wanted to tell Will I was gay since I was twelve. As twins, we shared everything back then: clothes, gadgets, thoughts, secrets. Everything except this. So when we met for lunch more than a year ago, I thought that finally coming out to him would close the distance that had grown between us. When we were kids, we created our own language, whispering to each other as our bewildered parents looked on. Now, at twenty-eight, we had never been further apart.

I asked him about his recent trip. He asked me about work. Short questions. One-word answers. Then an awkward pause.

Will was one of the last to know. Partly it was his fault. He is hard to pin down for brunch or a drink, and this was not the sort of conversation I wanted to have over the phone. I had actually been trying to tell him for more than a month, but he kept canceling at the last minute—a friend was in town, he'd met a girl.

But part of me was relieved. This was the talk I had feared the most. 4
Coming out is, in an unforgiving sense, an admission of fraud. Fraud
against yourself primarily, but also fraud against your family and friends.
So, once I resolved to tell my secret, I confessed to my most recent "victims" first. I told my friends from law school—those I had met just a few
years earlier and deceived the least—then I worked back through college
to the handful of high-school friends I still keep in touch with.

**I had wanted to tell Will
I was gay since I was
twelve. As twins,
we shared everything
back then: clothes,
gadgets, thoughts,
secrets. Everything
except this.**

Keeping my sexuality from my parents 5
had always seemed permissible, so our sit-
down chat did not stress me out as much as
it might have. We all mislead our parents.
"I'm too sick for school today." "No, I
wasn't drinking." "Yes, Mom, I'm fine.
Don't worry about me." That deception is
understood and, in some sense, expected.
But twins expect complete transparency,
however romantic the notion.

Although our lives unfolded along par- 6
allel tracks—we went to college together,
both moved to New York and had many of
the same friends—Will and I quietly drifted
apart. When he moved abroad for a year, we lost touch almost entirely.
Our mother and father didn't think this was strange, because like many
parents of twins, they wanted us to follow divergent paths. But friends
were baffled when we began to rely on third parties for updates on each
other's lives. "How's Will?" someone would ask. "You tell me," I would
respond. One mutual friend, sick of playing the intermediary, once sent me
an e-mail message with a carbon copy to Will. "Dave, meet Will, your
twin," it said. "Will, let me introduce you to Dave."

Now, here we were, at lunch, just the two of us. "There's something 7
I've been meaning to tell you," I said. "I'm gay." I looked at him closely, at
the edges of his mouth, the wrinkles around his eyes, for some hint of what
he was thinking.

"O.K.," he said evenly. 8

"I've been meaning to tell you for a while," I said. 9

"Uh-huh." He asked me a few questions but seemed slightly uneasy, as 10
if he wasn't sure he wanted to hear the answers. Do Mom and Dad know?
Are you seeing anyone? How long have you known you were gay? I
hesitated.

I've known since I was young, and to some degree, I thought Will had 11
always known. How else to explain my adolescent melancholy, my

withdrawal, the silence when the subject changed to girls, sex, and who was hot. As a teenager I watched, as if from a distance, as my demeanor went from outspoken to sullen. I had assumed, in the self-centered way kids often do, that everyone noticed this change—and that my brother had guessed the reason. To be fair, he asked me once in our twenties, after I had ended yet another brief relationship with a woman. "Of course I'm not gay," I told him, as if the notion were absurd.

"How long have you known?" he asked again.   12

"About fifteen years," I said. Will looked away.   13

Food arrived. We ate and talked about other things. Mom, Dad, the   14
mayor, and the weather. We asked for the check and agreed to get together again soon. No big questions, no heart to heart. Just disclosure, explanation, follow-up, conclusion. But what could I expect? I had shut him out for so long that I suppose ultimately he gave up. Telling my brother I was gay hadn't made us close, as I had naively hoped it would; instead it underscored just how much we had strayed apart.

As we left the restaurant, I felt the urge to apologize, not for being gay,   15
of course, but for the years I'd kept him in the dark, for his being among the last to know. He hailed a cab. It stopped. He stepped inside, the door still open.

"I'm sorry," I said.   16

He smiled. "No, I think it's great."   17

A nice gesture. Supportive. But I think he misunderstood.   18

A year later, we are still only creeping toward the intimacy everyone   19
expects us to have. Although we live three blocks away from each other, I can't say we see each other every week or even every two weeks. But with any luck, next year, I'll be the one updating our mutual friends on Will's life.

Thinking Critically about the Text

How do you think Will felt when David announced that he was gay? Do you think Will had any clue about David's sexual orientation? What in Will's response to David's announcement led you to this conclusion? Why do you think it has been so difficult for them to recapture the "intimacy everyone expects [them] to have" (paragraph 19) in the year following David's coming out to Will?

Questions on Subject

1. Why do you suppose Bardeen chose to keep his sexual orientation a secret from his brother? Why was this particular "coming-out" so difficult? Was Bardeen realistic in thinking that "Will had always known" (paragraph 11) that he was gay?

*bad-tempered, sulky, gloomy.

2. What does Bardeen mean when he says, "But twins expect complete transparency, however romantic the notion" (paragraph 5)?

3. Why does Bardeen feel the need to apologize to his brother as they part? Do you think his brother understood the meaning of the apology? Why, or why not?

4. What do you think Bardeen had hoped would happen after he confided his secret to his brother? Was this hope unrealistic?

5. What harm had Bardeen's secret done to his relationship with his brother? What is necessary to heal the relationship?

Questions on Strategy

1. Bardeen narrates his coming-out using the first-person pronoun *I*. (Glossary: *Point of View*) Why is the first person particularly appropriate for telling a story such as this one? Explain.

2. How has Bardeen organized his narrative? (Glossary: *Organization*) In paragraphs 3 through 6, Bardeen uses flashbacks to give readers a context for his relationship with his twin. What would have been lost or gained had he begun his essay with paragraphs 3 through 6?

3. During the lunch-meeting part of the narrative (paragraphs 7–17), Bardeen uses dialogue. (Glossary: *Dialogue*) What does he gain by doing this? Why do you suppose he uses dialogue sparingly elsewhere?

4. Bardeen uses a number of short sentences and deliberate sentence fragments. What effect do these have on you? Why do you suppose he uses some sentence fragments instead of complete sentences?

5. Bardeen's title plays on the old saying "too close for comfort." What does his title suggest to you? (Glossary: *Title*) How effectively does it capture the essence of his relationship with his brother? Explain.

6. In paragraphs 6 and 11, Bardeen uses comparison and contrast to highlight the similarities and differences between himself and Will. (Glossary: *Comparison and Contrast*) Which did you find more interesting and revealing, the similarities or differences? Why?

Questions on Diction and Vocabulary

1. How would you describe Bardeen's voice in this narrative? How is that voice established? What, if anything, does Bardeen's diction tell you about him as a person? (Glossary: *Diction*) Explain.

2. Bardeen says that "[c]oming out is, in an unforgiving sense, an admission of fraud" (paragraph 4). Why do you suppose he uses the word *fraud* to

describe how he felt about his coming-out? What does he mean when he says "in an unforgiving sense"? What other words might he have used instead of *fraud*?

3. Refer to your dictionary to determine the meanings of the following words as Bardeen uses them in this selection: *baffled* (paragraph 6), *melancholy* (11), *demeanor* (11), *sullen* (11), *intimacy* (19).

Classroom Activity Using Narration

Beginning at the beginning and ending at the end is not the only way to tell a story. Think of the individual incidents or events in a story that you would like to tell or perhaps one that you are already working on. Don't write the story itself; simply make a list of the events that you need to include. Be sure to identify at least six to ten key events in your story. Start by listing the events in chronological order. Now play with the arrangement of those events; try to develop one or two alternative sequences that include the use of flashback. Using your list of events, discuss with other class members how flashback can improve the dramatic impact of your narrative.

Writing Suggestions

1. Using your Preparing to Read response for this selection, write an essay about a secret you once had and how it affected relationships with those close to you. What exactly was your secret? Why did you decide to keep this information secret? How did you feel while you kept your secret? What happened when you revealed your secret? What insights into secrets do you have as a result of this experience?

2. In paragraph 4, Bardeen states, "So, once I resolved to tell my secret, I confessed to my most recent 'victims' first. I told my friends from law school — those I had met just a few years earlier and deceived the least — then I worked back through college to the handful of high-school friends I still keep in touch with." Write an essay in which you compare and contrast your level of honesty among your friends or a larger community and your level of honesty among your family or people with whom you are very close. (Glossary: *Comparison and Contrast*) Are there secrets you would be more likely to share with one group than another? If so, how would you classify those secrets? (Glossary: *Classification; Division*) Do you think it is easier to be honest with people who do or do not know you very well? Why?

3. The "coming out" photograph on the next page of college students at a gay rights rally was taken on October 11, 2003 — National Coming Out Day — in Austin, Texas. How do you "read" this photograph? (For a discussion of how to analyze photographs and other visual texts, see pages 15–19.) Why do you

suppose viewers' eyes are drawn to the young man's T-shirt? How do you interpret the message on his T-shirt? What significance, if any, do you attach to his being the only one wearing sunglasses? In your mind, is the young man being forthright, or is he holding back? Using Bardeen's essay, this photograph, and your own observations and experiences, write an essay about the mixed feelings and emotions as well as the potential misunderstandings attendant on "coming out."

Stranger Than True

BARRY WINSTON

Barry Winston is a practicing attorney in Chapel Hill, North Carolina. He was born in New York City in 1934 and served in the Marine Corps from 1953 to 1955. He later graduated from the University of North Carolina, from which he also received his law degree. His specialty is criminal law. He was admitted to the North Carolina Bar in 1961 and for almost fifty years has been an active defense lawyer. He is listed in the *Bar Register of Preeminent Lawyers*.

"Stranger Than True" was published in *Harper's* magazine in December 1986. In the story, Winston recounts his experience defending a young college graduate accused of driving while under the influence of alcohol and causing his sister's death. The story is characterized by Winston's energetic and strong voice. In commenting on his use of narrative detail, Winston says, "I could have made it twice as long, but it wouldn't have been as good a story." What do you think he meant by this comment?

Preparing to Read

The American judicial system works on the basis of the presumption of innocence. In short, you are innocent until proven guilty. But what about a situation in which all the evidence seems to point to a person's guilt? What's the purpose of a trial in such a case?

L et me tell you a story. A true story. The court records are all there if anyone wants to check. It's three years ago. I'm sitting in my office, staring out the window, when I get a call from a lawyer I hardly know. Tax lawyer. Some kid is in trouble and would I be interested in helping him out? He's charged with manslaughter, a felony, and driving under the influence. I tell him sure, have the kid call me.

So the kid calls and makes an appointment to see me. He's a nice kid, fresh out of college, and he's come down here to spend some time with his older sister, who's in med school. One day she tells him they're invited to a cookout with some friends of hers. She's going directly from class, and he's going to take her car and meet her there. It's way out in the country, but he gets there before she does, introduces himself around, and pops a beer. She shows up after a while and he pops another beer. Then he eats a hamburger and drinks a third beer. At some point his sister says, "Well, it's about time to go," and they head for the car.

And, the kid tells me, sitting there in my office, the next thing he remembers, he's waking up in a hospital room, hurting like hell, bandages and casts all over him, and somebody is telling him he's charged with manslaughter and DUI because he wrecked his sister's car, killed her in the process, and blew fourteen on the Breathalyzer. I ask him what the hell he means by "the next thing he remembers," and he looks me straight in the eye and says he can't remember anything from the time they leave the cookout until he wakes up in the hospital. He tells me the doctors say he has post-retrograde amnesia. I say of course I believe him, but I'm worried about finding a judge who'll believe him.

> The next thing he remembers, he's waking up in a hospital room, hurting like hell, bandages and casts all over him, and somebody is telling him he's charged with manslaughter and DUI . . .

I agree to represent him and send somebody for a copy of the wreck report. It says there are four witnesses: a couple in a car going the other way who passed the kid and his sister just before their car ran off the road, the guy whose front yard they landed in, and the trooper who investigated. I call the guy whose yard they ended up in. He isn't home. I leave word. Then I call the couple. The wife agrees to come in the next day with her husband. While I'm talking to her, the first guy calls. I call him back, introduce myself, tell him I'm representing the kid and need to talk to him about the accident. He hems and haws and I figure he's one of those people who think it's against the law to talk to defense lawyers. I say the D.A. will tell him it's O.K. to talk to me, but he doesn't have to. I give him the name and number of the D.A. and he says he'll call me back.

Then I go out and hunt up the trooper. He tells me the whole story. The kid and his sister are coming into town on Smith Level Road, after it turns from fifty-five to forty-five. The Thornes — the couple — are heading out of town. They say this sports car passes them, going the other way, right after that bad turn just south of the new subdivision. They say it's going like a striped-ass ape, at least sixty-five or seventy. Mrs. Thorne turns around to look and Mr. Thorne watches in the rearview mirror. They both see the same thing: halfway into the curve, the car runs off the road on the right, whips back onto the road, spins, runs off on the left, and disappears. They turn around in the first driveway they come to and start back, both terrified of what they're going to find. By this time, Trooper Johnson says, the guy whose front yard the car has ended up in has pulled the kid and his sister out of the wreck and started CPR on the girl. Turns out he's an emergency medical technician. Holloway, that's his name. Johnson tells me that Holloway says he's sitting in his front room, watching television, when he hears a hell of a crash in his yard. He runs outside and finds the car flipped over, and so he pulls the kid out from the driver's side, the girl from the other side. She dies in his arms.

And that, says Trooper Johnson, is that. The kid's blood/alcohol content was fourteen, he was going way too fast, *and* the girl is dead. He had to charge him. It's a shame, he seems a nice kid, it was his own sister and all, but what the hell can he do, right? 6

The next day the Thornes come in, and they confirm everything Johnson said. By now things are looking not so hot for my client, and I'm thinking it's about time to have a little chat with the D.A. But Holloway still hasn't called me back, so I call him. Not home. Leave word. No call. I wait a couple of days and call again. Finally I get him on the phone. He's very agitated, and won't talk to me except to say that he doesn't have to talk to me. 7

I know I better look for a deal, so I go to the D.A. He's very sympathetic. But. There's only so far you can get on sympathy. A young woman is dead, promising career cut short, all because somebody has too much to drink and drives. The kid has to pay. Not, the D.A. says, with jail time. But he's got to plead guilty to two misdemeanors: death by vehicle and driving under the influence. That means probation, a big fine. Several thousand dollars. Still, it's hard for me to criticize the D.A. After all, he's probably going to have the MADD mothers all over him because of reducing the felony to a misdemeanor. 8

On the day of the trial, I get to court a few minutes early. There are the Thornes and Trooper Johnson, and someone I assume is Holloway. Sure enough, when this guy sees me, he comes over and introduces himself and starts right in: "I just want you to know how serious all this drinking and driving really is," he says. "If those young people hadn't been drinking and driving that night, that poor young girl would be alive today." Now, I'm trying to hold my temper when I spot the D.A. I bolt across the room, grab him by the arm, and say, "We gotta talk. Why the hell have you got all those people here? That jerk Holloway. Surely to God you're not going to call him as a witness. This is a guilty plea! My client's parents are sitting out there. You don't need to put them through a dog-and-pony show." 9

The D.A. looks at me and says, "Man, I'm sorry, but in a case like this, I gotta put on witnesses. Weird Wally is on the bench. If I try to go without witnesses, he might throw me out." 10

The D.A. calls his first witness. Trooper Johnson identifies himself, tells about being called to the scene of the accident, and describes what he found when he got there and what everybody told him. After he finishes, the judge looks at me. "No questions," I say. Then the D.A. calls Holloway. He describes the noise, running out of the house, the upside-down car in his yard, pulling my client out of the window on the left side of the car and then going around to the other side for the girl. When he gets to this part, 11 he really hits his stride. He describes, in minute detail, the injuries he saw and what he did to try and save her life. And then he tells, breath by breath, how she died in his arms.

The D.A. says, "No further questions, your Honor." The judge looks at me. I shake my head, and he says to Holloway, "You may step down." 12

One of those awful silences hangs there, and nothing happens for a minute. Holloway doesn't move. Then he looks at me, and at the D.A., and then at the judge. He says, "Can I say something else, your Honor?" 13

All my bells are ringing at once, and my gut is screaming at me, Object! Object! I'm trying to decide in three quarters of a second whether it'll be worse to listen to a lecture on the evils of drink from this jerk Holloway or piss off the judge by objecting. But all I say is, "No objections, your Honor." The judge smiles at me, then at Holloway, and says, "Very well, Mr. Holloway. What did you wish to say?" 14

It all comes out in a rush. "Well, you see, your Honor," Holloway says, "it was just like I told Trooper Johnson. It all happened so fast. I heard the noise, and I came running out, and it was night, and I was excited, and the next morning, when I had a chance to think about it, I figured out what had happened, but by then I'd already told Trooper Johnson and I didn't know what to do, but you see, the car, it was upside down, and I did pull that boy out of the left-hand window, but don't you see, the car was upside down, and if you turned it over on its wheels like it's supposed to be, the left-hand side is really on the right-hand side, and your Honor, that boy wasn't driving that car at all. It was the girl that was driving, and when I had a chance to think about it the next morning, I realized that I'd told Trooper Johnson wrong, and I was scared and I didn't know what to do, and that's why"—and now he's looking right at me—"why I wouldn't talk to you." 15

Naturally, the defendant is allowed to withdraw his guilty plea. The charges are dismissed and the kid and his parents and I go into one of the back rooms in the courthouse and sit there looking at one another for a while. Finally, we recover enough to mumble some Oh my Gods and Thank yous and You're welcomes. And that's why I can stand to represent somebody when I know he's guilty. 16

Thinking Critically about the Text

Much abuse is heaped on lawyers who defend clients whose guilt seems obvious. How does Winston's story help explain why lawyers need to defend "guilty" clients?

Questions on Subject

1. Why does the D.A. bring in witnesses for a case that has been plea-bargained? What is ironic about that decision? (Glossary: *Irony*)

2. Why was Holloway reluctant to be interviewed by Winston about what he saw and did in the aftermath of the accident? What might he have been afraid of?

3. Why did Holloway finally ask to speak to the court? Why do you suppose Winston chose not to object to Holloway's request?

4. What do you think is the point of Winston's narrative?

Questions on Strategy

1. Winston establishes the context for his story in the first three paragraphs. What basic information does he give readers?

2. What details does Winston choose to include in the story? Why does he include them? Is there other information that you would like to have had? Why do you suppose Winston chose to omit that information?

3. Explain how Winston uses sentence variety to pace his narrative. What effect do his short sentences and sentence fragments have on you?

4. What does Winston gain as a writer by telling us that this is "a true story," one that we can check out in the court records?

5. During the courtroom scene (paragraphs 9–15), Winston relies heavily on dialogue. (Glossary: *Dialogue*) What does he gain by using dialogue? Why do you suppose he uses dialogue sparingly in the other parts of his narrative?

6. How does Winston use description to differentiate the four witnesses to the accident? (Glossary: *Description*) Why is it important for him to give his readers some idea of their differing characters?

Questions on Diction and Vocabulary

1. How would you characterize Winston's voice in this story? How is that voice established? (Glossary: *Voice*)

2. What, if anything, does Winston's diction tell you about Winston himself? (Glossary: *Diction*) What effect does his diction have on the tone of his narrative? (Glossary: *Tone*)

3. Refer to your dictionary to determine the meanings of the following words as Winston uses them in this selection: *felony* (paragraph 1), *agitated* (7), *misdemeanor* (8), *probation* (8), *bolt* (9).

Classroom Activity Using Narration

Effective narration uses strong verbs and clear, vivid description. Newspaper writers, because they must concisely and vividly evoke everyday events, are acutely aware of the need for effective narration. It is not enough for them to say that the city council discussed the resolution, the tornado happened, or the team won;

they must choose language that efficiently brings the discussion, the weather, and the game to life. For this reason, verbs such as *argued*, *tore*, *destroyed*, *buried*, *trounced*, and the like are common in the headlines of our local papers, and great care is taken to ensure that meaning is conveyed efficiently but accurately.

Sometimes these efforts go astray. As an exercise in both editing for and using strong verbs, consider the following real newspaper headlines — headlines that should have been reconsidered before the paper went to press. First, identify the source of the unintended humor in each headline. Then — as illustrated in the sample below — rewrite the headline using effective narration techniques.

Sample headline: Red Tape Holds Up New Bridges

Edited headline: ₋Red Tape ̲Holds Up̲ New Bridges
(Bureaucratic Delays)

New Study of Obesity Looks for Larger Test Group

Kids Make Nutritious Snacks

Local High School Dropouts Cut in Half

Hospitals Sued by 7 Foot Doctors

Police Begin Campaign to Run Down Jaywalkers

Typhoon Rips Through Cemetery: Hundreds Dead

Man Kills Self Before Shooting Wife and Daughter

Juvenile Court to Try Shooting Defendant

If Strike Isn't Settled Quickly, It May Last Awhile

Writing Suggestions

1. "Stranger Than True" is a first-person narrative told from the defense lawyer's point of view. Imagine that you are a newspaper reporter covering this case. What changes would you have to make in Winston's narrative to make it a news story? Make a list of the changes you would have to make, and then rewrite the story.

2. Holloway's revelation in the courtroom catches everyone by surprise. Analyze the chain of events in the accident and the assumptions that people made based on the accounts of those events. After reading the introduction to Chapter 11, "Cause and Effect Analysis," write a cause and effect essay in which you explain some of the possible reasons why Holloway's confession is so unexpected. (Glossary: *Cause and Effect Analysis*)

For Immigrant Family,
No Easy Journeys

JENNIFER 8. LEE

Jennifer 8. Lee was born in New York City in 1976 to Chinese immigrant parents. As a teenager, Lee gave herself her unusual middle name to bring her good fortune — something that has accompanied her throughout her career. Having grown up in New York City, Lee attended Harvard College, where she studied applied mathematics and economics and participated in the Asian American Association. Lee also worked tirelessly on the *Harvard Crimson* and a start-up magazine called *Diversity and Distinction*. Before graduating in 1999, Lee honed her journalism skills with internships at the *Washington Post*, the *Wall Street Journal*, the *Boston Globe*, and *Newsday*, among other publications. A fluent Mandarin speaker, Lee also studied international relations at Beijing University for a year on a Harvard-Yenching Fellowship. Lee began writing for the *New York Times* as a summer intern in 1999. By 2001, she was on staff as a reporter, most recently writing the *Times*'s local news blog, City Room. Although an expert on the world of Chinese food, Lee wrote on a wide variety of topics, ranging from poverty and the environment to politics, crime, and technology. Her book *The Fortune Cookie Chronicles: Adventures in the World of Chinese Food* was published in 2008.

In "For Immigrant Family, No Easy Journeys," first published in the *New York Times* on January 4, 2003, Lee tells the story of Yan Hua Zheng and her family. She describes their struggle-filled journey to America from Fujian, China. Settling first in New York City, Ms. Zheng is finally reunited with her whole family in rural Georgia a decade later. Notice that Lee narrates her story about this immigrant family as an observer, using the third-person point of view.

Preparing to Read

The word *immigrant* has many connotations. If you have moved to the United States from another country, what associations does the word have for you and your family? Alternatively, if you were born in the United States, what associations come to mind? Share your thoughts about the word *immigrant* with your classmates. How does one's perspective affect one's associations with the word? Explain.

Yan Hua Zheng was worried about the crabs: They might not survive a twenty-hour bus ride. She knew that her two daughters, who moved to the mountains of north Georgia two months earlier, missed fresh crab, a Fujianese favorite, but the crabs are no good unless they go into the pot alive.

So Ms. Zheng instead bought Chinese groceries that could endure her own journey to rural Georgia. She was moving from New York to reunite with her family. She rode the subway back home to Herald Square from Chinatown with orange and red shopping bags teeming with pickled radishes, dried mushrooms, shredded pork, and soy milk.

Packing to leave a city after a decade is hard. Leaving via Greyhound is even harder: Life has to be collapsed into bags that do not exceed 70 pounds. And a lifetime of experiences must be collapsed into the space of a single bus seat, to be expanded again only when the door opens and lets in the strangeness of a new environment, a new climate, a new stage of life.

> A lifetime of experiences must be collapsed into the space of a single bus seat, to be expanded again only when the door opens and lets in the strangeness of a new environment, a new climate, a new stage of life.

Ms. Zheng, thirty-nine, moved to Manhattan a decade ago from her hometown in Fujian, a coastal province in southeastern China. At Thanksgiving time, she was making the second leg of her life journey, to Hiawassee, a small town in the northeast corner of Georgia.

In the last decade, waves of rural immigrants from Fujian have come to New York City. Tens of thousands arrived illegally, paying $30,000, $50,000, and even more to organized gangs of smugglers—known as snakeheads—to buy their chance at the American dream. In New York, they crowded each other out, out of homes, out of jobs.

Now the Fujianese are fanning out from New York City: north to Boston, south to Virginia, west to Tennessee. Some, like Ms. Zheng's family, are landing in small towns in the rural South like Hiawassee. "Every state has a Chinese restaurant," she said, explaining the feasibility of such moves. "Americans depend on us to eat."

She was leaving the only place in the country that had an identity to the Fujianese: New York City. Other parts of the United States are not called Indiana or Virginia or Georgia. Instead they are collectively known as *waizhou*—Mandarin Chinese for "out of state."

For the Fujianese, *waizhou* is more than a geographic description. It is the white space left over where there is no New York, no Chinatown, no East Broadway. *Waizhou* is where fathers and sons go away for weeks and months at a time to work twelve-hour days in Chinese restaurants. *Waizhou* is crisscrossed by Greyhound bus routes and dotted with little towns, all of which either already have or could use a Chinese restaurant. *Waizhou* schools are better. In *waizhou*, supermarkets sell crab meat prepackaged in boxes.

Ms. Zheng was reluctant to leave, but her husband had insisted on   9
buying a Chinese restaurant in Hiawassee, a town of 850 people that prides
itself for being two hours away from everywhere, including Atlanta. He
argued that the restaurant could give them the financial and family stability
that eluded them in New York. Her husband and two daughters left months
before; now she was going with her young son in her lap to join them.

A SECOND MIGRATION

Ms. Zheng came to New York after paying $30,000 to snakeheads for a   10
fake passport and a plane ticket. She left her husband, John Ni, behind
with their four-year-old daughter, Jolin. Three years later, Mr. Ni left Jolin,
too. He was given asylum in the United States on religious grounds, and
that allowed his wife to become a legal resident as well.

He had no idea of how hard it would be to earn American money with   11
poor English skills. In Fujian, he had graduated from college and held a
low-stress job as an accountant. But in the United States, he worked as a
waiter, slowly learning the restaurant business. Ms. Zheng worked in garment
factories. Sometimes she even slept there, her head by the sewing machine.

They lived at 31st and Broadway, in a building filled with Fujianese   12
crowded four or five to a room. The building is a study in the art of vertical
living: bunk beds, wooden lofts, shelves that reach to the ceiling, boards
strung across pipes to create storage space. It is a building full of takeout
deliverymen. At night, the doorway is surrounded by dozens of chained
bicycles.

In 1998, they had another daughter, Nancy, whom they sent back to   13
China to be raised by her grandparents. A year later, they had a son. They
named him Jeffrey but called him Momo, from their local Chinese dialect
for "no hair." Ms. Zheng decided to keep him at her side.

A year and a half ago, Jolin got a visa and moved here, joining parents   14
she had not seen in ten years, in a one-room apartment. Nancy was brought
by her grandparents three months later.

John Ni was from the countryside and had never really felt comfort-   15
able with life in Manhattan, the crowds, the clutter, the smells. He was
tired of their family living in a single room where they cooked in a makeshift kitchen in the bathroom.

In July, the couple heard from a friend about a modest Chinese restau-   16
rant called China Grill for sale in Hiawassee, a town whose name Ms.
Zheng could barely pronounce. Mr. Ni went down to see the place. It was
in a strip mall, sandwiched between a Dairy Queen and a Subway sandwich shop. The eight tables were set with A.1. steak sauce and Chinese
zodiac place mats. The letters out front were in faux Chinese calligraphy.

Mr. Ni liked Hiawassee: It was small and the landscape reminded him   17
of home. For the same rent as they paid for their 250-square-foot room in
New York City, the family could get a 1,250-square-foot apartment with
two bedrooms, seven closets, and a washer and dryer. On the phone, he
told Jolin that she could go fishing in the nearby lake.

Hiawassee seemed safer than a big city, where stories of men being   18
beaten or killed while delivering food was a common currency among the
Fujianese. A relative of Ms. Zheng's was shot and killed in a restaurant
holdup a few years ago in Philadelphia. She hated the idea of living in the
middle of nowhere, but she relented.

In September, after borrowing money from friends and family, they   19
bought the restaurant, for $60,000. Mr. Ni went first, buying a 1992 Cutlass
Cierra for $1,300. Then he learned to drive.

Nancy and Jolin took the Greyhound down to Hiawassee in October;   20
Ms. Zheng stayed behind with Momo to deal with a crisis. Their apartment
had been robbed in August, and someone stole a safe with $10,000 in cash,
jewelry, and many legal papers — including birth certificates and passports.
Ms. Zheng was stuck here a little while longer untangling the mess.

In Georgia, business was slow — the tourist season in the Appalachians   21
was over — but the customers were friendly. One man gave Mr. Ni a fishing
rod. A local artist took the girls to register at school. On the first day of
classes, one of Jolin's classmates asked her if she was in New York on
September 11, 2001. She couldn't understand what the other child said.
Then a boy went up to the board and drew two buildings and a plane.

Jolin found *waizhou* boring, but she also found beauty. On her first   22
trip to Atlanta, she gazed out at fourteen lanes of densely packed car
lights — one river of red, one white — that flowed to and from the night
horizon on Interstate 85. "They look like ants moving up a mountain," she
said. "It's prettier than New York."

There was a wonderful place called "Wama," which was huge, and   23
sold everything from milk to underwear to televisions, at good prices. The
man at the door gave out yellow smiley stickers that said "WAL-MART."

But she was surprised by the Chinatowns in *waizhou*. The ones on   24
Atlanta's Buford Highway were U-shaped strip malls. And instead of
densely packed streets, the "Chinatowns" had huge parking lots that over-
flowed on weekends.

ATLANTA HAS FRESH CRABS

Greyhound doesn't stop in Hiawassee, so when she finally straightened out   25
everything in New York, Ms. Zheng bought a ticket for Gainesville,
Georgia — an hour of winding mountain roads away.

She left on November 26. On the way to the Port Authority bus ter- 26
minal, she passed bands practicing for the Macy's Thanksgiving Day
Parade in Herald Square. At the terminal, Ms. Zheng looked for her gate
with seven bags and a toddler in tow. A woman with a polka dot scarf waiting at the gate tried to be helpful. "Donde va?" she asked. Ms. Zheng
stared back.

Ms. Zheng sat near the front, next to the lady in the polka dot scarf, 27
because the back of buses made her carsick. When the Lincoln Tunnel spit
out the bus into New Jersey, Ms. Zheng held her son and looked back at
the Manhattan skyline. She had paid $30,000 to move to New York; she
had paid $59 to Greyhound to leave.

Momo, quickly tiring of his confined space, exasperated some other 28
passengers with his thorough exploration of the bus.

"Who has cold medicine to knock him out?" piped up one man. 29

"What he needs is a shot of rum—straight up," called out another 30
passenger.

Ms. Zheng did not understand what they were saying, but she could 31
read the tone of their voices.

The industrial landscape of Interstate 95 melted into the hollow 32
stretches of Interstate 85. Baltimore. Richmond, Virginia, where there was
a delay. Charlotte, North Carolina, where she had to change buses.
Spartanburg, North Carolina, Greenville, South Carolina. The hills and
trees along Interstate 85 reminded Ms. Zheng of her village and her father's
farm. The temperature rose, and there were leaves on the trees.

In the Charlotte bus depot, she met a Fujianese man on his way back 33
to Tennessee after a New York City vacation. He gave Ms. Zheng almost
$100 worth of seafood that he was afraid would spoil because his bus was
delayed.

The clams and abalone were still fresh, but the crabs had died between 34
Richmond and Charlotte. They were big ones, the kind that cost $7 a
pound.

After twenty-four hours, Ms. Zheng arrived at her final bus depot. She 35
waited and waited for her husband. A voice pierced through the crowd.
"Hello! Hello!"

Mr. Ni rushed up, scooped up his son, and hugged him. Husband and 36
wife looked at each other. They had not seen each other for two months.
There was no embrace.

It was 3 a.m. by the time they reached their home in Hiawassee, where 37
there was still some clean white mountain snow on the ground. Mr. Ni turned
on the bedroom light and shook his daughters. Jolin woke up, bleary-eyed.
She looked around and her face brightened when she realized who was
there. She immediately hugged her little brother. "He smells," she said.

Nancy continued to sleep on the mattress on the floor. "She's gotten 38
chubbier," Ms. Zheng observed, looking at her younger daughter. She'd
been eating snacks from the restaurant, Jolin explained.

Jolin dragged the bags in from the car. She jumped on fourteen vid- 39
eotapes her mother had brought of a popular Chinese serial opera. Mr. Ni
swung Momo around, laughing.

Ms. Zheng watched the two of them. For the first time in their lives, 40
the pieces of the family puzzle were complete. It was a family that barely
knew each other, but now had only each other to depend on.

After the restaurant closed the next night, the family had their first 41
dinner together in months. Ms. Zheng brought out the chilled clams from
Charlotte to go along with the stir-fried broccoli and sesame chicken. The
clam was good when dipped in wasabi mixed with soy sauce. But it wasn't
crab.

So at her first opportunity, Ms. Zheng endured a two-hour journey of 42
winding roads to Atlanta. (She threw up twice; New York subways are not
adequate preparation for winding roads.) She brought back two bags of
crabs and steamed them for dinner. "They are not much more expensive
than in New York," she said.

The family sat around the table. They had no need for crab crackers, 43
breaking the warm red shells with fingers and teeth. It was a lot of effort
for thin slivers of white crab meat and spoonsful of orange roe. But they
thought it was worth it. "Fujianese are not afraid of hard work," Jolin said.

Thinking Critically about the Text

What were your expectations after reading the title of Lee's narrative? Usually
when one thinks of immigration, one thinks of a journey. Were you surprised to
see that Lee used the plural *journeys* in the title? Just how difficult were Ms.
Zheng's and her family's journeys? What was the goal that kept the family sacrificing and forging ahead?

Questions on Subject

1. How old was Ms. Zheng when she first moved to Manhattan? Why was she
   willing to pay the "snakeheads" $30,000 to smuggle her into the United
   States? Why do you think the Chinese immigrants called these smugglers
   "snakeheads"?

2. When did her husband John Ni arrive in the United States? How did Mr. Ni and
   his wife become legal residents in the United States?

3. In paragraph 12, what does Lee mean when she says that the building at 31st
   and Broadway in New York City is "a study in the art of vertical living"?

4. Why did Mr. Ni want to buy a Chinese restaurant in rural Georgia? What did he like about Hiawassee once he had moved there? Why was Ms. Zheng reluctant to leave New York City?

5. How would you describe Ms. Zheng's reaction as she watched her husband swing their son Momo around? In what ways was Ms. Zheng's family "a family that barely knew each other" (paragraph 40)?

Questions on Strategy

1. How does Lee establish a context for her narrative in the selection's opening paragraphs?

2. Why do you suppose Lee uses the third-person point of view to narrate Yan Hua Zheng's story? What would have been gained or lost had she chosen to use the first-person point of view in her narration?

3. How has Lee organized her narration? Does she use a straightforward chronology or does she make use of flashback?

4. At various points in the narrative, Lee quotes Ms. Zheng and other members of her family; she even quotes several passengers on the bus from New York to Georgia. In what ways do these quotations enhance Lee's narrative? What would have been lost if she had not chosen to tell readers what the various people had said? Explain.

5. How effective did you find Lee's conclusion (paragraphs 42–43)? In what ways does her ending hark back to her opening paragraphs? How did you respond to Jolin's observation in the last sentence? Explain.

Questions on Diction and Vocabulary

1. Identify five or six transitional words or phrases that Lee uses to help readers connect and understand the sequence of events in her narrative or to see how much time has elapsed between events. How helpful did you find these transitional time markers?

2. What does the word *waizhou* mean in Mandarin Chinese? Why do the Fujianese use this word to refer to other parts of the United States that are not New York City? Explain.

3. Refer to a dictionary to determine the meanings of the following words as Lee uses them in this selection: *teeming* (paragraph 2), *eluded* (9), *asylum* (10), *calligraphy* (16), *exasperated* (28), *roe* (43).

Classroom Activity Using Narration

The number of words or paragraphs a writer devotes to the retelling of an event does not usually correspond to the number of minutes or hours or days the event took to happen. A writer may require multiple paragraphs to recount an important or complex ten- or twenty-minute encounter but then pass over several hours, days, or even years in several sentences. In narration, length has less to do with chronological real time than with the amount of emphasis the writer wants to give a particular incident. Identify several passages in Lee's essay where she uses multiple paragraphs to recount a relatively brief encounter or incident, and where she uses only a paragraph or two to cover a long period of time. What does this tell you about the relative importance of the material being narrated? Explain.

Writing Suggestions

1. Do you know someone who is part of an immigrant family? What has been their experience in moving to the United States? Why did they choose to leave their native country? How long did it take for them to feel at home in their adopted country? After interviewing one or more members of this immigrant family, write a narrative essay about their experience in coming to America, using the third-person point of view as Lee does in her essay.

2. The decision to relocate from New York City to Hiawassee, Georgia, was not an easy one. Lee tells us that "John Ni was from the countryside and had never really felt comfortable with life in Manhattan, the crowds, the clutter, the smells. He was tired of their family living in a single room where they cooked in a makeshift kitchen in the bathroom" (paragraph 15). His wife, on the other hand, was reluctant to leave Manhattan, a place she'd called home for a decade. "She was leaving the only place in the country that had an identity to the Fujianese" (7), and "she hated the idea of living in the middle of nowhere, but she relented" (18). Write an essay about the relationship between place and personal identity. How is your own identity tied to the place where you grew up or where you live now?

3. Jolin's closing remark that "Fujianese are not afraid of hard work" is a summary of her family's experience in the United States. How willing are you to work hard for something that you want? Write a narrative essay in which you recount a time you worked hard and sacrificed in order to meet a goal that was important to you. Be sure to create a context for your story and to clearly articulate the goal you were working toward. You may find it helpful to review your answer to the "Thinking Critically about the Text" questions for this selection (page 120) before beginning to write.

WRITING SUGGESTIONS FOR NARRATION

1. Using Malcolm X's, David P. Bardeen's, or Elisa Mala's essay as a model, narrate an experience that gave you a new awareness of yourself. Use enough telling detail in your narrative to help your reader visualize your experience and understand its significance for you. You may find the following suggestions helpful in choosing an experience to narrate in the first person:

   a. my greatest success
   b. my biggest failure
   c. my most embarrassing moment
   d. my happiest moment
   e. a truly frightening experience
   f. an experience that, in my eyes, turned a hero or an idol into an ordinary person
   g. an experience that turned an ordinary person I know into one of my heroes
   h. the experience that was the most important turning point in my life

2. Each of us can tell of an experience that has been unusually significant in teaching us about our relationship to society or to life's institutions — schools, social or service organizations, religious groups, government. Think about your past, and identify one experience that has been especially important for you in this way. After you have considered this event's significance, write an essay recounting it. In preparing to write your narrative, you might benefit from reading George Orwell's account of acting against his better judgment in "Shooting an Elephant" (pages 639–45). To bring your experience into focus and to help you decide what to include in your essay, ask yourself: Why is this experience important to me? What details are necessary for me to re-create the experience in an interesting and engaging way? How can my narrative be most effectively organized? What point of view will work best?

3. While growing up, we have all done something we know we should not have done. Sometimes we have gotten away with our transgressions, sometimes not. Sometimes our actions have no repercussions; sometimes they have very serious ones. Tell the story of one of your escapades, and explain why you have remembered it so well.

4. Many people love to tell stories (that is, they use narration) to illustrate an abstract point, to bring an idea down to a personal level, or to render an idea memorable. Often, the telling of such stories can be entertaining as well as instructive. Think about a belief or position that you hold dear (e.g., every

individual deserves respect, recycling matters, voluntarism creates community, people need artistic outlets, nature renews the individual), and try to capture that belief in a sentence or two. Then, narrate a story that illustrates your
belief or position.

5. **Writing with Sources.** As a way of gaining experience with third-person narration, write an article intended for your school or community newspaper in
   which you report on what happened at one of the following:

   a. the visit of a state or national figure to your campus or community
   b. a dormitory meeting
   c. a current event of local, state, or national significance
   d. an important sports event
   e. a current research project of one of your professors
   f. a campus gathering or performance
   g. an important development at a local business or at your place of
      employment

   You may find it helpful to read the third-person narrative about the invention of
   Coca-Cola (page 80) or Jennifer 8. Lee's "For Immigrant Family, No Easy
   Journeys" (pages 115–20) before starting to write your own narrative. In order
   to provide context for your article, consider interviewing one or more people
   involved and/or doing some background research on the object of your narrative. For models of and advice on integrating sources in your essay, see
   Chapters 14 and 15.

6. **Writing with Sources.** Imagine that you are a member of a campus organization seeking volunteers for a community project. Your job is to write a piece
   for the school newspaper to solicit help for your organization. To build support
   for the project, narrate one or more stories about the rewards of lending a
   hand to others within the community. In order to provide context for your
   article, consider interviewing one or more people who already volunteer or
   do some background research on the need for the community project. For
   models of and advice on integrating sources in your essay, see Chapters 14
   and 15.

7. Take some time to study Grant Snider's "Life in the Woods" reproduced at the
   beginning of this chapter (page 78).

   a. First, take a few minutes to describe what's going on in this illustration.
      Who is the character? Where is he or she? What happens? Next, consider
      how you know this. What aspects of the narrative are conveyed by written
      elements? What parts are conveyed by visual elements only?
   b. Write a short paper in which you discuss what you discovered about the
      differences between visual and written narratives.

8. **Writing with Sources.** Consider broadening and deepening your exploration of the differences between visual and written narratives by reading what others have to say about using visuals to convey meaning. (One good source for such discussion is Scott McCloud's *Understanding Comics*.) Alternatively, consider writing a paper in which you compare and contrast two genres (graphic novels and films, perhaps) used with a single work or two examples from the same genre (for instance, Gene Luen Yang's *American-Born Chinese* and Marjane Satrapi's *Persepolis*, two graphic novels). For models of and advice on integrating sources in your essay, see Chapters 14 and 15.

9. **Writing in the Workplace.** Imagine that you will be attending a national sales conference, representing the office where you work. For one of the opening small-group sessions, you have been asked to prepare a three-to-five-minute narrative in which you tell a revealing story about yourself as a way of introducing yourself to the group. What is it that you think others would be interested in knowing about you?

---

 e-Pages

Don't Tell, Martha!

LT. DAN CHOI

See how narration works on the Web. Go to bedfordstmartins.com/subjectand strategy for a video reading and study questions about Dan Choi's experience with the U.S. military's "Don't Ask, Don't Tell" policy.

CHAPTER 5

Description

WHAT IS DESCRIPTION?

DESCRIBING SOMETHING WITH WORDS IS OFTEN COMPARED TO PAINTING a verbal picture. Both verbal description (like a magazine article profiling a celebrity) and visual description (like a photograph, painting, or drawing accompanying the article) seek to transform fleeting perceptions into lasting images—through words in the case of an article and pixels, paints, or pencils in the case of a photograph, painting, or drawing. Both verbal and visual descriptions enable us to imaginatively experience the subject using some or all of our five senses. Both kinds of description convey information about a subject, telling us something we didn't know before. Both can convey a dominant impression of the subject. And, finally, both verbal and visual descriptions can be classed as primarily objective or subjective, depending on how much they reveal the perspective of the person doing the describing.

The photograph opposite—one of a series of portraits of Ella Watson, a custodial worker in a federal government building, taken by Gordon Parks in August 1942—is a good example of description conveyed through strictly visual cues, principally lighting and composition (the arrangement of the flag, mop, and broom, with an unsmiling Watson at the center).

DESCRIPTION IN WRITTEN TEXTS

Description is a key element in many kinds of written texts. Consider, for example, the following description by Bernd Heinrich from his book *One Man's Owl* (1987). In this selection, Heinrich describes trekking through the woods in search of owls. First, try to see, hear, smell, and feel the scene he describes: Form the jigsaw puzzle of words and details into a complete experience. Once you've accomplished this, define the dominant impression Heinrich creates.

Sets the scene with description of landscape	By mid-March in Vermont, the snow from the winter storms has already become crusty as the first midday thaws refreeze during the cold nights. A solid white cap compacts the snow, and you can walk on it without breaking through to your waist. The maple sap is starting to run on warm days, and one's blood quickens.
Describes sights and sounds of birds in early spring	Spring is just around the corner, and the birds act as if they know. The hairy and downy woodpeckers drum on dry branches and on the loose flakes of maple bark, and purple finches sing merrily from the spruces. This year the reedy voices of the pine siskins can be heard everywhere on the ridge where the hemlocks grow, as can the chickadees' two-note, plaintive song. Down in the bog, the first red-winged blackbirds have just returned, and they can be heard yodeling from the tops of dry cattails. Flocks of rusty blackbirds fly over in long skeins, heading north.
Reveals his position and relies on auditory details as night approaches	From where I stand at the edge of the woods overlooking Shelburne Bog, I feel a slight breeze and hear a moaning gust sweeping through the forest behind me. It is getting dark. There are eery creaking and scraping noises. Inside the pine forest it is becoming black, pitch black. The songbirds are silent. Only the sound of the wind can be heard above the distant honks of Canada geese flying below the now starry skies. Suddenly I hear a booming hollow "hoo-hoo-*hoo*-hoo—." The deep resonating hoot can send a chill down any spine, as indeed it has done to peoples of many cultures. But I know what the sound is, and it gives me great pleasure.

Heinrich could have described the scene with far fewer words, but that description would likely not have conveyed his dominant impression—one of comfort with the natural surroundings. Heinrich reads the landscape with subtle insight; he knows all the different birds and understands their springtime habits. The reader can imagine the smile on Heinrich's face when he hears the call of the owl.

USING DESCRIPTION AS A WRITING STRATEGY

Writers often use the strategy of description to inform—to provide readers with specific data. You may need to describe the results of a chemical reaction for a lab report, the style of a Renaissance painting for an art history term paper, the physical capabilities and limitations of a stroke patient for a case study, or the acting of Meryl Streep in a movie you want your friends to see. Such descriptions will sometimes be scientifically objective, sometimes intensely impressionistic. The approach you use will depend on the subject itself, the information you want to communicate about it, and the format in which the description appears.

Another important use of description is to create a mood or atmosphere or even to convey your own views — to develop a *dominant impression*. Pat Mora uses the strategy of description to capture the fierce determination and joy that Lobo, her spinster aunt, found in leading "[a] life of giving."

> Lobo was a woman of fierce feelings, of strong opinions. She was a woman who literally whistled while she worked. The best way to cheer her when she'd visit my young children was to ask for her help. Ask her to make a bed, fold laundry, set the table or dry dishes, and the whistling would begin as she moved about her task. Like all of us, she loved being needed. Understandable, then, that she muttered in annoyance when her body began to fail her. She was a woman who found self-definition and joy in visibly showing her family her love for us by bringing us hot *té de canela* (cinnamon tea) in the middle of the night to ease a cough, by bringing us comics and candy whenever she returned home. A life of giving.

Each of the descriptions in this chapter is distinguished by the strong dominant impression the writer creates.

There are essentially two types of description: objective and subjective. *Objective description* is as factual as possible, emphasizing the actual qualities of the subject being described while subordinating the writer's personal responses. For example, a witness to a mugging would try to give authorities a precise, objective description of the assailant, unaffected by emotional responses, so that a positive identification could be made. In the excerpt from his book, Bernd Heinrich objectively describes what he sees: "The hairy and downy woodpeckers drum on dry branches and on the loose flakes of maple bark, and purple finches sing merrily from the spruces."

Subjective or *impressionistic description*, on the other hand, conveys the writer's personal opinion or impression of the object, often in language rich in modifiers and figures of speech. A food critic describing a memorable meal would inevitably write about it impressionistically, using colorful or highly subjective language. (In fact, relatively few words in English can describe the subtleties of smell and taste in neutral terms.) In "A Woman on the Street," Jeannette Walls uses objective and subjective description techniques to capture a picture of her mother and what she sees as her dilemma.

Notice that with objective description, it is usually the person, place, or thing being described that stands out, whereas with subjective description the response of the person doing the describing is the most prominent feature. Most topics, however, lend themselves to both objective and subjective description, depending on the writer's purpose. You could write, for example, that you had "exactly four weeks" to finish a history term paper (objective) or that you had "all the time in the world" or "an outrageously short amount of time" (subjective). Each type of description can be accurate and useful in its own way.

Although descriptive writing can stand alone, and often does, it is also used with other types of writing. In a narrative, for example, descriptions provide the context for the story—and make the characters, settings, and events come alive. Description may also help to define an unusual object or animal, such as a giraffe, or to clarify the steps of a process, such as diagnosing an illness. Wherever it is used, good description creates vivid and specific pictures that clarify, create a mood, and build a dominant impression.

USING DESCRIPTION ACROSS THE DISCIPLINES

When writing essays in the academic disciplines, you will have many opportunities to use the strategy of description to both organize and strengthen the presentation of your ideas. To determine whether or not description is the right strategy for you in a particular paper, review the guidelines in Chapter 2 (Determining a Strategy for Developing Your Essay, pages 32–33). Consider the following examples:

History

1. **MAIN IDEA:** Roman medicine, while primitive in some ways, was in general very advanced.
2. **QUESTION:** What primitive beliefs and advanced thinking characterize Roman medicine?
3. **STRATEGY:** Description. The direction word *characterize* signals the need to describe Roman medical practices and beliefs.
4. **SUPPORTING STRATEGY:** Comparison and contrast might be used to set off Roman practices and beliefs from those in later periods of history.

Chemistry

1. **MAIN IDEA:** The chemical ingredients in acid rain are harmful to humans and the environment.
2. **QUESTION:** What are the components of acid rain?
3. **STRATEGY:** Description. The direction word *components* suggests the need for a description of acid rain, including as it does sulfuric acid, carbon monoxide, carbon dioxide, chlorofluorocarbons, and nitric acid.
4. **SUPPORTING STRATEGY:** Cause and effect might be used to show the harm caused by acid rain. Process analysis might be used to explain how acid rain develops.

Psychology

1. **MAIN IDEA:** Law enforcement officers who are under abnormal stress manifest certain symptoms.
2. **QUESTION:** What comprises the symptoms?
3. **STRATEGY:** Description. The direction word *comprises* suggests the need for a picture or description of the *symptoms*.
4. **SUPPORTING STRATEGY:** Comparison and contrast might be used to differentiate those officers suffering from stress. Process analysis might be used to explain how to carry out an examination to identify the symptoms of stress. Argumentation might be used to indicate the need for programs to test for excessive stress on the job.

SAMPLE STUDENT ESSAY USING DESCRIPTION AS A WRITING STRATEGY

Jim Tassé wrote the following essay while he was a student at the University of Vermont, where he majored in English and religion. Tassé hopes to teach eventually, perhaps at the college level, but his most immediate interests include biking and singing with a rock band. As his essay "Trailcheck" reveals, Tassé is an enthusiastic skier. His experience working on ski patrol during winter breaks provided him with the subject for a striking description.

Trailcheck

Jim Tassé

Context — early morning in January and preparations for Trailcheck

At a quarter to eight in the morning, the sharp cold of the midwinter night still hangs in the air of Smuggler's Notch. At the base of Madonna Mountain, we stamp our feet and turn up our collars while waiting for Dan to get the chairlift running.   1

Description of Trailcheck begins with explanation of what it is

Trailcheck always begins with this cold, sleepy wait — but it can continue in many different ways. The ski patrol has to make this first run every morning to assess the trail conditions before the mountain opens — and you never know what to expect on top of the Mad Dog, Madonna Mountain. Sometimes we take our first run down the sweet, light powder that fell the night before; sometimes we have to ski the rock-hard boiler-plate ice that formed when yesterday's mush froze. But there's always the cold — the dank, bleary cold of 8 a.m. in January.

Use of present tense gives immediacy to the description

I adjust my first-aid belt and heft my backpack up a little   2
higher, cinching it tight. I shiver, and pull my hat down a bit

lower. I am sleepy, cold, and impatient. Dan's finally got the lift running, and the first two patrollers, Chuck and Ken, get on. Three more chairs get filled, and then there's me. Looks like I'm riding up alone. The chairlift jars me a little more awake as it hits the back of my boots. I sit down and am scooped into the air.

Description of total experience is enhanced by appealing to reader's senses — especially touch, hearing, and sight

It's a cold ride up, and I snuggle my chin deep into my parka. The bumps of the chair going over the lift-tower rollers help keep me awake. Trees piled high and heavy with snow move silently past. Every so often, in sudden randomness, a branch lets go a slide and the air fills with snow dust as the avalanche crashes from branch to branch, finally landing with a soft thud on the ground. Snow dances in the air with kaleidoscopic colors, shining in the early daylight.

3

I imagine what it would have been like on the mountain on a similar day three hundred years ago. A day like this would have been just as beautiful, or maybe even more so—the silent mountain, all trees and cold and sunshine, with no men and no lifts. I think of the days when the fog rolls out of the notch, and the wind blows cold and damp, and the trees are close and dark in the mist, and I try to imagine how terrifyingly wild the mountain would have been centuries ago, before the white man came and installed the chairlift that takes me to the top so easily. I think how difficult it would have been to climb through the thick untamed forest that bristles out of the mountain's flanks, and I am glad I don't have to walk up Madonna this sleepy-eyed morning.

4

Well-selected details contribute to description of wintry mountain and magic of the day

I watch the woods pass, looking for the trails of small animals scrolled around the trees. Skiing should be nice with all the new snow. Arriving at the top, I throw up the safety bar, tip my skis up, make contact, stand, and ski clear of the lift. The view from the mountaintop is incredible. I can see over the slopes of Stowe, where another patrol is running trailcheck just as we are. Across the state, Mt. Washington hangs above the horizon like a mirage. Back toward Burlington, I can see the frozen lake sprawling like a white desert.

5

I toss my backpack full of lunch and books to Marty, who's going into the patrol shack to get the stove fired up. I stretch my legs a little as we share small talk, waiting for the mountain captain to say we can go down. I tighten my boots. Finally, Ken's radio crackles out the word, and I pull down my goggles and pole forward.

6

Opening sentence and two fragments following signal the end of the ride and the beginning of the Trailcheck

Wake up! The first run of the day. Trailcheck. Today the run is heaven—eight inches of light dry powder. My turns are relaxed giant slaloms that leave neat S's in the snow behind me. No need to worry about ice or rocks—the snow covers everything with an airy cushion that we float on, fly on, our skis barely on the ground. We split up at the first intersection, and I bear to the left, down the Glades. My skis gently hiss as they break the powder, splitting the snow like a boat on calm water. I blast through deep drifts of snow, sending gouts and geysers of snow up around me. The air sparkles with snow, breaking the light into flecks of color.

Strong action verbs bring the description alive

Contrast enhances description of the Trailcheck

What a day! Some mornings I ride up in fifteen-below-zero cold, only to ski down icy hardpack on which no new snow has fallen for days. There are rocks and other hazards to be noted and later marked with bamboo poles so skiers don't hit them. Fallen branches must be cleared from the trail. On days like that, when the snow is lousy and I have to worry about rocks gouging the bottoms of the skis, trailcheck is work—cold, necessary work done too early in the morning. But when the run is like today, the suffering is worthwhile.

Dominant impression of ecstatic playfulness emerges

I yelp with pleasure as I launch myself off a knoll and gently land in the soft whiteness, blasting down a chute of untracked powder that empties out into a flatter run. I can hear the other patroller whooping and yelling with me in the distance. Turns are effortless; a tiny shift of weight and the skis respond like wings. I come over the next pitch, moving fast, and my skis hit an unseen patch of ice; my tails slide, too late to get the edge in, and POOF! I tumble into the snow in an explosion of snow dust. For a second I lie panting. Then I wallow in ecstasy, scooping the handfuls of powder over myself, the sweet light snow tingling in the air. After a moment I hop up and continue down, sluicing the S-turns on the whipped-cream powder.

Concluding comment sums up the writer's experience in one word

Reaching the patrol room, I click off my skis and stamp the snow from myself. No longer do I feel the night's cold breath in the air—just the sting of the melting snow on my face. Ken looks at me as I drip and glisten over my trail report, and asks: "Good run, Jim?"

I grin at him and say, "Beau-ti-ful!"

7

8

9

10

11

> **Analyzing Jim Tassé's Description Essay:**
> **Questions for Discussion**
>
> 1. How does Tassé support his dominant impression in this essay?
> 2. How does Tassé *show* that the mountain is beautiful rather than simply *say* that it is?
> 3. How and where does Tassé indicate the importance of a trailcheck?

SUGGESTIONS FOR USING DESCRIPTION AS A WRITING STRATEGY

As you plan, write, and revise your essay of description, be mindful of the writing process guidelines described in Chapter 2. Pay particular attention to the basic requirements and essential ingredients of this writing strategy.

▶ Planning Your Description Essay

Planning is an essential part of writing a good description essay. You can save yourself a great deal of work by taking the time to think about key building blocks of your essay before you actually begin to write.

DETERMINE A PURPOSE. Begin by determining your purpose: Are you trying to inform, express your emotions, persuade, or entertain? While it is not necessary, or even desirable, to state your purpose explicitly, it is necessary that you have one that your readers recognize. If your readers do not see a purpose in your writing, they may be tempted to respond by asking, "So what?" Making your reason for writing clear in the first place will help you avoid this pitfall.

USE DESCRIPTION IN THE SERVICE OF AN IDEA. Your readers will want to know why you chose to describe what you did. You should always write description with a thesis in mind, an idea you want to convey to your readers. For example, you might describe a canoe trip as one of both serenity and exhilarating danger, which for you symbolize the contrasting aspects of nature. In his essay "A View from the Bridge" (see pages 8–10), Cherokee Paul McDonald uses description in the service of an idea, and that idea is description itself: McDonald needs to describe a fish so that a blind boy can "see" it. In the process of describing, the author comes to an epiphany: The act of describing the fish brings him closer to the essence of it. He realizes then that he has received from the boy more than he has given.

SHOW, DON'T TELL: USE SPECIFIC NOUNS AND ACTION VERBS. Inexperienced writers often believe that adjectives and adverbs are the basis for effective descriptions. They're right in one sense, but not wholly so. Al-

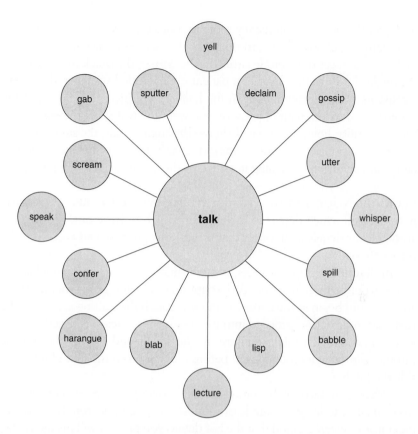

though strong adjectives and adverbs are crucial, description also depends on well-chosen nouns and verbs. *Vehicle* is not nearly as descriptive as something more specific—*Jeep, snowmobile,* or *Honda Civic.* Similarly, the verb *talk* does far less to describe the *way* something is said than do any of a host of possible substitutes (see the diagram on page 135). The more specific and strong you make your nouns and verbs, the more lively and interesting your descriptions will be.

When you have difficulty thinking of specific action nouns and verbs to use, reach for a thesaurus—but only if you are sure you can discern the best word for your purpose. Inexpensive paperback editions are available at any bookstore, and most word-processing programs have a thesaurus utility. A thesaurus will help you keep your descriptions from getting repetitive and will be invaluable when you need to find a specific word with just the right meaning.

◗ Organizing Your Description Essay

CREATE A DOMINANT IMPRESSION. After generating as many details as possible describing your subject, reread them and select those that will be most helpful in developing a dominant impression. Suppose that you wish to depict the hospital emergency room as a place of great tension. You will then naturally choose details to reinforce that sense of tension: the worried looks on the faces of a couple sitting in the corner, the quick movements of the medical staff as they tend to a patient on a wheeled stretcher, the urgent whisperings of two interns out in the hallway, the incessant paging of Dr. Thomas. If the dominant impression you want to create is of the emergency room's sterility, however, you will choose different details: the smell of disinfectant, the spotless white uniforms of the staff members, the stainless steel tables and chairs, the gleaming instruments the nurse hands to the physician.

ORGANIZE YOUR DETAILS TO CREATE A VIVID PICTURE.   Once you have decided which details to include and which to leave out, you need to arrange your details in an order that serves your purpose and is easy for the reader to follow.

In describing some subjects, it might make sense to imagine what the reader would experience first. A description of an emergency room, for example, could begin at the entrance, move through the waiting area, pass the registration desk, and proceed into the treatment cubicles. A description of a restaurant kitchen might conjure up the smells and sounds that escape through the swinging doors even before moving on to the first glimpse inside the kitchen.

Other patterns of organization include moving from general to specific, from smallest to largest, from least to most important, or from the usual to the unusual. Keep in mind that the last details you present will probably stay in the reader's mind the longest and that the first details will also have special force.

Before you begin your first draft, you may find it useful to sketch out an outline of your description. Here's a sample outline for Bernd Heinrich's description of his trek through the late winter landscape in search of owls (page 128).

Description of Shelburne Bog

Dominant impression: Comfort with the natural surroundings

Paragraph 1: Snow-crusted landscape in mid-March

Paragraph 2: Activity and sounds of the birds (e.g., woodpeckers, finches, chickadees, and red-winged blackbirds) described from the edge of the woods

Paragraph 3: Activity and sounds inside the pine forest behind the speaker, culminating with the familiar call of the owl

Such an outline can remind you of the dominant impression you want to create and can suggest which specific details may be most useful to you.

❱ Revising and Editing Your Description Essay

SHARE YOUR WORK WITH OTHERS.   Try sharing your draft with other students in your writing class to make sure that your description makes sense. Ask them if there are any parts that they do not understand. Have them tell you what they think is the point of your description. If their answers differ from what you intended, have them indicate which passages led them to their interpretation so that you can change your text accordingly. To maximize the effectiveness of conferences with your peers, use the guidelines presented on page 36. Feedback from these conferences often provides one or more places where you can start revising.

QUESTION YOUR OWN WORK WHILE REVISING AND EDITING.   Revision is best done by asking yourself key questions about what you have written. Begin by reading, preferably aloud, what you have written. Reading aloud forces you to pay attention to every single word, and you are more likely to catch lapses in the logical flow of thought. After you have read your paper through, answer the following questions for revising and editing, and make the necessary changes. For help with twelve common writing problems, see Chapter 16, "Editing for Grammar, Punctuation, and Sentence Style."

Questions for Revising and Editing: Description

1. Do I have a clear purpose for my description? Have I answered the "so what" question?

2. Is the subject of my description interesting and relevant to my audience?

3. What senses have I chosen to use to describe it? For example, what does it look like, sound like, or smell like? Does it have a texture or taste that is important to mention?

4. Which details must I include in my essay? Which are irrelevant or distracting to my purpose and should be discarded?

5. Have I achieved the dominant impression I wish to leave with my audience?

6. Does the organization I have chosen for my essay make it easy for the reader to follow my description?

7. How carefully have I chosen my descriptive words? Are my nouns and verbs strong and specific?

8. Have I used figurative language, if appropriate, to further strengthen my description?

9. Does my paper contain any errors in grammar, punctuation, or mechanics? Is my sentence style as clear, smooth, and persuasive as possible?

A Woman on the Street

JEANNETTE WALLS

Jeannette Walls was born in 1960 in Phoenix, Arizona, and later moved with her family from Phoenix to San Francisco, California, to Battle Mountain, Nevada, and to Welch, West Virginia. At the age of seventeen she entered Barnard College in New York City, graduating with honors in 1984. After college she interned and then became a reporter for the *Phoenix*, a small newspaper in Brooklyn, New York. Walls is best known for her gossip reporting on "The Scoop" on MSNBC (1998–2007) and for *The Glass Castle* (2005), a memoir of her childhood years growing up in a nomadic and, at times, homeless family. *The Glass Castle* remained on the *New York Times* best-seller list for more than 200 weeks, sold over 2.5 million copies, was translated into twenty-two languages, and has been optioned as a movie by Paramount. Walls has written two other books, *Dish: The Inside Story on the World of Gossip* (2000) and *Half-Broke Horses: A True-Life Novel* (2009).

In "A Woman on the Street," the first chapter of *The Glass Castle*, Walls describes a chance sighting of her mother scavenging in a Dumpster in New York City and a subsequent meeting to try to help "improve" her mother's homeless life.

Preparing to Read

Do you ever wonder about the homeless, their lives before becoming homeless, and their beliefs and values? Does the way we think about the homeless depend mostly on how we describe them, or are there real aspects of their lives that support our impressions? If you know someone who is homeless, what qualities does that person possess that others might not know?

I was sitting in a taxi, wondering if I had overdressed for the evening, when I looked out the window and saw Mom rooting through a Dumpster. It was just after dark. A blustery March wind whipped the steam coming out of the manholes, and people hurried along the sidewalks with their collars turned up. I was stuck in traffic two blocks from the party where I was heading.

Mom stood fifteen feet away. She had tied rags around her shoulders to keep out the spring chill and was picking through the trash while her dog, a black-and-white terrier mix, played at her feet. Mom's gestures were all familiar—the way she tilted her head and thrust out her lower lip when studying items of potential value that she'd hoisted out of the Dumpster, the way her eyes widened with childish glee when she found something she liked. Her long hair was streaked with gray, tangled and matted, and her eyes had sunk deep into their sockets, but still she reminded me of the mom she'd been when I was a kid, swan-diving off cliffs and painting in the desert and reading Shakespeare aloud. Her cheekbones were still high and strong, but the skin was parched and ruddy from all those winters and summers exposed to the elements. To the people walking by, she probably looked like any of the thousands of homeless people in New York City.

It had been months since I laid eyes on Mom, and when she looked up, 3 I was overcome with panic that she'd see me and call out my name, and that someone on the way to the same party would spot us together and Mom would introduce herself and my secret would be out.

I slid down in the seat and asked the driver to turn around and take me 4 home to Park Avenue.

The taxi pulled up in front of my building, the doorman held the door 5 for me, and the elevator man took me up to my floor. My husband was working late, as he did most nights, and the apartment was silent except for the click of my heels on the polished wood floor. I was still rattled from seeing Mom, the unexpectedness of coming across her, the sight of her rooting happily through the Dumpster. I put some Vivaldi on, hoping the music would settle me down.

I looked around the room. There were the turn-of-the-century bronze- 6 and-silver vases and the old books with worn leather spines that I'd collected at flea markets. There were the Georgian maps I'd had framed, the Persian rugs, and the overstuffed leather armchair I liked to sink into at the end of the day. I'd tried to make a home for myself here, tried to turn the apartment into the sort of place where the person I wanted to be would live. But I could never enjoy the room without worrying about Mom and Dad huddled on a sidewalk grate somewhere. I fretted about them, but I was embarrassed by them, too, and ashamed of myself for wearing pearls and living on Park Avenue while my parents were busy keeping warm and finding something to eat.

What could I do? I'd tried to help them 7 countless times, but Dad would insist they didn't need anything, and Mom would ask for something silly, like a perfume atomizer or a membership in a health club. They said that they were living the way they wanted to.

After ducking down in the taxi so Mom wouldn't see me, I hated 8
myself—hated my antiques, my clothes, and my apartment. I had to do
something, so I called a friend of Mom's and left a message. It was our
system of staying in touch. It always took Mom a few days to get back to
me, but when I heard from her, she sounded, as always, cheerful and casual, as though we'd had lunch the day before. I told her I wanted to see her
and suggested she drop by the apartment, but she wanted to go to a restaurant. She loved eating out, so we agreed to meet for lunch at her favorite
Chinese restaurant.

Mom was sitting at a booth, studying the menu, when I arrived. She'd 9
made an effort to fix herself up. She wore a bulky gray sweater with only a
few light stains, and black leather men's shoes. She'd washed her face, but
her neck and temples were still dark with grime.

She waved enthusiastically when she saw me. "It's my baby girl!" she 10
called out. I kissed her cheek. Mom had dumped all the plastic packets of
soy sauce and duck sauce and hot-and-spicy mustard from the table into
her purse. Now she emptied a wooden bowl of dried noodles into it as
well. "A little snack for later on," she explained.

We ordered. Mom chose the Seafood Delight. "You know how I love 11
my seafood," she said.

She started talking about Picasso. She'd seen a retrospective of his 12
work and decided he was hugely overrated. All the cubist stuff was gimmicky, as far as she was concerned. He hadn't really done anything worthwhile after his Rose Period.

"I'm worried about you," I said. "Tell me what I can do to help." 13

Her smile faded. "What makes you think I need your help?" 14

"I'm not rich," I said. "But I have some money. Tell me what it is you 15
need."

She thought for a moment. "I could use an electrolysis treatment." 16

"Be serious." 17

"I am serious. If a woman looks good, she feels good." 18

"Come on, Mom." I felt my shoulders tightening up, the way they 19
invariably did during these conversations. "I'm talking about something
that could help you change your life, make it better."

"You want to help me change my life?" Mom asked. "I'm fine. You're 20
the one who needs help. Your values are all confused."

"Mom, I saw you picking through trash in the East Village a few days 21
ago."

"Well, people in this country are too wasteful. It's my way of 22
recycling." She took a bite of her Seafood Delight. "Why didn't you say
hello?"

"I was too ashamed, Mom. I hid." 23

Mom pointed her chopsticks at me. "You see?" she said. "Right there. 24
That's exactly what I'm saying. You're way too easily embarrassed. Your
father and I are who we are. Accept it."

"And what am I supposed to tell people about my parents?" 25

"Just tell the truth," Mom said. "That's simple enough." 26

Thinking Critically about the Text

"A Woman on the Street" is a description of Walls's mother, but if you reflect on
what she has written, you soon realize that the essay is equally as much about her
as a daughter. Explain how Walls is able to "turn the tables" on herself, as it were.

Questions on Subject

1. Do you think Walls's mother is happy? Why, or why not?

2. Do you think Walls herself is happy? Why, or why not?

3. Is Walls's mother against material possessions? How do you know?

4. Why do you suppose Walls's mother refuses to go to her daughter's
   apartment?

5. In the end, what point is her mother trying to make Walls understand? What
   does she mean when she says to her daughter, "I'm fine. You're the one that
   needs help. Your values are all confused" (paragraph 20)? Are Walls's values
   confused? Explain.

Questions on Strategy

1. How does Walls describe her mother? What details does she reveal about her?

2. How does Walls describe herself? What details does she reveal about herself?

3. How does Walls use comparison and contrast in this selection? (Glossary:
   Comparison and Contrast)

4. Is Walls's essay arranged inductively or deductively? Explain. (Glossary: *Deduction*; *Induction*)

5. In your opinion, is Walls a reliable narrator? What evidence does she present
   to indicate that she is or is not telling the story truthfully to the best of her
   ability?

6. Why do you think Walls makes paragraph 4 a single sentence?

Questions on Diction and Vocabulary

1. Walls uses certain words and phrases to quickly draw distinctions between
   the life her mother is leading and the life she herself is leading. Point out a half
   dozen of those terms and phrases and explain how they work as a kind of
   descriptive shorthand.

2. In paragraph 16, is Walls's mother being straightforward or ironic when she says that she would like "an electrolysis treatment"? How do you know? (Glossary: *Irony*)

3. What do you think about Walls's title for this selection? Do you think it is the best title? Can you offer some alternatives that you think would work better? (Glossary: *Title*)

Classroom Activity Using Description

Think about your topic — the person, place, thought, or concept that lies at the center of your descriptive essay. Make a list of all the details that you could gather about it using your five senses, as well as those that simply come to mind when you consider your topic. Determine a dominant impression that you would like to create, and then choose those details from your list that will best help you form it. Your instructor may wish to have you and your classmates go over your lists in class and discuss how effective the items will be in building dominant impressions.

Writing Suggestions

1. In paragraph 6, Walls says of her own apartment, "I tried to make a home for myself here, tried to turn the apartment into the sort of place where the person I wanted to be would live." Write an essay in which you consider the idea that homelessness might be as much a state of mind as a physical reality. In other words, does one have to be without a home to be homeless? Can one be homeless living in a wonderful home with all its creature comforts? If you agree with this idea, what is it that makes a person have a sense of belonging, and a sense of warmth, comfort, safety, and satisfaction? Describe that life.

2. Walls's writing demonstrates that a writer need not include a lot of details to paint a picture, only the ones that will do the job. For example, she describes her own apartment in the first three sentences of paragraph 6 in a very revealing way. Describe your own room, whether at school or at home, using a minimum of details to convey a sense of the place in the manner that you want your reader to know it. Start with a list of all the objects that might be included and then winnow the list to the most telling and essential details for your purpose. Finally, be sure to make your description not an exercise in selectivity and brevity alone but one which, like Walls's essay, is part of a narrative that relies on your description to make your story work.

Remembering Lobo

PAT MORA

Pat Mora was born in El Paso, Texas, in 1942. She grew up in a mostly Spanish-speaking household greatly influenced by her four grandparents, who had fled to El Paso during the Mexican Revolution in the early part of the twentieth century. Speaking Spanish at home and English in public school, Mora received her B.A. from Texas Western College in 1963 and her M.A. from the University of Texas at El Paso in 1967. As a writer, lecturer, teacher, university administrator, and literacy advocate, Mora has spent her career speaking and writing about the value of family, Mexican American culture, and the desert. She is the author of over forty works of fiction and nonfiction for children and adults, among them collections of poetry such as *Chants* (1984), *Borders* (1986), and *Communion* (1991) that explore bicultural and bilingual themes. *House of Houses* (1997), perhaps her most important work, is a family memoir that uses the metaphor of a house to tell the generational story of her family in the span of a single year.

In "Remembering Lobo," taken from *Nepantla: Essays from the Middle* (1993), Mora offers us a poignant portrait of her Aunt Ignacia, better known to family members as *Lobo*. With telling details and touching devotion, Mora describes her aunt and shows how Lobo "taught [her] much about one of our greatest challenges as human beings: loving well."

Preparing to Read

Think about one of your favorite aunts or uncles or a dear family friend. What makes that person special to you? Is it that the person has a special affection for you? Is it because the person has special character traits that you'd like to emulate or think are in some way strange but appealing? Or is it that the person shares some family traits with your parents? Explain.

We called her *Lobo*. The word means "wolf" in Spanish, an odd name for a generous and loving aunt. Like all names it became synonymous with her, and to this day returns me to my childself. Although the name seemed perfectly natural to us and to our friends, it did cause frowns from strangers throughout the years. I particularly remember one hot afternoon when on a crowded streetcar between the border cities of El Paso and Juarez, I momentarily lost sight of her. "Lobo! Lobo!" I cried in panic. Annoyed faces peered at me, disappointed at such disrespect to a white-haired woman.

Actually the fault was hers. She lived with us for years, and when she arrived home from work in the evening, she'd knock on our front door and ask, *"¿Dónde están mis lobitos?"* "Where are my little wolves?"

Gradually she became our *lobo*, a spinster aunt who gathered the four of us around her, tying us to her for life by giving us all she had. Sometimes to tease her we would call her by her real name. *"¿Dónde está Ignacia?"* we would ask. Lobo would laugh and say, "She is a ghost."

We called her *Lobo*.

The word means "wolf"

in Spanish, an odd

name for a generous

and loving aunt.

To all of us in nuclear families today, the notion of an extended family under one roof seems archaic, complicated. We treasure our private space. I will always marvel at the generosity of my parents, who opened their door to both my grandmother and Lobo. No doubt I am drawn to the elderly because I grew up with two entirely different white-haired women who worried about me, tucked me in at night, made me tomato soup or hot *hierbabuena* (mint tea) when I was ill.

Lobo grew up in Mexico, the daughter of a circuit judge, my grandfather. She was a wonderful storyteller and over and over told us about the night her father, a widower, brought his grown daughters on a flatbed truck across the Rio Grande at the time of the Mexican Revolution. All their possessions were left in Mexico. Lobo had not been wealthy, but she had probably never expected to have to find a job and learn English.

When she lived with us, she worked in the linens section of a local department store. Her area was called "piece goods and bedding." Lobo never sewed, but she would talk about materials she sold, using words I never completely understood, such as *piqué* and *broadcloth*. Sometimes I still whisper such words just to remind myself of her. I'll always savor the way she would order "sweet milk" at restaurants. The precision of a speaker new to the language.

Lobo saved her money to take us out to dinner and a movie, to take us to Los Angeles in the summer, to buy us shiny black shoes for Christmas. Though she never married and never bore children, Lobo taught me much about one of our greatest challenges as human beings: loving well. I don't think she ever discussed the subject with me, but through the years she lived her love, and I was privileged to watch.

She died at ninety-four. She was no sweet, docile Mexican woman dying with perfect resignation. Some of her last words before drifting into semiconsciousness were loud words of annoyance at the incompetence of nurses and doctors.

"No sirven." "They're worthless," she'd say to me in Spanish.

"They don't know what they're doing. My throat is hurting and they're   10
taking X-rays. Tell them to take care of my throat first."

I was busy striving for my cherished middle-class politeness. "Shh,   11
shh," I'd say. "They're doing the best they can."

"Well, it's not good enough," she'd say, sitting up in anger.   12

Lobo was a woman of fierce feelings, of strong opinions. She was a   13
woman who literally whistled while she worked. The best way to cheer her
when she'd visit my young children was to ask for her help. Ask her to
make a bed, fold laundry, set the table, or dry dishes, and the whistling
would begin as she moved about her task. Like all of us, she loved being
needed. Understandable, then, that she muttered in annoyance when her
body began to fail her. She was a woman who found self-definition and joy
in visibly showing her family her love for us by bringing us hot *té de canela*
(cinnamon tea) in the middle of the night to ease a cough, by bringing us
comics and candy whenever she returned home. A life of giving.

One of my last memories of her is a visit I made to her on November 2,   14
El Día de los Muertos, or All Souls' Day. She was sitting in her rocking
chair, smiling wistfully. The source of the smile may seem a bit bizarre to a
U.S. audience. She was fondly remembering past visits to the local cemetery on this religious feast day.

"What a silly old woman I have become," she said. "Here I sit in my   15
rocking chair all day on All Souls' Day, sitting when I should be out there.
At the cemetery. Taking good care of *mis muertos*, my dead ones.

"What a time I used to have. I'd wake while it was still dark outside.   16
I'd hear the first morning birds, and my fingers would almost itch to begin.
By six I'd be having a hot bath, dressing carefully in black, wanting *mis
muertos* to be proud of me, proud to have me looking respectable and
proud to have their graves taken care of. I'd have my black coffee and
plenty of toast. You know the way I like it. Well browned and well but-
tered. I wanted to be ready to work hard.

"The bus ride to the other side of town was a long one, but I'd say a   17
rosary and plan my day. I'd hope that my perfume wasn't too strong and
yet would remind others that I was a lady.

"The air at the cemetery gates was full of chrysanthemums: that strong,   18
sharp, fall smell. I'd buy tin cans full of the gold and wine flowers. How I
liked seeing aunts and uncles who were also there to care for the graves of
their loved ones. We'd hug. Happy together.

"Then it was time to begin. The smell of chrysanthemums was like a   19
whiff of pure energy. I'd pull the heavy hose and wash the gravestones
over and over, listening to the water pelting away the desert sand. I always
brought newspaper. I'd kneel on the few patches of grass, and I'd scrub
and scrub, shining the gray stones, leaning back on my knees to rest for a bit

and then scrubbing again. Finally a relative from nearby would say, *'Ya, ya, Nacha,'* and laugh. Enough. I'd stop, blink my eyes to return from my trance. Slightly dazed, I'd stand slowly, place a can of chrysanthemums before each grave.

"Sometimes I would just stand there in the desert sun and listen. I'd 20 hear the quiet crying of people visiting new graves; I'd hear families exchanging gossip while they worked.

"One time I heard my aunt scolding her dead husband. She'd sweep 21 his gravestone and say, *'¿Porqué?* Why did you do this, you thoughtless man? Why did you go and leave me like this? You know I don't like to be alone. Why did you stop living?' Such a sight to see my aunt with her proper black hat and her fine dress and her carefully polished shoes muttering away for all to hear.

"To stifle my laughter, I had to cover my mouth with my hands." 22

Thinking Critically about the Text

Mora grew up living with an extended family that included her grandmother and aunt. Why does she "marvel at the generosity of [her] parents" in this regard (paragraph 4)? What concessions might her parents have made to help make their living arrangement work? What were the benefits of the arrangement for Mora in particular?

Questions on Subject

1. Why do you think Mora's aunt Ignacia wanted to be called "Lobo"?

2. What does Mora mean when she writes about the name Lobo: "Like all names it became synonymous with her, and to this day returns me to my childself" (paragraph 1)?

3. Mora writes in paragraph 13 that Lobo "found self-definition and joy in visibly showing her family her love." In what acts did Lobo specifically, according to Mora, exhibit her love?

4. Why was All Souls' Day so important to Lobo? Why was it important for her to go to the cemetery on this day?

5. When she was dying, Lobo became annoyed at her nurses. What was her problem? How does Mora inform us of Lobo's problem with her nurses? (Glossary: *Dialogue*)

Questions on Strategy

1. How does Mora show us Lobo's playful side?

2. How does the image of the "wolf" work in furthering Mora's purpose? (Glossary: *Figures of Speech*)

3. What advantage does Mora gain by using food, particularly drink, to help her describe Lobo? (Glossary: *Figures of Speech*)

4. Mora writes in paragraph 8 that Lobo was "no sweet, docile Mexican woman dying with perfect resignation." How does Mora show us this side of Lobo?

5. How does Mora show us Lobo's respect for All Souls' Day? (Glossary: *Dialogue; Illustration*)

Questions on Diction and Vocabulary

1. Why do you suppose Mora invents the term "childself" instead of using the word *childhood* (paragraph 1)? How does the new term help Mora accomplish her purpose?

2. What does Mora accomplish by adding some Spanish words and phrases to her description of Lobo?

3. Mora says in paragraph 6 that Lobo used words in referring to her job that she [Mora] "never completely understood." What were those words, and why did she not bother to find out their meanings? What magic qualities might they have had for Mora?

Classroom Activity Using Description

Organizational possibilities are many and varied, reflecting your purpose and the subject or object you are attempting to describe. Depending on your purpose you could present the same set of details and order them in several different ways. Suppose, for example, you wanted to describe a favorite teacher you had in high school. You could present your teacher's qualities according to a logical plan ranging from the least important to the most important, or you could describe her qualities in a chronological manner from the time you first met her to the time you had to leave her class. You could also organize your description according to her obvious physical attributes and then move on to describe the more complex parts of her personality, in effect moving from the outer to the inner person.

In order to see how this works, first make a list of descriptive features for an object of your choice and then organize them according to any two of the following principles:

Smallest to largest	Left to right
Least to most important	Easiest to most difficult to understand
Outside to inside	Specific to general
Far to near	

Writing Suggestions

1. Using Mora's essay as a model and your response to the Preparing to Read prompt for this selection, write a description of one of your favorite aunts or uncles or a special family friend. Keep in mind that effective description requires examples drawn from sense perceptions, telling details, thoughtful organization, showing and not telling, and the use of concrete nouns and strong action verbs, as well as figurative language. Above all, think about the dominant impression you wish to create and your larger purpose in describing the person you choose as your subject.

2. Mora returned the gift of love that her aunt bestowed on her by writing about Lobo and, in a sense, immortalized her. In similar fashion, describe a relative, friend, or even a stranger who has given you a character-building gift, whether it be perseverance, courage, dedication, honesty, or some other intangible trait — and how that gift was passed on to you by your subject. Describe how your subject was able to influence you so importantly and how you have put that gift to good use in your own life.

The Barrio

ROBERT RAMÍREZ

Robert Ramírez was born in 1949 and was raised in Edinburg, Texas, near the Mexican border. He graduated from the University of Texas–Pan American and then worked in several communications-related jobs before joining KGBT-TV in Harlingen, Texas, where he was an anchor. He then moved to finance and worked for a time in banking and as a development officer responsible for alumni fund-raising for his alma mater.

Ramírez's knowledge of the barrio allows him to paint an affectionate portrait of barrio life that nevertheless has a hard edge. His barrio is colorful but not romantic, and his description raises important societal issues as it describes the vibrant community. "The Barrio" was originally published in *Pain and Promise: The Chicano Today* (1972), edited by Edward Simmen.

Preparing to Read

Describe the neighborhood in which you grew up or the most memorable neighborhood you ever encountered. Did you like it? Why, or why not? How strong was the sense of community between neighbors? How did it contrast with other neighborhoods nearby?

The train, its metal wheels squealing as they spin along the silvery tracks, rolls slower now. Through the gaps between the cars blinks a streetlamp, and this pulsing light on a barrio street-corner beats slower, like a weary heartbeat, until the train shudders to a halt, the light goes out, and the barrio is deep asleep.

Throughout Aztlán (the Nahuatl term meaning "land to the north"), trains grumble along the edges of a sleeping people. From Lower California, through the blistering Southwest, down the Rio Grande to the muddy Gulf, the darkness and mystery of dreams engulf communities fenced off by railroads, canals, and expressways. Paradoxical communities, isolated from the rest of the town by concrete columned monuments of progress, yet stranded in the past. They are surrounded by change. It eludes their reach, in their own backyards, and the people, unable and unwilling to see the future, or even touch the present, perpetuate the past.

Leaning from the expressway or jolting across the tracks, one enters a different physical world permeated by a different attitude. The physical dimensions are impressive. It is a large section of town which extends for fifteen blocks north and south along the tracks, and then advances eastward, thinning into nothingness beyond the city limits. Within the invisible (yet sensible) walls of the barrio, are many, many people living in too few houses. The homes, however, are much more numerous than on the outside.

Members of the barrio describe the entire area as their home. It is a home, but it is more than this. The barrio is a refuge from the harshness and the coldness of the Anglo world. It is a forced refuge. The leprous people are isolated from the rest of the community and contained in their section of town. The stoical pariahs of the barrio accept their fate, and from the angry seeds of rejection grow the flowers of closeness between outcasts, not the thorns of bitterness and the mad desire to flee. There is no want to escape, for the feeling of the barrio is known only to its inhabitants, and the material needs of life can also be found here.   4

> The barrio is a refuge from the harshness and the coldness of the Anglo world.

The *tortillería* fires up its machinery three times a day, producing steaming, round, flat slices of barrio bread. In the winter, the warmth of the tortilla factory is a wool *sarape* in the chilly morning hours, but in the summer, it unbearably toasts every noontime customer.   5

The *panadería* sends its sweet messenger aroma down the dimly lit street, announcing the arrival of fresh, hot sugary *pan dulce*.   6

The small corner grocery serves the meal-to-meal needs of customers, and the owner, a part of the neighborhood, willingly gives credit to people unable to pay cash for foodstuffs.   7

The barbershop is a living room with hydraulic chairs, radio, and television, where old friends meet and speak of life as their salted hair falls aimlessly about them.   8

The pool hall is a junior level country club where *'chucos*, strangers in their own land, get together to shoot pool and rap, while veterans, unaware of the cracking, popping balls on the green felt, complacently play dominoes beneath rudely hung *Playboy* foldouts.   9

The *cantina* is the night spot of the barrio. It is the country club and the den where the rites of puberty are enacted. Here the young become men. It is in the taverns that the young dude shows his *machismo* through the quantity of beer he can hold, the stories of *rucas* he has had, and his willingness and ability to defend his image against hardened and scarred old lions.   10

No, there is no frantic wish to flee. It would be absurd to leave the familiar and nervously step into the strange and cold Anglo community when the needs of the Chicano can be met in the barrio.   11

The barrio is closeness. From the family living unit, familial rela- 12 tionships stretch out to immediate neighbors, down the block, around the corner, and to all parts of the barrio. The feeling of family, a rare and trea- surable sentiment, pervades and accounts for the inability of the people to leave. The barrio is this attitude manifested on the countenances of the people, on the faces of their homes, and in the gaiety of their gardens.

The color-splashed homes arrest your eyes, arouse your curiosity, and 13 make you wonder what life scenes are being played out in them. The flimsy, brightly colored, wood-frame houses ignore no neon-brilliant color. Houses trimmed in orange, chartreuse, lime-green, yellow, and mixtures of these and other hues beckon the beholder to reflect on the peculiarity of each home. Passing through this land is refreshing like Brubeck, not nar- cotizing like revolting rows of similar houses, which neither offend nor please.

In the evenings, the porches and front yards are occupied with men 14 calmly talking over the noise of children playing baseball in the unpaved extension of the living room, while the women cook supper or gossip with female neighbors as they water their *jardines*. The gardens mutely echo the expressive verses of the colorful houses. The denseness of multicolored plants and trees gives the house the appearance of an oasis or a tropical island hideaway, sheltered from the rest of the world.

Fences are common in the barrio, but they are fences and not the walls 15 of the Anglo community. On the western side of town, the high wooden fences between houses are thick, impenetrable walls, built to keep the neighbors at bay. In the barrio, the fences may be rusty, wire contraptions or thick green shrubs. In either case you can see through them and feel no sense of intrusion when you cross them.

Many lower-income families of the barrio manage to maintain a com- 16 fortable standard of living through the communal action of family members who contribute their wages to the head of the family. Economic need creates interdependence and closeness. Small barefooted boys sell papers on cool, dark Sunday mornings, deny themselves pleasantries, and give their earnings to *mamá*. The older the child, the greater the responsibility to help the head of the household provide for the rest of the family.

There are those, too, who for a number of reasons have not achieved a 17 relative sense of financial security. Perhaps it results from too many chil- dren too soon, but it is the homes of these people and their situation that numbs rather than charms. Their houses, aged and bent, oozing children, are fissures in the horn of plenty. Their wooden homes may have brick- pattern asbestos tile on the outer walls, but the tile is not convincing.

Unable to pay city taxes or incapable of influencing the city to live   18
up to its duty to serve all the citizens, the poorer barrio families remain
trapped in the nineteenth century and survive as best they can. The backyards have well-worn paths to the outhouses, which sit near the alley.
Running water is considered a luxury in some parts of the barrio. Decent
drainage is usually unknown, and when it rains, the water stands for days,
an incubator of health hazards and an avoidable nuisance. Streets, costly to
pave, remain rough, rocky trails. Tires do not last long, and the constant
rattling and shaking grind away a car's life and spread dust through screen
windows.

The houses and their *jardines*, the jollity of the people in an adverse   19
world, the brightly feathered alarm clock pecking away at supper and cautiously eyeing the children playing nearby, produce a mystifying sensation
at finding the noble savage alive in the twentieth century. It is easy to look
at the positive qualities of life in the barrio, and look at them with a dis-
tantly envious feeling. One wishes to experience the feelings of the barrio
and not the hardships. Remembering the illness, the hunger, the feeling of
time running out on you, the walls, both real and imagined, reflecting on
living in the past, one finds his envy becoming more elusive, until it has
vanished altogether.

Back now beyond the tracks, the train creaks and groans, the cars   20
jostle each other down the track, and as the light begins its pulsing, the barrio, with all its meanings, greets a new dawn with yawns and restless
stretchings.

Thinking Critically about the Text

Does Ramírez's essay leave you with a positive or negative image of the barrio?
Is it a place you would like to live, visit, or avoid? Explain your answer.

Questions on Subject

1. Based on Ramírez's essay, what is the barrio? Why do you think that Ramírez
   uses the image of the train to introduce and close his essay about the
   barrio?

2. Why do you think Ramírez refers to the barrios of the Southwest as "paradoxical communities" (paragraph 2)?

3. In paragraph 4, Ramírez states that residents consider the barrio something
   more than a home. What does he mean? In what ways is it more than just a
   place where they live?

4. Why are the color schemes of the houses in the barrio striking? How do they contrast with houses in other areas of town? (Glossary: *Comparison and Contrast*)

5. Many of the barrio residents are able to achieve financial security. How are they able to do this? What is life like for those who cannot?

Questions on Strategy

1. Explain Ramírez's use of the imagery of walls and fences to describe a sense of cultural isolation. What might this imagery symbolize?

2. Ramírez uses several metaphors throughout his essay. (Glossary: *Figures of Speech*) Identify them, and discuss how they contribute to the essay.

3. Ramírez begins his essay with a relatively positive picture of the barrio but ends on a more disheartening note. (Glossary: *Beginnings/Endings*) Why has he organized his essay this way? What might the effect have been if he had reversed the images?

4. Ramírez goes into detail about the many groups living in the barrio. How does his subtle use of division and classification add to his description of the barrio? (Glossary: *Classification; Division*) In what ways do the groups he identifies contribute to the unity of life in the barrio?

5. Ramírez invokes such warm images of the barrio that his statement that its inhabitants do not wish to leave seems benign. In the end, however, it has a somewhat ominous ring. How does the description of the barrio have two components, one good and one bad? What are the two sides of the barrio's embrace for the residents?

Questions on Diction and Vocabulary

1. Ramírez uses Spanish phrases throughout his essay. Why do you suppose he uses them? What is their effect on the reader? He also uses the words *home*, *refuge*, *family*, and *closeness*. In what ways, if any, are they essential to his purpose? (Glossary: *Purpose*)

2. Ramírez calls barrio residents "the leprous people" (paragraph 4). What does the word *leprous* connote in the context of this essay? (Glossary: *Connotation/ Denotation*) Why do you think Ramírez chose to use such a strong word to communicate the segregation of the community?

3. In paragraph 6, Ramírez uses personification when he calls the aroma of freshly baked sweet rolls a "messenger" who announces the arrival of the baked goods. Cite other words or phrases that Ramírez uses to give human characteristics to the barrio.

Classroom Activities Using Description

1. Using action verbs can make a major difference in the quality of your writing. Review a draft of a descriptive essay that you have written and look for at least three weak verbs — verbs that do not add very much descriptive punch — and make a list of at least three alternatives you could replace each one with. Be sure that the meaning of each of your alternative action verbs supports your meaning and fits the context in which you use it.

2. Examine the photo on this page carefully. Based on the visual details in the photograph, what can you say about the community? Which details suggest the area's ethnicity and socioeconomic status? What can you say about the pace of life as depicted in the photograph? From what you see, is this an appealing neighborhood, in your judgment? How does this scene differ from the portrait of a barrio that Ramírez paints in his essay?

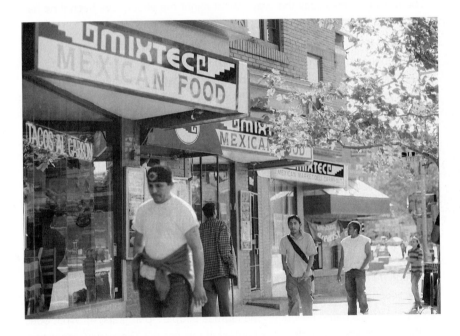

Writing Suggestions

1. Ramírez frames his essay with the image of a train rumbling past the sleeping residents. Using Ramírez's essay as a model, write a descriptive essay about the place you currently live and use a metaphorical image to frame your essay. (Glossary: *Figures of Speech*) What image is both a part of life where you live and an effective metaphor for it?

2. Write a comparison and contrast essay in which you compare where you live now with another residence. (Glossary: *Comparison and Contrast*) Where are you the most comfortable? What about your current surroundings do you like? What do you dislike? How does it compare with your hometown, your first apartment, or another place you have lived? If and when you move on, where do you hope to go?

Once More to the Lake

E. B. WHITE

Elwyn Brooks White (1899–1985) was born outside of New York City in the town of Mount Vernon. After serving in the army, he attended Cornell University and moved to Seattle to work as a reporter. He later returned to New York to work on the staff of the recently established *New Yorker*, for which he wrote everything from essays and editorials to cartoon captions. White eventually relocated to Maine, where he began farming. During this time, he wrote a column for *Harper's* that focused on his dual life as a writer and farmer; these essays were eventually collected and published in *One Man's Meat* (1944). White is well-known for his revision of William Strunk's writing guide *The Elements of Style* (1959), as well as for *Stuart Little* (1945) and *Charlotte's Web* (1952), children's stories that have both become classics.

"Once More to the Lake" is among the essays White wrote for *Harper's*. Published in 1941, White describes a childhood vacation spot to which he has returned as an adult with his son. As he witnesses what has changed and what has remained the same about the lake, he reflects on the passage of time and the inevitability of mortality.

Preparing to Read

If you have taken summer vacations to the beach, mountains, lake, or some other spot that is a favorite with you and your family, what stands out in your memory of the place you visited? How might you briefly describe it so that others can appreciate what made that place so special for you?

One summer, along about 1904, my father rented a camp on a lake in Maine and took us all there for the month of August. We all got ringworm from some kittens and had to rub Pond's Extract on our arms and legs night and morning, and my father rolled over in a canoe with all his clothes on; but outside of that the vacation was a success and from then on none of us ever thought there was any place in the world like that lake in Maine. We returned summer after summer—always on August 1st for one month. I have since become a salt-water man, but sometimes in summer there are days when the restlessness of the tides and the fearful cold of the sea water and the incessant wind which blows across the afternoon and into the evening make me wish for the placidity of a lake in the woods. A few weeks ago this feeling got so strong I bought myself a couple of bass hooks and a spinner and returned to the lake where we used to go, for a week's fishing and to revisit old haunts.

I took along my son, who had never had any fresh water up his nose   2 and who had seen lily pads only from train windows. On the journey over to the lake I began to wonder what it would be like. I wondered how time would have marred this unique, this holy spot—the coves and streams, the hills that the sun set behind, the camps and the paths behind the camps. I was sure that the tarred road would have found it out and I wondered in what other ways it would be desolated. It is strange how much you can remember about places like that once you allow your mind to return into the grooves which lead back. You remember one thing, and that suddenly reminds you of another thing. I guess I remembered clearest of all the early mornings, when the lake was cool and motionless, remembered how the bedroom smelled of the lumber it was made of and of the wet woods whose scent entered through the screen. The partitions in the camp were thin and did not extend clear to the top of the rooms, and as I was always the first up I would dress softly so as not to wake the others, and sneak out into the sweet outdoors and start out in the canoe, keeping close along the shore in the long shadows of the pines. I remembered being very careful never to rub my paddle against the gunwale for fear of disturbing the stillness of the cathedral.

The lake had never been what you would call a wild lake. There were   3 cottages sprinkled around the shores, and it was in farming country although the shores of the lake were quite heavily wooded. Some of the cottages were owned by nearby farmers, and you would live at the shore and eat your meals at the farmhouse. That's what our family did. But although it wasn't wild, it was a fairly large and undisturbed lake and there were places in it which, to a child at least, seemed infinitely remote and primeval.

I was right about the tar: it led to within half a mile of the shore. But   4 when I got back there, with my boy, and we settled into a camp near a farmhouse and into the kind of summertime I had known, I could tell that it was going to be pretty much the same as it had been before—I knew it, lying in bed the first morning, smelling the bedroom, and hearing the boy sneak quietly out and go off along the shore in a boat. I began to sustain the illusion that he was I, and therefore, by simple transposition, that I was my father. This sensation persisted, kept cropping up all the time we were there. It was not an entirely new feeling, but in this setting it grew much stronger. I seemed to be living a dual existence. I would be in the middle of some simple act, I would be picking up a bait box or laying down a table fork, or I would be saying something, and suddenly it would be not I but my father who was saying the words or making the gesture. It gave me a creepy sensation.

We went fishing the first morning. I felt the same damp moss cover- [5] ing the worms in the bait can, and saw the dragonfly alight on the tip of my rod as it hovered a few inches from the surface of the water. It was the arrival of this fly that convinced me beyond any doubt that everything was as it always had been, that the years were a mirage and there had been no years. The small waves were the same, chucking the rowboat under the chin as we fished at anchor, and the boat was the same boat, the same color green and the ribs broken in the same places, and under the floor-boards the same freshwater leavings and débris—the dead helgramite, the wisps of moss, the rusty discarded fishhook, the dried blood from yesterday's catch. We stared silently at the tips of our rods, at the dragon-flies that came and went. I lowered the tip of mine into the water, ten-tatively, pensively dislodging the fly, which darted two feet away, poised, darted two feet back, and came to rest again a little farther up the rod. There had been no years between the ducking of this dragonfly and the other one—the one that was part of memory. I looked at the boy, who was silently watching his fly, and it was my hands that held his rod, my eyes watching. I felt dizzy and didn't know which rod I was at the end of.

We caught two bass, hauling them in briskly as though they were [6] mackerel, pulling them over the side of the boat in a businesslike manner without any landing net, and stunning them with a blow on the back of the head. When we got back for a swim before lunch, the lake was exactly where we had left it, the same number of inches from the dock, and there was only the merest sugges-tion of a breeze. This seemed an utterly enchanted sea, this lake you could leave to its own devices for a few hours and come back to, and find that it had not stirred, this constant and trustworthy body of water. In the shallows, the dark, water-soaked sticks and twigs, smooth and old, were undulating in clusters on the bottom against the clean ribbed sand, and the track of the mussel was plain. A school of minnows swam by, each minnow with its small individ-ual shadow, doubling the attendance, so clear and sharp in the sunlight. Some of the other campers were in swimming, along the shore, one of them with a cake of soap, and the water felt thin and clear and unsubstan-tial. Over the years there had been this person with the cake of soap, this cultist, and here he was. There had been no years.

This seemed an utterly enchanted sea, this lake you could leave to its own devices for a few hours and come back to, and find that it had not stirred. . .

Up to the farmhouse to dinner through the teeming, dusty field, the road under our sneakers was only a two-track road. The middle track was missing, the one with the marks of the hooves and the splotches of dried, flaky manure. There had always been three tracks to choose from in choosing which track to walk in; now the choice was narrowed down to two. For a moment I missed terribly the middle alternative. But the way led past the tennis court, and something about the way it lay there in the sun reassured me; the tape had loosened along the backline, the alleys were green with plantains and other weeds, and the net (installed in June and removed in September) sagged in the dry noon, and the whole place steamed with midday heat and hunger and emptiness. There was a choice of pie for dessert, and one was blueberry and one was apple, and the waitresses were the same country girls, there having been no passage of time, only the illusion of it as in a dropped curtain—the waitresses were still fifteen; their hair had been washed, that was the only difference—they had been to the movies and seen the pretty girls with the clean hair. 7

Summertime, oh summertime, pattern of life indelible, the fade-proof lake, the woods unshatterable, the pasture with the sweet-fern and the juniper forever and ever, summer without end; this was the background, and the life along the shore was the design, the cottages with their innocent and tranquil design, their tiny docks with the flagpole and the American flag floating against the white clouds in the blue sky, the little paths over the roots of the trees leading from camp to camp and the paths leading back to the outhouses and the can of lime for sprinkling, and at the souvenir counters at the store the miniature birch-bark canoes and the post cards that showed things looking a little better than they looked. This was the American family at play, escaping the city heat, wondering whether the newcomers in the camp at the head of the cove were "common" or "nice," wondering whether it was true that the people who drove up for Sunday dinner at the farmhouse were turned away because there wasn't enough chicken. 8

It seemed to me, as I kept remembering all this, that those times and those summers had been infinitely precious and worth saving. There had been jollity and peace and goodness. The arriving (at the beginning of August) had been so big a business in itself, at the railway station the farm wagon drawn up, the first smell of the pine-laden air, the first glimpse of the smiling farmer, and the great importance of the trunks and your father's enormous authority in such matters, and the feel of the wagon under you for the long ten-mile haul, and at the top of the last long hill catching the first view of the lake after eleven months of not seeing this cherished body of water. The shouts and cries of the other campers when they saw you, and the trunks to be unpacked, to give up their rich burden. (Arriving was 9 less exciting nowadays, when you sneaked up in your car and parked it under a tree near the camp and took out the bags and in five minutes it was all over, no fuss, no loud wonderful fuss about trunks.)

Peace and goodness and jollity. The only thing that was wrong now, really, was the sound of the place, an unfamiliar nervous sound of the outboard motors. This was the note that jarred, the one thing that would sometimes break the illusion and set the years moving. In those other summertimes all motors were inboard; and when they were at a little distance, the noise they made was a sedative, an ingredient of summer sleep. They were one-cylinder and two-cylinder engines, and some were make-and-break and some were jump-spark, but they all made a sleepy sound across the lake. The one-lungers throbbed and fluttered, and the twin-cylinder ones purred and purred, and that was a quiet sound too. But now the campers all had outboards. In the daytime, in the hot mornings, these motors made a petulant, irritable sound; at night, in the still evening when the afterglow lit the water, they whined about one's ears like mosquitoes. My boy loved our rented outboard, and his great desire was to achieve singlehanded mastery over it, and authority, and he soon learned the trick of choking it a little (but not too much), and the adjustment of the needle valve. Watching him I would remember the things you could do with the old one-cylinder engine with the heavy flywheel, how you could have it eating out of your hand if you got really close to it spiritually. Motor boats in those days didn't have clutches, and you would make a landing by shutting off the motor at the proper time and coasting in with a dead rudder. But there was a way of reversing them, if you learned the trick, by cutting the switch and putting it on again exactly on the final dying revolution of the flywheel, so that it would kick back against compression and begin reversing. Approaching a dock in a strong following breeze, it was difficult to slow up sufficiently by the ordinary coasting method, and if a boy felt he had complete mastery over his motor, he was tempted to keep it running beyond its time and then reverse it a few feet from the dock. It took a cool nerve, because if you threw the switch a twentieth of a second too soon you could catch the flywheel when it still had speed enough to go up past center, and the boat would leap ahead, charging bull-fashion at the dock.

We had a good week at the camp. The bass were biting well and the sun shone endlessly, day after day. We would be tired at night and lie down in the accumulated heat of the little bedrooms after the long hot day and the breeze would stir almost imperceptibly outside and the smell of the swamp drift in through the rusty screens. Sleep would come easily and in the morning the red squirrel would be on the roof, tapping out his gay routine. I kept remembering everything, lying in bed in the mornings — the small steamboat that had a long rounded stern like the lip of a Ubangi, and how quietly she ran on the moonlight sails, when the older boys played their mandolins and the girls sang and we ate doughnuts dipped in sugar, and how sweet the music was on the water in the shining night, and what it had felt like to think about girls then. After breakfast we would go up to the store and the things were in the same place — the minnows in a bottle, the plugs and spinners disarranged and pawed over by the youngsters from the boys' camp, the fig newtons and the Beeman's gum. Outside, the road was tarred and cars stood in front of the store. Inside, all was just as it had always been, except there was more Coca-Cola and not so much Moxie and root beer and birch beer and sarsaparilla. We would walk out with a bottle of pop apiece and sometimes the pop would backfire up our noses and hurt. We explored the streams, quietly, where the turtles slid off the sunny logs and dug their way into the soft bottom; and we lay on the town wharf and fed worms to the tame bass. Everywhere we went I had trouble making out which was I, the one walking at my side, the one walking in my pants.

One afternoon while we were there at that lake a thunderstorm came 12 up. It was like the revival of an old melodrama that I had seen long ago with childish awe. The second-act climax of the drama of the electrical disturbance over a lake in America had not changed in any important respect. This was the big scene, still the big scene. The whole thing was so familiar, the first feeling of oppression and heat and a general air around camp of not wanting to go very far away. In midafternoon (it was all the same) a curious darkening of the sky, and a lull in everything that had made life tick; and then the way the boats suddenly swung the other way at their moorings with the coming of a breeze out of the new quarter, and the pre-monitory rumble. Then the kettle drum, then the snare, then the bass drum and cymbals, then crackling light against the dark, and the gods grinning and licking their chops in the hills. Afterward the calm, the rain steadily rustling in the calm lake, the return of light and hope and spirits, and the campers running out in joy and relief to go swimming in the rain, their bright cries perpetuating the deathless joke about how they were getting simply drenched, and the children screaming with delight at the new sensation of bathing in the rain, and the joke about getting drenched linking the generations in a strong indestructible chain. And the comedian who waded in carrying an umbrella.

When the others went swimming my son said he was going in too. He 13 pulled his dripping trunks from the line where they had hung all through the shower, and wrung them out. Languidly, and with no thought of going in, I watched him, his hard little body, skinny and bare, saw him wince slightly as he pulled up around his vitals the small, soggy, icy garment. As he buckled the swollen belt, suddenly my groin felt the chill of death.

Thinking Critically about the Text

Why do children and adults perceive things differently? Can we trust our childhood memories? How does White's adult visit to the lake match what he remembers from his boyhood summers? Are differences due to changes in him, the lake, or both? What predictions can you make about White's son?

Questions on Subject

1. Why does White decide to return to the lake as an adult?

2. What has changed about the lake since White's childhood? What has stayed the same? What meaning does White find in the differences he witnesses in the road, the waitresses, and the motorboats?

3. In paragraph 4, White says, "I began to sustain the illusion that my son was I, and therefore, by simple transposition, that I was my father." What prompts White to experience this "illusion," and how does the illusion shed light on his feelings about his trip to the lake?

4. White ends his piece on a somber note. Why does he feel "the chill of death" as he watches his son pull on his swim trunks? Did the close of the essay catch you by surprise, or did you feel prepared for it? Why?

Questions on Strategy

1. How do the first three paragraphs of the essay introduce the reader to what follows? (Glossary: *Beginnings*) What specific function does each of these paragraphs serve?

2. How does White organize his description of a late afternoon thunderstorm at the lake in paragraph 12? (Glossary: *Organization*) How does the old melodrama metaphor function in this description? (Glossary: *Figures of Speech*)

3. The dominant impression of the lake White creates as an adult differs from the dominant impression he creates there as a child. Describe each of these impressions. How exactly do they differ?

4. White narrates the essay in the first person. Rewrite a few of the paragraphs in the third person. In what ways does this change in point of view alter the essay? (Glossary: *Narration*)

5. How does White utilize comparison and contrast to develop his story?

Questions on Diction and Vocabulary

1. Comment on the connotations of each phrase. How do these connotations affect you as you read White's essay? What kind of mood do they evoke? (Glossary: *Connotation/Denotation*)

   a. "stillness of the cathedral" (paragraph 2)

   b. "infinitely remote and primeval" (3)

    c. "utterly enchanted sea" (6)

    d. "the woods unshatterable" (8)

    e. "nervous sound of . . . outboard motors" (10)

2. How would you describe the essay's tone? (Glossary: *Tone*) How does the tone manifest itself in White's diction? What does this tone suggest about White's attitude toward his visit to the lake?

3. Look up the meaning of the following words as they are used in the essay: *placidity* (paragraph 1), *haunts* (1), *partitions* (2), *primeval* (3), *transposition* (4), *tentatively* (5), *pensively* (5), *petulant* (10), *premonitory* (12).

Classroom Activity Using Description

In a group of three or four students, take turns describing some specific beautiful or remarkable place or thing as if your classmates were blind. You may actually want to bring an object to observe while your classmates cover their eyes. Help each other find the best words to create a vivid verbal picture. Write your description in a couple of brief paragraphs, retaining the informal style of your speaking voice.

Writing Suggestions

1. Write an essay about a time when you visited an important place from your past — an old home or school, a city you no longer live in, a vacation spot — that you hadn't been back to in a while. Describe the experience of returning to this place. What changed, and how did these changes affect you and your memories about this location? If possible, choose a spot you can actually revisit so that you may reflect on the ways that place has changed since you were last there.

2. Write an essay about your ideal vacation. Describe where you would choose to go and what you would do there. What would you hope to experience during this vacation? What do your hopes and desires about this vacation reveal about you?

Sister Flowers

MAYA ANGELOU

Best-selling author and poet Maya Angelou was born in 1928. She is an educator, historian, actress, playwright, civil rights activist, producer, and director. She is best known as the author of *I Know Why the Caged Bird Sings* (1970), the first book in a series that constitutes her recently completed autobiography, and for "On the Pulse of the Morning," a characteristically optimistic poem on the need for personal and national renewal that she read at President Clinton's inauguration in 1993. Starting with her beginnings in St. Louis in 1928, Angelou's autobiography presents a joyful triumph over hardships that test her courage and threaten her spirit. It includes the titles *All God's Children Need Traveling Shoes* (1986), *Wouldn't Take Anything for My Journey Now* (1993), and *Heart of a Woman* (1997). The sixth book in the series, *A Song Flung Up to Heaven*, was published in 2002. Angelou reflects on her often difficult relationship with her mother in *Mom & Me & Mom* (2013). Several volumes of her poetry were collected in *Complete Collected Poems of Maya Angelou* in 1994.

In the following excerpt from *I Know Why the Caged Bird Sings*, Angelou describes a family friend who had a major impact on her early life. As you read, notice the way Angelou describes Sister Flowers's physical presence, her stately manners, and the guidance she offered her as a youngster.

Preparing to Read

Think about a major crisis you had to face. Was there someone who came to your aid, offering solid advice and comforting support? How would you describe that person? What physical and personality traits characterize that person?

For nearly a year [after I was raped], I sopped around the house, the 1 Store, the school, and the church, like an old biscuit, dirty and inedible. Then I met, or rather got to know, the lady who threw me my first life line.

Mrs. Bertha Flowers was the aristocrat of Black Stamps. She had the 2 grace of control to appear warm in the coldest weather, and on the Arkansas summer days it seemed she had a private breeze which swirled around, cooling her. She was thin without the taut look of wiry people, and her printed voile dresses and flowered hats were as right for her as denim overalls for a farmer. She was our side's answer to the richest white woman in town.

Her skin was a rich black that would have peeled like a plum if snagged, 3 but then no one would have thought of getting close enough to Mrs.

Flowers to ruffle her dress, let alone snag her skin. She didn't encourage familiarity. She wore gloves too.

I don't think I ever saw Mrs. Flowers laugh, but she smiled often. A   4
slow widening of her thin black lips to show even, small white teeth, then the slow effortless closing. When she chose to smile on me, I always wanted to thank her. The action was so graceful and inclusively benign.*

She was one of the few gentlewomen I have ever known, and has   5
remained throughout my life the measure of what a human being can be.

Momma had a strange relationship with her. Most often when she   6
passed on the road in front of the Store, she spoke to Momma in that soft yet carrying voice, "Good day, Mrs. Henderson." Momma responded with "How you, Sister Flowers?"

Mrs. Flowers didn't belong to our church, nor was she Momma's   7
familiar. Why on earth did she insist on calling her Sister Flowers? Shame made me want to hide my face. Mrs. Flowers deserved better than to be called Sister. Then, Momma left out the verb. Why not ask, "How *are* you, *Mrs.* Flowers?" With the unbalanced passion of the young, I hated her for showing her ignorance to Mrs. Flowers. It didn't occur to me for many years that they were as alike as sisters, separated only by formal education.

Although I was upset, neither of the women was in the least shaken by   8
what I thought an unceremonious greeting. Mrs. Flowers would continue her easy gait up the hill to her little bungalow, and Momma kept on shelling peas or doing whatever had brought her to the front porch.

Occasionally, though, Mrs. Flowers would drift off the road and down   9
to the Store and Momma would say to me, "Sister, you go on and play." As she left I would hear the beginning of an intimate conversation. Momma persistently using the wrong verb, or none at all.

"Brother and Sister Wilcox is sho'ly the meanest—" "Is," Momma?   10
"Is"? Oh, please, not "is," Momma, for two or more. But they talked, and from the side of the building where I waited for the ground to open up and swallow me, I heard the soft-voiced Mrs. Flowers and the textured voice of my grandmother merging and melting. They were interrupted from time to time by giggles that must have come from Mrs. Flowers (Momma never giggled in her life). Then she was gone.

She appealed to me because she was like people I had never met per-   11
sonally. Like women in English novels who walked the moors (whatever they were) with their loyal dogs racing at a respectful distance. Like the women who sat in front of roaring fireplaces, drinking tea incessantly from silver trays full of scones and crumpets. Women who walked over the "heath" and read morocco-bound books and had two last names divided by a hyphen. It would be safe to say that she made me proud to be Negro, just by being herself.

*having a kindly disposition; gracious

She acted just as refined as whitefolks in the movies and books and she 12
was more beautiful, for none of them could have come near that warm color
without looking gray by comparison.

She acted just as refined as whitefolks in the movies and books and she was more beautiful, for none of them could have come near that warm color without looking gray by comparison.

It was fortunate that I never saw her 13
in the company of powhitefolks. For since
they tend to think of their whiteness as an
evenizer, I'm certain that I would have
had to hear her spoken to commonly as
Bertha, and my image of her would have
been shattered like the unmendable
Humpty-Dumpty.

One summer afternoon, sweet-milk 14
fresh in my memory, she stopped at the
Store to buy provisions. Another Negro
woman of her health and age would have
been expected to carry the paper sacks
home in one hand, but Momma said,
"Sister Flowers, I'll send Bailey up to your
house with these things."

She smiled that slow dragging smile, "Thank you, Mrs. Henderson. I'd 15
prefer Marguerite, though." My name was beautiful when she said it. "I've
been meaning to talk to her, anyway." They gave each other age-group looks.

Momma said, "Well, that's all right then. Sister, go and change your 16
dress. You going to Sister Flowers's."

The chifforobe was a maze. What on earth did one put on to go to 17
Mrs. Flowers's house? I knew I shouldn't put on a Sunday dress. It might
be sacrilegious. Certainly not a house dress, since I was already wearing a
fresh one. I chose a school dress, naturally. It was formal without suggesting that going to Mrs. Flowers's house was equivalent to attending church.

I trusted myself back into the Store. 18

"Now, don't you look nice." I had chosen the right thing, for once. . . . 19

There was a little path beside the rocky road, and Mrs. Flowers walked 20
in front swinging her arms and picking her way over the stones.

She said, without turning her head, to me, "I hear you're doing very 21
good school work, Marguerite, but that it's all written. The teachers report
that they have trouble getting you to talk in class." We passed the triangu-
lar farm on our left and the path widened to allow us to walk together. I
hung back in the separate unasked and unanswerable questions.

"Come and walk along with me, Marguerite." I couldn't have refused 22
even if I wanted to. She pronounced my name so nicely. Or more correctly,
she spoke each word with such clarity that I was certain a foreigner who
didn't understand English could have understood her.

"Now no one is going to make you talk—possibly no one can. But 23
bear in mind, language is man's way of communicating with his fellow man
and it is language alone which separates him from the lower animals." That
was a totally new idea to me, and I would need time to think about it.

"Your grandmother says you read a lot. Every chance you get. That's 24
good, but not good enough. Words mean more than what is set down on
paper. It takes the human voice to infuse them with the shades of deeper
meaning."

I memorized the part about the human voice infusing words. It seemed 25
so valid and poetic.

She said she was going to give me some books and that I not only must 26
read them, I must read them aloud. She suggested that I try to make a
sentence sound in as many different ways as possible.

"I'll accept no excuse if you return a book to me that has been badly 27
handled." My imagination boggled at the punishment I would deserve if in
fact I did abuse a book of Mrs. Flowers's. Death would be too kind and brief.

The odors in the house surprised me. Somehow I had never connected 28
Mrs. Flowers with food or eating or any other common experience of common people. There must have been an outhouse, too, but my mind never
recorded it.

The sweet scent of vanilla had met us as she opened the door. 29

"I made tea cookies this morning. You see, I had planned to invite you 30
for cookies and lemonade so we could have this little chat. The lemonade
is in the icebox."

It followed that Mrs. Flowers would have ice on an ordinary day, when 31
most families in our town bought ice late on Saturdays only a few times
during the summer to be used in the wooden ice-cream freezers.

She took the bags from me and disappeared through the kitchen door. 32
I looked around the room that I had never in my wildest fantasies imagined
I would see. Browned photographs leered* or threatened from the walls
and the white, freshly done curtains pushed against themselves and against
the wind. I wanted to gobble up the room entire and take it to Bailey, who
would help me analyze and enjoy it.

"Have a seat, Marguerite. Over there by the table." She carried a plat- 33
ter covered with a tea towel. Although she warned that she hadn't tried her
hand at baking sweets for some time, I was certain that like everything else
about her the cookies would be perfect.

They were flat round wafers, slightly browned on the edges and butter- 34
yellow in the center. With the cold lemonade they were sufficient for childhood's lifelong diet. Remembering my manners, I took nice little lady-like
bites off the edges. She said she had made them expressly for me and that
she had a few in the kitchen that I could take home to my brother. So I

* Sly look

jammed one whole cake in my mouth and the rough crumbs scratched the insides of my jaws, and if I hadn't had to swallow, it would have been a dream come true.

As I ate she began the first of what we later called "my lessons in living." She said that I must always be intolerant of ignorance but understanding of illiteracy. That some people, unable to go to school, were more educated and even more intelligent than college professors. She encouraged me to listen carefully to what country people called mother wit. That in those homely sayings was couched the collective wisdom of generations.

When I finished the cookies she brushed off the table and brought a thick, small book from the bookcase. I had read *A Tale of Two Cities* and found it up to my standards as a romantic novel. She opened the first page and I heard poetry for the first time in my life.

"It was the best of times and the worst of times . . ." Her voice slid in and curved down through and over the words. She was nearly singing. I wanted to look at the pages. Were they the same that I had read? Or were there notes, music, lined on the pages, as in a hymn book? Her sounds began cascading gently. I knew from listening to a thousand preachers that she was nearing the end of her reading, and I hadn't really heard, heard to understand, a single word.

"How do you like that?"

It occurred to me that she expected a response. The sweet vanilla flavor was still on my tongue and her reading was a wonder in my ears. I had to speak.

I said, "Yes, ma'am." It was the least I could do, but it was the most also.

"There's one more thing. Take this book of poems and memorize one for me. Next time you pay me a visit, I want you to recite."

I have tried often to search behind the sophistication of years for the enchantment I so easily found in those gifts. The essence escapes but its aura remains. To be allowed, no, invited, into the private lives of strangers, and to share their joys and fears, was a chance to exchange the Southern bitter wormwood for a cup of mead with Beowulf or a hot cup of tea and milk with Oliver Twist. When I said aloud, "It is a far, far better thing that I do, than I have ever done . . ." tears of love filled my eyes at my selflessness.

On that first day, I ran down the hill and into the road (few cars ever came along it) and had the good sense to stop running before I reached the Store.

I was liked, and what a difference it made. I was respected not as Mrs. Henderson's grandchild or Bailey's sister but for just being Marguerite Johnson.

Childhood's logic never asks to be proved (all conclusions are abso- 45
lute). I didn't question why Mrs. Flowers had singled me out for attention,
nor did it occur to me that Momma might have asked her to give me a little
talking to. All I cared about was that she had made tea cookies for *me* and
read to *me* from her favorite book. It was enough to prove that she liked me.

Thinking Critically about the Text

In paragraph 44, Marguerite indicates how important it was for her to be respected
and liked for "just being Marguerite Johnson." Why do you suppose she, in particular, feels that way? Why is it important for anyone to feel that way?

Questions on Subject

1. What is Angelou's main point in describing Sister Flowers? Why was Sister
   Flowers so important to her?

2. What does Angelou mean when she writes that Sister Flowers did not "encourage familiarity" (paragraph 3)?

3. Why does Sister Flowers think that reading is "good, but not good enough" for
   Marguerite (paragraph 24)?

4. What revelations about race relations in her community growing up does
   Angelou impart in this selection? What do those revelations add to the point
   Angelou is trying to make?

5. Why is being liked by Sister Flowers important to Marguerite?

Questions on Strategy

1. What dominant impression of Sister Flowers does Angelou create in this selection? (Glossary: *Dominant Impression*)

2. To which of the reader's senses does Angelou appeal in describing Sister
   Flowers? To which senses does she appeal in describing Sister Flowers's
   house?

3. At the end of her description of Sister Flowers, Angelou implies that at the
   time it did not occur to her that Sister Flowers might have been asked to give
   her "a little talking to" (paragraph 45). What clues in the description suggest
   that Momma asked Sister Flowers to befriend and draw out Marguerite? Why
   do you suppose Momma didn't take on that task herself?

4. Why does Angelou have Marguerite imagine the conversations that Momma
   and Sister Flowers have on several occasions instead of reporting them
   directly (paragraph 10)?

5. Comment on Angelou's reference to the issue of subject-verb agreement in
   paragraph 10. Does Momma need to use standard grammar to be understood? Why is Marguerite — who rarely speaks — so embarrassed?

Questions on Diction and Vocabulary

1. Angelou uses figures of speech in paragraphs 1 and 3. Explain how they work and what they add to her description of herself and Sister Flowers. (Glossary: *Figures of Speech*)

2. How do Momma and Sister Flowers differ in their manner of speaking? What annoys Marguerite about the way Momma speaks? Does Momma's speech annoy Sister Flowers? Why, or why not?

3. What do you think Sister Flowers means when she tells Marguerite that "words mean more than what is set down on paper" (paragraph 24)? Why is it important for Sister Flowers to tell Marguerite about this difference between reading and speaking?

Classroom Activity Using Description

One of the best ways to make a description memorable is to use figurative language such as a simile (making a comparison using *like* or *as*) or a metaphor (making a comparison without the use of *like* or *as*). Create a simile or metaphor that would be helpful in describing each item in the following list. To illustrate the activity, the first one has been completed for you.

1. a skyscraper: The skyscraper sparkled like a huge glass needle.

2. a huge explosion:

3. an intelligent student:

4. a crowded bus:

5. a slow-moving car:

6. a pillow:

7. a narrow alley:

8. a thick milkshake:

9. hot sun:

10. a dull knife:

Writing Suggestions

1. Sister Flowers is an excellent example of a person with grace, charm, spirit, intelligence, generosity, and high-mindedness — personality traits we ourselves might possess or are capable of possessing. Describe someone you know who has similar personality traits and try to imagine what might account for such traits. Can such qualities be learned from a role model? Can they be taught in the abstract?

2. Review your response to the Preparing to Read prompt for this selection. How would you describe the person who came along at just the right time to help you when you were having a personal crisis? Write a description of that person's physical and character traits. Be sure to select the details of your description carefully so that you create a dominant impression rather than simply offer a series of loosely related descriptive details.

WRITING SUGGESTIONS FOR DESCRIPTION

1. Most description is predominantly visual; that is, it appeals to our sense of sight. Good description, however, often goes beyond the visual; it appeals as well to one or more of the other senses — hearing, smell, taste, and touch. One way to heighten your awareness of these other senses is to purposefully deemphasize the visual impressions you receive. For example, while standing on a busy street corner, sitting in a classroom, or shopping in a supermarket, carefully note what you hear, smell, taste, or feel. (It may help if you close your eyes to eliminate visual distractions as you carry out this experiment.) Use these sense impressions to write a brief description of the street corner, the classroom, the supermarket, or another spot of your choosing.

2. Select one of the following topics, and write an objective description of it. Remember that your task in writing an objective description is to inform the reader about the object, not to convey to the reader the mood or feeling that the object evokes in you.

   a. a pine tree

   b. a personal computer

   c. a café

   d. a dictionary

   e. a fast-food restaurant

   f. a basketball

   g. the layout of your campus

   h. a movie theater

   i. a houseplant

   j. your room

3. Select one of the following places, and write a multiparagraph description that captures your subjective sense impressions of that particular place.

   a. a busy intersection

   b. a bakery

   c. a dorm room

   d. a factory

   e. a service station

   f. a zoo

   g. a cafeteria

   h. a farmers' market

   i. a concert hall

   j. a locker room

   k. a bank

   l. a library

4. At college you have the opportunity to meet many new people, students as well as teachers. In a letter to someone back home, describe one of your new acquaintances. Try to capture the essence of the person you choose and to explain why this person stands out from all the other people you have met at school.

5. This chapter on description focuses on people (Jeannette Walls and her mother, Lobo, and Sister Flowers) as well as places (a barrio and a lake). Write an essay in which you compare and contrast any two readings. Here are some questions to get you started:

a. If you choose to write on the selections by Walls, Mora, and Angelou, ask yourself what features of Walls's mother, Lobo, and Sister Flowers the authors concentrate on. What features do they leave out or downplay? Do they give equal attention to internal and external characteristics, or do they emphasize one over the other? Which person do you get to know best, and why?

b. If you choose to write on the selections by Ramírez and White, ask yourself whether you feel you come to know the lake or the barrio better. What techniques do the writers employ that contribute to a better understanding and appreciation? Which author makes better use of dominant impressions?

6. McDonald's "A View from the Bridge" on page 8 and the *Calvin and Hobbes* cartoon on page 174 are just two "fish stories" in the long and rich tradition of that genre. In their own ways, both the essay and the cartoon play on the ironic notion that fishing is a quiet sport but one in which the unexpected frequently occurs. (Glossary: *Irony*).

For the narrator in McDonald's story, there is the revelation of the difference between merely looking and truly seeing. For Calvin, there is that sudden splash in the water (this time, alas, not the sign of a great catch). Write an essay in which you tell a "fish story" of your own, one that reveals a larger, significant truth or life lesson. Pay particular attention to the pattern of organization you choose, and be sure to revise your essay to tighten up your use of the pattern. If possible, incorporate some elements of surprise as well.

7. **Writing with Sources.** Writers of description often rely on factual information to make their writing more substantial and interesting. Using facts, statistics, or other information found online or in your college library, write an essay describing one of the people, places, or things in the following list. Be sure that you focus your description, that you have a purpose for your description, and that you present your facts in an interesting manner.

a. the Statue of Liberty
b. the iPad
c. Lady Gaga
d. the Grand Canyon
e. the Great Wall of China
f. Hillary Rodham Clinton
g. LeBron James
h. the Tower of London
i. the sun
j. Disney World
k. the Hubble Space Telescope
l. Sonia Sotomayor
m. Jon Stewart
n. a local landmark

For models of and advice on integrating sources in your essay, see Chapters 14 and 15.

8. **Writing with Sources.** As a way of getting to know your campus, select a building, statue, sculpture, or other familiar landmark and research it. What is its

significance or meaning to your college or university? Are there any ceremonies or rituals associated with the object? What are its distinctive or unusual features? When was it erected? Who sponsored it? Is it currently being used as originally intended? Once you have completed your research, write a description of your subject in which you create a dominant impression of your landmark's importance to the campus community.

You and your classmates may wish to turn this particular assignment into a collaborative class project: the compilation of a booklet of essays that introduces readers to the unique physical and historic features of your campus. To avoid duplication, the class should make a list of campus landmarks, and students should sign up for the one that they would like to write about. For models of and advice on integrating sources in your essay, see Chapters 14 and 15.

9. **Writing with Sources.** Study the photograph by Gordon Parks that appears at the beginning of this chapter (page 126). First, respond to the photograph, answering the following questions: What does the image convey to you? How would you characterize the figure of the woman, the presence of the American flag and the broom and mop? Do you see any significance in how the woman and the inanimate objects are positioned in the photograph?

Next, do some research on Parks's work. (You might start by searching for the Library of Congress's online exhibit entitled "Ella Watson, U.S. Government Charwoman.") Be sure to find out why the photo is commonly called *American Gothic*. What is its connection to American painter Grant Wood's iconic painting of the same name? In what ways is Parks's photograph a parody of or commentary on Wood's painting?

Finally, write an essay describing the photograph and discussing its history and the message you think Parks means to convey. For models of and advice on integrating sources in your essay, see Chapters 14 and 15.

10. **Writing in the Workplace.** You are working for your local weekly newspaper and your boss has assigned you to do a profile of a local celebrity for their series on getting to know important people in the community. Interview your subject and describe the person both objectively and subjectively, telling of the person's background and achievements so as to make lively reading for the average weekly newspaper reader. What special qualities do you detect in your subject? What contributions has the person made to the community? What weaknesses has the person overcome? What triumphs has your subject achieved? What stands out for you about your subject, and what is it that readers will most want to know about this community figure?

---

e e-Pages

Tower of David

VOCATIV

See how description works on the Web. Go to bedfordstmartins.com/subjectand strategy for a video and study questions on life in the "world's tallest slum," an abandoned 45-story skyscraper in Caracas, Venezuela.

A FEW OF MY EARLY

CHILDHOOD FEARS

Your eyeballs can become glued to T.V.

Doing somersaults can break your head off.

Mom really did leave the store without me.

It will never be daytime again...

I'll never get my teddy bear back.

Something's going to come up the drain.

Peek-a-Boo will make dad disappear.

There's a spider around here somewhere.

I'm going to melt.

My uncle just pulled my nose off.

The ants are coming to get me.

The fingernail I bit off won't grow back.

This thing is going to pull my teeth out.

There's a monster in the closet.

There's a shark under the bed.

Mom will let go and this thing will flip over.

The bag may get mad and eat my hand.

This candle will light my hair on fire.

The furnace.

Churches.

The dog across the street.

"Tales Of Mere Existence" By Levni Yilmaz   www.ingredientx.com

CHAPTER 6

Illustration

WHAT IS ILLUSTRATION?

THE STRATEGY OF ILLUSTRATION USES EXAMPLES—FACTS, OPINIONS, samples, and anecdotes or stories—to make a general observation, assertion, or claim more vivid, understandable, and persuasive. We use examples all the time in everyday life to make our points clearer. How often have we asked for or given an example or two when something was not evident or clear? And many of the advertisements that bombard us daily use illustration—literally and as a strategy to support a claim.

The cartoon about childhood fears on the opposite page uses the strategy of illustration (as well as an effective narration about the artist's memories) to demonstrate the innocent, naïve perspective of childhood. The graphic presents twenty-one examples of things that frightened him because they were unknown, unseen, or little understood. As we mature and grow, our everyday world becomes less intimidating as we learn why things work, but to a child, things can be quite overwhelming.

ILLUSTRATION IN WRITTEN TEXTS

In the following paragraph from "Wandering through Winter," notice how naturalist Edwin Way Teale uses examples to illustrate his generalization that "country people" have many superstitions about how harsh the coming winter will be.

Topic sentence about weather superstitions frames entire paragraph	In the folklore of the country, numerous superstitions relate to winter weather. Back-country farmers examine their husks—the thicker the husk, the colder the winter. They watch the acorn crop—the more acorns, the more severe the season. They observe where white-faced hornets place their paper nests—the higher they are, the deeper will be the snow. They examine the size and shape and color of the spleens of butchered hogs for clues to the severity of the season. They keep track of the blooming of the dogwood in the spring—the more

Series of examples amplify and clarify topic sentence	abundant the blooms, the more bitter the cold in January. When chipmunks carry their tails high and squirrels have heavier fur, the superstitious gird themselves for a long, hard winter. Without any specific basis, a wider-than-usual black band on a woolly-bear caterpillar is accepted as a sign that winter will arrive early and stay late. Even the way a cat sits beside the stove carries its message to the credulous. According to the belief once widely held in the Ozarks, a cat sitting with its tail to the fire indicates very cold weather is on the way.

Teale uses nine separate examples to illustrate and explain his topic sentence about weather-related superstitions. These examples both demonstrate his knowledge of folk traditions and entertain us. As readers, we come away from Teale's paragraph thinking that he is an authority on his subject.

Teale's examples are a series of related but varied illustrations of his main point. Sometimes, however, just one sustained example can be equally effective if the example is representative and the writer develops it well. Here is one such example by basketball legend Bill Russell from his autobiographical *Second Wind*:

Topic sentence focuses on athletes slipping into a new gear	Every champion athlete has a moment when everything goes so perfectly for him he slips into a gear that he didn't know was there. It's easy to spot that perfect moment in a sport like track. I remember watching the 1968 Olympics in Mexico City, where the world record in the long jump was just under 27 feet. Then Bob Beamon flew
Extended example of Bob Beamon's record-shattering day exemplifies topic sentence	down the chute and leaped out over the pit in a majestic jump that I have seen replayed many times. There was an awed silence when the announcer said that Beamon's jump measured 29 feet 2¼ inches. Generally world records are broken by fractions of inches, but Beamon had exceeded the existing record by more than two feet. On learning what he had done, Beamon slumped down on the ground and cried. Most viewers' image of Beamon ends with the picture of
Example illustrates that even Beamon did not anticipate his own performance	him weeping on the ground, but in fact he got up and took some more jumps that day. I like to think that he did so because he had jumped for so long at his best that *even then* he didn't know what might come out of him. At the end of the day he wanted to be absolutely sure that he'd had his perfect day.

Few readers have experienced that "extra gear" that Russell describes, so he illustrates what he means with a single, extended example—in this case, an anecdote that gives substance to the idea he wants his readers to understand. Russell's example of Bob Beamon's record-breaking jump is not only concrete and specific, it is also memorable because it so aptly captures the essence of his topic sentence about athletic perfection. Without this extended example, Russell's claim that every great athlete "slips into a gear that he didn't know was there" would simply be a hollow statement.

USING ILLUSTRATION AS A WRITING STRATEGY

Illustrating a point with examples serves several purposes for writers. First, examples make writing more vivid and interesting. Writing that consists of loosely strung together generalizations is lifeless and difficult to read, regardless of the believability of the generalizations or our willingness to accept them. Good writers try to provide just the right kind and number of examples to make their ideas clear and convincing. For example, an essay about television bloopers will be dull and pointless without some examples of on-screen blunders—accidents, pratfalls, and "tips of the slongue," as one writer calls them. Likewise, a more serious essay on the dangers of drunk driving will have more impact if it is illustrated with descriptive examples of the victims' suffering and the grief of their family and friends.

Writers also use illustration to explain or clarify their ideas. All readers want specific information and feel that it is the writer's responsibility to provide it. Even if readers can provide examples themselves, they want to see what kind of evidence the writer can present. In an essay on political leadership for a history or political science class, for instance, the assertion "Successful leaders are often a product of their times" will certainly require further explanation. Such explanation could be provided effectively through examples: Franklin D. Roosevelt, Winston Churchill, Corazon Aquino, and Nelson Mandela all rose to power because their people were looking for leadership in a time of national crisis. Keep in mind, however, that the use of these specific examples paints a different picture of the term "successful leaders" than a different set of examples would; unlike leaders like Joseph Stalin, Adolf Hitler, and Benito Mussolini, who rose to power under similar circumstances, the first group of leaders exercised their power in the interest of the people.

Illustration is so useful and versatile a strategy that it is found in many different kinds of writing, such as reports, cover letters, editorials, applications, proposals, law briefs, and reviews. In fact, there is hardly an essay in this book that does not use illustration in one way or another.

USING ILLUSTRATION ACROSS THE DISCIPLINES

When writing essays in the academic disciplines, you will have many opportunities to use the strategy of illustration to both organize and strengthen the presentation of your ideas. To determine whether or not illustration is the right strategy for you in a particular paper, review the guidelines described in Chapter 2 (Determining a Strategy for Developing Your Essay, pages 32–33). Consider the following examples.

American Literature

1. **MAIN IDEA:** Mark Twain uses irony to speak out against racism in *The Adventures of Huckleberry Finn*.

2. **QUESTION:** Where does Mark Twain use irony to combat racism in *The Adventures of Huckleberry Finn*?

3. **STRATEGY:** Illustration. The direction words *uses* and *where* say "show me," and what better way to show than with solid, representative examples from the novel of Twain's use of irony to speak out against racism?

4. **SUPPORTING STRATEGY:** Argument. The examples can be used to argue in favor of a particular interpretation of Twain's work.

Criminal Justice

1. **MAIN IDEA:** America's criminal justice system neglects the families of capital offenders.

2. **QUESTION:** How has America's criminal justice system neglected the families of capital offenders?

3. **STRATEGY:** Illustration. Both the statement of the main idea and the question cry out for proof or evidence, and the best evidence would be a series of examples of the claimed neglect.

4. **SUPPORTING STRATEGY:** Process analysis. The paper might conclude with a possible remedy or solution—a step-by-step process for eliminating the current neglect.

Biology

1. **MAIN IDEA:** Cloning and other biotechnical discoveries give rise to serious moral and ethical issues that need our attention.

2. **QUESTION:** What are some of the moral and ethical issues raised by recent biotechnical discoveries that we need to address?

3. **STRATEGY:** Illustration. The direction words *what* and *some* call for examples of the moral and ethical issues raised by biotechnical discoveries.

4. **SUPPORTING STRATEGY:** Argument. The direction word *need* suggests that the examples should be both compelling and persuasive so that readers will want to address these issues.

SAMPLE STUDENT ESSAY USING ILLUSTRATION AS A WRITING STRATEGY

Diets and dieting fascinated Paula Kersch, especially because she and her friends were constantly trying out the popular plans. Eventually, however, Paula began wondering: If these diets really worked, why were people always looking for new ones to try? She also wondered if these diets posed any real risks, especially when she started thinking about the more extreme ones. She made a list of the various diets she and her friends had tried and then did some research on the Internet to see what she could learn about them. On the basis of what she discovered, she developed the following thesis: "If Americans knew more about the risks that accompany trendy diets and the seriousness of our obesity problem, perhaps they would not look for a quick fix but instead would adopt a weight-management plan that would help them achieve the desired results without compromising their health and their pocketbooks."

Before drafting her essay, Paula familiarized herself with the materials found in Chapter 14, "Writing with Sources," and Chapter 15, "A Brief Guide to Researching and Documenting Essays." What follows is the final draft of her essay. Notice how she uses examples of specific diet plans to explain her key points.

Title introduces paper topic	Weight Management: More Than a Matter of Good Looks Paula Kersch
Beginning engages reader by referring to common experience and observation	Americans are obsessed with their weight. Most Americans consider themselves in need of some type of diet, and, whether they're looking to lose those extra holiday pounds or the accumulation of a lifetime, there's plenty of help out there. Bookstore owners often stock an entire section with the latest diet books, and a quick search of the Internet reveals over 250 trendy diets that are currently in vogue. This help is there because dieting is big business in America. In fact, the U.S. Centers for Disease Control and Prevention reported in 2008 that "the dieting industry earned 55 billion dollars in 2006" (*Latest*). At the same time, most experts agree that fad diets don't work (Katz, "Pandemic"). Some estimate that a full 95% of fad diets fail (Hulse).
Thesis announces essay's focus — trendy diets can be dangerous	In the face of the staggering failure rate for most fad diets, why do these quick-loss plans remain so popular? If Americans knew more about the risks that accompany trendy diets and the seriousness of our obesity problem, perhaps they would not be so quick to look for a quick fix but instead would adopt a weight-management plan that would help them achieve the desired results without compromising their health and their pocketbooks.
	Most of the currently popular quick-weight-loss schemes appeal to Americans' desire for instant gratification. Who

1

2

3

wants to look forward to a year of losing a pound or less a week? Most of these diets fall into one of several categories: (1) fasts and detox cleanses, (2) plans that emphasize one food group while eliminating or minimizing others, and (3) diet pills and supplements. All of these crash-dieting methods produce results. People who try them lose pounds quickly just as the ads promise—the South Beach Diet boasts seven pounds in seven days and Dr. Simeons' HCG Weight Loss Protocol, thirty-four pounds in forty-three days. Sadly, however, virtually all dieters compromise their health and gain back the weight they lose—and then some.

People have been using water and juice fasts and cleanses since biblical times for both spiritual and physical reasons. Most regimens last only a few days, resulting in the rapid loss of five to seven pounds in some cases. The popular Master Cleanse—also known as the Lemonade Diet—developed by Stanley Burroughs in 1941 recommends a slightly longer fourteen-day program to achieve the desired detoxification and diet results (Ogunnaike). Because humans can go without food for longer periods of time if they have water, this regimen is not necessarily dangerous. However, some people push fasts and cleanses to unhealthy extremes. Even apart from the health risks, these extremes often fail to produce the desired long-term weight-loss results.

Although there is a technical difference between fasting and starving, metabolically the human body does not differentiate between the two. When a person fasts, the body has to rely on burning its own reserves for energy. Because the body does not know when its next meal might be coming, the body lowers its metabolism in order to conserve fuel, thus slowing weight loss. Also, while fasting may produce lost pounds on the scale, usually it is not the fat loss most dieters aim for. Short-term fasts result in large water losses, which are almost immediately regained once the fast is broken.

The longer a fast or cleanse continues, the greater the serious risk for muscle damage in the body because the body is not getting the nutrients it needs. Additionally, people are at risk of gaining even more weight than they lost after coming off a fast because their bodies will still be functioning at a slower metabolic rate, allowing more rapid weight gain on

Organization: numbers signal order in which schemes will be discussed

Examples of first category of trendy diets — fasts and cleanses — illustrate dangers and problems

Parenthetical in-text citation documents information about Master Cleanse

Explains in detail what happens during a fast

4

5

6

fewer calories. Repeated fasting can permanently alter the body's base metabolic rate.

One does not have to be a nutritionist to understand that if people eat only foods from one food group and do not eat any from others, their bodies will not be able to function correctly. Over the years there have been a number of high-protein low-carb diets that promise quick weight loss by emphasizing foods high in protein, while excluding most carbohydrates. The infamous Last-Chance Diet of the 1970s, with its emphasis on a liquid-protein drink and the exclusion of all other food, led to numerous heart attacks and over sixty deaths among users. The Atkins Diet, an enormously popular diet first developed in the 1970s and later updated in *Dr. Atkins's New Diet Revolution*, is another prime example of a diet that excludes large groups of foods. Meat and fat are emphasized to the exclusion of other foods, making the diet high in cholesterol. Neither medically sound nor nutritionally safe, this diet results in a rapid and dangerous drop in weight.

In spite of the fact that this and other low-carb diets—like the currently popular Dr. Arthur Agatston's *The South Beach Diet Supercharged* and *Dr. Gott's No Flour, No Sugar Diet*—can compromise a person's health, many people continue to follow these diets to shed their excess pounds. These and other trendy diets that emphasize single foods or food groups, like the Cabbage Soup Diet, the Grapefruit Diet, and the Apple Cider Vinegar Diet, have all been debunked as unhealthy and unrealistic solutions to a very real problem.

America's search for a quick, easy solution to the weight problem is perhaps epitomized best in the popularity of diet pills and supplements. In years gone by dieters have used thyroid hormone injections, amphetamines, and fen-phen—a combination of fenfluramine or dextenfluramine and phentermine—among other things. In September 1997, however, manufacturers took the "fen" drugs off the market at the request of the Food and Drug Administration (FDA) because fen-phen was linked to heart valve damage and death (Kolata). In May of 2009, the FDA recalled Hydroxycut, a popular dietary supplement containing ephedra, which caused liver damage.

Nevertheless, the search for a magic bullet to combat excess weight continues, motivated by the public's desire for more

Margin notes:

Introduces second category of trendy diets — plans that emphasize one food group while eliminating or minimizing others

Relevant and representative examples illustrate the range of "one food group" diets

Introduces third category of trendy diets — pills and supplements — and provides historical perspective

Paragraph numbers: 7, 8, 9, 10

attractive and healthy bodies and corporate America's pursuit of unimaginable profits if they are able to hit on the right formula. In June of 2008, GlaxoSmithKline first marketed Alli (pronounced "ally," as in supporter or friend), an over-the-counter version of the prescription-strength Xenical, an FDA-approved fat blocker. When used as recommended, Alli promises to increase weight loss by up to 50% over what might normally be lost by most people following a healthy diet and a regular exercise program. (Alli is not intended as a stand-alone solution for someone with a nutritionally unhealthy diet and no exercise regimen.)

Example explores promise of diet pill Alli in detail

While the future currently looks bright for Alli, it remains to be seen whether it will fulfill its promise. The FDA recommends that Alli not be used by children or for longer than two consecutive years—considerable restrictions. Alli also has some annoying side effects, among them "excessive flatulence, oily bowel movements, which can be difficult to control, and anal leakage" (Baldwin). Some may find these side effects minor deterrents, but others may not be willing to endure the embarrassment and inconvenience associated with them. Some critics allege that while Alli blocks the absorption of some fats, it may also block some important vitamins and minerals. Dr. Sidney Wolfe, director of Public Citizen's Health Research Group in Washington, DC, sees no reason to take Alli because "there are demonstrable short-term risks and no possibility of long-term benefit" (qtd. in Mann).

Discusses the drawbacks of using Alli

Quotation from medical authority supports reservations about using Alli

11

It is obvious from even this cursory examination of trendy dieting practices that "get-thin-quick" schemes typically offer little more than empty promises. According to experts, the key to real weight loss is not dieting: The best results come from long-term changes in lifestyle habits. Weight control is best achieved with commonsense eating, consisting of foods high in nutrition and low in fat and sugar, in conjunction with regular exercise. While this kind of weight control cannot offer fast results, it usually proves successful where diets ultimately fail. Here's why.

Weight management introduced as healthy alternative to "get-thin-quick" schemes

12

Losing weight in a healthy manner is a slow process. Most nutritionists suggest that a sensible goal is 2-4 pounds per month. When a person follows a sustainable eating and exercise program, that person's body will naturally start to slim down over time. Eating a well-balanced diet with foods from the four food groups gives the body all the essentials it needs. The high amounts of fiber in fruits, vegetables, and whole

Emphasis on eating well-balanced diet and exercising regularly

13

grains make the stomach feel full and satisfied. When the body receives the nutrients it needs, it functions better as well. It is common knowledge that depression, migraine headaches, and lethargy are often triggered by overindulgence or nutritional deficiencies. Once moderation is achieved and any deficiencies eliminated, ailments tend to disappear (United States, *Nutrition*).

Many trendy diets do not advocate exercise; some even claim that exercise is unnecessary. But working out is an essential ingredient in any good weight-management program. Exercise tones up the body and gives people more energy and a sense of well-being. Moderate exercise such as rapid walking can rev up the metabolism and help the body burn calories more efficiently. Regular exercise has the additional benefit of increasing over time the body's base metabolic rate so that more food may be eaten with no weight gain (United States, *Physical*).

14

Trendy dieting as practiced during the past two decades just has not worked. Fasting, one-food-group dieting, and diet pills and supplements often do more harm than good in terms of nutrition and general well-being. As a society, Americans must face the obesity problem head-on. If we do not, the consequences will be dire. Dr. David L. Katz, nutrition and weight-control expert and director of the Yale Prevention Research Center, warns that "by 2018 more than 100 million Americans will be obese, and we will be spending roughly $340 billion annually on obesity, a tripling of current levels that are already breaking the bank" ("Compelling" 3B). Long-term weight-management programs that incorporate healthy lifestyle habits offer a real solution where trendy diets fail. When overweight Americans forsake the lure of quick weight loss and understand all the negative aspects associated with these trendy diets, they will begin to get a handle on what they must do to tackle their weight problems.

15

Benefits of exercise explained

Conclusion explains that trendy diets will not solve America's problem with obesity

Quotation emphasizes gravity of the problem, lending support to the writer's position

Writer uses MLA style for works cited

Works Cited

Baldwin, Donovan. "Pros and Cons of the New Alli Diet Pill." *SearchWarp.com*. SearchWarp.com, 20 June 2007. Web. 20 Jan. 2010.

Hulse, Dean. "Fad Diets Popular but Have Major-League Failure Rate." *News for North Dakotans*. Agriculture Communication, North Dakota State U, 8 July 1999. Web. 10 Feb. 2010.

See pages
724–33 for more
models of MLA
entries

Katz, David L. "The Compelling Case for Obesity Control." *Naples Daily News*. 3 Jan. 2010: B1+. Print.

---. "Pandemic Obesity and the Contagion of Nutritional Nonsense." *Public Health Review* 31.1 (2003): 33-44. Web. 10 Feb. 2010.

Kolata, Gina. "Companies Recall 2 Top Diet Drugs at F.D.A.'s Urging." *New York Times*. New York Times, 16 Sept. 1997. Web. 8 Feb. 2010.

Mann, Denise. "All about Alli, the Weight Loss Pill." *WebMD*. WebMD, 2007. Web. 2 Feb. 2010.

Ogunnaike, Lola. "I Heard It through the Diet Grapevine." *New York Times*. New York Times, 10 Dec. 2006. Web. 9 Feb. 2010.

United States. Dept. of Health and Human Services. Centers for Disease Control and Prevention. *Latest CDC Data Show More Americans Report Being Obese. CDC Online Newsroom*. CDC, 17 July 2008. Web. 20 Jan. 2010.

---. *Nutrition for Everyone*. CDC. CDC, 14 Sept. 2009. Web. 9 Feb. 2010.

---. *Physical Activity for Everyone*. CDC. CDC, 14 Sept. 2009. Web. 9 Feb. 2010.

Analyzing Paula Kersch's Illustration Essay: Questions for Discussion

1. What points do Paula's examples illustrate or support?

2. Are her examples relevant and representative? Explain why or why not. What examples of your own can you think of to illustrate her points?

3. Which examples did you find most effective? Least effective? Why?

4. Paula used outside sources in her essay. What did these sources add to the essay?

5. How does Paula conclude her essay? In what ways is her conclusion connected to her beginning? Explain.

SUGGESTIONS FOR USING ILLUSTRATION AS A WRITING STRATEGY

As you plan, write, and revise your illustration essay, be mindful of the writing process guidelines described in Chapter 2 (see pages 23–47). Also, pay particular attention to the basic requirements and essential ingredients for this writing strategy.

▶ Planning Your Illustration Essay

Planning is an essential part of writing a good illustration essay. You can save yourself a great deal of effort by taking the time to think about the key building blocks of your essay before you actually begin to write.

FOCUS ON YOUR THESIS OR MAIN IDEA.   Begin by thinking of how you can make your ideas clearer and more persuasive by illustrating them with examples — facts, anecdotes, and specific details. Once you have established your thesis — the main point that you will develop in your essay — you should find examples that add clarity, color, and authority.

Consider the following thesis:

> Americans are a pain-conscious people who would rather get rid of pain than seek and cure its root causes.

This assertion is broad; it cries out for evidence or support. You could make it stronger and more meaningful through illustration. You might, for example, point to the sheer number of over-the-counter painkillers available and the different types of pain they address, or cite specific situations in which people you know have gone to the drugstore instead of to a doctor. In addition, you might cite sales figures for painkillers in the United States and compare them with sales figures in other countries.

GATHER MORE EXAMPLES THAN YOU CAN USE.   Before you begin to write, bring together as many examples as you can that are related to your subject — more than you can possibly use. An example may be anything from a fact or a statistic to an anecdote or a story; it may be stated in a few words — "India's population is now approaching 1.2 billion people" — or it may go on for several pages of elaborate description or explanation.

The kinds of examples you look for and where you look for them will depend, of course, on your subject and the point you want to make about it. If you plan to write about all the quirky, fascinating people who make up your family, you can gather your examples without leaving your room: descriptions of their habits and clothing, stories about their strange adventures, facts about their backgrounds, quotations from their conversations. If, however, you are writing an essay on book censorship in American public schools, you will need to do research in the library or on the Internet and read many sources to supply yourself with examples. Your essay might well include accounts drawn from newspapers; statistics published by librarians' or teachers' professional organizations; court transcripts and judicial opinions on censorship; and interviews with school board members, parents, book publishers, and even the authors whose work has been pulled off library shelves or kept out of the classroom. The range of sources and the variety of examples are limited only by your imagination and the time you can spend on research. (For models of and advice on integrating sources in your essay, see Chapters 14 and 15.)

Collecting an abundance of examples will allow you to choose the strongest and most representative ones for your essay, not merely the first ones that come to mind. Having enough material will also make it less likely that you will have to stop in mid-draft and hunt for additional examples, losing the rhythm of your work or the thread of your ideas. Moreover, the more examples you gather, the more you will learn about your subject and the easier it will be to write about it with authority.

CHOOSE RELEVANT EXAMPLES.   You must make sure that your examples are relevant. Do they clarify and support the points you want to make? Suppose the main point of your planned essay is that censorship currently runs rampant in American public education. A newspaper story about the banning of *Catcher in the Rye* and *The Merchant of Venice* from the local high school's English curriculum would clearly be relevant because it concerns book censorship at a public school. The fact that James Joyce's novel *Ulysses* was once banned as obscene and then vindicated in a famous trial, although a landmark case of censorship in American history, has nothing to do with book censorship in contemporary public schools. While the case of *Ulysses* might be a useful example for other discussions of censorship, it would not be relevant to your essay.

Sometimes more than one of your examples will be relevant. In such cases, choose the examples that are most closely related to your thesis. If you were working on an essay on how Americans cope with pain, a statistic indicating the sales of a particular drug in a given year might be useful; however, a statistic showing that over the past ten years painkiller sales in America have increased more rapidly than the population has would be directly relevant to the idea that Americans are a pain-conscious people and therefore more effective as an example. Examples may be interesting in and of themselves, but they only come alive when they illustrate and link important ideas that you are trying to promote.

BE SURE YOUR EXAMPLES ARE REPRESENTATIVE.   Besides being relevant, your examples should also be representative—that is, they should be typical of the main point or concept, indicative of a larger pattern rather than an uncommon or isolated occurrence. In an essay on pain referred to earlier, figures showing how many people use aspirin, and for what purposes, would be representative because aspirin is the most widely used painkiller in America. Statistics about a newly developed barbiturate (a highly specialized kind of painkiller) might show a tremendous increase in its use, but the example would not be representative because not many people use barbiturates. Giving the barbiturate example might even cause readers to wonder why aspirin, which is better known, was not used as an example.

If, while working on the censorship paper, you found reports on a dozen quiet administrative hearings and orderly court cases, but only one report of a sensational incident in which books were actually burned in a school parking lot, the latter incident, however dramatic, is clearly not a representative example. You might want to mention the book burning in your essay as an extreme example, but you should not present it as typical.

What if your examples do not support your point? Perhaps you have missed some important information and need to look further. It may be, though, that the problem is with the point itself. For example, suppose you intend your censorship paper to illustrate the following thesis: "Book censorship has seriously influenced American public education." However, you have not found very many examples in which specific books were actually censored or banned outright—most attempts at censorship were ultimately prevented or overturned in the courts. You might then have to revise your original thesis: "Although there have been many well-publicized attempts to censor books in public schools, actual censorship is relatively rare and less of a problem than is commonly thought."

▶ Organizing Your Illustration Essay

SEQUENCE YOUR EXAMPLES LOGICALLY. It is important to arrange your examples in an order that serves your purpose, is easy for readers to follow, and will have maximum effect. Some possible patterns of organization include chronological order and spatial order. Others include moving from the least to the most controversial, as in Martin Luther King Jr.'s "The Ways of Meeting Oppression" (pages 370–72); or from the least to the most important, as in Jo Goodwin Parker's "What Is Poverty?" (pages 403–07). Or you may hit on an order that "feels right" to you, as Edwin Way Teale did in his paragraph about winter superstitions (pages 177–78).

How many examples you include depends, of course, on the length and nature of the assignment. Before starting the first draft, you may find it helpful to work out your organization in a rough outline, using only enough words so that you can tell which example each entry refers to.

USE TRANSITIONS. While it is important to give the presentation of your examples an inherent logic, it is also important to link your examples to the topic sentences in your paragraphs and, indeed, to the thesis of your entire essay by using transitional words and expressions such as *for example, for instance, therefore, afterward, in other words, next,* and *finally*. Such structural devices will make the sequencing of the examples easy to follow.

❱ Revising and Editing Your Illustration Essay

SHARE YOUR WORK WITH OTHERS. You may find it particularly helpful to share the drafts of your essays with other students in your writing class. One of our students commented, "In total, I probably wrote five or six different versions of this essay. I shared them with members of the class, and their comments were extremely insightful. I remember one student's question in particular because she really got me to focus on the problems with fad diets. The students also helped me to see where I needed examples to explain what I was talking about. The very first draft that I wrote is completely different from the one I submitted in class." To maximize the effectiveness of peer conferences, utilize the suggestions on page 36. Feedback from these conferences often provides one or more places where you can start writing.

QUESTION YOUR OWN WORK WHILE REVISING AND EDITING. Revision is best done by asking yourself key questions about what you have written. Begin by reading your paper, preferably aloud. Reading aloud forces you to pay attention to every single word. You are more likely to catch lapses in the logical flow of thought. (For help with twelve common writing problems, see Chapter 16, "Editing for Grammar, Punctuation, and Sentence Style.")

After you have read your paper through, answer the following questions for revising and editing, and make the necessary changes.

Questions for Revising and Editing: Illustration

1. Is my topic well focused?

2. Does my thesis statement clearly identify my topic and make an assertion about it?

3. Are my examples well chosen to support my thesis? Are there other examples that might work better?

4. Are my examples representative? That is, are they typical of the main point or concept, rather than bizarre or atypical?

5. Do I have enough examples to be convincing? Do I have too many examples?

6. Have I developed my examples in enough detail so as to be clear to readers?

7. Have I organized my examples in some logical pattern, and is that pattern clear to readers?

8. Does the essay accomplish my purpose?

9. Are my topic sentences strong? Are my paragraphs unified?

10. Does my paper contain any errors in grammar, punctuation, or mechanics? Is my sentence style as clear, smooth, and persuasive as possible?

Be Specific

NATALIE GOLDBERG

Author Natalie Goldberg has made a specialty of writing about writing. Her first and best-known work, *Writing Down the Bones: Freeing the Writer Within*, was published in 1986. Goldberg's advice to would-be writers is, on the one hand, practical and pithy; on the other, it is almost mystical in its call to know and appreciate the world. In a 2007 interview with Shara Stewart for *Ascent* magazine, Goldberg remarked that "[w]riting and Zen for me are completely interconnected. The relationship is seamless for me. . . . Writing is a practice for me, like someone else would do sitting or walking. Writing is a true spiritual practice." "Be Specific," the excerpt that appears below, is representative of the book as a whole. Amid widespread acclaim for the book, one critic commented, "Goldberg teaches us not only how to write better, but how to live better." *Writing Down the Bones* was followed by four more books about writing: *Wild Mind: Living the Writer's Life* (1990), *Living Color: A Writer Paints Her World* (1996), *Thunder and Lightning: Cracking Open the Writer's Craft* (2000), and *The Essential Writer's Notebook* (2001). Altogether, over a million copies of these books are now in print. Goldberg has also written fiction; her first novel, *Banana Rose*, was published in 1994. Her most recent books are *Top of My Lungs* (2002), a collection of poetry and paintings; *The Great Failure: My Unexpected Path to Truth* (2004), a memoir; *Old Friend from Far Away: The Practice of Writing Memoir* (2008); and *The True Secret of Writing: Connecting Life with Language* (2013).

Notice the way in which Goldberg demonstrates her advice to be specific in the following selection.

Preparing to Read

Suppose someone says to you, "I walked in the woods." What do you envision? Write down what you see in your mind's eye. Now suppose someone says, "I walked in the redwood forest." Again, write what you see. What's different about your two descriptions, and why?

Be specific. Don't say "fruit." Tell what kind of fruit — "It is a 1 pomegranate." Give things the dignity of their names. Just as with human beings, it is rude to say, "Hey, girl, get in line." That "girl" has a name. (As a matter of fact, if she's at least twenty years old, she's a woman, not a "girl" at all.) Things, too, have names. It is much better to say "the geranium in the window" than "the flower in the window." "Geranium" — that one word gives us a much more specific picture. It penetrates more deeply into the beingness of that flower. It immediately gives us the scene by the window — red petals, green circular leaves, all straining toward sunlight.

Don't say "fruit." Tell what kind of fruit — "It is a pomegranate." Give things the dignity of their names.

About ten years ago I decided I had to learn the names of plants and flowers in my environment. I bought a book on them and walked down the tree-lined streets of Boulder, examining leaf, bark, and seed, trying to match them up with their descriptions and names in the book. Maple, elm, oak, locust. I usually tried to cheat by asking people working in their yards the names of the flowers and trees growing there. I was amazed how few people had any idea of the names of the live beings inhabiting their little plot of land.

When we know the name of something, it brings us closer to the ground. It takes the blur out of our mind; it connects us to the earth. If I walk down the street and see "dogwood," "forsythia," I feel more friendly toward the environment. I am noticing what is around me and can name it. It makes me more awake.

If you read the poems of William Carlos Williams, you will see how specific he is about plants, trees, flowers — chicory, daisy, locust, poplar, quince, primrose, black-eyed Susan, lilacs — each has its own integrity. Williams says, "Write what's in front of your nose." It's good for us to know what is in front of our noses. Not just "daisy," but how the flower is in the season we are looking at it — "The dayseye hugging the earth / in August . . . brownedged, / green and pointed scales / armor his yellow."[1] Continue to hone your awareness: to the name, to the month, to the day, and finally to the moment.

Williams also says: "No idea, but in things." Study what is "in front of your nose." By saying "geranium" instead of "flower," you are penetrating more deeply into the present and being there. The closer we can get to what's in front of our nose, the more it can teach us everything. "To see the World in a Grain of Sand, and a heaven in a Wild Flower . . ."[2]

In writing groups and classes, too, it is good to quickly learn the names of all the other group members. It helps to ground you in the group and make you more attentive to each other's work.

Learn the names of everything: birds, cheese, tractors, cars, buildings. A writer is all at once everything — an architect, French cook, farmer — and at the same time, a writer is none of these things.

[1] William Carlos Williams, "Daisy," in *The Collected Earlier Poems* (New York: New Directions, 1938).
[2] William Blake, "The Auguries of Innocence."

Thinking Critically about the Text

Natalie Goldberg found that she wasn't the only one in her neighborhood who didn't know the names of local trees and flowers. Would you be able to name many? How might you go about learning them? (Consider why Goldberg says it was "cheating" to ask people the names of their flowers and trees.) What would you gain by knowing them?

Questions on Subject

1. In paragraphs 3, 5, and 6, Goldberg cites a number of advantages to be gained by knowing the names of things. Review these advantages. What are they? Do they ring true?

2. Throughout the essay, Goldberg instructs readers to be specific and to be aware of the world around them. Of what besides names are the readers advised to be aware? Why?

Questions on Strategy

1. How does Goldberg "specifically" follow the advice she gives writers in this essay?

2. Goldberg makes several lists of the names of things. What purpose do these lists serve? How does she use these specifics to illustrate her point?

3. What specific audience is Goldberg addressing in this essay? (Glossary: *Audience*) How do you know?

4. The strategies of definition and illustration are closely intertwined in this essay; to name a thing precisely, after all, is to take the first step in defining it. (Glossary: *Definition*) What central concept is defined by Goldberg's many illustrations of naming? How might a writer use illustration to make definitions richer and more meaningful?

Questions on Diction and Vocabulary

1. Goldberg says that to name an object gives it dignity (paragraph 1) and integrity (4). What does she mean in each case?

2. In paragraph 1, Goldberg writes, "It [the word *geranium*] penetrates more deeply into the beingness of that flower." The word *beingness* does not appear in the dictionary. Where does it come from? Why does Goldberg use it, and what does she mean by her statement?

3. In his poem "Daisy," quoted in paragraph 4, William Carlos Williams calls the flower "dayseye." How does this spelling reinforce the central idea of the paragraph? Of the essay as a whole?

4. Refer to your dictionary to determine the meanings of the following words as Goldberg uses them in this selection: *pomegranate* (paragraph 1), *integrity* (4).

Classroom Activity Using Illustration

Specific examples are always more effective and convincing than general ones. A useful exercise in learning to be specific is to see the words we use for people, places, objects, and ideas as being positioned somewhere on a continuum of specificity. In the following chart, notice how the words become more specific as you move from left to right:

More General	General	Specific	More Specific
Organism	Reptile	Snake	Coral snake
Food	Sandwich	Corned beef sandwich	Reuben

Fill in the missing part for each of the following lists:

More General	General	Specific	More Specific
Writing instrument		Fountain pen	Waterman fountain pen
Vehicle	Car		1958 Chevrolet Impala
Book	Reference book	Dictionary	
American		Navaho	Laguna Pueblo
	Oral medicine	Gel capsule	Tylenol Gel Caps
School	High school	Technical high school	
Celebrity	Male celebrity		Brad Pitt

Writing Suggestions

1. Write a brief essay advising your readers of something they should do. Title your essay, as Goldberg does, with a directive ("Be Specific"). Tell your readers how they can improve their lives by taking your advice, and give strong examples of the behavior you are recommending.

2. Goldberg likes William Carlos Williams's statement, "No idea, but in things" (paragraph 5). Using this line as both a title and a thesis, write your own argument for the use of the specific over the general in a certain field — journalism, history, political science, biology, or literature, for example. (Glossary: *Argument*) Be sure to support your argument with relevant, representative examples.

In Praise of Copycats

KAL RAUSTIALA AND
CHRIS SPRIGMAN

A graduate of Duke University in 1988, Kal Raustiala received his Ph.D. in political science from the University of San Diego in 1996 and his J.D. from Harvard Law School in 1999. After graduating, he was a fellow at the Brookings Institution and a Peccei Scholar at the International Institute for Applied Systems. Raustiala has been a visiting professor at Harvard Law School, Columbia Law School, Princeton University, and the University of Chicago Law School and has published widely in scholarly journals as well as the *New York Times*, the *Financial Times*, and the *New Yorker*. He joined the faculty at the UCLA School of Law in 2004 and since 2007 has also served as the director of the UCLA Ronald W. Burkle Center for International Relations.

Chris Sprigman is a 1988 graduate of the University of Pennsylvania. He received his J.D. from the University of Chicago Law School in 1993. Following graduation, Sprigman taught at the law school of the University of the Witwatersrand, in Johannesburg, South Africa. Later he served in the Antitrust Division of the United States Department of Justice and practiced law in Washington, D.C. In 2003 he became a fellow at the Center for Internet and Society at Stanford Law School, and in 2005, he joined the faculty at the University of Virginia School of Law.

Starting in 2006, Raustiala and Sprigman teamed up on a number of projects involving the relationship between intellectual property rights and creativity. Together they authored "The Piracy Paradox: The Puzzling Irrelevance of Intellectual Property in Fashion Design" for the *Virginia Law Review* (2006) and "The Piracy Paradox Revisited" for the *Stanford Law Review* (2009). Their work culminated in the publication of *The Knockoff Economy: How Imitation Sparks Innovation* in September 2012.

The following article, adapted from the book *The Knockoff Economy*, first appeared in the *Wall Street Journal* on August 10, 2012. Here they argue that creativity and innovation can not only survive in the face of copying, but also can flourish. Notice how they use examples from finance, fashion, food, and sports to support this thesis and explain how and why this happens.

Preparing to Read

What is your attitude toward companies copying or imitating one another? Do you see any relationship between imitation and innovation in the world of fashion or technology? Do you think copying or imitating serves any useful purpose? Explain.

Critics called it "Bogle's folly." In 1976, John Bogle introduced the first index fund through his new company, the Vanguard Group. The idea was based on research for his senior thesis in economics at Princeton, in which he showed that, on average, professional money managers failed to beat the rate of return of the overall market. (The thesis, written in 1950, earned him an A+.)

Wall Street veterans initially scoffed at the fund, which tracked the Standard & Poor's 500 Index. Who would be content with hitting the market average? But the critics were quickly proven wrong. Vanguard grew explosively, and it is now the largest mutual fund company in the nation. Mr. Bogle's ideas have been widely copied by rival firms. Until recently, competitors were free to copy financial innovations—and as a result, index funds are now a huge business for Wall Street.

The conventional wisdom today is that copying is bad for creativity. If we allow people to copy new inventions, the thinking goes, no one will create them in the first place. Copycats do none of the work of developing new ideas but capture much of the benefit. That is the reason behind patents and copyrights: Copying destroys the incentive to innovate.

Except when it doesn't. There are many creative industries, like finance, that lack protection against copying (or did for a long time). A closer look at these fields shows that plenty of innovation takes place even when others are free to copy. There are many examples of successful industries that survive despite extensive copying. In fact, some even *thrive* because they are so open to copying.

Consider the fashion industry, which is virtually synonymous with the word "knockoff." Faviana, a New York fashion firm, makes its business model clear on its website. Faviana cheerfully replicates the work of major designers, providing what it calls "bling on a budget." As CEO Omid Moradi says on the site, "Ten minutes after any big awards telecast, the Faviana design team is already working on our newest 'celebrity look-alike gowns.'"

Faviana isn't alone. Anyone who has spent time in a Forever 21 store, or who reads fashion magazines, knows that the industry is full of knockoffs. And all this copying is completely legal, because copyright law doesn't cover apparel design. Yet far from killing creativity and destroying the market, the industry is prospering.

How is that possible? Because copying accelerates the fashion cycle, banishing old designs to the dustbin of history (perhaps to be dusted off and reintroduced later) and sending the fashion-conscious off in search of the new, new thing. Trends are the cornerstone of contemporary fashion, and legal copying allows them to develop and spread. Fashion—and finance—show that sometimes sharing an idea is more valuable than monopolizing it.

Copying can even serve as advertising. When an innovation is imi- 8
tated, more people see it and experience it, which helps to create
"buzz"—the notion that a particular thing has status and is especially
worth having. Copies can also become trial versions of the original. A 2009
Harvard Business School study found that many women who buy knockoff handbags soon move up to the real thing. Copies act as a kind of gate-
way drug to the harder (or, at least, more expensive) stuff.

The world of cuisine is similar. As any frequent restaurant-goer knows, 9
great dishes migrate from place to place. (Ever had a molten chocolate
cake?) And that is because no one can own a recipe or monopolize a terrific dish. Recipes and food are, like fashion designs, simply outside the
scope of copyright. But that doesn't stop the most ambitious chefs from
developing new dishes. The food world is
more creative today than ever before.

Great innovations often build on existing ones — and that requires the freedom to copy.

In cuisine, as in fashion, copying is a 10
critical part of the creative process. Chefs
sometimes get annoyed when others copy
their dishes without attribution. But many
of the world's most talented chefs, such as
the French Laundry's Thomas Keller, are
firm believers in an open approach to innovation. Mr. Keller's salmon tar-
tare cornets have been widely imitated. But that hasn't changed his views
on the merits of shared ideas. The freedom to copy, to tweak, and to
improve on a good idea is what makes it go from good to great. Along the
way it provides inspiration to others and serves to advertise, for those in
the know, the prowess of the originator.

Even football illustrates the power of copying. With myriad possibili- 11
ties for formations and plays, football strategy is always changing—but
none of it is protected against copycats. This hardly discourages great
coaches from innovating. Exhibit No. 1 is the West Coast Offense, which
relies on quick, short passes to control the ball and gain incremental yard-
age. The idea was the brainchild of Bill Walsh, who in the 1960s coached
the Cincinnati Bengals, then a recently formed and hapless NFL expansion
team. Cincinnati, he said, "was probably the worst-stocked franchise in the
history of the NFL. So in putting the team together, I personally was trying
to find a way we could compete."

His way was to develop a new style of offense. Later, when he 12
was coach of the 49ers, Mr. Walsh's ideas helped to lead the team to
three Super Bowl wins. Traditionalists at first dismissed his offense as
a gimmick. But no one could dispute its success. Eventually, it was imitated by the Green Bay Packers, the Philadelphia Eagles and many other
teams.

Why do football coaches invest long hours in developing innovative 13 strategies, even when they know that their rivals will imitate them as soon as they prove successful?

The rewards of winning can be immense, especially at the highest lev- 14 els of the game. Even a temporary advantage, lasting a week or perhaps a whole season, is worth pursuing.

More important, in sports there are practical barriers to immediately 15 copying a successful new tactic. The first time a play, formation or strategy is used, it can create a big element of surprise. After that, opponents can reverse engineer the idea relatively quickly. More difficult is the process of rebuilding a team to take full advantage of the innovation. This takes time. Economists refer to this window as the first-mover advantage.

In the case of Major League Baseball, as Michael Lewis showed in 16 "Moneyball," the Oakland A's won for a time with their number-crunching strategy, but the team faced a host of imitators after a few seasons. This dynamic of innovation by competitive underdogs is by no means limited to sports—from software to warfare, competition sparks creativity, even when copying is sure to follow.

We live in a world in which copying is getting easier. It certainly can 17 cause harm, and some rules to protect creations are necessary. But copying has an upside too. Great innovations often build on existing ones—and that requires the freedom to copy.

Thinking Critically about the Text

After having read this selection, has your attitude toward copying changed? Do you agree that "the freedom to copy, to tweak, and to improve on a good idea is what makes it go from good to great" (paragraph 10)?

Questions on Subject

1. According to Raustiala and Sprigman, how exactly does copying help spur creativity and innovation?

2. What is "bling on a budget" (paragraph 5)? Why haven't knockoffs killed the fashion industry?

3. In paragraph 13, Raustiala and Sprigman ask an interesting question. How would you answer their question? How do they answer it?

4. What exactly is "the first-mover advantage" (paragraph 15)? How does this term from economics apply to the sports world? The fashion industry?

Questions on Strategy

1. Raustiala and Sprigman begin their essay with the example of John Bogle and the "first index fund." How does this example serve to introduce their

thesis? (Glossary: *Thesis*) Considering the publication in which this essay appeared, how appropriate is this example for their audience? (Glossary: *Audience*)

2. What three main examples do Raustiala and Sprigman use to demonstrate that innovation happens despite widespread copying? Which example did you find most convincing? Explain.

3. In paragraph 5, the authors quote Faviana CEO Omid Moradi. What in your opinion does this quotation add to the discussion of knockoffs in the fashion industry? Explain.

4. How does the question that opens paragraph 7 function in the context of the essay?

5. How have Raustiala and Sprigman organized their essay? (Glossary: *Organization*) How do the authors ensure the smooth transition from one major example to another? (Glossary: *Transitions*)

Questions on Diction and Vocabulary

1. How did you react to the word *copycats* in Raustiala and Sprigman's title? Why do you suppose that they chose this word and not, say, *copying* or *imitators*? Explain. (Glossary: *Connotation/Denotation*)

2. Identify the figure of speech in paragraph 8. (Glossary: *Figures of Speech*). How does it work in the context of the paragraph in which it appears?

3. Refer to a dictionary to determine the meanings of the following words as Raustiala and Sprigman use them in this selection: *folly* (paragraph 1), *index fund* (1), *scoffed* (2), *virtually* (5), *replicates* (5), *cornerstone* (7), *migrate* (9), *prowess* (10), *myriad* (11), *incremental* (11), *hapless* (11).

Classroom Activity Using Illustration

Linton Weeks begins his essay "Burdens of the Modern Beast" (*Washington Post*, February 8, 2006) by contrasting the people in two old photographs with people of today. Carefully consider how Weeks uses examples in these opening five paragraphs to enhance the contrast and to introduce the central point of his essay.

> Slogging around with a backpack, a notebook, and a bottle of water, you stop for a while and stare at the historic black-and-white photographs in the National Museum of American History. You know, the ones depicting Americans going about their everyday lives: waiting for District trolley cars circa 1900, for instance, or people crisscrossing Pennsylvania Avenue in 1905.
>
> Notice something missing? That's right: stuff.
>
> The people — all ages, all colors, all genders — are not carrying any backpacks or water bottles. They are not schlepping cell phones, cradling coffee

cups, or lugging laptops. They have no bags — shopping, tote, or diaper. Besides a small purse here or a walking cane or umbrella there, they are unburdened: footloose and fingers free.

Now walk outside and take a look around. People on the same city streets are loaded down. They are laden with books, newspapers, Gatorade jugs, personal stereos, knapsacks, briefcases, and canvas totes with high-heel shoes inside. They have iPods strapped to upper arms, fanny packs buckled around waists, and house keys Velcroed to shoelaces.

Perhaps it's because we are multitaskers. Or because we're insecure. Maybe we are becoming more independent. Whatever the reasons, we are more and more burdened by our belongings.

What is your reaction to Weeks's examples? What would have been lost had he relied on generalizations to make his point? Identify any examples you would consider "more specific" than some of the other examples. Why do you suppose Weeks did not make all his examples as specific as he could have? Explain.

Writing Suggestions

1. Raustiala and Sprigman conclude their essay by arguing that "Great innovations often build on existing ones — and that requires the freedom to copy" (paragraph 17). They also recognize that copying "certainly can cause harm, and some rules to protect creations are necessary." Write an essay in which you explore the downside of copying. What types of industries need regulation or protection from copying? What kinds of harm can copying and imitation cause? Be sure to use specific examples to illustrate your key points.

2. **Writing with Sources.** Raustiala and Sprigman claim that "there are many examples of successful industries that survive despite extensive copying. In fact, some even *thrive* because they are so open to copying" (paragraph 4). To test their claim, take a close look at the world of fast foods, phones, automobiles, computers, televisions, or sports equipment. Using examples from one or more of these industries, write an essay in which you argue for or against their position. For models of and advice on integrating sources in your essay, see Chapters 14 and 15.

If You Had One Day
with Someone Who's Gone

MITCH ALBOM

Journalist and author Mitch Albom was born in Passaic,
New Jersey, in 1958. He earned a degree in sociology
from Brandeis University in 1979 and master's degrees
in journalism and business administration from Columbia University in 1981 and 1982. Starting in 1985, after
working for newspapers in New York and Florida, Albom
landed a staff position at the *Detroit Free Press*, where he
writes a regular sports column. Over the years he has
earned a loyal following of Detroit sports fans both as a
columnist and as a host of radio and television sports talk shows. His reputation as
a sportswriter blossomed with the publication of *The Live Albom: The Best of* Detroit
Free Press *Sports* (1988–1995), four volumes of his sports column. With the University of Michigan's legendary football coach Bo Schembechler, he wrote *Bo: The Bo
Schembechler Story* (1989) and, when Michigan won the national championship in
basketball, he authored *Fab Five: Basketball, Trash Talk, and the American Dream* (1993).
But it was the publication of *Tuesdays with Morrie: An Old Man, a Young Man, and Life's
Greatest Lesson* (1997), the story of Albom's weekly visits with his former sociology
professor Morrie Schwartz, that catapulted Albom onto the national stage. Albom
followed this work of nonfiction with *Have a Little Faith: A True Story* (2009) and three
novels: *The Five People You Meet in Heaven* (2003), *For One More Day* (2006), and *The
Time Keeper* (2012), all of which have been national best-sellers. Albom's books have
sold more than 30 million copies worldwide. In addition to numerous sportswriting
awards, Albom has received humanitarian awards for his work with Dream Team, A
Time to Help, Caring Athletes Team for Children's and Henry Ford Hospitals, Forgotten Harvest, and National Hospice.

In "If You Had One Day with Someone Who's Gone," an essay first published in
Parade magazine on September 17, 2006, Albom uses the illustrative stories of five
people to find out what they would do if they were granted one more day with a loved
one. His examples led him to a surprising life lesson.

Preparing to Read

Have you ever lost or become disconnected from someone you loved or were close
to — a family member or childhood friend? What were the circumstances that separated you? What would you most like to do with this person if you could be recon-
nected for a whole day?

Her world shattered in a telephone call. My mother was fifteen years old. "Your father is dead," her aunt told her.

Dead? How could he be dead? Hadn't she seen him the night before, when she kissed him goodnight? Hadn't he given her two new words to look up in the dictionary? Dead?

"You're a liar," my mother said.

But it wasn't a lie. Her father, my grandfather, had collapsed that morning from a massive heart attack. No final hugs. No goodbye. Just a phone call. And he was gone.

Have you ever lost someone you love and wanted one more conversation, one more day to make up for the time when you thought they would be here forever? I wrote that sentence as part of a new novel. Only after I finished did I realize that, my whole life, I had wondered this question of my mother.

> Have you ever lost someone you love and wanted one more conversation, one more day to make up for the time when you thought they would be here forever?

So, finally, I asked her.

"One more day with my father?" she said. Her voice seemed to tumble back into some strange, misty place. It had been six decades since their last day together. Murray had wanted his little girl, Rhoda, to be a doctor. He had wanted her to stay single and go to medical school. But after his death, my mother had to survive. She had to look after a younger brother and a depressed mother. She finished high school and married the first boy she ever dated. She never finished college.

"I guess, if I saw my father again, I would first apologize for not becoming a doctor," she answered. "But I would say that I became a different kind of doctor, someone who helped the family whenever they had problems.

"My father was my pal, and I would tell him I missed having a pal around the house after he was gone. I would tell him that my mother lived a long life and was comfortable at the end. And I would show him my family—his grandchildren and his great-grandchildren—of which I am the proudest. I hope he'd be proud of me, too."

My mother admitted that she cried when she first saw the movie *Ghost*, where Patrick Swayze "comes back to life" for a few minutes to be with his girlfriend. She couldn't help but wish for time like that with her father. I began to pose this scenario to other people—friends, colleagues, readers. How would they spend a day with a departed loved one? Their responses said a lot about what we long for.

Almost everyone wanted to once again "tell them how much I loved them"—even though these were people they had loved their whole lives on Earth. 11

Others wanted to relive little things. Michael Carroll, from San Antonio, Texas, wrote that he and his departed father "would head for the racetrack, then off to Dad's favorite hamburger place to eat and chat about old times." 12

Cathy Koncurat of Bel Air, Maryland, imagined a reunion with her best friend, who died after mysteriously falling into an icy river. People had always wondered what happened. "But if I had one more day with her, those questions wouldn't be important. Instead, I'd like to spend it the way we did when we were girls—shopping, seeing a movie, getting our hair done." 13

Some might say, "That's such an ordinary day." 14

Maybe that's the point. 15

Rabbi Gerald Wolpe has spent nearly fifty years on the pulpit and is a senior fellow at the University of Pennsylvania's Center for Bioethics. Yet, at some moment every day, he is an eleven-year-old boy who lost his dad to a sudden heart attack in 1938. 16

"My father is a prisoner of my memory," he said. "Would he even recognize me today?" Rabbi Wolpe can still picture the man, a former vaudevillian, taking him to Boston Braves baseball games or singing him a bedtime prayer. 17

Help me always do the right
Bless me every day and night.

If granted one more day, Rabbi Wolpe said, he "would share the good and the bad. My father needed to know things. For example, as a boy, he threw a snowball at his brother and hit him between the eyes. His brother went blind. My father went to his death feeling guilty for that. 18

"But we now know his brother suffered an illness that made him susceptible to losing his vision. I would want to say, 'Dad, look. It wasn't your fault.'" 19

At funerals, Rabbi Wolpe often hears mourners lament missed moments: "I never apologized. My last words were in anger. *If only I could have one more chance.*" 20

Maury De Young, a pastor in Kentwood, Michigan, hears similar things in his church. But De Young can sadly relate. His own son, Derrick, was killed in a car accident a few years ago, at age sixteen, the night before his big football game. There was no advance notice. No chance for goodbye. 21

"If I had one more day with him?" De Young said, wistfully. "I'd start it off with a long, long hug. Then we'd go for a walk, maybe to our cottage in the woods." 22

De Young had gone to those woods after Derrick's death. He'd sat 23
under a tree and wept. His faith had carried him through. And it eases his
pain now, he said, "because I know Derrick is in heaven."

Still, there are questions. Derrick's football number was 42. The day 24
after his accident, his team, with heavy hearts, won a playoff game by scoring 42 points. And the next week, the team won the state title by scoring—
yes—42 points.

"I'd like to ask my son," De Young whispered, "if he had something to 25
do with that."

We often fantasize about a perfect day—something exotic and far 26
away. But when it comes to those we miss, we desperately want one more
familiar meal, even one more argument. What does this teach us? That the
ordinary is precious. That the normal day is a treasure.

Think about it. When you haven't seen a loved one in a long time, the 27
first few hours of catching up feel like a giddy gift, don't they? That's the
gift we wish for when we can't catch up anymore. That feeling of connection. It could be a bedside chat, a walk in the woods, even a few words
from the dictionary.

I asked my mother if she still recalled those two words her father had 28
assigned her on the last night of his life.

"Oh, yes," she said quickly. "They were 'detrimental' and 'inculcate.' 29
I'll never forget them."

Then she sighed, yearning for a day she didn't have and words 30
she never used. And it made me want to savor every day with her even
more.

Thinking Critically about the Text

Albom shares with us the stories of five people who lost a loved one. In each case,
the loss was sudden and unexpected. How did the suddenness of the loss affect
each of the survivors? In what ways do you think sudden loss is different from
losing someone to a terminal illness or old age? Explain.

Questions on Subject

1. Why did Albom's mother cry when she first viewed the movie *Ghost*?

2. When asked how they would spend a day with a departed loved one — if that
   were possible — how did people respond? What life lesson does Albom draw
   from these responses in his conclusion?

3. What do you think Rabbi Wolpe meant when he said, "My father is a prisoner
   of my memory" (paragraph 17)?

4. What does it say about Albom's mother and the relationship she had with her father when it's revealed that she still remembers the two vocabulary words her father gave her the night before he died six decades ago? Explain.

Questions on Strategy

1. Albom opens his essay with the story of his mother losing her father when she was fifteen years old. How effective did you find this beginning? How is Albom's conclusion connected to this beginning? (Glossary: *Beginnings/ Endings*)

2. Paragraph 5 starts with the rhetorical question "Have you ever lost someone you love and wanted one more conversation, one more day to make up for the time when you thought they would be here forever?" (Glossary: *Rhetorical Question*) How does this question function in the context of Albom's essay?

3. How did Albom find the examples he uses in this essay? In what ways are Albom's examples both relevant and representative?

4. Albom often repeats key words or ideas to make the transition from one paragraph to the next. Identify several places where he has done this particularly well. What other transitional devices or expressions does he use? (Glossary: *Transitions*)

5. Why do you suppose Albom uses several one-sentence paragraphs? What would be lost had he tacked the sentence "So, finally, I asked her" (paragraph 6) on the end of the previous paragraph?

Questions on Diction and Vocabulary

1. Albom lets most of the people in his examples speak for themselves. What does he gain by letting people tell their own stories instead of telling us what they said? Explain.

2. What, if anything, does Albom's diction tell you about Albom himself? (Glossary: *Diction*) Do you think Albom's diction and tone are appropriate for his subject? (Glossary: *Tone*) Explain.

3. Refer to your dictionary to determine the meanings of the following words as Albom uses them in this selection: *scenario* (paragraph 10), *vaudevillian* (17), *lament* (20), *wistfully* (22), *giddy* (27), *detrimental* (29), *inculcate* (29).

Classroom Activity Using Illustration

Suppose you are writing an essay about the career choices that members of your extended family have made to see what trends or influences you could discover. Using your own extended family (great-grandparents, grandparents, parents, aunts and uncles, siblings) as potential material, make several lists of examples — for instance, one for family members who worked in agriculture or one of the trades, a second for those who worked in education, a third for those who worked in one of the professions, and a fourth for those who worked in the service sector.

Writing Suggestions

1. Has someone close to you — a parent, grandparent, relative, or friend — died, or has someone moved away whom you would like to see again if only for a day? Write an essay in which you first tell us something about your relationship with the person you are missing and then describe what you would do with that person for one whole day.

2. What do you value most about your relationships with family members? Do you have a special relationship with one particular parent, sibling, aunt or uncle, or grandparent? How would you describe the relationship you have with this person? What specifically do you get from him or her? Write an essay about your relationship with this family member, using relevant and representative examples to illustrate why you value having the person in your life.

Hot Dogs and Wild Geese

FIROOZEH DUMAS

Firoozeh Dumas was born in Abadan, Iran, in 1965. When she was seven, she and her family moved to Whittier, California. Two years later, they moved back to Iran, this time living in Ahvaz and Tehran, but after several years returned to Southern California. As a young adult, Dumas studied at the University of California, Berkeley, where she met her husband, François Dumas, a Frenchman, whom she married after graduation. In 2001, she started writing about life in Iran and the United States as a way of preserving this family history and culture for her children. The resulting memoir, *Funny in Farsi: A Memoir of Growing Up Iranian in America,* was published in 2003. She builds on her first book in *Laughing Without an Accent: Adventures of a Global Citizen* (2008), a collection of tender and humorous vignettes about the melding of cultures and the struggles of immigrants living in the United States. She is also the author of *A Vision of Hope: Addressing Prejudice and Stereotyping in the Wake of 9/11* (2006).

In "Hot Dogs and Wild Geese," a chapter from *Funny in Farsi*, Dumas discusses the frustrating but often humorous troubles she and her Iranian family had with the English language when they first moved to the United States over thirty years ago. After years of struggling with the English language, Dumas's parents found comfort in "the wave of immigration that has brought Iranian television, newspapers, and supermarkets to America." As you read Dumas's essay, notice how she uses multiple examples to illustrate her parents' missteps with language and how those detailed examples make her essay humorous and lively.

Preparing to Read

If your first language is English, it is now possible to go to many places in the world and get along pretty well speaking English, no matter what other languages are spoken in the host country. If you were to emigrate, how hard would you work to learn the predominant language of your chosen country? What advantages would there be in learning that language, even if you could get by in English? In the United States are there any incentives for immigrants to learn English? Should there be?

M oving to America was both exciting and frightening, but we found great comfort in knowing that my father spoke English. Having spent years regaling us with stories about his graduate years in America, he had left us with the distinct impression that America was his second home. My mother and I planned to stick close to him, letting him guide us through the exotic American landscape that he knew so well. We counted on him not only to translate the language but also to translate the culture, to be a link to this most foreign of lands. He was to be our own private Rosetta stone.

Once we reached America, we wondered whether perhaps my father had confused his life in America with someone else's. Judging from the bewildered looks of store cashiers, gas station attendants, and waiters, my father spoke a version of English not yet shared with the rest of America. His attempts to find a "vater closet" in a department store would usually lead us to the drinking fountain or the home furnishings section. Asking my father to ask the waitress the definition of "sloppy Joe" or "Tater Tots" was no problem. His translations, however, were highly suspect. Waitresses would spend several minutes responding to my father's questions, and these responses, in turn, would be translated as "She doesn't know." Thanks to my father's translations, we stayed away from hot dogs, catfish, and hush puppies, and no amount of caviar in the sea would have convinced us to try mud pie.

We wondered how my father had managed to spend several years attending school in America yet remain so utterly befuddled by Americans. We soon discovered that his college years had been spent mainly in the library, where he had managed to avoid contact with all Americans except his engineering professors. As long as the conversation was limited to vectors, surface tension, and fluid mechanics, my father was Fred Astaire with words. But one step outside the scintillating world of petroleum engineering and he had two left tongues.

My father's only other regular contact in college had been his roommate, a Pakistani who spent his days preparing curry. Since neither spoke English but both liked curries, they got along splendidly. The person who had assigned them together had probably hoped they would either learn English or invent a common language for the occasion. Neither happened.

My father's inability to understand spoken English was matched only by his efforts to deny the problem. His constant attempts at communicating with Americans seemed at first noble and adventurous, then annoying. Somewhere between his thick Persian accent and his use of vocabulary found in pre–World War II British textbooks, my father spoke a private language. That nobody understood him hurt his pride, so what he lacked in speaking ability, he made up for by reading. He was the only person who actually read each and every document before he signed it. Buying a washing machine from Sears might take the average American thirty minutes, but by the time my father had finished reading the warranties, terms of contracts, and credit information, the store was closing and the janitor was asking us to please step aside so he could finish mopping the floor.

My mother's approach to learning English consisted of daily lessons with Monty Hall and Bob Barker. Her devotion to *Let's Make a Deal* and

The Price Is Right was evident in her newfound ability to recite useless information. After a few months of television viewing, she could correctly tell us whether a coffeemaker cost more or less than $19.99. How many boxes of Hamburger Helper, Swanson's TV dinners, or Turtle Wax could one buy without spending a penny more than twenty dollars? She knew that, too. Strolling down the grocery aisle, she rejoiced in her celebrity sightings—Lipton tea! Campbell's tomato soup! Betty Crocker Rich & Creamy Frosting! Every day, she would tell us the day's wins and losses on the game shows. "He almost won the boat, but the wife picked curtain number two and they ended up with a six-foot chicken statue." The bad prizes on *Let's Make a Deal* sounded far more intriguing than the good ones. Who would want the matching La-Z-Boy recliners when they could have the adult-size crib and high-chair set?

My mother soon decided that the easiest way for her to communicate [7] with Americans was to use me as an interpreter. My brother Farshid, with his schedule full of soccer, wrestling, and karate, was too busy to be recruited for this dubious honor. At an age when most parents are guiding their kids toward independence, my mother was hanging on to me for dear life. I had to accompany her to the grocery store, the hairdresser, the doctor, and every place else that a kid wouldn't want to go. My reward for doing this was the constant praise of every American we encountered. Hearing a seven-year-old translate Farsi into English and vice versa made quite an impression on everyone. People lavished compliments on me. "You must be very, very smart, a genius maybe." I always responded by assuring them that if they ever moved to another country, they, too, would learn the language. (What I wanted to say was that I wished I could be at home watching *The Brady Bunch* instead of translating the qualities of various facial moisturizers.) My mother had her own response to the compliments: "Americans are easily impressed."

> My parents still don't understand why teenagers want to be cool so they can be hot.

I always encouraged my mother to learn English, but her talents lay [8] elsewhere. Since she had never learned English in school, she had no idea of its grammar. She would speak entire paragraphs without using any verbs. She referred to everyone and everything as "it," leaving the listener wondering whether she was talking about her husband or the kitchen table. Even if she did speak a sentence more or less correctly, her accent made it incomprehensible. "W" and "th" gave her the most difficulty. As if God were playing a linguistic joke on us, we lived in "Vee-tee-er" (Whittier), we shopped at "Veetvood" (Whitwood) Plaza, I attended "Leffingvell" School, and our neighbor was none other than "Valter Villiams."

Despite little progress on my mother's part, I continually encouraged her. Rather than teach her English vocabulary and grammar, I eventually decided to teach her entire sentences to repeat. I assumed that once she got used to speaking correctly, I could be removed, like training wheels, and she would continue coasting. I was wrong.

Noticing some insects in our house one day, my mother asked me to call the exterminator. I looked up the number, then told my mother to call and say, "We have silverfish in our house." My mother grumbled, dialed the number, and said, "Please come rrright a-vay. Goldfeeesh all over dee house." The exterminator told her he'd be over as soon as he found his fishing pole.

A few weeks later, our washing machine broke. A repairman was summoned and the leaky pipe was quickly replaced. My mother wanted to know how to remove the black stain left by the leak. "Y'all are gonna hafta use some elbow grease," he said. I thanked him and paid him and walked with my mother to the hardware store. After searching fruitlessly for elbow grease, I asked the salesclerk for help. "It removes stains," I added. The manager was called.

Once the manager finished laughing, he gave us the disappointing explanation. My mother and I walked home empty-handed. That, I later learned, is what Americans call a wild-goose chase.

Now that my parents have lived in America for thirty years, their English has improved somewhat, but not as much as one would hope. It's not entirely their fault; English is a confusing language. When my father paid his friend's daughter the compliment of calling her homely, he meant she would be a great housewife. When he complained about horny drivers, he was referring to their tendency to honk. And my parents still don't understand why teenagers want to be cool so they can be hot.

I no longer encourage my parents to learn English. I've given up. Instead, I'm grateful for the wave of immigration that has brought Iranian television, newspapers, and supermarkets to America. Now, when my mother wants to ask the grocer whether he has any more eggplants in the back that are a little darker and more firm, because the ones he has out aren't right for *khoresht bademjun*, she can do so in Farsi, all by herself. And for that, I say hallelujah, a word that needs no translation.

Thinking Critically about the Text

Dumas uses a number of detailed examples to describe her parents' struggles with the English language. What new appreciation of the English language do you have after reading of problems her parents had with adapting to an English-speaking world?

Questions on Subject

1. What were your expectations when you first saw the title of this essay? (Glossary: *Title*) After reading the essay, how appropriate do you think her title is for her subject? Explain.

2. Dumas confesses that "moving to America was both exciting and frightening," but dealing with a new language was not one of the challenges that concerned her. What expectations did Dumas and her mother have before arriving in America? What does Dumas mean when she says that her father "was to be our own private Rosetta stone" (paragraph 1)?

3. What did she discover about her father's English once she and her mother were in America? How well did Dumas herself deal with English as a second language? How did her parents cope with English?

4. Dumas says she "always encouraged my mother to learn English" (paragraph 8). What success did she have with her mother? Why did Dumas eventually give up trying to help her parents learn English?

5. How did Dumas's mother solve her problem of communicating with Americans?

Questions on Strategy

1. What is the thesis or main idea of Dumas's essay, and where does she present it? (Glossary: *Thesis*)

2. How does Dumas account for her father's inability to use English with the America public? Did you find her use of examples in paragraph 2 to illustrate her father's problems helpful? Explain.

3. In paragraphs 6–12, Dumas provides multiple examples of her mother's struggles with English. Which of the examples did you find most effective? Do you think she provided too many examples? Too few? Or just the right number?

4. How has Dumas organized her essay? (Glossary: *Organization*)

5. How does Dumas introduce humor into her essay? For example, what accounts for the humor in paragraphs 10–12? How else could she have approached her subject if not humorously? Explain.

Questions on Diction and Vocabulary

1. Identify the extended metaphor that Dumas uses in paragraph 3 and explain how it works for readers. (Glossary: *Figures of Speech*)

2. What does Dumas mean when she likens herself to "training wheels" in paragraph 9?

3. How would you describe Dumas's voice in this selection? (Glossary: *Voice*) What in her diction led you to your conclusion?

4. Refer to a dictionary to determine the meanings of the following words as Dumas uses them in this selection: *regaling* (paragraph 1), *scintillating* (3), *dubious* (7), *lavished* (7).

Classroom Activity Using Illustration

The Web site thingsarefine.org, sponsored by the Portland-based advertising agency Borders Perrin Norrander (BPN), features the following text on its home page:

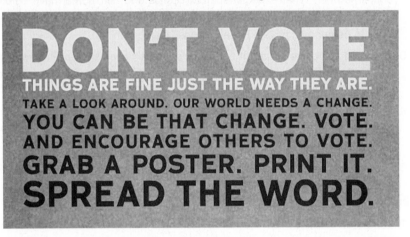

After considering this text, take a look at one of the downloadable posters on the site, such as the one reproduced on page 213.

After considering the Web site's message and the poster, answer the following questions: What does BPN want to persuade viewers to do? In the poster, what example does BPN use to suggest what's "fine" (or not) in the United States right now? Is the example persuasive? In small groups, discuss your answers. What conclusions about BPN's use of illustration did you come to?

Writing Suggestions

1. In paragraph 13, Dumas excuses her parents' struggles with English: "It's not entirely their fault; English is a confusing language." Using that statement as a starting point, write an essay in which you recount several of your own frustrating experiences with language. Make a list of the things that you find confusing about the English language before you begin. Make sure to use specific examples, like the ones Dumas uses, to support each of your main points.

2. For many immigrants, the process of assimilating into American society and culture can, as Dumas observes, be "both exciting and frightening" (paragraph 1). Make two lists: one of the exciting prospects of arriving and settling into a new country, and another of the frightening prospects of finding your way in a different or unknown place. Use examples from your own experience, observation, or reading to write an essay in which you support Dumas's observation.

How to Give Orders Like a Man

DEBORAH TANNEN

Deborah Tannen, professor of linguistics at Georgetown University, was born in 1945 in Brooklyn, New York. Tannen received her B.A. in English from the State University of New York at Binghamton in 1966 and taught English in Greece until 1968. She then earned an M.A. in English literature from Wayne State University in 1970. While pursuing her Ph.D. in linguistics at the University of California–Berkeley, she received several prizes for her poetry and short fiction. Her work has appeared in *New York, Vogue,* and the *New York Times Magazine.* In addition, she has authored three best-selling books on how people communicate: *You Just Don't Understand* (1990), *That's Not What I Meant* (1991), and *Talking from Nine to Five* (1994). The success of these books attests to the public's interest in language, especially when it pertains to gender differences. Tannen's other books include *The Argument Culture: Stopping America's War of Words* (1998), *I Only Say This Because I Love You: Talking to Your Parents, Partners, Sibs, and Kids When You're All Adults* (2002), *You're Wearing That? Mothers and Daughters in Conversation* (2006), and most recently *You Were Always Mom's Favorite: Sisters in Conversation Throughout Their Lives* (2009). Her research led Tannen to conclude that "in some ways, siblings and especially sisters are more influential in your childhood than your parents."

In this essay, first published in the *New York Times Magazine* in August 1994, Tannen looks at the variety of ways in which orders are given and received. Interestingly, she concludes that, contrary to popular belief, directness is not necessarily logical or effective and indirectness is not necessarily manipulative or insecure.

Preparing to Read

Write about a time in your life when you were ordered to do something. Who gave you the order — a friend, a parent, maybe a teacher? Did the person's relationship to you affect how you carried out the order? Did it make a difference to you whether the order giver was male or female? Why?

A university president was expecting a visit from a member of the board of trustees. When her secretary buzzed to tell her that the board member had arrived, she left her office and entered the reception area to greet him. Before ushering him into her office, she handed her secretary a sheet of paper and said: "I've just finished drafting this letter. Do you think you could type it right away? I'd like to get it out before lunch. And would you please do me a favor and hold all calls while I'm meeting with Mr. Smith?"

When they sat down behind the closed door of her office, Mr. Smith   2
began by telling her that he thought she had spoken inappropriately to her
secretary. "Don't forget," he said. "*You're* the president!"

Putting aside the question of the appropriateness of his admonishing   3
the president on her way of speaking, it is revealing—and representative
of many Americans' assumptions—that the indirect way in which the university president told her secretary what to do struck him as self-
deprecating. He took it as evidence that she didn't think she had the right
to make demands of her secretary. He probably thought he was giving her
a needed pep talk, bolstering her self-confidence.

> I challenge the assumption that talking in an indirect way necessarily reveals powerlessness, lack of self-confidence, or anything else about the character of the speaker.

I challenge the assumption that talking   4
in an indirect way necessarily reveals pow-
erlessness, lack of self-confidence, or anything else about the character of the
speaker. Indirectness is a fundamental element in human communication. It is also
one of the elements that varies most from
one culture to another, and one that can
cause confusion and misunderstanding
when speakers have different habits with
regard to using it. I also want to dispel the
assumption that American women tend to
be more indirect than American men.
Women and men are both indirect, but in
addition to differences associated with their backgrounds—regional, ethnic, and class—they tend to be indirect in different situations and in different ways.

At work, we need to get others to do things, and we all have different   5
ways of accomplishing this. Any individual's ways will vary depending on
who is being addressed—a boss, a peer, or a subordinate. At one extreme
are bald commands. At the other are requests so indirect that they don't
sound like requests at all, but are just a statement of need or a description
of a situation. People with direct styles of asking others to do things perceive indirect requests—if they perceive them as requests at all—as
manipulative. But this is often just a way of blaming others for our discomfort with their styles.

The indirect style is no more manipulative than making a telephone   6
call, asking "Is Rachel there?" and expecting whoever answers the phone
to put Rachel on. Only a child is likely to answer "Yes" and continue holding the phone—not out of orneriness but because of inexperience with the
conventional meaning of the question. (A mischievous adult might do it to
tease.) Those who feel that indirect orders are illogical or manipulative do
not recognize the conventional nature of indirect requests.

Issuing orders indirectly can be the prerogative of those in power. 7
Imagine, for example, a master who says "It's cold in here" and expects a
servant to make a move to close a window, while a servant who says the
same thing is not likely to see his employer rise to correct the situation and
make him more comfortable. Indeed, a Frenchman raised in Brittany tells
me that his family never gave bald commands to their servants but always
communicated orders in indirect and highly polite ways. This pattern renders less surprising the finding of David Bellinger and Jean Berko Gleason
that fathers' speech to their young children had a higher incidence than
mothers' of both direct imperatives like "Turn the bolt with the wrench"
and indirect orders like "The wheel is going to fall off."

The use of indirectness can hardly be understood without the cross- 8
cultural perspective. Many Americans find it self-evident that directness is
logical and aligned with power while indirectness is akin to dishonesty and
reflects subservience. But for speakers raised in most of the world's cultures, varieties of indirectness are the norm in communication. This is the
pattern found by a Japanese sociolinguist, Kunihiko Harada, in his analysis of a conversation he recorded between a Japanese boss and a subordinate.

The markers of superior status were clear. One speaker was a Japanese 9
man in his late 40s who managed the local branch of a Japanese private
school in the United States. His conversational partner was a Japanese
American woman in her early 20s who worked at the school. By virtue of
his job, his age, and his native fluency in the language being taught, the
man was in the superior position. Yet when he addressed the woman, he
frequently used polite language and almost always used indirectness. For
example, he had tried and failed to find a photography store that would
make a black-and-white print from a color negative for a brochure they
were producing. He let her know that he wanted her to take over the task
by stating the situation and allowed her to volunteer to do it: (This is a
translation of the Japanese conversation.)

> On this matter, that, that, on the leaflet? This photo, I'm thinking of
> changing it to black-and-white and making it clearer. . . . I went to a photo
> shop and asked them. They said they didn't do black-and-white. I asked if
> they knew any place that did. They said they didn't know. They weren't
> very helpful, but anyway, a place must be found, the negative brought to it,
> the picture developed.

Harada observes, "Given the fact that there are some duties to be 10
performed and that there are two parties present, the subordinate is supposed to assume that those are his or her obligation." It was precisely
because of his higher status that the boss was free to choose whether to

speak formally or informally, to assert his power or to play it down and build rapport—an option not available to the subordinate, who would have seemed cheeky if she had chosen a style that enhanced friendliness and closeness.

The same pattern was found by a Chinese sociolinguist, Yuling Pan, in a meeting of officials involved in a neighborhood youth program. All spoke in ways that reflected their place in the hierarchy. A subordinate addressing a superior always spoke in a deferential way, but a superior addressing a subordinate could either be authoritarian, demonstrating his power, or friendly, establishing rapport. The ones in power had the option of choosing which style to use. In this spirit, I have been told by people who prefer their bosses to give orders indirectly that those who issue bald commands must be pretty insecure; otherwise why would they have to bolster their egos by throwing their weight around?   11

I am not inclined to accept that those who give orders directly are really insecure and powerless, any more than I want to accept that judgment of those who give indirect orders. The conclusion to be drawn is that ways of talking should not be taken as obvious evidence of inner psychological states like insecurity or lack of confidence. Considering the many influences on conversational style, individuals have a wide range of ways of getting things done and expressing their emotional states. Personality characteristics like insecurity cannot be linked to ways of speaking in an automatic, self-evident way.   12

Those who expect orders to be given indirectly are offended when they come unadorned. One woman said that when her boss gives her instructions, she feels she should click her heels, salute, and say "Yes, boss!" His directions strike her as so imperious as to border on the militaristic. Yet I received a letter from a man telling me that indirect orders were a fundamental part of his military training. He wrote: 13

> Many years ago, when I was in the Navy, I was training to be a radio technician. One class I was in was taught by a chief radioman, a regular Navy man who had been to sea, and who was then in his third hitch. The students, about twenty of us, were fresh out of boot camp, with no sea duty and little knowledge of real Navy life. One day in class the chief said it was hot in the room. The students didn't react, except perhaps to nod in agreement. The chief repeated himself: "It's hot in this room." Again there was no reaction from the students.
>
> Then the chief explained. He wasn't looking for agreement or discussion from us. When he said that the room was hot, he expected us to do something about it—like opening the window. He tried it one more time, and this time all of us left our workbenches and headed for the windows. We had learned. And we had many opportunities to apply what we had learned.

This letter especially intrigued me because "It's cold in here" is the   14
standard sentence used by linguists to illustrate an indirect way of getting
someone to do something—as I used it earlier. In this example, it is the
very obviousness and rigidity of the military hierarchy that makes the statement of a problem sufficient to trigger corrective action on the part of
subordinates.

A man who had worked at the Pentagon reinforced the view that the   15
burden of interpretation is on subordinates in the military—and he
noticed the difference when he moved to a position in the private sector. He
was frustrated when he'd say to his new secretary, for example, "Do we
have a list of invitees?" and be told, "I don't know; we probably do" rather
than "I'll get it for you." Indeed, he explained, at the Pentagon, such a question would likely be heard as a reproach that the list was not already on
his desk.

The suggestion that indirectness is associated with the military must   16
come as a surprise to many. But everyone is indirect, meaning more than is
put into words and deriving meaning from words that are never actually
said. It's a matter of where, when, and how we each tend to be indirect and
look for hidden meanings. But indirectness has a built-in liability. There is
a risk that the other will either miss or choose to ignore your meaning.

On January 13, 1982, a freezing cold, snowy day in Washington, Air   17
Florida Flight 90 took off from National Airport, but could not get the
lift it needed to keep climbing. It crashed into a bridge linking Washington
to the state of Virginia and plunged into the Potomac. Of the seventy-nine
people on board, all but five perished, many floundering and drowning in
the icy water while horror-stricken bystanders watched helplessly from the
river's edge and millions more watched, aghast, on their television screens.
Experts later concluded that the plane had waited too long after deicing to
take off. Fresh buildup of ice on the wings and engine brought the plane
down. How could the pilot and co-pilot have made such a blunder? Didn't
at least one of them realize it was dangerous to take off under these conditions?

Charlotte Linde, a linguist at the Institute for Research on Learning in   18
Palo Alto, Califorina, has studied the "black box" recordings of cockpit
conversations that preceded crashes as well as tape recordings of conversations that took place among crews during flight simulations in which problems were presented. Among the black box conversations she studied was
the one between the pilot and co-pilot just before the Air Florida crash.
The pilot, it turned out, had little experience flying in icy weather. The co-
pilot had a bit more, and it became heartbreakingly clear on analysis that
he had tried to warn the pilot, but he did so indirectly.

The co-pilot repeatedly called attention to the bad weather and to ice   19
building up on other planes:

> Co-pilot: Look how the ice is just hanging on his, ah, back, back there,
> see that?
> . . .
> Co-pilot: See all those icicles on the back there and everything?
> Captain: Yeah.

He expressed concern early on about the long waiting time between   20
deicing:

> Co-pilot: Boy, this is a, this is a losing battle here on trying to deice those
> things, it [gives] you a false feeling of security, that's all that does.

Shortly after they were given clearance to take off, he again expressed   21
concern:

> Co-pilot: Let's check these tops again since we been setting here awhile.
> Captain: I think we get to go here in a minute.

When they were about to take off, the co-pilot called attention to the   22
engine instrument readings, which were not normal:

> Co-pilot: That don't seem right, does it? [three-second pause] Ah, that's
> not right. . . .
> Captain: Yes, it is, there's eighty.
> Co-pilot: Naw, I don't think that's right. [seven-second pause] Ah,
> maybe it is.
> Captain: Hundred and twenty.
> Co-pilot: I don't know.

The takeoff proceeded, and thirty-seven seconds later the pilot and   23
co-pilot exchanged their last words.

The co-pilot had repeatedly called the pilot's attention to dangerous   24
conditions but did not directly suggest they abort the takeoff. In Linde's
judgment, he was expressing his concern indirectly, and the captain didn't
pick up on it—with tragic results.

That the co-pilot was trying to warn the captain indirectly is supported   25
by evidence from another airline accident—a relatively minor one—
investigated by Linde that also involved the unsuccessful use of indirectness.

On July 9, 1978, Allegheny Airlines Flight 453 was landing at Monroe   26
County Airport in Rochester, when it overran the runway by 728 feet.
Everyone survived. This meant that the captain and co-pilot could be
interviewed. It turned out that the plane had been flying too fast for a safe

landing. The captain should have realized this and flown around a second time, decreasing his speed before trying to land. The captain said he simply had not been aware that he was going too fast. But the co-pilot told interviewers that he "tried to warn the captain in subtle ways, like mentioning the possibility of a tail wind and the slowness of flap extension." His exact words were recorded in the black box. The crosshatches indicate words deleted by the National Transportation Safety Board and were probably expletives:

> Co-pilot: Yeah, it looks like you got a tail wind here.
> Captain: Yeah.
> [?]: Yeah [it] moves awfully # slow.
> Co-pilot: Yeah the # flaps are slower than a #.
> Captain: We'll make it, gonna have to add power.
> Co-pilot: I know.

The co-pilot thought the captain would understand that if there was a tail wind, it would result in the plane going too fast, and if the flaps were slow, they would be inadequate to break the speed sufficiently for a safe landing. He thought the captain would then correct for the error by not trying to land. But the captain said he didn't interpret the co-pilot's remarks to mean they were going too fast.   27

Linde believes it is not a coincidence that the people being indirect in these conversations were the co-pilots. In her analyses of flight-crew conversations she found it was typical for the speech of subordinates to be more mitigated—polite, tentative, or indirect. She also found that topics broached in a mitigated way were more likely to fail, and that captains were more likely to ignore hints from their crew members than the other way around. These findings are evidence that not only can indirectness and other forms of mitigation be misunderstood, but they are also easier to ignore.   28

In the Air Florida case, it is doubtful that the captain did not realize what the co-pilot was suggesting when he said, "Let's check these tops again since we been setting here awhile" (though it seems safe to assume he did not realize the gravity of the co-pilot's concern). But the indirectness of the co-pilot's phrasing certainly made it easier for the pilot to ignore it. In this sense, the captain's response, "I think we get to go here in a minute," was an indirect way of saying, "I'd rather not." In view of these patterns, the flight crews of some airlines are now given training to express their concerns, even to superiors, in more direct ways.   29

The conclusion that people should learn to express themselves more directly has a ring of truth to it—especially for Americans. But direct communication is not necessarily always preferable. If more direct expression   30 is better communication, then the most direct-speaking crews should be the best ones. Linde was surprised to find in her research that crews that used the most mitigated speech were often judged the best crews. As part of the study of talk among cockpit crews in flight simulations, the trainers observed and rated the performances of the simulation crews. The crews they rated top in performance had a higher rate of mitigation than crews they judged to be poor.

This finding seems at odds with the role played by indirectness in the examples of crashes that we just saw. Linde concluded that since every utterance functions on two levels—the referential (what it says) and the relational (what it implies about the speaker's relationships), crews that attend to the relational level will be better crews. A similar explanation was suggested by Kunihiko Harada. He believes that the secret of successful communication lies not in teaching subordinates to be more direct, but in teaching higher-ups to be more sensitive to indirect meaning. In other words, the crashes resulted not only because the co-pilots tried to alert the captains to danger indirectly but also because the captains were not attuned to the co-pilots' hints. What made for successful performance among the best crews might have been the ability—or willingness—of listeners to pick up on hints, just as members of families or longstanding couples come to understand each other's meaning without anyone being particularly explicit.

It is not surprising that a Japanese sociolinguist came up with this explanation; what he described is the Japanese system, by which good communication is believed to take place when meaning is gleaned without being stated directly—or at all.

While Americans believe that "the squeaky wheel gets the grease" (so it's best to speak up), the Japanese say, "The nail that sticks out gets hammered back in" (so it's best to remain silent if you don't want to be hit on the head). Many Japanese scholars writing in English have tried to explain to bewildered Americans the ethics of a culture in which silence is often given greater value than speech, and ideas are believed to be best communicated without being explicitly stated. Key concepts in Japanese give a flavor of the attitudes toward language that they reveal—and set in relief the strategies that Americans encounter at work when talking to other Americans.

Takie Sugiyama Lebra, a Japanese-born anthropologist, explains that one of the most basic values in Japanese culture is *omoiyari*, which she translates as "empathy." Because of *omoiyari*, it should not be necessary to state one's meaning explicitly; people should be able to sense each other's meaning intuitively. Lebra explains that it is typical for a Japanese speaker to let sentences trail off rather than complete them because expressing ideas before knowing how they will be received seems intrusive. "Only an insensitive, uncouth person needs a direct, verbal, complete message," Lebra says.

Sasshi, the anticipation of another's message through insightful guess-work, is considered an indication of maturity. 35

Considering the value placed on direct communication by Americans in general, and especially by American businesspeople, it is easy to imagine that many American readers may scoff at such conversational habits. But the success of Japanese businesses makes it impossible to continue to maintain that there is anything inherently inefficient about such conversational conventions. With indirectness, as with all aspects of conversational style, our own habitual style seems to make sense—seems polite, right, and good. The light cast by the habits and assumptions of another culture can help us see our way to the flexibility and respect for other styles that is the only best way of speaking. 36

Thinking Critically about the Text

In her essay, Tannen states that "indirectness is a fundamental element in human communication" (paragraph 4). Do you agree with Tannen on this point? What does she mean when she says that it is just as important to notice what we do not say as what we actually say?

Questions on Subject

1. How does Tannen define indirect speech? What does she see as the built-in liability of indirect speech? Do you see comparable liability inherent in direct speech?

2. Tannen doesn't contest a finding that fathers had a higher incidence of both direct imperatives and indirect orders than mothers did. How does she interpret these results?

3. Why do you think Tannen doesn't tell her audience how to deal with an insecure boss?

4. Why is it typical for Japanese speakers to let their sentences trail off?

Questions on Strategy

1. What is Tannen's thesis, and where does she present it? (Glossary: *Thesis*)

2. Tannen mostly uses examples in which men give direct orders. In what ways do these examples support her thesis?

3. For what audience has Tannen written this essay? Does this help to explain why she focuses primarily on indirect communication? Why, or why not? (Glossary: *Audience*)

4. Tannen gives two examples of flight accidents that resulted from indirect speech, yet she then explains that top-performing flight teams used indirect speech more often than poorly performing teams. How do these seemingly contradictory examples support the author's argument?

5. Explain how Tannen uses comparison and contrast to document the assertion that "indirectness is a fundamental element in human communication. It is also one of the elements that varies most from one culture to another, and one that can cause confusion and misunderstanding when speakers have different habits with regard to using it" (paragraph 4). (Glossary: *Comparison and Contrast*) How does this strategy enhance or support the dominant strategy of illustration in the essay?

Questions on Diction and Vocabulary

1. In paragraph 13, what irony does Tannen point out in the popular understanding of the word *militaristic*? (Glossary: *Irony*)

2. How would you describe Tannen's diction in this essay? (Glossary: *Diction*) Does she ever get too scientific for the general reader? If so, where do you think her language gets too technical? Why do you think she uses such language?

3. Refer to your dictionary to determine the meanings of the following words as Tannen uses them in this selection: *admonishing* (paragraph 3), *self-deprecating* (3), *manipulative* (5), *prerogative* (7), *subservience* (8), *cheeky* (10), *deferential* (11), *imperious* (13), *liability* (16), *mitigated* (28), *broached* (28), *gleaned* (32), *relief* (33), *empathy* (34).

Classroom Activity Using Illustration

Once you have established what examples you will use in a paper, you need to decide how you will organize them. Here are some major patterns of organization you may want to use:

- Chronological (oldest to newest, or the reverse)
- Spatial (top to bottom, left to right, inside to outside, and so forth)
- Most familiar to least familiar, or the reverse
- Easiest to most difficult to comprehend
- Easiest to most difficult to accept or carry out
- According to similarities or differences

Use one or more of these patterns to organize the examples in the paper you are currently working on, or to organize the lists of examples of career choice in your extended family that you generated for the classroom activity accompanying the Albom essay on page 205.

Writing Suggestions

1. Tannen concludes that "the light cast by the habits and assumptions of another culture can help us see our way to the flexibility and respect for other styles that is the only best way of speaking" (paragraph 36). Write an essay in which you use concrete examples from your own experience, observation, or readings to agree or disagree with her conclusion.

2. Write an essay comparing the command styles of two people — either people you know or fictional characters. You might consider your parents, professors, coaches, television characters, or characters from movies or novels. What conclusions can you draw from your analysis? (Glossary: *Comparison and Contrast*) Illustrate your essay with clear examples of the two command styles.

WRITING SUGGESTIONS FOR ILLUSTRATION

1. Write an essay on one of the following statements, using examples to illustrate your ideas. You should be able to draw some of your examples from personal experience and firsthand observations.

   a. Fads never go out of style.
   b. Television has produced a number of "classic" programs.
   c. Every college campus has its own unique slang terms.
   d. Making excuses sometimes seems like a national pastime.
   e. A liberal arts education can have many practical applications.
   f. All good teachers (or doctors, secretaries, auto mechanics, sales representatives) have certain traits in common.
   g. Television talk shows are an accurate (or inaccurate) reflection of our society.
   h. Good literature always teaches us something about our humanity.
   i. Grades are not always a good indication of what has been learned.
   j. Recycling starts with the individual.

2. College students are not often given credit for the community volunteer work they do. Write a letter to the editor of your local newspaper in which you demonstrate, with several extended examples, the beneficial impact that you and your fellow students have had on the community.

3. How do advertisers portray older people in their advertisements? Based on your analysis of some real ads, how fair are advertisers to senior citizens? What tactics do advertisers use to sell their products to senior citizens? Write an essay in which you use actual ads to illustrate two or three such tactics.

4. Most students would agree that in order to be happy and "well adjusted," people need to learn how to relieve stress and to relax. What strategies do you and your friends use to relax? What have been the benefits of these relaxation techniques for you? Write an article for the school newspaper in which you give examples of several of these techniques and encourage your fellow students to try them.

5. The Internet has profoundly altered the way people around the world communicate and share information. One area in which significant change is especially evident is education. While having so much information at your fingertips can be exciting, such technology is not without its problems. What are the advantages and disadvantages of the Internet for teachers and students? Write an essay in which you analyze the Internet's educational value. Document your assessment with specific examples.

6. Some people think it's important to look their best and, therefore, give careful attention to the clothing they wear. Others do not seem to care. How much stock do you put in the old saying, "Clothes make the person"? Use examples of the people on your own campus or in your community to argue your position.

7. **Writing with Sources.** Write an essay on one of the following statements, using examples to illustrate your ideas. Draw your examples from a variety of sources: your library's print and Internet resources, interviews, and information gathered from lectures and the media. As you plan your essay, consider whether you will want to use a series of short examples or one or more extended examples.

   a. Much has been (or should still be) done to eliminate barriers for the physically handicapped.
   b. Nature's oddities are numerous.
   c. Throughout history, dire predictions have been made about the end of the world.
   d. The past predictions of science fiction are today's realities.
   e. The world has not seen an absence of warfare since World War II.
   f. Young executives have developed many innovative management strategies.
   g. A great work of art may come out of an artist's most difficult period.
   h. The misjudgments of our presidents can be useful lessons in leadership.
   i. Genius is 10 percent talent and 90 percent hard work.
   j. Drugs have taken an economic toll on American business.
   k. Democracy has attracted renewed interest in countries outside of the United States.

   For models of and advice on integrating sources in your essay, see Chapters 14 and 15.

8. **Writing with Sources.** Take some time to study the twenty-one panel comic that opens this chapter (page 176). What's going on in the illustration? How much of what's going on is conveyed by the written text, and how much by the visual text? How effective do you find the visual? Do some research online or in your library to learn about the role of imagination in childhood, and then write an essay about the importance of imagination and creativity in cognitive development.

   Before starting your research and drafting your essay, you will find it helpful to become familiar with Chapter 14, "Writing with Sources," and Chapter 15, "A Brief Guide to Researching and Documenting Essays."

9. **Writing in the Workplace.** Your boss at your internship asks you to evaluate one aspect of the company's operation (customer service, advertising/promotion, internal communications, employee morale, community service, etc.). After selecting an aspect of the company you wish to evaluate and talking with customers and/or other employees, write a memo to your boss in which you use examples to document your findings.

 e-Pages

Did You Know?

XPLANE

See how illustration works on the Web. Go to bedfordstmartins.com/subjectand strategy for a video and study questions exploring how media, information, and technology converge in the modern world.

HOW PASTRIES BECOME PLASTIC

Food waste
Muffins, pastries, cakes and breads collected from bakeries

+

Fungus
Added to the starchy food to break down chemical bonds

Bacteria
Added to the sugars to produce other chemicals

+

Sugars and a nitrogen compound
Released after fungus enzymes digest the food waste

Succinic acid
One of a few versatile ingredients created by the bacteria

=

Bioplastics
Formed using succinic acid (among other chemicals) and used to make eco-friendly laundry-detergent bottles, car parts and more

CHAPTER 7

Process Analysis

WHAT IS PROCESS ANALYSIS?

THE STRATEGY OF PROCESS ANALYSIS INVOLVES SEPARATING AN EVENT, an operation, or a cycle of development into distinct steps, describing each step precisely, and arranging the steps in their proper order.

Whenever you explain how something occurs or how it can (and should) be done—how plants create oxygen, how to make ice cream, or merely how to get to your house—you are using process analysis. Recipes are a form of process analysis; so are the instruction and assembly manuals for the many technological devices we use around the house; and so are posters telling us what to do in case of fire, choking, or other emergency. The graphically illustrated explanation on the opposite page is a little different, however. Showing the process whereby stale and unused baked goods collected from bakeries are turned into plastics, it's not a directional process analysis, but an informational one. Rather than a recipe for how specifically to make it happen, the presentation explains how the process is carried out.

PROCESS ANALYSIS IN WRITTEN TEXTS

Each year, thousands of books and magazine articles tell us how to make home repairs, how to lose weight and get physically fit, how to improve our memories, how to play better tennis, how to manage our money. They try to satisfy our curiosity about how television shows are made, how jet airplanes work, and how monkeys, bees, or whales mate. People simply want to know how things work and how to do things for themselves, so it's not surprising that process analysis is one of the most widespread and popular forms of writing today.

Here is a process analysis written by Bernard Gladstone to explain how to light a fire in a fireplace.

First sentence establishes purpose: how to build a fire in a fireplace	Though "experts" differ as to the best technique to follow when building a fire, one generally accepted method consists of first laying a generous amount of crumpled newspaper on the hearth

<table>
<tr><td>First paragraph takes us through six steps: the result is a wood-and-paper structure</td><td>between the andirons. Kindling wood is then spread generously over this layer of newspaper and one of the thickest logs is placed across the back of the andirons. This should be as close to the back of the fireplace as possible, but not quite touching it. A second log is then placed an inch or so in front of this, and a few additional sticks of kindling are laid across these two. A third log is then placed on top to form a sort of pyramid with air space between all logs so that flames can lick freely up between them.</td></tr>
</table>

First paragraph takes us through six steps: the result is a wood-and-paper structure

between the andirons. Kindling wood is then spread generously over this layer of newspaper and one of the thickest logs is placed across the back of the andirons. This should be as close to the back of the fireplace as possible, but not quite touching it. A second log is then placed an inch or so in front of this, and a few additional sticks of kindling are laid across these two. A third log is then placed on top to form a sort of pyramid with air space between all logs so that flames can lick freely up between them.

Next three paragraphs present three common mistakes

A mistake frequently made is in building the fire too far forward so that the rear wall of the fireplace does not get properly heated. A heated back wall helps increase the draft and tends to suck smoke and flames rearward with less chance of sparks or smoke spurting out into the room.

Another common mistake often made by the inexperienced fire-tender is to try to build a fire with only one or two logs, instead of using at least three. A single log is difficult to ignite properly, and even two logs do not provide an efficient bed with adequate fuel burning capacity.

Use of too many logs, on the other hand, is also a common fault and can prove hazardous. Building too big a fire can create more smoke and draft than the chimney can safely handle, increasing the possibility of sparks or smoke being thrown out into the room. For best results, the homeowner should start with three medium-sized logs as described above, then add additional logs as needed if the fire is to be kept burning.

Conclusion reinforces his directions for building a fire

USING PROCESS ANALYSIS AS A WRITING STRATEGY

Process analysis resembles narration because both strategies present a series of events occurring over time. But a narration is the story of how things happened in a particular way, during one particular period of time; process analysis relates how things always happen — or always should happen — in essentially the same way time after time.

There are essentially two major reasons for writing a process analysis: to give directions, known as *directional process analysis*, and to inform, known as *informational process analysis*. Writers often combine one of these reasons with other rhetorical strategies to evaluate the process in question; this is known as *evaluative process analysis*. Let's take a look at each of these forms more closely.

▶ Directional Process Analysis

Writers use directional process analysis to provide readers with the necessary steps to achieve a desired result. The directions may be as simple as the instructions on a frozen-food package ("Heat in microwave on high for six to eight minutes. Rotate one-quarter turn halfway through cooking time, stir, and serve") or as complex as the operator's manual for a personal computer. Mortimer Adler proposes a method for getting the most out of reading in his essay "How to Mark a Book." First he compares what he sees as the "two ways in which one can own a book" and classifies book lovers into three categories. Then he presents his directions for how one should make marginal comments to get the most out of a book. In a brief selection on pages 229–30, Bernard Gladstone explains step-by-step how to build a fire in a fireplace. No matter their length or complexity, however, all directions have the same purpose: to guide the reader through a clear and logically ordered series of steps toward a particular goal.

▶ Informational Process Analysis

This strategy deals not with processes that readers are able to perform for themselves, but with processes that readers are curious about or would like to understand better: how presidents are elected, how plants reproduce, how an elevator works, how the brain processes and generates language. In the following selection from his *Lives Around Us*, Alan Devoe explains what happens to an animal when it goes into hibernation.

> When the temperature of the September days falls below 50 degrees or so, the woodchuck becomes too drowsy to come forth from his burrow in the chilly dusk to forage. He remains in the deep nest-chamber, lethargic, hardly moving. Gradually, with the passing of hours or days, his coarse-furred body curls into a semicircle, like a fetus, nose-tip touching tail. The small legs are tucked in, the hand-like clawed forefeet folded. The woodchuck has become a compact ball. Presently the temperature of his body begins to fall.
>
> In normal life the woodchuck's temperature, though fluctuant, averages about 97 degrees. Now, as he lies tight-curled in a ball with the winter sleep stealing over him, this body heat drops ten degrees, twenty degrees, thirty. Finally, by the time the snow is on the ground and the woodchuck's winter dormancy has become complete, his temperature is only 38 or 40. With the falling of the body heat there is a slowing of his heartbeat and his respiration. In normal life he breathes thirty or forty times each minute; when he is excited, as many as a hundred times. Now he breathes slower and slower: ten times a minute, five times a minute, once a minute, and at last only ten or twelve times in an hour. His heartbeat is a twentieth of normal. He has entered fully into the oblivion of hibernation.

The process Devoe describes is natural to woodchucks but not to humans, so obviously he cannot be giving instructions. Rather, he has created an informational process analysis to help us understand what happens during the remarkable process of hibernation. Using transitional expressions and time markers, Devoe shows us that the process lasts for weeks, even months. He connects the progress of hibernation with changes in the weather because the woodchuck's body responds to the dropping temperature as autumn sets in rather than to the passage of specific periods of time.

❱ Evaluative Process Analysis

People often want to understand processes in order to evaluate and improve them by making them simpler, quicker, safer, or more efficient. They may also wish to analyze processes to understand them more deeply or accurately. In explaining how to build a fire in a fireplace, Bernard Gladstone presents three common mistakes to avoid when trying to make a fire.

USING PROCESS ANALYSIS ACROSS THE DISCIPLINES

When writing essays in the academic disciplines, you will have many opportunities to use the strategy of process analysis to both organize and strengthen the presentation of your ideas. To determine whether or not process analysis is the right strategy for you in a particular paper, review the guidelines described in Chapter 2 (Determining a Strategy for Developing Your Essay, pages 32–33). Consider the following examples:

Psychology

1. **MAIN IDEA:** Most people go through a predictable grief process when a friend or loved one dies.
2. **QUESTION:** What are the steps in the grieving process?
3. **STRATEGY:** Process Analysis. The word *steps* signals the need to list the stages of the grieving process.
4. **SUPPORTING STRATEGY:** Description. Each step might be described and be accompanied by descriptions of the subject's behavior throughout the process.

Biology

1. **MAIN IDEA:** Human blood samples can be tested to determine their blood groups.
2. **QUESTION:** What steps are followed in typing human blood?
3. **STRATEGY:** Process Analysis. The word *steps* suggests a sequence of activities that is to be followed in testing blood.
4. **SUPPORTING STRATEGY:** Comparison and Contrast; Classification. Comparison and contrast might be used to differentiate blood characteristics and chemistry. Classification might be used to place samples in various categories.

Folklore

1. **MAIN IDEA:** Folklorists use several main methods for gathering their data.

2. **QUESTION:** How do folklorists go about collecting data?

3. **STRATEGY:** Process Analysis. The words *how do* and *go about* suggest process analysis.

4. **SUPPORTING STRATEGY:** llustration and Argumentation. Illustration can give examples of particular data and how it is collected. Argumentation might support one method over others.

SAMPLE STUDENT ESSAY USING PROCESS ANALYSIS AS A WRITING STRATEGY

Shoshanna Lew was born in Pinetop, Arizona, and was a double major in English and music at the University of Vermont. After graduation, she continued her studies in musicology at graduate school. In this informative essay, Lew explains the process for selecting people to serve on juries in New York City. Notice, as you read, how she manages to explain clearly the steps in the process, as well as accommodate two audiences, those who would welcome jury duty and those who would rather be doing just about anything else.

Title introduces mixed feelings about prospect of jury duty

How (Not) to Be Selected for Jury Duty
Shoshanna Lew

Opening sentence is effective with just one word

"SUMMONS." The red-lettered envelope slipped out from behind the junk mail and magazines. At first, I thought it must be for one of my parents, but, when I looked closer, I realized that it was *my* name on the jury duty notice. I didn't even know eighteen-year-old college students were *eligible* for jury duty, but a quick Google search told me otherwise. Great, for my summer vacation, I'd be trapped inside a jury box listening to dull testimony, or worse, examining grotesque photos of bullet wounds à la a CSI episode. On the upside, the $44 a day for serving was more than what I was making at my summer internship.

1

Thesis: jury selection is a multistep process

Jury selection in New York City is a multistep process. It starts bright and early with a video extolling the virtues of the justice system in which each potential juror is participating

2

by simply showing up on the appointed day and time. After the video finishes, the bailiff in charge of the jury pool collects everyone's cards and fields the requests of people to postpone or be exempt from their civic duty. Doctors' letters appear out of handbags and suited businesspeople wave their Blackberries to show that they are far too busy to be on a jury. As the bailiff— who determines the fate of each potential juror—dismisses people, the crowd thins down to those who will be eligible to be called to juries in the next three days. Since it is summer, my full-time student status doesn't let me off the hook. Once this process is complete, the remaining people begin doing what they will do for most of their time: They wait.

Explains exemption process

From the jury room, the courthouse looks nothing like the ones on television. Presumably—according to our introductory video—somewhere in the building lawyers are making arguments before judges, settling cases out of court, or succeeding in getting charges dropped. But in the jury room, folks read, watch television (CNN only), or nap. Suddenly, an announcement comes over the intercom. A case has been called; jury members will be empaneled—meaning a select group from the jury pool will be questioned, and some selected to sit on the jury—in fifteen minutes.

3

Once the bailiff is informed that a jury is being called, he brings out a bin containing cards, one for each potential juror. Just like the bins used in raffles at county fairs, the bailiff turns the crank several times and begins to pull out names. The bailiff assigns each person a number, and the lucky raffle winners are escorted into the jury room where they sit in the order they were called and fill out questionnaires. Beyond the basics of name and address, jurists provide level of education, place of birth, and employment information, and disclose whether or not they have relatives working in medical, legal, or insurance professions. (Bring a family tree with you on jury duty day. You'll be asked to explain jobs of any relation!)

Bailiff presents jurors' cards

4

Unlike John Grisham's legal thrillers, in which a dramatic jury questioning occurs in a courtroom with a judge and court reporter (and some rhetorical fireworks), a real jury selection may or may not happen in front of a judge. After the lawyers acquaint themselves with the potential jurists' questionnaires, they ask all the jurors if they have any philosophical objections to the American legal system and the role of a jury

Organization: paragraph addresses general questions asked of all jurors

5

Unity: paragraph
stays on topic of
questions asked
of all jurors

in it. These questions focus on beliefs about the justice system, but are phrased to weed out only those people with the
strongest opinions *against* the American justice system. (This
is a good time to find your inner anarchist.) The lawyers also
want to make sure that no panelist has any connection to a
party to the case—be it the plaintiff, the defendant, the lawyers in the case, or others affiliated with the attorneys' firms.

Organization:
plaintiff's
lawyer's
questions

Once these preliminaries have been dealt with, the actual   6
questioning begins. First, the lawyer for the plaintiff—the person with the legal complaint—presents the basis for the lawsuit. Then, the plaintiff's lawyer questions the jurors. He asks
questions of the entire group, and he also addresses jurors
about specific information on their questionnaires. Much of
the questioning is meant to illuminate potential biases that
jury members might harbor. For instance, doctors can expect
to face intense scrutiny if they are being considered for a mal-
practice case. Jurors will also be questioned about their ability
to put aside connections they have to the participants in the
case— such as a shared profession or common alma mater—
and be objective in weighing evidence.

Organization:
defense
attorney's
questions

When the plaintiff's lawyer has finished posing questions,   7
the defense attorney—who represents the person being sued—
takes her turn. Again, the potential jurors hear a short summary of the case but from the defense's perspective. Once
more, the lawyer asks specific jurors about their backgrounds
and directs inquiries to the entire group. During this part of
the process people begin to be dismissed from the case. At this
point, you'll probably wish for some courtroom drama to break
up the monotony of the day, but you're not likely to see a war
of words. Despite the numerous jokes intimating otherwise,
lawyers tend to remain polite, if not cordial, during jury selection. If you are lucky enough to be one of the later jurors to be
questioned, you'll have plenty of time to figure out what answers will give you the best chance of being dismissed from
or accepted to—if that's your goal—the jury.

Organization:
final jury
selection is
made

Finally, the lawyers pick their jury. Even though they dismiss   8
some people based on their answers to questions as the inquiries are made, they make their final "picks" only after the defense
finishes its part. After conferring privately, the lawyers provide a
bailiff with their list of jurors and the bailiff announces the final
outcome to the panel. In the reverse of a playground kickball

game, the bailiff first names the people who will not be on the jury. Those who are left at the end make up Team Jury.

Conclusion: why attorneys may have chosen as they did

It's difficult to know why the lawyers choose the people they do. My guess is that they look for people who seem the least likely to let their emotions play a part in weighing evidence and for those with the stamina to spend more than a week listening to dense testimony. Jury selection doesn't have the theatricality of *Law and Order*, but it is clear that the lawyers are invested in assembling the fairest jury possible—not simply the one most likely to rule in their favor—out of the candidates pulled from that raffle bin.

9

Analyzing Shoshanna Lew's Process Analysis Essay: Questions for Discussion

1. Lew shifts from the past tense (paragraph 1) to the present tense (2–9) in her essay. Why is it important for her to put the actual jury selection process in the present tense?

2. Try explaining Lew's analysis of the jury selection process to a friend. Is it more or less complex than you first thought? Did you leave any parts of the process out? Did you get the activities out of order? Explain.

3. Lew's title indicates that some people may want to serve on a jury while others may not. Serving on a jury is an important civic responsibility, so why do you think there are mixed feelings about it? How do you feel about the prospect of serving on a jury?

SUGGESTIONS FOR USING PROCESS ANALYSIS AS A WRITING STRATEGY

As you plan and revise your process analysis essay, be mindful of the writing guidelines described in Chapter 2. Pay particular attention to the basic requirements and essential ingredients of this strategy.

▌ Planning Your Process Analysis Essay

KNOW THE PROCESS YOU ARE WRITING ABOUT. Be sure that you have more than a vague or general grasp of the process you are writing about: Make sure you can analyze it fully, from beginning to end. You can sometimes convince yourself that you understand an entire process when, in fact, your understanding is somewhat superficial. If you do outside research, it's a good idea to read explanations by several authorities on the subject. If you were analyzing the process by which children learn language, for example, you wouldn't want to rely on only one expert's account. Turning to more than one account not only reinforces your understanding of key points in the process, but it also points out various ways the process is performed; you may want to consider these alternatives in your writing.

HAVE A CLEAR PURPOSE. Giving directions for administering cardio-pulmonary resuscitation and explaining how the El Niño phenomenon unfolds are worthy purposes for writing a process analysis paper. Many process analysis papers go beyond these fundamental purposes, however. They lay out processes to evaluate them, to suggest alternative steps, to point out shortcomings in generally accepted practices, and to suggest improvements. In short, process analysis papers are frequently persuasive or argumentative. Be sure to decide what you want your writing to do before you begin.

▶ Organizing and Writing Your Process Analysis Essay

ORGANIZE THE PROCESS INTO STEPS. As much as possible, make each step a simple and well-defined action, preferably a single action. To guide yourself in doing so, write a scratch outline listing the steps. Here, for example, is an outline of Bernard Gladstone's directions for building a fire.

Process Analysis of Building a Fire in a Fireplace

1. Put down crumpled newspaper.
2. Lay kindling.
3. Place back log near rear wall but not touching.
4. Place next log an inch forward from the first one.
5. Bridge logs with kindling.
6. Place third log on top of kindling bridge.

Next, check your outline to make sure that the steps are in the right order and that none has been omitted. Then analyze your outline more carefully. Are any steps so complex that they need to be described in some detail—or perhaps divided into more steps? Will you need to explain the purpose of a certain step because the reason for it is not obvious? Especially in an informational process analysis, two steps may take place at the same time; perhaps they are performed by different people or different parts of the body. Does your outline make this clear? (One solution is to assign both steps the same number but divide them into substeps by labeling one of them "A" and the other "B.") When you feel certain that the steps of the process are complete and correct, ask yourself two more questions. Will the reader need any other information to understand the process—definitions of unusual terms, for example, or descriptions of special equipment? Should you anticipate common mistakes or misunderstandings and discuss them, as Gladstone does? If so, be sure to add an appropriate note or two to your scratch outline as a reminder.

USE TRANSITIONS TO LINK THE STEPS. Transitional words and phrases like *then*, *next*, *after doing this*, and *during the summer months* can both emphasize and clarify the sequence of steps in your process analysis. The same is true of sequence markers like *first*, *second*, *third*, and so on. Devoe uses such words to make clear which stages in the hibernation process are simultaneous and which are not; Gladstone includes an occasional *first* or *then* to alert us to shifts from one step to the next.

▶ Revising and Editing Your Process Analysis Essay

ENERGIZE YOUR WRITING: USE THE ACTIVE VOICE AND STRONG ACTION VERBS. Writers prefer the active voice because it stresses the doer of an action, is lively and emphatic, and uses strong descriptive verbs. The passive voice, on the other hand, stresses what was done rather than who did it and uses forms of the weak verb *to be*.

> active   The coaches analyzed the game film, and the fullback decided to rededicate herself to playing defense.

> passive   A game film analysis was performed by the coaches, and a rededication to playing defense was decided on by the fullback.

Sometimes, however, the doer of an action is unknown or less important than the recipient of an action. In this case, it is acceptable to use the passive voice.

> The Earth's moon was formed more than 4 billion years ago.

When you revise your drafts, scan your sentences for passive constructions and weak verbs. Put your sentences into the active voice and find strong action verbs to replace weak verbs. Instead of the weak verb *run*, use *fly*, *gallop*, *hustle*, *jog*, *race*, *rush*, *scamper*, *scoot*, *scramble*, *tear*, or *trot*, for example. Instead of the weak verb *say*, use *declare*, *express*, *muse*, *mutter*, *pronounce*, *report*, *respond*, *recite*, *reply*, *snarl*, or *utter*, for example. Forms of the verb *to be* (*is*, *are*, *was*, *were*, *will be*, *should be*) are weak and non-descriptive and, therefore, should be avoided whenever possible. Here are some other common weak verbs you should replace with strong action verbs in your writing:

have, had, has	do	determine
make	use	become
concern	get	go
reflect	involve	appear
provide		

USE CONSISTENT VERB TENSE. A verb's tense indicates when an action is taking place: some time in the past, right now, or in the future. Using verb tense consistently helps your readers understand time changes in your writing. Inconsistent verb tenses—or *shifts*—within a sentence confuse readers and are especially noticeable in narration and process analysis writing, which are sequence—and time—oriented. Generally, you should write in the past or present tense and maintain that tense throughout your sentence.

> inconsistent   I mixed the eggs and sugar and then add the flour.

Mixed is past tense; *add* is present tense.

> corrected   I mix the eggs and sugar and then add the flour.

The sentence is now consistently in the present tense. The sentence can also be revised to be consistently in the past tense.

> corrected   I mixed the eggs and sugar and then added the flour.

Here's another example:

> inconsistent   The painter studied the scene and pulls a fan brush decisively from her cup.

Studied is past tense, indicating an action that has already taken place; *pulls* is present tense, indicating an action taking place now.

> corrected   The painter studies the scene and pulls a fan brush decisively from her cup.

> corrected   The painter studied the scene and pulled a fan brush decisively from her cup.

SHARE YOUR DRAFTS WITH OTHERS. Try sharing the drafts of your essays with other students in your writing class to make sure that your process analysis works. Ask them if there are any steps in the process that they do not understand. Have them tell you what they think is the point of your essay. If their answers differ from what you intended, have them indicate the passages that led them to their interpretations so that you can change your text accordingly. To maximize the effectiveness of conferences with your peers, utilize the guidelines presented on page 36. Feedback from these conferences often provides places where you can start revising.

QUESTION YOUR OWN WORK WHILE REVISING AND EDITING. Revision is best done by asking yourself key questions about what you have written. Begin by reading, preferably aloud, what you have written. Reading aloud forces you to pay attention to every single word, and you are more likely to catch lapses in the logical flow of thought. After you have read your paper through, answer the following questions for revising and editing and make the necessary changes.

Questions for Revising and Editing: Process Analysis

1. Do I have a thorough knowledge of the process I chose to write about?

2. Have I clearly informed readers about how to perform the process (directional process analysis), or have I explained how a process occurs (informational process analysis)? Does my choice reflect the overall purpose of my process analysis paper?

3. Have I divided the process into clear, readily understandable steps?

4. Did I pay particular attention to transitional words to take readers from one step to the next?

5. Are all my sentences in the active voice? Have I used strong action verbs?

6. Is my tense consistent?

7. Have I succeeded in tailoring my diction to my audience's familiarity with the subject?

8. Are my pronoun antecedents clear?

9. How did readers of my draft respond to my essay? Did they find any confusing passages or any missing steps?

10. Have I avoided errors in grammar, punctuation, and mechanics? Is my sentence style as clear, smooth, and persuasive as possible?

How to Mark a Book

MORTIMER ADLER

Writer, editor, and educator Mortimer Adler (1902–2001) was born in New York City. A high school dropout, Adler completed the undergraduate program at Columbia University in three years, but he did not graduate because he refused to take the mandatory swimming test. Adler is recognized for his editorial work on the *Encyclopaedia Britannica* and for his leadership of the Great Books Program at the University of Chicago, where adults from all walks of life gathered twice a month to read and discuss the classics.

In the following essay, which first appeared in the *Saturday Review of Literature* in 1940, Adler offers a timeless lesson: He explains how to take full ownership of a book by marking it up, by making it "a part of yourself."

Preparing to Read

When you read a book that you must understand thoroughly and remember for a class or for your own purposes, what techniques do you use to help you understand what you are reading? What helps you remember important parts of the book and improve your understanding of what the author is saying?

Y ou know you have to read "between the lines" to get the most out of anything. I want to persuade you to do something equally important in the course of your reading. I want to persuade you to "write between the lines." Unless you do, you are not likely to do the most efficient kind of reading.

I contend, quite bluntly, that marking up a book is not an act of mutilation but of love.

You shouldn't mark up a book which isn't yours. Librarians (or your friends) who lend you books expect you to keep them clean, and you should. If you decide that I am right about the usefulness of marking books, you will have to buy them. Most of the world's great books are available today in reprint editions.

There are two ways in which one can own a book. The first is the property right you establish by paying for it, just as you pay for clothes and furniture. But this act of purchase is only the prelude to possession. Full ownership comes only when you have made it a part of yourself, and the best way to make yourself a part of it is by writing in it. An illustration may make the point clear. You buy a beefsteak and transfer it from the butcher's icebox to your own. But you do not own the beefsteak in the most important sense until you consume it and get it into your bloodstream. I am arguing that books, too, must be absorbed in your bloodstream to do you any good.

Confusion about what it means to *own* a book leads people to a false reverence for paper, binding, and type—a respect for the physical thing—the craft of the printer rather than the genius of the author. They forget that it is possible for a man to acquire the idea, to possess the beauty, which a great book contains, without staking his claim by pasting his bookplate inside the cover. Having a fine library doesn't prove that its owner has a mind enriched by books; it proves nothing more than that he, his father, or his wife, was rich enough to buy them.

> Marking up a book is not an act of mutilation but of love.

There are three kinds of book owners. The first has all the standard sets and best-sellers—unread, untouched. (This deluded individual owns woodpulp and ink, not books.) The second has a great many books—a few of them read through, most of them dipped into, but all of them as clean and shiny as the day they were bought. (This person would probably like to make books his own, but is restrained by a false respect for their physical appearance.) The third has a few books or many—every one of them dog-eared and dilapidated, shaken and loosened by continual use, marked and scribbled in from front to back. (This man owns books.)

Is it false respect, you may ask, to preserve intact and unblemished a beautifully printed book, an elegantly bound edition? Of course not. I'd no more scribble all over a first edition of *Paradise Lost* than I'd give my baby a set of crayons and an original Rembrandt! I wouldn't mark up a painting or a statue. Its soul, so to speak, is inseparable from its body. And the beauty of a rare edition or of a richly manufactured volume is like that of a painting or a statue.

But the soul of a book *can* be separated from its body. A book is more like the score of a piece of music than it is like a painting. No great musician confuses a symphony with the printed sheets of music. Arturo Toscanini reveres Brahms, but Toscanini's score of the C-minor Symphony is so thoroughly marked up that no one but the maestro himself can read it. The reason why a great conductor makes notations on his musical scores—marks them up again and again each time he returns to study them—is the reason why you should mark your books. If your respect for magnificent binding or typography gets in the way, buy yourself a cheap edition and pay your respects to the author.

Why is marking up a book indispensable to reading? First, it keeps you awake. (And I don't mean merely conscious; I mean wide awake.) In the second place, reading, if it is active, is thinking, and thinking tends to express itself in words, spoken or written. The marked book is usually the thought-through book. Finally, writing helps you remember the thoughts you had, or the thoughts the author expressed. Let me develop these three points.

If reading is to accomplish anything more than passing time, it must be active. You can't let your eyes glide across the lines of a book and come up with an understanding of what you have read. Now an ordinary piece of light fiction, like say, *Gone with the Wind*, doesn't require the most active kind of reading. The books you read for pleasure can be read in a state of relaxation, and nothing is lost. But a great book, rich in ideas and beauty, a book that raises and tries to answer great fundamental questions, demands the most active reading of which you are capable. You don't absorb the ideas of John Dewey[1] the way you absorb the crooning of Mr. Vallee.[2] You have to reach for them. That you cannot do while you're asleep.

If, when you've finished reading a book, the pages are filled with your notes, you know that you read actively. The most famous active reader of great books I know is President Hutchins, of the University of Chicago. He also has the hardest schedule of business activities of any man I know. He invariably reads with a pencil, and sometimes, when he picks up a book and pencil in the evening, he finds himself, instead of making intelligent notes, drawing what he calls "caviar factories" on the margins. When that happens, he puts the book down. He knows he's too tired to read, and he's just wasting time.

But, you may ask, why is writing necessary? Well, the physical act of writing, with your own hand, brings words and sentences more sharply before your mind and preserves them better in your memory. To set down your reaction to important words and sentences you have read, and the questions they have raised in your mind, is to preserve those reactions and sharpen those questions.

Even if you wrote on a scratch pad, and threw the paper away when you had finished writing, your grasp of the book would be surer. But you don't have to throw the paper away. The margins (top and bottom, as well as side), the end-papers, the very space between the lines, are all available. They aren't sacred. And, best of all, your marks and notes become an integral part of the book and stay there forever. You can pick up the book the following week or year, and there are all your points of agreement,

10

11

12

13

[1]John Dewey (1859–1952) was an educational philosopher who had a profound influence on learning through experimentation. — Eds.
[2]Rudy Vallee (1901–1986) was a popular singer of the 1920s and '30s, famous for his crooning high notes. — Eds.

disagreement, doubt, and inquiry. It's like resuming an interrupted conversation with the advantage of being able to pick up where you left off.

And that is exactly what reading a book should be: a conversation 14 between you and the author. Presumably he knows more about the subject than you do; naturally, you'll have the proper humility as you approach him. But don't let anybody tell you that a reader is supposed to be solely on the receiving end. Understanding is a two-way operation; learning doesn't consist in being an empty receptacle. The learner has to question himself and question the teacher. He even has to argue with the teacher, once he understands what the teacher is saying. And marking a book is literally an expression of your differences, or agreements of opinion, with the author.

There are all kinds of devices for marking a book intelligently and 15 fruitfully. Here's the way I do it:

1. *Underlining:* of major points, of important or forceful statements. 16

2. *Vertical lines at the margin:* to emphasize a statement already 17 underlined.

3. *Star, asterisk, or other doo-dad at the margin:* to be used sparingly, to 18 emphasize the ten or twenty most important statements in the book. (You may want to fold the bottom corner of each page on which you use such marks. It won't hurt the sturdy paper on which most modern books are printed, and you will be able to take the book off the shelf at any time and, by opening it at the folded-corner page, refresh your recollection of the book.)

4. *Numbers in the margin:* to indicate the sequence of points the author 19 makes in developing a single argument.

5. *Numbers of other pages in the margin:* to indicate where else in the 20 book the author made points relevant to the point marked; to tie up the ideas in a book, which, though they may be separated by many pages, belong together.

6. *Circling:* of key words or phrases. 21

7. *Writing in the margin, or at the top or bottom of the page, for the sake* 22 *of:* recording questions (and perhaps answers) which a passage raised in your mind; reducing a complicated discussion to a simple statement; recording the sequence of major points right through the book. I use the end-papers at the back of the book to make a personal index of the author's points in the order of their appearance.

The front end-papers are, to me, the most important. Some people 23 reserve them for a fancy bookplate. I reserve them for fancy thinking. After I have finished reading the book and making my personal index on the back end-papers, I turn to the front and try to outline the book, not page by page, or point by point (I've already done that at the back), but as an integrated structure, with a basic unity and an order of parts. This outline is, to me, the measure of my understanding of the work.

If you're a die-hard anti-book-marker, you may object that the margins, the space between the lines, and the end-papers don't give you room enough. All right. How about using a scratch pad slightly smaller than the page-size of the book—so that the edges of the sheets won't protrude? Make your index, outlines, and even your notes on the pad, and then insert these sheets permanently inside the front and back covers of the book. 24

Or, you may say that this business of marking books is going to slow up your reading. It probably will. That's one of the reasons for doing it. Most of us have been taken in by the notion that speed of reading is a measure of our intelligence. There is no such thing as the right speed for intelligent reading. Some things should be read quickly and effortlessly, and some should be read slowly and even laboriously. The sign of intelligence in reading is the ability to read different things differently according to their worth. In the case of good books, the point is not to see how many of them you can get through, but rather how many can get through you—how many you can make your own. A few friends are better than a thousand acquaintances. If this be your aim, as it should be, you will not be impatient if it takes more time and effort to read a great book than it does a newspaper. 25

You may have one final objection to marking books. You can't lend them to your friends because nobody else can read them without being distracted by your notes. Furthermore, you won't want to lend them because a marked copy is a kind of intellectual diary, and lending it is almost like giving your mind away. 26

If your friend wishes to read your *Plutarch's Lives, Shakespeare*, or *The Federalist Papers*, tell him gently but firmly to buy a copy. You will lend him your car or your coat—but your books are as much a part of you as your head or your heart. 27

Thinking Critically about the Text

After you have read Adler's essay, compare your answer to the Preparing to Read prompt with Adler's guidelines for reading. What are the most significant differences between Adler's guidelines and your own? How can you better make the books you read part of yourself?

Questions on Subject

1. What are the three kinds of book owners Adler identifies? What are their differences?

2. According to Adler, why is marking up a book indispensable to reading? Do you agree with his three arguments? (Glossary: *Argument*) Why, or why not?

3. What does Adler mean when he writes "the soul of a book *can* be separated from its body" (paragraph 8)? Is the separation a good thing? Explain.

4. Adler says that reading a book should be a conversation between the reader and the author. What characteristics does he say the conversation should have? How does marking a book help in carrying on and preserving the conversation?

5. What kinds of devices do you use for "marking a book intelligently and fruit- fully" (paragraph 15)? How useful do you find these devices?

Questions on Strategy

1. In the first paragraph, Adler writes, "I want to persuade you to do something equally important in the course of your reading. I want to persuade you to 'write between the lines.'" What assumptions does Adler make about his audience when he chooses to use the parallel structure of "I want to persuade you . . ."? (Glossary: *Audience; Parallelism*) Is stating his intention so blatantly an effective way of presenting his argument? (Glossary: *Argument*) Why, or why not?

2. Adler expresses himself very clearly throughout the essay, and his topic sen- tences are carefully crafted. (Glossary: *Topic Sentence*) Reread the topic sen- tences for paragraphs 3–6, and identify how each introduces the main idea for the paragraph and unifies it.

3. Throughout the essay, Adler provides the reader with a number of verbal cues ("There are two ways," "Let me develop these three points"). What do these verbal cues indicate about the organizational connections of the essay? (Glossary: *Organization*) Explain how Adler's organization creates an essay that logically follows from sentence to sentence and from paragraph to paragraph.

4. Summarize in your own words Adler's process analysis about how one should mark a book. Explain how Adler's process analysis is also an argument for the correct way to read. (Glossary: *Argument*)

5. Adler's process analysis is also a description of an event or a sequence of events (how to read). Does he claim that his recommended reading process will aid the reader's understanding, increase the reader's interest, or both?

Questions on Diction and Vocabulary

1. Adler makes an analogy that links reading books with the statement "A few friends are better than a thousand acquaintances" (paragraph 25). (Glossary: *Analogy*) Explain how this analogy works. Why is this analogy important to Adler's overall argument?

2. Throughout the essay, Adler uses the personal pronoun *I* to describe his read- ing experience. (Glossary: *Point of View*) How does this personalized voice help or hinder the explanation of the process of reading?

3. What does Adler mean by the phrase "active reading"?

Classroom Activity Using Process Analysis

This exercise requires that you work in pairs. Draw a simple geometric design, such as the one below, without letting your partner see your drawing.

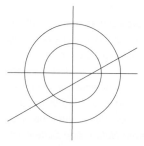

With the finished design in front of you, write a set of directions that will allow your partner to reproduce it accurately. Before writing your directions, ask yourself how you will convey the context for your instructions, where you will begin, and how what you write may help your partner or lead your partner astray. As your partner attempts to draw the design from your instructions, do not offer any verbal advice. Let your directions speak for themselves. Once you have finished, compare your drawing to the one your partner has produced. Discuss the results with your partner and, if time allows, with the entire class.

Writing Suggestions

1. Write a directional process analysis in which you present your techniques for getting the most enjoyment out of a common activity. For example, perhaps you have a set routine you follow for spending an evening watching television — preparing popcorn, checking what's on, clearing off the coffee table, finding the remote control, settling into your favorite chair, and so on. Choose from the following topics:

   a. how to listen to music
   b. how to eat an ice-cream cone
   c. how to reduce stress
   d. how to wash a dog
   e. how to play a sport or game

2. Adler devotes a large portion of his essay to persuading his audience that marking books is a worthwhile task. (Glossary: *Persuasion*) Write an essay in which you instruct your audience about how to do something they do not necessarily wish to do or they do not think they need to do. For instance, before explaining how to buy the best MP3 player, you may need to convince readers that they *should* buy an MP3 player. Write your directional process analysis after making a convincing argument for the validity of the process you wish to present. (Glossary: *Argument*)

Young Love

TIFFANY O'CALLAGHAN

Tiffany O'Callaghan (née Sharples) was born in 1981 in New Haven, Connecticut. She earned a bachelor of arts in English and Writing from Colgate University and a master of science in journalism from the Medill School of Journalism at Northwestern University. She is currently an editor at *New Scientist* magazine in London and was previously a writer for *Time* magazine. Her work has also been featured in *Nature* and *Slate.com*. She specializes in health, medical, and social science reporting. When asked if she had any advice for young writers, she offered, "Don't expect to get everything right the first time. That's what revision is for."

In the following article, which first appeared in the January 28, 2008, issue of *Time* magazine, O'Callaghan writes, "Most Western romance research involves Western cultures, where things may move at a very different pace from that of, say, the Far East or the Muslim world. While not all of the studies yield universal truths, they all suggest that people are wired to pick up their love skills in very specific stages."

Preparing to Read

Do you remember the first time you fell in love? What was it like? Were you frightened? Intrigued? Exhilarated? Bewildered?

There's a very thin line between being thrilled and being terrified, and Candice Feiring saw both emotions on her son's face. The sixth grader had just gotten off the phone with a girl in his class who called to ask if he'd like to go to the movies—just the two of them. It sounded a whole lot like a date to him. "Don't I have something to do tomorrow?" he asked his mother. A psychologist and an editor of *The Development of Romantic Relationships in Adolescence*, Feiring was uniquely prepared to field that question and give her son the answer that, for now, he needed. "I think you're too young to go out one-on-one," she said. His face broke into a relieved grin.

A year later, even a month later, Feiring's adolescent son might have reacted very differently to being told he was not ready to date. That moment-to-moment mutability of his interest in—never mind his readiness for—courtship is only one tiny part of the exhilarating, exhausting, confounding path all humans travel as they make their halting way into the world of love. From the moment we're born—when the world is mostly sensation, and nothing much matters beyond a full belly, a warm embrace, and a clean diaper—until we finally emerge into adulthood and understand the rich mix of tactile, sexual, and emotional experiences that come with loving another adult, we are in a constant state of learning and rehearsing. Along with language, romance may be one of the hardest skills we'll ever be called on to acquire. But while we're more or less fluent in speech by the time we're five, romance takes a lot longer. Most Western romance research involves Western cultures, where things may move at a very different pace from that of, say, the Far East or the Muslim world. While not all of the studies yield universal truths, they all suggest that people are wired to pick up their love skills in very specific stages.

> Along with language, romance may be one of the hardest skills we'll ever be called on to acquire.

INFANCY AND BABYHOOD

Babies may not have much to do right after they're born, but the stakes are vitally high that they do it right. One of the first skills newborns must learn is how to woo the adults in their world. "For a baby literally you're going to be dead without love, so getting people around you to love you is a really good strategy," says Alison Gopnik, a cognitive psychologist at the University of California, Berkeley. 3

Babies do this much the way adults do: by flirting. Within a couple of months, infants may move and coo, bob, and blink in concert with anyone who's paying attention to them. Smiling is a critical and cleverly timed part of this phase. Babies usually manage a first smile by the time they're six weeks old, which, coincidentally or not, is about the time the novelty of a newborn has worn off and sleep-deprived parents are craving some peace. A smile can be a powerful way to win them back. 4

Even before we know how to turn on the charm, touch and chemistry are bonding us firmly to our parents—and bonding them to us. Oxytocin—a hormone sometimes called the cuddle chemical—surges in new mothers and, to a lesser extent, in new fathers, making their baby instantly irresistible to them. One thing grown-ups particularly can't resist doing is picking a baby up, and that, too, is a key to survival. "Babies need physical contact with human hands to grow and thrive," says Lisa Diamond, a psychologist at the University of Utah. Years of data have shown that premature babies who are regularly touched fare much better than those who aren't. 5

As babies seduce and adults respond, a sophisticated dynamic develops. Mothers learn to synch their behavior with their newborn's, so that 6 they offer a smile when their baby smiles, food when their baby's hungry. That's a pleasingly reciprocal deal, and while adults are already aware that when you give pleasure and comfort, you get it in return, it's news for the baby. "Babies are building up ideas about how close relationships work," says Gopnik.

TODDLERHOOD AND PRESCHOOL

When kids reach two, mom and dad aren't paying quite the same attention they used to. You feed yourself, you play on your own, you get held less often. That's not to say you need your parents less—and you're not shy about letting them know it. Children from ages two to five have yet to develop what's known as a theory of mind—the understanding that other people have hidden thoughts that are different from yours and that you can conceal your thoughts, too. Without that knowledge, kids conceal nothing. "They love you," says Gopnik, "and they really, really express it."

At the same time, kids are learning something about sensual pleasures. They explore their bodies more, discovering that certain areas yield more electrifying feelings than others. This simultaneous emotional development and physical experience can lead to surprising behavior. "Three- and four-year-olds are very sexual beings," says Gopnik, "and a lot of that is directed at their parents." Some of this can get generalized to other adults, too, as when a small child develops a crush on a teacher or seems to flirt with an aunt or uncle. While a number of things are at work when this happens, the most important is playacting and the valuable rehearsal for later life it provides. "Kids are trying to play out a set of roles and be more like adults," says psychologist Andrew Collins of the University of Minnesota's Institute of Child Development.

The same kind of training behavior can show up with playmates and friends, often accompanied by unexpectedly powerful feelings. Social psychologist Elaine Hatfield of the University of Hawaii is best known for cocreating the Passionate Love Scale, a questionnaire with which she can gauge feelings of romantic connectedness in adults. She has modified the test to elicit similar information from children. In early work, she studied 114 boys and 122 girls, some as young as four, presenting them with statements like "I am always thinking about _____" or "I would rather be with _____ than anybody else." The kids filled in the name of someone they loved, and Hatfield asked them to rate the intensity of feelings with stacks of checkers: the higher the stack, the more they felt. In some instances, the kids became overwhelmed with emotion, as in the case of a five-year-old girl who wept at the thought of a boy she would never see again. "Little kids fall in love, too," Hatfield says plainly.

SCHOOL AGE AND PUBERTY

As with so much else in childhood, things get more complicated once kids 10
reach the social incubator of elementary school. Nowhere near sexually
mature, they nonetheless become sexually active—in their own fashion.
The opposite-sex teasing and chasing that are rife on playgrounds may give
teachers headaches, but they teach boys and girls a lot. The games, after all,
are about pursuit and emotional arousal, two critical elements of sex.
"There are a lot of erotic forms of play," says Barrie Thorne, a sociologist
at the University of California, Berkeley, and the author of *Gender Play:
Boys and Girls in School.* "It can be titillating, and it may involve sexual
meaning, but it comes and goes."

More enduring—for a while at least—is the gender segregation that 11
begins at this age. Boys and girls who once played in mixed groups at
school begin to drift apart into single-sex camps, drawing social boundaries that will stay in place for years. In her 1986 study that is still cited
today, Thorne looked at 802 elementary-school students from California
and Massachusetts to determine just what goes on behind these gender
fortifications and why they're established in the first place.

To no one's surprise, both groups spend a lot of time talking and think- 12
ing about the opposite sex, but they do it in very different ways. Boys
experiment more with sexually explicit vocabulary and, later, sexual fantasies. Girls focus more heavily—but hardly exclusively—on romantic fantasies. The two-gender world they'll eventually reenter will be a lot more
complex than that, but for now, the boys are simply practicing being
boys—albeit in a very rudimentary way—and the girls are practicing
being girls. "Among the boys, for example, there's a lot of bragging talk,"
says Thorne. "You're supposed to be powerful and not vulnerable."

When puberty hits, the wall between the worlds begins to crumble— 13
a bit. Surging hormones make the opposite sex irresistible, but the rap-
prochement happens collectively, with single-gender groups beginning to
merge into coed social circles within which individual boys and girls can
flirt and experiment. Generally, kids who pair off with a love interest and
begin dating will hold on to a return ticket to the mixed-gender group.
Jennifer Connolly, a psychologist at York University in Toronto, studied
174 high school students in grades nine to eleven and found that when
things go awry with couples, the kids are quickly absorbed back into the
coed circle, with the old single-sex group increasingly eclipsed. "Once the
progression has started," Connolly says, "we don't see kids retreating back
into only same-gender interaction."

Almost all of these early relationships are, not surprisingly, short- 14
lived—and a good thing, too. If the purpose is to pick a mate for life,

you're hardly likely to find a suitable one on your very first go. What's more, even if you did get lucky, you'd almost certainly not have the emotional wherewithal to keep the relationship going. Adults often lament the love they had and lost in high school and wonder what would have happened if they had met just a few years later. But the only way to acquire the skills to conduct a lifetime relationship is to practice on ones you may destroy in the process. "Kids don't really have a sense of working to preserve a relationship," Connolly says. "Adolescence is a time for experimentation."

Sexual experimentation is a big part of that—and it's a part that's especially fraught. Pregnancy and sexually transmitted diseases are just two of the things that make sex perilous. There are also emotional conflicts kids bring into their early experiences with intimacy. Psychologists have long warned that children who grow up in a hostile home or one in which warmth is withheld are likelier to start having sex earlier and engage in it more frequently. In a [2008] study . . . , Trish Williams, a neuropsychology fellow at Alberta Children's Hospital, studied a group of 1,959 kids ages eleven to thirteen and did find a striking correlation between a volatile home and earlier sexual behavior. A few of the children had had intercourse at as young an age as twelve, and while the number of sexually active kids wasn't high—just 2 percent of the total—the cause was clear. "Hostile parenting is highly associated with problem behavior," says Williams.

Even kids without such emotional scarring can be pretty undiscriminating in their sexual choices. Two studies conducted by sociologist Wendy Manning in 2005 and 2006 showed that while 75 percent of kids have their first sexual experience with a partner they're dating—a figure that may bring at least some comfort to worried parents—more than 60 percent will eventually have sex with someone with whom they're not in any kind of meaningful dating relationship. Hooking up—very informal sex between two people with no intent of pursuing a deeper relationship—takes this casualness even further. A 2004 study Manning worked on showed that the overwhelming majority of hookups involve alcohol use—an impairer of sexual judgment if ever there was one—and according to the work of other researchers, more than half the times kids hook up, they do not use a condom. Manning's studies suggest that hooking up prevents kids from practicing the interpersonal skills they'll need in a permanent relationship and may lead to lowered expectations of what those relationships should be like—and a greater willingness to settle for less.

For all these perils, the fact is, most people manage to shake off even such high-stakes behavior and find a satisfying life partner, and that says something about the resilience of humans as romantic creatures. In the United States, by the time we're eighteen, about 80 percent of us have had at least one meaningful romantic relationship. As adults, up to 75 percent of us marry. Certainly, nature doesn't make things easy. From babyhood on, it equips us with the tools we'll need for the hardest social role we'll ever play—the role of romantic—and then chooses the moment when we're drunk on the hormones of adolescence and least confident in ourselves to push us on stage to perform. That we go on at all is a mark of our courage. That we learn the part so well is a mark of how much is at stake.

Thinking Critically about the Text

Respond to O'Callaghan's statement in paragraph 2 that "romance may be one of the hardest skills we'll ever be called on to acquire." Explain why you agree or disagree.

Questions on Subject

1. What role does flirting play in all stages of human development? Why is it so important?

2. How do children rehearse for adult roles (paragraph 8)?

3. Why does O'Callaghan say that romantic relationships in puberty are "almost all . . . , not surprisingly, short-lived — and a good thing, too" (paragraph 14)?

4. Men and women who "hook up" often use alcohol and fail to use condoms, according to researchers. What does hooking up also prevent kids from doing, according to O'Callaghan (paragraph 16)?

5. What role does hostile parenting play in early sexual behavior, according to neuropsychologist Trish Williams (paragraph 15)?

Questions on Strategy

1. On what principle has O'Callaghan organized her explanation of the process whereby we learn to love? (Glossary: *Organization*)

2. How effective is the beginning of O'Callaghan's essay? Explain. (Glossary: *Beginnings/Endings*)

3. Comment on the author's use of research. Where and how has she used outside authorities to support her claims? (Glossary: *Evidence*) How have those outside sources enhanced her essay? Does she cite too many outside authorities? Explain.

4. Does the fact that many marriages end in divorce factor into the overall picture that O'Callaghan paints regarding romantic love? Do you think she has purposely left divorce statistics out of the essay? Would such a discussion be appropriate given her title? Explain.

5. Do you think anything is lost — perhaps the mystery of love itself — in O'Callaghan's objective analysis of the process we go through as we learn to love? Explain.

Questions on Diction and Vocabulary

1. O'Callaghan uses the metaphor of life as a stage in her final paragraph. Is the metaphor an effective one, in your opinion? (Glossary: *Figures of Speech*)

2. How would you characterize O'Callaghan's tone in this essay? Do you find it appropriate for her purpose and audience? Explain. (Glossary: *Audience; Tone*)

Classroom Activity Using Process Analysis

Perhaps one of the most universally memorable activities of childhood is making a paper airplane. Carefully read wikiHow's online instructions for making one at www.wikiHow.com/make-a-paper-airplane. Then construct your own airplane, using the wikiHow instructions, and fly it. How far, if at all, did it fly? How helpful did you find the illustrations that accompany the written instructions? Based on your results, what revisions to the instructions would you make? Why?

Writing Suggestions

1. Write an essay using directional process analysis for a "simple" task that could prove disastrous if not explained precisely — for example, changing a tire, putting out a kitchen fire, driving a manual-transmission car, packing for a camping trip, or testing for and eliminating lead or radon in your home. Be sure to explain why your directions are the best and what could happen if readers don't follow them exactly.

2. **Writing with Sources.** How are love skills learned in non-Western cultures? Choose a non-Western culture that interests you — for example, Japanese, Afghan, or Turkish — and do some research on it. Then write an essay modeled on O'Callaghan's that examines the process by which babies, children, and young adults learn their romantic roles in that society. For models of and advice on integrating sources in your essay, see Chapters 14 and 15.

Eating Industrial Meat

MICHAEL POLLAN

Writer, journalist, and educator Michael Pollan was born in 1955 and grew up on Long Island. In 1977 he graduated from Bennington College. He attended Mansfield College, Oxford University, and received a master's in English from Columbia University in 1981. As a writer, Pollan is fascinated by food, agriculture, gardening, drugs, and architecture — those places where the human and natural worlds intersect. Running throughout Pollan's work is the belief that eating is our most deeply significant interaction with the natural world. His award-winning nonfiction books include *Second Nature: A Gardener's Education* (1991), *A Place of My Own: The Education of an Amateur Builder* (1997), *The Botany of Desire: A Plant's Eye View of the World* (2001), *The Omnivore's Dilemma: A Natural History of Four Meals* (2006), *In Defense of Food: An Eater's Manifesto* (2008), and *Cooked: A Natural History of Transformation* (2013). Since 1987 Pollan has been a contributing writer to the *New York Times Magazine,* and his articles on various food-related topics have appeared in *Esquire, Harper's, Gourmet, Condé Nast Traveler, Mother Jones,* and *Vogue.* He has taught at the University of Pittsburgh and the University of Wisconsin and is currently the John S. and James L. Knight Professor of Journalism at the University of California, Berkeley, where he directs the Knight Program in Science and Environmental Journalism.

In the following selection, excerpted from *The Omnivore's Dilemma,* Pollan examines the process of bringing beef to market. His focus is one steer in particular, number 534, as it's being held in a feedlot in Kansas to gain weight before being slaughtered. As you read, pay special attention to the far-ranging connections and implications of what he's learned about the way we have industrialized cattle farming in this country.

Preparing to Read

Reflect on the origins of the food you eat. Do you know where it comes from? Do you have any sense of how it is farmed or manufactured? If you are a meat eater, do you ever think about what the creatures you eat have themselves eaten? If you know very little about the origins of the food you eat, does that lack of knowledge affect you?

M y first impression of pen 63, where my steer [534] is spending his last five months, was, *Not a bad little piece of real estate, all considered.* The pen is far enough from the feed mill to be fairly quiet and it has a water view of what I thought was a pond or reservoir until I noticed the brown scum. The body of water is what is known, in the geography of CAFOs,[1] as a manure lagoon. I asked the feedlot manager why they didn't just spray the liquefied manure on neighboring farms. The farmers don't want it, he explained. The nitrogen and phosphorus levels are so high that spraying the crops would kill them. He didn't say that feedlot wastes also contain heavy metals and hormone residues, persistent chemicals that end up in waterways downstream, where scientists have found fish and amphibians exhibiting abnormal sex characteristics. CAFOs like Poky transform what at the proper scale would be a precious source of fertility—cow manure—into toxic waste.

2 The pen 534 lives in is surprisingly spacious, about the size of a hockey rink, with a concrete feed bunk along the road, and a fresh water trough out back. I climbed over the railing and joined the ninety steers, which, en masse, retreated a few lumbering steps, and then stopped to see what I would do.

3 I had on the same carrot-colored sweater I'd worn to the ranch in South Dakota, hoping to elicit some glint of recognition from my steer. I couldn't find him at first; all the faces staring at me were either completely black or bore an unfamiliar pattern of white marks. And then I spotted him—the three white blazes—way off in the back. As I gingerly stepped toward him the quietly shuffling mass of black cowhide between us parted, and there stood 534 and I, staring dumbly at one another. Glint of recognition? None, none whatsoever. I told myself not to take it personally; 534 and his pen mates have been bred for their marbling, after all, not their ability to form attachments.

4 I noticed that 534's eyes looked a little bloodshot. Dr. Metzin had told me that some animals are irritated by feedlot dust. The problem is especially serious in the summer months, when the animals kick up clouds of the stuff and workers have to spray the pens with water to keep it down. I had to remind myself that this is not ordinary dirt dust, inasmuch as the dirt in a feedyard is not ordinary dirt; no, this is fecal dust. But apart from the air quality, how did feedlot life seem to be agreeing with 534? I don't know enough about the emotional life of a steer to say with confidence that 534 was miserable, bored, or indifferent, but I would not say he looked happy.

5 He's clearly eating well, though. My steer had put on a couple hundred pounds since we'd last met, and he looked it: thicker across the shoulder and round as a barrel through the middle. He carried himself more like a steer now than a calf, even though his first birthday was still two months away. Dr. Metzin complimented me on his size and conformation. "That's a handsome-looking beef you got there." (Shucks.)

6 If I stared at my steer hard enough, I could imagine the white lines of the butcher's chart dissecting his black hide: rump roast, flank steak, standing

[1]Concentrated Animal Feeding Operations—Eds.

rib, tenderloin, brisket. One way of looking at 534—the feedlot way, the industrial way—was as a most impressive machine for turning number 2 field corn into cuts of beef. Every day between now and his slaughter in six months, 534 will convert thirty-two pounds of feed into four pounds of gain—new muscle, fat, and bone. This at least is how 534 appears in the computer program I'd seen at the mill: the ratio of feed to gain that determines his efficiency. (Compared to other food animals, cattle are terribly inefficient: The ratio of feed to flesh in chicken, the most efficient animal by this measure, is two pounds of corn to one of meat, which is why chicken costs less than beef.) Poky Feeders is indeed a factory, transforming—as fast as bovinely possible—cheap raw materials into a less cheap finished product, through the mechanism of bovine metabolism.

> If I stared at my steer hard enough, I could imagine the white lines of the butcher's chart dissecting his black hide: rump roast, flank steak, standing rib, tenderloin, brisket.

Yet metaphors of the factory and the machine obscure as much as they reveal about the creature standing before me. He has, of course, another, quite different identity—as an animal, I mean, connected as all animals must be to certain other animals and plants and microbes, as well as to the earth and the sun. He's a link in a food chain, a thread in a far-reaching web of ecological relationships. Looked at from this perspective, everything going on in this cattle pen appears quite different, and not nearly as far removed from our world as this manure-encrusted patch of ground here in Nowhere, Kansas, might suggest. 7

For one thing, the health of these animals is inextricably linked to our own by that web of relationships. The unnaturally rich diet of corn that undermines a steer's health fattens his flesh in a way that undermines the health of the humans who will eat it. The antibiotics these animals consume with their corn at this very moment are selecting, in their gut and wherever else in the environment they end up, for new strains of resistant bacteria that will someday infect us and withstand the drugs we depend on to treat that infection. We inhabit the same microbial ecosystem as the animals we eat, and whatever happens in it also happens to us. 8

Then there's the deep pile of manure on which I stand, in which 534 sleeps. We don't know much about the hormones in it—where they will end up, or what they might do once they get there—but we do know something about the bacteria, which can find their way from the manure on the ground to his hide and from there into our hamburgers. The speed at which these animals will be slaughtered and processed—four hundred an hour at the plant where 534 will go—means that sooner or later some of 9 the manure caked on these hides gets into the meat we eat. One of the bacteria that almost certainly resides in the manure I'm standing in is particularly lethal to humans. *Escherichia coli* 0157:H7 is a relatively new strain of the common intestinal bacteria (no one had seen it before 1980) that thrives in feedlot cattle, 40 percent of which carry it in their gut. Ingesting as few as ten of these microbes can cause a fatal infection; they produce a toxin that destroys human kidneys.

Most of the microbes that reside in the gut of a cow and find their way   10
into our food get killed off by the strong acids in our stomachs, since they evolved to live in the neutral pH environment of the rumen. But the rumen of a corn-fed feedlot steer is nearly as acidic as our own stomachs, and in this new, man-made environment new acid-resistant strains of *E. coli*, of which 0157:H7 is one, have evolved—yet another creature recruited by nature to absorb the excess biomass coming off the Farm Belt. The problem with these bugs is that they can shake off the acid bath in our stomachs—and then go on to kill us. By acidifying the rumen with corn we've broken down one of our food chain's most important barriers to infection. Yet another solution turned into a problem.

We've recently discovered that this process of acidification can be   11
reversed, and that doing so can greatly diminish the threat from *E. coli* 0157:H7. Jim Russell, a USDA microbiologist on the faculty at Cornell, has found that switching a cow's diet from corn to grass or hay for a few days prior to slaughter reduces the population of *E. coli* 0157:H7 in the animal's gut by as much as 80 percent. But such a solution (*Grass?!*) is considered wildly impractical by the cattle industry and (therefore) by the USDA. Their preferred solution for dealing with bacterial contamination is irradiation—essentially, to try to sterilize the manure getting into the meat.

So much comes back to corn, this cheap feed that turns out in so many   12
ways to be not cheap at all. While I stood in pen 63 a dump truck pulled up alongside the feed bunk and released a golden stream of feed. The black mass of cowhide moved toward the trough for lunch. The $1.60 a day I'm paying for three meals a day here is a bargain only by the narrowest of calculations. It doesn't take into account, for example, the cost to the public health of antibiotic resistance or food poisoning by *E. coli* 0157:H7. It doesn't take into account the cost to taxpayers of the farm subsidies that keep Poky's raw materials cheap. And it certainly doesn't take into account all the many environmental costs incurred by cheap corn.

I stood alongside 534 as he lowered his big head into the stream of   13
fresh grain. How absurd, I thought, the two of us standing hock-deep in manure in this godforsaken place, overlooking a manure lagoon in the middle of nowhere somewhere in Kansas. Godforsaken perhaps, and yet not apart, I realized, as I thought of the other places connected to this

place by the river of commodity corn. Follow the corn from this bunk back to the fields where it grows and I'd find myself back in the middle of that 125,000-mile-square monoculture, under a steady rain of pesticide and fertilizer. Keep going, and I could follow the nitrogen runoff from that fertilizer all the way down the Mississippi into the Gulf of Mexico, adding its poison to an eight-thousand-square-mile zone so starved of oxygen nothing but algae can live in it. And then go farther still, follow the fertilizer (and the diesel fuel and the petrochemical pesticides) needed to grow the corn all the way to the oil fields of the Persian Gulf.

I don't have a sufficiently vivid imagination to look at my steer and see 14 a barrel of oil, but petroleum is one of the most important ingredients in the production of modern meat, and the Persian Gulf is surely a link in the food chain that passes through this (or any) feedlot. Steer 534 started his life part of a food chain that derived all of its energy from the sun, which nourished the grasses that nourished him and his mother. When 534 moved from ranch to feedlot, from grass to corn, he joined an industrial food chain powered by fossil fuel—and therefore defended by the U.S. military, another never-counted cost of cheap food. (One-fifth of America's petroleum consumption goes to producing and transporting our food.) After I got home from Kansas, I asked an economist who specializes in agriculture and energy if it might be possible to calculate precisely how much petroleum it will take to grow my steer to slaughter weight. Assuming 534 continues to eat twenty-five pounds of corn a day and reaches a weight of twelve hundred pounds, he will have consumed in his lifetime the equivalent of thirty-five gallons of oil—nearly a barrel.

So this is what commodity corn can do to a cow: industrialize the mir- 15 acle of nature that is a ruminant, taking this sunlight- and prairie grass-powered organism and turning it into the last thing we need: another fossil fuel machine. This one, however, is able to suffer.

Standing there in the pen alongside my steer, I couldn't imagine ever 16 wanting to eat the flesh of one of these protein machines. Hungry was the last thing I felt. Yet I'm sure that after enough time goes by, and the stink of this place is gone from my nostrils, I will eat feedlot beef again. Eating industrial meat takes an almost heroic act of not knowing or, now, forgetting. But I left Poky determined to follow this meat to a meal on a table somewhere, to see this food chain at least that far. I was curious to know what feedlot beef would taste like now, if I could taste the corn or even, since taste is as much a matter of what's in the head as it is about molecules dancing on the tongue, some hint of the petroleum. "You are what you eat" is a truism hard to argue with, and yet it is, as a visit to a feedlot suggests, incomplete, for you are what what you eat eats, too. And what we are, or have become, is not just meat but number 2 corn and oil.

Thinking Critically about the Text

Pollan writes at the beginning of his essay that his first impression of the feedlot was that it was *"Not a bad little piece of real estate, all considered."* What facts undermine his first impression?

Questions on Subject

1. Why don't farmers want the liquefied manure from feedlots? What does that fact tell you about industrialized beef?
2. A butcher might look at 534 as an array of cuts of meat. Identify some of the other perspectives by which farm animals such as 534 are viewed.
3. What discovery has recently been made regarding reversing the acidification of the rumen of steers? Explain how it works.
4. Why do the cattle industry and the USDA find feeding grass to cattle impractical?
5. Why does the cheap corn fed to cows turn out to be not cheap after all, according to Pollan?

Questions on Strategy

1. How does Pollan organize his essay? (Glossary: *Organization*) Explain why his organization seems most appropriate for his subject.
2. Explain the process by which bacteria enter cattle and end up in the hamburgers we eat.
3. Explain the process by which a natural barrier to infection is diminished by feeding corn to cows.
4. How has Pollan used transitions to move from paragraph to paragraph in his essay? (Glossary: *Transitions*) Cite several examples and explain how they work.
5. How does Pollan connect what's happening to 534 to the oil fields of the Persian Gulf?

Questions on Diction and Vocabulary

1. In paragraph 3, Pollan writes, "534 and his pen mates have been bred for their marbling, after all, not their ability to form attachments." What does he mean by *marbling*?
2. Pollan ends paragraph 5 with "(Shucks)." How are we meant to interpret that expression? (Glossary: *Irony*)
3. What does Pollan mean when he writes in paragraph 7, "Yet metaphors of the factory and the machine obscure as much as they reveal about the creature standing before me." (Glossary: *Figures of Speech*)

Classroom Activity Using Process Analysis

Most do-it-yourself jobs require that you follow a set process to achieve the best results. Make a list of the steps involved in accomplishing one of the following household tasks:

    a. baking chocolate chip cookies
    b. transplanting a plant
    c. replacing a lock
    d. packing a suitcase
    e. mowing a lawn
    f. washing a pile of dirty towels

Compare your list with those of other students who focused on the same task. How do the lists differ? What could be improved?

Writing Suggestions

1. In an essay, write, as Pollan does, about the web of interconnectedness among processes that might at first seem unrelated. Pollan writes, for example, about the unintended consequences that arise when we pursue food-production practices and processes that run counter to the laws of nature. For your essay, consider an entirely different arena — the world of the Internet, for example, and the unintended consequences of our pursuit of maximum technological connectivity.

2. **Writing with Sources.** Pollan focuses his attention on the processes by which we raise cattle and bring them to market. By explaining those processes as they are carried out by the large industrial meat producers, he intends to provide us with information we need in order to make decisions about our economy, our environment, and our health. Do some research on other areas of food production — fruit growing or milk production, for example — and explain the processes involved. Write an essay in which you describe what the implications of the process might be for our economy, environment, or health. For models of and advice on integrating sources in your essay, see Chapters 14 and 15.

Are Butterflies Two Different Animals in One? The Death and Resurrection Theory

ROBERT KRULWICH

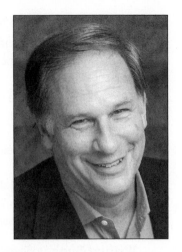

Robert Krulwich is a journalist with a special ability to make complicated topics clear to his radio and television audiences. He graduated from Earlham College in 1969 with a B.A. in history and then went on to earn his J.D. degree from Columbia Law School in 1974. Two months afterward, Krulwich abandoned his idea of becoming a lawyer and began covering the Watergate hearings for Pacifica Radio. Since that time he has worked for such companies as ABC, CBS, National Public Radio, *Rolling Stone*, and *TV Guide*, contributing a wide variety of materials to shows such as *Nightline*, *World News Today*, *Frontline*, *NOVA*, *NOW with Bill Moyers*, *Good Morning America*, and *Prime Time Live*. He has won many awards for his work, among them the Extraordinary Communicator Award from the National Cancer Institute in 2000, an Emmy, a Dupont Award, and a George Polk Award.

In "Are Butterflies Two Different Animals in One? The Death and Resurrection Theory," posted on the NPR.org blog "Krulwich Wonders" on August 1, 2012, the author considers a fascinating and shocking theory about the process involved when caterpillars turn into moths and butterflies or, as the case might be, when a caterpillar dies and a moth or butterfly is born.

As you read, pay attention to the tone and style of the piece, which is informal and conversational commentary, not a news report. In fact, since it originally appeared on a blog, Krulwich was able to add additional notes in response to his readers. That postscript (entitled "On the Other Hand . . .") is also included here.

Preparing to Read

Have you, like many before you, been fascinated to learn that moths and butterflies start out their lives as caterpillars? What did you think as you learned about their miraculous transformation from wormlike critters to creatures of flight and stunning beauty? Did you wonder how this could happen?

Here's a dangerous, crazy thought from an otherwise sober (and very eminent) biologist, Bernd Heinrich. He's thinking about moths and butterflies, and how they radically change shape as they grow, from little wormy, caterpillar critters to airborne beauties. Why, he wondered, do these flying animals begin their lives as wingless, crawling worms? Baby ducks have wings. Baby bats have wings. Why not baby butterflies?

His answer—and I'm quoting him here—knocked me silly. 2

"[T]he radical change that occurs," he says, "does indeed arguably 3 involve death followed by reincarnation."

What? 4

So he says it again: "[T]he adult forms of these insects are actually new 5 organisms."

I'm sorry. Maybe I didn't hear that right . . . 6

"In effect, the animal is a chimera, an amalgam of two, where the first 7 one lives and dies . . . and then the other emerges."

What he's saying is, while a moth appears to be one animal, with a 8 wormy start and a flying finish, it's *actually two animals*—two in one! We start with a baby caterpillar that lives a full life and then dies, dissolves. There's a pause. Then a new animal, the moth, springs to life, from the same cells, reincarnated.

According to this theory, long, long ago, two very different animals, 9 one destined to be wormy, the other destined to take wing, accidentally mated, and somehow their genes learned to live side by side in their descendants. But their genes never really integrated. They are sharing a DNA molecule like two folks sharing a car, except halfway through the trip, one driver dissolves and up pops his totally different successor. Driver No. 2 emerges from the body of driver No. 1.

Really? 10

When this theory was first proposed (not by Bernd, but by an English 11 zoologist), eminent scientists scoffed.

Said Duke biologist Fred Nijhout, this idea fits better in "*The National* 12 *Enquirer* than the National Academy (of Sciences)." Said paleontologist Conrad Labandiera, "You must be kidding!"

But Donald Williamson, a zoologist from the University of Liverpool 13 in England, wasn't kidding. And if Bernd Heinrich is now warming to this notion, it's time to take a closer look at Death and Resurrection in insects.

THE DEATH AND RESURRECTION CYCLE?

Many insects begin life as worm-shaped, leggy, tubular thingies that spend 14 lots of time eating. We call them grubs or maggots or caterpillars, and they are programmed by a set of genes that sit in their DNA, spelled out in chemical letters, A, C, T and G.

For example, imagine that this animal has a sixteen-gene sequence of 15 A C T G G A C T T G A A C T G A, but that only the first eight (A C T G G A C T) are the "caterpillar" instruction genes. The eight remaining instruction genes are, temporarily, silent.

These seven panels show a process of development, from a caterpillar to a monarch butterfly.

So the caterpillar grows and grows until one day, it spins itself a silk 16
coverlet (a cocoon) or a harder pupa or chrysalis container that dangles off a twig and it goes . . . well, silent.

This phase is, as Heinrich puts it, "a deathlike intermission." Inside, 17
these caterpillars shrink, shed their skin, their organs dissolve. Their insides turn to mush. Most of their cells die. But lurking in the goo are a few cells (the so-called adult or "imaginal" cells) that at this moment jump into action, reorganize all the free-floating proteins and other nutrients and turn what was once caterpillar into . . . here comes the resurrection . . . a moth!

What's happened, says Heinrich, is that the caterpillar section of the 18
DNA has been turned off, and the butterfly instructions have been turned on.

"[T]here are indeed two very different sets of genetic instructions at 19
work," he writes, and this switch, turning "caterpillar" off, turning "butterfly" on, means that "most of one body dies and the new life is resurrected in a new body."

TWO IN ONE

There is no controversy about the mechanics I just described; it's the expla- 20
nation that's new and controversial. The old view was that over millions of years, animals evolved this habit of switching from one set of instructions to the other. The new view is that this is not one animal gradually changing shape, but rather instructions for two different animals sandwiched together and this change is so radical, says Bernd, "with no continuity from one to the next, that the adult forms of these insects are *actually new organisms*."

If cross-species matings were once possible, who knows what you could die and turn into?

A caterpillar is born and dies; a butterfly is resurrected from its juices. 21
It's a stunning idea. (But with all kinds of problems: How to explain 22
two very different creatures from different ancient species "mating"?

Usually, they can't do that. How do you get DNA to not mix, so that the two creatures stay distinct? How do you define "death"?)

But still, I can't stop thinking about this. If cross-species matings were 23 once possible, who knows what you could die and turn into? Could dandelions dream of becoming spruce trees? Could tadpoles, instead of morphing into frogs, become catfish? This is silly, I know, but radical metamorphoses, from tadpoles to frogs, maggots to flies, grubs to beetles, remain largely mysterious, so new explanations are intriguing, even if they startle. (Especially if they startle.)

ON THE OTHER HAND . . .

I have a postscript to this blog. Yes, Bernd Heinrich is intrigued by Donald 24 Williamson's Death and Resurrection thesis, and yes the strangeness of this theory makes it fun to write about. But there is, of course, an alternate possibility: that this idea is just plain wrong. I mentioned that Donald Williamson's paper was very controversial when it was first published. It still is. A few hours after this post went up, I was sent a critique of Williamson's work written by two scientists, Michael Hart and Richard Grosberg.

They think there is no credible evidence for this idea of ancient mating 25 between different species, and that, to summarize their view, they think Williamson's theory is scientifically indefensible. So far, however, Williamson's original paper has not been retracted, which is what happens when an idea is so off, or so insupportable that it is no longer scientifically plausible. (However another subsequent Williamson paper—describing another possible ancient mating—has been retracted from a different journal.)

So, what we have here is one of my favorite scientists embracing an 26 idea that a great many other scientists find noxious and wrong. "You must be kidding!" is still the cry from many men and women who do cell and developmental biology for a living. Eventually, somebody's face will be red. Maybe Bernd's. Maybe the other guys'. That's how science works. But I think you should know that wondering about butterflies and moths can get feisty.

Thinking Critically about the Text

If the distinguished biologist Bernd Heinrich and the scientists that have gone before him are correct about moths and butterflies being examples of creatures that somehow resurrect themselves, what possibilities, if any, do their theories and examples imply?

Questions on Subject

1. Krulwich writes in paragraph 1, "Here's a dangerous, crazy thought from an otherwise sober (and very eminent) biologist, Bernd Heinrich." Why dangerous? Why crazy?

2. How do you explain in your own words the theory that moths and butterflies are actually two different animals in one and not one animal metamorphosing into another?

3. Does it matter that Bernd Heinrich was not the first scientist to put forth the theory of death and resurrection in the case of caterpillars and moths and butterflies? Why, or why not?

4. In paragraph 15, Krulwich divides a string of genes into two groups and says that the eight instruction genes in the second group "are, temporarily, silent." What instructions is he referring to? Why does he say "temporarily silent"?

5. According to Heinrich, what is "a deathlike intermission"?

6. What gives Krulwich trouble in understanding Heinrich's theory of two animals in one? Can you venture any possible answers to his questions?

Questions on Strategy

1. In paragraph 1, Krulwich repeats the same basic sentence pattern when he writes, "Baby ducks have wings. Baby bats have wings." (Glossary: *Parallelism*) Why do you suppose he did not simply write, "Baby ducks and bats have wings"?

2. Is the analogy about the car that Krulwich uses in paragraph 9 a good one in your opinion? (Glossary: *Analogy*) Why does it work or fail to work for you?

3. Krulwich uses some very short sentences in his essay. To what extent are they effective? What does he accomplish by using them?

4. Krulwich shares with his reader his own fascination and questions regarding the processes he is attempting to explain with first-person narrative interjections. Are these helpful to your understanding? How might your understanding change if his explanations of the theory of two-creatures-in-one were approached from a third-person perspective? Explain.

Questions on Diction and Vocabulary

1. In paragraph 7, Krulwich uses the word *chimera* to refer to the caterpillar/butterfly. Investigate the word *chimera* further. Is it an appropriate term to use in this instance? Why, or why not?

2. What are the so-called "imaginal cells"? Why is the term appropriate for them?

3. Switching DNA on and off is an easy way to refer to the end of one organism and the start of a new organism, but do we really know what the switching processes are? Explain.

4. In paragraph 23, Krulwich asks, "Could dandelions dream of becoming spruce trees?" Why do you suppose he uses the verb *dream*?

Classroom Activity Using Process Analysis

Consider the analogy about the car that Krulwich uses in paragraph 9. (Glossary: *Analogy*) Why does it work or fail to work for you? Analogies are a useful device in any writing that aims to explain, and they can be especially helpful in explaining natural processes, especially those that are often difficult for us to see and understand. In a classroom discussion, briefly develop analogies for the following: digestion, decomposition, combustion, volcanic eruption, fermentation, photosynthesis, greenhouse effect, or some other natural process.

Writing Suggestions

1. Krulwich's article is really an informal report where he informs us of Heinrich's work on the theory that caterpillars and butterflies may be two separate creatures and not the metamorphosis of a single creature. Reflect on other coursework involving a natural process and write a similar report on what excites you about that process. Think about processes that most readers would not be familiar with, or ones in which recent discoveries have been made, or yet others about which thinking has recently changed. Write an essay on one of the following or on a subject of your own choosing:

   a. weight gain
   b. climate change
   c. genome research
   d. wireless technology
   e. brain mapping
   f. infectious diseases

2. *New York* magazine wrote of Robert Krulwich that he is "the man who simplifies without being simple." Let's assume that as a college student you have been invited by a friend who teaches eighth grade to explain how something works. You, of course, want to be honest with your material and accurate with your information, and neither talk down to nor talk over the heads of the students in the class. Here are some possible subjects for you to consider: how dependence on PEDs (performance-enhancing drugs) can lead to serious health problems, how wireless communications work, how our privacy is being threatened by our own electronic devices, how contact sports can lead to lifelong health problems, or how vaccinations can reduce childhood diseases. Write an essay on one of these topics for an audience of eighth-graders.

Campus Racism 101

NIKKI GIOVANNI

Yolanda Cornelia "Nikki" Giovanni was born in Knox-
ville, Tennessee, in 1943 and was raised in Ohio. After
graduating from Fisk University, she organized the Black
Arts Festival in Cincinnati and then entered graduate
school at the University of Pennsylvania. Her first book
of poetry, *Black Feeling, Black Talk*, was published in
1968 and began a lifetime of writing that reflects on the
African American identity. Recent books of poetry include the anthologies *Selected Poems of Nikki Giovanni*
(1996), *Love Poems* (1997), *Blues for All the Changes: New
Poems* (1999), *Quilting the Black-Eyed Pea: Poems and
Not Quite Poems* (2002), *The Collected Poetry of Nikki Giovanni* (2003), and *Aco-
lytes: Poems* (2007). Her honors include the Langston Hughes Award for Distinguished Contributions to Arts and Letters in 1996, the NAACP Image Award for
Literature in 1998, and Woman of the Year awards from several magazines, including
Essence, Mademoiselle, and *Ladies Home Journal.* She is currently professor of English
and Gloria D. Smith Professor of Black Studies at Virginia Tech.

The following selection, taken from her nonfiction work *Racism 101*, instructs
black students about how to succeed at predominantly white colleges.

Preparing to Read

How would you characterize race relations at your school? How much do white and
minority students interact, and what, in your experience, is the tone of those interactions? What is being done within the institution to address any problems or to foster
greater respect and understanding?

There is a bumper sticker that reads: TOO BAD IGNORANCE ISN'T PAIN-   1
FUL. I like that. But ignorance is. We just seldom attribute the pain
to it or even recognize it when we see it. Like the postcard on my
corkboard. It shows a young man in a very hip jacket smoking a
cigarette. In the background is a high school with the American flag waving.
The caption says: "Too cool for school. Yet too stupid for the real world."
Out of the mouth of the young man is a bubble enclosing the words "Maybe
I'll start a band." There could be a postcard showing a jock in a uniform saying, "I don't need school. I'm going to the NFL or NBA." Or one showing a
young man or woman studying and a group of young people saying, "So you
want to be white." Or something equally demeaning. We need to quit it.

I am a professor of English at Virginia Tech. I've been here for four   2
years, though for only two years with academic rank. I am tenured, which

means I have a teaching position for life, a rarity on a predominantly white campus. Whether from malice or ignorance, people who think I should be at a predominantly Black institution will ask, "Why are you at Tech?" Because it's here. And so are Black students. But even if Black students weren't here, it's painfully obvious that this nation and this world cannot allow white students to go through higher education without interacting with Blacks in authoritative positions. It is equally clear that predominantly Black colleges cannot accommodate the numbers of Black students who want and need an education.

Is it difficult to attend a predominantly white college? Compared with what? Being passed over for promotion because you lack credentials? Being turned down for jobs because you are not college-educated? Joining the armed forces or going to jail because you cannot find an alternative to the streets? Let's have a little perspective here. Where can you go and what can you do that frees you from interacting with the white American mentality? You're going to interact; the only question is, will you be in some control of yourself and your actions, or will you be controlled by others? I'm going to recommend self-control.

What's the difference between prison and college? They both prescribe your behavior for a given period of time. They both allow you to read books and develop your writing. They both give you time alone to think and time with your peers to talk about issues. But four years of prison doesn't give you a passport to greater opportunities. Most likely that time only gives you greater knowledge of how to get back in. Four years of college gives you an opportunity not only to lift yourself but to serve your people effectively. What's the difference when you are called nigger in college from when you are called nigger in prison? In college you can, though I admit with effort, follow procedures to have those students who called you nigger kicked out or suspended. You can bring issues to public attention without risking your life. But mostly, college is and always has been the future. We, neither less nor more than other people, need knowledge. There are discomforts attached to attending predominantly white colleges, though no more so than living in a racist world. Here are some rules to follow that may help:

There are discomforts attached to attending predominantly white colleges, though no more so than living in a racist world.

Go to class. No matter how you feel. No matter how you think the professor feels about you. It's important to have a consistent presence in the classroom. If nothing else, the professor will know you care enough and are serious enough to be there.

Meet your professors. Extend your hand (give a firm handshake) and tell them your name. Ask them what you need to do to make an A. You may never make an A, but you have put them on notice that you are serious about getting good grades.

Do assignments on time. Typed or computer-generated. You have the syllabus. Follow it, and turn those papers in. If for some reason you can't complete an assignment on time, let your professor know before it is due and work out a new due date—then meet it.

Go back to see your professor. Tell him or her your name again. If an assignment received less than an A, ask why, and find out what you need to do to improve the next assignment.

Yes, your professor is busy. So are you. So are your parents who are working to pay or help with your tuition. Ask early what you need to do if you feel you are starting to get into academic trouble. Do not wait until you are failing.

Understand that there will be professors who do not like you; there may even be professors who are racist or sexist or both. You must discriminate among your professors to see who will give you the help you need. You may not simply say, "They are all against me." They aren't. They mostly don't care. Since you are the one who wants to be educated, find the people who want to help.

Don't defeat yourself. Cultivate your friends. Know your enemies. You cannot undo hundreds of years of prejudicial thinking. Think for yourself and speak up. Raise your hand in class. Say what you believe no matter how awkward you may think it sounds. You will improve in your articulation and confidence.

Participate in some campus activity. Join the newspaper staff. Run for office. Join a dorm council. Do something that involves you on campus. You are going to be there for four years, so let your presence be known, if not felt.

You will inevitably run into some white classmates who are troubling because they often say stupid things, ask stupid questions—and expect an answer. Here are some comebacks to some of the most common inquiries and comments:

Q: What's it like to grow up in a ghetto?
A: I don't know.

Q: (from the teacher) Can you give us the Black perspective on Toni Morrison, Huck Finn, slavery, Martin Luther King Jr., and others?
A: I can give you *my* perspective. (Do not take the burden of 22 million people on your shoulders. Remind everyone that you are an individual, and don't speak for the race or any other individual within it.)

Q: Why do all the Black people sit together in the dining hall? 18

A: Why do all the white students sit together? 19

Q: Why should there be an African American studies course? 20

A: Because white Americans have not adequately studied the contri- 21
butions of Africans and African Americans. Both Black and white students
need to know our total common history.

Q: Why are there so many scholarships for "minority" students? 22

A: Because they wouldn't give my great-grandparents their forty 23
acres and the mule.

Q: How can whites understand Black history, culture, literature, and 24
so forth?

A: The same way we understand white history, culture, literature, 25
and so forth. That is why we're in school: to learn.

Q: Should whites take African American studies courses? 26

A: Of course. We take white-studies courses, though the universities 27
don't call them that.

Comment: When I see groups of Black people on campus, it's really 28
intimidating.

Comeback: I understand what you mean. I'm frightened when I see 29
white students congregating.

Comment: It's not fair. It's easier for you guys to get into college than 30
for other people.

Comeback: If it's so easy, why aren't there more of us? 31

Comment: It's not our fault that America is the way it is. 32

Comeback: It's not our fault, either, but both of us have a responsi- 33
bility to make changes.

It's really very simple. Educational progress is a national concern; edu- 34
cation is a private one. Your job is not to educate white people; it is to
obtain an education. If you take the racial world on your shoulders, you
will not get the job done. Deal with yourself as an individual worthy of
respect, and make everyone else deal with you the same way. College is a
little like playing grown-up. Practice what you want to be. You have been
telling your parents you are grown. Now is your chance to act like it.

Thinking Critically about the Text

Giovanni concludes her essay by pointing out the nature of the "job" black students have undertaken, focusing on what it does *not* involve for them. For you,
does the "job" of being a student involve more than just getting an education? If

so, what other priorities do you have, and what additional challenges do they present? If not, explain your situation. How well are you able to put other things aside to achieve your educational goals?

Questions on Subject

1. Who is Giovanni's audience? When does the intended audience first become clear? (Glossary: *Audience*)

2. Why does Giovanni dismiss the notion that it is difficult being a black student at a predominantly white college? What contexts does she use to support her contention?

3. The rules Giovanni presents to help black students succeed at white colleges offer a lot of sound advice for any student at any college. Why does Giovanni use what could be considered general information in her essay?

4. On what topic does Giovanni provide sample questions and answers for her readers? Why is the topic important to her readers?

Questions on Strategy

1. What is Giovanni arguing for in this essay? (Glossary: *Argument*) What is her thesis? (Glossary: *Thesis*)

2. Giovanni begins her essay with staccato rhythm. Short sentences appear throughout the essay, but they are emphasized in the beginning. (Glossary: *Beginnings/Endings*) Reread paragraph 1. What does Giovanni accomplish with her rapid-fire delivery? Why is it appropriate for the subject matter?

3. What does Giovanni gain by including her short personal narrative in paragraph 2? (Glossary: *Narration*) Why is it necessary to know her personal history and current situation?

4. After beginning her essay with straight prose, Giovanni uses a list with full explanations and a series of Q&A examples to outline strategies to help black students cope at predominantly white colleges. Why did Giovanni use these techniques to convey her material? How might they add to the usefulness of the essay for the reader?

5. What does Giovanni mean when she says, "Educational progress is a national concern; education is a private one" (paragraph 34)? What is the difference between "educational progress" and "education"? In what ways is this point important to her purpose? (Glossary: *Purpose*)

Questions on Diction and Vocabulary

1. How did you first react to Giovanni's title, "Campus Racism 101"? What did it connote to you? (Glossary: *Connotation/Denotation*) After reading the essay, do you think the title is appropriate? Explain your answer.

2. Giovanni uses the word *stupid* on two occasions. The first use (paragraph 1), "too stupid for the real world," provides a context for how she views the word, while the second characterizes what white students sometimes ask or say to black students. The second use (paragraph 13) is a little jarring — often these days the characterization is softened to "insensitive" or "thoughtless." The use of *stupid* implies a more active ignorance on the part of the questioner. What does Giovanni gain by using the word? Do you think it is meant to be pejorative toward the white students? Explain your answer.

3. How would you describe the author's tone in this essay? (Glossary: *Tone*) Is it angry, firm, moderate, instructional, or something else? Explain.

Classroom Activity Using Process Analysis

After finishing the first draft of your process analysis essay, have someone else in your writing class read it. If you are writing a directional analysis, ask your reader to follow the instructions and then tell you whether he or she was able to understand each step and, if possible, perform it satisfactorily. Was the desired result achieved? If not, examine your process step by step, looking for errors and omissions that would explain the unsatisfactory result.

Writing Suggestions

1. What specific strategies do you employ to do well in your classes? Do you ask the professor what is needed for an A and make sure you attend every class, as Giovanni suggests in her essay? Do you take meticulous notes, study every day, just cram the night before exams, or have a lucky shirt for test days? Write a process analysis in which you present your method for success in school in a way that others could emulate, should they so choose.

2. In Giovanni's Q&A section, she replies to the question, "Why are there so many scholarships for 'minority' students?" with the answer, "Because they wouldn't give my great-grandparents their forty acres and the mule" (paragraphs 22–23). Write an argumentative essay in which you react to both Giovanni's answer and the situation as a whole. Do you think qualified minority students should receive preferential treatment for admissions and financial aid? If you argue no, what other strategies would you support to address the current educational inequities between whites and blacks?

3. **Writing with Sources.** Giovanni's essay covers a subject — African Americans attending predominantly white colleges — that has a relatively short history in many areas of the country. Although African Americans have a long history of success in higher education in the Northeast, where they were admitted to some schools as early as the 1820s, it has only been in the last five decades that the final barriers to college attendance have been removed nationwide. The battle over education rights became one of the most

important components of the civil rights movement and led to some of the most contentious showdowns.

The photograph below shows James Meredith as he attempts to become the first African American to enter the University of Mississippi on October 1, 1962. His efforts resulted in riots that caused two deaths and 160 injuries. Meredith graduated from Ole Miss in 1964 and then went on to Columbia University and earned a degree in law.

What evidence of determination do you see on the faces and in the body language of both those who wished to keep James Meredith from entering the university and those who were his supporters? Notice that the photograph reveals a sort of mirror image, with the opposing sides reflecting each other's confrontational attitudes.

Research the background and precipitating circumstances of Meredith's admittance to the University of Mississippi, and write an essay explaining the process he went through to make his case heard and accepted by authorities in the civil rights movement, the federal government, the state of Mississippi, and the university. For models of and advice on integrating sources in your essay, see Chapters 14 and 15.

WRITING SUGGESTIONS FOR PROCESS ANALYSIS

1. Write a directional or evaluative process analysis on one of the following topics:

   a. how to copy a CD
   b. how to adjust bicycle brakes
   c. how to save photos you take on your smartphone
   d. how to throw a party
   e. how to use the memory function on a calculator
   f. how to add, drop, or change a course
   g. how to play a particular card game
   h. how to wash a sweater
   i. how to stop spam
   j. how to build a Web page
   k. how to select a major course of study
   l. how to safely dispose of old electronics
   m. how to rent an apartment
   n. how to develop confidence
   o. how to wrap a present
   p. how to change the oil in a car
   q. how to do a magic trick

2. Think about your favorite pastime or activity. Write an essay in which you explain one or more of the processes you follow in participating in that activity. For example, if basketball is your hobby, how do you go about making a layup? If you are a photographer, how do you develop and print a picture following traditional methods? If you are an actor, how do you go about learning your lines? If cooking is your passion, how do you get ready to prepare a particular dish? Do you follow standard procedures, or do you personalize the process in some way?

3. All college students have to register for courses each term. What is the registration process like at your college? Do you find any part of the process unnecessarily frustrating or annoying? In a letter to your campus newspaper or an appropriate administrator, evaluate your school's current registration procedure, offering suggestions for making the process more efficient and pleasurable.

4. Writing to a person who is a computer novice, explain how to do a Web search. Be sure to define key terms and to illustrate the steps in your process with screen shots of search directories and search results.

5. Based on an idea similar to the one contained in the cartoon below, write a humorous process analysis essay with the thesis "Nothing is ever as simple as it looks."

"And that's how you make a peanut butter sandwich."

6. **Writing with Sources.** Do some research, and then write an informational or evaluative process analysis on one of the following topics:
   a. how your heart functions
   b. how a U.S. president is elected
   c. how ice cream is made
   d. how a hurricane forms
   e. how hailstones form
   f. how a volcano erupts
   g. how the human circulatory system works
   h. how a camera works
   i. how photosynthesis takes place
   j. how an atomic bomb or reactor works
   k. how fertilizer is made

    l. how a refrigerator works

    m. how water evaporates

    n. how flowers bloom

    o. how a recession occurs

    p. how an automobile is made

    q. how a bill becomes law in your state

For models of and advice on integrating sources in your essay, see Chapters 14 and 15.

7. **Writing with Sources.** Although each of us hopes never to be in a natural disaster such as an earthquake or a major flood, many of us have been or could be, and it is important that people know what to do. Do some research on the topic, and then write an essay in which you explain the steps that a person should follow to protect life and property during and in the aftermath of a particular natural disaster. For models of and advice on integrating sources in your essay, see Chapters 14 and 15.

8. **Writing with Sources.** If you are scientifically minded or simply want to know more about evolution, research some subprocesses that contribute to the evolutionary process, using books, journals, articles, videos, and online resources. Some of the subprocesses that you may want to pursue include adaptation, selection, divergence, genetic drift, natural selection, mutation, and bipedalism. Consider an educated, general-interest reader to be your audience, so be sure to define technical terms. For models of and advice on integrating sources in your essay, see Chapters 14 and 15.

9. **Writing with Sources.** The opening illustration for this chapter on page 228 is an informational process analysis about how baked goods are recycled into plastics. Do some research in your library or online, and write a set of detailed directions for carrying out that process. You will need to explain how to get the ingredients, how much of each ingredient is needed, and the types of required equipment and machinery, as well as explicit directions for carrying out the process. As with any good set of directions, you will need not only to say what to do, but also what not to do. Mention where the process can go wrong at any and every point and what the components and ingredients should look like at each step. For models of and advice on integrating sources in your essay, see Chapters 14 and 15.

10. **Writing in the Workplace.** You have just been hired to be the person in charge of small gift giving for a local nonprofit organization. Among your various responsibilities is the writing of letters of acknowledgment for gifts to the organization. Prepare several letters thanking donors. One should be a

general letter suitable for most donors. The second letter should be one in which the donor makes the gift in memory of someone and wants that person's family to be notified of the gift. You will need to make up a name for your organization, a fictitious name for the donor, and one for the person in whose memory the gift is being made. Before starting to draft your letter, think about what needs to be said in each situation. Also be sure to carefully consider the tone of your letter in each case.

 e-Pages

How to Compost in Your Apartment
SUSTAINABLE AMERICA

See how process analysis works on the Web. Go to bedfordstmartins.com/subjectandstrategy for an infographic and study questions examining the steps, tips, and advantages of composting food waste.

REBUILDING PROGRESS IN NEW ORLEANS

BEFORE HURRICANE KATRINA **2 YEARS LATER ('07)** **3 YEARS LATER ('08)** **4 YEARS LATER ('09)**

Households Actively receiving mail in Orleans Parish

198,232

133,966

142,240

152,904

Labor force In New Orleans metropolitan area

638,912

517,539

539,723

534,451*

Child care centers Open in Orleans Parish

275

98

117

142

Single family home sales In New Orleans metropolitan area

1,376

1,064

830

792*

Permits for new residential housing units In Orleans Parish, June

85

774

100

89

*Preliminary

CHAPTER 8

Comparison and Contrast

WHAT ARE COMPARISON AND CONTRAST?

A COMPARISON PRESENTS TWO OR MORE SUBJECTS (PEOPLE, IDEAS, OR objects), considers them together, and shows in what ways they are alike; a contrast shows how they differ. These two perspectives, apparently in contradiction to each other, actually work so often in conjunction that they are commonly considered a single strategy, called *comparison and contrast* or simply *comparison* for short.

Comparison and contrast are so much a part of daily life that we are often not aware of using them. Whenever you make a choice—what to wear, where to eat, what college to attend, what career to pursue—you implicitly use comparison and contrast to evaluate your options and arrive at your decision.

The graphic on the opposite page uses visual comparison and contrast to clearly demonstrate rebuilding progress in New Orleans after Hurricane Katrina. The chart establishes points or areas of comparison, such as "households receiving mail," "child care centers open," and "single family home sales." Then, using pre–Hurricane Katrina statistics as a baseline, the visual charts comparative statistics in each area for "2 years later ('07)," "3 years later ('08)," and "4 years later ('09)." Thus we can see that in the two years immediately following Katrina the number of households receiving mail dropped from 198,232 to 133,966. This number increased to 142,240 in 2008 and 152,904 in 2009 as residents moved back to Orleans Parish. In what other areas do you see progress being made? (Do you think the point of the graphic *is* that progress is being made? If not, what is the point?)

COMPARISON AND CONTRAST IN WRITTEN TEXTS

The strategy of comparison and contrast is most commonly used in writing when the subjects under discussion belong to the same class or general category: four makes of car, for example, or two candidates for Senate. (See

Chapter 9, "Division and Classification," for a more complete discussion of classes.) Such subjects are said to be *comparable*, or to have a strong basis for comparison.

▶ Point-by-Point and Block Comparison

There are two basic ways to organize comparison and contrast essays. In the first, *point-by-point comparison*, the author starts by comparing both subjects in terms of a particular point, then moves on to a second point and compares both subjects, then moves on to a third point, and so on. The other way to organize a comparison is called *block comparison*. In this pattern, the information about one subject is gathered into a block, which is followed by a block of comparable information about the second subject.

Each pattern of comparison has advantages and disadvantages. Point-by-point comparison allows the reader to grasp fairly easily the specific points of comparison the author is making; it may be harder, though, to pull together the details and convey a distinct impression of what each subject is like. The block comparison guarantees that each subject will receive a more unified discussion; however, the points of comparison between them may be less clear.

The first of the following two annotated passages illustrates a point-by-point comparison. This selection, a comparison of President Franklin Roosevelt and his vice-presidential running mate Harry Truman of Missouri, is from historian David McCullough's Pulitzer Prize–winning biography *Truman* (1992).

Point-by-point comparison identifies central similarities

Both were men of exceptional determination, with great reserves of personal courage and cheerfulness. They were alike, too, in their enjoyment of people. (The human race, Truman once told a reporter, was an "excellent outfit.") Each had an active sense of humor and was inclined to be dubious of those who did not. But Roosevelt, who loved stories, loved also to laugh at his own, while Truman was more of a listener and laughed best when somebody else told "a good one." Roosevelt enjoyed flattery, Truman was made uneasy by

Point-by-point contrast introduces several differences

it. Roosevelt loved the subtleties of human relations. He was a master of the circuitous solution to problems, of the pleasing if ambiguous answer to difficult questions. He was sensitive to nuances in a way Harry Truman never was and never would be. Truman, with his rural Missouri background, and partly, too, because of the limits of his education, was inclined to see things in far simpler terms, as right or wrong, wise or foolish. He dealt little in abstractions. His answers

Development of key difference

to questions, even complicated questions, were nearly always direct and assured, plainly said, and followed often by a conclusive "And that's all there is to it," an old Missouri expression, when in truth there may have been a great deal more "to it."

Point-by-point comparison and contrast of each man's life struggles and experiences

Each of them had been tested by his own painful struggle, Roosevelt with crippling polio, Truman with debt, failure, obscurity, and the heavy stigma of the Pendergasts. Roosevelt liked to quote the admonition of his old headmaster at Groton, Dr. Endicott Peabody: "Things in life will not always run smoothly. Sometimes we will be rising toward the heights—then all will seem to reverse itself and start downward. The great fact to remember is that the trend of civilization is forever upward. . . . " Assuredly Truman would have subscribed to the same vision. They were two optimists at heart, each in his way faithful to the old creed of human progress. But there had been nothing in Roosevelt's experience like the night young Harry held the lantern as his mother underwent surgery, nothing like the Argonne, or Truman's desperate fight for political survival in 1940.

In the following example from *Harper's* magazine, Otto Friedrich uses a block format to contrast a newspaper story with a newsmagazine story.

Subjects of comparison: Newspaper story and magazine story belong to the same class

There is an essential difference between a news story, as understood by a newspaperman or a wire-service writer, and a newsmagazine story. The chief purpose of the conventional news story is to tell what happened. It starts with the most important information and continues into increasingly inconsequential details, not only because the reader may not read beyond the first paragraph, but because an editor working on galley proofs a few minutes before press time likes to be able to cut freely from the end of the story.

Block comparison: Each paragraph deals with one type of story

A newsmagazine is very different. It is written to be read consecutively from beginning to end, and each of its stories is designed, following the critical theories of Edgar Allan Poe, to create one emotional effect. The news, what happened that week, may be told in the beginning, the middle, or the end; for the purpose is not to throw information at the reader but to seduce him into reading the whole story, and into accepting the dramatic (and often political) point being made.

In this selection, Friedrich has two purposes: to offer information that explains the differences between a newspaper story and a newsmagazine story and to persuade readers that magazine stories tend to be more biased than newspaper stories.

▶ Analogy: A Special Form of Comparison and Contrast

When the subject under discussion is unfamiliar, complex, or abstract, the resourceful writer may use a special form of comparison called *analogy* to help readers understand the difficult subject. Whereas most comparisons analyze items within the same class, analogies compare two largely dissimilar subjects to look for illuminating similarities. In addition, while the typical comparison seeks to illuminate specific features of both subjects, the primary purpose of analogy is to clarify one subject that is complex or unfamiliar by pointing out its similarities to a more familiar or concrete subject.

If, for example, your purpose were to explain the craft of fiction writing, you might note its similarities to the craft of carpentry. In this case, you would be drawing an analogy, because the two subjects clearly belong to different classes. You would be using the concrete work of the carpenter to help readers understand the more abstract work of the novelist. You can use analogy in one or two paragraphs to clarify a particular aspect of the larger topic, or you can use it as the organizational strategy for an entire essay.

In the following example from *The Mysterious Sky* (1960), observe how Lester Del Rey explains the functions of Earth's atmosphere (a subject that people have difficulty with because they can't "see" it) by making an analogy to an ordinary window.

> The atmosphere of Earth acts like any window in serving two very important functions. It lets light in and it permits us to look out. It also serves as a shield to keep out dangerous or uncomfortable things. A normal glazed window lets us keep our houses warm by keeping out cold air, and it prevents rain, dirt, and unwelcome insects and animals from coming in. As we have already seen, Earth's atmospheric window also helps to keep our planet at a comfortable temperature by holding back radiated heat and protecting us from dangerous levels of ultraviolet light.

You'll notice that Del Rey's analogy establishes no direct relationship between the subjects under comparison. The analogy is effective precisely because it enables the reader to visualize the atmosphere, which is unobservable, by comparing it to something quite different—a window—that is familiar and concrete.

USING COMPARISON AND CONTRAST AS A WRITING STRATEGY

To compare one thing or idea with another, to discover the similarities and differences between them, is one of the most basic human strategies for learning, evaluating, and making decisions. Because it serves so many fundamental purposes, comparison and contrast is a particularly useful strategy for the writer. It may be the primary mode for essay writers who seek to educate or persuade the reader; to evaluate things, people, or events; and to differentiate between apparently similar subjects or to reconcile the differences between dissimilar ones.

Comparison and contrast may be combined readily with other writing strategies and often serve to sharpen, clarify, and add interest to essays written in a different primary mode. For example, an essay of argumentation gains credibility when the writer contrasts desirable and undesirable reasons or examples. In the Declaration of Independence (pages 509–12), Thomas Jefferson effectively contrasts the actual behavior of the English king with the ideals of a democratic society. In "I Have a Dream" (pages 522–26), Martin Luther King Jr. compares 1960s America with the promise of what it ought to be to argue that the realization of the dream of freedom for all American citizens is long overdue. Likewise, Richard Lederer, in "The Case for Short Words" (pages 516–19), uses comparison and contrast to showcase the virtues of one-syllable words when measured against their multisyllabic counterparts.

Many descriptive essays rely heavily on comparison and contrast; one of the most effective ways to describe any person, place, or thing is to show how it is like another model of the same class and how it differs. Robert Ramírez ("The Barrio," page 149) describes his Hispanic neighborhood as contrasted with "the harshness and the coldness of the Anglo world." Definition is also clarified and enriched by the use of comparison and contrast. Virtually all the essays in Chapter 10 employ comparison and contrast to enhance and refine the definitions being developed.

USING COMPARISON AND CONTRAST ACROSS THE DISCIPLINES

When writing essays in the academic disciplines, you will have many opportunities to use the strategy of comparison and contrast to both organize and strengthen the presentation of your ideas. To determine whether or not comparison and contrast is the right strategy for you in a particular paper, review the guidelines described in Chapter 2 (Determining a Strategy for Developing Your Essay, pages 32–33). Consider the following examples:

Music

1. **MAIN IDEA:** The music of the Romantic period sharply contrasts with the music of the earlier Classical period.
2. **QUESTION:** What are the key differences between the music of the Romantic and the Classical periods?
3. **STRATEGY:** Comparison and Contrast. The direction words *contrasts* and *differences* call for a discussion distinguishing characteristics of the two periods in music history.

4. **SUPPORTING STRATEGIES:** Definition and Illustration. It might be helpful to define the key terms *Romanticism* and *Classicism* and to illustrate each of the differences with examples from representative Romantic composers (Brahms, Chopin, Schubert, and Tchaikovsky) and Classical composers (Beethoven, Haydn, and Mozart).

Political Science

1. **MAIN IDEA:** Though very different people, Winston Churchill and Franklin D. Roosevelt shared many larger-than-life leadership qualities during World War II, a period of doubt and crisis.
2. **QUESTION:** What are the similarities between Winston Churchill and Franklin D. Roosevelt as world leaders?
3. **STRATEGY:** Comparison and Contrast. The direction words *shared* and *similarities* require a discussion of the leadership traits displayed by both men.
4. **SUPPORTING STRATEGY:** Definition. It might prove helpful to define *leader* and/or *leadership* to establish a context for this comparison.

Physics

1. **MAIN IDEA:** Compare and contrast the three classes of levers—simple machines used to amplify force.
2. **QUESTION:** What are the similarities and differences among the three classes of levers?
3. **STRATEGY:** Comparison and Contrast. The direction words *compare*, *contrast*, *similarities*, and *differences* say it all.
4. **SUPPORTING STRATEGY:** Illustration. Readers will certainly appreciate familiar examples—pliers, nutcracker, and tongs—of the three classes of levers, examples that both clarify and emphasize the similarities and differences.

SAMPLE STUDENT ESSAY USING COMPARISON AND CONTRAST AS A WRITING STRATEGY

A studio art major from Pittsburgh, Pennsylvania, Barbara Bowman has a special interest in photography. In her writing courses, Bowman has discovered many similarities between the writing process and the process that an artist follows. Her essay "Guns and Cameras," however, explores similarities of another kind: those between hunting with a gun and hunting with a camera.

Guns and Cameras

Barbara Bowman

Introduces objects being compared

With a growing number of animals heading toward extinction and with the idea of protecting such animals on game reserves increasing in popularity, photographic safaris are replacing hunting safaris. This may seem odd because of the obvious differences between guns and cameras. Shooting is aggressive, photography is passive; shooting eliminates, photography preserves. However, some hunters are willing to trade their guns for cameras because of similarities in the way the equipment is used, as well as in the relationship among equipment, user, and "prey." 1

Brief point-by-point contrast

Thesis

Block organization: first block about the hunter

The hunter has a deep interest in the apparatus he uses to kill his prey. He carries various types of guns, different kinds of ammunition, and special sights and telescopes to increase his chances of success. He knows the mechanics of his guns and understands how and why they work. This fascination with the hardware of his sport is practical—it helps him achieve his goal—but it frequently becomes an end, almost a hobby in itself. 2

Point A: equipment

Point B: stalking

Not until the very end of the long process of stalking an animal does a game hunter use his gun. First he enters into the animal's world. He studies his prey, its habitat, its daily habits, its watering holes and feeding areas, its migration patterns, its enemies and allies, its diet and food chain. Eventually the hunter himself becomes animal-like, instinctively sensing the habits and moves of his prey. Of course, this instinct gives the hunter a better chance of killing the animal; he knows where and when he will get the best shot. But it gives him more than that. Hunting is not just pulling the trigger and killing the prey. Much of it is a multifaceted and ritualistic identification with nature. 3

Point C: the result

After the kill, the hunter can do a number of things with his trophy. He can sell the meat or eat it himself. He can hang the animal's head on the wall or lay its hide on the floor or even sell these objects. But any of these uses is a luxury, and its cost is high. An animal has been destroyed; a life has been eliminated. 4

Second block about the photographer

Like the hunter, the photographer has a great interest in the tools he uses. He carries various types of cameras, lenses, 5

Point A:
equipment

and film to help him get the picture he wants. He understands the way cameras work, the uses of telephoto and micro lenses, and often the technical procedures of printing and developing. Of course, the time and interest a photographer invests in these mechanical aspects of his art allow him to capture and produce the image he wants. But as with the hunter, these mechanics can and often do become fascinating in themselves.

Point B: stalking

The wildlife photographer also needs to stalk his "prey" with knowledge and skill in order to get an accurate "shot." Like the hunter, he has to understand the animal's patterns, characteristics, and habitat; he must become animal-like in order to succeed. And like the hunter's, his pursuit is much more prolonged and complicated than the shot itself. The stalking processes are almost identical and give many of the same satisfactions.   6

Point C:
the result

The successful photographer also has something tangible to show for his efforts. A still picture of an animal can be displayed in a home, a gallery, a shop; it can be printed in a publication, as a postcard, or as a poster. In fact, a single photograph can be used in all these ways at once; it can be reproduced countless times. And despite all these ways of using his "trophies," the photographer continues to preserve his prey.   7

Conclusion: The
two activities
are similar and
give the same
satisfaction, so
why kill?

Photography is obviously the less violent and to many the more acceptable method for obtaining a trophy of a wild animal. People no longer need to hunt in order to feed or clothe themselves, and hunting for "sport" seems to be barbaric. Luckily, the excitement of pursuing an animal, learning its habits and patterns, outsmarting it on its own level, and finally "getting" it can all be done with a camera. So why use guns?   8

Analyzing Barbara Bowman's Comparison and Contrast Essay: Questions for Discussion

1. What is Bowman's thesis in this essay?

2. What are her main points of comparison between hunting with a gun and hunting with a camera?

3. How has Bowman organized her comparison? Why do you suppose she decided on this option? Explain.

4. How else could she have organized her essay? Would this alternative organization have been as effective as the one she used? Explain.

5. How does Bowman conclude her essay? In what ways is her conclusion a reflection of her thesis?

SUGGESTIONS FOR USING COMPARISON AND CONTRAST AS A WRITING STRATEGY

As you plan, write, and revise your comparison and contrast essay, be mindful of the writing process guidelines described in Chapter 2 (see pages 23–40). Also, pay particular attention to the basic requirements and essential ingredients for this writing strategy.

▶ Planning Your Comparison and Contrast Essay

Planning is an essential part of writing a good comparison and contrast essay. You can save yourself a great deal of aggravation by taking the time to think about the key components of your essay before you actually begin to write.

Many college assignments ask you to use the strategy of comparison and contrast. As you read an assignment, look for one or more of the words that suggest the use of this strategy. When you are asked to *compare* and *contrast* one item with another or to identify the *similarities* and *differences* between two items, you should use comparison and contrast. Other assignments might ask you to determine which of two options is *better* or to select the *best* solution to a particular problem. Again, the strategy of comparison and contrast will help you make this evaluation and arrive at a sound, logical conclusion.

As you start planning and writing a comparison and contrast essay, keep in mind the basic requirements of this writing strategy.

COMPARE SUBJECTS FROM THE SAME CLASS. Remember that the subjects of your comparison should be in the same class or general category so that you can establish a clear basis for comparison. (There are any number of possible classes, such as particular types of persons, places, and things, as well as occupations, activities, philosophies, points in history, and even concepts and ideas.) If your subject is difficult, complex, or unobservable, you may find that analogy, a special form of comparison, is the most effective strategy to explain that subject. Remember, also, that if the similarities and differences between the subjects are too obvious, your reader is certain to lose interest quickly.

DETERMINE YOUR PURPOSE, AND FOCUS ON IT. Suppose you choose to compare and contrast solar energy with wind energy. It is clear that both are members of the same class—energy—so there is a basis for comparing them; there also seem to be enough interesting differences to make a comparison and contrast possible. But before going any further, you must ask yourself why you want to compare and contrast these particular subjects. What audience do you seek to address? Do you want to inform, to emphasize, to explain, to evaluate, to persuade? Do you have more than one purpose? Whatever your purpose, it will influence the content and organization of your comparison.

In comparing and contrasting solar and wind energy, you will certainly provide factual information, yet you will probably also want to evaluate the two energy sources to determine whether either is a practical means of producing energy. You may also want to persuade your readers that one technology is superior to the other.

FORMULATE A THESIS STATEMENT.   Once you have your purpose clearly in mind, formulate a preliminary thesis statement. At this early stage in the writing process, the thesis statement is not cast in stone; you may well want to modify it later on, as a result of research and further consideration of your subject. A preliminary thesis statement has two functions: First, it fixes your direction so that you will be less tempted to stray into byways while doing research and writing drafts; second, establishing the central point of the essay makes it easier for you to gather supporting material and to organize your essay.

Suppose, for example, that you live in the Champlain Valley of Vermont, one of the cloudiest areas of the country, where the wind whistles along the corridor between the Green Mountains and the Adirondacks. If you were exploring possible alternative energy sources for the area, your purpose might be to persuade readers of a local environmental journal that wind is preferable to sun as a source of energy for this region. The thesis statement for this essay will certainly differ from that of a writer for a national newsmagazine whose goal is to offer general information about alternative energy sources to a broad readership.

CHOOSE THE POINTS OF COMPARISON.   *Points of comparison* are the qualities and features of your subjects on which you base your comparison. For some comparisons, you will find the information you need in your own head; for others, you will have to search for that information in the library or on the Internet.

At this stage, if you know only a little about the subjects of your comparison, you may have only a few hazy ideas for points of comparison. Perhaps wind energy means no more to you than an image of giant windmills lined up on a California ridge, and solar energy brings to mind only the reflective, glassy roof on a Colorado ski lodge. Even so, it is possible to list points of comparison that will be relevant to your subjects and your purpose. Here, for example, are important points of comparison in considering energy sources:

Cost

Efficiency

Convenience

Environmental impact

A tentative list of points will help you by suggesting the kind of information you need to gather for your comparison and contrast. You should always remain alert, however, for other factors you may not have thought of. For example, as you conduct research, you may find that maintenance requirements are another important factor in considering energy systems, and thus you might add that point to your list.

▶ Organizing and Writing Your Comparison and Contrast Essay

CHOOSE AN ORGANIZATIONAL PATTERN THAT FITS YOUR MATERIAL. Once you have gathered the necessary information, you should decide which organizational pattern, block or point-by-point, will best serve your purpose. In deciding which pattern to use, you may find it helpful to jot down a scratch outline before beginning your draft.

Block organization works best when the two objects of comparison are relatively straightforward and when the points of comparison are rather general, few in number, and can be stated succinctly. As a scratch outline illustrates, block organization makes for a unified discussion of each object, which can help your readers understand the information you have to give them.

Block Organization

BLOCK ONE **Solar Energy**
Point 1. Cost
Point 2. Efficiency
Point 3. Convenience
Point 4. Maintenance requirements
Point 5. Environmental impact

BLOCK TWO **Wind Energy**
Point 1. Cost
Point 2. Efficiency
Point 3. Convenience
Point 4. Maintenance requirements
Point 5. Environmental impact

If your essay will be more than two or three pages long, however, block organization may be a poor choice: By the time your readers come to your discussion of the costs of wind energy, they may well have forgotten what you had to say about solar energy costs several pages earlier. In this case, you would do better to use point-by-point organization.

Point-by-Point Organization

POINT ONE   **Cost**
  Subject 1. Solar energy
  Subject 2. Wind energy

POINT TWO   **Efficiency**
  Subject 1. Solar energy
  Subject 2. Wind energy

POINT THREE   **Convenience**
  Subject 1. Solar energy
  Subject 2. Wind energy

POINT FOUR   **Maintenance Requirements**
  Subject 1. Solar energy
  Subject 2. Wind energy

POINT FIVE   **Environmental Impact**
  Subject 1. Solar energy
  Subject 2. Wind energy

USE PARALLEL CONSTRUCTIONS FOR EMPHASIS. Use parallel grammatical structures to emphasize the similarities and differences between the items being compared. Parallelism is the repetition of word order or grammatical form either within a single sentence or in several sentences that develop the same central idea. As a rhetorical device, parallel structure can aid coherence and add emphasis. Franklin Roosevelt's famous Depression-era statement "I see one-third of a nation *ill-housed, ill-clad,* and *ill-nourished*" illustrates effective parallelism. Look for opportunities to use parallel constructions with (1) paired items or items in a series, (2) correlative conjunctions, and (3) the words *as* or *than*.

DRAW A CONCLUSION FROM YOUR COMPARISON. Only after you have gathered your information and made your comparisons will you be ready to decide on a conclusion. When drawing your essay to its conclusion, remember your purpose in writing, the claim made in your thesis statement, and your audience and emphasis.

Perhaps, having presented information about both technologies, your comparison shows that solar and wind energy are both feasible, with solar energy having a slight edge on most points. If your purpose has been evaluation for a general audience, you might conclude, "Both solar and wind energy are practical alternatives to conventional energy sources." If you asserted in your thesis statement that one of the technologies is superior to the other, your comparison will support a more persuasive conclusion. For the general audience, you might say, "While both solar and wind energy are practical technologies, solar energy now seems the better investment." However, for a readership made up of residents of the cloudy Champlain Valley, you might conclude, "While both solar and wind energy are practical technologies, wind energy makes more economic sense for investors in northwest Vermont."

▶ Revising and Editing Your Comparison and Contrast Essay

SHARE YOUR DRAFTS WITH OTHERS. Try sharing the drafts of your essays with other students in your writing class to make sure that your comparison and contrast works. Ask them if there are any parts of your essay that they do not understand. Have them tell you what they think your point is. If their answers differ from what you intended, have them tell you what led them to their interpretations so that you can revise accordingly. To maximize the effectiveness of conferences with your peers, use the guidelines presented on page 36. Feedback from these conferences often provides one or more places where you can start revising.

QUESTION YOUR OWN WORK WHILE REVISING AND EDITING. Revision is best done by asking yourself key questions about what you have written. Begin by reading, preferably aloud, what you have written. Reading aloud forces you to pay attention to every single word, and you are more likely to catch lapses in the logical flow of thought. For help with twelve common writing problems, see Chapter 16, "Editing for Grammar, Punctuation, and Sentence Style."

After you have read your paper through, answer the questions for revising and editing on page 294 and make the necessary changes.

Questions for Revising and Editing: Comparison and Contrast

1. Are the subjects of my comparison comparable; that is, do they belong to the same class of items (for example, two cars, two advertisements, two landscape paintings) so that there is a clear basis for comparison?

2. Are there any complex or abstract concepts that might be clarified by using an analogy?

3. Is the purpose of my comparison clearly stated?

4. Have I presented a clear thesis statement?

5. Have I chosen my points of comparison well? Have I avoided obvious points of comparison, concentrating instead on similarities between obviously different items or differences between essentially similar items?

6. Have I developed my points of comparison in sufficient detail so that my readers can appreciate my thinking?

7. Have I chosen the best pattern — block or point-by-point — to organize my information?

8. Have I drawn a conclusion that is in line with my thesis and purpose?

9. Have I used parallel constructions correctly in my sentences?

10. Have I avoided other errors in grammar, punctuation, and mechanics? Is my sentence style as clear, smooth, and persuasive as possible?

Neat People vs. Sloppy People

SUZANNE BRITT

Born in Winston-Salem, North Carolina, Suzanne Britt now makes her home in Raleigh. She graduated from Salem College and Washington University, where she received her M.A. in English. A poet and essayist, Britt has been a columnist for the Raleigh *News and Observer* and *Stars and Stripes*, European edition. Her work appears regularly in *North Carolina Gardens and Homes*, the *New York Times*, *Newsweek*, and the *Boston Globe*. Her essays have been collected in two books, *Skinny People Are Dull and Crunchy Like Carrots* (1982) and *Show and Tell* (1982). She is the author of *A Writer's Rhetoric* (1988), a college textbook, and *Images: A Centennial Journey* (1991), a history of Meredith College, the small independent women's college in Raleigh where Britt teaches English and continues to write.

The following essay was taken from *Show and Tell*, a book Britt humorously describes as a report on her journey into "the awful cave of self: You shout your name and voices come back in exultant response, telling you their names." Here, mingling humor with a touch of seriousness, Britt examines the differences between neat and sloppy people and gives us some insights about several important personality traits.

Preparing to Read

Many people in our society are fond of comparing people, places, and things. Often, these comparisons are premature and even damaging. Consider the ways people judge others based on clothes, appearance, or hearsay. Write about a time in your life when you made such a comparison about someone or something. Did your initial judgment hold up? If not, why did it change?

've finally figured out the difference between neat people and sloppy people. The distinction is, as always, moral. Neat people are lazier and meaner than sloppy people. 1

Sloppy people, you see, are not really sloppy. Their sloppiness is merely the unfortunate consequence of their extreme moral rectitude. Sloppy people carry in their mind's eye a heavenly vision, a precise plan, that is so stupendous, so perfect, it can't be achieved in this world or the next. 2

Sloppy people live in Never-Never Land. Someday is their métier.[1] Someday they are planning to alphabetize all their books and set up home 3

---

[1] Activity or work for which a person is especially suited. — Eds.

catalogs. Someday they will go through their wardrobes and mark certain items for tentative mending and certain items for passing on to relatives of similar shape and size. Someday sloppy people will make family scrapbooks into which they will put newspaper clippings, postcards, locks of hair, and the dried corsage from their senior prom. Someday they will file everything on the surface of their desks, including the cash receipts from coffee purchases at the snack shop. Someday they will sit down and read all the back issues of *The New Yorker*.

> I've finally figured out the difference between neat people and sloppy people. The distinction is, as always, moral.

For all these noble reasons and more, sloppy people never get neat. 4 They aim too high and wide. They save everything, planning someday to file, order, and straighten out the world. But while these ambitious plans take clearer and clearer shape in their heads, the books spill from the shelves onto the floor, the clothes pile up in the hamper and closet, the family mementos accumulate in every drawer, the surface of the desk is buried under mounds of paper and the unread magazines threaten to reach the ceiling.

Sloppy people can't bear to part with anything. They give loving atten- 5 tion to every detail. When sloppy people say they're going to tackle the surface of the desk, they really mean it. Not a paper will go unturned; not a rubber band will go unboxed. Four hours or two weeks into the excavation, the desk looks exactly the same, primarily because the sloppy person is meticulously creating new piles of papers with new headings and scrupulously stopping to read all of the old book catalogs before he throws them away. A neat person would just bulldoze the desk.

Neat people are bums and clods at heart. They have cavalier attitudes 6 toward possessions, including family heirlooms. Everything is just another dust-catcher to them. If anything collects dust, it's got to go and that's that. Neat people will toy with the idea of throwing the children out of the house just to cut down on the clutter.

Neat people don't care about process. They like results. What they 7 want to do is get the whole thing over with so they can sit down and watch the rasslin' on TV. Neat people operate on two unvarying principles: Never handle any item twice, and throw everything away.

The only thing messy in a neat person's house is the trash can. 8 The minute something comes to a neat person's hand, he will look at it, try to decide if it has immediate use and, finding none, throw it in the trash.

Neat people are especially vicious with mail. They never go through 9 their mail unless they are standing directly over a trash can. If the trash can is beside the mailbox, even better. All ads, catalogs, pleas for charitable contributions, church bulletins, and money-saving coupons go straight into the trash can without being opened. All letters from home, postcards from Europe, bills, and paychecks are opened, immediately responded to, then dropped in the trash can. Neat people keep their receipts only for tax purposes. That's it. No sentimental salvaging of birthday cards or the last letter a dying relative ever wrote. Into the trash it goes.

Neat people place neatness above everything, even economics. 10 They are incredibly wasteful. Neat people throw away several toys every time they walk through the den. I knew a neat person once who threw away a perfectly good dish drainer because it had mold on it. The drainer was too much trouble to wash. And neat people sell their furniture when they move. They will sell a La-Z-Boy recliner while you are reclining in it.

Neat people are no good to borrow from. Neat people buy everything 11 in expensive little single portions. They get their flour and sugar in two-pound bags. They wouldn't consider clipping a coupon, saving a leftover, reusing plastic nondairy whipped cream containers, or rinsing off tin foil and draping it over the unmoldy dish drainer. You can never borrow a neat person's newspaper to see what's playing at the movies. Neat people have the paper all wadded up and in the trash by 7:05 A.M.

Neat people cut a clean swath through the organic as well as the inor- 12 ganic world. People, animals, and things are all one to them. They are so insensitive. After they've finished with the pantry, the medicine cabinet, and the attic, they will throw out the red geranium (too many leaves), sell the dog (too many fleas), and send the children off to boarding school (too many scuff marks on the hardwood floors).

Thinking Critically about the Text

Suzanne Britt reduces people to two types: sloppy and neat. What does she see as the defining characteristics of each type? Do you consider yourself a sloppy or a neat person? Perhaps you are neither. If this is the case, make up your own category, and explain why Britt's categories are not broad enough.

Questions on Subject

1. Why do you suppose Britt characterizes the distinction between sloppy and neat people as a "moral" one (paragraph 1)? What is she really poking fun at with this reference? (Glossary: *Irony*)

2. In your own words, what is the "heavenly vision," the "precise plan," Britt refers to in paragraph 2? How does Britt use this idea to explain why sloppy people can never be neat?

3. Exaggeration, as Britt uses it, is only effective if it is based on some shared idea of the truth. What commonly understood ideas about sloppy and neat people does Britt rely on? Do you agree with her? Why, or why not?

Questions on Strategy

1. Note Britt's use of transitions as she moves from trait to trait. (Glossary: *Transitions*) How well does she use transitions to achieve unity in her essay? Explain.

2. One of the ways Britt achieves a sense of the ridiculous in her essay is to switch the commonly accepted attributes of sloppy and neat people. Cite examples of this technique, and discuss the ways in which it adds to her essay. What does it reveal to the reader about her purpose in writing the essay? (Glossary: *Purpose*)

3. Britt uses block comparison to point out the differences between sloppy and neat people. Make a side-by-side list of the traits of sloppy and neat people. After reviewing your list, determine any ways in which sloppy and neat people may be similar. Why do you suppose Britt does not include any of the ways in which they are the same?

4. Why do you think Britt has chosen to use a block comparison? What would have been gained or lost had she used a point-by-point system of contrast?

5. Throughout the essay, Britt uses numerous examples to show the differences between sloppy and neat people. (Glossary: *Illustration*) Cite five examples that Britt uses to exemplify these points. How effective do you find Britt's use of examples? What do they add to her comparison and contrast essay?

Questions on Diction and Vocabulary

1. Cite examples of Britt's diction that indicate her change of tone when she is talking about either sloppy or neat people. (Glossary: *Diction; Tone*)

2. How would you characterize Britt's vocabulary in the essay — easy or difficult? What does her choice of vocabulary say about her intended audience? In which places does Britt use precise word choice to particularly good effect?

3. Refer to your dictionary to determine the meanings of the following words as Britt uses them in this selection: *rectitude* (paragraph 2), *tentative* (3), *meticulously* (5), *heirlooms* (6), *salvaging* (9), *swath* (12).

Classroom Activity Using Comparison and Contrast

Using the sample outlines on pages 291–92 as models, prepare both block and point-by-point outlines for one of the following topics:

1. dogs and cats as pets
2. print media and electronic media

3. an economy car and a luxury car
4. your local newspaper and the *New York Times*
5. a high school teacher and a college teacher

Explain any advantages of one organizational plan over the other.

Writing Suggestions

1. Write an essay in which you describe yourself as either sloppy or neat. In what ways does your behavior compare or contrast with the traits Britt offers? You may follow Britt's definition of sloppy and neat, or you may come up with your own.

2. Take some time to reflect on a relationship in your life — perhaps one with a friend, a family member, or a teacher. Write an essay in which you discuss what it is about you and that other person that makes the relationship work. You may find it helpful to think of a relationship that doesn't work to better understand why the relationship you're writing about does work. What discoveries about yourself did you make while working on this essay? Explain. (Glossary: *Description*)

Which Diet Works?

MARK BITTMAN

Food journalist and author Mark Bittman was born in New York City in 1950 and is a graduate of Clark University. Since 1980 he has been a professional food writer. In 1987 he was named senior writer and later editor of *Cook's Illustrated* magazine, and in 1990 he joined the staff of the *New York Times*. Bittman willingly admits that "I'm not a chef, and I never have been. And though I've cooked with some of the best-known chefs in the world, I've never had formal training, and I've never worked in a restaurant. None of which has gotten in the way of my mission to get people cooking simply, comfortably, and well." He is an avid home cook, and for thirteen years he wrote the *Times*'s "Minimalist" column on food and dining. Its popularity led to the publication of three cookbooks: *The Minimalist Cooks at Home* (2000), *The Minimalist Cooks Dinner* (2001), and *The Minimalist Entertains* (2003). In 2005 Bittman hosted two popular PBS series: *Bittman Takes on America's Chef* and *The Best Recipes in the World*. Each series later led to a successful cookbook. Bittman has also written the award-winning cookbooks *How to Cook Everything* (1998, Revised in 2008) and *How to Cook Everything Vegetarian* (2007). In 2009 Bittman published *Food Matters*, a book about food and our environmental challenges, lifestyle diseases, and overproduction and overconsumption of meat and refined carbohydrates. The following year, he published *The Food Matters Cookbook* based on those principles.

Bittman's "Which Diet Works?" was first published in his "Opinionator" column in the *New York Times* on June 26, 2012. Here he uses comparison and contrast to analyze the various merits of three widely followed diet plans. Notice how he doesn't jump to what at first appear like obvious conclusions, instead opting to listen to scientist David Ludwig's interpretation of the results.

Preparing to Read

Take a moment to reflect on your experiences with food. How would you describe your daily diet and eating habits? What types of food do you like to eat, and what motivates those choices? Do you try to eat a nutritionally balanced diet, or are you a fast-food junkie? What label best describes the foods you eat: "low-fat," "low-carb," "high-protein," or something else? If you've ever dieted or considered dieting, what was your experience like?

ne of the challenges of arguing that hyperprocessed carbohydrates are largely responsible for the obesity pandemic ("epidemic" is no longer a strong enough word, say many experts) is the notion that "a calorie is a calorie."   1

Accept that, and you buy into the contention that consuming 100 calories' worth of sugar water (like Coke or Gatorade), white bread, or French fries is the same as eating 100 calories of broccoli or beans. And Big Food—which has little interest in selling broccoli or beans—would have you believe that if you expend enough energy to work off those 100 calories, it simply doesn't matter. 2

> Big Food—which has little interest in selling broccoli or beans—would have you believe that if you expend enough energy to work off those 100 calories, [calorie type] simply doesn't matter.

There's an increasing body of evidence, however, that calories from highly processed carbohydrates like white flour (and of course sugar) provide calories that the body treats differently, spiking both blood sugar and insulin and causing us to retain fat instead of burning it off. 3

In other words, all calories are not alike. 4

You might need a little background here: To differentiate "bad" carbs from "good," scientists use the term "glycemic index" (or "load") to express the effect of the carbs on blood sugar. High-glycemic diets cause problems by dramatically increasing blood sugar and insulin after meals; low-glycemic diets don't. Highly processed carbohydrates (even highly processed whole grains, like instant oatmeal and fluffy whole-grain breads) tend to make for higher-glycemic diets; less-processed grains, fruits, non-starchy vegetables, legumes, and nuts—along with fat and protein—make for a lower-glycemic diet. 5

A new study published Tuesday in the *Journal of the American Medical Association* adds powerfully to the notion that low-glycemic diets are the way forward. (Or, actually, backward, since the low-glycemic diet is largely traditional.) The work took place at the New Balance Foundation Obesity Prevention Center of Boston Children's Hospital, and looked at people's ability to maintain weight loss, which is far more difficult than losing weight. (Few people maintain even a small portion of their weight loss after dieting.) To do this, the researchers—led by the center's associate director Cara Ebbeling and director David Ludwig—put three groups of people on diets to lose 10 to 15 percent of their body weight. 6

They then assigned each of the dieters, in random order, to follow four weeks each of three diets with the same number of calories. One was a standard low-fat diet: 60 percent carbohydrates—with an emphasis on fruits, vegetables, and whole grains (but not unprocessed ones)—20 percent from protein and 20 percent from fat. This is the low-fat diet that has been reigning "wisdom" for the last thirty years or more. 7

Another was an ultra-low-carb diet (for convenience, we'll call this 8 "Atkins"), of 10 percent of calories from carbs, 60 percent from fat, and 30 percent from protein. And the third was a low-glycemic diet, with 40 percent carbs—minimally processed grains, fruit, vegetables, and legumes—40 percent fat, and 20 percent protein.

The results were impressive. Those on the "Atkins" diet burned 350 9 calories more per day—the equivalent of an hour of moderate exercise—than those on the standard low-fat diet. Those on the low-glycemic diet burned 150 calories more, roughly equivalent to an hour of light exercise.

Three conclusions you can draw on the face of this: One is that the 10 kind of calories you eat does matter. Two, as Ludwig concludes, is that "the low-fat diet that has been the primary approach for more than a generation is actually the worst for most outcomes, with the worst effects on insulin resistance, triglycerides, and HDL, or good cholesterol." And three, we should all be eating an "Atkins" diet.

But not so fast; the "Atkins" diet also had marked problems. It raised 11 levels of CRP (c-reactive protein), which is a measure of chronic inflammation, and cortisol, a hormone that mediates stress. "Both of these," says Ludwig, "are tightly linked to long-term heart risk and mortality."

His conclusion, then? "The 'Atkins' diet gives you the biggest meta- 12 bolic benefit initially, but there are long-term downsides, and in practice, people have trouble sticking to low-carb diets. Over the long term, the low-glycemic diet appears to work the best, because you don't have to eliminate an entire class of nutrients, which our research suggests is not only hard from a psychological perspective but may be wrong from a biological perspective."

Almost every diet, from the radical no-carb-at-all notions to the tame 13 (and sane) "Healthy Eating Plate" from Harvard, agrees on at least this notion: reduce, or even come close to eliminating, the amount of hyperprocessed carbohydrates in your diet, because, quite simply, they're bad for you. And if you look at statistics, at least a quarter of our calories come from added sugars (7 percent from beverages alone), white flour, white rice, white pasta—are you seeing a pattern here? (Oh, and white potatoes. And beer.)

So what's Ludwig's overall advice? "It's time to reacquaint ourselves 14 with minimally processed carbs. If you take three servings of refined carbohydrates and substitute one of fruit, one of beans, and one of nuts, you could eliminate 50 percent of diet-related disease in the United States. These relatively modest changes can provide great benefit."

The message is pretty simple: Unprocessed foods give you a better 15 chance of idealizing your weight—and your health. Because all calories are not created equal.

Thinking Critically about the Text

Why do you think Bittman favors the low-glycemic diet? Do you agree with his conclusion? What does he mean when he talks about "minimally processed carbs" (paragraph 14)? How much of your diet consists of "hyperprocessed carbohydrates" (13), and how difficult do you think it would be to eliminate these foods from your own diet?

Questions on Subject

1. According to Bittman, what is "one of the challenges of arguing that hyperprocessed carbohydrates are largely responsible for the obesity pandemic" (paragraph 1)? How does he counter that argument?

2. What is the difference between "good" carbs and "bad" carbs? How does the human body react to these two different types of carbs? Why do you suppose Bittman felt the need to explain this difference in paragraph 5?

3. Briefly describe the three diets that the participants in the New Balance Foundation study ate. What are the key similarities and differences among the three?

4. What three conclusions does Bittman initially draw from the results of the New Balance Foundation study? How does he modify his initial conclusions?

Questions on Strategy

1. How did you react to Bittman's opening four paragraphs? Why is it important for him to establish the fact that "all calories are not alike" (paragraph 4) in his introduction? Why do you suppose Bittman chose to make paragraph 4 a one-sentence paragraph?

2. What is Bittman's purpose in writing this essay? (Glossary: *Purpose*)

3. To what end does Bittman use the new study reported in the *Journal of the American Medical Association*?

4. In paragraphs 10, 11, 12, and 14, Bittman directly quotes David Ludwig, director of the New Balance Foundation Obesity Prevention Center of Boston Children's Hospital. What does each of these quotations add to Bittman's essay? What, if anything, would have been lost had Bittman chosen to paraphrase or summarize this information in his own words? Explain.

5. How has Bittman organized his essay? (Glossary: *Organization*) You may find it helpful to outline the essay paragraph-by-paragraph to see the organizational pattern.

6. How is Bittman's conclusion related to his beginning? (Glossary: *Beginnings/ Endings*)

Questions on Diction and Vocabulary

1. What do you think Bittman means when he uses the label "Big Food" in paragraph 2? What connotations does "Big Food" have for you? Explain.

2. How would you describe Bittman's tone in this essay — serious, conversational, humorous, angry, confrontational? What about his choice of words led you to this conclusion? How did you react to his many parenthetical comments? Explain.

3. Refer to your dictionary to determine the meanings of the following words as Bittman uses them in this selection: *hyperprocessed* (paragraph 1), *pandemic* (1), *legumes* (5), *glycemic* (5), *reigning* (7), *mediates* (11), *metabolic* (12).

Classroom Activity Using Comparison and Contrast

When flu season is upon us, it is helpful to know the difference between normal cold symptoms and flu symptoms. Consider the following point-by-point comparison of the common cold and the flu from WebMD (www.webmd.com/cold-and-flu/flu-guide/is-it-cold-flu):

Symptoms	Cold	Flu
Fever	Rare	Characteristic; high (100–102 degrees F); lasts three to four days
Headache	Rare	Prominent
General Aches, pains	Slight	Usual; often severe
Fatigue, weakness	Quite mild	Can last up to two to three weeks
Extreme exhaustion	Never	Early and prominent
Stuffy nose	Common	Sometimes
Sneezing	Usual	Sometimes
Sore throat	Common	Sometimes
Chest discomfort, cough	Mild to moderate; hacking cough	Common; can become severe

What are the most important differences in symptoms between a cold and the flu? Why do you think people often confuse a cold with the flu? Did you find this chart helpful? Do you think that this visual presentation of the comparison is more or less effective than a two-paragraph discursive presentation? Explain. What, if anything, do you think could be done to enhance the chart's effectiveness?

Writing Suggestions

1. Select one of the following topics, and write an essay of comparison and contrast.

a. two restaurants		f. English muffin and bagel
b. two brands of pizza		g. fresh tuna and canned tuna
c. hot dog and bratwurst		h. sweet potato fries and onion rings
d. two desserts		i. ice cream and frozen yogurt
e. two soft drinks		

   Carefully think about your purpose in writing your essay and your organizational pattern before you start composing.

2. **Writing with Sources.** In the wake of all the media attention given to America's obesity problem and lawsuits claiming that fast-food restaurants are negligent about warning their customers about potential health problems associated with their products, what have America's fast-food chains done to improve their tarnished image and to attract customers? Have any of them made an effort to change the ingredients in their current food products? Have any of them introduced new, healthier product lines? If so, what claims are made for these modified and new products? Is it possible to get a meal that you could describe as "low-fat," "ultra-low-carb," or "low-glycemic"? Using resources that you find in your library or online as well as your own observations of fast-food restaurants, analyze the responses to public scrutiny made by a fast-food chain like Wendy's, Kentucky Fried Chicken, Dunkin' Donuts, Burger King, Krispy Kreme, McDonald's, Subway, or another chain of your choosing. You may find it helpful to visit that fast-food franchise and talk to the manager about changes in the restaurant's menu options, portion sizes, and advertising. For models of and advice on integrating sources in your essay, see Chapters 14 and 15.

3. **Writing with Sources.** What, for you, are the connotations of the words *natural*, *fresh*, *local*, and *organic*? Do you believe that these words are inherently deceptive? What do you think you are buying when you purchase a product with one or more of these words on its label? Should these words be regulated in advertisements for food products? Using advertisements for food products and/or actual text on food packaging, analyze how these words and words like them are used. Write an essay either for or against regulation, using examples from the ads or product packaging to support your position. For models of and advice on integrating sources in your essay, see Chapters 14 and 15.

Two Ways to Belong in America

BHARATI MUKHERJEE

The prominent Indian American writer and university professor Bharati Mukherjee was born into a wealthy family in Calcutta (now Kolkata), India, in 1940. Shortly after India gained its independence, her family relocated to England. In the 1950s, she returned to India, where she earned her bachelor's degree at the University of Calcutta in 1959 and a master's degree from the University of Baroda in 1961. Later she pursued her long-held desire to become a writer by earning a master of fine arts degree at the University of Iowa and eventually a doctorate in English and comparative literature. After marrying an American, Clark Blaise, she moved with her husband to Canada, where they lived for fourteen years until legislation there against South Asians led them to move back to the United States.

Before joining the faculty at the University of California, Berkeley, Mukherjee taught at McGill University, Skidmore College, Queens College, and the City University of New York. Currently her work centers on writing and the theme of immigration, particularly as it concerns women, immigration policy, and cultural alienation. With her husband, she has authored *Days and Nights in Calcutta* (1977) and *The Sorrow and the Terror: The Haunting Legacy of the Air India Tragedy* (1987). In addition, she has published eight novels, including *The Tiger's Daughter* (1971), *Wife* (1975), *Darkness* (1985), *Jasmine* (1989), *The Holder of the World* (1993), *The Tree Bride* (2004), and *Miss New India* (2011); two collections of short stories, *Darkness* (1985) and *The Middleman and Other Stories* (1988), for which she won the National Book Critics Circle Award; and two works of nonfiction, *Political Culture and Leadership in India* (1991) and *Regionalism in Indian Perspective* (1992).

The following essay was first published in the *New York Times* in 1996 in response to new legislation championed by then–vice president Al Gore, which provided for expedited routes to citizenship for legal immigrants living in the United States. As you read Mukherjee's essay, notice the way she has organized the contrasting views she and her sister have toward various aspects of living as either a legal immigrant or a citizen.

Preparing to Read

The word *immigrant* has many connotations. What associations does the word have for you? If you were to move to another country, how do you think it would feel to be considered an immigrant?

This is a tale of two sisters from Calcutta, Mira and Bharati, who have lived in the United States for some thirty-five years, but who find themselves on different sides in the current debate over the status of immigrants. I am an American citizen and she is not. I am moved that thousands of long-term residents are finally taking the oath of citizenship. She is not.

Mira arrived in Detroit in 1960 to study child psychology and preschool education. I followed her a year later to study creative writing at the University of Iowa. When we left India, we were almost identical in appearance and attitude. We dressed alike, in saris; we expressed identical views on politics, social issues, love, and marriage in the same Calcutta convent-school accent. We would endure our two years in America, secure our degrees, then return to India to marry the grooms of our father's choosing.

Instead, Mira married an Indian student in 1962 who was getting his business administration degree at Wayne State University. They soon acquired the labor certifications necessary for the green card of hassle-free residence and employment.

Mira still lives in Detroit, works in the Southfield, Michigan, school system, and has become nationally recognized for her contributions in the fields of preschool education and parent-teacher relationships. After thirty-six years as a legal immigrant in this country, she clings passionately to her Indian citizenship and hopes to go home to India when she retires.

In Iowa City in 1963, I married a fellow student, an American of Canadian parentage. Because of the accident of his North Dakota birth, I bypassed labor-certification requirements and the race-related "quota" system that favored the applicant's country of origin over his or her merit. I was prepared for (and even welcomed) the emotional strain that came with marrying outside my ethnic community. In thirty-three years of marriage, we have lived in every part of North America. By choosing a husband who was not my father's selection, I was opting for fluidity, self-invention, blue jeans, and T-shirts, and renouncing three thousand years (at least) of caste-observant, "pure culture" marriage in the Mukherjee family. My books have often been read as unapologetic (and in some quarters overenthusiastic) texts for cultural and psychological "mongrelization." It's a word I celebrate.

Mira and I have stayed sisterly close by phone. In our regular Sunday morning conversations, we are unguardedly affectionate. I am her only blood relative on this continent. We expect to see each other through the looming crises of aging and ill health without being asked. Long before Vice President Gore's "Citizenship USA" drive, we'd had our polite arguments over the ethics of retaining an overseas citizenship while expecting the permanent protection and economic benefits that come with living and working in America.

Like well-raised sisters, we never said what was really on our minds, 7
but we probably pitied one another. She, for the lack of structure in my
life, the erasure of Indianness, the absence of an unvarying daily core. I, for
the narrowness of her perspective, her uninvolvement with the mythic
depths or the superficial pop culture of this society. But, now, with the
scapegoating of "aliens" (documented or illegal) on the increase, and the
targeting of long-term legal immigrants like Mira for new scrutiny and new
self-consciousness, she and I find ourselves unable to maintain the same
polite discretion. We were always unacknowledged adversaries, and we are
now, more than ever, sisters.

"I feel used," Mira raged on the phone the other night. "I feel manipu- 8
lated and discarded. This is such an unfair way to treat a person who
was invited to stay and work here because of her talent. My employer
went to the INS and petitioned for the labor certification. For over thirty
years, I've invested my creativity and professional skills into the improvement of *this* country's preschool system. I've obeyed all the rules, I've paid
my taxes, I love my work, I love my students, I love the friends I've made.
How dare America now change its rules in midstream? If America wants
to make new rules curtailing benefits of legal immigrants, they should
apply only to immigrants who arrive after those rules are already in place."

To my ears, it sounded like the description of a long-enduring, com- 9
fortable yet loveless marriage, without risk or recklessness. Have we the
right to demand, and to expect, that we be loved? (That, to me, is the
subtext of the arguments by immigration advocates.) My sister is an expatriate, professionally generous and creative, socially courteous and gracious, and that's as far as her Americanization can go. She is here to
maintain an identity, not to transform it.

I asked her if she would follow the example of others who have decided 10
to become citizens because of the anti-immigration bills in Congress. And
here, she surprised me. "If America wants to play the manipulative game,
I'll play it, too," she snapped. "I'll become a U.S. citizen for now, then
change back to Indian when I'm ready to go home. I feel some kind of
irrational attachment to India that I don't to America. Until all this hysteria
against legal immigrants, I was totally happy. Having my green card meant
I could visit any place in the world I wanted to and then come back to a job
that's satisfying and that I do very well."

In one family, from two sisters alike as peas in a pod, there could not 11
be a wider divergence of immigrant experience. America spoke to me — I
married it — I embraced the demotion from expatriate aristocrat to immigrant nobody, surrendering those thousands of years of "pure culture," the
saris, the delightfully accented English. She retained them all. Which of us
is the freak?

Mira's voice, I realize, is the voice not just of the immigrant South 12
Asian community but of an immigrant community of the millions who
have stayed rooted in one job, one city, one house, one ancestral culture,
one cuisine, for the entirety of their productive years. She speaks for greater
numbers than I possibly can. Only the fluency of her English and the anger, rather
than fear, born of confidence from her education, differentiate her from the seamstresses, the domestics, the technicians, the shop owners, the millions of hardworking but effectively silenced documented immigrants as well as their less fortunate "illegal" brothers and sisters.

> I embraced the demotion from expatriate aristocrat to immigrant nobody, surrendering those thousands of years of "pure culture," the saris, the delightfully accented English.

Nearly twenty years ago, when I was liv- 13
ing in my husband's ancestral homeland of Canada, I was always well-employed but never allowed to feel part of the local Quebec or larger Canadian society. Then, through a Green Paper that invited a national referendum on the unwanted side effects of
"nontraditional" immigration, the government officially turned against its
immigrant communities, particularly those from South Asia.

I felt then the same sense of betrayal that Mira feels now. I will never 14
forget the pain of that sudden turning, and the casual racist outbursts the
Green Paper elicited. That sense of betrayal had its desired effect and
drove me, and thousands like me, from the country.

Mira and I differ, however, in the ways in which we hope to interact 15
with the country that we have chosen to live in. She is happier to live in
America as an expatriate Indian than as an immigrant American. I need to
feel like a part of the community I have adopted (as I tried to feel in Canada
as well). I need to put roots down, to vote and make the difference that I
can. The price that the immigrant willingly pays, and that the exile avoids,
is the trauma of self-transformation.

Thinking Critically about the Text

What do you think Mukherjee's sister means when she says in paragraph 10, "If
America wants to play the manipulative game, I'll play it, too"? How do you react
to her plans? Explain.

Questions on Subject

1. What is Mukherjee's thesis? (Glossary: *Thesis*) Where does she present it?

2. What arguments does Mukherjee make for becoming an American citizen? What arguments does her sister make for retaining Indian citizenship?

3. Why do you think Mukherjee's sister feels "used" by attempts to change American laws regarding benefits for legal noncitizens?

4. At the end of paragraph 11, Mukherjee asks a question. How does she answer it? How would you answer it?

5. What does Mukherjee mean when she says, "The price that the immigrant willingly pays, and that the exile avoids, is the trauma of self-transformation" (paragraph 15)?

6. In your eyes, which sister made the right decision? Explain.

Questions on Strategy

1. How has Mukherjee organized her essay? Is it block comparison, point-by-point comparison, or some combination of the two?

2. Why is the pattern of organization that Mukherjee uses appropriate for her subject and purpose? (Glossary: *Purpose; Subject*)

3. Mukherjee chooses to let her sister, Mira, speak for herself in this essay. What do you think would have been lost had Mukherjee simply reported what Mira felt and believed? Explain.

Questions on Diction and Vocabulary

1. Mukherjee uses the word *mongrelization* in paragraph 5. What do you think she means by this word, and why does she "celebrate" it?

2. Mukherjee uses quotation marks around a number of words — "quota" (paragraph 5), "pure culture" (5, 11), "aliens" (7), "illegal" (12), "nontraditional" (13). What does she gain by using the quotation marks?

3. How does Mukherjee use "marriage" to describe the essential differences between Mira's and her relationship to America?

4. Refer to your dictionary to determine the meanings of the following words as Mukherjee uses them in this selection: *caste* (paragraph 5), *ethics* (6), *scapegoating* (7), *subtext* (9), *expatriate* (15).

Classroom Activity Using Comparison and Contrast

Consider the cartoon on page 311.

How is it possible for two people with similar backgrounds to have completely different views about something? And why are we so fascinated by differences when we were expecting similarities or by similarities when we were expecting differences? Explain.

"Conversation? I thought we were just meeting for coffee."

Writing Suggestions

1. Mukherjee writes about her relationship with her sister by saying, "[W]e never said what was really on our minds, but we probably pitied one another" (paragraph 7). Such differences are often played out on a larger scale when immigrants who assimilate into American life are confronted by those who choose to retain their ethnic identity; these tensions can lead to name-calling and even aggressive prejudice within immigrant communities. Write an essay about an ethnic or cultural community you are familiar with, comparing and contrasting lifestyle choices its members make as they try to find a comfortable place in American society.

2. Mukherjee presents her sister's reasons for not becoming a citizen and supports them with statements that her sister has made. Imagine that you are Mira Mukherjee. Write a counterargument to the argument presented by Bharati, giving your reasons for remaining an Indian citizen. Remember that you have already broken with tradition by marrying a man not of your "father's choosing" and that the "trauma of self-transformation" that Bharati raises in the conclusion of her essay is much deeper and more complicated than she has represented it to be. Can you say that you are holding to tradition when you are not? Can you engage in a challenging self-transformation if it is not genuinely motivated?

The Difference between "Sick" and "Evil"

ANDREW VACHSS

Crime fiction writer and attorney Andrew Vachss was born in New York City in 1942. He received his B.A. from Case Western Reserve University in 1965. Before graduating from the New England School of Law in 1975, Vachss held a number of positions all related to child protection, ranging from a New York City social services caseworker to director of a maximum-security prison for aggressive violent juvenile offenders. As a lawyer, he exclusively represents children and youths. He also serves as a child protection consultant. Vachss has written more than twenty-five novels, two collections of short stories, three plays, and two works of nonfiction. He is perhaps best known as the author of the award-winning Burke series of hard-boiled crime mysteries. The central character, an unlicensed investigator named Burke, is an ex-con and a deeply conflicted person. Vachss describes him as "the prototypical abused child: hypervigilant, distrustful. He's so committed to his family of choice — not his DNA-biological family, which tortured him, or the state which raised him, but to the family he chose — that homicide is a natural consequence of injuring of that family." Vachss lectures widely on issues relating to child protection and has written articles on the subject for *Esquire*, *Playboy*, the *New York Times*, and *Parade*. He is also a founder and national advisory board member of PROTECT: The National Association to Protect Children.

In the following article, which first appeared in *Parade* on July 14, 2002, Andrew Vachss issues a call to action to protect America's children in the wake of the pedophile priest scandal. Here he asks the fundamental question: "Are those who abuse their positions of trust to prey upon children — a category certainly not limited to those in religious orders — sick . . . or are they evil?" To answer this question, Vachss believes that we need to establish a clear understanding of the differences between the words *sick* and *evil*, two words that the public often uses synonymously.

Preparing to Read

How do you define *evil*? What kinds of behavior or things do you use the word *evil* to describe? Identify several historical figures whom you consider evil, and briefly describe what makes them evil.

T he shock waves caused by the recent exposures of so-called "pedophile priests" have reverberated throughout America. But beneath our anger and revulsion, a fundamental question pulsates: Are those who abuse their positions of trust to prey upon children—a category certainly not limited to those in religious orders—sick . . . or are they evil?

We need the answer to that fundamental question. Because, without the truth, we cannot act. And until we act, nothing will change.

My job is protecting children. It has taken me from big cities to rural outposts, from ghettos to penthouses, and from courtrooms to genocidal battlefields. But whatever the venue, the truth remains constant: Some humans intentionally hurt children. They commit unspeakable acts—for their pleasure, their profit, or both.

Many people who hear of my cases against humans who rape, torture, and package children for sale or rent immediately respond with, "That's sick!" Crimes against children seem so grotesquely abnormal that the most obvious explanation is that the perpetrator must be mentally ill—helpless in the grip of a force beyond his or her control.

But that very natural reaction has, inadvertently, created a special category of "blameless predator." That confusion of "sick" with "sickening" is the single greatest barrier to our primary biological and ethical mandate: the protection of our children.

The difference between sick and evil cannot be dismissed with facile eye-of-the-beholder rhetoric. There are specific criteria we can employ to give us the answers in every case, every time.

Sickness is a condition. Evil is a behavior. Evil is a matter of choice.

Some of those answers are self-evident and beyond dispute: A mother who puts her baby in the oven because she hears voices commanding her to bake the devil out of the child's spirit is sick; and a mother who sells or rents her baby to child pornographers is evil. But most cases of child sexual abuse—especially those whose "nonviolent" perpetrators come from within the child's circle of trust—seem, on their surface, to be far more complex.

That complexity is an illusion. The truth is as simple as it is terrifying:

Sickness is a condition.

Evil is a behavior.

Evil is always a matter of choice. Evil is not thought; it is conduct. And that conduct is always volitional.

And just as evil is always a choice, sickness is always the absence of choice. Sickness happens. Evil is inflicted.

Until we perceive the difference clearly, we will continue to give aid and comfort to our most pernicious enemies. We, as a society, decide whether something is sick or evil. Either decision confers an obligation upon us. Sickness should be treated. Evil must be fought.

If a person has desires or fantasies about sexually exploiting children, that individual may be sick. (Indeed, if such desires are disturbing, as opposed to gratifying, to the individual, there may even be a "cure.") But if the individual chooses to act upon those feelings, that conduct is evil. People are not what they think; they are what they do. 14

Our society distrusts the term *evil*. It has an almost biblical ring to it—something we believe in (or not), but never actually understand. We prefer scientific-sounding terms, such as *sociopath*. But sociopathy is not a mental condition; it is a specific cluster of behaviors. The diagnosis is only made from actual criminal conduct. 15

No reputable psychiatrist claims to be able to cure a sociopath—or, for that matter, a predatory pedophile. Even the most optimistic professionals do not aim to change such a person's thoughts and feelings. What they hope is that the predator can learn self-control, leading to a change in behavior. 16

Such hopes ignore the inescapable fact that the overwhelming majority of those who prey upon children don't want to change their behavior—they want only to minimize the consequences of being caught at it. 17

In the animal kingdom, there is a food chain—predators and prey. But among humans, there is no such natural order. Among our species, predators select themselves for that role. 18

Psychology has given us many insights of great value. But it has also clouded our vision with euphemisms. To say a person suffers from the "disease" of pedophilia is to absolve the predator of responsibility for his behavior. 19

Imagine if an attorney, defending someone accused of committing a dozen holdups, told the jury his poor client was suffering from "armed-robberia." That jury would decide that the only crazy person in the courtroom was the lawyer. 20

When a perpetrator claims to be sick, the *timing* of that claim is critical to discovering the truth. Predatory pedophiles carefully insinuate themselves into positions of trust. They select their prey and approach cautiously. Gradually, sometimes over a period of years, they gain greater control over their victims. Eventually, they leave dozens of permanently damaged children in their wake. 21

But only when they are caught do predatory pedophiles declare themselves to be sick. And the higher the victim count, the sicker (and, therefore less responsible), they claim to be. 22

In too many cases, a veil of secrecy and protection then descends. The predator's own organization appoints itself judge and jury. The perpetrator is deemed sick, and sent off for in-house "treatment." The truth is never made public. And when some secret tribunal decides a cure has been achieved, the perpetrator's rights and privileges are restored, and he or she is given a new assignment. 23

In fact, such privileged predators actually are assisted. They enter new 24
communities with the blessing of their own organization, their history and
propensities kept secret. As a direct result, unsuspecting parents entrust
their children to them. Inevitably, the predator eventually resumes his or
her conduct and preys upon children again. And when that conduct comes
to light, the claim of "sickness" re-emerges as well.

Too often, our society contorts itself to excuse such predators. We 25
are so eager to call those who sexually abuse children "sick," so quick to
understand their demons. Why? Because sickness not only offers the possibility of finding a cure but also assures us that the predator didn't really
mean it. After all, it is human nature to try to understand inhuman
conduct.

Conversely, the concept of evil terrifies us. The idea that some humans 26
choose to prey upon our children is frightening, and their demonstrated
skill at camouflage only heightens this fear.

For some, the question, "Does evil exist?" is philosophical. But for 27
those who have confronted or been victimized by predatory pedophiles,
there is no question at all. We are what we do.

Just as conduct is a choice, so is our present helplessness. We may be 28
powerless to change the arrogance of those who believe they alone should
have the power to decide whether predatory pedophiles are "sick," or
when they are "cured." But, as with the perpetrators themselves, we do
have the power to change their behavior.

In every state, laws designate certain professions that regularly come 29
into contact with children—such as teachers, doctors, social workers, and
day-care employees—as "mandated reporters." Such personnel are required to report reasonable suspicion of child abuse when it comes to their
attention. Failure to do so is a crime.

Until now, we have exempted religious organizations from mandated- 30
reporter laws. Recent events have proven the catastrophic consequences of
this exemption. We must demand—now—that our legislators close this
pathway to evil.

A predatory pedophile who is recycled into an unsuspecting commu- 31
nity enters it cloaked with a protection no other sex offender enjoys. If
members of religious orders were mandated reporters, we would not have
to rely on their good-faith belief that a predator is cured. We could make
our own informed decisions on this most vital issue.

Modifying the law in this way would not interfere with priest-penitent 32
privileges: When child victims or their parents disclose abuse, they are not
confessing, they are crying for help. Neither confidentiality nor religious
freedom would in any way be compromised by mandatory reporting.

Changing the laws so that religious orders join the ranks of mandated 33
reporters is the right thing to do. And the time is right now.

Thinking Critically about the Text

Vachss believes that "our society distrusts the term *evil*" (paragraph 15). Do you agree? Why is the concept of evil such a difficult one to understand when it comes to human behavior?

Questions on Subject

1. What question does Vachss ask in his opening paragraph? Why does he believe that it is important for us to find an answer?

2. What for Vachss is the essential difference between "sick" and "evil"? What criteria does he offer to help his readers understand the difference? How does the public's confusion with "sick" and "sickening" muddy the waters?

3. What does Vachss mean when he says that "psychology has given us many insights of great value. But it has also clouded our vision with euphemisms" (paragraph 19)?

4. Why does Vachss believe that the "timing" of one's claim to be sick is critical to uncovering the truth (paragraph 21)?

5. Why does Vachss believe that people are so willing to call sex offenders sick instead of evil? Do you agree? What is the danger of letting evil pass as a sickness?

6. What action does Vachss want his readers to take after reading his article? Did you find Vachss's argument compelling? Why, or why not?

Questions on Strategy

1. What is Vachss's thesis, and where is it stated? (Glossary: *Thesis*)

2. What experience or expertise qualifies Vachss to write about this subject?

3. What is Vachss's purpose in writing this essay? (Glossary: *Purpose*) How do you know?

4. How does Vachss develop the essential differences between "sick" and "evil" in paragraphs 6 through 14? How effectively does he use examples to illustrate these differences? (Glossary: *Illustration*)

5. In paragraph 20, Vachss uses the analogy of a lawyer defending a robber to give his readers insight into the "'disease' of pedophilia" presented in the previous paragraph. How effective or convincing do you find his analogy? (Glossary: *Analogy*)

6. Why do you suppose Vachss devotes so much space to discussing the concept of "evil" when he discusses evil behavior?

Questions on Diction and Vocabulary

1. Vachss adds interest and vitality to his opening two sentences with the strong action verbs *reverberated* and *pulsates*. (Glossary: *Verb*) Identify other strong

verbs that Vachss uses and explain what they add to the appeal of his writing.

2. In paragraph 5, Vachss uses the oxymoron "blameless predator" as a label for perpetrators who are somehow excused by society for their crimes because they are mentally ill. How did you react when you first read about the blameless predators we have inadvertently created? What does Vachss find inherently wrong about the concept of a predator who is deemed blameless? Explain.

3. Refer to your dictionary to determine the meanings of the following words as Vachss uses them in this selection: *revulsion* (paragraph 1), *venue* (3), *mandate* (5), *facile* (6), *pernicious* (13), *sociopath* (15), *insinuate* (21), *propensities* (24).

Classroom Activity Using Comparison and Contrast

After reviewing the discussion of analogy in the introduction to this chapter (pages 283–84) and Vachss's analogy in paragraphs 18–20, create an analogy to explain one of the following:

1. your relationship with one of your teachers or coaches
2. the essence of a game that you enjoy playing
3. a scientific or sociological principle or idea
4. a creative activity such as writing, weaving, painting, or composing music

Share your analogy with other members of your class, and discuss how well the analogies work.

Writing Suggestions

1. As Vachss demonstrates in his discussion of "sick" and "evil," important decisions and actions hinge on establishing a clear understanding of the similarities and/or differences in the terminology that we use. Using his essay as a model, write an essay in which you compare and contrast one of the following pairs of terms or a pair of your own choosing:

smart and intelligent	professional and amateur	normal and abnormal
weird and eccentric	manager and leader	public and private

2. What is your position on capital punishment? Who has the right to take the life of another? Ideally, knowing what the punishment will be should deter people from doing the wrong thing in the first place, but does the death penalty really act as a deterrent? Are certain punishments more effective as deterrents than others? In this context, consider the message in the cartoon on page 318, which highlights the great irony that is inherent in capital punishment. Write an essay in which you compare and contrast the arguments for and against the death penalty.

"Maybe this will teach you that it's morally wrong to kill people!"

3. **Writing with Sources.** For more than three decades, lawyer Andrew Vachss has advocated for children victimized by adult predators. His article in *Parade* on July 14, 2002, was written in response to the handling of the so-called pedophile priests in America. However, as Vachss points out, there are other instances of people who intentionally hurt children, people who "rape, torture, and package children for sale or rent." In your library or online, research one such case that has recently been in the news. What was the nature of the crime against the children? Would you label the perpetrator "sick" or "evil"? Why? How was the perpetrator of the crime punished? Do you agree with the way the perpetrator was handled? Write an essay in which you report your findings. For models of and advice on integrating sources in your essay, see Chapters 14 and 15.

Grant and Lee: A Study in Contrasts

BRUCE CATTON

Arguably the most prolific and popular Civil War historian, Bruce Catton (1899–1978) was born in Petoskey, Michigan, and attended Oberlin College. Early in his career, Catton worked as a reporter for various newspapers, among them the *Cleveland Plain Dealer.* His interest in history led him to write about the Civil War. His books on the subject include *Mr. Lincoln's Army* (1951), *Glory Road* (1952), *A Stillness at Appomattox* (1953), *This Hallowed Ground* (1956), *The Coming Fury* (1961), *Never Call Retreat* (1965), and *Gettysburg: The Final Fury* (1974). Catton won both the Pulitzer Prize and the National Book Award in 1954. A fellow historian once wrote, "There is a near-magic power of imagination in Catton's work that seem[s] to project him physically into the battlefields, along the dusty roads, and to the campfires of another age."

The following selection was included in *The American Story,* a collection of historical essays edited by Earl Schenk Miers. In this essay, Catton considers "two great Americans, Grant and Lee — very different, yet under everything very much alike."

Preparing to Read

What do you know about America's Civil War and the roles played by Ulysses S. Grant and Robert E. Lee in that monumental struggle? For you, what does each of these men represent? Do you consider either of them to be an American hero? Explain.

When Ulysses S. Grant and Robert E. Lee met in the parlor of a modest house at Appomattox Court House, Virginia, on April 9, 1865, to work out the terms for the surrender of Lee's Army of Northern Virginia, a great chapter in American life came to a close, and a great new chapter began.

These men were bringing the Civil War to its virtual finish. To be sure, other armies had yet to surrender, and for a few days the fugitive Confederate government would struggle desperately and vainly, trying to find some way to go on living now that its chief support was gone. But in effect it was all over when Grant and Lee signed the papers. And the little room where they wrote out the terms was the scene of one of the poignant, dramatic contrasts in American history.

They were two strong men, these oddly different generals, and they represented the strengths of two conflicting currents that, through them, had come into final collision.

Back of Robert E. Lee was the notion that the old aristocratic concept might somehow survive and be dominant in American life.

Lee was tidewater Virginia, and in his background were family, culture, and tradition . . . the age of chivalry transplanted to a New World which was making its own legends and its own myths. He embodied a way of life that had come down through the age of knighthood and the English country squire. America was a land that was beginning all over again, dedicated to nothing much more complicated than the rather hazy belief that all men had equal rights and should have an equal chance in the world. In such a land Lee stood for the feeling that it was somehow of advantage to human society to have a pronounced inequality in the social structure. There should be a leisure class, backed by ownership of land; in turn, society itself should be keyed to the land as the chief source of wealth and influence. It would bring forth (according to this ideal) a class of men with a strong sense of obligation to the community; men who lived not to gain advantage for themselves, but to meet the solemn obligations which had been laid on them by the very fact that they were privileged. From them the country would get its leadership;

Robert E. Lee

to them it could look for the higher values—of thought, of conduct, of personal deportment—to give it strength and value.

Lee embodied the noblest elements of this aristocratic ideal. Through 6
him, the landed nobility justified itself. For four years, the Southern states had fought a desperate war to uphold the ideals for which Lee stood. In the end, it almost seemed as if the Confederacy fought for Lee; as if he himself was the Confederacy . . . the best thing that the way of life for which the Confederacy stood could ever have to offer. He had passed into legend before Appomattox. Thousands of tired, underfed, poorly clothed Confederate soldiers, long since past the simple enthusiasm of the early days of the struggle, somehow considered Lee the symbol of everything for which they had been willing to die. But they could not quite put this feeling into words. If the Lost Cause, sanctified by so much heroism and so many deaths, had a living justification, its justification was General Lee.

> They were two strong men, these oddly different generals, and they represented the strengths of two conflicting currents that, through them, had come into final collision.

Grant, the son of a tanner on the Western frontier, was everything Lee 7
was not. He had come up the hard way and embodied nothing in particular except the eternal toughness and sinewy fiber of the men who grew up beyond the mountains. He was one of a body of men who owed reverence and obeisance to no one, who were self-reliant to a fault, who cared hardly anything for the past but who had a sharp eye for the future.

These frontier men were the precise opposite of the tidewater aristo- 8
crats. Back of them, in the great surge that had taken people over the Alleghenies and into the opening Western country, there was a deep, implicit dissatisfaction with a past that had settled into grooves. They stood for democracy, not from any reasoned conclusion about the proper ordering of human society, but simply because they had grown up in the middle of democracy and knew how it worked. Their society might have privileges, but they would be privileges each man had won for himself. Forms and patterns meant nothing. No man was born to anything, except perhaps to a chance to show how far he could rise. Life was competition.

Yet along with this feeling had come a deep sense of belonging to a 9
national community. The Westerner who developed a farm, opened a shop, or set up in business as a trader, could hope to prosper only as his own community prospered—and his community ran from the Atlantic to the Pacific and from Canada down to Mexico. If the land was settled, with

Ulysses S. Grant

towns and highways and accessible markets, he could better himself. He
saw his fate in terms of the nation's own destiny. As its horizons expanded,
so did his. He had, in other words, an acute dollars-and-cents stake in the
continued growth and development of his country.

And that, perhaps, is where the contrast between Grant and Lee   10
becomes most striking. The Virginia aristocrat, inevitably, saw himself in
relation to his own region. He lived in a static society which could endure
almost anything except change. Instinctively, his first loyalty would go to
the locality in which that society existed. He would fight to the limit of
endurance to defend it, because in defending it he was defending everything that gave his own life its deepest meaning.

The Westerner, on the other hand, would fight with an equal tenacity   11
for the broader concept of society. He fought so because everything he
lived by was tied to growth, expansion and a constantly widening horizon.
What he lived by would survive or fall with the nation itself. He could not
possibly stand by unmoved in the face of an attempt to destroy the Union.
He would combat it with everything he had, because he could only see it
as an effort to cut the ground out from under his feet.

So Grant and Lee were in complete contrast, representing two dia- 12
metrically opposed elements in American life. Grant was the modern man
emerging; beyond him, ready to come on the stage, was the great age of
steel and machinery, of crowded cities and a restless burgeoning vitality.
Lee might have ridden down from the old age of chivalry, lance in hand,
silken banner fluttering over his head. Each man was the perfect champion of his cause, drawing both his strengths and his weaknesses from the
people he led.

Yet it was not all contrast, after all. Different as they were—in back- 13
ground, in personality, in underlying aspiration—these two great soldiers
had much in common. Under everything else, they were marvelous fight-
ers. Furthermore, their fighting qualities were really very much alike.

Each man had, to begin with, the great virtue of utter tenacity and 14
fidelity. Grant fought his way down the Mississippi Valley in spite of acute
personal discouragement and profound military handicaps. Lee hung on in
the trenches at Petersburg after hope itself had died. In each man there
was an indomitable quality . . . the born fighter's refusal to give up as long
as he can still remain on his feet and lift his two fists.

Daring and resourcefulness they had, too; the ability to think faster 15
and move faster than the enemy. These were the qualities which gave Lee
the dazzling campaigns of Second Manassas and Chancellorsville and won
Vicksburg for Grant.

Lastly, and perhaps greatest of all, there was the ability, at the end, 16
to turn quickly from war to peace once the fighting was over. Out of
the way these two men behaved at Appomattox came the possibility of a
peace of reconciliation. It was a possibility not wholly realized, in the
years to come, but which did, in the end, help the two sections to become
one nation again . . . after a war whose bitterness might have seemed
to make such a reunion wholly impossible. No part of either man's
life became him more than the part he played in their brief meeting in
the McLean house at Appomattox. Their behavior there put all succeeding generations of Americans in their debt. Two great Americans, Grant
and Lee—very different, yet under everything very much alike. Their
encounter at Appomattox was one of the great moments of American
history.

Thinking Critically about the Text

Catton concludes with the claim that Grant and Lee's "encounter at Appomattox
was one of the great moments of American history" (paragraph 16). How does
Catton prepare readers for this claim? What, for Catton, do these two Civil War
generals represent, and what does he see as the implications for the country of
Lee's surrender?

Questions on Subject

1. In paragraphs 10–12, Catton discusses what he considers to be the most striking contrast between Grant and Lee. What is that difference?

2. List the similarities that Catton sees between Grant and Lee. Which similarity does Catton believe is most important? Why?

3. What attitudes and ideas does Catton describe to support his view that the culture of tidewater Virginia was a throwback to the "age of chivalry" (paragraph 5)?

4. Catton says that Grant was "the modern man emerging" (paragraph 12). How does he support that statement? Do you agree?

Questions on Strategy

1. What would have been lost had Catton looked at the similarities between Grant and Lee before looking at the differences? Would anything have been gained?

2. How does Catton organize the body of his essay (paragraphs 3–16)? When answering this question, you may find it helpful to summarize the point of comparison in each paragraph and to label whether the paragraph concerns Lee, Grant, or both. (Glossary: *Organization*)

3. Catton makes clear transitions between paragraphs. Identify the transitional devices he uses to lead readers from one paragraph to the next throughout the essay. As a reader, how do these transitions help you? (Glossary: *Transitions*) Explain.

4. How does Catton use both description and cause and effect analysis to enhance his comparison and contrast of Grant and Lee? In what ways does description serve to sharpen the differences between these generals? How does Catton use cause and effect analysis to explain their respective natures? Cite several examples of Catton's use of each strategy to illustrate your answer. (Glossary: *Cause and Effect Analysis; Description*)

Questions on Diction and Vocabulary

1. Identify at least two metaphors that Catton uses, and explain what each contributes to his comparison. (Glossary: *Figures of Speech*)

2. Refer to your dictionary to determine the meanings of the following words as Catton uses them in this selection: *poignant* (paragraph 2), *chivalry* (5), *sanctified* (6), *sinewy* (7), *obeisance* (7), *tidewater* (8), *tenacity* (11), *aspiration* (13).

Classroom Activity Using Comparison and Contrast

Carefully read the following paragraphs from Stephen E. Ambrose's book *Crazy Horse and Custer: The Parallel Lives of Two American Warriors* (1975) and then answer the questions that follow.

> It was bravery, above and beyond all other qualities, that Custer and Crazy Horse had in common. Each man was an outstanding warrior in war-mad societies. Thousands upon thousands of Custer's fellow whites had as much opportunity as he did to demonstrate their courage, just as all of Crazy Horse's associates had countless opportunities to show that they equaled him in bravery. But no white warrior, save his younger brother, Tom, could outdo Custer, just as no Indian warrior, save his younger brother, Little Hawk, could outdo Crazy Horse. And for both white and red societies, no masculine virtue was more admired than bravery. To survive, both societies felt they had to have men willing to put their lives on the line. For men who were willing to do so, no reward was too great, even though there were vast differences in the way each society honored its heroes.
>
> Beyond their bravery, Custer and Crazy Horse were individualists, each standing out from the crowd in his separate way. Custer wore outlandish uniforms, let his hair fall in long, flowing golden locks across his shoulders, surrounded himself with pet animals and admirers, and in general did all he could to draw attention to himself. Crazy Horse's individualism pushed him in the opposite direction — he wore a single feather in his hair when going into battle, rather than a war bonnet. Custer's vast energy set him apart from most of his fellows; the Sioux distinguished Crazy Horse from other warriors because of Crazy Horse's quietness and introspection. Both men lived in societies in which drugs, especially alcohol, were widely used, but neither Custer nor Crazy Horse drank. Most of all, of course, each man stood out in battle as a great risk taker.

What is Ambrose's point in these two paragraphs? How does he use comparison and contrast to make this point? How has he organized his paragraphs?

Writing Suggestions

1. Catton gives readers few details of the physical appearance of Grant and Lee, but the portraits that accompany this essay do show us what these men looked like. (For a discussion of how to analyze photographs and other visual texts, see pages 15–19.) Write a brief essay in which you compare and contrast the men you see in the portraits. How closely does your assessment of each general match the "picture" Catton presents in his essay? How would you describe the appearance — both dress and posture — of these two generals? What details in the photographs are most telling for you? Explain why. In what ways can Grant and Lee be said to represent the way of life associated with the side each commanded? Explain.

2. In the persons of Grant and Lee, Catton sees the "final collision" (paragraph 3) between two ways of living and thinking — the "age of steel and machinery" (12) conquering the "age of chivalry" (5). As we approach the 150th anniversary of the conclusion to the Civil War, what do you see as the dominant ways of living and thinking in the current "age of information"? Do today's lifestyles appear to be on a collision course with one another, or do you think they can coexist? Write an essay in which you present your position and defend it using appropriate examples.

3. **Writing with Sources.** Write an essay in which you compare and contrast two world leaders, sports figures, or celebrities whose careers have at some point crossed in a dramatic or decisive way. Examples include Hillary Rodham Clinton and Barack Obama; Ronald Reagan and Mikhail Gorbachev; Serena Williams and Maria Sharapova; Brad Pitt and Angelina Jolie; Marilyn Monroe and Joe DiMaggio; Taylor Swift and Justin Bieber. Use library resources and the Internet to research your two famous people. For models of and advice on integrating sources in your essay, see Chapters 14 and 15.

WRITING SUGGESTIONS FOR COMPARISON AND CONTRAST

1. Write an essay in which you compare and contrast two objects, people, or events to show at least one of the following.

   a. their important differences
   b. their significant similarities
   c. their relative value
   d. their distinctive qualities

2. Select a topic from the list that follows. Write an essay using comparison and contrast as your primary means of development. Be sure that your essay has a definite purpose and a clear direction.

   a. two methods of dieting
   b. two television situation comedies
   c. two types of summer employment
   d. two people who display different attitudes toward responsibility
   e. two restaurants
   f. two courses in the same subject area
   g. two friends who exemplify different lifestyles
   h. two network television or local news programs
   i. two professional quarterbacks
   j. two ways of studying for an exam
   k. two rooms in which you have classes
   l. two of your favorite magazines
   m. two attitudes toward death
   n. two ways to heat a home

3. Use one of the following "before and after" situations as the basis for an essay of comparison and contrast.

   a. before and after an examination
   b. before and after seeing a movie
   c. before and after reading an important book
   d. before and after dieting
   e. before and after a long trip

4. Most of us have seen something important in our lives — a person, place, or thing — undergo a significant change, either in the subject itself or in our own perception of it. Write an essay comparing and contrasting the person, place, or thing before and after the change. There are many possibilities to consider. Perhaps a bucolic vista of open fields has become a shopping mall; perhaps

a favorite athletic team has gone from glory to shame; perhaps a loved one has been altered by decisions, events, or illness.

5. Interview a professor who has taught for many years at your college or university. Ask the professor to compare and contrast the college as it was when he or she first taught there with the way it is now; encourage reminiscence and evaluation. Combine strategies of description, comparison and contrast, and possibly definition as you write your essay. (Glossary: *Definition; Description*)

6. **Writing with Sources.** Five of the essays in this book deal, more or less directly, with issues related to the definition, achievement, or nature of manhood in America. The essays are "How to Give Orders Like a Man" (page 214) by Deborah Tannen; "Grant and Lee: A Study in Contrasts" by Bruce Catton (page 319); "What Does 'Boys Will Be Boys' Really Mean?" by Deborah M. Roffman (page 416); "How Boys Become Men" by Jon Katz (page 451); and "Shooting an Elephant" by George Orwell (page 639). Read these essays, and discuss with classmates the broad issues they raise. Choose one aspect of the topic of particular interest to you, and study the three or four essays that seem to bear most directly on this topic. Write an essay in which you compare, contrast, and evaluate the assertions in these essays. For models of and advice on integrating sources in your essay, see Chapters 14 and 15.

7. **Writing with Sources.** Study the "Rebuilding Progress in New Orleans" chart reproduced at the beginning of this chapter (page 280). In what areas is the most progress being made? What areas seem to be lagging behind? What conclusions, if any, can you draw about the recovery of New Orleans from Hurricane Katrina? After doing research in your library as well as on the Internet, write an essay in which you report on current efforts to revitalize New Orleans. What still needs to be done? What's being done to reduce or eliminate the chance of a Katrina-like catastrophe happening again? For models of and advice on integrating sources in your essay, see Chapters 14 and 15.

8. **Writing in the Workplace.** Imagine that you were recently hired to work in a small insurance business that employs five people. Your boss asks you to research and make a recommendation about the purchase of a new printer or copier for the office. Explore different office machines online, or visit an office equipment store and talk with a salesperson about what printers or copiers might be appropriate for a five-person office. Decide which two or three printers or copiers best fill the bill, and then write a memo to your boss in which you compare and contrast the features of the top candidates, concluding with

your recommendation of which model to purchase. In addition to research at retail outlets, you might find it helpful to visit the Web sites of different manufacturers to learn the specifications and capabilities of each machine. For models of and advice on integrating sources in your essay, see Chapters 14 and 15.

---

 e-Pages

One Small Step for Man

DEVIN HAHN

See how comparison and contrast works on the Web. Go to bedfordstmartins.com/subjectandstrategy for a video and study questions exploring how anthropology professor Jeremy DeSilva compares human and chimpanzee fossils in his research.

Smithsonian
National Museum of Natural History

2 Second Floor

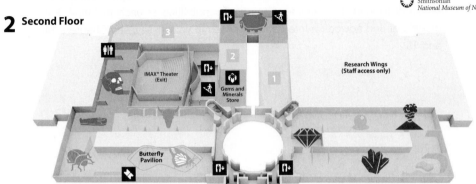

3

2

1

Research Wings
(Staff access only)

IMAX® Theater
(Exit)

Gems and
Minerals
Store

Butterfly
Pavilion

1 First Floor

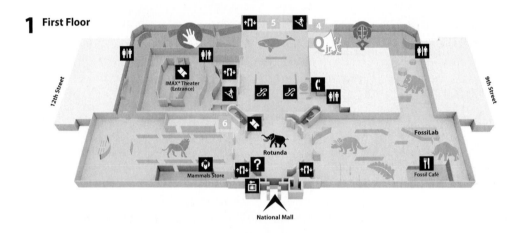

5

4

12th Street

9th Street

IMAX® Theater
(Entrance)

Rotunda

FossiLab

Fossil Café

6

Mammals Store

National Mall

G Ground Floor

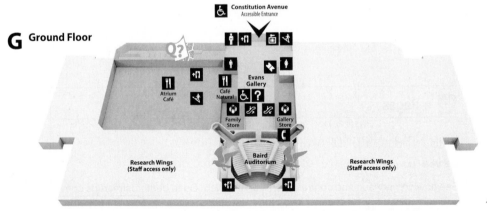

Constitution Avenue
Accessible Entrance

Evans
Gallery

Atrium
Café

Café
Natural

Family
Store

Gallery
Store

Research Wings
(Staff access only)

Baird
Auditorium

Research Wings
(Staff access only)

North

Division and Classification

WHAT ARE DIVISION AND CLASSIFICATION?

Like comparison and contrast, division and classification are separate yet closely related operations. Division involves breaking down a single large unit into smaller subunits or separating a group of items into discrete categories. Classification, on the other hand, entails placing individual items into established categories. Division, then, takes apart, whereas classification groups together. But even though the two processes can operate separately, they tend to be used together.

The floor plan of the National Museum of Natural History (opposite) illustrates division and classification at work. The museum has divided its three floors into sections and further divided those sections between exhibits and staff-only research space. The layout of the exhibits suggests how different categories relate to one another. For instance, the butterfly pavilion is located within an area dedicated to bugs and insects. Visitors to the museum can quickly glance at the depiction of the floor plan, get a simplified understanding of the natural world, and learn where to go to see representative examples of a particular class of objects from that world. The principles of division and classification have provided an easy way for museumgoers to make sense out of what would otherwise be an overwhelming conglomeration of objects.

DIVISION AND CLASSIFICATION IN WRITTEN TEXTS

In writing, division can be the most effective method for making sense of one large, complex, or multifaceted entity. Consider, for example, the following passage from E. B. White's *Here is New York,* in which he discusses New Yorkers and their city.

Division into categories occurs in opening sentence	There are roughly three New Yorks. There is, first, the New York of the man or woman who was born here, who takes the city for granted and accepts its size and its turbulence as natural and inevitable.

Second, there is the New York of the commuter—the city that is devoured by locusts each day and spat out each night. Third, there is the New York of the person who was born somewhere else and came to New York in quest of something. Of these three trembling cities the greatest is the last—the city of final destination, the city that is a goal. It is this third city that accounts for New York's highstrung disposition, its poetical deportment, its dedication to the arts, and its incomparable achievements. Commuters give the city its tidal restlessness; natives give it solidarity and continuity; but the settlers give it passion. And whether it is a farmer arriving from Italy to set up a small grocery store in a slum, or a young girl arriving from a small town in Mississippi to escape the indignity of being observed by her neighbors, or a boy arriving from the Corn Belt with a manuscript in his suitcase and a pain in his heart, it makes no difference: each embraces New York with the intense excitement of first love, each absorbs New York with the fresh eyes of an adventurer, each generates heat and light to dwarf the Consolidated Edison Company.

Author explains the nature of people in each category

In his opening sentences, White suggests a principle for dividing the population of New York, establishing his three categories on the basis of a person's relationship to the city. There is the New York of the native, the New York of the commuter, and the New York of the immigrant. White's divisions help him make a point about the character of New York City, depicting its restlessness, its solidarity, and its passion.

In contrast to breaking a large idea into parts, classification can be used to draw connections between disparate elements based on a common category—price, for example. Often, classification is used in conjunction with another rhetorical strategy, such as comparison and contrast. Consider, for example, how in the following passage from Toni Cade Bambara's "The Lesson" she classifies a toy in F.A.O. Schwarz and other items in the thirty-five-dollar category to compare the relative value of things in the life of two girls, Sylvia and Sugar.

Me and Sugar at the back of the train watchin the tracks whizzin by large then small then getting gobbled up in the dark. I'm thinkin about this tricky toy I saw in the store. A clown that somersaults on a bar then does chin-ups just cause you yank lightly at his leg. Cost $35. I could see me askin my mother for a $35 birthday clown. "You wanna who that costs what?" she'd say, cocking her head to the side to get a better view of the hole in my head. Thirty-five dollars could buy new bunk beds for Junior and Gretchen's boy. Thirty-five dollars and the whole household could go visit Grand-daddy Nelson in the country. Thirty-five dollars would pay for the rent and the piano

Classification used along with comparison and contrast

bill, too. Who are these people that spend that much for performing clowns and $1000 for toy sailboats? What kinda work they do and how they live and how come we ain't in on it?

Another example may help clarify how division and classification work hand in hand. Suppose a sociologist wants to determine whether the socioeconomic status of the people in a particular neighborhood has any influence on their voting behavior. Having decided on her purpose, the sociologist chooses as her subject the fifteen families living on Maple Street. Her goal then becomes to group these families in a way that will be relevant to her purpose: (1) according to socioeconomic status (low-income earners, middle-income earners, and high-income earners) and (2) according to voting behavior (voters and nonvoters).

In confidential interviews with each family, the sociologist begins to classify each family according to her established categories. Her work leads her to construct the following diagram, which allows her to visualize her division and classification system and its essential components: the subject, her bases or principles of division, the subclasses or categories that derive from these principles, and her conclusion.

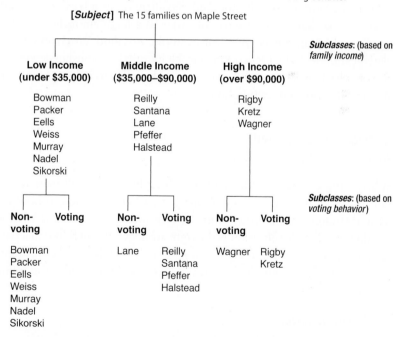

Purpose: To study the relationship between socioeconomic status and voting behavior

[*Subject*] The 15 families on Maple Street

Low Income (under $35,000)	Middle Income ($35,000–$90,000)	High Income (over $90,000)	*Subclasses*: (based on family income)
Bowman Packer Eells Weiss Murray Nadel Sikorski	Reilly Santana Lane Pfeffer Halstead	Rigby Kretz Wagner	

Non-voting	Voting	Non-voting	Voting	Non-voting	Voting	*Subclasses*: (based on voting behavior)
Bowman Packer Eells Weiss Murray Nadel Sikorski		Lane	Reilly Santana Pfeffer Halstead	Wagner	Rigby Kretz	

Conclusion: On Maple Street there seems to be a relationship between socioeconomic status and voting behavior: The low-income families are nonvoters.

USING DIVISION AND CLASSIFICATION AS A WRITING STRATEGY

As the work of the Maple Street sociologist shows, division and classification are used primarily to demonstrate a particular point about the subject under discussion. In a paper about the emphasis a television network places on reaching various audiences, you could begin by dividing prime-time programming into suitable subclasses: shows primarily for adults, shows for families, shows for children, and so forth. You could then classify each of that network's programs into one of these categories, analyze this data, and draw your conclusions about which audiences the network tries hardest to reach.

Another purpose of division and classification is to help writers and readers make choices. A voter may classify politicians on the basis of their attitudes toward nuclear energy or abortion; the technology magazine *Wired* classifies smartphones on the basis of available memory, screen size, processor speed, camera pixels, and carrier availability; high school seniors classify colleges and universities on the basis of prestige, geographic location, programs available, and tuition fees. In such cases, division and classification have an absolutely practical end: making a decision about whom to vote for, which laptop to buy, and where to apply for admission to college.

Finally, writers use division and classification as a basic organizational strategy, one that brings a sense of order to a large amorphous whole. As you'll see later in this chapter, for example, Rosalind Wiseman's system of classification in "The Queen Bee and Her Court" establishes seven categories of roles played by young girls in school cliques to help us better understand how those cliques function.

USING DIVISION AND CLASSIFICATION ACROSS THE DISCIPLINES

When writing essays in the academic disciplines, you will have many opportunities to use the strategy of division and classification to both organize and strengthen the presentation of your ideas. To determine whether or not division and classification is the right strategy for you to use in a particular paper, review the guidelines described in Chapter 2 (Determining a Strategy for Developing Your Essay, pages 32–33). Consider the following examples:

Earth Sciences

1. **MAIN IDEA:** Pollution is a far-reaching and unwieldy subject.
2. **QUESTION:** On what basis can we divide pollution into its various categories and what examples of pollution can we place into each category?

3. **STRATEGY:** Division and Classification. This strategy involves two activities: dividing into categories and placing items in their appropriate categories. The word *divide* signals the need to separate pollution into manageable groupings. The word *examples* and the phrase *place into each category* signal the need to classify types of pollution into appropriate categories.

4. **SUPPORTING STRATEGY:** Argumentation is often used to support both the rationale for categorization and classification itself.

Education

1. **MAIN IDEA:** Children's learning disabilities fall into three major groups.

2. **QUESTION:** What are the major types of learning disabilities into which children fall?

3. **STRATEGY:** Division and Classification. The words *major types* suggest the need to divide learning problems into major categories. The words *fall into* suggest that every learning disability can be classified into one of the three categories.

4. **SUPPORTING STRATEGY:** Argumentation could be used to persuade readers that the categories of problems discussed are major and to persuade them that a knowledge of these three major types of problems can be useful to teachers and parents in helping a child.

Political Science

1. **MAIN IDEA:** There are four types of U.S. presidents.

2. **QUESTION:** On what basis or bases do we group U.S. presidents?

3. **STRATEGY:** Division and Classification. The words *basis* or *bases* signals the need to establish criteria for dividing all our presidents. The word *group* suggests the need to classify the presidents according to the established groupings.

4. **SUPPORTING STRATEGY:** Illustration can be used to provide examples of various presidents.

SAMPLE STUDENT ESSAY USING DIVISION AND CLASSIFICATION AS A WRITING STRATEGY

In the following essay student Gerald Dromos makes sense of the different types of textspeak users he knows by dividing that large class into five basic categories: the heavy user, the anti-texter, and three categories he discerns between those two extremes. By establishing and placing users into those categories, he not only makes sense of an undifferentiated mass for himself but also helps us to see it more clearly. Additionally, he predicts that his division and classification of generationally determined textspeakers will be helpful in spotting new trends as new technology develops.

NYM's Talk

Gerald Dromos

It's a cliché to say that technology is shaping our language at an unprecedented rate. In fact, "textspeak" has become so commonplace that even the biggest names in print dictionaries annually scramble to include the latest texting terms in their newest editions. While some call textspeak a universal language, others see it as the demise of "proper" communication. But the divide between these two camps is more a gradation than a distinct line. Users of textspeak can be divided into five basic categories. They range from those "Hip2Text"— people so quick to code and decode common phrases that they already decided "NYM" must mean "Not Your Mother"— to the Anti-Texter, whose revulsion for texting compelled them to scoff at this essay's title. Three other significant categories of textspeak users fill the murky space between, those we might call Econotexters, KPCers (Keep Parents Clueless), and CPUers (Clueless Parent Users).

Thesis: textspeakers can be divided into five basic categories

[marginal note beside paragraph 1]

Most of us know someone we would classify as Hip2Text, or, more accurately, H2T, as they are likely to prefer. H2Ters are the vanguard of textspeak and likely in their late teens to late twenties; they are the people who are so immersed in texting that for them it is somewhere between sport and art. They revel in the thrill of stumping another H2Ter and bask in the awe of being able to convey sentences' worth of discussion in a few keystrokes. The quickest way to identify a true H2Ter is likely by listening to them converse, since even their speech is dominated by texting acronyms. These are generally younger speakers, likely under thirty, who seamlessly toss in LOL, OMG, and TTYS without even blinking. H2Ters don't think twice about speaking these acronyms aloud because, for them, the acronyms are fundamental vocabulary.

Organization: first type, Hip2Texters, are introduced

Illustration: Hip2Texters are described

Anti-Texters are the antithesis of H2Ters. In our own lives, they are likely grandparents and other older relatives of retirement age who left the workforce before the switch from

Organization: second type, AntiTexters, are introduced

1

2

3

Illustration:
Anti-Texters are
described

memo to e-mail, from phone to IM. Now part of a world in which texting seems inescapable, their practical response is exclusion. While some elect to avoid these medium and slang changes in their own lives, others are simply unable to keep up with the pace of change or the dexterity required for touch-to-type devices. Their Anti-Text stance may signify some degree of fear about a fast-moving cultural change that puts them out of touch with their grandchildren, and, to some degree, even their children who may have moved to communicating by text more frequently than by phone. While rendered as laughable "holdouts" in the television sitcom, the Anti-Texters we know personally may show us the value in another personality: the Econotexter, a person who is empathetic to the H2Ter and the Anti-Texter and is willing to adapt to and learn from both.

Organization:
third type,
Econotexters,
are introduced

Illustration:
Econotexters
are described

Unlike the H2Ter or the Anti-Texter, Econotexters are sensible texters age thirty and over who balance their textspeak with practical concerns for clarity. In other words, they recognize that while using an abbreviation might save time in the immediate future, it might take just as long to later "decode" the encoded message for the recipient. Econotexters are likely to understand and quickly decode what H2Ters say, but they adopt only the most recognizable textspeak as acceptable shorthand. They are folks who are nearly as "in the know" as H2Ters—in fact, they may have been H2Ters a few years ago—but now use textspeak discerningly, seeing it more as a tool than a marvel, as more of a time-saving helper than the definition of hip. They are the people who largely define and adopt the "common text phrase." In fact, arguably comprising the largest portion of types of textspeakers, Econotexters' textspeak is what generates Web pages such as Netlingo.com and Noslang.com, both of which serve as online dictionaries for commonly texted acronyms.

4

Organization:
fourth and fifth
types, KPCers
and CPUers,
are introduced

Illustration:
KPCers and
CPUers are
described

The fourth and fifth categories of textspeakers are interrelated. We might call them the KPCers and the CPUers, or those wishing to Keep Parents Clueless and their Clueless Parents. KPCers are a class of tween and teen textspeakers who adopt much of the textspeak employed by H2Ters with the intent of confusing their parents. KPCers, generally under eighteen and still living at home, adopt further slang that they translate to textspeak to disguise plans their parents would

5

disapprove of if discussed openly. KPCers' textspeak might be considered "Pig Latin[1] nouveau," as its purpose is less about the awe of fast communication or the fewest keystrokes as it is about disguising meaning from parental plan-thwarters. By contrast, CPUer parents, likely in their mid- to late forties, are just out of the age-typical range of the Econotexters, and much less in tune with the H2Ters. Although still in the workforce, they largely communicate with similarly aged peers who likely prefer e-mail to IM, putting them in less contact with the Econotexter's daily acronyms. CPUers might have years of experience with traditional acronyms such as FYI (For Your Information) and may have even added obvious newcomers such as "LOL" and "OMG" to their repertoire, but "TBH" and "L8R" may give them pause. Still, CPUers' ready access to computers and adeptness at looking up common textspeak makes them a potential threat to KPCers' desire for privacy. This may, in turn, speed up the KPCers' protective slang-to-textspeak conversion.

Conclusion: the purpose and usefulness of the classification is explained

Given the pace at which technological devices enabling textspeak are pushed into the marketplace, it is likely that in the next decade another category or two of textspeak users will emerge. For example, as speech-to-text transcription becomes a standard device feature, certain consistent translation flubs may become permanent slang, or, as devices become smaller, our repertoire of standard letter-based abbreviations may become even larger. For now, these remain fairly standard, generationally determined classifications. Understanding both what divides each textspeak user from the other and the similar traits within each category will help us identify new trends within each group, leading us to form new classes of speakers. In a time when even the definitive source of definitions and etymology among Western speakers, the *Oxford English Dictionary*, recognized in March 2011 the need to add entries for LOL and OMG, we know that textspeak is here to stay. It may not be your mother's talk, but it is becoming an integral and acceptable part of our communication.

6

[1] A form of language play originating in the nineteenth century and often used by children to disguise the discussion.

Analyzing Gerald Dromos's Division and Classification Essay: Questions for Discussion

1. What categories does Dromos use to classify his subject? Brainstorm about other categories of textspeak users that might exist. Could these alternate categories be used to make a similar point?

2. How did Dromos organize the categories in his essay? Is his organization effective, or could he have chosen a better way?

3. What other strategies might Dromos have used to strengthen his essay? Be specific about the benefits of each strategy.

SUGGESTIONS FOR USING DIVISION AND CLASSIFICATION AS A WRITING STRATEGY

As you plan, write, and revise your division and classification essay, be mindful of the writing process guidelines described in Chapter 2. Pay particular attention to the basic requirements and essential ingredients of this writing strategy.

❱ Planning Your Division and Classification Essay

Planning is an essential part of writing a good division and classification essay. You can save yourself a great deal of trouble by taking the time to think about the key building blocks of your essay before you actually begin to write.

DETERMINE YOUR PURPOSE, AND FOCUS ON IT. The principle you use to divide your subject into categories depends on your larger purpose. It is crucial, then, that you determine a clear purpose for your division and classification before you begin to examine your subject in detail. For example, in studying the student body at your school, you might have any number of purposes, such as discovering how much time your classmates spend in the library during the week, explaining how financial aid is distributed, discussing the most popular movies or music on campus, or describing styles of dorm-room decor. The categories into which you divide the student body will vary according to your purpose.

Let's say, for example, that you are in charge of writing an editorial for your school newspaper that will make people aware of how they might reduce the amount of trash going to the landfill. Having established your purpose, your next task might be to identify the different ways objects could be handled to avoid sending them to the landfill. For instance, you might decide that there are four basic ways to prevent things from ending up in the trash. Then, you could establish a sequence or order of importance in which they should be addressed. Your first draft might start something like the following:

Over the course of the last semester, more trash was removed from our campus than in any semester in history. But was it all trash that had to go to the landfill? For example, many of us love to wear fleece vests, but did you know that they are made from recycled plastic bottles? Much of what is considered trash need not go to the landfill at all. There are four ways we can prevent trash from being sent to the landfill. I call them the four R's. First, we can all reduce the amount of individually packaged goods that we send to the landfill by buying frequently used items in family-size or bulk containers. Next, we can reuse those containers, as well as other items, either for their original purpose or for another. Be creative. After a while, though, things will wear out after repeated use. Then it's a good time to try to restore them. If that, too, can no longer be done, then they should be recycled. Only after these options have failed should items be considered "real" trash and be removed to the landfill. Using the four R's—Reduce, Reuse, Restore, Recycle—we can reduce the amount of trash our campus sends to the landfill every semester.

This introduction clearly expresses the purpose of the editorial: to change readers' behavior regarding the amount of "trash" they throw out.

As this example shows, classification and division can be used to persuade readers toward or away from certain types of actions. As we will see in the essay "The Ways of Meeting Oppression" later in this chapter, Martin Luther King Jr., by identifying three categories of protest, is able to cite historical precedents to argue against violent forms of protest and in favor of nonviolent ones. (Argumentation, one of the most powerful rhetorical modes, will be explained in detail in Chapter 12.)

FORMULATE A THESIS STATEMENT. When writing a division and classification essay, be sure that your thesis statement clearly presents the categories that you will be using to make your point. Here are two examples from this chapter.

- "*The same thing is true of Muppet Theory, a little-known, poorly understood philosophy that holds that every living human can be classified according to one simple metric: Every one of us is either a Chaos Muppet or an Order Muppet.*" This thesis statement, from the essay by Dahlia Lithwick (page 344), presents the subject—every one of us—and the two categories, one of which each of us falls into, according to Lithwick.

- "*Because girls' social hierarchies are complicated and overwhelming in their detail, I'm going to take you through a general breakdown of the different positions in the clique.*" This thesis statement is from Rosalind Wiseman's "The Queen Bee and Her Court" (page 349). From this opening statement, the reader knows exactly what Wiseman intends to discuss and how.

When you begin to formulate your thesis statement, keep these examples in mind. You could also look for other examples of thesis statements in the essays throughout this book. As you begin to develop your thesis statement, ask yourself the following questions: "What is my point?," "What categories will be most useful in making my point?" If you can't answer these questions, write some ideas down, and try to determine your main point from these ideas.

Once you have settled on an idea, go back to the two questions above, and write down your answers to them. Then combine the answers into a single thesis statement. (Your thesis statement does not necessarily have to be one sentence; making it one sentence, though, can be an effective way of focusing both your point and your categories.)

▶ Organizing and Writing Your Division and Classification Essay

ESTABLISH VALID CATEGORIES.   When establishing categories, make sure that they meet three criteria:

- *The categories must be appropriate to your purpose.* In determining the factors affecting financial aid distribution among students at a particular school, you might consider family income, academic major, and athletic participation, but obviously you would not consider style of dress or preferred brand of toothpaste.
- *The categories must be consistent and mutually exclusive.* For example, dividing the student body into the classes of men, women, and athletes would be illogical because athletes can be either male or female. Instead, you could divide the student body into male athletes, female athletes, male nonathletes, and female nonathletes.
- *The categories must be complete, and they must account for all the members or aspects of your subject.* In dividing the student body according to place of birth, it would be inaccurate to consider only states in the United States; such a division would not account for foreign students or citizens born outside the country.

You may often find that a diagram (such as the one of families on Maple Street, shown on page 333), a chart, or a table can help you visualize your organization and help you make sure that your categories are appropriate, mutually exclusive, and complete.

Division and classification essays, when sensibly planned, can generally be organized with little trouble; the essay's chief divisions will reflect the classes into which you have divided the subject. A scratch outline can help you see those divisions and plan your presentation. For example, here is an outline of student Gerald Dromos's essay "NYM's Talk" about different types of textspeakers:

Five Types of Textspeakers:

1. Hip2Texter
   a. Under age 30
   b. Very fluent in textspeak; constant user

2. Anti-Texter
   a. Retirement age
   b. Avoids textspeak altogether and unlikely to understand it

3. Econotexter
   a. Over age 30
   b. Fluent in textspeak but tailors usage to audience and urgency

4. KPCer (Keep Parents Clueless)
   a. Under age 18; lives at home
   b. Deliberately invents and uses unconventional shorthand as secret code

5. CPUer (Clueless Parent User)
   a. Mid-to-late 40s
   b. Knows only basic or dated acronyms; unlikely to use them

Such an outline clearly reveals the essay's overall structure.

STATE YOUR CONCLUSION.   Your essay's purpose will determine the kinds of conclusions you reach. For example, a study of the student body of your college might show that 35 percent of male athletes are receiving scholarships, compared with 20 percent of female athletes, 15 percent of male nonathletes, and 10 percent of female nonathletes. These facts could provide a conclusion in themselves, or they might be the basis for a more controversial assertion about your school's athletic program. A study of dorm-room decor might conclude with the observation that juniors and seniors tend to have more elaborate rooms than first-year students. Your conclusion will depend on the way you work back and forth between the various classes you establish and the individual items available for you to classify.

▶ Revising and Editing Your Division and Classification Essay

LISTEN TO WHAT YOUR CLASSMATES HAVE TO SAY. The importance of student peer conferences cannot be stressed enough, particularly as you revise and edit your essay. Often, others in your class will immediately see problems that you can't see yourself because you are too close to your essay. For example, they might see that the basis for your classification needs adjustment, that there are inconsistencies in your categories, that you need more and better transitions to link the discussions of your categories, or that you may need more examples. So take advantage of suggestions where you judge them to be valid, and make revisions accordingly. For questions on peer conferences, see page 36.

QUESTION YOUR OWN WORK WHILE REVISING AND EDITING. Revision is best done by asking yourself key questions about what you have written. Begin by reading, preferably aloud, what you have written. Reading aloud forces you to pay attention to every single word, and you are more likely to catch lapses in the logical flow of thought. After you have read your paper through, answer the following questions for revising and editing and make the necessary changes.

For help with twelve common writing problems, see Chapter 16, "Editing for Grammar, Punctuation, and Sentence Style."

Questions for Revising and Editing: Division and Classification

1. Is my subject a coherent entity that readily lends itself to analysis by division and classification?

2. Does the manner in which I divide my subject into categories help me achieve my purpose in writing the essay?

3. Does my thesis statement clearly identify the number and type of categories I will be using in my essay?

4. Do I stay focused on my subject and stay within the limits of my categories throughout my essay?

5. Do my categories meet the following three criteria: Are they appropriate to my purpose, consistent and mutually exclusive, and complete?

6. Have I organized my essay in a way that makes it easy for the reader to understand my categories and how they relate to my purpose?

7. Are there other rhetorical strategies that I can use to help me achieve my purpose?

8. Is my use of headings and subheadings consistent? Could I use headings and subheadings to clarify the organization of my essay?

9. Does my paper contain any errors in grammar, punctuation, or mechanics? Is my sentence style as clear, smooth, and persuasive as possible?

Chaos Theory: A Unified Theory of Muppet Types

DAHLIA LITHWICK

Dahlia Lithwick is a senior editor and legal correspondent for *Slate*. She was born in Ottawa, Ontario, Canada. In 1990 she graduated from Yale with a B.A. degree in English. While at Yale she debated on the American Parliamentary Debate Association circuit, ultimately placing as a runner-up for the National Debate Team of the Year. In 1996 she earned her J.D. from Stanford Law School and then clerked for Judge Proctor Hug on the United States Supreme Court of Appeals for the Ninth Circuit in Reno, Nevada. Her work has appeared in the *New York Times*, the *New Republic*, the *Washington Post*, *Elle*, and the *American Prospect*, and she has been a guest on National Public Radio's newsmagazine *Day to Day*. Along with Brandt Goldstein she is the author of *Me v. Everybody: Absurd Contracts for an Absurd World* (2003), a legal humor book. In 2001 Lithwick was awarded the Online Journalism Award for Online Commentary for her "Supreme Court Dispatches."

In the following essay, first published in *Slate* on June 8, 2012, Lithwick classifies all humans as belonging to either of two classes: Chaos Muppets or Order Muppets. Of course, her division and classification essay is a spoof . . . or maybe not.

Preparing to Read

Where along a scale ranging from chaos to order might you characterize yourself? Are you happy with where you are on the scale? Why, or why not?

E very once in a while, an idea comes along that changes the way we   1
all look at ourselves forever. Before Descartes, nobody knew they
were thinking. They all believed they were just mulling. Until Karl
Marx, everyone totally hated one another but nobody knew quite
why. And before Freud, nobody understood that all of humanity could be
classified into one of two simple types: people who don't yet know they want
to sleep with their mothers, and people who already know they want to sleep
with their mothers. These dialectics can change and shape who we are so
profoundly, it's hard to imagine life before the paradigm at all.

The same thing is true of Muppet Theory, a little-known, poorly   2
understood philosophy that holds that every living human can be classified
according to one simple metric: Every one of us is either a Chaos Muppet
or an Order Muppet.

Chaos Muppets are out of control, emotional, volatile. They tend toward   3
the blue and fuzzy. They make their way through life in a swirling maelstrom
of food crumbs, small flaming objects, and the letter C. Cookie Monster,
Ernie, Grover, Gonzo, Dr. Bunsen Honeydew, and—paradigmatically—
Animal, are all Chaos Muppets. Zelda Fitzgerald was a Chaos Muppet. So,
I must tell you, is Justice Stephen Breyer.

Order Muppets—and I'm thinking about Bert, Scooter, Sam the   4
Eagle, Kermit the Frog, and the blue guy who is perennially harassed by
Grover at restaurants (the Order Muppet Everyman)—tend to be neu-
rotic, highly regimented, averse to surprises, and may sport monstrously
large eyebrows. They sometimes resent the responsibility of the world
weighing on their felt shoulders, but they secretly revel in the knowledge
that they keep the show running. Your first-grade teacher was probably an
Order Muppet. So is Chief Justice John Roberts. It's not that any one type
of Muppet is inherently better than the other. (Order Muppets do seem to
attract the ladies, but then Chaos Muppets collect the chicken harems.) It's
simply the case that the key to a happy marriage, a well-functioning family,
and a productive place of work lies in carefully calibrating the ratio of
Chaos Muppets to Order Muppets within any closed system. That, and
always letting the Chaos Muppets do the driving.

> Be it "Pigs in Space,"
> Oscar's garbage can,
> or producing a hit
> Broadway show in
> nineteen hours, it's
> always crucial to get
> the ratio of Order-to-
> Chaos exactly right.

Think about your basic Muppet work-   5
places: Be it "Pigs in Space," Oscar's garbage can, or producing a hit Broadway show
in nineteen hours, it's always crucial to get
the ratio of Order-to-Chaos exactly right.
One possible explanation for the blossoming dysfunctionality of the current Supreme
Court is that the Order Muppets have all
but taken over. With exception of Justices
Breyer and Antonin Scalia, the Order Muppets are running the show completely. (The
jury is still out on whether Elena Kagan may
prove a Chaos Muppet.) Remember the old
rule of thumb: Too many Order Muppets
means no cookies for anyone.

It's hard to be ruthlessly honest when evaluating one's own Muppet   6
classification. As is the case when going shopping for white pants, your
best bet is probably just to trust a friend. It's not enough to judge by career
choice or pastimes. For instance: Order Muppets are musical. So are Chaos
Muppets. Some initial clues can be garnered by scrutinizing your CD
storage system and spice racks. Chaos Muppets may well be able to recite
the alphabet, but they don't alphabetize anything willingly and usually

only do so in exchange for cookies. If your house catches on fire, as you practice a death-defying leap through a flaming hoop while reciting Hamlet, you're most probably a Chaos Muppet anyhow. But if your house catches on fire and you know precisely how to rescue your Schumann CDs in under fifteen seconds, you're an Order Muppet.

Perhaps the best determinant of your Muppet Classification, however, is your partner: Order Muppets tend to pick Chaos Muppets for their life partners, cookies notwithstanding. Thus, if you're in a long-term relationship with a Chaos Muppet, there's a pretty good chance you're Bert. If you're married to an Order Muppet, you may well be the Swedish Chef. And by all that is holy, don't marry your same type if you can help it. That's where Baby Elmos come from.

Here's the part where some of you will pen earnest missives explaining how all this maps perfectly onto all the new brain science about the inherent neurological differences between Republicans and Democrats. Please don't. This is really just me having fun. Also I am (basically) a Chaos Muppet and will probably lose your mail anyhow.

There's just one other thing you should know before you start describing yourself and others exclusively according to the Muppet System. There's an enormous amount of false consciousness at work here (Thanks Karl Marx!!!) and many of us are prone to profound misdiagnoses. My seven-year-old told me last night that he is most definitely a Chaos Muppet. He's not. To tell the truth he and I are both Faux Chaos Muppets—Chaos on the outside, but with hard, rigid, inflexible caramel centers. Like Dr. Bunsen Honeydew, we sow chaos throughout the land. But like the good doctor, we do so in an effort to better organize the world.

I leave you now to make your own determinations, about your personal Muppet typology and whether your marriage is on firm ground. I leave you as well with this one brief parting observation: Mahna Mahna.

Thank you.

Thinking Critically about the Text

Why do you suppose Lithwick wrote this humorous sketch? What truth, if any, do you see in her division and classification? Has she oversimplified the topic of personality types, or does she have it just about right? Explain.

Questions on Subject

1. Do you need to be a fan of the Muppets to really appreciate Lithwick's humor? Explain.

2. Do you believe in Muppet Theory? Can you immediately identify your relatives and friends as Chaos and Order Muppets?

3. What is Muppet Theory?

4. What does Lithwick mean when she writes in paragraph 5, "it's always crucial to get the ratio of Order-to-Chaos exactly right"?

5. Can you think of life before learning about Chaos and Order Muppets? Does knowing about Muppet Theory make your life easier? Explain.

Questions on Strategy

1. What is Lithwick's thesis in this essay? (Glossary: *Thesis*)

2. What is Lithwick's purpose in using justices on the United States Supreme Court as some of her examples? Is she making fun of the court?

3. Why does Lithwick alert us to the fact that her classification system can't use career choices or pastimes as a basis of whether someone is a Chaos Muppet or an Order Muppet?

4. What's your choice for two or three of Lithwick's most humorous lines in this selection? Why do you find them humorous?

Questions on Diction and Vocabulary

1. Lithwick uses the words *Mahna, Mahna* to conclude paragraph 10. To what do these words refer?

2. Consult your dictionary for the meanings of the following words and phrases as they are used in this selection: *mulling* (paragraph 1), *dialectics* (1), *paradigm* (1), *swirling maelstrom* (3), *blossoming dysfunctionality* (5), *false consciousness* (9), *typology* (10).

Classroom Activity Using Division and Classification

Visit a local supermarket and select one of the many areas (frozen foods, dairy products, cereals, soft drinks, meat, produce) for an exercise in classification. First, establish the general class of products in the area you have selected by determining the features that distinguish one subclass from another. Next place the products from your selected area in appropriate subclasses within your classification system. Finally, share your classification system and how it works with members of your class. Be prepared to answer questions your classmates may have about the decisions you made.

Writing Suggestions

1. Lithwick's essay can be a very useful model for your own essay of division and classification. She successfully composes an essay that not only humorously considers a part of our popular culture but also insightfully teaches us something about ourselves and those around us. Choose a topic and try writing a similar essay — one that not only entertains, but also makes an observation or two that teaches.

2. Write a division and classification essay in which you categorize the kinds of television programs you watch. Think not only of classes but also of subclasses of programming. For example, you may claim that the only types of programs you watch are documentaries, situation comedies, and sports but within the sports category you realize you only watch NFL games and not college games. You may only watch basketball, but only college and not NBA games. By looking at subclasses as well as classes, you will come to a much more detailed understanding of your television-viewing habits.

The Queen Bee and Her Court

ROSALIND WISEMAN

Rosalind Wiseman was born in 1969 in Philadelphia, Pennsylvania. She received her B.A. in political science from Occidental College in Los Angeles, California, in 1988. Wiseman is the cofounder and president of the Empower Program, a nonprofit organization certified through the Program for Young Negotiators at Harvard University, whose mission is "to work with youth to end the culture of violence." Wiseman's articles have appeared in *Principal Leadership* magazine, *Educational Digest*, and *New York Newsday*, and she has spoken extensively in the media about young people and violence. Her books include *Defending Ourselves: A Guide to Prevention, Self-Defense, and Recovery from Rape* (1995); *Queen Bees and Wannabes: Helping Your Daughter Survive Cliques, Gossip, Boyfriends, and Other Realities of Adolescence* (2002), on which the film *Mean Girls* (2004) is based; and *Queen Bee Moms and Kingpin Dads* (2007), a book about the social pecking orders of parents. Wiseman has also written and developed the *Owning Up Curriculum* (2009), which encourages students to take responsibility — as perpetrators, bystanders, and targets — for unethical behavior.

In "The Queen Bee and Her Court," an excerpt from *Queen Bees and Wannabes,* Wiseman divides and classifies young schoolgirls into various hierarchical social classes dominated by the "Queen Bee."

Preparing to Read

How did the various cliques work in your elementary school and high school? What roles did you play within those cliques? Did the existence of cliques bother you, or did you regard them as merely a reflection of society as a whole?

We need to give girls credit for the sophistication of their social structures. Our best politicians and diplomats couldn't do better than a teen girl does in understanding the social intrigue and political landscape that lead to power. Cliques are sophisticated, complex, and multilayered, and every girl has a role within them. However, positions in cliques aren't static. Especially from the sixth to eighth grade, a girl can lose her position to another girl, and she can move up and down the social totem pole. Also, your daughter doesn't have to be in the "popular" group to have these roles within her group of friends. Because girls' social hierarchies are complicated and overwhelming in their detail, I'm going to take you through a general breakdown of the different positions in the clique. However, when you talk to your daughter about cliques, encourage her to come up with her own names and create roles she thinks I've missed. If you can answer yes to the majority of items for each role, you've identified your daughter. So, here are the different roles that your daughter and her friends might play:

Queen Bee

Sidekick

Banker

Floater

Torn Bystander

Pleaser/Wannabe/Messenger

Target

THE QUEEN BEE

For the girl whose popularity is based on fear and control, think of a combination of the Queen of Hearts in *Alice in Wonderland* and Barbie. I call her the Queen Bee. Through a combination of charisma, force, money, looks, will, and manipulation, this girl reigns supreme over the other girls and weakens their friendships with others, thereby strengthening her own power and influence. Indeed, she appears omnipotent. Never underestimate her power over other girls (and boys as well). She can and will silence her peers with a look. If your daughter's the Queen Bee and you could spy on her, you would (or should) be mortified by how she treats other girls.

Your Daughter Is a Queen Bee If . . .

- Her friends do what she wants to do.
- She isn't intimidated by any other girl in her class.
- Her complaints about other girls are limited to the lame things they did or said.
- When she's young, you have to convince her to invite everyone to her birthday party. When she does invite everyone you want, she ignores and excludes some of her guests. (When she's older, you lose your privilege to tell her who she can invite.)
- She can persuade her peers to do just about anything she wants.
- She can argue anyone down, including friends, peers, teachers, and parents.

- She's charming to adults, a female Eddie Haskell.
- She can make another girl feel "anointed" by declaring her a special friend.
- She's affectionate, but often that affection is deployed to demonstrate her rejection of another girl. For example, she sees two girls in her group, one she's pleased with and one she isn't. When she sees them, she'll throw her arms around one and insist that they sit together and barely say anything to the other.
- She won't (or is very reluctant to) take responsibility when she hurts someone's feelings.
- If she thinks she's been wronged she feels she has the right to seek revenge. She has an eye-for-an-eye worldview.

> She thinks she's better than everyone else. She's in control, intimidating, smart, caring, and has the power to make others feel good or bad. She'll make stuff up about people and everyone will believe her.   —ANNE, 15   4

Who was the Queen Bee in your junior and/or high school? (If you were the Queen Bee, it's okay to admit it.) Remember how much power she had? Keep in mind that Queen Bees are good at slipping under adults' radar (including parents, teachers, and myself). Some of the nicest girls in my classes, who speak the most eloquently about how terrible they feel when girls are mean to each other, turn out to be the most cruel.   5

Our best politicians and diplomats couldn't do better than a teen girl does in understanding the social intrigue and political landscape that lead to power.

> We're like an army.   —AMANDA, 13   6

Most Queen Bees aren't willing to recognize the cruelty of their actions. They believe their behavior is justified because of something done to them first. Justifications usually begin with, "For no reason, this girl got really upset about not being in the group. I mean we told her nicely and she just wasn't getting the hint. We tried to be nice but she just wasn't listening." When a Queen Bee does this, she's completely bypassing what she did and defining right and wrong by whether the individual was loyal (i.e., not challenging her authority).   7

If that sinking feeling in your stomach is because you just realized your daughter is a Queen Bee, congratulate yourself. Honesty is the first step to parenting an adolescent successfully.   8

What Does She Gain by Being a Queen Bee?

She feels power and control over her environment. She's the center of   9
attention and people pay homage to her.

What Does She Lose by Being a Queen Bee?

A real sense of self. She's so busy maintaining her image that she loses herself   10
in the process. She can be incredibly cynical about her friendships with both
boys and girls ("They're only sucking up to me because I'm popular; they
don't really like me."). She's vulnerable to having intimate relationships where
she believes her image is dependent on the relationship. She may easily feel
that she can't admit to anyone when she's in over her head because her reputation dictates that she always has everything and everyone in control.

THE SIDEKICK

She's the lieutenant or second in command, the girl who's closest to the   11
Queen Bee and will back her no matter what because her power depends
on the confidence she gets from the Queen Bee. All girls in a clique tend to
dress similarly, but the Sidekick wears the most identical clothes and shares
the mannerisms and overall style closest to the Queen Bee. Together they
appear to other girls as an impenetrable force. They commonly bully and
silence other girls to forward their own agenda. These girls are usually the
first to focus on boys and are often attracted to older boys. This is particularly true in seventh and eighth grade (and their behavior is even worse if
they're physically mature and going to high school parties). The difference
between the two is if you separate the Sidekick from the Queen Bee, the
Sidekick can alter her behavior for the better, while the Queen Bee would
be more likely to find another Sidekick and begin again.

Your Daughter Is a Sidekick If . . .

- She has a best friend (the Queen Bee) who tells her what to do, think,   12
  dress, etc.
- The best friend is your daughter's authority figure, not you.
- She feels like it's the two of them and everyone else is a Wannabe.
- You think her best friend pushes her around.

   She notices everything about the Queen Bee. She will do everything the   13
   Queen Bee says and wants to be her. She lies for the Queen Bee but she
   isn't as pretty as the Queen Bee.   —MADELINE, 14

What Does She Gain by Being a Sidekick?

Power over other girls that she wouldn't have without the Queen Bee. She 14
also gains a close friend (whom you may not like) who makes her feel popular and included.

What Does She Lose by Being a Sidekick?

The right to express her personal opinions. If she sticks around the Queen 15
Bee too long, she may forget she even has her own opinion.

THE BANKER

Information about each other is currency in Girl World. The Banker cre- 16
ates chaos everywhere she goes by banking information about girls in her
social sphere and dispensing it at strategic intervals for her own benefit.
For instance, if a girl has said something negative about another girl, the
Banker will casually mention it to someone in conversation because she
knows it's going to cause a conflict and strengthen her status as someone
"in the know." She can get girls to trust her because when she pumps them
for information it doesn't seem like gossip; instead, she does it in an innocent, I'm-trying-to-be-your-friend way.

> Her power lies in getting girls to confide in her. Once they figure out 17
> she can't be trusted, it's too late because she already has information
> on them, and in order to keep her from revealing things, girls will be nice
> to her. —LEIGH, 17

The Banker is almost as powerful as the Queen Bee, but it's easy to mistake 18
her for the Messenger. She's usually quiet and withdrawn in front of adults
and can be physically immature in comparison to her friends. This is the
girl who sneaks under adult radar all the time because she seems so cute
and harmless.

Your Daughter Is a Banker If . . .

- She is extremely secretive. 19
- She thinks in complex, strategic ways.
- She seems to be friends with everyone; some girls even treat her like
  a pet.
- She's rarely the subject of fights.
- She's rarely excluded from the group.

What Does She Gain by Being a Banker?

Power and security. The Banker is very confusing to other girls because she seems harmless and yet everyone is afraid of her. [20]

What Does She Lose by Being a Banker?

Once other girls figure out what she's doing, they don't trust her. With her utilitarian mind-set, she can forget to look to other girls as a trusted resource. [21]

> The girls can't oust the Banker from the clique because she has information on everyone and could make or break reputations based on the information she knows. —CHARLOTTE, 15 [22]

THE FLOATER

You can usually spot this girl because she doesn't associate with only one clique. She has friends in different groups and can move freely among them. She usually has protective characteristics that shield her from other girls' cruelty—for example, she's beautiful but not too beautiful, nice, not terribly sophisticated, and avoids conflicts. She's more likely to have higher self-esteem because she doesn't base her self-worth on how well she's accepted by one group. Because she has influence over other girls but doesn't use it to make them feel bad, I call her the Floater. Girls want to be the Floater because she has confidence, people genuinely like her, and she's nice to everyone. She has the respect of other girls because she doesn't rule by meanness. When backed into a corner, the Floater is one of the few girls who will actually stand up to the Queen Bee. While Floaters have some power, they don't have the same influence and impact as Queen Bees. Why? Because Floaters don't gain anything by sowing seeds of discontent and insecurity among the other girls; Queen Bees do. [23]

> I have always felt that many potential Floaters are either swallowed up by the popular crowd or choose not to identify with popular people at all and instead create their own groups. In every girl there is a Floater who wants to get out. —JOANNA, 17 [24]

> I don't think there are *real* Floaters. Maybe I'm just bitter, but most of the time they are too good to be true. —LIZA, 17 [25]

Your Daughter Is a Floater If . . .

- She doesn't want to exclude people; you aren't always having fights with her about spending time with people she considers "losers." [26]

- Her friends are comfortable around her and don't seem intimidated; she's not "winning" all the conversations.
- She's not exclusively tied to one group of friends; she may have a jock group she hangs with, then the kids in the band, then her friends in the neighborhood.
- She can bring another person into a group on her own with some success.

What Does She Gain by Being a Floater?

Her peers like her for who she is as a person. She'll be less likely to sacrifice herself to gain and keep social status.

27

What Does She Lose by Being a Floater?

Nothing! Count yourself truly blessed that she's your daughter.

28

If you're thinking this is your daughter, wait. It isn't that I don't believe you, but please read all the roles before making your final decision. We all want to believe the best about the people we love, but sometimes our love blinds us to reality. I've met countless parents who truly believe their daughters are Floaters, and they're not. It should go without saying that just because your daughter isn't a Floater doesn't mean she won't become an amazing young woman and/or that you haven't done a good job raising her. But if you insist on seeing her in a way that she isn't, you won't be able to be as good a parent as she needs you to be.

29

THE TORN BYSTANDER

She's constantly conflicted between doing the right thing and her allegiance to the clique. As a result, she's the one most likely to be caught in the middle of a conflict between two girls or two groups of girls. She'll often rationalize or apologize for the Queen Bee and Sidekick's behavior, but she knows it's wrong. She often feels more uncomfortable around boys, but can be very easily influenced by the clique to do what it wants (for example, getting together with a boy they decide is right for her). The status she gets from the group is very important, and the thought of standing up to the more powerful girls in the clique is terrifying. She's honest enough with herself (and maybe with you as well) to know that she doesn't like what the Queen Bee does but feels powerless to stop it.

30

Your Daughter Is a Torn Bystander If . . .

- She's always finding herself in situations where she has to choose be- 31 tween friends.
- She tries to accommodate everyone.
- She's not good at saying no to her friends.
- She wants everyone "to get along."
- She can't imagine standing up to anyone she has a conflict with; she goes along to get along.

> She's confused and insecure because her reputation is over if she doesn't 32 stick with the Queen Bee, but she can be really cool when she's alone.
>
> —ANNE, 13

What Does She Gain by Being a Torn Bystander?

By associating herself with more powerful girls, she has access to popular- 33 ity, high social status, and boys.

What Does She Lose by Being a Torn Bystander?

She has to sacrifice a great deal. She may not try new things or she may stop 34 doing things she's interested in (plays, band, "geeky" clubs, etc.) because her friends make fun of her. She may dumb herself down to get along with others. This doesn't mean her grades will suffer, although they could. Lots of girls hide their academic accomplishments from their peers for this reason. ("I know I totally failed that test.") It more likely means that she presents herself as less intelligent than she is. This is merely irritating when she's a teen, but literally stupid when she's an adult in a job interview.

THE PLEASER/WANNABE/MESSENGER

Almost all girls are pleasers and wannabes; some are just more obvious 35 than others. This is one of the more fascinating roles. She can be in the clique or on the perimeter trying to get in. She will do anything to be in the good graces of the Queen Bee and the Sidekick. She'll enthusiastically back them up no matter what. She'll mimic their clothes, style, and anything else she thinks will increase her position in the group. She's a careful observer, especially of the girls in power. She's motivated above all else to please the person who's standing above her on the social totem pole. She can easily get herself into messy conflicts with other people because she'll change her mind depending on who she's interacting with.

As a Pleaser/Wannabe/Messenger her security in the clique is precarious   36
and depends on her doing the Queen Bee's "dirty work," such as spreading
gossip about a Target. While the Banker gathers information to further her
own causes, the Pleaser/Wannabe/Messenger does it to service the Queen
Bee and get in her good graces and feel important. But she can easily be
dropped and ridiculed if she's seen as trying too hard to fit in. (One of the
worst accusations you can make of a teen is to say she's trying too hard. In
Girl World, all actions must appear effortless.) The Queen Bee and Sidekick
enjoy the convenience of making her their servant, but they love talking
behind her back. ("Can you believe what a suck-up she is? That's so pathetic.")

When there's a fight between two girls or two groups of girls, she often   37
serves as a go-between. Her status immediately rises when she's in active
duty as a Messenger. It's also the most powerful position she can attain,
which means she has a self-interest in creating and maintaining conflicts
between girls so she doesn't get laid off.

Your Daughter Is a Pleaser/Wannabe/Messenger If . . .

- Other girls' opinions and wants are more important than her own.   38
- Her opinions on dress, style, friends, and "in" celebrities constantly
  change.
- She can't tell the difference between what she wants and what the
  group wants.
- She's desperate to have the "right" look (clothes, hair, etc.).
- She'll stop doing things she likes because she fears the clique's dis-
  approval.
- She's always in the middle of a conflict.
- She feels better about herself when the other girls are coming to her for
  help, advice, or when she's doing their dirty work.
- She loves to gossip — the phone and e-mail are her lifeline.

What Does She Gain by Being a Pleaser?

The feeling that she belongs; she's in the middle of the action and has   39
power over girls.

What Does She Lose by Being a Pleaser?

Personal authenticity — she hasn't figured out who she is or what she val-   40
ues. She's constantly anticipating what people want from her and doesn't
ask herself what she wants in return. She feels insecure about her

friendships—do girls really like her, or do they only value her for the gossip she trades in? She has trouble developing personal boundaries and the ability to communicate them to others.

> She's insecure and you can't trust her. —CARRIE, 14 41

THE TARGET

She's the victim, set up by the other girls to be humiliated, made fun of, 42
excluded. Targets are assumed to be out of the clique, one of the class "losers." While this is sometimes true, it's not always the case. Just because a girl is in the clique doesn't mean she can't be targeted by the other members. Often the social hierarchy of the clique is maintained precisely by having someone clearly at the bottom of the group's totem pole. Girls outside the clique tend to become Targets because they've challenged the clique or because their style of dress, behavior, and such are outside the norms acceptable to the clique. Girls inside the clique tend to become Targets if they've challenged someone higher on the social totem pole (i.e., the Queen Bee, Sidekick, or Banker) and need to be taken down a peg.

Your Daughter Is a Target If . . .

- She feels helpless to stop the girls' behavior. 43
- She feels she has no allies. No one will back her up.
- She feels isolated.
- She can mask her hurt by rejecting people first, saying she doesn't like anyone.

This role can be harder to figure out than you would think, and your daugh- 44
ter may be too embarrassed to tell you. She might admit she feels excluded, or she might just withdraw from you and "not want to talk about it."

> Targets don't want to tell their parents because they don't want their par- 45
> ents to think they're a loser or a nobody. —JENNIFER, 16

What Does She Gain by Being a Target?

This may seem like an odd question, but being a Target can have some hid- 46
den benefits. There's nothing like being targeted to teach your daughter about empathy and understanding for people who are bullied and/or discriminated against. Being a Target can also give her objectivity. She can see the costs of fitting in and decide she's better off outside the clique because

at least she can be true to herself and/or find good friends who like her for who she is, not for her social standing.

What Does She Lose by Being a Target?

She feels totally helpless in the face of other girls' cruelty. She feels ashamed 47
of being rejected by the other girls because of who she is. She'll be tempted
to change herself in order to fit in. She feels vulnerable and unable to affect
the outcome of her situation. She could become so anxious that she can't
concentrate on schoolwork.

> I didn't understand why I was so unhappy in sixth grade. I couldn't have 48
> told my parents that girls were being mean to me.   —ERIN, 17

> Girls will almost always withdraw instead of telling a parent. —CLAIRE, 14 49

> If a girl's stuck in a degrading clique, it's the same as when she's later in a 50
> bad relationship. She doesn't expect to be treated any better. —ELLEN, 15

OK, now you know the different roles girls play in cliques. The next ques- 51
tions are: How were these roles created in the first place? Who and what
determine these positions and power plays? Why are girls able to get away
with treating each other so badly?

It isn't really that big a secret. As girls become teens, the world becomes 52
a much bigger, scarier place. Many girls go from a small elementary school
to a much larger, more impersonal institutional school.

In elementary school, students are usually based in one room, with one 53
teacher. The principal sees them on a daily basis and parents are often
active in the school's activities, going on field trips, bringing food for bake
sales, and volunteering in after-school programs. By the end of fifth or
sixth grade, girls are beginning to prepare to leave this safe, comfy haven
of elementary school. They alternatively look forward to and dread moving
on to middle school or junior high.

Then comes the first day at the middle school or junior high—and every- 54
thing changes. Adults, in our profound wisdom, place them in a setting where
they're overwhelmed by the number of students, and they become nameless
faces with ID security cards. If you ever want to remember what it feels like,
go to your daughter's school and hang out in the hall when the bell rings right
before a lunch period (you probably have lots of times to choose from since
most schools have so many students that they need multiple lunch periods,
which means some students eat their midday meal at ten a.m.). When the bell
rings, walk from one end of the hall to the other. It's hard enough simply navigating through this noisy throng. Now imagine navigating the same hallway
and caring what each person thinks of you as you walk by.

We put our girls in this strange new environment at exactly the same   55
time that they're obsessively microanalyzing social cues, rules, and regulations and therefore are at their most insecure. Don't underestimate how
difficult and frightening this is for girls, and give your daughter credit for
getting out of bed in the morning.

Thinking Critically about the Text

How real for you is the social classification system that Wiseman establishes in
this selection? If you are a woman, where would you place your younger self in the
hierarchy? Were you a Queen Bee, a Banker, a Floater? If you are a young man,
do you think a similar classification would work for boys as well? Explain.

Questions on Subject

1. What characteristics does the Queen Bee possess, according to Wiseman? Would you agree or disagree with her assessment of the girl at the top
   of the social totem pole? Would you add or subtract any characteristics?
   Explain.

2. Throughout her essay, Wiseman includes quoted passages in which young girls
   offer their own accounts of the characters. How effective do you find these passages? What do they add, if anything, to Wiseman's classification system?

3. For every character type Wiseman includes a formulaic set of questions: "What
   does she gain by being an X?" and "What does she lose by being an X?" Why
   do you suppose she uses that formula? (Glossary: *Cause and Effect Analysis*)

4. Wiseman states that each character in the hierarchy gains from her position —
   even the Target. Do you agree? Explain.

5. What explanation does Wiseman give for the development of cliques?
   (Glossary: *Cause and Effect Analysis*)

Questions on Strategy

1. What does Wiseman mean when she writes that "cliques are sophisticated,
   complex, and multilayered, and every girl has a role within them" (paragraph
   1)? Is that statement her thesis? (Glossary: *Thesis*)

2. What does Wiseman hope to gain when she advises that "when you talk to
   your daughter about cliques, encourage her to come up with her own names
   and create roles she thinks I've missed" (paragraph 1)? Why is her advice a
   useful strategy, given her subject and audience? (Glossary: *Audience; Subject*)

3. Into what classes does Wiseman divide all young girls in her classification
   system?

4. Explain how Wiseman has organized her essay. (Glossary: *Organization*) Is that
   organizational pattern effective? Explain.

5. Wiseman's division and classification is supported by her use of definition, illustration, and comparison and contrast. (Glossary: *Comparison and Contrast; Definition; Illustration*) How do these supporting strategies strengthen Wiseman's essay?

Questions on Diction and Vocabulary

1. How effective is Wiseman's title? (Glossary: *Title*) How effective are the names she gives each class in her classification? Would you change any of those names? If so, why?

2. What is Wiseman's attitude toward cliques? (Glossary: *Attitude*) What in her diction indicates that attitude? (Glossary: *Diction*)

3. Refer to your dictionary to determine the meanings of the following words as Wiseman uses them in this selection: *clique* (paragraph 1), *omnipotent* (2), *mortified* (2), *anointed* (3), *cynical* (10), *agenda* (11), *utilitarian* (21), *oust* (22), *rationalize* (30), *perimeter* (35), *precarious* (36).

Classroom Activity Using Division and Classification

Think about how you might classify people in one of the following groups:

athletes

dieters

television viewers

sports fans

college students

Compare your method of classification with the method used by others in your class who chose the same category. What conclusions can you draw from the differences?

Writing Suggestions

1. Rosalind Wiseman offers her classification system for the roles that young girls play in cliques. Her system is based on interviews with young girls, their friends, their teachers, and their mothers. But girls are not the only ones who belong to cliques. What about boys' cliques? Write a classification essay in which you divide and classify schoolboys on the basis of their behavioral characteristics and the roles they play within cliques. Review Wiseman's organization. Model your organization on hers, modify her design, or create an entirely new approach.

2. What about parents? Can we classify them into some recognizable and meaningful classes and subclasses? Jim Fay of the Love and Logic Institute in Golden, Colorado, thinks so. He classifies parents into three groups: the

Consultant who "provides guidance," the Helicopter "who hovers over children and rescues them from the hostile world in which they live," and the Drill Sergeant "who commands and directs the lives of children." Think about your parents and talk to your friends, the students in your class, and others to gather opinions about the various parenting approaches that people demonstrate. Use the information to write an essay in which you classify parents. Be sure to define each class clearly and provide examples of their members' behavior. (Glossary: *Definition; Illustration*)

3. The photograph below depicts a common scene of a group of girls sitting, talking, and passing the time together. How do you "read" this photograph? What might the girls' facial expressions, body language, hairstyles, and dress tell you about them as individuals? As members of the group? What does their configuration on the steps tell you about the girls as a group? About their roles in the group? Write an essay in which you analyze the photograph and speculate about this group of girls and the dynamics that may hold them together as well as separate them.

The Truth about Lying

JUDITH VIORST

Judith Viorst, poet, journalist, author of children's books, and novelist, was born in 1931. She has chron- icled her life in such books as *It's Hard to Be Hip Over Thirty and Other Tragedies of Married Life* (1968), *How Did I Get to Be Forty and Other Atrocities* (1976), and *When Did I Stop Being Twenty and Other Injustices: Selected Prose from Single to Mid-Life* (1987). In 1981, she went back to school, taking courses at the Washington Psychoana- lytic Institute. This study, along with her personal expe- rience of psychoanalysis, helped to inspire *Necessary Losses* (1986), a popular and critical success. Combin- ing theory, poetry, interviews, and anecdotes, Viorst approaches personal growth as a shedding of illusions. Her recent work includes *I'm Too Young to Be Seventy: And Other Delusions* (2005).

In this essay, first published in the March 1981 issue of *Redbook*, the author ap- proaches lying with delicacy and candor as she carefully classifies the different types of lies we all encounter.

Preparing to Read

Lying happens every day in our society, whether it is a politician hiding behind a sub- tly worded statement or a guest fibbing to a host about the quality of a meal. What, for you, constitutes lying? Are all lies the same? In other words, are there different degrees or types of lying?

've been wanting to write on a subject that intrigues and challenges me: 1 the subject of lying. I've found it very difficult to do. Everyone I've talked to has a quite intense and personal but often rather intolerant point of view about what we can—and can never *never*—tell lies about. I've finally reached the conclusion that I can't present any ultimate conclusions, for too many people would promptly disagree. Instead, I'd like to present a series of moral puzzles, all concerned with lying. I'll tell you what I think about them. Do you agree?

SOCIAL LIES

Most of the people I've talked with say that they find social lying accept-   2 able and necessary. They think it's the civilized way for folks to behave. Without these little white lies, they say, our relationships would be short and brutish and nasty. It's arrogant, they say, to insist on being so incorruptible and so brave that you cause other people unnecessary embarrassment or pain by compulsively assailing them with your honesty. I basically agree. What about you?

Will you say to people, when it simply isn't true, "I like your new   3
hairdo," "You're looking much better," "It's so nice to see you," "I had a
wonderful time"?

Will you praise hideous presents and homely kids?   4

Will you decline invitations with "We're busy that night—so sorry we   5
can't come," when the truth is you'd rather stay home than dine with the
So-and-sos?

And even though, as I do, you may prefer the polite evasion of "You   6
really cooked up a storm" instead of "The soup"—which tastes like warmed-
over coffee—"is wonderful," will you, if you must, proclaim it wonderful?

There's one man I know who absolutely refuses to tell social lies. "I   7
can't play that game," he says; "I'm simply not made that way." And his
answer to the argument that saying nice things to someone doesn't cost
anything is, "Yes, it does—it destroys your credibility." Now, he won't,
unsolicited, offer his views on the painting you just bought, but you don't
ask his frank opinion unless you want *frank*, and his silence at those
moments when the rest of us liars are muttering, "Isn't it lovely?" is, for the
most part, eloquent enough. My friend does not indulge in what he calls
"flattery, false praise, and mellifluous comments." When others tell fibs he
will not go along. He says that social lying is lying, that little white lies are
still lies. And he feels that telling lies is morally wrong. What about you?

PEACE-KEEPING LIES

Many people tell peace-keeping lies; lies designed to avoid irritation or argu-   8
ment; lies designed to shelter the liar from possible blame or pain; lies (or so
it is rationalized) designed to keep trouble at bay without hurting anyone.

I tell these lies at times, and yet I always feel they're wrong. I under-   9
stand why we tell them, but still they feel wrong. And whenever I lie so that
someone won't disapprove of me or think less of me or holler at me, I feel
I'm a bit of a coward, I feel I'm dodging responsibility, I feel . . . guilty.
What about you?

Do you, when you're late for a date because you overslept, say that   10
you're late because you got caught in a traffic jam?

Do you, when you forget to call a friend, say that you called several   11
times but the line was busy?

Do you, when you didn't remember that it was your father's birthday,   12
say that his present must be delayed in the mail?

And when you're planning a weekend in New York City and you're   13
not in the mood to visit your mother, who lives there, do you conceal—with

a lie, if you must—the fact that you'll be in New York? Or do you have the courage—or is it the cruelty?—to say, "I'll be in New York, but sorry—I don't plan on seeing you"?

(Dave and his wife Elaine have two quite different points of view on 14 this very subject. He calls her a coward. She says she's being wise. He says she must assert her right to visit New York sometimes and not see her mother. To which she always patiently replies: "Why should we have useless fights? My mother's too old to change. We get along much better when I lie to her.")

Finally, do you keep the peace by telling your husband lies on the sub- 15 ject of money? Do you reduce what you really paid for your shoes? And in general do you find yourself ready, willing and able to lie to him when you make absurd mistakes or lose or break things?

"I used to have a romantic idea that part of intimacy was confessing 16 every dumb thing that you did to your husband. But after a couple of years of that," says Laura, "have I changed my mind!"

And having changed her mind, she finds herself telling peace-keeping 17 lies. And yes, I tell them, too. What about you?

PROTECTIVE LIES

Protective lies are lies folks tell—often quite serious lies—because they're 18 convinced that the truth would be too damaging. They lie because they feel there are certain human values that supersede the wrong of having lied. They lie, not for personal gain, but because they believe it's for the good of the person they're lying to. They lie to those they love, to those who trust them most of all, on the grounds that breaking this trust is justified.

They may lie to their children on money or marital matters. 19

They may lie to the dying about the state of their health. 20

They may lie about adultery, and not—or so they insist—to save their 21 own hide, but to save the heart and the pride of the men they are married to.

They may lie to their closest friend because the truth about her talents 22 or son or psyche would be—or so they insist—utterly devastating.

I sometimes tell such lies, but I'm aware that it's quite presumptuous 23 to claim I know what's best for others to know. That's called playing God. That's called manipulation and control. And we never can be sure, once we start to juggle lies, just where they'll land, exactly where they'll roll.

And furthermore, we may find ourselves lying in order to back up the 24 lies that are backing up the lie we initially told.

And furthermore—let's be honest—if conditions were reversed, we 25 certainly wouldn't want anyone lying to us.

Yet, having said all that, I still believe that there are times when protec- 26 tive lies must nonetheless be told. What about you?

If your Dad had a very bad heart and you had to tell him some bad 27
family news, which would you choose: to tell him the truth or lie?

If your former husband failed to send his monthly child-support check 28
and in other ways behaved like a total rat, would you allow your children—
who believed he was simply wonderful—to continue to believe that he
was wonderful?

If your dearly beloved brother selected a wife whom you deeply dis- 29
liked, would you reveal your feelings or would you fake it?

And if you were asked, after making love, "And how was that for 30
you?" would you reply, if it wasn't too good, "Not too good"?

Now, some would call a sex lie unimportant, little more than social 31
lying, a simple act of courtesy that makes all human intercourse run
smoothly. And some would say all sex lies are bad news and unacceptably
protective. Because, says Ruth, "a man with an ego that fragile doesn't
need your lies—he needs a psychiatrist." Still others feel that sex lies are
indeed protective lies, more serious than simple social lying, and yet at
times they tell them on the grounds that when it comes to matters sexual,
everybody's ego is somewhat fragile.

"If most of the time things go well in sex," says Sue, "I think you're 32
allowed to dissemble when they don't. I can't believe it's good to say, 'Last
night was four stars, darling, but tonight's performance rates only a half.'"

I'm inclined to agree with Sue. What about you? 33

TRUST-KEEPING LIES

Another group of lies are trust-keeping lies, lies that involve triangulation, 34
with A (that's you) telling lies to B on behalf of C (whose trust you'd promised to keep). Most people concede that once you've agreed not to betray
a friend's confidence, you can't betray it, even if you must lie. But I've
talked with people who don't want you telling them anything that they
might be called on to lie about.

"I don't tell lies for myself," says Fran, "and I don't want to have to tell 35
them for other people." Which means, she agrees, that if her best friend is
having an affair, she absolutely doesn't want to know about it.

"Are you saying," her best friend asks, "that if I went off with a lover 36
and I asked you to tell my husband I'd been with you, that you wouldn't lie
for me, that you'd betray me?"

Fran is very pained but very adamant. "I wouldn't want to betray you, 37
so . . . don't ask me."

Fran's best friend is shocked. What about you? 38

Do you believe you can have close friends if you're not prepared to 39
receive their deepest secrets?

Do you believe you must always lie for your friends? 40

Do you believe, if your friend tells a secret that turns out to be quite 41 immoral or illegal, that once you've promised to keep it, you must keep it?

And what if your friend were your boss—if you were perhaps one of 42 the President's men—would you betray or lie for him over, say, Watergate?

As you can see, these issues get terribly sticky. 43

It's my belief that once we've promised to keep a trust, we must tell lies 44 to keep it. I also believe that we can't tell Watergate lies. And if these two statements strike you as quite contradictory, you're right—they're quite contradictory. But for now they're the best I can do. What about you?

Some say that truth will out and thus you might as well tell the truth. 45 Some say you can't regain the trust that lies lose. Some say that even though the truth may never be revealed, our lies pervert and damage our relationships. Some say . . . well, here's what some of them have to say.

"I'm a coward," says Grace, "about telling close people important, 46 difficult truths. I find that I'm unable to carry it off. And so if something is bothering me, it keeps building up inside till I end up just not seeing them anymore."

"I lie to my husband on sexual things, but I'm furious," says Joyce, 47 "that he's too insensitive to know I'm lying."

"I suffer most from the misconception that children can't take the 48 truth," says Emily. "But I'm starting to see that what's harder and more damaging for them is being told lies, is not being told the truth."

"I'm afraid," says Joan, "that we often wind up feeling a bit of contempt for the people we lie to." 49

And then there are those who have no talent for lying. 50

"I'm willing to lie. But just as a last resort — the truth's always better."

"Over the years, I tried to lie," a friend 51 of mine explained, "but I always got found out and I always got punished. I guess I gave myself away because I feel guilty about any kind of lying. It looks as if I'm stuck with telling the truth."

For those of us, however, who are good 52 at telling lies, for those of us who lie and don't get caught, the question of whether or not to lie can be a hard and serious moral problem. I liked the remark of a friend of mine who said, "I'm willing to lie. But just as a last resort—the truth's always better."

"Because," he explained, "though others may completely accept the 53 lie I'm telling, I don't."

I tend to feel that way, too. 54

What about you? 55

Thinking Critically about the Text

The title of the essay plays with the relationship between lies and the truth. Viorst discusses lies that help to conceal the truth, but she's quick to point out that not all lies are malicious. Look at her subsections about "protective lies" (paragraphs 18–33) and "trust-keeping lies" (34–44). Do you think that these lies are necessary, or would it be easier to tell the truth? Explain.

Questions on Subject

1. Why is Viorst wary of giving advice on the subject of lying?

2. Viorst admits to contradicting herself in her section on "trust-keeping lies." Where else do you see her contradicting herself?

3. In telling a "protective lie," what assumption about the person hearing the lie does Viorst make? Would you make the same assumption? Why, or why not?

4. What's the difference between a "peace-keeping lie" and a "protective lie"?

Questions on Strategy

1. Into what main categories does Viorst divide lying? Do you agree with her division, or do some of her categories seem to overlap? Explain.

2. Viorst recognizes that many people have steadfast views on lying. What accommodations does she make for this audience? (Glossary: *Audience*) How does she challenge this audience?

3. There are at least two parties involved in a lie — the liar and the listener. How much significance does the author give to each of these parties? How does she make the distinction?

4. Viorst presents the reader with a series of examples or moral puzzles. How do these puzzles encourage further thought on the subject of lying? Are they successful? Why, or why not?

5. Viorst chooses an unconventional way to conclude her essay by showing different people's opinions of lying. What do you think she's doing in this last section, beginning in paragraph 45? Does this ending intensify any of the points she has made? Explain. (Glossary: *Beginnings/Endings*)

6. Viorst wants us to see that a lie is not a lie is not a lie is not a lie (i.e., that not all lies are the same). To clarify the various types of lies, she uses division and classification. She also uses illustration to show the reasons people lie. (Glossary: *Illustration*) Using several of the examples that work best for you, discuss how Viorst's use of illustration strengthens and enhances her classification.

Questions on Diction and Vocabulary

1. How would you characterize Viorst's diction in this essay? (Glossary: *Diction*) Consider the essay's subject and audience. (Glossary: *Audience; Subject*) Cite specific examples of her word choice to support your conclusions.

2. Refer to your dictionary to determine the meanings of the following words as Viorst uses them in this selection: *mellifluous* (paragraph 7), *supersede* (18), *dissemble* (32).

Classroom Activity Using Division and Classification

Consider the following classes of items and determine at least two principles of division that could be used for each class. Then write a paragraph or two in which you classify one of the groups of items according to a single principle of division. For example, in discussing crime one could use the seriousness of the crime or the type of crime as principles of division. If the seriousness of the crime were used, this might yield two categories: felonies and misdemeanors. If the types of crime were used, this would yield categories such as burglary, murder, arson, fraud, rape, and drug dealing.

movies

college professors

social sciences

roommates

professional sports

Writing Suggestions

1. Viorst wrote this essay for *Redbook*, which is usually considered a women's magazine. If you were writing this essay for a male audience, would you change the examples? If so, how would you change them? If not, why not? Do you think men are more likely to tell lies of a certain category? Explain. Write an essay in which you discuss whether men and women share similar perspectives about lying. (Glossary: *Comparison and Contrast*)

2. Write an essay of division and classification on the subject of friends. How many different types of friends do you recognize? On what basis do you differentiate them? Do you make distinctions among them on the basis of gender? Are some friends more important, more useful, more intimate, more convenient, more trustworthy, more reliable, more supportive, more lasting than others? Are you more willing to share your most personal thoughts and feelings with some friends than with others? Be sure to establish a context for why you are writing about friends and putting forth an essay that divides and classifies them. Conclude with an insightful statement drawn from your thesis, the division and classification you establish, and the examples you provide.

The Ways of Meeting Oppression

MARTIN LUTHER KING JR.

Martin Luther King Jr. (1929–1968) was the son of a Baptist minister. Ordained at the age of eighteen, King went on to study at Morehouse College, Crozer Theological Seminary, Boston University, and Chicago Theological Seminary. He came to prominence in 1955 in Montgomery, Alabama, when he led a successful boycott against the city's segregated bus system. A powerful orator and writer, King went on to become the leading spokesperson for the civil rights movement during the 1950s and 1960s. In 1964, he was awarded the Nobel Peace Prize for his policy of nonviolent resistance to racial injustice, a policy that he explains in the following selection. King was assassinated in April 1968 after speaking at a rally in Memphis, Tennessee.

This selection is excerpted from the book *Stride Toward Freedom* (1958). Notice how King classifies the three ways oppressed people throughout history have reacted to their oppressors and how his organization prepares the reader for his conclusion.

Preparing to Read

Summarize what you know about the civil rights movement of the late 1950s and early 1960s. What were the movement's goals? What tactics did its leaders use? How successful were those tactics? How did this movement change American society?

Oppressed people deal with their oppression in three characteristic ways. One way is acquiescence: The oppressed resign themselves to their doom. They tacitly adjust themselves to oppression, and thereby become conditioned to it. In every movement toward freedom some of the oppressed prefer to remain oppressed. Almost 2,800 years ago Moses set out to lead the children of Israel from the slavery of Egypt to the freedom of the promised land. He soon discovered that slaves do not always welcome their deliverers. They become accustomed to being slaves. They would rather bear those ills they have, as Shakespeare pointed out, than flee to others that they know not of. They prefer the "fleshpots of Egypt" to the ordeals of emancipation.

There is such a thing as the freedom of exhaustion. Some people are so worn down by the yoke of oppression that they give up. A few years ago in the slum areas of Atlanta, a Negro guitarist used to sing almost daily: "Been down so long that down don't bother me." This is the type of negative freedom and resignation that often engulfs the life of the oppressed.

But this is not the way out. To accept passively an unjust system is to cooperate with that system; thereby the oppressed become as evil as the oppressor. Noncooperation with evil is as much a moral obligation as is cooperation with good. The oppressed must never allow the conscience of the oppressor to slumber. Religion reminds every man that he is his brother's keeper. To accept injustice or segregation passively is to say to the oppressor that his actions are morally right. It is a way of allowing his conscience to fall asleep. At this moment the oppressed fails to be his brother's keeper. So acquiescence—while often the easier way—is not the moral way. It is the way of the coward. The Negro cannot win the respect of his oppressor by acquiescing; he merely increases the oppressor's arrogance and contempt. Acquiescence is interpreted as proof of the Negro's inferiority. The Negro cannot win the respect of the white people of the south or the peoples of the world if he is willing to sell the future of his children for his personal and immediate comfort and safety.

> The problem is not a purely racial one, with Negroes set against whites. In the end, it's not a struggle between people at all, but a tension between justice and injustice.

A second way that oppressed people sometimes deal with oppression is to resort to physical violence and corroding hatred. Violence often brings about momentary results. Nations have frequently won their independence in battle. But in spite of temporary victories, violence never brings permanent peace. It solves no social problem; it merely creates new and more complicated ones.

Violence as a way of achieving racial justice is both impractical and immoral. It is impractical because it is a descending spiral ending in destruction for all. The old law of an eye for an eye leaves everybody blind. It is immoral because it seeks to humiliate the opponent rather than win his understanding; it seeks to annihilate rather than to convert. Violence is immoral because it thrives on hatred rather than love. It destroys community and makes brotherhood impossible. It leaves society in monologue rather than dialogue. Violence ends by defeating itself. It creates bitterness in the survivors and brutality in the destroyers. A voice echoes through time saying to every potential Peter, "Put up your sword." History is cluttered with the wreckage of nations that failed to follow this command.

If the American Negro and other victims of oppression succumb to the temptation of using violence in the struggle for freedom, future generations will be the recipients of a desolate night of bitterness, and our chief legacy to them will be an endless reign of meaningless chaos. Violence is not the way.

The third way open to oppressed people in their quest for freedom is the way of nonviolent resistance. Like the synthesis in Hegelian philosophy, the principle of nonviolent resistance seeks to reconcile the truths of two opposites—the acquiescence and violence—while avoiding the extremes and immoralities of both. The nonviolent resister agrees with the person who acquiesces that one should not be physically aggressive toward his opponent; but he balances the equation by agreeing with the person of violence that evil must be resisted. He avoids the nonresistance of the former and the violent resistance of the latter. With nonviolent resistance, no individual or group need submit to any wrong, nor need anyone resort to violence in order to right a wrong. 7

It seems to me that this is the method that must guide the actions of the Negro in the present crisis in race relations. Through nonviolent resistance the Negro will be able to rise to the noble height of opposing the unjust system while loving the perpetrators of the system. The Negro must work passionately and unrelentingly for full stature as a citizen, but he must not use inferior methods to gain it. He must never come to terms with falsehood, malice, hate, or destruction. 8

Nonviolent resistance makes it possible for the Negro to remain in the South and struggle for his rights. The Negro's problem will not be solved by running away. He cannot listen to the glib suggestion of those who would urge him to migrate en masse to other sections of the country. By grasping his great opportunity in the South he can make a lasting contribution to the moral strength of the nation and set a sublime example of courage for generations yet unborn. 9

By nonviolent resistance, the Negro can also enlist all men of good will in his struggle for equality. The problem is not a purely racial one, with Negroes set against whites. In the end, it is not a struggle between people at all, but a tension between justice and injustice. Nonviolent resistance is not aimed against oppressors but against oppression. Under its banner consciences, not racial groups, are enlisted. 10

Thinking Critically about the Text

Find the definition of *oppress* or *oppression* in the dictionary. Exactly what does King mean when he speaks of people being "oppressed" in the South in twentieth-century America? Do you think that people are still being oppressed in America today? Explain.

Questions on Subject

1. What does King mean by the phrase "freedom of exhaustion" (paragraph 2)? Why is he scathing in his assessment of people who succumb to such a condition in response to oppression?

2. According to King, what is the role of religion in the battle against oppression?

3. Why does King advocate the avoidance of violence in fighting oppression, despite the short-term success violence often achieves for the victors? How do such victories affect the future?

4. According to King, how does nonviolent resistance transform a racial issue into one of conscience?

Questions on Strategy

1. King's essay is easy to read and understand, and everything in it relates to his purpose. (Glossary: *Purpose*) What is that purpose? Summarize how each paragraph supports his purpose. How does the essay's organization help King achieve his purpose? (Glossary: *Organization*)

2. King says that "nonviolent resistance is not aimed against oppressors but against oppression" (paragraph 10). What does he mean by this? Why does he deflect anger and resentment away from a concrete example, the oppressors, to an abstract concept, oppression? (Glossary: *Concrete/Abstract*) How does this choice support his purpose? (Glossary: *Purpose*)

3. King evokes the names of Moses, Shakespeare, and Hegel in his essay. What does this tell you about his intended audience? (Glossary: *Audience*) Why does King address the audience in this way?

4. King uses division and classification to help him argue his point in this essay. What other rhetorical strategies does King use? How does each strategy, including division and classification and argument, contribute to the effectiveness of the essay?

Questions on Diction and Vocabulary

1. In his discussion about overcoming oppression with violence, King says that "future generations will be the recipients of a desolate night of bitterness" (paragraph 6). What image do his words evoke for you? Why do you think he chooses to use a striking metaphor here, instead of a less poetic statement? (Glossary: *Figures of Speech*)

2. King urges Negroes to avoid "falsehood, malice, hate, or destruction" (paragraph 8) in their quest to gain full stature as citizens. How does each of these terms relate to his earlier argument about avoiding violence? How does each enhance or add new meaning to his earlier argument?

3. Refer to your dictionary to determine the meanings of the following words as King uses them in this selection: *acquiescence* (paragraph 1), *tacitly* (1), *yoke* (2), *perpetrators* (8), *glib* (9), *sublime* (9).

Classroom Activity Using Division and Classification

Be prepared to discuss in class why you believe division and classification are important strategies or ways of thinking in everyday life. Explain, for example, how useful the two complementary strategies are for you as you go shopping in the supermarket for items on your shopping list or look for particular textbooks in your college bookstore.

Writing Suggestions

1. Write a division and classification essay in which you follow King's model. Identify three methods that you can use to achieve a goal — study for a test, apply to graduate school, or interview for a job, for example. Choose one method to advocate; then frame your essay so that the division and classification strategy helps you make your point.

2. Toward the end of his essay, King states, "By grasping his great opportunity in the South [the Negro] can make a lasting contribution to the moral strength of the nation and set a sublime example of courage for generations yet unborn" (paragraph 9). With your classmates, discuss whether the movement that King led achieved its goal of solving many of the underlying racial tensions and inequities in the United States. In terms of equality, what has happened in the United States since King's famous "I Have a Dream" speech (page 522)? Write a paper in which you argue for or against the idea that King's "dream" is alive and well. (Glossary: *Argument*)

"Beam Us Up, Mr. Scott": Why Misquotations Catch On

MARIA KONNIKOVA

Maria Konnikova is a writer whose work has appeared in such publications as the *Atlantic*, the *New York Times*, *Slate*, the *New Republic*, the *Paris Review*, the *Boston Globe*, *Scientific American*, *Scientific MIND*, and the *Observer*. Born in Moscow, Russia, she arrived in the United States when she was four years old and went on to study creative writing, government, and psychology at Harvard, where she graduated magna cum laude. She is currently a doctoral candidate in psychology at Columbia University. Literature and psychology are the subjects of Konnikova's *Scientific American* column "Literally Psyched." The two disciplines also form the basis of her first book, *Mastermind: How to Think Like Sherlock Holmes* (2013), a study of how the great sleuth's thought processes can be understood by the study of modem neuroscience and be used to help us think clearly and creatively.

In " 'Beam Us Up, Mr. Scott': Why Misquotations Catch On," first published in the *Atlantic* on August 15, 2012, Konnikova classifies a vast number of misremembered quotations from books, movies, and speeches to help illuminate why people use them inaccurately.

Preparing to Read

The more books we read, the more television shows and movies we watch, the more we remember lines that characters speak. Why do we remember them? Do we remember them accurately?

Misquotations are often stickier than actual quotes," Abraham Lincoln once joked. He didn't really, of course—but he'd be a great spokesperson of the sentiment, given how often his words have been misremembered, miscast, passed down from person to person in a way that little resembles any of his actual statements. (Actually, Mark Twain would be a better candidate for that one. Didn't he say basically everything?)

In the world of speeches and orations, especially historical ones, the persistent misquotation is understandable. You hear a speech. You misremember or mishear a line as something more colorful than it was. If you're a journalist—especially in the pre-recording age, when all notes were taken by hand—you might then type that misremembrance into an article. Multiple versions circulate. And so on.

But in the modern age, where basically everything is track-downable, what's our excuse? Why do misquotes arise—and why are they so persistent and hard to eradicate? 3

The persistence part is simple, especially with the rise of the Internet. It has become far easier to share—and incorrect information is just as sharable as valid information. The more something is shared, the more hits it gets, the more difficult it becomes to verify, and so forth. It becomes easier to just quote and hope for the best. But why do we misquote in the first place? 4

> In the modern age, where basically everything is track-downable, what's our excuse? Why do misquotes arise — and why are they so persistent and hard to eradicate?

Have you noticed how incorrect quotes often just *sound* right—sometimes, more right than actual quotations? There's a reason for that. Our brains really like fluency, or the experience of cognitive ease (as opposed to cognitive strain) in taking in and retrieving information. The more fluent the experience of reading a quote—or the easier it is to grasp, the smoother it sounds, the more readily it comes to mind—the less likely we are to question the actual quotation. Those right-sounding misquotes are just taking that tendency to the next step: cleaning up, so to speak, quotations so that they are more mellifluous, more all-around quotable, easier to store and recall at a later point. We might not even be misquoting on purpose, but once we do, the result tends to be catchier than the original. 5

In some cases, it's a simple question of word order. "Methinks the lady doth protest too much" has an easier rhythm than the actual, "The lady doth protest too much, methinks." The change certainly matters if you're a poet, or preserving the integrity of Shakespeare. But at least it does no real harm to the meaning. 6

In some, it's a simplification or contraction of something that's a bit messier to remember without it. "Beam me up, Scotty!" was never actually uttered by any *Star Trek* character. "Beam us up, Mr. Scott!" was, in the 1968 "Gamesters of Triskelion." Likewise, Humphrey Bogart's iconic "Play it again, Sam" was in reality, "If she can stand it, I can. Play it." Note how in both cases, the sense remains basically the same. The adjustments are minor ones. They aren't blatant misquotations so much as attempts to, on some level, make things sound the way they *should* sound. These misquotes are in the category of, "right, that's what I wanted to say—and maybe even how I wanted to say it." 7

There are, of course, simplifications that are more perfidious and sneaky. The famous "power corrupts; absolute power corrupts absolutely," 8 for one, diverges in just one tiny way from Lord Acton's original phrasing: "Power tends to corrupt; absolute power corrupts absolutely." Modifiers like "should" aren't as pretty—or as striking—as absolutes. Rhetorically, the first one surely sounds better (hence, our enhanced memory of it and taste for its correctness). But the gulf between it and the real thing is vast. What one little word can do. (Here's another example: The line from Tennyson's "Charge of the Light Brigade" that is often quoted as "theirs but to do or die" is instead "theirs but to do *and* die." That "and" might be small, but it makes all the difference.)

The last misquotation type in the "more fluent" category is the most 9 blatant. It actually reworks to a great extent the original line, usually by shortening or simplifying it—and while the result is doubtless superior from a purely oratorical perspective (as in, it sounds more dramatic and is more likely to lodge itself in your mind), it also departs to an alarming extent from the original. Take the oft-quoted Thomas Carlyle gem, from his life of Frederick the Great: "Genius is an infinite capacity for taking pains." Isn't that nice? A simple, strong definition. Except, Carlyle wrote, "The good plan itself, this comes not of its own accord; it is the fruit of genius (which means transcendent capacity of taking trouble, first of all)." Not quite the same thing, is it? (But just try to bring the real monster of a phrase to mind when you need a good quote to drive a point home.)

It's not too far from that elaborate paraphrasing to, more literally, put- 10 ting words into the mouths of unsuspecting quote victims. Marie Antoinette's "let them eat cake" would be one of the most famous lines in history were it not for the fact that she never actually said it. The line comes instead from Book 6 of Jean-Jacques Rousseau's *Confessions*, written several years before Marie Antoinette ever came to Versailles—and its speaker is never actually named but rather referred to as a "great princess." (Oh, and it's not cake; it's brioche.)

And poor Mark Twain. He seems to have said everything there is to say 11 in the world. Several of my favorite lines turn out to be purely apocryphal, like "I would rather go to bed with Lillian Russell stark naked than with Ulysses S. Grant in full military regalia" and "Giving up smoking is easy. I've done it hundreds of times." Several other bon mots are actually not original to Twain, but rather quoted by him (Twain, to his credit, always gave the source; his listeners and readers paid less careful attention.) "There are three kinds of lies: lies, damn lies, and statistics," for instance, was, according to Twain, an invention of Benjamin Disraeli's, and "Wagner's music is better than it sounds" originated with Edgar Wilson Nye. Twain was a witty man, but, alas, he didn't say it all. (But the quotes, like Lincoln's, stick because they make sense; the greater the cognitive ease, the more superficial and less suspicious the thinking. Why question if we have no reason to think anything is wrong?)

Then, there are those quotes that aren't technically wrong—except they become attributed to a literary character when they were really said by his film counterpart. These, too, aren't malicious; in many cases, our minds simply misremember. Especially if a film's line has that fluency that our memories so love, we might forget entirely that the source was the movie and not the book. Into that bucket falls Sherlock Holmes's most memorable line, "Elementary, my dear Watson," which was never written by Arthur Conan Doyle but came instead from the 1929 film. (Though it's the first Holmes line that likely comes to mind for most fans.) There, too, we put Dracula's famed "I want to suck your blood"—not words ever penned by Bram Stoker.

And finally, we come to a category of misquotation that has everything to do with our sensory perception: We misquote because we actually, physically misread or mishear (our eyes see what they want or expect to see; our ears hear what, in turn, sounds right to them)—and the result makes so much sense that it sticks.

In "The Mourning Bride," William Congreve makes a beautiful observation of music's appeal: "Music hath charms to soothe the savage beast." Actually, the word in question is breast. But see how close the two look? How easy it would be to read "beast" after "savage." The former almost cues the latter in mind. We think of savage beasts all the time. Savage breasts, not so much.

But perhaps the most frequent victim of this type of error is William Shakespeare, whose lines often look and sound like something else—and something that is frequently easier to recall later on than the original. In *Hamlet*, we often hear the prince described as "to the manor born." Only, when Hamlet refers to himself, it's as born to the *manner*. On its own, that makes little sense, a likely reason for the manor's persistence. But take it in full context—"But to my mind, though I am native here / And to the manner born, it is a custom / More honour'd in the breach than the observance"—and it becomes quite clear what the prince is trying to say.

And how often does one hear the evil cackling of the *Macbeth* witches, "Bubble bubble, toil and trouble"? In the play, of course, the proper line is "Double, double"—but the two sound remarkably similar (especially with a British accent), and we're talking about a cauldron here, right? So bubbling makes a great deal of sense.

There is, too, that well-known line from the *Merchant of Venice*, that admonition that "all that glitters is not gold." (Sometimes, it's also quoted as "also that glistens.") In reality, nothing is glittering or glistening. What Shakespeare wrote was, "All that *glisters* is not gold." But it's easy to see how the misquotation might arise—and the replacements certainly sound better to the modern ear, and make more sense.

That's the thing about misquotations. They tend, for the most part, to arise not out of malice or intentional misrepresentation but out of understandable cognitive processes. (That, and improper punctuation. Remember Jessica Dovey, the inadvertent heir to Martin Luther King?) And the more understandable a process, the more likely it is to play out in similar fashion for multiple people—and the more likely the misquotation is to spring up at various times and in various places, instead of being immediately corrected.

Of course, the other common reason for misquoting is simple laziness. We think we remember something and so we just write it down, rather than spend time checking. Or, we like the way a phrase sounds or the message it has and so we just assume our (likely online) source is correct—and the more sites there are with the mistake, the more persuasive it becomes—instead of painfully tracking down the original to verify it for ourselves.

So how do you spot that misquote? There's (sadly) no effortless way to go about it. The most we can do is to always be skeptical of ourselves, especially if something sounds too right or fluent or spot on. Because the better it sounds, the more likely it is to be a little off. That, and check quotes before we perpetuate them in cyberspace or print. Otherwise, we might end up like Bob Dylan, who once remarked, "I've misquoted myself so many times, I don't know what I've said." (He totally could have said that, right?)

Thinking Critically about the Text

In preparation for a classroom discussion on accuracy in using quoted material, check all of Konnikova's quotations in your school library or on the Internet to see how accurately she uses them in her essay. Be ready to report your findings to the class.

Questions on Subject

1. Why, according to Konnikova, do misquotations persist? Why can't we stamp them out?

2. To what does Konnikova attribute most misquotations of Shakespeare?

3. In paragraph 18, Konnikova makes a reference to Jessica Dovey and Martin Luther King Jr. What is that reference all about? How can you find out? What does the story behind the reference have to do with the points that Konnikova makes in her essay?

4. Why does finding the same information in multiple sources still not prevent us from perpetuating misquotations?

5. What did Bob Dylan mean when he said (or "could have said"), "I've misquoted myself so many times, I don't know what I've said"?

Questions on Strategy

1. What do you think that Konnikova hoped to achieve in writing her essay? (Glossary: *Purpose*)

2. What is Konnikova's thesis in this essay? (Glossary: *Thesis*) Where does she state it?

3. Into what classes does Konnikova divide and classify misremembered quotations?

4. Check out the *Atlantic*'s description of itself on the Internet; or, if possible, peruse a few copies of the magazine the next time you're at a newsstand or library. What makes Konnikova's essay a good one for the *Atlantic*'s reading audience?

5. The aside or parenthetical phrase is a characteristic of Konnikova's style. How does she use asides and to what effect?

Questions on Diction and Vocabulary

1. In paragraph 5, Konnikova talks about misquotations sometimes being catchier. What makes something catchy?

2. In paragraph 8, Konnikova says that some simplifications are "perfidious and sneaky." What does she mean by these two words? Do you think that they are appropriate in the context she uses them? Explain.

3. In paragraph 1, Konnikova writes, "Misquotations are often stickier than actual quotes." At the end of paragraph 13, she also uses the word *sticks*. What does she mean by her use of *stickier* and *sticks*? Have you ever used these words in this way? Might you now?

Classroom Activity Using Division and Classification

Divide each item in the following list into at least three different categories, and be prepared to explain your principle of division. For example, you can use a number of different principles of division with newspapers. Here are five, together with the categories that result in each case: the medium in which they appear (online, print, or both); how partisan they are (left, center, or right); the coverage they give (national, local, or both); their subscription structure (free, monthly payment, or annual payment); their degree of specialization (sports, technology, the arts); and so forth.

1. instructors
2. restaurants
3. writers
4. coaches

Writing Suggestions

1. Some authors use division and classification to generate new ways of understanding topics, and some use division and classification to revisit subjects of lasting interest on which they wish to offer fresh insights. Select a topic for your essay, and then decide which approach you want to take. If you think you are writing an original classification, you may want to check the Internet to see that no one, in fact, has dealt with it already. If you are writing a classification that has been treated before (for example, types of love, types of lies, types of college slang, types of poetry, types of science fiction, types of humor, types of dance, types of students), you will want to learn all you can about the way other writers have treated your subject. Naturally, you will want to offer some fresh insights for even tried-and-true classifications, rather than simply offering fresh examples of what others have already found to be true.

2. Division and classification is often used to probe deeper into a body of information in an attempt to understand it in a more detailed manner. For example, it's not *simply* a disease or weather pattern we might refer to, but rather a *specific kind* of disease or weather. Such information allows us to treat a disease more specifically, or to warn a population more accurately of an impending weather-related threat. Anything that is undifferentiated is difficult to talk about intelligently. The principle of division and classification — as well as the specific classes and subclasses that you establish about any situation — makes the world more understandable. Select a body of information that you want to understand in a more detailed manner, and then write an essay of division and classification explaining clearly why your system of division and classification is important.

WRITING SUGGESTIONS FOR DIVISION AND CLASSIFICATION

1. To write a meaningful classification essay, you must analyze a body of unorganized material, arranging it for a particular purpose. (Glossary: *Purpose*) For example, to identify for a buyer the most economical cars currently on the market, you might initially determine which cars can be purchased for under $25,000 and which cost between $25,000 and $35,000. Then, using a second basis of selection — fuel economy — you could determine which cars have the best gas mileage within each price range.

   Select one of the following subjects, and write a classification essay. Be sure that your purpose is clearly explained and that your bases of selection are chosen and ordered in accordance with your purpose.

   a. attitudes toward physical fitness
   b. contemporary American music
   c. reading materials
   d. reasons for going to college
   e. attitudes toward the religious or spiritual side of life
   f. choosing a hobby
   g. television comedies
   h. college professors
   i. local restaurants
   j. choosing a career
   k. college courses
   l. recreational activities
   m. ways of financing a college education
   n. parties or other social events

2. We sometimes resist classifying other people because it can seem like "pigeonholing" or stereotyping individuals unfairly. In an essay, compare and contrast two or more ways of classifying people, including at least one that you would call legitimate and one that you would call misleading. (Glossary: *Comparison and Contrast*) What conclusions can you draw about the difference between useful classifications and damaging stereotypes?

3. Use division and classification to explain your school or town. What categories might you use? Would you divide your subject into different types of people? Would you classify people by their spending habits? What are the other ways in which you might explain your school or town? What other rhetorical strategies might you incorporate to strengthen your presentation? You

might want to look at the Web site of your school or town to find out what categories it uses to present itself.

4. The cartoon below was created by Bernard Schoenbaum and first appeared in the *New Yorker* on September 19, 1994.

While it's meant to be amusing, the cartoon's classification of books according to reader's attention span does provide more than a moment's comic relief: Readers usually do prefer certain types of books, from more to less challenging, depending on what they hope to achieve by reading. Write an essay in which you divide and classify book readers according to a system of your own devising.

5. **Writing with Sources.** Do some research on the last presidential election or another political campaign that interests you. Reread or watch online major news coverage of the last days of the election, and identify at least three qualities that were mentioned most often for the two final contenders. What categories or classes do these qualities belong to? Write an essay in which you discuss how this division and classification of the candidates' qualities might have contributed to the winner's victory. Also consider who did the dividing: Was it the media? The public? For models of and advice on integrating sources in your essay, see Chapters 14 and 15.

6. **Writing with Sources.** The opening illustration for this chapter on page 330 is an excerpt of a floor plan from the National Museum of Natural History, a part of the Smithsonian Institution. Search "Floor Plans of the Smithsonian National Museum of Natural History" online to examine the full version, which is not only color-coded but also contains a key to the meaning of each icon. Then, using the terms "museum floor plan," search online for other, similarly formatted layouts. Consider museums that you've visited in the past or museums you hope to visit in the future. Look at a few different plans, and then select one with exhibit categories that interest you. Brainstorm a list of things that might appear in each category, and write a paragraph about why those items would be a good fit for the museum's overall purpose, focus, and audience. Be sure to reference specific parts of your floor plan in your explanation. For models of and advice on integrating sources in your essay, see Chapters 14 and 15.

7. **Writing in the Workplace.** You are starting a new business, either a nonprofit charitable organization in which you are looking for donors or a for-profit business for which you need customers. Develop a fund-raising plan or a marketing plan in which you divide and classify your potential donors and customers. Be sure that your plan identifies the classes and subclasses of donors and customers that would maximize your desired outcome. When classifying, consider such demographics as age, sex, income, race, ethnicity, location, and likely proficiency with social media.

---

 e-Pages

Social Media Demographics
Who's Using Which Sites?

FLOWTOWN

See how division and classification works on the Web. Go to bedfordstmartins .com/subjectandstrategy for an infographic and study questions comparing who uses such social-media platforms as Facebook, Twitter, Digg, and Reddit.

Espresso
[ess-press-oh]

Espresso Macchiato
[ess-press-oh mock-e-ah-toe]

Espresso con Panna
[ess-press-oh kon pawn-nah]

Caffé Latte
[caf-ay lah-tey]

Flat White

Cafe Breve
[caf-ay brev-ay]

Cappuccino
[kap-oo-chee-noh]

Caffé Mocha
[caf-ay moh-kuh]

Americano
[uh-mer-i-kan-oh]

CHAPTER 10

Definition

WHAT IS DEFINITION?

IF YOU HAVE EVER USED A DICTIONARY, YOU ARE ALREADY FAMILIAR with the concept of definition. The job of explaining the meanings of words and phrases is not limited to the dictionary alone, however: We use definition all the time in our everyday lives to make our points clearer. How often have you been asked what you mean when a word or phrase you're using is ambiguous, unusual, or simply unfamiliar to your listener? We can only communicate with one another clearly and effectively when we all define the words we use in the same way — and that is not always easy.

Visuals can come to our aid in definition, as the chart on the page opposite shows. While we could certainly define the various coffee drinks using words alone, the illustration gives a quick, at-a-glance indication of their basic components. A chart like this one displayed at a specialty coffee shop would eliminate all ambiguity in ordering.

DEFINITION IN WRITTEN TEXTS

Unlike the relative proportions of coffee, milk, and water in various coffee drinks, understanding and explaining complex concepts is often impossible without using precise, detailed, verbal definitions. These definitions can take on many different forms depending, in part, on the purpose of the definition and on what is being defined.

For example, let's look at how Robert Keith Miller attempts to define *discrimination* in his essay called "Discrimination Is a Virtue," which first appeared in *Newsweek*.

> We have a word in English which means "the ability to tell differences." That word is *discrimination*. But within the last [fifty] years, this word has been so frequently misused that an entire generation has grown up believing that "discrimination" means "racism." People are always proclaiming that

"discrimination" is something that should be done away with. Should that ever happen, it would prove to be our undoing.

Discrimination means discernment; it means the ability to perceive the truth, to use good judgment and to profit accordingly. The *Oxford English Dictionary* traces this meaning of the word back to 1648 and demonstrates that for the next 300 years, "discrimination" was a virtue, not a vice. Thus, when a character in a nineteenth-century novel makes a happy marriage, Dickens has another character remark, "It does credit to your discrimination that you should have found such a very excellent young woman."

Of course, "the ability to tell differences" assumes that differences exist, and this is unsettling for a culture obsessed with the notion of equality. The contemporary belief that discrimination is a vice stems from the compound "discriminate against." What we need to remember, however, is that some things deserve to be judged harshly: We should not leave our kingdoms to the selfish and the wicked.

Discrimination is wrong only when someone or something is discriminated against because of prejudice. But to use the word in that sense, as so many people do, is to destroy its true meaning. If you discriminate against something because of general preconceptions rather than particular insights, then you are not discriminating—bias has clouded the clarity of vision that discrimination demands.

How does Miller define *discrimination*? He mainly uses a technique called *extended definition*, a definition that requires a full discussion. This is only one of many types of definition that you could use to explain what a word or an idea means to you. The following paragraphs identify and explain several other types.

A *formal definition*—a definition such as that found in a dictionary—explains the meaning of a word by assigning it to a class and then differentiating it from other members of that class.

TERM		CLASS	DIFFERENTIATION
Music	is	sound	made by voices or instruments and characterized by melody, harmony, or rhythm.

Note how crucial the differentiation is here: There are many sounds—from the roar of a passing jet airplane to the fizz of soda in a glass—that must be excluded for the definition to be precise and useful. Dictionary entries often follow the class-differentiation pattern of the formal definition.

A *synonymous definition* explains a word by pairing it with another word of similar but perhaps more limited meaning.

Music is melody.

Synonymous definition is almost never as precise as formal definition because few words share exactly the same meaning. But when the word being defined is reasonably familiar and somewhat broad, a well-chosen synonym can provide readers with a surer sense of its meaning in context.

A *negative definition* explains a word by saying what it does not mean.

> Music is not silence, and it is not noise.

Such a definition must obviously be incomplete: There are sounds that are neither silence nor noise and yet are not music—quiet conversation, for example. But specifying what something is *not* often helps to clarify other statements about what it is.

An *etymological definition* also seldom stands alone, but by tracing a word's origins it helps readers understand its meaning. *Etymology* itself is defined as the study of the history of a linguistic form—the history of words.

> Music is descended from the Greek word *mousikē*, meaning literally "the art of the Muse."

The Muses, according to Greek mythology, were deities and the sources of inspiration in the arts. Thus the etymology suggests why we think of music as an art and as the product of inspiration. Etymological definitions often reveal surprising sources that suggest new ways of looking at ideas or objects.

A *stipulative definition* is a definition invented by a writer to convey a special or unexpected sense of an existing and often familiar word.

> Music is a language, but a language of the intangible, a kind of soul-language.   —EDWARD MACDOWELL

> Music is the arithmetic of sounds.   —CLAUDE DEBUSSY

Although these two examples seem to disagree with each other, and perhaps also with your idea of what music is, note that neither is arbitrary. (That is, neither assigns to the word *music* a completely foreign meaning, as Humpty Dumpty did in *Through the Looking-Glass* when he defined *glory* as "a nice knock-down argument.") The stipulative definitions by MacDowell and Debussy help explain each composer's conception of the subject and can lead, of course, to further elaboration. Stipulative definitions almost always provide the basis for a more complex discussion. These definitions are often the subjects of an extended definition.

Extended definition, like the definition of *discrimination* given by Robert Keith Miller on pages 387–88, is used when a word, or the idea it stands for, requires more than a sentence of explanation. *Extended definition* may employ any of the definition techniques mentioned above, as well as the strategies discussed in other chapters. For example, an extended definition of music might provide *examples*, ranging from African drumming to a Bach fugue to a Bruce Springsteen song, to develop a fuller and more vivid sense of what music is. A writer might *describe* music in detail by showing its characteristic features, or explain the *process* of composing music, or *compare and contrast* music with language (according to MacDowell's stipulative definition) or arithmetic (according to Debussy's). Each of these strategies helps make the meaning of a writer's words and ideas clear.

In his extended definition of the word *discrimination*, Miller uses a very brief formal definition of *discrimination* [term]: "the ability [class] to tell differences [differentiation]." He then offers a negative definition (discrimination is not racism) and a synonymous definition (discrimination is discernment). Next he cites the entry in a great historical dictionary of English to support his claim, and he quotes an example to illustrate his definition. He concludes by contrasting the word *discrimination* with the compound "discriminate against." Each of these techniques helps make the case that the most precise meaning of *discrimination* is in direct opposition to its common usage today.

USING DEFINITION AS A WRITING STRATEGY

Since most readers have dictionaries, it might seem that writers would hardly ever have to define their terms with formal definitions. In fact, writers don't necessarily do so all the time, even when using an unusual word like *tergiversation*, which few readers have in their active vocabularies; if readers don't know it, the reasoning goes, let them look it up. But there are times when a formal definition is quite necessary. One of these times is when a writer uses a word so specialized or so new that it simply won't be in dictionaries; another is when a writer must use a number of unfamiliar technical terms within only a few sentences. Also, when a word has several different meanings or may mean different things to different people, writers will often state exactly the sense in which they are using the word. In each of these cases, definition serves the purpose of achieving clarity.

But writers also sometimes use definition, particularly extended definition, to explain the essential nature of the things and ideas they write about. For example, consider E. B. White's definition of *democracy*, which first appeared in the *New Yorker* on July 3, 1943.

> We received a letter from the Writers' War Board the other day asking for a statement on "The Meaning of Democracy." It presumably is our duty to comply with such a request, and it is certainly our pleasure.
>
> Surely the Board knows what democracy is. It is the line that forms on the right. It is the *don't* in "don't shove." It is the hole in the stuffed shirt

through which the sawdust slowly trickles; it is the dent in the high hat. Democracy is the recurrent suspicion that more than half of the people are right more than half of the time. It is the feeling of privacy in the voting booths, the feeling of communion in the libraries, the feeling of vitality everywhere. Democracy is a letter to the editor. Democracy is the score at the beginning of the ninth. It is an idea which hasn't been disproved yet, a song the words of which have not gone bad. It's the mustard on the hot dog and the cream in the rationed coffee. Democracy is a request from a War Board, in the middle of a morning in the middle of a war, wanting to know what democracy is.

Such writing goes beyond answering the question, "What does _____ mean exactly?" to tackle the much broader and deeper question "What is _____, and what does it represent?"

Although exploring a term and what it represents is often the primary object of such a definition, sometimes writers go beyond giving a formal definition; they also use extended definitions to make persuasive points. Take the Miller essay, for example (pages 387–88). The subject of Miller's extended definition is clearly the word *discrimination*. His purpose, however, is less immediately obvious. At first it appears that he wants only to explain what the word means. But by the third sentence he is distinguishing what it does not mean, and at the end it's clear he's trying to persuade readers to use the word correctly and thus to discriminate more sharply and justly themselves.

USING DEFINITION ACROSS THE DISCIPLINES

When writing essays in the academic disciplines, you will have many opportunities to use the strategy of definition to both organize and strengthen the presentation of your ideas. To determine whether or not definition is the right strategy for you in a particular paper, use the guidelines described in Chapter 2 (Determining a Strategy for Developing Your Essay, pages 32–33). Consider the following examples:

Philosophy

1. **MAIN IDEA:** A person of integrity is more than just an honest person.
2. **QUESTION:** What does it mean to have *integrity*?
3. **STRATEGY:** Definition. The direction words *mean* and *is more than* call for a complete explanation of the meaning of the word *integrity*.
4. **SUPPORTING STRATEGY:** Comparison and Contrast. To clarify the definition of *integrity*, it might be helpful to differentiate a person of integrity from a moral person or an ethical person.

Economics

1. **MAIN IDEA:** One way to understand the swings in the United States economy is to know the meaning of inflation.

2. **QUESTION:** What is inflation?

3. **STRATEGY:** Definition. The direction words *meaning* and *is* point us toward the strategy of definition—the word *inflation* needs to be explained.

4. **SUPPORTING STRATEGY:** Cause and Effect Analysis. In explaining the meaning of *inflation*, it would be interesting to explore economic factors that cause inflation as well as the effects of inflation on the economy.

Astronomy

1. **MAIN IDEA:** With the demotion of Pluto from planet to "dwarf planet" or plutoid, astronomers have given new attention to the definition of *planet*.

2. **QUESTION:** What is a planet?

3. **STRATEGY:** Definition. The direction words *definition* and *is* call for an extended definition of the word *planet*. For clarification purposes, it would be helpful to define *asteroid* as well.

4. **SUPPORTING STRATEGIES:** Illustration; Cause and Effect Analysis. The definition of *planet* could be supported with several concrete examples of planets as well as an explanation of why astronomers thought a new definition was necessary.

SAMPLE STUDENT ESSAY USING DEFINITION AS A WRITING STRATEGY

Originally a native of New York City, Howard Solomon Jr. studied in France as part of the American Field Services Intercultural Program in high school, and he majored in French at the University of Vermont. Solomon's other interests include foreign affairs, languages, photography, and cycling; in his wildest dreams, he imagines becoming an international lawyer. For the following essay, Solomon began by interviewing twenty students in his dormitory, collecting information and opinions that he eventually brought together with his own experiences to develop a definition of *best friends.*

Best Friends

Howard Solomon Jr.

Introduction: brief definition of *best friend*

Best friends, even when they are not a part of people's day-to-day lives, are essential to their well-being. They supply the companionship, help, security, and love that all people

1

need. It is not easy to put into words exactly what a best friend is, because the matter is so personal. People can benefit, however, from thinking about their best friends—who they are, what characteristics they share, and why they are so important—in order to gain a better understanding of themselves and their relationships.

Purpose: in defining best friend, writer comes to new understanding of self and relationships

When interviewed for their opinions about the qualities they most valued in their own best friends, twenty people in a University of Vermont dormitory agreed on three traits: reciprocity, honesty, and love. Reciprocity means that one can always rely on a best friend in times of need. A favor doesn't necessarily have to be returned, but best friends will return it anyway, because they want to. Best friends are willing to help each other for the sake of helping and not just for personal gain. One woman interviewed said that life seemed more secure because she knew her best friend was there if she ever needed help.

Organization: sequence of interview questions

3-part answer to question 1: What qualities do you value in a best friend?

Defines reciprocity between best friends

Honesty in a best friendship is the sharing of feelings openly and without reserve. All people interviewed said they could rely on their best friends as confidants: They could share problems with their best friends and ask for advice. They also felt that, even if best friends were critical of each other, they would never be hurtful or spiteful.

Defines honesty between best friends

Love is probably the most important quality of a best friend relationship, according to the interview group. They very much prized the affection and enjoyment they felt in the company of their best friends. One man described it as a "gut reaction," and all said it was a different feeling from being with other friends. Private jokes, looks, and gestures create personal communication between best friends that is at a very high level—many times one person knows what the other is thinking without anything being said. The specifics differ, but almost everyone agreed that a special feeling exists, which is best described as love.

Describes feelings of love between best friends

When asked who could be a best friend and who could not, most of those interviewed stated that it was impossible for parents, other relatives, and people of the opposite sex (especially husbands or wives) to be best friends. One woman said such people were "too inhibitive." Only two of those interviewed, both of whom were men, disagree—each had a female best friend. However, they seem to be an exception. Most of the people interviewed thought that their best friends were

Answers to question 2: Who can be a best friend?

Interprets informants' responses

2

3

4

5

not demanding, while relatives and partners of the opposite sex can be very demanding.

Answers to question 3: How many best friends can a person have?

To the question of how many best friends one can have, about half of the sample responded that it is possible to have several best friends, although very few people can do so; others said it was possible to have only a very few best friends; and still others felt they could have just one. It was interesting to see how ideas varied on this question. Although best friends may be no less special for one person than another, people do define the concept differently. 6

Answers to question 4: How long does it take to become a best friend?

Regarding how long it takes to become best friends and how long the relationship lasts, all were in agreement. "It is a long hard process which takes a lot of time," one woman explained. "It isn't something that can happen overnight," suggested another. One man said, "You usually know the person very well before you consider him your best friend. In fact you know everything about him, his bad points as well as his good points, so there is little likelihood that you can come into conflict with him." In addition, everyone thought that once a person has become a best friend, he or she remains so for the rest of one's life. 7

Quotes informants to capture their thoughts and feelings accurately

Highlights an important difference in responses from men and women

During the course of the interviews one important and unexpected difference emerged between men and women. The men all said that a best friend usually possessed one quality that stood out above all others—an easygoing manner or humor or sympathy, for example. One of them said that he looked not for loyalty but for honesty, for someone who was truthful, because it was so rare to find this quality in anyone. The women, however, all responded that they looked for a well-rounded person who had many good qualities. One woman said that a person who had just one good quality and not several would be "too boring to associate with." If this difference holds true beyond my sample, it means that men and women have quite different definitions of their best friends. 8

Personal example: tells what he learned about best friends at the time of his father's death

On a personal note, I have always wondered why my own best friends were so important to me; it wasn't until recently that something happened to make me really understand my relationship with them. My father died, and this was a crisis for me. Most of my friends gave me their condolences, but my best friends did more than that: They actually supported me. They called long distance to see how I was and what I needed, to try 9 to help me work out my problems, or simply to talk. Two of my best friends even took time from their spring break and, along with two other best friends, attended my father's memorial service. None of my other friends came. Since then, these are the only people who have continued to worry about me and talk to me about my father. I know that whenever I need someone they will be there and willing to help me. I know also that whenever they need help I will be ready to do the same for them.

Conclusion: personal definition of *best friend*

Thesis

Yet, like the people I interviewed, I don't value my best 10 friends just for what they do for me. I simply enjoy their company more than anyone else's. We talk, joke, play sports, and do all kinds of things when we are together. I never feel ill at ease with them, even after we've been apart for a while. As with virtually all of those I interviewed, the most important thing for me about best friends is the knowledge that I am never alone, that there are others in the world who care about my well-being as much as I do about theirs. Viewed in this light, having a best friend seems more like a necessity than it does a luxury reserved for the lucky few.

Analyzing Howard Solomon Jr.'s Definition Essay: Questions for Discussion

1. How does Solomon define *best friend* in his opening paragraph?
2. According to the people Solomon surveyed, what three qualities are valued most in a best friend?
3. Which of these qualities is considered the most important? Why?
4. How do men's and women's definitions of *best friend* differ? Do you agree with Solomon's interviewees?
5. In what ways do Solomon's interviews enhance his own definition of *best friend*?
6. In the final analysis, why does Solomon think people value their best friends so much?

SUGGESTIONS FOR USING DEFINITION AS A WRITING STRATEGY

As you plan, write, and revise your definition essay, be mindful of the writing process guidelines described in Chapter 2. Also, pay particular attention to the basic requirements and essential ingredients for this writing strategy.

❱ Planning Your Definition Essay

Planning is an essential part of writing a good definition essay. You can save yourself a great deal of work by taking the time to think about the key components of your essay before you actually begin to write.

DETERMINE YOUR PURPOSE.   Whatever your subject, make sure you have a clear sense of your purpose. Why are you writing a definition? If it's only to explain what a word or phrase means, you'll probably run out of things to say in a few sentences, or you'll find that a good dictionary has already said them for you. An effective extended definition should attempt to explain the essential nature of a thing or an idea, whether it be *photosynthesis* or *spring fever* or *Republicanism* or *prison* or *common sense*.

Often the challenge of writing a paper using the rhetorical strategy of definition is in getting your audience to understand your particular perception of the term or idea you are trying to define and explain. Take, for example, the following selection from a student essay. For many years, the citizens of Quebec, one of Canada's ten provinces, have been debating and voting on the issue of secession from Canada. At the core of this volatile issue is the essential question of Canadian identity. As you will see from the student's introduction, the Quebecois define Canadian identity very differently from the way other Canadians define it.

Quebecois Are Canadians

The peaceful formation of Canada as an independent nation has led to the current identity crisis in Quebec. The Quebecois perceive themselves to be different from all other Canadians because of their French ancestry and their unique history as both rulers and minorities in Canada. In an attempt to create a unified Canada the government has tried to establish a common Canadian culture through the building of a transcontinental railroad, a nationalized medical system, a national arts program, a national agenda, and the required use of both French and English in all publications and on all signs. As the twenty-first century begins, however, Canadians, especially the Quebecois, continue to grapple with the issue of what it means to be a Canadian, and unless some consensus can be reached on the definition of the Canadian identity, Quebec's attempt to secede from Canada may succeed.

This introductory paragraph establishes the need to define the terms *Canadians* and *Quebecois*. The emphasis on these two terms implies that another rhetorical strategy—comparison and contrast—will likely come into play. The writer might go on to use other strategies, such as description or illustration, to highlight common characteristics or differences between the Canadians and Quebecois. Judging from the title, it is clear that an argument will be made that Quebecois are Canadians.

When you decide on your topic, consider an idea or term that you would like to clarify or explain to someone. For example, Howard Solomon Jr. hit on the idea of defining what a best friend is. He recalls that "a friend of mine had become a best friend, and I was trying to figure out what had happened, what was different. So I decided to explore what was on my mind." At the beginning, you should have at least a general idea of what your subject means to you, as well as a sense of the audience you are writing your definition for and the impact you want your definition to achieve. The following advice will guide you as you plan and draft your essay.

FORMULATE A THESIS STATEMENT. A strong, clear thesis statement is critical in any essay. When writing an essay using extended definition, you should formulate a thesis statement that states clearly both the word or idea that you want to define or explain and the way in which you are going to present your thoughts. Here are two examples from this chapter.

> **thesis** We have a word in English which means "the ability to tell differences." That word is *discrimination*. But within the last [fifty] years, this word has been so frequently misused that an entire generation has grown up believing that "discrimination" means "racism."
>
> [Robert Keith Miller's thesis statement tells us that he will be discussing the word *discrimination* and how it is not the same as racism.]

> **thesis** As the twenty-first century begins, however, Canadians, especially the Quebecois, continue to grapple with the issue of what it means to be a Canadian, and unless some consensus can be reached on the definition of the Canadian identity, Quebec's attempt to secede from Canada may succeed.
>
> [The student writer makes it clear that the identity of both the Canadians and the Quebecois will be defined. The thesis statement also conveys a sense of the urgency of discussing these definitions and the possible consequences.]

As you begin to develop your thesis statement, ask yourself, "What is my point?" Next ask yourself, "What types of definitions will be most useful in making my point?" If you can't answer these questions yet, write some ideas down and try to determine your main point from these ideas.

Once you have settled on an idea, go back to the two questions above and write down your answers to them. Then combine the answers into a single-sentence thesis statement. Your eventual thesis statement does not have to be one sentence, but this exercise can be an effective way of focusing your point.

CONSIDER YOUR AUDIENCE. What do your readers know? If you're an economics major in an undergraduate writing course, you can safely assume that you know your subject better than most of your readers do, and so you will have to explain even very basic terms and ideas. If, however, you're writing a paper for your course in econometrics, your most important reader—the one who grades your paper—won't even slow down at your references to *monetary aggregates* and *Philips Curves*—provided, of course, that you use them correctly, showing that you know what they mean.

CHOOSE A TYPE OF DEFINITION THAT FITS YOUR SUBJECT. How you choose to develop your definition depends on your subject, your purpose, and your readers. Many inexperienced writers believe that any extended definition, no matter what the subject, should begin with a formal "dictionary" definition. This is not necessarily so; you will find that few of the essays in this chapter include formal definitions.

Instead, their authors assume that their readers have dictionaries and know how to use them. If, however, you think your readers do require a formal definition at some point, don't simply quote from a dictionary. Unless you have some very good reason for doing otherwise, put the definition into your own words—words that suit your approach and the probable readers of your essay. (Certainly, in an essay about photosynthesis, nonscientists would be baffled by an opening such as this: "The dictionary defines *photosynthesis* as 'the process by which chlorophyll-containing cells in green plants convert incident light to chemical energy and synthesize organic compounds from inorganic compounds, especially carbohydrates from carbon dioxide and water, with the simultaneous release of oxygen.'") There's another advantage to using your own words: You won't have to write "The dictionary defines . . ." or "According to *Webster's* . . ."; stock phrases like these almost immediately put the reader's mind to sleep.

Certain concepts, such as *liberalism* and *discrimination*, lend themselves to different interpretations, depending on the writer's point of view. While readers may agree in general about what such subjects mean, there will be much disagreement over particulars and therefore room for you to propose and defend your own definitions.

Solomon remembers the difficulties he had getting started with his essay on best friends:

> The first draft I wrote was nothing. I tried to get a start with the dictionary definition, but it didn't help—it just put into two words what really needs hundreds of words to explain, and the words it used had to be defined, too. My teacher suggested I might get going better if I talked about my topic with other people. I decided to make it semiformal, so I made up a list of a few specific questions—five questions—and went to twenty people I knew and asked them questions like, "What qualities do your best friends have?" and "What are some of the things they've done for you?" I took notes on the answers, and I was surprised when so many of them agreed. It isn't a scientific sampling, but the results helped me get started.

▶ Organizing and Writing Your Definition Essay

DEVELOP AN ORGANIZATIONAL PLAN.   Once you have gathered all the information you will need for your extended definition essay, you will want to settle on an organizational plan that suits your purpose and your materials. If you want to show that one definition of *family* is better than others, for example, you might want to lead with the definitions you plan to discard and end with the one you want your readers to accept.

Howard Solomon Jr. can trace several distinct stages that his paper went through before he settled on the plan of organizing his examples around the items on his interview questionnaire.

> Doing this paper showed me that writing isn't all that easy. Boy, I went through so many drafts—adding some things, taking out some things, reorganizing. At one point half the paper was a definition of *friends*, so I could contrast them with the definition of *best friends*. That wasn't necessary. Then the personal stuff came in late. In fact, my father died after I'd begun writing the paper, so that paragraph came in almost last of all. On the next-to-last draft everything was there, but it was put together in a sort of random way—not completely random, one idea would lead to the next and then the next—but there was a lot of circling around. My teacher pointed this out and suggested I outline what I'd written and work on the outline. So I tried it, and I saw what the problem was and what I had to do. It was just a matter of getting my examples into an order that corresponded to my interview questions.

USE OTHER RHETORICAL STRATEGIES TO SUPPORT YOUR DEFINITION. Although definition can be used effectively as a separate rhetorical strategy, it is generally used alongside other writing strategies. Photosynthesis, for example, is a natural process, so one logical strategy for defining it would be *process analysis*; readers who know little about biology may better understand photosynthesis if you draw an *analogy* with the eating and breathing of human beings. *Common sense* is an abstract concept, so its meaning could certainly be *illustrated* with concrete *examples*; in addition, its special nature might emerge more sharply through *comparison and contrast* with other ways of thinking. To define a salt marsh, you might choose a typical marsh and *describe* it. To define economic inflation or a particular disease, you might discuss its *causes and effects*. In the end, only one requirement limits your choice of supporting strategy: The strategy must help you define your term.

As you read the essays in this chapter, consider all of the writing strategies that the authors have used to support their definitions. Solomon, for example, builds his definition essay around the many examples he garnered from his interviews with other students and from his own personal experiences. As you read the other essays and note the supporting strategies authors use when defining their subjects, ask yourself the following: How do you think these other strategies have added to or changed the style of the essay? Are there strategies that you might have added or taken out? What strategies, if any, do you think you might use to strengthen your definition essay?

▶ Revising and Editing Your Definition Essay

SHARE YOUR DRAFTS WITH OTHERS.   Try sharing the drafts of your essay with other students in your writing class to make sure that your definition works. Ask them if there are any parts that they do not understand. Have them tell you what they think is the point of your essay. If their answers differ from what you intended, have them indicate the passages that led them to their interpretations so that you can change your text accordingly. To maximize the effectiveness of conferences with your peers, use the guidelines presented on page 36. Feedback from these conferences often provides one or more places where you can start revising.

SELECT WORDS THAT ACCURATELY DENOTE AND CONNOTE WHAT YOU WANT TO SAY.   The *denotation* of a word is its literal meaning or dictionary definition. Most of the time you will have no trouble with denotation, but problems can occur when words are close in meaning or sound a lot alike.

accept	*v.*, to receive
except	*prep.*, to exclude
affect	*v.*, to influence
effect	*n.*, the result; *v.*, to produce, bring into existence
anecdote	*n.*, a short narrative
antidote	*n.*, a medicine for countering effects of poison

coarse	*adj.*, rough; crude
course	*n.*, a route, a program of instruction
disinterested	*adj.*, free of self-interest or bias
uninterested	*adj.*, without interest
eminent	*adj.*, outstanding, as in reputation
immanent	*adj.*, remaining within, inherent
imminent	*adj.*, about to happen
principal	*n.*, a school official; in finance, a capital sum; *adj.*, most important
principle	*n.*, a basic law or rule of conduct
than	*conj.*, used in comparisons
then	*adv.*, at that time

Consult your dictionary if you are not sure you are using the correct word.

Words have connotative values as well as denotative meanings. *Connotations* are the associations or emotional overtones that words have acquired. For example, the word *hostage* denotes a person who is given or held as security for the fulfillment of certain conditions or terms, but it connotes images of suffering, loneliness, torture, fear, deprivation, starvation, anxiety, as well as other images based on our individual associations. Because many words in English are synonyms or have the same meanings—*strength, potency, force,* and *might* all denote "power"—your task as a writer in any given situation is to choose the word with the connotations that best suit your purpose.

USE SPECIFIC AND CONCRETE WORDS.   Words can be classified as relatively general or specific, abstract or concrete. *General words* name groups or classes of objects, qualities, or actions. *Specific words* name individual objects, qualities, or actions within a class or group. For example, *dessert* is more specific than *food*, but more general than *pie*. And *pie* is more general than *blueberry pie*.

Abstract words refer to ideas, concepts, qualities, and conditions—*love, anger, beauty, youth, wisdom, honesty, patriotism,* and *liberty,* for example. *Concrete words,* on the other hand, name things you can see, hear, taste, touch, or smell. *Corn bread, rocking chair, sailboat, nitrogen, computer, rain, horse,* and *coffee* are all concrete words.

General and abstract words generally fail to create in the reader's mind the kind of vivid response that concrete, specific words do. Always question the words you choose. Notice how Jo Goodwin Parker uses concrete, specific diction in the opening sentences of many paragraphs in her essay "What Is Poverty?" to paint a powerful verbal picture of what poverty is:

> Poverty is getting up every morning from a dirt- and illness-stained mattress. . . .
> Poverty is being tired. . . .

Poverty is dirt. . . .

Poverty is staying up all night on cold nights to watch the fire, knowing one spark on the newspaper covering the walls means your sleeping children die in flames. — Jo Goodwin Parker, "What Is Poverty?," pages 403–07

Collectively, these specific and concrete words create a memorable definition of the abstraction *poverty*.

QUESTION YOUR OWN WORK WHILE REVISING AND EDITING. Revision is best done by asking yourself key questions about what you have written. Begin by reading, preferably aloud, what you have written. Reading aloud forces you to pay attention to every single word, and you are more likely to catch lapses in the logical flow of thought. After you have read your paper through, answer the following questions for revising and editing, and make the necessary changes.

For help with twelve common writing problems, see Chapter 16, "Editing for Grammar, Punctuation, and Sentence Style."

Questions for Revising and Editing: Definition

1. Have I selected a subject in which there is some controversy or at least a difference of opinion about the definitions of key words?

2. Is the purpose of my definition clearly stated?

3. Have I presented a clear thesis statement?

4. Have I considered my audience? Do I oversimplify material for knowledgeable people or complicate material for beginners?

5. Have I used the types of definitions (*formal definition, synonymous definition, negative definition, etymological definition, stipulative definition,* and *extended definition*) that are most useful in making my point?

6. Is my definition essay easy to follow? That is, is there a clear organizational principle (chronological or logical, for example)?

7. Have I used other rhetorical strategies — such as illustration, comparison and contrast, and cause and effect analysis — as needed and appropriate to enhance my definition?

8. Does my conclusion stem logically from my thesis statement and purpose?

9. Have I used precise language to convey my meaning? Have I used words that are specific and concrete?

10. Have I avoided errors in grammar, punctuation, and mechanics? Is my sentence style as clear, smooth, and persuasive as possible?

What Is Poverty?

JO GOODWIN PARKER

All we know about Jo Goodwin Parker comes from the account of professor George Henderson, who received the following essay from Parker while he was compiling a selection of readings intended for future educators planning to teach in rural communities. This selection, which Henderson subsequently included in *America's Other Children: Public Schools Outside Suburbs* (1971), has been identified as the text of a speech given in De Land, Florida, on December 27, 1965. Although Henderson has not shared any biographical information on the author, it may be useful to consider her identity. While Parker may be who she claims to be — one of the rural poor who eke out a difficult living just beyond view of America's middle-class majority — it is also possible that she is instead a spokesperson for these individuals, families, and communities, writing not from her own experience, but from long and sympathetic observation. In either case, her definition of *poverty* is so detailed and forceful that it conveys, even to those who have never known it, the nature of poverty.

Preparing to Read

What does it mean to you to be poor? What do you see as some of the effects of poverty on people?

You ask me what is poverty? Listen to me. Here I am, dirty, smelly, and with no "proper" underwear on and with the stench of my rotting teeth near you. I will tell you. Listen to me. Listen without pity. I cannot use your pity. Listen with understanding. Put yourself in my dirty, worn-out, ill-fitting shoes, and hear me.

Poverty is getting up every morning from a dirt- and illness-stained mattress. The sheets have long since been used for diapers. Poverty is living in a smell that never leaves. This is a smell of urine, sour milk, and spoiling food sometimes joined with the strong smell of long-cooked onions. Onions are cheap. If you have smelled this smell, you did not know how it came. It is the smell of the outdoor privy. It is the smell of young children who cannot walk the long dark way in the night. It is the smell of the mattresses where years of "accidents" have happened. It is the smell of the milk which has gone sour because the refrigerator long has not worked, and it costs money to get it fixed. It is the smell of rotting garbage. I could bury it, but where is the shovel? Shovels cost money.

Poverty is being tired. I have always been tired. They told me at the hospital when the last baby came that I had chronic anemia caused from poor diet, a bad case of worms, and that I needed a corrective operation. I listened politely—the poor are always polite. The poor always listen. They don't say that there is no money for iron pills, or better food, or worm medicine. The idea of an operation is frightening and costs so much that, if I had dared, I would have laughed. Who takes care of my children? Recovery from an operation takes a long time. I have three children. When I left them with "Granny" the last time I had a job, I came home to find the baby covered with fly specks, and a diaper that had not been changed since I left. When the dried diaper came off, bits of my baby's flesh came with it. My other child was playing with a sharp bit of broken glass, and my oldest was playing alone at the edge of a lake. I made twenty-two dollars a week, and a good nursery school costs twenty dollars a week for three children. I quit my job.

> Poverty is getting up every morning from a dirt- and illness-stained mattress. The sheets have long since been used for diapers. Poverty is living in a smell that never leaves.

Poverty is dirt. You say in your clean clothes coming from your clean house, "Anybody can be clean." Let me explain about housekeeping with no money. For breakfast I give my children grits with no oleo or cornbread without eggs and oleo. This does not use up many dishes. What dishes there are, I wash in cold water and with no soap. Even the cheapest soap has to be saved for the baby's diapers. Look at my hands, so cracked and red. Once I saved for two months to buy a jar of Vaseline for my hands and the baby's diaper rash. When I had saved enough, I went to buy it and the price had gone up two cents. The baby and I suffered on. I have to decide every day if I can bear to put my cracked, sore hands into the cold water and strong soap. But you ask, why not hot water? Fuel costs money. If you have a wood fire it costs money. If you burn electricity, it costs money. Hot water is a luxury. I do not have luxuries. I know you will be surprised when I tell you how young I am. I look so much older. My back has been bent over the wash tubs for so long, I cannot remember when I ever did anything else. Every night I wash every stitch my school-age child has on and just hope her clothes will be dry by morning.

Poverty is staying up all night on cold nights to watch the fire, knowing one spark on the newspaper covering the walls means your sleeping children die in flames. In summer poverty is watching gnats and flies devour your baby's tears when he cries. The screens are torn and you pay so little rent you know they will never be fixed. Poverty means insects in your food, in your nose, in your eyes, and crawling over you when you sleep. Poverty is hoping it never rains because diapers won't dry when it rains and soon you are using newspapers. Poverty is seeing your children forever with runny noses. Paper handkerchiefs cost money and all your rags you need for other things. Even more costly are antihistamines. Poverty is cooking without food and cleaning without soap.

Poverty is asking for help. Have you ever had to ask for help, knowing your children will suffer unless you get it? Think about asking for a loan from a relative, if this is the only way you can imagine asking for help. I will tell you how it feels. You find out where the office is that you are supposed to visit. You circle that block four or five times. Thinking of your children, you go in. Everyone is very busy. Finally, someone comes out and you tell her that you need help. That never is the person you need to see. You go see another person, and after spilling the whole shame of your poverty all over the desk between you, you find that this isn't the right office after all—you must repeat the whole process, and it never is any easier at the next place.

You have asked for help, and after all it has a cost. You are again told to wait. You are told why, but you don't really hear because of the red cloud of shame and the rising black cloud of despair.

Poverty is remembering. It is remembering quitting school in junior high because "nice" children had been so cruel about my clothes and my smell. The attendance officer came. My mother told him I was pregnant. I wasn't but she thought that I could get a job and help out. I had jobs off and on, but never long enough to learn anything. Mostly I remember being married. I was so young then. I am still young. For a time, we had all the things you have. There was a little house in another town, with hot water and everything. Then my husband lost his job. There was unemployment insurance for a while and what few jobs I could get. Soon, all our nice things were repossessed and we moved back here. I was pregnant then. This house didn't look so bad when we first moved in. Every week it gets worse. Nothing is ever fixed. We now had no money. There were a few odd jobs for my husband, but everything went for food then, as it does now. I don't know how we lived through three years and three babies, but we did. I'll tell you something, after the last baby I destroyed my marriage. It had been a good one, but could you keep on bringing children in this dirt? Did you ever think how much it costs for any kind of birth control? I knew my husband was leaving the day he left, but there were no good-byes between us. I hope he has been able to climb out of this mess somewhere. He never could hope with us to drag him down.

That's when I asked for help. When I got it, you know how much it was? It was, and is, seventy-eight dollars a month for the four of us; that is all I ever can get. Now you know why there is no soap, no needles and thread, no hot water, no aspirin, no worm medicine, no hand cream, no shampoo. None of these things forever and ever and ever. So that you can see clearly, I pay twenty dollars a month rent, and most of the rest goes for food. For grits and cornmeal, and rice and milk and beans. I try my best to use only the minimum electricity. If I use more, there is that much less for food.

Poverty is looking into a black future. Your children won't play with 10 my boys. They will turn to other boys who steal to get what they want. I can already see them behind the bars of their prison instead of behind the bars of my poverty. Or they will turn to the freedom of alcohol or drugs, and find themselves enslaved. And my daughter? At best, there is for her a life like mine.

But you say to me, there are schools. Yes, there are schools. My chil- 11 dren have no extra books, no magazines, no extra pencils, or crayons, or paper and the most important of all, they do not have health. They have worms, they have infections, they have pinkeye all summer. They do not sleep well on the floor, or with me in my one bed. They do not suffer from hunger, my seventy-eight dollars keeps us alive, but they do suffer from malnutrition. Oh yes, I do remember what I was taught about health in school. It doesn't do much good. In some places there is a surplus com- modities program. Not here. The county said it cost too much. There is a school lunch program. But I have two children who will already be dam- aged by the time they get to school.

But, you say to me, there are health clinics. Yes, there are health clinics 12 and they are in the towns. I live out here eight miles from town. I can walk that far (even if it is sixteen miles both ways), but can my little children? My neighbor will take me when he goes; but he expects to get paid, *one way or another.* I bet you know my neighbor. He is that large man who spends his time at the gas station, the barbershop, and the corner store complaining about the government spending money on the immoral moth- ers of illegitimate children.

Poverty is an acid that drips on pride until all pride is worn away. 13 Poverty is a chisel that chips on honor until honor is worn away. Some of you say that you would do *something* in my situation, and maybe you would, for the first week or the first month, but for year after year after year?

Even the poor can dream. A dream of a time when there is money. 14 Money for the right kinds of food, for worm medicine, for iron pills, for toothbrushes, for hand cream, for a hammer and nails and a bit of screen- ing, for a shovel, for a bit of paint, for some sheeting, for needles and thread. Money to pay *in money* for a trip to town. And, oh, money for hot water and money for soap. A dream of when asking for help does not eat away the last bit of pride. When the office you visit is as nice as the offices of other governmental agencies, when there are enough workers to help you quickly, when workers do not quit in defeat and despair. When you have to tell your story to only one person, and that person can send you for other help and you don't have to prove your poverty over and over and over again.

I have come out of my despair to tell you this. Remember I did not come from another place or another time. Others like me are all around you. Look at us with an angry heart, anger that will help you help me. Anger that will let you tell of me. The poor are always silent. Can you be silent, too?

15

Thinking Critically about the Text

Throughout the essay, Parker describes the feelings and emotions associated with her poverty. Have you ever witnessed or observed people in Parker's situation? What was your reaction?

Questions on Subject

1. Why didn't Parker have the operation that was recommended for her? Why did she quit her job?

2. In Parker's view, what makes asking for help such a difficult and painful experience? What compels her to do so anyway?

3. Why did Parker's husband leave her? How does she justify her attitude toward his leaving? (Glossary: *Attitude*)

4. In paragraph 12, Parker says the following about a neighbor giving her a ride to the nearest health clinic: "My neighbor will take me when he goes; but he expects to get paid, *one way or another.* I bet you know my neighbor." What is she implying in these sentences and in the rest of the paragraph?

5. What are the chances that the dreams described in paragraph 14 will come true? What do you think Parker would say?

Questions on Strategy

1. What is Parker's purpose in defining poverty as she does? (Glossary: *Purpose*) Why has she cast her essay in the form of an extended definition? What effect does this have on the reader?

2. What techniques of definition does Parker use? What is missing that you would expect to find in a more general and impersonal definition of poverty? Why does Parker leave such information out?

3. Parker repeats words and phrases throughout this essay. Choose several examples, and explain their impact on you. (Glossary: *Coherence*)

4. In depicting poverty, Parker uses description to create vivid verbal pictures, and she illustrates the various aspects of poverty with examples drawn from

her experience. (Glossary: *Description; Illustration*) What are the most striking details she uses? How do you account for the emotional impact of the details and images she has selected? In what ways do description and illustration enhance her definition of poverty?

Questions on Diction and Vocabulary

1. Although her essay is written for the most part in simple, straightforward language, Parker does make use of an occasional striking figure of speech. (Glossary: *Figures of Speech*) Identify at least three such figures — you might begin with those in paragraph 13 (for example, "Poverty is an acid") — and explain their effect on the reader.

2. In paragraph 10, Parker states that "poverty is looking into a black future." How does this language characterize her children's future?

3. How would you characterize Parker's tone and her style? (Glossary: *Style; Tone*) How do you respond to her use of the pronoun *you*? Point to specific examples of her diction and descriptions as support for your view. (Glossary: *Diction*)

4. Refer to your dictionary to determine the meanings of the following words as Parker uses them in this selection: *chronic* (paragraph 3), *anemia* (3), *grits* (4), *oleo* (4), *antihistamines* (5).

Classroom Activity Using Definition

Without consulting a dictionary, try writing a formal definition for one of the following terms by putting it in a class and then differentiating it from other words in the class. (See page 388 for a discussion of formal definitions together with examples.)

tortilla chips	trombone
psychology	*American Idol*
robin	Catholicism
anger	secretary

Once you have completed your definition, compare it with the definition found in a dictionary. What conclusions can you draw? Explain.

Writing Suggestions

1. Using Parker's essay as a model, write an extended definition of a topic about which you have some expertise. Choose as your subject a particular environment (suburbia, the inner city, a dormitory, a shared living area), a way of living (as the child of divorce, as a person with a disability, as a working student), or a topic of your own choosing. If you prefer, you can adopt a persona instead of writing from your own perspective.

2. **Writing with Sources.** Write a proposal or a plan of action that will make people aware of poverty or some other social problem in your community.

How do you define the problem? What needs to be done to increase awareness of it? What practical steps would you propose be undertaken once the public is made aware of the situation? You will likely need to do some research in the library or online in order to garner support for your proposal. For models of and advice on integrating sources in your essay, see Chapters 14 and 15.

Steal This MP3 File:
What Is Theft?

G. ANTHONY GORRY

G. Anthony Gorry is a medical educator and information technology specialist. He received his B.S. from Yale University in 1962 and pursued graduate study at the University of California–Berkeley, where he earned his M.S. in chemical engineering in 1963, and at the Massachusetts Institute of Technology (MIT), where he received his Ph.D. in computer science in 1967. Gorry has taught at MIT and Baylor College of Medicine and is currently the Friedkin Professor of Management and a professor of computer science at Rice University. He is the author of numerous journal articles on management information systems and problem identification. Since 1997 he has served as a director for Ore Pharmaceutical Holdings, Inc.

In the following article, which first appeared in the *Chronicle of Higher Education* on May 23, 2003, Gorry recounts an experience he had in one of his information technology courses in order to demonstrate how technology might be shaping the attitude of today's youth. He senses that the meaning of *theft* may be shifting in our ever-changing world.

Preparing to Read

What for you constitutes theft? Do you recall ever stealing anything? Did you get caught? Did you have to return the item or make restitution? How did you feel about the incident at the time? How do you feel about it now?

Sometimes when my students don't see life the way I do, I recall the complaint from *Bye Bye Birdie*, "What's the matter with kids today?" Then I remember that the "kids" in my class are children of the information age. In large part, technology has made them what they are, shaping their world and what they know. For my students, the advance of technology is expected, but for me, it remains both remarkable and somewhat unsettling.

In one course I teach, the students and I explore the effects of information technology on society. Our different perspectives on technology lead to engaging and challenging discussions that reveal some of the ways in which technology is shaping the attitudes of young people. An example is our discussion of intellectual property in the information age, of crucial importance to the entertainment business.

In recent years, many users of the Internet have launched an assault on the music business. Armed with tools for "ripping" music from compact discs and setting it "free" in cyberspace, they can disseminate online count-less copies of a digitally encoded song. Music companies, along with some artists, have tried to stop this perceived pillaging of intellectual property by legal and technical means. The industry has had some success with legal actions against companies that provide the infrastructure for file sharing, but enthusiasm for sharing music is growing, and new file-sharing services continue to appear.

The Recording Industry Association of America . . . filed lawsuits   4
against four college students, seeking huge damages for "an emporium of music piracy" run on campus networks. However, the industry settled those lawsuits less than a week after a federal judge in California ruled against the association in another case, affirming that two of the Internet's most popular music-swapping services are not responsible for copyright infringements by their users. (In the settlement, the students admitted no wrongdoing but agreed to pay amounts ranging from $12,000 to $17,500 in annual installments over several years and to shut down their file-sharing systems.)

[I]n the case of digital music, where the material is disconnected from the physical moorings of conventional stores and copying is so easy, many of my students see matters differently.

With so many Internet users currently   5
sharing music, legal maneuvers alone seem unlikely to protect the industry's way of doing business. Therefore, the music indus-try has turned to the technology itself, seek-ing to create media that cannot be copied or can be copied only in prescribed cir-cumstances. Finding the right technology for such a defense, however, is not easy. Defensive technology must not prevent legitimate uses of the media by customers, yet it must somehow ward off attacks by those seeking to "liberate" the content to the Internet. And each announcement of a defensive technology spurs development of means to circumvent it.

In apparent frustration, some companies have introduced defective   6
copies of their music into the file-sharing environment of the Internet, hoping to discourage widespread downloading of music. But so far, the industry's multifaceted defense has failed. Sales of CDs continue to decline. And now video ripping and sharing has emerged on the Internet, threaten-ing to upset another industry in the same way.

Music companies might have more success if they focused on the users   7
instead of the courts and technology. When they characterize file sharing as theft, they overlook the interplay of technology and behavior that has

altered the very idea of theft, at least among young people. I got a clear demonstration of that change in a class discussion that began with the matter of a stolen book.

During the '60s, I was a graduate student at a university where student activism had raised tensions on and around the campus. In the midst of debates, demonstrations, and protests, a football player was caught leaving the campus store with a book he had not bought. Because he was well known, his misadventure made the school newspaper. What seemed to be a simple case of theft, however, took on greater significance. A number of groups with little connection to athletics rose to his defense, claiming that he had been entrapped: The university required that he have the book, the publisher charged an unfairly high price, and the bookstore put the book right in front of him, tempting him to steal it. So who could blame him?

Well, my students could. They thought it was clear that he had stolen the book. But an MP3 file played from my laptop evoked a different response. Had I stolen the song? Not really, because a student had given me the file as a gift. Well, was that file stolen property? Was it like the book stolen from the campus bookstore so many years ago? No again, because it was a copy, not the original, which presumably was with the student. But then what should we make of the typical admonition on compact-disc covers that unauthorized duplication is illegal? Surely the MP3 file was a duplication of the original. To what extent is copying stealing?

The readings for the class amply demonstrated the complexity of the legal, technical, and economic issues surrounding intellectual property in the information age and gave the students much to talk about. Some students argued that existing regulations are simply inadequate at a time when all information "wants to be free" and when liberating technology is at hand. Others pointed to differences in the economics of the music and book businesses. In the end, the students who saw theft in the removal of the book back in the '60s did not see stealing in the unauthorized copying of music. For me, that was the most memorable aspect of the class because it illustrates how technology affects what we take to be moral behavior.

The technology of copying is closely related to the idea of theft. For example, my students would not take books from a store, but they do not consider photocopying a few pages of a book to be theft. They would not copy an entire book, however, perhaps because they vaguely acknowledge intellectual-property rights but probably more because copying would be cumbersome and time-consuming. They would buy the book instead. In that case, the very awkwardness of the copying aligns their actions with moral guidelines and legal standards.

But in the case of digital music, where the material is disconnected from the physical moorings of conventional stores and copying is so easy, many of my students see matters differently. They freely copy and share music. And they copy and share software, even though such copying is often illegal. If their books were digital and thus could be copied with comparable ease, they most likely would copy and share them.

Of course, the Digital Millennium Copyright Act, along with other 13 laws, prohibits such copying. So we could just say that theft is theft, and complain with the song, "Why can't they be like we were, perfect in every way? . . . Oh, what's the matter with kids today?" But had we had the same digital technology when we were young, we probably would have engaged in the same copying and sharing of software, digital music, and video that are so common among students today. We should not confuse lack of tools with righteousness.

The music industry would be foolish to put its faith in new protective 14 schemes and devices alone. Protective technology cannot undo the changes that previous technology has caused. Should the industry aggressively pursue legal defenses like the suits against the four college students? Such highly publicized actions may be legally sound and may even slow music sharing in certain settings, but they cannot stop the transformation of the music business. The technology of sharing is too widespread, and my students (and their younger siblings) no longer agree with the music companies about right and wrong. Even some of the companies with big stakes in recorded music seem to have recognized that lawsuits and technical defenses won't work. Sony, for example, sells computers with "ripping and burning" capabilities, MP3 players, and other devices that gain much of their appeal from music sharing. And the AOL part of AOL Time Warner is promoting its new broadband service for faster downloads, which many people will use to share music sold by the Warner part of the company.

The lesson from my classroom is that digital technology has unalter- 15 ably changed the way a growing number of customers think about recorded music. If the music industry is to prosper, it must change, too—perhaps offering repositories of digital music for downloading (like Apple's . . . iTunes Music Store), gaining revenue from the scope and quality of its holdings, and from a variety of new products and relationships, as yet largely undefined. Such a transformation will be excruciating for the industry, requiring the abandonment of previously profitable business practices with no certain prospect of success. So it is not surprising that the industry has responded aggressively, with strong legal actions, to the spread of file sharing. But by that response, the industry is risking its relationship with a vital segment of its market. Treating customers like thieves is a certain recipe for failure.

Thinking Critically about the Text

Where do you stand on file sharing? Like Gorry's students, do you freely copy and share music or software? Do you consider all such sharing acceptable, or is there some point where it turns into theft? Explain.

Questions on Subject

1. What is intellectual property, and how is it different from other types of property?

2. How has the music industry tried to stop "music piracy" on the Internet? What has been the success of their efforts?

3. Do you think the football player caught leaving the campus store with a book was guilty of stealing, or are you persuaded by the argument that "he had been entrapped" (paragraph 8)? Explain.

4. What does Gorry mean when he says that "the technology of copying is closely related to the idea of theft" (paragraph 11)?

5. What advice do Gorry and his students have for the music industry? Is this advice realistic? Explain. What suggestions would you like to add?

Questions on Strategy

1. What is Gorry's thesis, and where is it stated? (Glossary: *Thesis*)

2. Gorry's purpose is to show that there has recently been a shift in what the Internet generation believes constitutes theft. (Glossary: *Purpose*) How well does he accomplish his purpose?

3. What examples does Gorry use to develop his definition of theft? (Glossary: *Illustration*) How does he use these examples to illustrate the shift in meaning that he believes has occurred?

4. With what authority does Gorry write on the subjects of intellectual property, technology, and theft?

5. Gorry uses lyrics from the movie *Bye Bye Birdie* to introduce his essay and start his conclusion. (Glossary: *Beginnings/Endings*) Are these just gimmicky quotations, or do they contribute to the substance of Gorry's essay?

6. Gorry ends paragraph 8 with the question "So who could blame him?" and then begins paragraph 9 with the response "Well, my students could," thus making a smooth transition from one paragraph to the next. (Glossary: *Transitions*) What other transitional devices does Gorry use to add coherence to his essay? (Glossary: *Coherence*)

Questions on Diction and Vocabulary

1. Who is Gorry's intended audience? (Glossary: *Audience*) To whom does the pronoun *we* in paragraph 13 refer? What other evidence in Gorry's diction do you find to support your conclusion about his audience?

2. How would you describe Gorry's diction — formal, objective, conversational, jargon-filled? (Glossary: *Technical Language*) Point out specific words and phrases that led you to this conclusion.

3. Refer to your dictionary to determine the meanings of the following words as Gorry uses them in this selection: *disseminate* (paragraph 3), *encoded* (3), *emporium* (4), *infringements* (4), *repositories* (15).

Classroom Activity Using Definition

Definitions are often dependent on one's perspective, as Gorry illustrates with the word *theft* in his essay. Discuss with your classmates other words or terms — such as *success, failure, wealth, poverty, cheap, expensive, happiness, loneliness, want, need* — whose definitions often are dependent on one's perspective. Write brief definitions for several of these words from your perspective. Share your definitions with other members of your class. What differences in perspective, if any, are apparent in the definitions?

Writing Suggestions

1. Although it is not always immediately apparent, English is constantly changing because it is a living language. New words come into the lexicon, and others become obsolete. Some words like *theft* change over time to reflect society's thinking and behavior. Another word whose definition has ignited recent debate is *marriage*. Using Gorry's essay as a model, write a paper in which you define a word whose meaning has changed over the past decade.

2. Gorry is very aware of how information technology is shaping our attitudes about the world. We're living at a time when digital technology makes it not only possible but also surprisingly easy for us to copy and share software, music, e-books, and video. Gorry does not condemn such behavior out of hand; instead, he warns that "we should not confuse lack of tools with righteousness" (paragraph 13). Write an essay in which you explore some of the ways today's technology has shaped your attitudes, especially as it "affects what we take to be moral behavior" (10). Be sure to support your key points with examples from your own reading or experience. (Glossary: *Illustration*)

What Does "Boys Will Be Boys" Really Mean?

DEBORAH M. ROFFMAN

A nationally certified sexuality and family life educator, Deborah M. Roffman was born in 1948 in Baltimore, Maryland. She graduated from Goucher College in 1968 and later received an M.S. in community health education from Towson University. Since 1975, Roffman has worked with scores of public and private schools on curriculum, faculty development, and parent education issues. Her work in health and sex education has been featured in the *New York Times, Baltimore Sun, Chicago Tribune, Boston Globe, Los Angeles Times, Education Week, Teacher* magazine, and *Parents* magazine. A former associate editor of the *Journal of Sex Education and Therapy*, she has appeared on an HBO special on parenting, on National Public Radio, on *The Early Show*, and on *The O'Reilly Factor*. In addition, Roffman was featured, in December of 2002, in a story on teenage sexuality on ABC's *20/20*. In 2001 Roffman published her first book, *Sex and Sensibility: The Thinking Parent's Guide to Talking Sense about Sex*, followed in 2002 by *But How'd I Get in There in the First Place?: Talking to Your Young Children about Sex*. Of the latter book, one reviewer wrote, "Roffman is a powerful advocate for children, understanding that in a society that gives confusing and exploitative messages about sexuality, children are desperate for communication from the caring adults in their lives." Her most recent book is *Talk to Me First: Everything You Need to Know to Become Your Kids' "Go-To" Person about Sex* (2012). Currently Roffman lives in Baltimore, where she teaches human sexuality education in grades 4 through 12.

The following essay was first published in the *Washington Post* on February 5, 2006. Roffman reports that the reaction to this article was overwhelming. "Many people thanked me for underscoring the point that boys and men are also treated disrespectfully in our culture and in some ways even more disrespectfully than girls and women, because of the gender-role stereotyping that defines them in even animalistic terms." Here she takes a common expression — "boys will be boys" — and asks us to think about what it really means and how that message affects boys in our society. Her conclusions will surprise those who have come to take the meaning of the expression for granted.

Preparing to Read

When you hear the expression "boys will be boys," what comes to mind? What traits or characteristics about boys and men does the expression imply for you?

Three of my seventh-grade students asked the other week if we might view a recent episode of the Fox TV cartoon show *Family Guy* in our human sexuality class. It's about reproduction, they said, and besides, it's funny. Not having seen it, I said I'd have to check it out.

Well, there must be something wrong with my sense of humor because most of the episode made me want to alternately scream and cry.

It centers on Stewie, a sexist, foul-mouthed preschooler who hates his mother, fantasizes killing her off in violent ways, and wants to prevent his parents from making a new baby—until he realizes that he might get to have a sibling as nasty as he is. Then he starts encouraging his parents' lovemaking. At one point he peers into their room and tells his dad to "Give it to her good, old man." When his father leaves the bed he orders him to "Come here this instant you fat [expletive] and do her!"

Of course I know that this is farce, but I announced the next day that no, we wouldn't be taking class time to view the episode, titled "Emission Impossible." When I asked my students why they thought that was, they guessed: The language? The women dressed like "bimbos"? The implied sexual acts? The mistreatment of the mother?

Nope, nope, nope, I replied. I didn't love any of that, either, but it was the less obvious images and messages that got my attention, the ones that kids your age *are* less likely to notice. It's not so much that the boy is always *being* bad—sometimes that sort of thing can seem so outrageous it's funny. It's the underlying assumption in the show, and often in our society, that boys, by nature, are bad.

> It's not so much that the boy is always *being* bad — sometimes that sort of thing can seem so outrageous it's funny. It's the underlying assumption . . . that boys, by nature, are bad.

I said I thought the "boys will be bad" message of the show was a terribly disrespectful one, and I wouldn't use my classroom in any way to reinforce it. It was a good moment: Recognizing for the first time the irony that maybe it was they who were really being demeaned, some of the boys got mad, even indignant.

You can hear and see evidence of this long-standing folk "wisdom" about boys almost everywhere, from the gender-typed assumptions people make about young boys to the resigned attitude or blind eye adults so often turn to disrespectful or insensitive male behavior. Two years ago, when Justin Timberlake grabbed at Janet Jackson's breast during the Super Bowl halftime, he got a free pass while she was excoriated. As the mother of two sons and teacher of thousands of boys, the reaction to that incident made me furious, but perhaps not for the reason you may think: I understood it paradoxically as a twisted kind of compliment to women and a hidden and powerful indictment of men. Is the female in such instances the only one from whom we think we can expect responsible behavior?

That incident and so many others explain why, no matter how demean- 8 ing today's culture may seem toward girls and women, I've always understood it to be fundamentally more disrespectful of boys and men—a point that escapes many of us because we typically think of men as always having the upper hand.

Consider, though, what "boys will be boys" thinking implies about the 9 true nature of boys. I often ask groups of adults or students what inherent traits or characteristics the expression implies. The answers typically are astonishingly negative: Boys are messy, immature, and selfish; hormone-driven and insensitive; irresponsible and troublemaking; rebellious, rude, aggressive, and disrespectful—even violent, predatory, and animal-like.

Is this a window into what we truly think, at least unconsciously, of the 10 male of the species? Is it possible that deep inside we really think they simply can't be expected to do any better than this? How else to explain the very low bar we continue to set for their behavior, particularly when it comes to girls, women, and sex? At a talk I gave recently, a woman in the audience asked, only half in jest, "Is it okay to instruct my daughters that when it comes to sex, teenage boys are animals?" Do we stop to think how easily these kinds of remarks can become self-fulfilling prophecies or permission-giving of the worst kind?

Thanks to popular culture, unfortunately, it only gets worse. Not too 11 long ago, I confiscated a hat from a student's head that read, "I'm a Pimp." This once-derogatory term is a complimentary handle these days for boys whom girls consider "hot." I asked the boy whether he would wear a hat that said "I'm a Rapist." Totally offended, he looked at me as if I had three heads. "Duh," I said. "Do you have any idea what real pimps do to keep their 'girls' in line?" Yet the term—like "slut" for girls—has been glamorized and legitimized by TV, movies, and popular music to such an extent that kids now bandy it about freely.

Just as fish don't know they're in water, young people today, who've 12 been swimming all their formative years in the cesspool that is American popular culture, are often maddeningly incapable of seeing how none of this is in their social, sexual, or personal best interest.

Adults I work with tend to be a lot less clueless. They are sick and tired 13 of watching the advertising and entertainment industries shamelessly pimp the increasingly naked bodies of American women and girls to sell everything from Internet service to floor tiles (I've got the ads to prove it).

Yet from my perspective, these same adults aren't nearly as clued in 14
about how destructive these ubiquitous images and messages can be for
boys. It, too, often takes patient coaching for them to see "boys will be
boys" for what it is—an insidious and long-neglected character issue:
People who think of and treat others as objects, in any way, are not kind,
decent people. It's bad enough that boys are being trained by the culture
to think that behaving in these ways is "cool"; it's outrageous and much
more disturbing that many of the immediate adults in their lives can't see
it, and may even buy into it.

The "boys will be bad" stereotype no doubt derives from a time when 15
men were the exclusively entitled gender: Many did behave badly, simply
because they could. (Interestingly, that's pretty much how Bill Clinton in
hindsight ultimately explained his poor behavior in the Lewinsky affair.)
For today's boys, however, the low expectations set for them socially and
sexually have less to do with any real entitlement than with the blinders we
wear to these antiquated and degrading gender myths.

I think, too, that the staying power of these myths has to do with the 16
fact that as stereotypes go, they can be remarkably invisible. I've long asked
students to bring in print advertisements using sex to sell products or
showing people as sex objects. No surprise that in the vast majority of ads
I receive, women are the focus, not men.

And yet, as I try to teach my students, there's always at least one invis- 17
ible man present—looking at the advertisement. The messages being
delivered to and/or about him are equally if not more powerful.

In one of my least favorite examples, a magazine ad for a video game 18
(brought to me by a sixth-grade boy) depicts a highly sexualized woman
with a dominatrix air brandishing a weapon. The heading reads, "Bet
you'd like to get your hands on these!," meaning her breasts, er, the game
controllers. And the man or boy not in the picture but looking on? The ad
implies that he's just another low-life guy who lives and breathes to ogle
and grab every large-breasted woman he sees.

Many boys I've talked with are pretty savvy about the permission- 19
giving that "boys will be bad" affords and use it to their advantage in their
relationships with adults. "Well, they really don't expect as much from us
as they do from girls," said one tenth-grade boy. "It makes it easier to get
away with a lot of stuff."

Others play it sexually to their advantage, knowing that in a system 20
where boys are expected to want sex but not necessarily to be responsible
about it, the girl will probably face the consequences if anything happens.
As long as girls can still be called sluts, the sexual double standard—and
its lack of accountability for boys—will rule.

Most boys I know are grateful when they finally get clued in to all this. 21
A fifth-grade boy once told me that the worst insult anyone could possibly
give him would be to call him a girl. When I walked him through what he
seemed to be saying—that girls are inferior to him—he was suddenly
ashamed that he could have thought such a thing. "I'm a better person
than that," he said.

Just as we've adjusted the bar for girls in academics and athletics, we 22
need to let boys know that, in the sexual and social arenas, we've been
shortchanging them by setting the bar so low. We need to explain why the
notion that "boys will be boys" embodies a bogus and ultimately corrupting set of expectations that are unacceptable.

We'll know we've succeeded when girls and boys better recognize 23
sexual and social mistreatment and become angry and personally offended
whenever anyone dares use the word *slut* against any girl, call any boy a
pimp, or suggest that anyone reduce themselves or others to a sexual object.

We'll also know when boys call one another more often on disrespect- 24
ful behavior, instead of being congratulatory, because they will have the
self-respect and confidence that comes with being held to and holding
themselves to high standards.

Thinking Critically about the Text

Why is it important that Roffman ask her readers to think about what the expression "boys will be boys" really means? What does she think the expression
means? What does she mean when she says, "We need to explain why the notion
that 'boys will be boys' embodies a bogus and ultimately corrupting set of expectations that are unacceptable" (paragraph 22)?

Questions on Subject

1. Why did Roffman's students think she did not want to show the episode of
   Family Guy in class? How does she respond to their answers? What about the
   show does Roffman find objectionable?

2. How did some of the boys react when Roffman revealed her reason for not viewing the show in class? In what ways was it "a good moment" (paragraph 6)?

3. In paragraph 7, Roffman uses the now infamous Justin Timberlake and Janet
   Jackson "wardrobe malfunction" incident during the Super Bowl halftime fes-
   tivities as an example of "this longstanding folk 'wisdom' about boys." In what
   ways does she find this episode demeaning and disrespectful of boys and
   men? Do you agree?

4. What about America's advertising and entertainment industries does Roffman
   find objectionable? What does she find disturbing about adult responses
   to the images and messages in so much current advertising and entertainment?

5. What does Roffman see as the source of the "boys will be bad" stereotype? Why does she believe this stereotype has such staying power?

Questions on Strategy

1. Roffman opens her essay with an anecdote about seventh-graders asking to view and discuss an episode of *Family Guy* in their human sexuality class. How effective did you find this introduction? (Glossary: *Beginnings/Endings*)

2. What is Roffman's purpose in writing this essay? (Glossary: *Purpose*)

3. In paragraph 10, Roffman asks a series of questions. How do these questions function in the context of her essay? How did you answer these questions when you first read them?

4. Identify the analogy that Roffman uses in paragraph 12. (Glossary: *Analogy*) How does this strategy help her explain the plight of today's young people? Explain.

Questions on Diction and Vocabulary

1. Who is Roffman's intended audience? (Glossary: *Audience*) To whom do the pronouns *you* in paragraph 7 and *us* and *we* in paragraph 8 refer? What other evidence in Roffman's diction do you find to support your conclusion about her audience?

2. In paragraph 9, Roffman lists the negative traits and characteristics of boys suggested by the expression "boys will be boys." What connotations do you associate with each of the descriptors? (Glossary: *Connotation/Denotation*) What order, if any, do you see in her list? Explain.

3. Refer to your dictionary to determine the meanings of the following words as Roffman uses them in this selection: *sibling* (paragraph 3), *expletive* (3), *farce* (4), *irony* (6), *excoriated* (7), *paradoxically* (7), *bandy* (11), *cesspool* (12), *ubiquitous* (14), *insidious* (14).

Classroom Activity Using Definition

Consider the following *Grand Avenue* strip by Steve Breen and Mike Thompson.

What insights into the nature of definition does the cartoon give you? If you were asked to help Michael, what advice or suggestions would you give him?

Writing Suggestions

1. When discussing people, we often resort to personality labels to identify or define them — *leader, procrastinator, workaholic, obsessive-compulsive, liar, addict, athlete, genius, mentor,* and so on. But such labels can be misleading because one person's idea of what a leader or a workaholic is doesn't necessarily match another person's idea. Write an essay in which you explain the defining characteristics for one of these personality types or for one personality type of your own choosing. Be sure to use examples to illustrate each of the defining characteristics.

2. **Writing with Sources.** In analyzing "print advertisements using sex to sell products or showing people as sex objects" (paragraph 16), Roffman recounts how she and her students discovered that, while most of the ads focused on women, "there's always at least one invisible man present — looking at the advertisement" (17). They conclude that what these ads say or imply about this invisible man is not very flattering. Collect several print advertisements that use sex to promote products or show women or men as sex objects, and analyze one of them. What insights, if any, does this advertisement offer about how popular culture portrays and defines both men and women? How do you think Roffman would interpret or analyze your advertisement? Write a paper in which you report your findings and conclusions. For models of and advice on integrating sources in your essay, see Chapters 14 and 15.

Ain't I a Woman?

SOJOURNER TRUTH

Sojourner Truth was born into slavery and named Isabella in Ulster County, New York, in 1797. After her escape from slavery in 1827, she went to New York City and underwent a profound religious transformation. She worked as a domestic servant, and as an evangelist she tried to reform prostitutes. Adopting the name Sojourner Truth in 1843, she became a traveling preacher and abolitionist, frequently appearing with Frederick Douglass. Although she never learned to write, Truth's compelling presence gripped her audience as she spoke eloquently about emancipation and women's rights. After the Civil War and until her death in 1883, she worked to provide education and employment for emancipated slaves.

At the Women's Rights Convention in Akron, Ohio, in May 1851, Truth extemporaneously delivered the following speech to a nearly all-white audience. The version we reprint was transcribed by Elizabeth Cady Stanton.

Preparing to Read

What comes to mind when you hear the word *speech*? Have you ever attended a rally or convention and heard speeches given on behalf of a social cause or political issue? What were your impressions of the speakers and their speeches?

Well, children, where there is so much racket there must be something out of kilter. I think that 'twixt the Negroes of the South and the women of the North, all talking about rights, the white men will be in a fix pretty soon. But what's all this here talking about? 1

That man over there says that women need to be helped into carriages, and lifted over ditches, and to have the best place everywhere. Nobody ever helps me into carriages, or over mud-puddles, or gives me any best place! And ain't I a woman? Look at me! Look at my arm! I have ploughed and planted, and gathered into barns, and no man could head me! And ain't I a woman? I could work as much and eat as much as a man—when I could get it—and bear the lash as well! And ain't I a woman? I have borne thirteen children, and seen them most all sold off to slavery, and when I cried out with my mother's grief, none but Jesus heard me! And ain't I a woman? 2

> Nobody ever helps me into carriages, or over mud-puddles, or gives me any best place!

Then they talk about this thing in the head; what's this they call it? 3
[Intellect, someone whispers.] That's it, honey. What's that got to do with women's rights or negro's rights? If my cup won't hold but a pint, and yours holds a quart, wouldn't you be mean not to let me have my little half-measure full?

Then that little man in black there, he says women can't have as much 4
rights as men, 'cause Christ wasn't a woman! Where did your Christ come from? Where did your Christ come from? From God and a woman! Man had nothing to do with Him.

If the first woman God ever made was strong enough to turn the world 5
upside down all alone, these women together ought to be able to turn it back, and get it right side up again! And now they is asking to do it, the men better let them.

Obliged to you for hearing me, and now old Sojourner ain't got noth- 6
ing more to say.

Thinking Critically about the Text

What are your immediate impressions of Truth's speech? Now take a minute to read her speech again, this time aloud. What are your impressions now? Are they different, and if so, how and why? What aspects of her speech are memorable?

Questions on Subject

1. What does Truth mean when she says, "Where there is so much racket there must be something out of kilter" (paragraph 1)? Why does Truth believe that white men are going to find themselves in a "fix" (1)?

2. What does Truth put forth as her "credentials" as a woman?

3. How does Truth counter the argument that "women can't have as much rights as men, 'cause Christ wasn't a woman" (paragraph 4)?

Questions on Strategy

1. What is Truth's purpose in this essay? (Glossary: *Purpose*) Why is it important for her to define what a woman is for her audience? (Glossary: *Audience*)

2. How does Truth use the comments of "that man over there" (paragraph 2) and "that little man in black" (4) to help her establish her definition of *woman*?

3. What, for you, is the effect of Truth's repetition of the question "And ain't I a woman?" four times? (Glossary: *Rhetorical Question*) What other questions does she ask? Why do you suppose Truth doesn't provide answers to the questions in paragraph 3, but does for the question in paragraph 4?

4. How would you characterize Truth's tone in this speech? (Glossary: *Tone*) What phrases in the speech suggest that tone to you?

5. Explain how Truth uses comparison and contrast to help establish her definition of *woman*, especially in paragraph 2. (Glossary: *Comparison and Contrast*)

Questions on Diction and Vocabulary

1. How would you describe Truth's diction in this speech? What does her diction reveal about her character and background?

2. Refer to your dictionary to determine the meanings of the following words as Truth uses them in this selection: *kilter* (paragraph 1), *ditches* (2), *intellect* (3), *obliged* (6).

Classroom Activity Using Definition

In a letter to the editor of the *New York Times*, Nancy Stevens, president of a small New York City advertising agency, argues against using the word *guys* to address women. She believes that the "use of *guy* to mean 'person' is so insidious that I'll bet most women don't notice they are being called 'guys,' or, if they do, find it somehow flattering to be one of them." Do you find such usage objectionable? Why, or why not? How is the use of *guy* to mean "person" different from using *gal* to mean "person"? How do you think Truth would react to the use of the word *guys* to refer to women? What light does your dictionary shed on this issue of definition?

Writing Suggestions

1. Sojourner Truth spoke out against the injustice she saw around her. In arguing for the rights of women, she found it helpful to define *woman* in order to make her point. What social cause do you find most compelling today? Human rights? Climate change? Domestic abuse? Alcoholism? Gay marriage? Racism? Select an issue about which you have strong feelings. Now carefully identify all key terms that you must define before arguing your position. Write an essay in which you use definition to make your point convincingly.

2. Sojourner Truth's speech holds out hope for the future. She envisions a future in which women join together to take charge and "turn [the world] back, and get it right side up again" (paragraph 5). What she envisioned has, to some extent, come to pass. For example, today the distinction between "women's work" and "men's work" has blurred or even vanished in some fields. Write an essay in which you speculate about how Truth would react to the world as we know it, and, more specifically, to the world depicted in the photograph on page 426. What do you think would please her? What would disappoint her? What do you think she would want to change about our society? Explain your reasoning.

The Genius of Jobs

WALTER ISAACSON

Newspaper reporter, magazine editor, author, and television executive Walter Isaacson was born in 1952 in New Orleans, Louisiana. He graduated from Harvard University in 1974 with a degree in history and literature and went on to Oxford University as a Rhodes Scholar, where in 1976 he received a graduate degree in Philosophy, Politics, and Economics (PPE). Isaacson launched his career in journalism with the *Sunday Times* of London and later returned to New Orleans where he put in a short stint with the *Times Picayune/States-Item*, covering local politics before joining *Time* magazine. His career at *Time* spanned more than two decades, starting as a reporter covering Ronald Reagan's 1980 campaign and ending as managing editor. In 2001 he became chairman and CEO of CNN. Currently, he is president and CEO of the Aspen Institute, an international forum interested in environmental and economic issues, and chairman of the board of Teach for America. In 1986 Isaacson teamed up with Evan Thomas to write *The Wise Men: Six Friends and the World They Made*, the story of American statesmen and the cold war. Isaacson is perhaps best known for his best-selling biographies: *Kissinger: A Biography* (1992), *Benjamin Franklin: An American Life* (2003), *Einstein: His Life and Universe* (2007), and *Steve Jobs* (2011). In 2009 he published *American Sketches: Great Leaders, Creative Thinkers, and Heroes of a Hurricane*, a collection of his essays, and in 2010 he edited *Profiles in Leadership: Historians on the Elusive Quality of Greatness*.

In the following selection, which was first published in the *New York Times* on October 29, 2011, Isaacson reflects on the Silicon Valley giant Steve Jobs and what it was that set him apart from his contemporaries. Notice how he uses the examples of Bill Gates, Albert Einstein, and Benjamin Franklin to identify and refine the defining qualities of Steve Jobs's genius.

Preparing to Read

Think of a person you know whom you consider to be smart. What, for you, are the defining characteristics of this person's intelligence? Would you describe this person as being more "book smart," "street smart," or some combination of the two? Explain.

One of the questions I wrestled with when writing about Steve Jobs was how smart he was. On the surface, this should not have been much of an issue. You'd assume the obvious answer was: He was really, really smart. Maybe even worth three or four reallys. After all, he was the most innovative and successful business leader of our era and embodied the Silicon Valley dream writ large: He created a start-up in his parents' garage and built it into the world's most valuable company.

But I remember having dinner with him a few months ago around his kitchen table, as he did almost every evening with his wife and kids. Someone brought up one of those brainteasers involving a monkey's having to carry a load of bananas across a desert, with a set of restrictions about how far and how many he could carry at one time, and you were supposed to figure out how long it would take. Mr. Jobs tossed out a few intuitive guesses but showed no interest in grappling with the problem rigorously. I thought about how Bill Gates would have gone click-click-click and logically nailed the answer in 15 seconds, and also how Mr. Gates devoured science books as a vacation pleasure. But then something else occurred to me: Mr. Gates never made the iPod. Instead, he made the Zune.

> He created a start-up in his parents' garage and built it into the world's most valuable company.

So was Mr. Jobs smart? Not conventionally. Instead, he was a genius. That may seem like a silly word game, but in fact his success dramatizes an interesting distinction between intelligence and genius. His imaginative leaps were instinctive, unexpected, and at times magical. They were sparked by intuition, not analytic rigor. Trained in Zen Buddhism, Mr. Jobs came to value experiential wisdom over empirical analysis. He didn't study data or crunch numbers but like a pathfinder, he could sniff the winds and sense what lay ahead.

He told me he began to appreciate the power of intuition, in contrast to what he called "Western rational thought," when he wandered around India after dropping out of college. "The people in the Indian countryside don't use their intellect like we do," he said. "They use their intuition instead . . . Intuition is a very powerful thing, more powerful than intellect, in my opinion. That's had a big impact on my work."

Mr. Jobs's intuition was based not on conventional learning but on experiential wisdom. He also had a lot of imagination and knew how to apply it. As Einstein said, "Imagination is more important than knowledge."

Einstein is, of course, the true exemplar of genius. He had contemporaries who could probably match him in pure intellectual firepower when it came to mathematical and analytic processing. Henri Poincaré, for example, first came up with some of the components of special relativity, and David Hilbert was able to grind out equations for general relativity around the same time Einstein did. But neither had the imaginative genius to make the full creative leap at the core of their theories, namely that there is no such thing as absolute time and that gravity is a warping of the fabric of space-time. (O.K., it's not that simple, but that's why he was Einstein and we're not.)

Einstein had the elusive qualities of genius, which included that intuition and imagination that allowed him to think differently (or, as Mr. Jobs's ads said, to Think Different). Although he was not particularly religious, Einstein described this intuitive genius as the ability to read the mind of God. When assessing a theory, he would ask himself, Is this the way that God would design the universe? And he expressed his discomfort with quantum mechanics, which is based on the idea that probability plays a governing role in the universe by declaring that he could not believe God would play dice. (At one physics conference, Niels Bohr was prompted to urge Einstein to quit telling God what to do.)

Both Einstein and Mr. Jobs were very visual thinkers. The road to relativity began when the teenage Einstein kept trying to picture what it would be like to ride alongside a light beam. Mr. Jobs spent time almost every afternoon walking around the studio of his brilliant design chief Jony Ive and fingering foam models of the products they were developing.

Mr. Jobs's genius wasn't, as even his fanboys admit, in the same quantum orbit as Einstein's. So it's probably best to ratchet the rhetoric down a notch and call it ingenuity. Bill Gates is super-smart, but Steve Jobs was super-ingenious. The primary distinction, I think, is the ability to apply creativity and aesthetic sensibilities to a challenge.

In the world of invention and innovation, that means combining an appreciation of the humanities with an understanding of science — connecting artistry to technology, poetry to processors. This was Mr. Jobs's specialty. "I always thought of myself as a humanities person as a kid, but I liked electronics," he said. "Then I read something that one of my heroes, Edwin Land of Polaroid, said about the importance of people who could stand at the intersection of humanities and sciences, and I decided that's what I wanted to do."

The ability to merge creativity with technology depends on one's ability to be emotionally attuned to others. Mr. Jobs could be petulant and unkind in dealing with other people, which caused some to think he lacked basic emotional awareness. In fact, it was the opposite. He could size people up, understand their inner thoughts, cajole them, intimidate them, target their deepest vulnerabilities, and delight them at will. He knew, intuitively, how to create products that pleased, interfaces that were friendly, and marketing messages that were enticing.

In the annals of ingenuity, new ideas are only part of the equation. Genius requires execution. When others produced boxy computers with intimidating interfaces that confronted users with unfriendly green prompts that said things like "C:\>," Mr. Jobs saw there was a market for an interface like a sunny playroom. Hence, the Macintosh. Sure, Xerox came up with the graphical desktop metaphor, but the personal computer it built was a flop and it did not spark the home computer revolution. Between conception and creation, T. S. Eliot observed, there falls the shadow.

In some ways, Mr. Jobs's ingenuity reminds me of that of Benjamin   13
Franklin, one of my other biography subjects. Among the founders, Franklin was not the most profound thinker—that distinction goes to Jefferson or Madison or Hamilton. But he was ingenious.

This depended, in part, on his ability to intuit the relationships between   14
different things. When he invented the battery, he experimented with it to produce sparks that he and his friends used to kill a turkey for their end-of-season feast. In his journal, he recorded all the similarities between such sparks and lightning during a thunderstorm, then declared "Let the experiment be made." So he flew a kite in the rain, drew electricity from the heavens, and ended up inventing the lightning rod. Like Mr. Jobs, Franklin enjoyed the concept of applied creativity—taking clever ideas and smart designs and applying them to useful devices.

China and India are likely to produce many rigorous analytical think-   15
ers and knowledgeable technologists. But smart and educated people don't always spawn innovation. America's advantage, if it continues to have one, will be that it can produce people who are also more creative and imaginative, those who know how to stand at the intersection of the humanities and the sciences. That is the formula for true innovation, as Steve Jobs's career showed.

Thinking Critically about the Text

In paragraph 10, Jobs says that he remembers reading what the inventor of the Polaroid camera had said "about the importance of people who could stand at the intersection of humanities and sciences." What does it mean to be a person who can stand at the intersection of the humanities and the sciences? In what ways was Steve Jobs just such a person?

Questions on Subject

1. Why do you think Isaacson had trouble determining how smart Steve Jobs was? What insight does the story in paragraph 2 suggest about Jobs's smartness? Explain.

2. For Isaacson, in what ways were Steve Jobs and Bill Gates different? What implicit judgment does Isaacson make when he says, "But then something else occurred to me: Mr. Gates never made the iPod. Instead, he made the Zune" (paragraph 2)?

3. According to Isaacson, what is the basic difference between "intelligence" and "genius"? What does Isaacson mean when he says Jobs's "imaginative leaps were instinctive, unexpected, and at times magical" (paragraph 3)? How is "ingenuity" related to "genius"?

4. For Isaacson, who is the quintessential genius? How does Steve Jobs compare with this iconic figure?

5. In paragraph 12, Isaacson paraphrases T. S. Eliot, who once observed that "Between conception and creation . . . there falls the shadow." What is the meaning of Eliot's words, and how do they apply to Steve Jobs?

Questions on Strategy

1. With what authority does Isaacson write about the genius of Steve Jobs?

2. How do the examples of Einstein and Franklin help Isaacson refine his definition of *genius*?

3. Isaacson starts the third paragraph with a short dramatic question. How does this question function in the context of the essay as a whole?

4. How does Isaacson illustrate the idea "Genius requires execution" (paragraph 12)? How does this example serve to flesh out the picture of Jobs's genius?

5. How has Isaacson organized his essay? (Glossary: *Organization*) Why, for example, does he discuss Einstein before he does Franklin?

6. What kinds of transitional words and devices does Isaacson use to help one paragraph run smoothly into the next? (Glossary: *Transitions*)

Questions on Diction and Vocabulary

1. Would you describe Isaacson's diction as being more formal or informal? Point to his word choices that support your conclusion.

2. In paragraph 7, Isaacson says, "Einstein had the elusive qualities of genius, which included that intuition and imagination that allowed him to think differently (or, as Mr. Jobs's ads said, to Think Different)." What is intuitive or imaginative about Apple's award-winning "Think Different" advertising campaign? Explain.

3. Refer to your dictionary to determine the meanings of the following words as Isaacson uses them in this selection: *rigor* (paragraph 3), *exemplar* (6), *rachet* (9), *ingenuity* (9), *petulant* (11), *cajole* (11), *interfaces* (12), *spawn* (15).

Classroom Activity Using Definition

One approach to defining something is through negative definition — explaining a word or phrase by what it does *not* mean (see also page 389). For example, in paragraph 9, notice how Isaacson uses negative definition to eliminate misunderstandings about Jobs's genius: "Mr. Jobs's genius wasn't, as even his fanboys admit, in the same quantum orbit as Einstein's. So it's probably best to rachet the rhetoric down a notch and call it ingenuity." In doing so he both clarifies and emphasizes his statements about what Jobs's genius is.

Try your hand at negative definition, using one or more of the following words. Be sure that when you specify what something is *not*, you help clarify what it *is*.

terrorism	patriotism	kindness	secret
marriage	happiness	loyalty	bipartisanship

Writing Suggestions

1. Using Isaacson's essay as a model, write a short essay in which you define one of the abstract terms in the Classroom Activity above or another similar term of your own choosing. Before beginning to write, you may find it helpful to review what you and your classmates discussed in the Classroom Activity for this selection.

2. In paragraph 5, Isaacson quotes Einstein, who said, "Imagination is more important than knowledge." What does Einstein mean? Using examples from your own reading, observation, and experience, write an essay in which you support Isaacson's conclusion that "Smart and educated people don't always spawn innovation" (15).

3. **Writing with Sources.** Shortly after Steve Jobs returned to Apple in 1996, he launched Apple's "Think Different" advertising campaign. The campaign was quickly hailed for rejuvenating Apple's image and restoring its reputation within the technology industry. Go online and find images from the campaign, which featured photographs of iconic and creative individuals like Albert Einstein, Amelia Earhart, Jim Henson, and Jimi Hendrix. Then, use that research to write an essay in which you explore some of the reasons why you believe the "Think Different" campaign was so successful. How do you account for the huge impact of the rather simple, uncomplicated appearing ads? In what ways does this ad campaign capture the essence of what Walter Isaacson would call the genius of Jobs? For models of and advice on integrating sources in your essay, see Chapters 14 and 15.

WRITING SUGGESTIONS FOR DEFINITION

1. Some of the most pressing social issues in American life today are further complicated by imprecise definitions of critical terms. Various medical cases, for example, have brought worldwide attention to the legal and medical definitions of the word *death*. Debates continue about the meanings of other controversial words, such as these:

a. values	i. remedial
b. minority (ethnic)	j. insanity
c. alcoholism	k. forgiveness
d. cheating	l. sex
e. pornography	m. success
f. kidnapping	n. happiness
g. lying	o. life
h. censorship	p. equality

   Select one of these words, and write an essay in which you discuss not only the definition of the term but also the problems associated with defining it.

2. Write an essay in which you define one of the words listed below by telling not only what it is but also what it is *not*. (For example, one could say that "poetry is that which cannot be expressed in any other way.") Remember, however, that defining by negation does not relieve you of the responsibility of defining the term in other ways as well.

a. intelligence	g. family
b. leadership	h. style
c. fear	i. loyalty
d. patriotism	j. selflessness
e. wealth	k. creativity
f. failure	l. humor

3. Consider the sample introduction to the essay defining Quebecois and Canadian identity (page 396). Think about your school, town, or country's identity. How would you define its essential character? Choose a place that is important in your life, and write an essay defining its character and its significance to you.

4. **Writing with Sources.** Karl Marx defined *capitalism* as an economic system in which the bourgeois owners of the means of production exploit the proletariat for their own selfish gain. How would you define *capitalism*? Write an essay defining *capitalism* that includes all six types of definition: formal, synonymous,

negative, etymological, stipulative, and extended. Do some research in the library or online to help you with your definitions. For models of and advice on integrating sources in your essay, see Chapters 14 and 15.

5. The opening visual for this chapter on page 386 defines various types of coffee drinks using a highly graphic style. Visual definitions can be an excellent complement to text-only definitions because our brains are often able to process them more quickly. Using the coffee-drinks image as a model, create a coherent set of visual definitions for types of pasta. Search online or in your library or supermarket to find the names of six to twelve different pasta shapes or dough. You may want to combine a few select words with your images to clearly distinguish what your illustration represents, as was done in the coffee-drinks image. To create your visual, either sketch by hand or use photo and graphics applications, keeping in mind that simple visuals often have greater resonance with viewers. Once your visual definitions are complete, write a paragraph explaining what your visual would uniquely add to a set of more traditional, text-only definitions. In what ways might the images affect your choice of pasta to purchase, prepare, or eat?

6. **Writing with Sources.** In discussing the power of labels that define identity, psychiatrist Thomas Szasz once wrote:

> The struggle for definition is veritably the struggle for life itself. In the typical western two men fight desperately for the possession of a gun that has been thrown to the ground: Whoever reaches the weapon first, shoots and lives; his adversary is shot and dies. In ordinary life, the struggle is not for guns but for words: Whoever first defines the situation is the victor; his adversary, the victim. . . . In short, he who first seizes the word imposes reality on the other; he who defines thus dominates and lives; and he who is defined is subjugated and may be killed.
> — From *The Second Sin*

Take some time to think about words like *gay*, *retarded*, or *jock*, whose meaning in our culture has become contested — that is, challenged by some who are offended by the way(s) in which those words are used (for information on campaigns that attempt to educate the public on these issues, see ThinkB4YouSpeak.com and r-word.org). What other defining labels have you encountered or observed? After doing some research in your library as well as on the Internet, write an essay in which you explore the power of labels to define. For models of and advice on integrating sources in your essay, see Chapters 14 and 15.

7. **Writing in the Workplace.** One of the most pressing social issues in American life today is same-sex marriage. The issue is being discussed in our nation's state legislatures and courts. One of the major complicating factors is that the word *marriage* means different things to different people. Suppose for a

minute that you are a lawyer arguing either for or against the rights of gay individuals to marry. In preparation for your court appearance, write a definition essay to explain your understanding of marriage and what it means to be married. To make your definition clearer to your reader, you might consider describing a marriage with which you are personally familiar. Perhaps it would be helpful to compare and contrast two or more different marriages. (Glossary: *Comparison and Contrast*) You could also incorporate a relevant narrative or an example to make your definition more persuasive.

---

 e-Pages

Not Your Parents' American Dream
The Pursuit of a New National Ideal
GOOD

See how definition works on the Web. Go to <u>bedfordstmartins.com/</u> <u>subjectandstrategy</u> for an infographic and study questions about the evolving meaning of the American dream.

WHERE
DID ALL THE MONEY GO ?

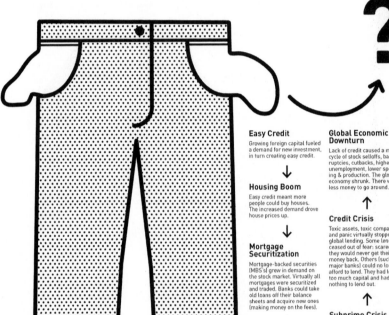

Easy Credit

Growing foreign capital fueled a demand for new investment, in turn creating easy credit.

↓

Housing Boom

Easy credit meant more people could buy houses. The increased demand drove house prices up.

↓

Mortgage Securitization

Mortgage-backed securities (MBS's) grew in demand on the stock market. Virtually all mortgages were securitized and traded. Banks could take old loans off their balance sheets and acquire new ones (making money on the fees).

↓

Market Saturation

The easy credit allowed everyone who wanted a house to get one. MBS's still were in high demand as "safe bets."

↓

Lowered Loan Standards

Lenders had to find a way to create yet more loans, so they lowered the requirements for who could get one. The loans were quickly sold off, so the lender did not bear any risk in the case of a default. It did not matter whom they were lending to or whether the money would be repaid. The lenders and brokers just collected their fees and created the MBS's for the market demand.

Global Economic Downturn

Lack of credit caused a mad cycle of stock selloffs, bankruptcies, cutbacks, higher unemployment, lower spending & production. The global economy shrunk. There was less money to go around.

↑

Credit Crisis

Toxic assets, toxic companies, and panic virtually stopped global lending. Some lenders ceased out of fear: scared that they would never get their money back. Others (such as major banks) could no longer afford to lend. They had lost too much capital and had nothing to lend out.

↑

Subprime Crisis

Throughout the housing boom, the financial market operated with the assumption that house prices would not fall. Assets that were thought to be safe were only safe because they were backed by houses of increasing value. When the prices did fall, the entire system was turned on its head.

↑

House Prices Fall

The average household income did not increase as house prices soared. Even with the easy loans, people could not afford houses anymore and stopped buying. More houses were still being built so the supply kept growing, but the demand dropped. House prices fell. Drastically.

CHAPTER 11

Cause and Effect Analysis

WHAT IS CAUSE AND EFFECT ANALYSIS?

PEOPLE EXHIBIT THEIR NATURAL CURIOSITY ABOUT THE WORLD BY asking questions. These questions represent a fundamental human need to find out how things work. Whenever a question asks *why*, answering it will require discovering a *cause* or a series of causes for a particular *effect*; whenever a question asks *what if*, its answer will point out the effect or effects that can result from a particular cause. Cause and effect analysis, then, explores the relationship between events or circumstances and the outcomes that result from them.

The illustration opposite is an excerpt from an analysis that attempts to explain a persistent question people have about the United States' current economic woes: Where did all the money go? The complex causal chain that "turned our country's pockets inside out" is represented with a combination of text and graphics explaining that easy credit, the initial cause, led to a chain of events culminating in the global economic downturn, with its multitude of disastrous consequences that Americans and people around the world are still feeling in all aspects of their lives.

CAUSE AND EFFECT ANALYSIS IN WRITTEN TEXTS

You will have frequent opportunity to use cause and effect analysis in your college writing. For example, a history instructor might ask you to explain the causes of the Six-Day War between Israel and its neighbors. In a paper for an American literature course, you might try to determine why *Huckleberry Finn* has sparked so much controversy in a number of schools and communities. On an environmental studies exam, you might have to speculate about the long-term effects acid rain will have on the ecology of northeastern Canada and the United States. Demonstrating an understanding of cause and effect is crucial to the process of learning.

One common use of the strategy is for the writer to identify a particular causal agent or circumstance and then discuss the consequences or effects it has had or may have. In the following passage from *Telephone* by John Brooks, it is clear from the first sentence that the author is primarily concerned with the effects that the telephone has had or may have had on modern life.

<table>
<tr>
<td>

First sentence establishes purpose in the form of a question

</td>
<td>

What has the telephone done to us, or for us, in the hundred years of its existence? A few effects suggest themselves at once. It has saved lives by getting rapid word of illness, injury, or famine from remote places. By joining with the elevator to make possible the multistory residence or office building, it has made possible—for better or worse—the modern city. By bringing about a quantum leap in the speed and ease with which information moves from place to place, it has greatly accelerated the rate of scientific and technologi-

</td>
</tr>
<tr>
<td>

A series of effects with the telephone as cause

</td>
<td>

cal change and growth in industry. Beyond doubt it has crippled if not killed the ancient art of letter writing. It has made living alone possible for persons with normal social impulses; by so doing, it has played a role in one of the greatest social changes of this century, the breakup of the multigenerational household. It has made the waging of war chillingly more efficient than formerly. Perhaps (though not provably) it has prevented wars that might have arisen out of international misunderstanding caused by written communication. Or perhaps—again not provably—by magnifying and extending irrational personal conflicts based on voice contact, it has caused wars. Certainly it has extended the scope of human conflicts, since it impartially disseminates the useful knowledge of scientists and the babble of bores, the affection of the affectionate and the malice of the malicious.

</td>
</tr>
</table>

The bulk of Brooks's paragraph is devoted to answering the very question he poses in his opening sentence: "What has the telephone done to us, or for us, in the hundred years of its existence?" Notice that even though many of the effects Brooks discusses are verifiable or probable, he is willing to admit that he is speculating about those effects that he cannot prove.

A second common use of the strategy is to reverse the forms by first examining the effect; the writer describes an important event or problem (effect) and then examines the possible reasons (causes) for it. For example, experts might trace the causes of poverty to any or all of the following: poor education, a nonprogressive tax system, declining commitment to social services, inflation, discrimination, or even the welfare system that is designed to help those most in need.

A third use of the strategy is for the writer to explore a complex causal chain. In this selection from his book *The Politics of Energy*, Barry Commoner examines the series of malfunctions that led to the near disaster at the Three Mile Island nuclear facility in Harrisburg, Pennsylvania.

On March 28, 1979, at 3:53 a.m., a pump at the Harrisburg plant failed. Because the pump failed, the reactor's heat was not drawn off in the heat exchanger and the very hot water in the primary loop overheated. The pressure in the loop increased, opening a release valve that was supposed to counteract such an event. But the valve stuck open and the primary loop system lost so much water (which ended up as a highly radioactive pool, six feet deep, on the floor of the reactor building) that it was unable to carry off all the heat generated within the reactor core. Under these circumstances, the intense heat held within the reactor could, in theory, melt its fuel rods, and the resulting "meltdown" could then carry a hugely radioactive mass through the floor of the reactor. The reactor's emergency cooling system, which is designed to prevent this disaster, was then automatically activated, but when it was, apparently, turned off too soon, some of the fuel rods overheated. This produced a bubble of hydrogen gas at the top of the reactor. (The hydrogen is dissolved in the water in order to react with oxygen that is produced when the intense reactor radiation splits water molecules into their atomic constituents. When heated, the dissolved hydrogen bubbles out of the solution.) This bubble blocked the flow of cooling water so that despite the action of the emergency cooling system the reactor core was again in danger of melting down. Another danger was that the gas might contain enough oxygen to cause an explosion that could rupture the huge containers that surround the reactor and release a deadly cloud of radioactive material into the surrounding countryside. Working desperately, technicians were able to gradually reduce the size of the gas bubble using a special apparatus brought in from the atomic laboratory at Oak Ridge, Tennessee, and the danger of a catastrophic release of radioactive materials subsided. But the sealed-off plant was now so radioactive that no one could enter it for many months—or, according to some observers, for years—without being exposed to a lethal dose of radiation.

Tracing a causal chain, as Commoner does here, is similar to narration. The writer must organize the events sequentially to show clearly how each event leads to the next.

In a causal chain, an initial cause brings about a particular effect, which in turn becomes the immediate cause of a further effect, and so on, bringing about a series of effects that also act as new causes. The so-called domino effect is a good illustration of the idea of a causal chain; the simple tipping over of a domino (initial cause) can result in the toppling of any number of dominoes down the line (series of effects). For example, before a salesperson approaches an important client about a big sale, she prepares extensively for the meeting (initial cause). Her preparation causes her to impress the client (effect A), which guarantees her the big sale (effect B), which in turn results in her promotion to district sales manager (effect C). The sale she made is the most immediate and the most obvious cause of her promotion, but it is possible to trace the chain back to its more essential cause: her hard work preparing for the meeting.

While the ultimate purpose of cause and effect analysis may seem simple—to know or to understand why something happens—determining causes and effects is often a thought-provoking and complex strategy. One reason for this complexity is that some causes are less obvious than others. *Immediate causes* are readily apparent because they are closest in time to the effect; the immediate cause of a flood, for example, may be the collapse of a dam. However, *remote causes* may be just as important, even though they are not as apparent and are perhaps even hidden. The remote (and, in fact, primary) cause of the flood might have been an engineering error or the use of substandard building materials or the failure of personnel to relieve the pressure on the dam caused by unseasonably heavy rains. In many cases, it is necessary to look beyond the most immediate causes to discover the true underlying sources of an event.

A second reason for the complexity of this strategy is the difficulty of distinguishing between possible and actual causes, as well as between possible and actual effects. An upset stomach may be caused by spoiled food, but it may also be caused by overeating, by flu, by nervousness, by pregnancy, or by a combination of factors. Similarly, an increase in the cost of electricity may have multiple effects: higher profits for utility companies, fewer sales of electrical appliances, higher prices for other products that depend on electricity in their manufacture, even the development of alternative sources of energy. Making reasonable choices among the various possibilities requires thought and care.

USING CAUSE AND EFFECT ANALYSIS AS A WRITING STRATEGY

Writers may use cause and effect analysis for three essential purposes: to inform, to speculate, and to argue. Most commonly, they will want to inform—to help their readers understand some identifiable fact. A state wildlife biologist, for example, might wish to tell the public about the effects severe winter weather has had on the state's deer herds. Similarly, in a newsletter, a member of Congress might explain to his or her constituency the reasons changes are being made in the Social Security system.

Cause and effect analysis may also allow writers to speculate—to consider what might be or what might have been. To satisfy the board of trustees, for example, a university treasurer might discuss the impact an increase in tuition will have on the school's budget. A columnist for *People* magazine might speculate about the reasons for a new singer's sudden popularity. Similarly, pollsters estimate the effects that various voter groups will have on future elections, and historians evaluate how the current presidency will continue to influence American government in the coming decades.

Finally, cause and effect analysis provides an excellent basis from which to argue a given position or point of view. An editorial writer, for example, could argue that bringing a professional basketball team into the area would have many positive effects on the local economy and on the community as a whole. Educators who think that video games are a cause of delinquency and poor school performance have argued in newspapers and professional journals against the widespread acceptance of such games.

USING CAUSE AND EFFECT ANALYSIS ACROSS THE DISCIPLINES

When writing essays in the academic disciplines, you will have many opportunities to use the strategy of cause and effect analysis to both organize and strengthen the presentation of your ideas. To determine whether or not cause and effect analysis is the right strategy for you in a particular paper, use the guidelines described in Chapter 2 (Determining a Strategy for Developing Your Essay, pages 32–33). Consider the following examples:

Native American History

1. **MAIN IDEA:** Treaties between Native American groups and the U.S. government had various negative effects on the Native Americans involved.

2. **QUESTION:** What have been some of the most harmful results for Native Americans of treaties between Native American groups and the U.S. government?

3. **STRATEGY:** Cause and Effect Analysis. The word *results* signals that this study needs to examine the harmful effects of the provisions of the treaties.

4. **SUPPORTING STRATEGY:** Illustration. Examples need to be given of both treaties and their consequences.

Nutrition

1. **MAIN IDEA:** A major factor to be considered when examining why people suffer from poor nutrition is poverty.

2. **QUESTION:** What is the relationship between poverty and nutrition?

3. **STRATEGY:** Cause and Effect Analysis. The word *relationship* signals a linkage between poverty and nutrition. The writer has to determine what is meant by poverty and poor nutrition in this country or in the countries examined.

4. **SUPPORTING STRATEGY:** Definition. Precise definitions will first be necessary in order for the writer to make valid judgments concerning the causal relationship in question.

Nursing

1. **MAIN IDEA:** Alzheimer's disease is the progressive loss of brain nerve cells, causing gradual loss of memory, concentration, understanding, and in some cases sanity.

2. **QUESTION:** What role does the overproduction of a protein that destroys nerve cells play in the development of Alzheimer's disease, and what causes the overproduction in the first place?

3. **STRATEGY:** Cause and Effect Analysis. The words *role*, *play*, and *causes* signal that the issue here is determining and explaining how Alzheimer's disease originates.

4. **SUPPORTING STRATEGY:** Process Analysis. Describing how Alzheimer's operates will be essential to making the reader understand its causes and effects.

SAMPLE STUDENT ESSAY USING CAUSE AND EFFECT ANALYSIS AS A WRITING STRATEGY

Born in Brooklyn, New York, Kevin Cunningham spent most of his life in Flemington, New Jersey. While enrolled in the mechanical engineering program at the University of Vermont, Cunningham shared an apartment near the Burlington waterfront with several other students. There he became interested in the effects that upscale real estate development—or gentrification—would have on his neighborhood. Such development is not unique to Burlington; it is happening in the older sections of cities across the country. After gathering information for his essay by talking with people who live in the neighborhood, Cunningham found it useful to discuss both the causes and the effects of gentrification in his well-unified essay.

Gentrification
Kevin Cunningham

Epigraph sets the theme

I went back to Ohio, and my city was gone. . . .
—Chrissie Hynde, of the Pretenders

My city is in Vermont, not Ohio, but soon my city might be
gone, too. Or maybe it's I who will be gone. My street, Lakeview
Terrace, lies unobtrusively in the old northwest part of Burlington and is notable, as its name suggests, for spectacular views
of Lake Champlain framed by the Adirondacks. It's not that the
neighborhood is going to seed, though—quite the contrary.

Thesis
Recently it has been discovered, and now it is on the verge of
being gentrified. For some of us who live here, that's bad.

Well-organized and unified paragraph: describes life cycle of city neighborhoods
Cities are often assigned human characteristics, one of which
is a life cycle: They have a birth, a youth, a middle age, and an
old age. A neighborhood is built and settled by young, vibrant
people, proud of their sturdy new homes. Together, residents
and houses mature, as families grow larger and extensions get
built on. Eventually, though, the neighborhood begins to show
its age. Buildings sag a little, houses aren't repainted as quickly,
and maintenance slips. The neighborhood may grow poorer, as
the young and upwardly mobile find new jobs and move away,
while the older and less successful inhabitants remain.

Decay, renewal, or redevelopment awaits aging neighborhoods
One of three fates awaits the aging neighborhood. Decay
may continue until the neighborhood becomes a slum. It may
face urban renewal, with old buildings being razed, and ugly,
new apartment houses taking their place. Finally, it may undergo redevelopment, in which government encourages the
upgrading of existing housing stock by offering low-interest
loans or outright grants. This last possibility would mean that
the original character of the neighborhood may be retained or
restored, allowing the city to keep part of its identity.

Organization: example of Hoboken, New Jersey
An example of redevelopment at its best is Hoboken, New
Jersey. In the early 1970s Hoboken was a dying city, with run-
down housing and many abandoned buildings. However, low-
interest loans enabled some younger residents to begin to
refurbish their homes, and soon the area began to show signs

Effects of redevelopment on Hoboken
of renewed vigor. Outsiders moved in and rebuilt some of the
abandoned houses. Today, whole blocks have been restored,

1

2

3

4

and neighborhood life is active again. The city does well, too, because property values are higher and so are property taxes. There, at least for my neighborhood, is the rub.

Transition: writer moves from example of Hoboken to his Lakeview Terrace neighborhood

Lakeview Terrace is a demographic potpourri of students and families, young professionals and elderly retirees, home-owners and renters. It's a quiet street where kids can play safely and the neighbors know each other. Most of the houses are fairly old and look it, but already some redevelopment has begun. Recently, several old houses were bought by a real es-tate company, rebuilt, and sold as condominiums; the new residents drive BMWs and keep to themselves. The house where I live is owned by a young professional couple—he's an architect—and they have renovated the place to what it must have looked like when it was new. They did a nice job, too. These two kinds of development are the main forms of gentri-fication, and so far they have done no real harm.

Describes "gentrification" to date

The city is about to start a major property tax reappraisal, however. Because of the renovations, the houses on Lakeview Terrace are currently worth more than they used to be; soon there will be a big jump in property taxes. That's when a lot of people will be hurt—possibly even evicted from their own neighborhood.

Redevelopment causes property values to increase, which causes property taxes to rise

Clem is a retired General Electric employee who has lived on Lakeview for over thirty years and who owns his home. About three years ago some condos were built on the lot next door, which didn't please Clem—he says they just don't fit in. With higher property taxes, however, it may be Clem who no longer fits in. At the very least, since he's on a fixed income, he will have to make sacrifices in order to stay. Ryan works as a mailman and also owns his Lakeview Terrace home, which is across the street from the houses that were converted into condos: same cause, same effect.

Organization: effects of gentrification on local property owners

Then there are those who rent. As landlords have to pay higher property taxes, they will naturally raise rents at least as much (and maybe more, if they've spent money on renova-tions of their own). Some renters won't be able to afford the increase and will have to leave. "Some renters" almost certainly includes me, as well as others who have lived on Lakeview Terrace much longer than I have. In fact, the exodus has al-ready begun, with the people who were displaced by the condo conversions.

Organization: effects of gentrification on renters

5

6

7

8

Conclusion   Of course, many people would consider what's happening   9
on Lakeview Terrace a genuine improvement in every way, resulting not only in better-looking houses but also in a better class
of people. I dispute that. The new people may be more affluent
than those they displace, but certainly not "better," not by any
Restatement   standard that matters. Gentrification may do wonders for a
of thesis   neighborhood's aesthetics, but it certainly can be hard on its soul.

Analyzing Kevin Cunningham's Cause and Effect Analysis: Questions for Discussion

1. According to Cunningham, in what way are cities like humans? What does he describe as the three possible outcomes for aging neighborhoods?

2. Cunningham presents this causal chain: Redevelopment (cause) increases property values (effect), which in turn increases property taxes upon reassessment by the city (effect), which leads to the displacement of poorer residents (effect). What other effects of redevelopment can you think of?

3. Cunningham decries the gentrification of his neighborhood, but a neighborhood descending into disrepair is not a desirable alternative. What do you think Cunningham would like to see happen on Lakeview Terrace? How can a neighborhood fend off decay while still maintaining its "soul"?

4. Would the essay have benefited if Cunningham had proposed and speculated about a viable alternative to gentrification? Explain.

SUGGESTIONS FOR USING CAUSE AND EFFECT ANALYSIS AS A WRITING STRATEGY

As you plan, write, and revise your cause and effect analysis, be mindful of the writing process guidelines described in Chapter 2. Pay particular attention to the basic requirements and essential ingredients of this writing strategy.

▌ Planning Your Cause and Effect Analysis

ESTABLISH YOUR FOCUS.   Decide whether your essay will propose causes, talk about effects, or analyze both causes and effects. Any research you do and any questions you ask will depend on how you wish to concentrate your attention. For example, let's say that as a reporter for the school paper, you are writing a story about a fire that destroyed an apartment building in the neighborhood, killing four people. In planning your story, you might focus on the cause of the fire: Was there more than one cause? Was carelessness to blame? Was the fire of suspicious origin? You might focus on the effects of the fire: How much damage was done to the building? How many people were left homeless? What was the impact on the families of the four victims? Or you might cover both the reasons for this tragic event and its ultimate effects, setting up a sort of causal chain. Such focus is crucial as you gather information. For example, student Kevin Cunningham decided early on that he wanted to explore what would happen to his neighborhood (the effects) if gentrification continued.

DETERMINE YOUR PURPOSE.   Once you begin to draft your essay and as you continue to refine it, make sure your purpose is clear. Do you wish your cause and effect analysis to be primarily informative, speculative, or argumentative? An informative essay allows readers to say, "I learned something from this. I didn't know that the fire was caused by faulty wiring." A speculative essay suggests to readers new possibilities: "That never occurred to me before. The apartment house could indeed be replaced by an office building." An argumentative essay convinces readers that some sort of action should be taken: "I have to agree—fire inspections should occur more regularly in our neighborhood." In his essay on gentrification, Cunningham uses cause and effect analysis to question the value of redevelopment by examining what it does to the soul of a neighborhood. Whatever your purpose, be sure to provide the information necessary to carry it through.

FORMULATE A THESIS STATEMENT.   All essays need a strong, clear thesis statement. When you are writing an essay using cause and effect, your thesis statement should clearly present either a cause and its effect(s) or an effect and its cause(s). As a third approach, your essay could focus on a complex causal chain of events. Here are a few examples from this chapter:

- *"What has the telephone done to us, or for us, in the hundred years of its existence?"* (page 438) This opening sentence signals that the essay will explore the effects of a single cause, the telephone.
- *"On March 28, 1979, at 3:53 a.m., a pump at the Harrisburg plant failed."* (page 439) Here, the pump failure introduces a causal chain of events leading to the disaster at Three Mile Island.
- *"Recently [our neighborhood] has been discovered, and now it is on the verge of being gentrified. For some of us who live here, that's bad."* (page 443) The first sentence asserts how one trend followed another while the second gives the author's opinion of those trends.

When you begin to formulate your thesis statement, keep these examples in mind. You can find other examples of thesis statements in the essays throughout this book. As you begin to develop your thesis statement, ask yourself, "What is my point?" Next, ask yourself, "What approach to a cause and effect essay will be most useful in making my point?" If you can't answer these questions yet, write some ideas down and try to determine your main point from these ideas.

▶ Organizing and Writing Your Cause and Effect Analysis

AVOID OVERSIMPLIFICATION AND ERRORS OF LOGIC. Sound and thoughtful reasoning, while present in all good writing, is central to any analysis of cause and effect. Writers of convincing cause and effect analysis must examine their material objectively and develop their essays carefully, taking into account any potential objections that readers might raise. Therefore, do not jump to conclusions or let your prejudices interfere with the logic of your interpretation or the completeness of your presentation. In gathering information for his essay, Kevin Cunningham discovered that he had to distinguish between cause and effect and mere coincidence:

> You have to know your subject, and you have to be honest. For example, my downstairs neighbors moved out last month because the rent was raised. Somebody who didn't know the situation might say, "See? Gentrification." But that wasn't the reason—it's that heating costs went up. This is New England, and we had a cold winter; gentrification had nothing to do with it. It's something that is just beginning to happen, and it's going to have a big effect, but we haven't actually felt many of the effects here yet.

Be sure that you do not oversimplify the cause and effect relationship you are writing about. A good working assumption is that most important matters cannot be traced to a single verifiable cause; similarly, a cause or set of causes rarely produces a single isolated effect. To be believable, your analysis of your topic must demonstrate a thorough understanding of the surrounding circumstances; there is nothing less convincing than the single-minded determination to show one particular connection. For example, someone writing about how the passage of a tough new crime bill (cause) has led to a decrease in arrests in a particular area (effect) will have little credibility unless other possible causes—socioeconomic conditions, seasonal fluctuations in crime, the size and budget of the police force, and so on—are also examined and taken into account. Of course, to achieve coherence, you will want to emphasize the important causes or the most significant effects: Just be careful not to lose your reader's trust by insisting on an oversimplified "X leads to Y" relationship.

The other common problem in cause and effect analysis is lack of evidence in establishing a cause or an effect. This error is known as the "after this, therefore because of this" fallacy (in Latin, *post hoc, ergo propter hoc*). In attempting to discover an explanation for a particular event or circumstance, a writer may point to something that merely preceded it in time, assuming a causal connection where none has in fact been proven. For example, if you have dinner out one evening and the next day come down with stomach cramps, you may blame your illness on the restaurant where you ate the night before; you do so without justification, however, if your only proof is the fact that you ate there beforehand. More evidence would be required to establish a causal relationship. The *post hoc, ergo propter hoc* fallacy is often harmlessly foolish ("I failed the exam because I lost my lucky key chain"). It can, however, lead writers into serious errors of judgment and blind them to more reasonable explanations of cause and effect. And, like oversimplification, such mistakes in logic can undercut a reader's confidence. Make sure that the causal relationships you cite are, in fact, based on demonstrable evidence and not merely on a temporal connection.

USE OTHER RHETORICAL STRATEGIES.   Although cause and effect analysis can be used effectively as a separate writing strategy, it is more common for essays to combine different strategies. For example, in an essay about a soccer team's victories, you might use comparison and contrast to highlight the differences between the team's play in the two losses and in five victories. Narration from interviews might also be used to add interest and color. An essay about the Internet might incorporate the strategy of argumentation as well as definition to defend the openness and effectiveness of the Internet. The argument could analyze exactly how the benefits outweigh the drawbacks, while definition could be used to focus the subject matter to better achieve your purpose. By combining strategies, you can gain both clarity and forcefulness in your writing.

Be aware, however, that you must always keep the purpose of your essay and the tone you wish to adopt in the front of your mind when combining strategies. Without careful planning, using more than one rhetorical strategy can alter both the direction and the tone of your essay in ways that detract from, rather than contribute to, your ability to achieve your purpose.

As you read the essays in this chapter, consider all of the writing strategies the authors have used to support their cause and effect analysis. How have these other strategies added to or changed the style of the essay? Are there strategies that you might have added or taken out? What strategies, if any, do you think you might use to strengthen your cause and effect essay?

▶ Revising and Editing Your Cause and Effect Analysis

SELECT WORDS THAT STRIKE A BALANCED TONE.   Be careful to neither overstate nor understate your position. Avoid exaggerations like "there can be no question" and "the evidence speaks for itself." Such diction is usually annoying and undermines your interpretation. Instead, allow your analysis of the facts to convince readers of the cause and effect relationship you wish to suggest. At the same time, no analytical writer convinces by continually understating or qualifying information with words and phrases such as *it seems that*, *perhaps*, *maybe*, *I think*, *sometimes*, *most often*, *nearly always*, or *in my opinion*. While it may be your intention to appear reasonable, overusing such qualifying words can make you sound unclear or indecisive, and it renders your analysis less convincing. Present your case forcefully, but do so honestly and sensibly.

SHARE YOUR DRAFT WITH OTHERS.   Try sharing the draft of your essay with other students in your writing class to make sure that your analysis makes sense. Ask them if there are any parts that they do not understand. Have them tell you what they think is the point of your analysis. If their answers differ from what you intended, have them indicate the passages that led them to their interpretations so that you can change your text accordingly. To maximize the effectiveness of conferences with your peers, use the guidelines presented on page 36. Feedback from these conferences often provides one or more places where you can start revising.

QUESTION YOUR OWN WORK WHILE REVISING AND EDITING.   Revision is best done by asking yourself key questions about what you have written. Begin by reading, preferably aloud, what you have written. Reading aloud forces you to pay attention to every word, and you are more likely to catch lapses in the logic. After you have read your paper through, answer the questions for revising and editing below and on the following page, and make the necessary changes.

For help with twelve common writing problems, see Chapter 16, "Editing for Grammar, Punctuation, and Sentence Style."

Questions for Revising and Editing: Cause and Effect Analysis

1. Why do I want to use cause and effect: to inform, to speculate, or to argue? Does my analysis help me achieve my purpose?

2. Is my topic manageable for the essay I wish to write? Have I effectively established my focus?

3. Does my thesis statement clearly state either the cause and its effects or the effect and its causes?

4. Have I identified the nature of my cause and effect scenario? Is there a causal chain? Have I identified immediate and remote causes? Have I distinguished between possible and actual causes and effects?

(continued on next page)

(continued from previous page)

5. Have I been able to avoid oversimplifying the cause and effect relationship I am writing about? Are there any errors in my logic?

6. Is my tone balanced, neither overstating nor understating my position?

7. Is there another rhetorical strategy that I can use with cause and effect to assist me in achieving my purpose? If so, have I been able to implement it with care so that I have not altered either the direction or the tone of my essay?

8. Have I taken every opportunity to use words and phrases that signal cause and effect relationships?

9. Have I used *affect* and *effect* properly?

10. Have I avoided the phrase *the reason is because*?

11. Have I avoided errors in grammar, punctuation, and mechanics? Is my sentence style as clear, smooth, and persuasive as possible?

How Boys Become Men

JON KATZ

Journalist and novelist Jon Katz was born in 1947. He writes with a keen understanding of life in contemporary suburban America. Each of his four mystery novels is a volume in the Suburban Detective Mystery series: *The Family Stalker* (1994), *Death by Station Wagon* (1994), *The Father's Club* (1996), and *The Last Housewife* (1996). The best known of these novels, *The Last Housewife*, won critical praise for its insights into the pressures and conflicts experienced by young professional couples in their efforts to achieve the American dream. Katz is also the author of *Media Rants: Postpolitics in the Digital Nation* (1997), a collection of his newspaper columns dealing primarily with the role and influence of the media in the public life of modern America; *Virtuous Reality: How Americans Surrendered Discussion of Moral Values to Opportunists, Nitwits, and Blockheads Like William Bennett* (1998); and *Geeks: How Two Lost Boys Rode the Internet Out of Idaho* (2000). Since 2000, he has written six books about dogs.

In the following essay, first published in January 1993 in *Glamour*, Katz explains why many men appear insensitive.

Preparing to Read

How important are childhood experiences to the development of identity? How do the rituals of the playground, the slumber party, and the neighborhood gang help mold us as men and women? Write about one or two examples from your own experience.

Two nine-year-old boys, neighbors and friends, were walking home from school. The one in the bright blue windbreaker was laughing and swinging a heavy-looking book bag toward the head of his friend, who kept ducking and stepping back. "What's the matter?" asked the kid with the bag, whooshing it over his head. "You chicken?"

His friend stopped, stood still, and braced himself. The bag slammed into the side of his face, the thump audible all the way across the street where I stood watching. The impact knocked him to the ground, where he lay mildly stunned for a second. Then he struggled up, rubbing the side of his head. "See?" he said proudly. "I'm no chicken."

No. A chicken would probably have had the sense to get out of the way. This boy was already well on the road to becoming a *man*, having learned one of the central ethics of his gender: Experience pain rather than show fear.

Women tend to see men as a giant problem in need of solution. They tell us that we're remote and uncommunicative, that we need to demonstrate less machismo and more commitment, more humanity. But if you don't understand something about boys, you can't understand why men are the way we are, why we find it so difficult to make friends or to acknowledge our fears and problems. 4

Boys live in a world with its own Code of Conduct, a set of ruthless, unspoken, and unyielding rules: 5

> Don't be a goody-goody.
> Never rat. If your parents ask about bruises, shrug.
> Never admit fear. Ride the roller coaster, join the fistfight, do what you have to do. Asking for help is for sissies.
> Empathy is for nerds. You can help your best buddy, under certain circumstances. Everyone else is on his own.
> Never discuss anything of substance with anybody. Grunt, shrug, dump on teachers, laugh at wimps, talk about comic books. Anything else is risky.

Boys are rewarded for throwing hard. Most other activities—reading, befriending girls, or just thinking—are considered weird. And if there's one thing boys don't want to be, it's weird. 6

More than anything else, boys are supposed to learn how to handle themselves. I remember the bitter fifth-grade conflict I touched off by elbowing aside a bigger boy named Barry and seizing the cafeteria's last carton of chocolate milk. Teased for getting aced out by a wimp, he had to reclaim his place in the pack. Our fistfight, at recess, ended with my knees buckling and my lip bleeding while my friends, sympathetic but out of range, watched resignedly. 7

When I got home, my mother took one look at my swollen face and screamed. I wouldn't tell her anything, but when my father got home I cracked and confessed, pleading with them to do nothing. Instead, they called Barry's parents, who restricted his television for a week. 8

The following morning, Barry and six of his pals stepped out from behind a stand of trees. "It's the rat," said Barry. 9

I bled a little more. *Rat* was scrawled in crayon across my desk. 10

They were waiting for me after school for a number of afternoons to follow. I tried varying my routes and avoiding bushes and hedges. It usually didn't work. 11

I was as ashamed for telling as I was frightened. "You did ask for it," said my best friend. Frontier Justice has nothing on Boy Justice. 12

In panic, I appealed to a cousin who was several years older. He followed me home from school, and when Barry's gang surrounded me, he 13 came barreling toward us. "Stay away from my cousin," he shouted, "or I'll kill you."

After they were gone, however, my cousin could barely stop laugh-ing. "You were afraid of *them*?" he howled. "They barely came up to my waist." 14

Men remember receiving little mercy as boys; maybe that's why it's sometimes difficult for them to show any. 15

"I know lots of men who had happy childhoods, but none who have happy memories of the way other boys treated them," says a friend. "It's a macho marathon from third grade up, when you start butting each other in the stomach." 16

Women tend to see men as a giant problem in need of solution.

"The thing is," adds another friend, "you learn early on to hide what you feel. It's never safe to say, 'I'm scared.' My girl-friend asks me why I don't talk more about what I'm feeling. I've gotten better at it, but it will *never* come naturally." 17

You don't need to be a shrink to see how the lessons boys learn affect their behavior as men. Men are being asked, more and more, to show sen-sitivity, but they dread the very word. They struggle to build their increas-ingly uncertain work lives but will deny they're in trouble. They want love, affection, and support but don't know how to ask for them. They hide their weaknesses and fears from all, even those they care for. They've learned to be wary of intervening when they see others in trouble. They often still balk at being stigmatized as weird. 18

Some men get shocked into sensitivity—when they lose their jobs, their wives, or their lovers. Others learn it through a strong marriage, or through their own children. 19

It may be a long while, however, before male culture evolves to the point that boys can learn more from one another than how to hit curve balls. Last month, walking my dog past the playground near my house, I saw three boys encircling a fourth, laughing and pushing him. He was skinny and rumpled, and he looked frightened. One boy knelt behind him while another pushed him from the front, a trick familiar to any former boy. He fell backward. 20

When the others ran off, he brushed the dirt off his elbows and walked toward the swings. His eyes were moist and he was struggling for control. 21

"Hi," I said through the chain-link fence. "How ya doing?" 22

"Fine," he said quickly, kicking his legs out and beginning his swing. 23

Thinking Critically about the Text

Do you agree with Katz that men in general are less communicative, less sensitive, and less sympathetic in their behavior than women? Why, or why not? Where does "Boy Justice" originate?

Questions on Subject

1. Why, according to Katz, do "women tend to see men as a giant problem in need of solution" (paragraph 4)?

2. In paragraph 3, Katz states that one of the "central ethics" of his gender is "Experience pain rather than show fear." Would you agree with Katz?

3. What is it that boys are supposed to learn "more than anything else" (paragraph 7)? What do you think girls are supposed to learn more than anything else?

4. In paragraph 12, what does Katz mean when he says, "Frontier Justice has nothing on Boy Justice"?

5. How, according to Katz, do some men finally achieve sensitivity? Can you think of other softening influences on adult males?

Questions on Strategy

1. This essay was originally published in *Glamour* magazine. Can you find any places where Katz addresses himself specifically to an audience of young women? Where? (Glossary: *Audience*)

2. Early in the essay, Katz refers to men as "we," but later he refers to men as "they." What is the purpose of this change?

3. Notice that in paragraphs 16 and 17, Katz quotes two friends on the nature of male development. Why is the location of these quotes crucial to the structure of the essay?

4. Katz illustrates his thesis with three anecdotes. Identify each of them. Where in the essay is each located? How do they differ? How does each enhance the author's message? (Glossary: *Narration*)

5. What irony is expressed by the boy's answer "Fine" in paragraph 23? (Glossary: *Irony*)

Questions on Diction and Vocabulary

1. In paragraph 3, Katz identifies what he describes as "one of the central ethics" of his gender. Why does he call it an ethic rather than a rule?

2. What connotations do the words *chicken* and *weird* have for you? (Glossary: *Connotation/Denotation*)

3. Are you familiar with the word *rat* as Katz uses it? What does it mean? Check your dictionary for what it says about *rat* as a noun and as a verb.

Classroom Activity Using Cause and Effect Analysis

Think about what might be necessary to write an essay similar to Katz's but entitled "How Girls Become Women." If we assume, as Katz does, that who men are is the product of their early experiences as boys, what in a woman's character might be caused by the experiences girls have growing up in our society? Share your thoughts with others in your class.

Writing Suggestions

1. Write an essay patterned on "How Boys Become Men," showing the causes and effects surrounding females growing up in American culture. In preparing to write, it may be helpful to review your response to the Preparing to Read prompt as well as ideas generated by the Classroom Activity for this selection. You might come to the conclusion that women do not have a standard way of growing up; you could also write a cause and effect essay supporting this idea. Either way, be sure to include convincing examples.

2. **Writing with Sources.** The subject of the differences between men and women perpetually spawns discussion and debate, and a spate of recently published and widely read books have commented seriously on relationship issues. Read one of these books. (*Men Are from Mars, Women Are from Venus* by John Gray and *You Just Don't Understand* by Deborah Tannen are good examples.) Write a review presenting and evaluating the major thesis of the book you have chosen. What issues make male-female relations so problematic? What can be done to bridge the "gender gap" that so many experts, books, and teachers struggle to explain? For models of and advice on integrating sources in your essay, see Chapters 14 and 15.

Is Anorexia a Cultural Disease?

CARRIE ARNOLD

Carrie Arnold is a freelance science writer who has covered such subjects as neuroscience, geology, genetics, biochemistry, nanotechnology, and microbiology. She earned her B.A. in chemistry and math from Hope College in 2002, her Masters of Public Health from the University of Michigan in 2005, and her M.A. in science writing from the Johns Hopkins University in 2008. In 2008 she wrote press releases and scientific summaries for the Proceedings of the National Academy of Sciences and a year later began publishing articles on breakthroughs in science for the *Washington Post*, *Earth* magazine, *Scientific American Mind*, and the *Johns Hopkins Public Health* magazine. A recovering anorexia nervosa patient, she has written three books on the subject: *Running on Empty: A Diary of Anorexia and Recovery* (2004); *Next to Nothing: A Firsthand Account of One Teenager's Experience with an Eating Disorder* (2007); and *Decoding Anorexia: How Breakthroughs in Science Offer Hope for Eating Disorders* (2012).

In the following article, first published in *Slate* on September 27, 2012, Arnold argues that environmental factors such as super-thin fashion models and digitally altered magazine photos are too often blamed as the cause of anorexia, especially by the media. While there is some evidence that fashion and celebrity cultures are responsible for the risk of developing the disorder, Arnold believes anorexia is a real illness and that its causes and effects deserve to be treated as such.

Preparing to Read

How much, if any, do you think our cultural emphasis on being thin is a contributing cause of anorexia? What role does the advertising industry play in causing low self-esteem and body dissatisfaction, especially in young women?

From the outside, my eating disorder looked a lot like vanity run 1 amok. It looked like a diet or an obsession with the size of my thighs. I spewed self- and body-hatred to friends and family for well over a decade. Anorexia may have looked like a disorder brought about by the fashion industry, by a desire to be thin and model-perfect that got out of hand.

Except that it wasn't. I wasn't being vain when I craned my neck trying 2 to check out my butt in the mirror—I truly had no idea what size I was anymore. I was so afraid of calories that I refused to use lip balm and, at one point, was unable to drink water. I was terrified of gaining weight, but I couldn't explain why.

As I lay in yet another hospital bed hooked up to yet another set of IVs and heart monitors, the idea of eating disorders as a cultural disorder struck me as utterly ludicrous. I didn't read fashion magazines, and altering my appearance wasn't what drove me to start restricting my food intake. I just wanted to feel better; I thought cutting out snacks might be a good way to make that happen. The more I read, the more I came to understand that culture is only a small part of an eating disorder. Much of my eating disorder, I learned, was driven by my own history of anxiety and depression, by my tendency to focus on the details at the expense of the big picture, and by hunger circuits gone awry. The overwhelming amount of misinformation about eating disorders—what they are and what causes them—drove me to write my latest book, *Decoding Anorexia: How Breakthroughs in Science Offer Hope for Eating Disorders.*

Efforts to fight eating disorders still target cultural phenomena, especially images of overly thin, digitally altered models. Last month, the Academy for Eating Disorders and the Binge Eating Disorders Association issued a press release condemning the high-end department store Barneys for giving beloved Disney characters a makeover. Minnie Mouse and Daisy Duck were stretched like taffy to appear emaciated in honor of Barneys' holiday ad campaign. The eating disorders groups wrote:

> Viewership of such images is associated with low self-esteem and body dissatisfaction in young girls and women, placing them at risk for development of body image disturbances and eating disorders. These conditions can have devastating psychological as well as medical consequences. This campaign runs counter to efforts across the globe to improve both the health of runway models and the representation of body image by the fashion industry.

All of which is technically true. But when you look at the research literature, several studies indicate that environmental factors such as emaciated models are actually a minor factor in what puts people at risk of an eating disorder. A 2000 study published in the *American Journal of Psychiatry* found that about 60 percent (and up to 85 percent) of a person's risk for developing anorexia was due to genetics. A 2006 follow-up study in the *Archives of General Psychiatry* found that only 5 percent of a person's risk of developing anorexia came from shared environmental factors like models and magazine culture. A far greater environmental risk (which the study estimated constituted 35 percent of someone's risk of anorexia) came from what researchers call non-shared environmental factors, which are unique to each individual, such as being bullied on the playground or being infected with a bacterium like *Streptococcus*. (Several very small studies have linked the sudden onset of anorexia and obsessive-compulsive symptoms to an autoimmune reaction to strep infections.)

Eating disorders existed long before the advent of supermodels. Researchers believe the "starving saints" of the Middle Ages, like Catherine of Siena, had anorexia. Reports from ancient history indicate that wealthy Romans would force themselves to vomit during feasts, to make room in their stomachs for yet another course. In modern times, anorexia has been reported in rural Africa and in Amish and Mennonite communities, none of which are inundated with images of overly thin women. Nor does culture explain the fact that all Americans are bombarded with these images but only a very tiny portion ever develop a clinical eating disorder.

Frankly, I think the Barneys' creation of Skinny Minnie and her newly svelte compatriots is ridiculous. They look absurd and freakish. I think we should be aware of and speak out against the thin body ideal, the sexualization of children, and the use of digitally altered images in advertising. I think we should do this regardless of the link to eating disorders. My objection to the AED and BEDA's response is that it reinforces an "I wanna look like a model" model for how we think of eating disorders. It implies that eating disorders are seen as issues for white, upper-class women, which means that these life-threatening disorders often go undetected and untreated in men, the poor, and minorities.

How sufferers, their families, and our culture at large think about eating disorders sets the agenda for treatment, research, and funding. Until a 2008 lawsuit in New Jersey established that anorexia and bulimia were biologically based mental illnesses, it was legal for insurance companies to deny necessary and lifesaving care. The message to sufferers? *You're not that bad off. You're just making this up. Get over it.*

Too many people can't. Eating disorders have the highest mortality rate of all psychiatric illnesses. Up to 1 in 5 chronic anorexia sufferers will die as a direct result of their illness. Recovery from anorexia is typically thought of as the rule of thirds: One-third of sufferers get better, one-third have periods of recovery interrupted by relapse, and one-third remain chronically ill or die.

Although research into eating disorders is improving, it is still dramatically underfunded compared to other neuropsychiatric conditions. The National Institute of Mental Health estimates that 4.4 percent of the U.S. population, or about 13 million Americans, currently suffers from an eating disorder, and eating disorders receive about $27 million in research funding from the government. That's about $2 per affected person, for a disease that costs the economy billions of dollars in treatment costs and loss of productivity. Schizophrenia, in comparison, receives $110 per affected person in research funding.

The lack of research funding means that it's been difficult to develop   11
new treatments for eating disorders and test them in clinical trials. Several types of psychotherapy have been found effective in the treatment of bulimia and binge-eating disorder, although many sufferers have difficulty maintaining recovery even with state-of-the-art treatment. Thus far, no therapies have been clinically proven for adults with anorexia. Because many of those with anorexia are scared of the idea of eating more and gaining weight, they tend to be reluctant to show up for treatment and follow through with a clinical trial. Researchers have found a type of treatment known as family-based treatment, which uses the family as an ally in fighting their child's eating disorder, to be effective in children, teens, and young adults with anorexia or bulimia.

> Recovery from anorexia is typically thought of as the rule of thirds: One-third of sufferers get better, one-third have periods of recovery interrupted by relapse, and one-third remain chronically ill or die.

The message from AED and BEDA is   12
technically correct: More and more children are dieting, whether in response to thin models, obesity prevention efforts, or both. Dieting is potentially dangerous because food restriction can set off a chain of events in a vulnerable person's brain and body. For most people, diets end after a modest weight loss (and are, more often than not, followed by a regain of the lost weight, plus a few "bonus" pounds as a reward for playing). For the 1 percent to 5 percent of the population that has a genetic vulnerability to an eating disorder, that innocent attempt at weight loss, "healthy eating," or other situation that results in fewer calories being eaten than necessary, can trigger a life-threatening eating disorder.

However, focusing on purported cultural "causes" of eating disorders   13
leaves out the much bigger, more multifaceted picture of what these disorders are. Eating disorders result from a complex interplay between genes and environment; it's not *just* culture. Yet most media coverage of eating disorders focuses on these types of cultural factors. Well over half of the eating disorder stories I see are about celebrities. Celebrities suffer from eating disorders, too, but they are a small fraction of the total number of sufferers out there. Eating disorders aren't solely about wanting to be thin. They aren't about celebrity culture or the supermodel *du jour*. They are real illnesses that ruin lives.

Thinking Critically about the Text

Has Arnold changed your mind in any way about how the fashion industry develops or encourages anorexia? If so, how?

Questions on Subject

1. Why did Arnold come to "regard the idea of eating disorders as a cultural disorder" as "ridiculous"?

2. What drove Arnold to write her own book on eating disorders?

3. According to the *American Journal of Psychiatry*, what role does genetics play in the development of anorexia?

4. Why is it important for us to realize that anorexia also affects men, the poor, and minorities?

5. What specifically concerns Arnold about the low level of funding for eating disorders?

6. What is family-based treatment? What problems do researchers think it helps to solve?

Questions on Strategy

1. What is Arnold arguing for in this essay? (Glossary: *Argument*)

2. What is her thesis? (Glossary: *Thesis*) Where does she place her thesis within her essay? Is it well-placed in your opinion? Why, or why not?

3. How do the historic and geographic diversity references in paragraph 7 help Arnold to argue her thesis?

4. Identify three or four transitions that Arnold uses between paragraphs in this essay, and explain how they serve to link her paragraphs and build unity in her essay. (Glossary: *Transitions*; *Unity*)

5. Why is Arnold's sentence such a fitting conclusion given her thesis and the evidence she presents? (Glossary: *Ending*)

Questions on Diction and Vocabulary

1. By using the "I" pronoun Arnold personally enters into her subject matter. Do you think that approach is valid and useful in her case? Why, or why not?

2. How would you describe Arnold's tone in this essay? How does she establish that tone? Do you find it an appropriate tone for the essay she writes? Why, or why not? (Glossary: *Tone*)

Classroom Activity Using Cause and Effect

As a class, discuss the causal chains that might have led to one of the following situations:

> a ban on drinking water in your community
>
> a car that won't start
>
> an increase in voter participation in local elections

What questions need to be asked and answered? For example, if math scores on standardized tests have improved recently in your local high school, was it the school board, the parents, the teachers, or someone else who asked for changes to be made? Was more time allotted to the teaching of math? Were improved teaching materials provided? What other causes might have been in play and in what order might they have occurred?

Writing Suggestions

1. Some cause and effect analyses approach complicated issues and situations from a relatively new perspective. Alternatively, some revisit well-accepted analyses from a new and different perspective or with a new emphasis. Arnold's approach to anorexia nervosa, for example, places a lot of weight on the psychological aspects of the disorder and less on the near-universal and very popular acceptance of cultural phenomena as the cause of the disorder. Look at a well-accepted cause and effect situation and write an essay modeled on Arnold's approach. In your view, what has been overlooked and needs to be rethought? What different emphases need to be introduced and advanced? You might wish to look, for example, at the causes and effects of gun-related violence in our schools, fad diets, teen auto accidents, voter apathy, underage drinking, bullying in schools, steroid use among school-age athletes, violence against women, or harmful food additives.

2. Write an essay in which you argue, as Arnold believes, that dieting for children is a bad idea. Of particular importance will be how you handle the question of the alarming incidence of obesity in America's children. Is the rate of obesity increasing, declining, or stable? If the rate is changing, what accounts for the change? What, if anything, changes if we include organic or low-fat diets or diets related to childhood diseases, disorders, and allergies? Do those situations alter the prohibition on childhood diets?

iPod World:
The End of Society?

ANDREW SULLIVAN

Andrew Sullivan was born in 1963 in South Godstone, Surrey, England, to Irish parents. He earned his B.A. degree in modern history at Magdalene College, Oxford, and his master's degree and Ph.D. in government at Harvard. Sullivan began his career in journalism at the *New Republic* and later wrote for the *New York Times Magazine*. A gay, Catholic, conservative, and often controversial commentator, Sullivan has made history as a blogger. His *The Daily Dish* blog became popular post–9/11 and received over 50,000 hits a day by 2005. He moved the blog to *The Atlantic* in 2007, and then again to *The Daily Beast* in 2011, before moving it to a reader-supported stand-alone site in 2013. Sullivan has written several books: *Virtually Normal: An Argument about Homosexuality* (1995); *Love Undetectable: Notes on Friendship, Sex and Survival* (1998); and *The Conservative Soul: How We Lost It, How to Get It Back* (2006).

In "iPod World: The End of Society?," which was first published in the *New York Times Magazine* on February 20, 2005, Sullivan examines the effects, both positive and negative, of the proliferation of iPods in our society.

Preparing to Read

If you are an iPod owner, what is attractive to you about the device? What does it allow you to do? What does it prevent you from having to do? Do you feel any sense of isolation when using your iPod? Do you think that your use of an iPod represents anything unique in our history? If so, what? If you do not have an iPod, what has prevented you from entering "iPod World"?

I was visiting New York City last week and noticed something I'd never   1
thought I'd say about the big city. Yes, nightlife is pretty much dead (and I'm in no way the first to notice that). But daylife—that insane mishmash of yells, chatter, clatter, hustle, and chutzpah that makes New York the urban equivalent of methamphetamine—was also a little different. It was just a little quieter. Yes, the suburbanization of Manhattan is now far-gone, its downtown a Disney-like string of malls, riverside parks, and pretty upper-middle-class villages. But there was something else as well. And as I looked across the throngs on the pavements, I began to see why. There were little white wires hanging down from their ears, tucked into pockets or purses or jackets. The eyes were a little vacant. Each was in

his or her own little musical world, walking to their own soundtrack, stars in their own music video, almost oblivious to the world around them. These are the iPod people.

> Even without the white wires, you can tell who they are. They walk down the street in their own MP3 cocoon, bumping into others, deaf to small social cues, shutting out anyone not in their bubble.

Even without the white wires, you can tell who they are. They walk down the street in their own MP3 cocoon, bumping into others, deaf to small social cues, shutting out anyone not in their bubble. Every now and again, some start unconsciously emitting strange tuneless squawks, like a badly-tuned radio, and their fingers snap or their arms twitch to some strange soundless rhythm. When others say, "Excuse me," there's no response. "Hi." Ditto. It's strange to be among so many people and hear so little. Except that each one is hearing so much.

Yes, I might as well fess up. I'm one of them. I witnessed the glazed New York looks through my own glazed pupils, my own white wires peeping out of my eardrums. I joined the cult a few years ago: the sect of the little white box worshippers. Every now and again, I go to church—those huge, luminous Apple stores, pews in the rear, the clerics in their monastic uniforms all bustling around, or sitting behind the "Genius Bars," like priests waiting to hear confessions. Others began, like I did, with a Walkman—and then another kind of clunkier MP3 player. But the sleekness of the iPod won me over. Unlike previous models, it actually gave me my entire musical collection to rearrange as I saw fit—on the fly, in my pocket. What was once an occasional musical diversion became a compulsive obsession. Now I have my iTunes in my iMac for my iPod in my iWorld. It's Narcissus's heaven: We've finally put the "i" into Me.

And, like all addictive cults, it's spreading. There are now 22 million iPod owners in the United States and Apple is now becoming a mass market company for the first time. Walk through any U.S. airport these days, and you will see person after person gliding through the social ether as if on autopilot. Get on a subway, and you're surrounded by a bunch of Stepford commuters, all sealed off from each other, staring into mid-space as if anesthetized by technology. Don't ask, don't tell, don't overhear, don't observe. Just tune in and tune out.

It wouldn't be so worrisome if it weren't part of something even bigger. Americans are beginning to narrowcast their own lives. You get your news from your favorite blogs, the ones that won't challenge your own view of the world. You tune in to a paid satellite radio service that also aims directly at a small market — for New Age fanatics, or liberal talk, or Christian rock. Television is all cable. Culture is all subculture. Your cell phones can receive e-mail feeds of your favorite blogger's latest thoughts — seconds after he has posted them — or sports scores for your own team, or stock quotes of just your portfolio. Technology has given us finally a universe entirely for ourselves — where the serendipity of meeting a new stranger, or hearing a piece of music we would never choose for ourselves, or an opinion that might actually force us to change our mind about something are all effectively banished. Atomization by little white boxes and cell phones. Society without the social. Others who are chosen — not met at random.

Human beings have never lived like this before. Yes, we have always   6 had homes or retreats or places where we went to relax or unwind or shut the world out. But we didn't walk around the world like hermit crabs with our isolation surgically attached. Music in particular was once the preserve of the living room or the concert hall. It was sometimes solitary but it was primarily a shared experience, something that brought people together, gave them the comfort of knowing that others too understood the pleasure of that Brahms symphony or that Beatles album.

But music is as atomized now as living is. And it's also secret. That   7 bloke next to you on the bus could be listening to heavy metal or Gregorian chant. You'll never know. And so, bit by bit, you'll never really know him. And by his very white wires, he is indicating he doesn't really want to know you.

What do we get from this? The awareness of more music, more often.   8 The chance to slip away for a while from everydayness, to give our lives our own sound track, to still the monotony of the commute, to listen more closely and carefully to music that can lift you up and keep you going. We become masters of our own interests, more connected to people like us over the Internet, more instantly in touch with anything we want or need or think we want and think we need. Ever tried a stairmaster in silence? And why not listen to a Haydn trio while in line at Tesco?

But what are we missing? That hilarious shard of an overheard conver-   9 sation that stays with you all day; the child whose chatter on the sidewalk takes you back to your own early memories; birdsong; weather; accents; the laughter of others; and those thoughts that come not by filling your head with selected diversion, but by allowing your mind to wander aimlessly through the regular background noise of human and mechanical life. External stimulation can crowd out the interior mind. Even the boredom that we flee has its uses. We are forced to find our own means to overcome it. And so we enrich our life from within, rather than from the static of white wires.

It's hard to give up, though, isn't it? Not so long ago, I was on a trip 10 and realized I had left my iPod behind. Panic. But then something else. I noticed the rhythms of others again, the sound of the airplane, the opinions of the cabby, the small social cues that had been obscured before. I noticed how others related to each other. And I felt just a little bit connected again. And a little more aware. Try it. There's a world out there. And it has a sound track all its own.

Thinking Critically about the Text

Sullivan's title asks whether "iPod world" represents the end of society. Do you think Sullivan answers his own question? If so, how and where in the text does he do so? If not, why might Sullivan have left the question for us to answer? Explain.

Questions on Subject

1. What is Sullivan's thesis in this essay? (Glossary: *Thesis*)

2. What does Sullivan see as the benefits of iPod world? What does he see as the drawbacks?

3. What does Sullivan mean when he writes in paragraph 5, "Culture is all subculture"?

4. What suggestion does Sullivan make at the conclusion of his essay? Is his suggestion an appropriate conclusion for his essay? (Glossary: *Beginnings/Endings*)

Questions on Strategy

1. What particular features of the iPod lead to the effects Sullivan points out?

2. In paragraph 3, Sullivan equates iPod world to a cult or religion. How does his analogy work? (Glossary: *Analogy*)

3. Sullivan writes in paragraph 6, "Human beings have never lived like this before." How does he use comparison and contrast to help make his point? (Glossary: *Comparison and Contrast*)

4. Cite several examples where Sullivan uses irony in his essay. (Glossary: *Irony*) To what effect does he use this rhetorical device?

5. In his final paragraph Sullivan gives us a brief example of cause and effect at work. What happens when he forgets to take his iPod on a trip?

Questions on Diction and Vocabulary

1. Reread paragraph 7. If you didn't already know that Sullivan was an Englishman, would you be able to tell from his diction in this paragraph? Explain.

2. Sullivan uses the words *atomization* (paragraph 5) and *atomized* (7). What does he mean by their use, and why do these words work so well for him?

3. How would you characterize Sullivan's style in this essay? Is it formal or informal, chatty or preachy, journalistic or academic, or something else? Support your answer with examples from the text. (Glossary: *Style*)

Classroom Activity Using Cause and Effect Analysis

In preparation for a classroom discussion, use your iPod or MP3 player for a morning as you go about your daily campus activities. In the afternoon, do not use the device at all. Make a brief list of the effects of both using and not using the device as a prompt for your later classroom discussion.

Writing Suggestions

1. Study the photo below. It is one of a series of poster advertisements for the iPod on which someone has written an interpretation of the meaning of the *i* in *iPod*. Write an argument for or against the idea expressed in the handwritten comment: "The *i* stands for ISOLATION." Feel free to use the ideas and statements that Andrew Sullivan uses in his essay as prompts, quotations, and evidence in your own work, but do not simply parrot what Sullivan has to say. Reach out in new and creative ways to express the causal relationship between the iPod and isolation.

2. Every time a new technological advance has been made that is widely accepted — telephone, radio, television, video, DVDs, cell phones, and similar devices — there are those who decry the innovation as the end of society as we know it. Write an essay in which you argue either that the iPod is just such a device or that it is different from the others in significant ways. Be sure to include clear explanations that are based in cause and effect analysis.

3. An underlying concern, and perhaps a theme, in Sullivan's essay is that music plays a vital role in our sense of well-being. Each person with an iPod plays, in effect, a personally programmed and designed sound track for his or her life. Write an essay in which you examine music as a cause in your life and the way it affects you.

The Real Computer Virus

CARL M. CANNON

Carl M. Cannon was born in San Francisco and majored in journalism at the University of Colorado. For twenty years he worked on a number of newspapers covering local and state politics, education, crime, and race relations. His reporting was instrumental in securing the freedom of a man in Georgia and a man in California who had both been wrongly convicted of murder. In 1989 Cannon's reporting on the Loma Prieta earthquake for the *San Jose Mercury* won him a Pulitzer Prize. Since 1998, Cannon has been a staff writer for the prestigious *National Journal,* where he is now the White House correspondent. Cannon's books include *Boy Genius* (2003), a biography of George W. Bush's advisor Karl Rove, which he wrote with Lou Dubose and Jan Reid; and *The Pursuit of Happiness in Times of War* (2003), which examines the meaning and history of Thomas Jefferson's influential and quintessentially American phrase.

In the following excerpt from "The Real Computer Virus," which first appeared in *American Journalism Review* in April 2001, Cannon writes about the problems of obtaining accurate information on the Internet and correcting the misinformation frequently found and spread there.

Preparing to Read

How do you go about fact-checking information from the Internet? Do you check to see who writes or sponsors the Web sites you visit? Do you use more than one or two sources for the information you need? Have you ever had reason to doubt the accuracy of information you have used in an assignment?

The Internet is an invaluable information-gathering tool for journalists. It also has an unmatched capacity for distributing misinformation, which all too often winds up in the mainstream media.

To commemorate Independence Day last year, *Boston Globe* columnist Jeff Jacoby came up with an idea that seemed pretty straightforward. Just explain to his readers what happened to the brave men who signed the Declaration of Independence.

This column caused big trouble for Jacoby when it was discovered that he had lifted the idea and some of its language from a ubiquitous e-mail making the rounds. It touched a particular nerve at the *Globe*, which had recently forced two well-regarded columnists to resign for making up quotes and characters. Jacoby was suspended for four months without pay, generating a fair amount of controversy, much of it because he was the primary conservative voice at an identifiably liberal paper.

But there was a more fundamental issue at play than Jacoby's failure to attribute the information in the column: Much of what the e-mail contained was factually incorrect. To his credit, Jacoby recognized this flaw and tried, with some success, to correct it. Ann Landers, however, didn't. She got the same e-mail and simply ran it verbatim in her column.   4

Passing along what she described as a "perfect" Independence Day column sent to her from "Ellen" in New Jersey, Ann Landers's epistle began this way: 5

Have you ever wondered what happened to the 56 men who signed the Declaration of Independence?   6

Five signers were captured by the British as traitors and tortured before they died. Twelve had their homes ransacked and burned. Two lost their sons who served in the Revolutionary Army. . . . Nine of the 56 fought and died from wounds or hardships of the Revolutionary War. They pledged their lives, their fortunes, and their sacred honor.   7

Landers's column—like Ellen's e-mail—goes on from that point to list names and explain the purported fates of many of the men. But this was not the "perfect" column Landers thought it was, for the simple reason that much of the information in it is simply false—as any Revolutionary War scholar would know readily.   8

I know because I interviewed some of them. R. J. Rockefeller, director of reference services at the Maryland State Archives, reveals that none of the signers was tortured to death by the British. E. Brooke Harlowe, a political scientist at the College of St. Catherine in St. Paul, Minnesota, reports that 2 of the 56 were wounded in battle, rather than 9 being killed. Brown University historian Gordon S. Wood points out that although the e-mail claims that for signer Thomas McKean "poverty was his reward," McKean actually ended up being governor of Pennsylvania and lived in material comfort until age 83.   9

And so on. What Landers was passing along was a collection of myths and partial truths that had been circulating since at least 1995, and which has made its way into print in newspaper op-eds and letters-to-the-editor pages and onto the radio airwaves many times before. Mark Twain supposedly said, in a less technologically challenging time, that a lie can make it halfway 'round the world before the truth gets its boots on. The Internet gives untruth a head start it surely never needed. And what a head start: If an e-mailer sends a message to 10 people and each person who receives it passes it on to 10 more, by the ninth transmission this missive could reach a billion people.   10

This is the real computer virus: misinformation. Despite years of warnings, this malady keeps creeping its way into the newsprint and onto the airwaves of mainstream news outlets.   11

One of the things that makes the Internet so appealing is that anyone   12
can pull things off of it. The other side of the coin is that anyone can put anything on it. This poses a particular challenge for reporters who are taught in journalism school to give more weight to the written word (get the official records!) than to something they hear—say, word-of-mouth at the corner barber shop. But the Web has both official documents and idle gossip, and reporters using it as a research tool—or even a tip sheet—do not always know the difference.

> Mark Twain supposedly said . . . that a lie can make it halfway 'round the world before the truth gets its boots on. The Internet gives untruth a head start it surely never needed.

"Journalists should be really skepti-   13
cal of everything they read online," says Sreenath Sreenivasan, a professor at the Columbia University Graduate School of Journalism. "They should be very aware of where they are on the Web, just the way they would be if they were on the street."

They aren't always.   14

In November 1998, the *New York Times* pulled off the Web—and   15
published—a series of riotously funny Chinese translations of actual Hollywood hits. *The Crying Game* became "Oh No! My Girlfriend Has a Penis!" *My Best Friend's Wedding* became "Help! My Pretend Boyfriend Is Gay." *Batman and Robin* was "Come to My Cave and Wear this Rubber Codpiece, Cute Boy."

If those seemed, in the old newsroom phrase, too good to check, it's   16
because they were. They came from an irreverent Web site called TopFive .com, which bills itself as offering "dangerously original humor."

But even after the *Times* issued a red-faced correction, the "transla-   17
tions" kept showing up. On January 5, 1999, Peter Jennings read the spoof of the title of the movie *Babe* ("The Happy Dumpling-To-Be Who Talks and Solves Agricultural Problems") as if it were factual. Jennings issued a correction 13 days later for his *World News Tonight* gaffe, but that didn't stop things. On April 16, 1999, some of the bogus translations showed up on CNN's *Showbiz Today*. On June 10, a *Los Angeles Times* staff writer threw one of the TopFive.com titles into his sports column. In Hong Kong, he claimed, the title *Field of Dreams* was "Imaginary Dead Ballplayers in a Cornfield."

"What journalists need to do is learn to distinguish between the crap   18
on the Web and the good stuff," says Yale University researcher and lecturer Fred Shapiro. "It's a crucial skill and one that some journalists need to be taught."

Even before President Clinton stirred up controversy with a slew of late-term pardons and commutations, I researched and wrote a 4,000-word article on the historical and legal underpinnings of a U.S. president's power to grant pardons, commutations, and clemency orders. One pertinent constitutional question was whether there are any real restrictions on the presidential pardon authority. 19

Logging onto Lexis-Nexis, I found several relevant, in-depth law review articles. Some of them cited Internet links to the original cases being cited. In fact these were highlighted "hyperlinks," meaning that with a single click of my mouse I was able to read the controlling Supreme Court cases dating back to Reconstruction. Within seconds of clicking on those Supreme Court links, I was gazing at the actual words of Salmon P. Chase, the chief justice appointed by Abraham Lincoln. Justice Chase answered my question rather unequivocally: "To the executive alone is entrusted the power of pardon," he wrote with simple eloquence, "and it is granted without limit." 20

This is not an isolated example. I cover the White House for *National Journal* and, like many of my colleagues, I have developed an utter reliance on the Internet. I do research and interviews online, find phone numbers, check facts and spellings, and research the clips. I can read court cases online, check presidential transcripts, find the true source of quotes, and delve into history. 21

Some days this is a tool that feels like a magic wand. The riches of the Web are as vast as the journalist's imagination. 22

The point of these examples is that the Internet has rapidly become such a valuable research tool that it's hard to remember how we did our jobs without it. Need that killer Shakespeare reference to truth-telling from *As You Like It* to spice up that Clinton legacy piece? Log on and find it. Fact-checking the Bible verses slung around by the candidates during the 2000 presidential election? The Bible is not only on the Web but is searchable with a couple of keystrokes. Attorney general John Ashcroft's Senate voting record is there, too, along with his controversial interview with *Southern Partisan* magazine. 23

Yet in recent months I have found myself quietly checking the validity of almost everything I find in cyberspace and whenever possible doing it the old-fashioned way: consulting reference books in libraries, calling professors or original sources on the phone, double-checking everything. I don't trust the information on the Net very much anymore. It turns out the same technology that gives reporters access to the intellectual richness of the ages also makes misinformation ubiquitous. It shouldn't come as a surprise, but a tool this powerful must be handled with care. 24

These problems are only going to get worse unless Net users—and journalists—get a whole lot more careful. According to the Nielsen/ 25

NetRatings released on February 15, 168 million Americans logged onto the Web in the first month of the new millennium.

Seven years ago, *American Journalism Review* warned that an over- 26
reliance on Lexis-Nexis was leading to a "misinformation explosion." Since that time, the number of journalists using the data retrieval service has increased exponentially; at many news organizations, libraries have been phased out and reporters do their own searches. This has led, predictably, to an entire subgenre of phony quotes and statistics that won't die.

Sometimes the proliferation of errors carries serious implications. A 27
couple of years ago, Diane Sawyer concluded a *PrimeTime Live* interview with Ellen DeGeneres the night her lesbian television character "came out" by reciting what Sawyer called "a government statistic": gay teenagers are "three times as likely to attempt suicide" as straight teenagers.

This factoid, which Sawyer said was provided to her by DeGeneres, is 28
a crock.

Sleuthing by a diligent reporter named Delia M. Rios of Newhouse 29
News Service revealed that this figure is not a government statistic, but rather the opinion of a single San Francisco social worker. In fact, a high-level interagency panel made up of physicians and researchers from the U.S. Department of Health and Human Services, the Centers for Disease Control, the National Institute of Mental Health, and other organizations concluded that there is no evidence that "sexual orientation and suicidality are linked in some direct or indirect manner."

Yet, the bogus stat is still routinely cited by certain gay-rights activists, 30
and thanks to Internet-assisted databases, has made its way into the *New York Times*, the *Chicago Tribune*, the *Los Angeles Times*—and onto prime time network television.

Joyce Hunter, onetime president of the National Lesbian and Gay 31
Health Association, insists that the available evidence suggests that both gay and straight teens are, instead, emotionally resilient people who "go on to develop a positive sense of self and who go on with their lives." Other clinicians fear that this misinformation could turn into a self-fulfilling prophecy. Peter Muehrer of the National Institutes of Health says he worries that a public hysteria over gay-teen suicide could contribute to "suicide contagion," in which troubled gay teens come to see suicide as a practical, almost normal, way out of their identity struggles.

Junk science on the Web—or junk history—has a way of oozing into 32
the mainstream media, often because it proves irresistible to disc jockeys and radio talk-show hosts. The same is true of conspiracy theories and faulty understanding of the law, particularly when the incendiary subject of race relations is involved.

An e-mail marked "URGENT! URGENT! URGENT!" flew like the   33
wind through the African American community for more than two years.
It warned that blacks' "right to vote" will expire in 2007. The impetus for
the e-mail was the impending expiration of the Voting Rights Act, which
has since been renewed and, in any event, no longer has anything to do
with guaranteeing anyone the right to vote.

Nonetheless, the preposterous claim was reiterated by callers to   34
African American radio talk shows. Eventually, it prompted an official
rebuttal by the Justice Department and a public disavowal by the
Congressional Black Caucus. "The Web has good, useful information,"
observes David Bositis, senior political analyst for the Joint Center for
Political and Economic Studies. "But it also has a lot of garbage."

This particular cyberrumor was eventually traced to a naive but well-   35
intentioned college student from Chicago, who toured the South on a pro-
motional trip sponsored by the NAACP. The mistaken notion that blacks'
right to vote depends on the whims of Congress was given wide circulation
in a guest column in *USA Today* by Camille O. Cosby, wife of entertainer
Bill Cosby.

"Congress once again will decide whether African Americans will be   36
allowed to vote," she wrote, echoing the e-mail. "No other Americans are
subjected to this oppressive nonsense."

Black leaders went to great lengths to dispel this hoax, but it energized   37
black voters. The ensuing higher-than-normal black turnout in the 1998
midterm elections helped Democrats at the polls, led to House Speaker
Newt Gingrich's demise, and may have saved Bill Clinton's job. Could the
e-mail hoax have played a role?

Other hoaxes are not so accidental. Last year, as the presidential   38
campaign began heating up, I received an e-mail from a fellow journalist
alerting me to an anti–Al Gore Web site she thought contained valuable
information. It included a litany of silly statements attributed to Gore.
Some of them were accurate, but several of them I recognized as being
utterances of former vice president Dan Quayle. Others were statements
never said by either Gore or Quayle.

On October 3, 1999, when liberal movie star Warren Beatty spoke to   39
Americans for Democratic Action about his political views, he said that he
wasn't the only one who worried that corporations were a threat to democracy. Beatty said that Abraham Lincoln himself had warned that corporations are "more despotic than monarchy," adding that Lincoln also said
"the money power preys upon the nation in times of peace, and it con-
spires against it in times of adversity." Beatty's populist version of Lincoln
hardly squares with his career as a corporate attorney—he represented
Illinois Central Railroad before he ran for public office—but that didn't

faze modern journalists. "That Lincoln stuff just amazed me," gushed *Newsweek*'s Jonathan Alter on *Rivera Live*. Alter wrote that Beatty's "harshest attacks . . . were actually quotes from a speech by Abraham Lincoln."

Actually, they weren't. Lincoln's official biographer once called the 40 quote "a bold, unblushing forgery." And in a piece for History News Service, an online site that often debunks faulty history, Lincoln scholar Matthew Pinsker said this particular fake Lincoln citation has been around since 1896. In his speech at the 1992 Republican National Convention, Ronald Reagan attributed phony conservative sentiments to Honest Abe, including, "You cannot help the weak by punishing the strong," and "You cannot help the poor by destroying the rich."

This example underscores a couple of important caveats about the 41 Web. First, bogus quotes were around a long time before the Internet. Moreover, the Net itself is often a useful tool for those trying to correct canards.

A postscript: Three years ago, while discussing with reporters the pit- 42 falls of the Internet, Hillary Rodham Clinton employed the line often attributed to Twain—and cited earlier in this piece—about a lie making its way halfway 'round the world before the truth could get its boots on. "Well, today," she added, "the lie can be twice around the world before the truth gets out of bed to find its boots." While fact-checking this article, I had reason to call Fred Shapiro at Yale. Perhaps because Mrs. Clinton never mentioned Twain—she attributed it to an "old saying"—my interest was piqued, and I asked Shapiro if he'd ever heard the aphorism. "I have just been intensively researching Twain quotes, and didn't come across this one," he replied. "I would assume that Twain did not say it."

Uh-oh. That sent me back into research mode. What I found is that the 43 "Twain" quote has been around. According to a 1996 article by James Bennet of the *New York Times*, Mrs. Clinton (and Al Gore as well) used the line, with attribution to Twain. Other politicians have credited it to Twain as well. Clintonite Paul Begala, writing last year in the *Orlando Sentinel*, used it, giving Twain full credit. So did Republican stalwart Haley Barbour in a *Roll Call* op-ed. In a 1999 column in the *Chattanooga Times*, a writer named L. M. Boyd gave credit for the quote to "the sage Israel Zangwill," adding that famed CBS newsman Edward R. Murrow used it all the time.

On the Internet, the responses were even more varied. Several Web 44 sites credited Twain while others attributed the quote to Will Rogers; Reagan-era interior secretary James Watt; Winston Churchill; another former British prime minister, James Callaghan; and, in one case, merely to "a French proverb."

Possibly all of these sources uttered it at one time or another. Callaghan 45 seems to have done so on November 1, 1976, in an address to the House of Commons. But he attributed the line to the man who is probably its rightful author: a Baptist preacher from England named Charles Haddon Spurgeon, a contemporary of Twain who, according to *Benham's Book of Quotations*, wrote this line: "A lie travels 'round the world, while Truth is putting on her boots."

Amen.

46

Thinking Critically about the Text

In paragraph 12, Cannon states, "One of the things that makes the Internet so appealing is that anyone can pull things off of it. The other side of the coin is that anyone can put anything on it." Do you agree? Why, or why not?

Questions on Subject

1. Cannon writes that one cause of journalists' errors is that they don't have much time to check their sources for accuracy. How do you respond?

2. What false understanding of the law in a cyberrumor led to a great deal of anxiety among African Americans?

3. What are the causes of errors in the information found on the Internet, according to Cannon?

4. If, as Cannon argues, the Web is a terrible source for accurate information, what can be done about the increasing numbers of people who have come to rely on it?

5. Have Cannon's ideas about the accuracy of information retrieved from the Web altered your own research methods? Why, or why not?

Questions on Strategy

1. What is Cannon arguing for in this essay? (Glossary: *Argument*) What is his thesis? (Glossary: *Thesis*)

2. What evidence does Cannon cite to support the fact that misinformation on the Internet can be downright dangerous? (Glossary: *Evidence*; *Illustration*)

3. How does Cannon use cause and effect analysis in his essay? Cite several examples.

4. Cannon begins with the story of Jeff Jacoby and the *Boston Globe*. Why is this a particularly good example for the beginning of his article? (Glossary: *Beginnings/Endings*)

5. Cannon ends with a postscript about the quotation falsely attributed to Mark Twain: "A lie can make it halfway 'round the world before the truth gets its boots on." Why is this an apt way of ending his essay? (Glossary: *Beginnings/ Endings*)

Questions on Diction and Vocabulary

1. How appropriate is "The Real Computer Virus" as a title? (Glossary: *Title*) Is the comparison of misinformation to a computer virus appropriate? (Glossary: *Analogy*) Why, or why not?

2. What is Cannon's tone in this essay? (Glossary: *Tone*) What evidence do you have for your assessment?

3. Cannon labels paragraphs 42–46 "A postscript." Why is that label appropriate?

Classroom Activity Using Cause and Effect Analysis

In preparation for writing a cause and effect analysis, list two effects on society and two effects on personal behavior for one of the following items: television talk shows, online shopping, all-sports channels, reality television programs, television advertising, fast food, or another item of your choosing. For example, a cell phone could be said to have the following effects:

Society
Fewer highway fatalities due to quicker response to accidents
Expansion of the economy

Personal Behavior
Higher personal phone bills
Risks to driving safety (where cell phone use is allowed)

Be prepared to discuss your answers with the class.

Writing Suggestions

1. "According to the Nielsen/NetRatings released on February 15, 168 million Americans logged on to the Web in the first month of the new millennium" (paragraph 25). Why does Cannon cite this figure? (Glossary: *Evidence*) What does he mean when he says, "These problems are only going to get worse unless Net users — and journalists — get a whole lot more careful" (25)? Write an essay in which you discuss possible effects of misinformation on an increasingly Web-savvy and Web-dependent public. How do incidents of incorrect reporting, such as those Cannon discusses, affect public trust of the media? What skills will people need to better judge what they read both online and off? What measures could be implemented to ensure that information is accurate and reliable? What would the other effects of such measures be?

2. Cannon discusses how the Internet, electronic databases, and e-mail can be used to spread *misinformation* and *disinformation*. What do these two terms mean? (Glossary: *Definition*) What examples does Cannon cite as evidence of each? (Glossary: *Evidence; Illustration*) Write an essay in which you explore the differences between misinformation and disinformation. (Glossary: *Comparison and Contrast*) In your opinion, which poses the greater threat? Why?

The Downside of Diversity

MICHAEL JONAS

Michael Jonas, who has been a journalist since the early 1980s, is executive editor of *CommonWealth* magazine, a quarterly focused on politics, ideas, and civic life in Massachusetts. Jonas was born in 1959 in Ann Arbor, Michigan, and received his B.A. in history from Hampshire College in 1981. Before joining the *CommonWealth* staff in 2001, Jonas was a contributing writer for the magazine. His cover story for *CommonWealth*'s Fall 1999 issue on youth antiviolence workers was selected for a PASS (Prevention for a Safer Society) Award from the National Council on Crime and Delinquency. His 2009 article on the centralization of power in the Massachusetts House of Representatives won an award for commentary and analysis from Capitolbeat, the national organization of state capitol reporters and editors.

In the following article, first published August 5, 2007, on Boston.com, the Web presence of the *Boston Globe*, Jonas reports on a Harvard political scientist who finds that diversity hurts civic life. "Be fearless in your willingness to probe difficult questions and write uncomfortable truths," comments Jonas. "Not only do I hope my article does this, but it is, in many ways, what Robert Putnam, the Harvard scholar whose study I write about, confronted himself in publishing research results that are at odds with what he would have hoped to find."

Preparing to Read

Do you think that people who live in ethnically diverse communities demonstrate stronger or weaker civic engagement and interconnectedness than people who live in homogeneous communities? What are your reasons for thinking as you do?

It has become increasingly popular to speak of racial and ethnic diversity as a civic strength. From multicultural festivals to pronouncements from political leaders, the message is the same: Our differences make us stronger.

But a massive new study, based on detailed interviews of nearly 30,000 people across America, has concluded just the opposite. Harvard political scientist Robert Putnam—famous for *Bowling Alone*, his 2000 book on declining civic engagement—has found that the greater the diversity in a community, the fewer people vote and the less they volunteer, the less they give to charity and work on community projects. In the most diverse communities, neighbors trust one another about half as much as they do in the most homogeneous settings. The study, the largest ever on civic engagement in America, found that virtually all measures of civic health are lower in more diverse settings.

"The extent of the effect is shocking," says Scott Page, a University of Michigan political scientist. 3

The study comes at a time when the future of the American melting pot is the focus of intense political debate, from immigration to race-based admissions to schools, and it poses challenges to advocates on all sides of the issues. The study is already being cited by some conservatives as proof of the harm large-scale immigration causes to the nation's social fabric. But with demographic trends already pushing the nation inexorably toward greater diversity, the real question may yet lie ahead: how to handle the unsettling social changes that Putnam's research predicts. 4

"We can't ignore the findings," says Ali Noorani, executive director of the Massachusetts Immigrant and Refugee Advocacy Coalition. "The big question we have to ask ourselves is, what do we do about it; what are the next steps?" 5

The study is part of a fascinating new portrait of diversity emerging from recent scholarship. Diversity, it shows, makes us uncomfortable—but discomfort, it turns out, isn't always a bad thing. Unease with differences helps explain why teams of engineers from different cultures may be ideally suited to solve a vexing problem. Culture clashes can produce a dynamic give-and-take, generating a solution that may have eluded a group of people with more similar backgrounds and approaches. At the same time, though, Putnam's work adds to a growing body of research indicating that more diverse populations seem to extend themselves less on behalf of collective needs and goals. 6

His findings on the downsides of diversity have also posed a challenge for Putnam, a liberal academic whose own values put him squarely in the prodiversity camp. Suddenly finding himself the bearer of bad news, Putnam has struggled with how to present his work. He gathered the initial raw data in 2000 and issued a press release the following year outlining the results. He then spent several years testing other possible explanations. 7

When he finally published a detailed scholarly analysis in June in the journal *Scandinavian Political Studies*, he faced criticism for straying from data into advocacy. His paper argues strongly that the negative effects of diversity can be remedied and says history suggests that ethnic diversity may eventually fade as a sharp line of social demarcation. 8

"Having aligned himself with the central planners intent on sustaining such social engineering, Putnam concludes the facts with a stern pep talk," wrote conservative commentator Ilana Mercer, in a recent *Orange Country Register* op-ed titled "Greater diversity equals more misery." 9

Putnam has long staked out ground as both a researcher and a civic player, someone willing to describe social problems and then have a hand in addressing them. He says social science should be "simultaneously rigorous and relevant," meeting high research standards while also "speaking to concerns of our fellow citizens." But on a topic as charged as ethnicity and race, Putnam worries that many people hear only what they want to. 10

"It would be unfortunate if a politically correct progressivism were to deny the reality of the challenge to social solidarity posed by diversity," he writes in the new report. "It would be equally unfortunate if an ahistorical and ethnocentric conservatism were to deny that addressing that challenge is both feasible and desirable." 11

Birds of different feathers may sometimes flock together, but they are also less likely to look out for one another.

Putnam is the nation's premier guru of civic engagement. After studying civic life in Italy in the 1970s and 1980s, Putnam turned his attention to the United States, publishing an influential journal article on civic engagement in 1995 that he expanded five years later into the best-selling *Bowling Alone*. The book sounded a national wake-up call on what Putnam called a sharp drop in civic connections among Americans. It won him audiences with presidents Bill Clinton and George W. Bush and made him one of the country's best-known social scientists. 12

Putnam claims the United States has experienced a pronounced decline in *social capital*, a term he helped popularize. Social capital refers to the social networks—whether friendships or religious congregations or neighborhood associations—that he says are key indicators of civic well-being. When social capital is high, says Putnam, communities are better places to live. Neighborhoods are safer; people are healthier; and more citizens vote. 13

The results of his new study come from a survey Putnam directed among residents in forty-one U.S. communities, including Boston. Residents were sorted into the four principal categories used by the U.S. Census: black, white, Hispanic, and Asian. They were asked how much they trusted their neighbors and those of each racial category and questioned about a long list of civic attitudes and practices, including their views on local government, their involvement in community projects, and their friendships. What emerged in more diverse communities was a bleak picture of civic desolation, affecting everything from political engagement to the state of social ties. 14

Putnam knew he had provocative findings on his hands. He worried about coming under some of the same liberal attacks that greeted Daniel 15

Patrick Moynihan's landmark 1965 report on the social costs associated with the breakdown of the black family. There is always the risk of being pilloried as the bearer of "an inconvenient truth," says Putnam.

After releasing the initial results in 2001, Putnam says he spent time 16 "kicking the tires really hard" to be sure the study had it right. Putnam realized, for instance, that more diverse communities tended to be larger, have greater income ranges, higher crime rates, and more mobility among their residents—all factors that could depress social capital independent of any impact ethnic diversity might have.

"People would say, 'I bet you forgot about X,'" Putnam says of the 17 string of suggestions from colleagues. "There were twenty or thirty Xs."

But even after statistically taking them all into account, the connection 18 remained strong: Higher diversity meant lower social capital. In his findings, Putnam writes that those in more diverse communities tend to "distrust their neighbors, regardless of the color of their skin, to withdraw even from close friends, to expect the worst from their community and its leaders, to volunteer less, give less to charity and work on community projects less often, to register to vote less, to agitate for social reform more but have less faith that they can actually make a difference, and to huddle unhappily in front of the television."

"People living in ethnically diverse settings appear to 'hunker 19 down'—that is, to pull in like a turtle," Putnam writes.

In documenting that hunkering down, Putnam challenged the two 20 dominant schools of thought on ethnic and racial diversity, the "contact" theory and the "conflict" theory. Under the contact theory, more time spent with those of other backgrounds leads to greater understanding and harmony between groups. Under the conflict theory, that proximity produces tension and discord.

Putnam's findings reject both theories. In more diverse communities, he 21 says, there were neither great bonds formed across group lines nor heightened ethnic tensions, but a general civic malaise. And in perhaps the most surprising result of all, levels of trust were not only lower between groups in more diverse settings, but even among members of the same group.

"Diversity, at least in the short run," he writes, "seems to bring out the 22 turtle in all of us."

The overall findings may be jarring during a time when it's become 23 commonplace to sing the praises of diverse communities, but researchers in the field say they shouldn't be.

"It's an important addition to a growing body of evidence on the chal- 24 lenges created by diversity," says Harvard economist Edward Glaeser.

In a recent study, Glaeser and colleague Alberto Alesina demonstrated 25 that roughly half the difference in social welfare spending between the

United States and Europe—Europe spends far more—can be attributed to the greater ethnic diversity of the U.S. population. Glaeser says lower national social welfare spending in the United States is a "macro" version of the decreased civic engagement Putnam found in more diverse communities within the country.

Economists Matthew Kahn of UCLA and Dora Costa of MIT reviewed fifteen recent studies in a 2003 paper, all of which linked diversity with lower levels of social capital. Greater ethnic diversity was linked, for example, to lower school funding, census response rates, and trust in others. Kahn and Costa's own research documented higher desertion rates in the Civil War among Union Army soldiers serving in companies whose soldiers varied more by age, occupation, and birthplace. 26

Birds of different feathers may sometimes flock together, but they are also less likely to look out for one another. "Everyone is a little self-conscious that this is not politically correct stuff," says Kahn. 27

So how to explain New York, London, Rio de Janeiro, Los Angeles— the great melting-pot cities that drive the world's creative and financial economies? 28

The image of civic lassitude dragging down more diverse communities is at odds with the vigor often associated with urban centers, where ethnic diversity is greatest. It turns out there is a flip side to the discomfort diversity can cause. If ethnic diversity, at least in the short run, is a liability for social connectedness, a parallel line of emerging research suggests it can be a big asset when it comes to driving productivity and innovation. In high-skill workplace settings, says Scott Page, the University of Michigan political scientist, the different ways of thinking among people from different cultures can be a boon. 29

"Because they see the world and think about the world differently than you, that's challenging," says Page, author of *The Difference: How the Power of Diversity Creates Better Groups, Firms, Schools, and Societies.* "But by hanging out with people different than you, you're likely to get more insights. Diverse teams tend to be more productive." 30

In other words, those in more diverse communities may do more bowling alone, but the creative tensions unleashed by those differences in the workplace may vault those same places to the cutting edge of the economy and of creative culture. 31

Page calls it the "diversity paradox." He thinks the contrasting positive and negative effects of diversity can coexist in communities, but "there's got to be a limit." If civic engagement falls off too far, he says, it's easy to imagine the positive effects of diversity beginning to wane as well. "That's what's unsettling about his findings," Page says of Putnam's new work. 32

Meanwhile, by drawing a portrait of civic engagement in which more   33
homogeneous communities seem much healthier, some of Putnam's worst
fears about how his results could be used have been realized. A stream of
conservative commentary has begun—from places like the Manhattan
Institute and the *American Conservative*—highlighting the harm the study
suggests will come from large-scale immigration. But Putnam says he's also
received hundreds of complimentary e-mails laced with bigoted language.
"It certainly is not pleasant when David Duke's Web site hails me as the
guy who found out racism is good," he says.

In the final quarter of his paper, Putnam puts the diversity challenge   34
in a broader context by describing how social identity can change over
time. Experience shows that social divisions can eventually give way to
"more encompassing identities" that create a "new, more capacious sense
of 'we,'" he writes.

Growing up in the 1950s in a small midwestern town, Putnam knew   35
the religion of virtually every member of his high school graduating class
because, he says, such information was crucial to the question of "who was
a possible mate or date." The importance of marrying within one's faith, he
says, has largely faded since then, at least among many mainline Protestants,
Catholics, and Jews.

While acknowledging that racial and ethnic divisions may prove more   36
stubborn, Putnam argues that such examples bode well for the long-term
prospects for social capital in a multiethnic America.

In his paper, Putnam cites the work done by Page and others, and uses   37
it to help frame his conclusion that increasing diversity in America is not
only inevitable, but ultimately valuable and enriching. As for smoothing
over the divisions that hinder civic engagement, Putnam argues that
Americans can help that process along through targeted efforts. He suggests expanding support for English-language instruction and investing in
community centers and other places that allow for "meaningful interaction
across ethnic lines."

Some critics have found his prescriptions underwhelming. And in   38
offering ideas for mitigating his findings, Putnam has drawn scorn for stepping out of the role of dispassionate researcher. "You're just supposed to
tell your peers what you found," says John Leo, senior fellow at the
Manhattan Institute, a conservative think tank. "I don't expect academics
to fret about these matters."

But fretting about the state of American civic health is exactly what   39
Putnam has spent more than a decade doing. While continuing to research
questions involving social capital, he has directed the Saguaro Seminar, a project he started at Harvard's Kennedy School of Government that promotes
efforts throughout the country to increase civic connections in communities.

"Social scientists are both scientists and citizens," says Alan Wolfe, 40
director of the Boisi Center for Religion and American Public Life at
Boston College, who sees nothing wrong in Putnam's efforts to affect some
of the phenomena he studies.

Wolfe says what is unusual is that Putnam has published findings as a 41
social scientist that are not the ones he would have wished for as a civic
leader. There are plenty of social scientists, says Wolfe, who never produce
research results at odds with their own worldview.

"The problem too often," says Wolfe, "is people are never uncomfort- 42
able about their findings."

Thinking Critically about the Text

If ethnic diversity seems to be a liability, at least in the short term, why does Putnam think it's "ultimately valuable and enriching" (paragraph 37)?

Questions on Subject

1. What are the effects of greater social diversity that Putnam's research reveals?
   What's being lost and gained? How serious are the losses, as Putnam sees
   them?

2. Putnam coined the term *social capital*. What does he mean by the term?
   (Glossary: *Definition*)

3. Why did Putnam worry about the effects that his research might have on his
   fellow social scientists and on the public at large?

4. What evidence related to the world's most vibrant cities seems to contradict
   the findings in Putnam's study? (Glossary: *Evidence*)

5. What are Putnam's suggestions for increasing social capital within diverse ethnic communities? Do you think those efforts are worthwhile? Why, or why not?

Questions on Strategy

1. How does cause and effect work in Jonas's essay? Does it work only on the
   level of diversity and its effects?

2. In paragraph 38, conservative think-tank fellow John Leo is scornful of
   Putnam's role as an advocate for diversity. Do you agree with Leo's criticism
   of Putnam? Why, or why not?

3. Jonas uses a number of very short, one- or two-sentence paragraphs. Examine several of them and explain why you think he uses them. Could Jonas
   have combined these short paragraphs with other paragraphs? Explain.

4. Examine Jonas's essay for examples of his use of outside authorities and
   evidence. How have these outside sources helped him to provide perspective
   on the issues he discusses? (Glossary: *Evidence*)

5. Is Jonas objective about the results and implications of Putnam's research, or does he reveal his own attitude about them? (Glossary: *Attitude*) Explain.

Questions on Diction and Vocabulary

1. One of Putnam's earlier works was *Bowling Alone*, a book that studied the gradual change from earlier decades in American culture, in which bowling was a very social activity, to more recent times, in which bowling has become one primarily engaged in by solitary individuals. Why was that metaphor a good one for the loss of social capital he wrote about? (Glossary: *Figures of Speech*)

2. Putnam says in paragraph 19 that "people living in ethnically diverse settings appear to 'hunker down' — that is, to pull in like a turtle." What figure of speech does his statement contain and what does it mean? (Glossary: *Figures of Speech*)

Classroom Activity Using Cause and Effect Analysis

Determining causes and effects requires careful thought. Establishing a causal chain of events is no less demanding, but it can also bring clarity and understanding to many complex issues. Consider the following example involving the H1N1 virus, or swine flu:

> **ultimate cause** According to the Centers for Disease Control (CDC), this virus was originally referred to as "swine flu" because laboratory testing showed that many of the genes in this new virus were very similar to influenza viruses that normally occur in pigs (swine) in North America. But further study has shown that this new virus is very different from what normally circulates in North American pigs. It has two genes from flu viruses that normally circulate in pigs in Europe and Asia and bird (avian) genes and human genes. Scientists call this a "quadruple reassortant" virus.

> **immediate cause** Contact with surfaces that have the flu virus on them and then touching the mouth or nose or eyes

> **effect** Influenza (fever, cough, sore throat, runny or stuffy nose, body aches, headache, chills and fatigue, possible vomiting and diarrhea)

> **effect** Possible death; possible pandemic

Develop a causal chain for each of the cause and effect pairs listed below. Then mix two of the pairs (for example, develop a causal chain for vacation/anxiety). Be prepared to discuss your answers with the class.

terror/alert	making a speech/anxiety
vacation/relaxation	climate change/technological innovation

Writing Suggestions

1. In the note that precedes this selection, Jonas suggests that you "be fearless in your willingness to probe difficult questions and write uncomfortable truths." Write an essay in which you examine more deeply the implications of Jonas's advice. Why does he consider it good and necessary advice to follow? What might be the difficult-to-deal-with effects of following that advice? Before writing, you may wish to read Steven Pinker's "In Defense of Dangerous Ideas" (page 529) for examples of what Jonas means and for a source of probing ideas about this topic.

2. Write an essay in which you examine your own ideas about diversity at all levels. What do you think its benefits and its negative aspects are? How might we as Americans work to achieve more social integration and understanding? In thinking about your topic you might want to consider the lessons that American history has taught us about how waves of immigrants gradually learned to live in mutually beneficial settings. Consider as well the measures that have been taken legally, socially, economically, and in other ways to maintain respect for diversity as well as social cohesion.

WRITING SUGGESTIONS FOR CAUSE AND EFFECT ANALYSIS

1. Write an essay in which you analyze the most significant reasons for your decision to attend college. You may wish to discuss your family background, your high school experience, people and events that influenced your decision, and your goals in college as well as in later life.

2. It is interesting to think of ourselves in terms of the influences that have caused us to be who we are. Write an essay in which you discuss two or three of what you consider the most important influences on your life. Following are some areas you may wish to consider in planning and writing your paper.

   a. a parent
   b. a book or movie
   c. a member of the clergy
   d. a teacher
   e. a friend
   f. a hero
   g. a youth organization
   h. a coach
   i. your neighborhood
   j. your ethnic background

3. Write an essay about a recent achievement of yours or about an important achievement in your community. Explain the causes of this success. Look at all of the underlying elements involved in the accomplishment, and explain how you selected the one main cause or the causal chain that led to the achievement. To do this, you will probably want to use the rhetorical strategy of comparison and contrast. You might also use exemplification and process analysis to explain the connection between your cause and its effect.

4. **Writing with Sources.** Decisions often involve cause and effect relationships; that is, a person usually weighs the possible results of an action before deciding to act. Write an essay in which you consider the possible effects that would result from one decision or another in one of the following controversies. You will need to do some research in the library or online in order to support your conclusions.

   a. taxing cars on the basis of fuel consumption
   b. reinstituting the military draft
   c. legalizing marijuana
   d. mandatory licensing of handguns

e. raising the mandatory fuel efficiency rating of cars

f. cloning humans

g. abolishing grades for college courses

h. raising the minimum wage

i. mandatory community service (one year) for all eighteen-year-olds

j. banning the use of pesticides on produce

k. requiring an ethics course in college

For models of and advice on integrating sources in your essay, see Chapters 14 and 15.

5. **Writing with Sources.** Review the graphic that opens this chapter (page 436). Take any one of the topics in the causal chain put forth in the graphic — for example, the housing boom, mortgage securitization, subprime crisis, or global economic downturn — and write an essay in which you dig deeper into the topic, exploring further causes and effects. For example, what caused "easy credit" to become available? How did foreign investors infuse our financial institutions with money? In examining mortgage securitization further, what did banks do that destabilized the mortgage system as we know it? What checks and balances or regulations did the government provide in this area of banking? Why did they fail? What causes (immediate and ultimate), effects, and causal chains do you see in the events?

For any of these topics you will need to do further research in print and online sources to understand and report on your findings. For models of and advice on integrating sources in your essay, see Chapters 14 and 15.

6. **Writing in the Workplace.** A position paper gives advice on an issue and may incorporate any combination of the different development methods you're studying in this book. Most likely, however, it will place the greatest emphasis on cause and effect analysis and argumentation. The purpose of a position paper is to make a case for a way of regarding a topic and for taking action on it. Rather than a review of research that explores all that's been said about a topic or issue, or an essay that allows you to show your own thinking about it, the position paper presents a question, considers the pros and cons of various courses of action, and makes a recommendation that the author thinks is best.

You are an executive at the Javro Coffee Roasters Company and the Board of Directors is interested in moving toward a fair-trade business model. Fair trade means selling coffee from beans that are raised on environmentally sustainable plantations, where workers are paid according to a fair and equitable wage scale, and where all business transactions are transparent and ethical. At the board's request, write a position paper on the feasibility of pursuing the fair-trade model, the pros and cons of the approach, and your recommendation about whether Javro should adopt it.

e-Pages

Texting While Walking

CASEY NEISTAT

See how cause and effect works on the Web. Go to bedfordstmartins.com/subjectandstrategy for a tongue-in-cheek video and study questions about the hazards of texting while walking.

I AM NOT A SOUVENIR

Thousands of marine turtles are slaughtered every year for their shells and skins, which are made into jewelry, leather goods and souvenirs for tourists.

Find out what you can do to stop wildlife crime.

STOP WILDLIFE CRIME
IT'S DEAD SERIOUS

worldwildlife.org/wildlifecrime

CHAPTER 12

Argumentation

WHAT IS ARGUMENTATION?

THE WORD *ARGUMENT* PROBABLY FIRST BRINGS TO MIND DISAGREE-
ments and disputes. Occasionally, such disputes are constructive. More
often, though, disputes like these are inconclusive and result only in anger
over your opponent's stubbornness or in the frustration of realizing that you
have failed to make your position understood.

Reasoned argument is something else again entirely. In reasoned argument, we attempt to convince listeners or readers to agree with a particular
point of view, to make a particular decision, or to pursue a particular course
of action. Such arguments involve the presentation of well-chosen evidence
and the artful control of language or other persuasive tools. Arguments need
not be written to be effective, however; oral argument, if well planned and
well delivered, can be equally effective, as can primarily visual arguments.

For an example of argument that combines text and visuals, consider
the antipoaching public service advertisement on the opposite page. This
ad, created by the World Wildlife Fund, uses a photograph and an emphatic
text headline to make its argument: The lives of turtles matter, and it's not
right to hunt and kill them in order to turn their bodies into sellable trinkets
and commodities. The declarative headline ("I Am . . .") personifies the turtle, reminding viewers that each animal has a unique personality. Ultimately,
the ad encourages viewers to be responsible, thoughtful, and respectful consumers that refuse to perpetuate the cycle of wildlife crime.

ARGUMENT IN WRITTEN TEXTS

Written arguments must be carefully planned. The writer must settle in advance on a specific thesis or proposition rather than grope toward one, as in
a dispute. There is a greater need for organization, for choosing the most
effective types of evidence from all that is available, for determining the
strategies of rhetoric, language, and style that will best suit the argument's
subject, purpose, thesis, and effect on the intended audience.

Most strong arguments are constructed around an effective thesis statement. Take, for example, the following opening to the essay "The Case for Short Words" by Richard Lederer (page 516).

> **Thesis statement**
>
> When you speak and write, there is no law that says you have to use big words. Short words are as good as long ones, and short, old words—like *sun* and *grass* and *home*—are best of all. A lot of small words, more than you might think, can meet your needs with a strength, grace, and charm that large words do not have.
>
> **Several examples support the thesis**
>
> Big words can make the way dark for those who read what you write and hear what you say. Small words cast their clear light on big things—night and day, love and hate, war and peace, and life and death. Big words at times seem strange to the eye and the ear and the mind and the heart. Small words are the ones we seem to have known from the time we were born, like the hearth fire that warms the home.

Note how Lederer uses examples to support his thesis statement. When you read the whole essay, you will want to check whether Lederer's argument is well reasoned and carefully organized. You will also want to check that his argument is logical and persuasive. A strong argument will have all of these qualities.

▶ Persuasive and Logical Argument

Most people who specialize in the study of argument identify two essential categories: persuasion and logic.

Persuasive argument relies primarily on appeals to emotion, to the subconscious, even to bias and prejudice. These appeals involve diction, slanting, figurative language, analogy, rhythmic patterns of speech, and a tone that encourages a positive, active response. Examples of persuasive argument are found in the claims of advertisers and in the speech making of politicians and social activists.

Logical argument, on the other hand, appeals primarily to the mind—to the audience's intellectual faculties, understanding, and knowledge. Such appeals depend on the reasoned movement from assertion to evidence to conclusion and on an almost mathematical system of proof and counterproof. Logical argument, unlike persuasion, does not normally impel its audience to action. Logical argument is commonly found in scientific or philosophical articles, in legal decisions, and in technical proposals.

Most arguments, however, are neither purely persuasive nor purely logical in nature. A well-written newspaper editorial that supports a controversial piece of legislation or that proposes a solution to a local problem, for example, will rest on a logical arrangement of assertions and evidence but will employ striking diction and other persuasive patterns of language to make it more effective. Thus the kinds of appeals a writer emphasizes depend on the nature of the topic, the thesis or proposition of the argument, the various kinds of support (e.g., evidence, opinions, examples, facts, statistics) offered, and a thoughtful consideration of the audience. Knowing the differences between persuasive and logical arguments is, then, essential in learning both to read and to write arguments.

Some additional types of arguments that are helpful in expanding your understanding of this strategy are described below.

▶ Informational, or Exploratory, Argument

It is often useful to provide a comprehensive review of the various facets of an issue. This is done to inform an audience, especially one that may not understand why the issue is controversial in the first place, and to help that audience take a position. An example of this kind of argument is Steven Pinker's "In Defense of Dangerous Ideas" (page 529). The writer of this type of argument does not take a position but aims, instead, to render the positions taken by the various sides in accurate and clear language. Your instructors may occasionally call for this kind of argumentative writing as a way of teaching you to explore the complexity of a particular issue.

▶ Focused Argument

This kind of argument has only one objective: to change the audience's mind about a controversial issue. Nicholas D. Kristof and Sheryl WuDunn, in "Two Cheers for Sweatshops" (page 539), focus on the idea that sweatshops, rather than being absolutely inhuman and intolerable for workers as has been argued so effectively by their critics, may actually be a positive force in helping millions of poor workers, especially in Southeast Asia, climb up from their desperate economic circumstances. Being comprehensive or taking the broad view is not the objective here. If opposing viewpoints are considered, it is usually to show their inadequacies and thereby to strengthen the writer's own position. This kind of argument is what we usually think of when we think of traditional argument.

▶ Action-Oriented Argument

This type of argument is highly persuasive and attempts to accomplish a specific task. This is the loud car salesperson on your television, the over-the-top subscription solicitation in your mail, the vote-for-me-because-I-am-the-only-candidate-who-can-lower-your-taxes type of argument. The language is emotionally charged, and buzzwords designed to arouse the emotions of the audience may even be used, along with such propaganda devices as glittering generalities (broad, sweeping statements) and bandwagonism ("Everyone else is voting for me—don't be left out").

▶ Quiet, or Subtle, Argument

Some arguments do not immediately appear to the audience to be arguments at all. They set out to be informative and objective, but when closely examined, they reveal that the author has consciously, or perhaps subconsciously, shaped and slanted the evidence in such a manner as to favor a particular position. Such shaping may be the result of choices in diction that bend the audience to the writer's perspective, or they may be the result of decisions not to include certain types of evidence while admitting others. Such arguments can, of course, be quite convincing, as there are always those who distrust obvious efforts to convince them, preferring to make their own decisions on the issues. This kind of argument is perhaps best demonstrated by Kate Suarez in her essay "Celebrity Obsession: Is It Healthy Behavior?" (page 499). She argues for a saner approach to celebrity worship in general, but we may also infer that she has an especially meaningful message for those of us caught up in such a world.

▶ Reconciliation Argument

Increasingly popular today is a form of argument in which the writer attempts to explore all facets of an issue to find common ground or areas of agreement. Of course, one way of viewing that common ground is to see it as a new argumentative thrust, a new assertion, about which there may yet be more debate. The object, nevertheless, is to lessen stridency and the hardening of positions and to mediate opposing views into a rational and, where appropriate, even practical outcome. Martin Luther King Jr.'s speech "I Have a Dream" (page 522) is perhaps the greatest example of a reconciliation argument of the past century.

USING ARGUMENTATION AS A WRITING STRATEGY

Reasoned arguments are limited to assertions about which there is a legitimate and recognized difference of opinion. It is unlikely that anyone will ever need to convince a reader that falling in love is a rare and intense experience, that crime rates should be reduced, or that computers are changing the world. Not everyone would agree, however, that women experience love more intensely than men do, that the death penalty reduces the incidence of crime, or that computers are changing the world for the worse; these assertions are arguable and admit differing perspectives. Similarly, a leading heart specialist might argue in a popular magazine that too many doctors are advising patients to have pacemakers implanted when they are not necessary; the editorial writer for a small-town newspaper could urge that a local agency supplying food to poor families be given a larger percentage of the town's budget; and in a lengthy and complex book, a foreign-policy specialist might attempt to prove that the current administration exhibits no consistent policy in its relationship with other countries and that the State Department is in need of overhauling.

No matter what forum it uses and no matter what its structure, an argument has as its chief purpose the detailed setting forth of a particular point of view and the rebuttal of any opposing views.

▶ The Classical Appeals

Classical thinkers believed that there are three key components in all rhetorical situations or attempts to communicate: the *speaker* (and for us the *writer*) who comments about a *subject* to an *audience*. For purposes of discussion we can isolate each of these three entities, but in actual rhetorical situations they are inseparable, each inextricably tied to and influencing the other two. The ancients also recognized the importance of qualities attached to each of these components that are especially significant in the case of argumentation: *ethos*, which is related to the speaker; *logos*, which is related to the subject; and *pathos*, which is related to the audience. Let's look a little closer at each of these.

Ethos (Greek for "character") has to do with the authority, the credibility, and, to a certain extent, the morals of the speaker or writer. In other words, *ethos* is the speaker's character as perceived by the audience, often based on shared values. Aristotle and Cicero, classical rhetoricians, believed that it was important for the speaker to be credible and to argue for a worthwhile cause. Putting one's argumentative skills in the service of a questionable cause was simply not acceptable. But how did one establish credibility? Sometimes it was gained through achievements outside the rhetorical arena. That is, the speaker had experience with an issue, had argued the subject before, and had been judged to be sincere and honest.

In the case of your own writing, establishing such credentials is not always possible, so you will need to be more concerned than usual with presenting your argument reasonably, sincerely, and in language untainted by excessive emotionalism. Finally, it is well worth remembering that you should always show respect for your audience in your writing.

Logos (Greek for "word"), related as it is to the subject, is the effective presentation of the argument itself. It refers to the speaker's grasp of the subject—his or her knowledge. Is the thesis or claim a worthwhile one? Is it logical, consistent, and well-buttressed by supporting evidence? Is the evidence itself factual, reliable, and convincing? Finally, is the argument so thoughtfully organized and so clearly presented that it has an impact on the audience and could change opinions? Indeed, this aspect of argumentation is the most difficult to accomplish but is, at the same time, the most rewarding.

Pathos (Greek for "emotion") has the most to do with the audience. The essential question is, How does the speaker or writer present an argument or a persuasive essay to maximize its appeal for a given audience? One way, of course, is to appeal to the audience's emotions through the artful and strategic use of well-crafted language. Certain buzzwords, slanted diction, or emotionally loaded language may become either rallying cries or causes of resentment in an argument.

▶ Considering Audience

It is worth remembering at this point that you can never be certain who your audience is; readers range along a spectrum from extremely friendly and sympathetic to extremely hostile and resistant, with a myriad of possibilities in between. The friendly audience will welcome new information and support the writer's position; the hostile audience will look for just the opposite: flaws in logic and examples of dishonest manipulation. With many arguments, there is the potential for a considerable audience of interested parties who are uncommitted. If the targeted audience is judged to be friendly, then the writer needs to be logical, but should feel free to use emotional appeals. If the audience is thought to be hostile, the *logos* must be the writer's immediate concern, and the language should be straightforward and objective. The greatest caution, subtlety, and critical thinking must be applied to the attempt to win over an uncommitted audience.

▶ Argumentation and Other Rhetorical Strategies

In general, writers of argument are interested in explaining aspects of a subject as well as in advocating a particular view. Consequently, they frequently use the other rhetorical strategies in a supportive role. In your efforts to argue convincingly, you may find it necessary to define, to compare and contrast, to analyze causes and effects, to classify, to describe, and to narrate. (For more information on the use of other strategies in argumentation, see Use Other Rhetorical Strategies, page 506.) Nevertheless, it is the writer's attempt to convince, not explain, that is of primary importance in an argumentative essay. In this respect, it is helpful to know that there are two basic patterns of thinking and of presenting our thoughts that are followed in argumentation: *induction* and *deduction*.

▶ Inductive and Deductive Reasoning

Inductive reasoning moves from a set of specific examples to a general statement or principle. As long as the evidence is accurate, pertinent, complete, and sufficient to represent the assertion, the conclusion of an inductive argument can be regarded as valid; if, however, you can spot inaccuracies in the evidence or can point to contrary evidence, you have good reason to doubt the assertion as it stands. Inductive reasoning is the most common of argumentative structures.

Deductive reasoning, more formal and complex than inductive reasoning, moves from an overall premise, rule, or generalization to a more specific conclusion. Deductive logic follows the pattern of the *syllogism*, a simple three-part argument consisting of a major premise, a minor premise, and a conclusion. For example, notice how the following syllogism works.

a. All humans are mortal. (*Major premise*)
b. Catalina is a human. (*Minor premise*)
c. Catalina is mortal. (*Conclusion*)

The conclusion here is true because both premises are true and the logic of the syllogism is valid.

Obviously, a syllogism will fail to work if either of the premises is untrue.

a. All living creatures are mammals. (*Major premise*)
b. A lobster is a living creature. (*Minor premise*)
c. A lobster is a mammal. (*Conclusion*)

The problem is immediately apparent. The major premise is obviously false: There are many living creatures that are not mammals, and a lobster happens to be one of them. Consequently, the conclusion is invalid.

Syllogisms, however, can fail in other ways, even if both premises are objectively true. Such failures occur most often when the arguer jumps to a conclusion without taking obvious exceptions into account.

a. All college students read books. (*Major premise*)
b. Larry reads books. (*Minor premise*)
c. Larry is a college student. (*Conclusion*)

Both the premises in this syllogism are true, but the syllogism is still invalid because it does not take into account that other people besides college students read books. The problem is in the way the major premise has been interpreted: If the minor premise were instead "Larry is a college student," then the valid conclusion "Larry reads books" would logically follow.

It is fairly easy to see the problems in a deductive argument when its premises and conclusion are rendered in the form of a syllogism. It is often more difficult to see errors in logic when the argument is presented discursively, or within the context of a long essay. If you can reduce the argument to its syllogistic form, however, you will have much less difficulty testing its validity. Similarly, if you can isolate and examine out of context the evidence provided to support an inductive assertion, you can more readily evaluate the written inductive argument.

Consider this excerpt from "The Draft: Why the Country Needs It," an article by James Fallows that first appeared in the *Atlantic* in 1980:

> The Vietnam draft was unfair racially, economically, educationally. By every one of those measures, the volunteer Army is less representative still. Libertarians argue that military service should be a matter of choice, but the plain fact is that service in the volunteer force is too frequently dictated by economics. Army enlisted ranks E1 through E4, the privates and corporals, the cannon fodder, the ones who will fight and die, are 36 percent black now. By the Army's own projections, they will be 42 percent black in three years. When other "minorities" are taken into account, we will have, for the first time, an army whose fighting members are mainly "non-majority," or more bluntly, a black and brown army defending a mainly white nation. The military has been an avenue of opportunity of many young blacks. They may well be first-class fighting men. They do not represent the nation.
>
> Such a selective sharing of the burden has destructive spiritual effects in a nation based on the democratic creed. But its practical implications can be quite as grave. The effect of a fair, representative draft is to hold the public hostage to the consequences of its decisions, much as the children's presence in the public schools focuses parents' attention on the quality of the schools. If the citizens are willing to countenance a decision that means that someone's child may die, they may contemplate more deeply if there is the possibility that the child will be theirs. Indeed, I would like to extend this principle even further. Young men of nineteen are rightly suspicious of the congressmen and columnists who urge them to the fore. I wish there were a practical way to resurrect provisions of the amended Selective Service Act of 1940, which raised the draft age to forty-four. Such a gesture might symbolize the desire to offset the historic injustice of the Vietnam draft, as well as suggest the possibility that, when a bellicose columnist recommends dispatching the American forces to Pakistan, he might also realize that he could end up as a gunner in a tank.

Here Fallows presents an inductive argument against the volunteer army and in favor of reinstating a draft. His argument can be summarized as follows:

Assertion: The volunteer army is racially and economically unfair.

Evidence: He points to the disproportionate percentage of blacks in the army, as well as to projections indicating that, within three years of the article's publication, more than half of the army's fighting members will be nonwhite.

Conclusion: "Such a selective sharing of the burden has destructive spiritual effects in a nation based on the democratic creed." Not until there is a fair, representative draft will the powerful majority be held accountable for any decision to go to war.

Fallows's inductive scheme here is, in fact, very effective. The evidence is convincing, and the conclusion is strong. But his argument also depends on a more complicated deductive syllogism.

a. The democratic ideal requires equal representation in the responsibilities of citizenship. (*Major premise*)

b. Military service is a responsibility of citizenship. (*Minor premise*)

c. The democratic ideal requires equal representation in military service. (*Conclusion*)

To attack Fallows's argument, it would be necessary to deny one of his premises.

Fallows also employs a number of other persuasive techniques, including an analogy: "The effect of a fair, representative draft is to hold the public hostage to the consequences of its decisions, much as the children's presence in the public schools focuses parents' attention on the quality of the schools." The use of such an analogy proves nothing, but it can force readers to reconsider their viewpoint and can make them more open-minded. The same is true of Fallows's almost entirely unserious suggestion about raising the draft age to forty-four. Like most writers, Fallows uses persuasive arguments to complement his more important logical ones.

USING ARGUMENTATION ACROSS THE DISCIPLINES

When writing essays in the academic disciplines, you will have many opportunities to use the strategy of argumentation to both organize and strengthen the presentation of your ideas. To determine whether or not argumentation is the right strategy for you in a particular paper, use the guidelines described in Chapter 2 (Determining a Strategy for Developing Your Essay, pages 32–33). Consider the following examples, which illustrate how this four-step method works for typical college papers:

Ethics

1. **MAIN IDEA:** Suicide is an end-of-life option.

2. **QUESTION:** Should a person be allowed to end his or her life when no longer able to maintain an acceptable quality of life?

3. **STRATEGY:** Argumentation. The question "Should a person be allowed" triggers a pro/con argument. The writer argues for or against laws that allow physician-assisted suicide, for example.

4. **SUPPORTING STRATEGY:** Definition should be used to clarify what is meant by the expression "quality of life." Cause and effect analysis should be used to determine, for example, at what point a person has lost a desirable "quality of life."

Environmental Studies

1. **MAIN IDEA:** The burning of fossil fuels is creating greenhouse gas emissions that are, in turn, causing global warming.

2. **QUESTION:** What can we do to reduce emissions from the burning of fossil fuels?

3. **STRATEGY:** Argumentation. The question "What can we do?" suggests an answer in the form of an argument. The writer might want to argue for higher taxes on fossil fuels, or for the installation of smokestack scrubbers.

4. **SUPPORTING STRATEGY:** Cause and effect analysis will be necessary to show how burning fossil fuels increases greenhouse emissions and how higher taxes and smokestack scrubbers will work to reduce harmful gases.

Biology

1. **MAIN IDEA:** The use of animals in biomedical research is crucial.

2. **QUESTION:** Should there be a ban on the use of animals in biomedical research?

3. **STRATEGY:** Argumentation. The word *should* signals a pro/con debate: Animals should/should not be used in biomedical research.

4. **SUPPORTING STRATEGY:** Comparison and contrast might be used to help make the case that alternatives to the use of animals are better/ worse than using animals.

SAMPLE STUDENT ESSAY USING ARGUMENTATION AS A WRITING STRATEGY

Student Kate Suarez begins her argumentation essay by questioning what she refers to as her "newest obsession," celebrity comings and goings. She was worried about how her fascination with celebrities might be affecting her character. Might it be "unhealthy?" she asks. In attempting to answer her question, she considers arguments both pro and con, supported by evidence from outside experts, before stating her own thesis at the conclusion of her essay: "we can use celebrities to see both ourselves and our communities just a bit clearer."

Title hints at writer's position	Celebrity Obsession: Is It Healthy Behavior? Kate Suarez
Writer explains personal experience	Celebrities are my newest obsession. I've always perused photos of young Hollywood stars, but lately I check tabloid blogs three times a day. I forward photos of young actresses in studded heels to friends, asking, *Can I pull this off?* Each "Get It for Less" guide is my ticket to instant celebrity style. To say that my time would be better spent studying the *New York Times* and catching up on current events misses the point that celebrity culture is its own full world of events. Still, with it taking over so much of my day, I find myself wondering whether an obsession with celebrity—or even a passing interest—might be unhealthy.
Writer identifies central question: Is celebrity obsession harmful or healthy?	
First argument: celebrity worship is practiced at expense of real-life experiences	It's easy to let sensationalized celebrity stories dominate our everyday conversations. In a recent blog post in the *Huffington Post, Celebrity, Inc.* author Jo Piazza blamed our constant stream of celebrity news for our false sense of closeness to celebrities. Even though they're technically strangers to us, we're incredibly comfortable chatting about and sharing their tweets, Facebook posts, and *TMZ* controversies. However, those chats can come at the expense of real interpersonal connections with those around us. Rather than sharing our own thoughts or feelings, we talk about our favorite celebrities as though they are close acquaintances or friends, which distracts us from our own experiences and gets in the way of knowing the people in our lives.
Counter-argument: the unifying force of celebrity worship can be beneficial	Yet defenders of celebrity culture maintain that this casual conversation fosters a feeling of national closeness. They suggest that it doesn't matter what we're talking about, just that we're talking about the same thing. Older, traditional forms of entertainment like movies, books, plays, and television shows have become so numerous that we're all watching and reading different things. In contrast, the narrow focus of celebrity news means that we all share the same knowledge. Neal Gabler, author of *Life: The Movie: How Entertainment Conquered Reality,* calls celebrities "America's modern denominators," explaining,
Writer cites source to support idea that celebrity worship is a unifying force	

1

2

3

as disparate and stratified as Americans are, practically all of them seem to share an intense engagement, or at the very least an acquaintance, with the sagas of Jon and Kate or Brad and Angelina or Jennifer and whomever, which is oddly comforting. (2)

Whether the story is love lost or found, the breakdown of a career, or even a death, sharing the same emotions unifies us. When a pop icon like Michael Jackson dies, everyone has something to say, and we listen to each other. It's real dialogue, and it's an exercise in communication that helps us tackle more serious social or political issues. We're reminded that we're all in this together.

Critics of celebrity don't deny this aspect of community building, but they do wonder how much sincerity is behind it. The average consumer might downplay the influence of celebrities on her life, but Piazza counters that our consumption of celebrity news has exceeded a healthy level. Consuming so much celebrity news tricks us into false belief and emulation, both psychologically and economically:

> Our obsession has gone beyond mere escapism. The noise that celebrities create in our brains is helping to turn us into zombies who look to celebrities as role models and often blindly follow their advice. (1)

We are seduced by the glitz and glamour of each celebrity narrative, often failing to understand that beyond the headlines and online ads, much of what we view as celebrity "real life" is constructed and fake. In fact, celebrities' very public status guarantees that everything they eat, drink, wear, and drive is on display, making them desirable company spokespeople. Companies are willing to pay for that kind of automatic attention and audience, and celebrities are happy for the increased exposure and additional cash. This makes the promoted product irrelevant, except to the consumer audience that is all too ready to imitate a celebrity's buying habits. Thus, when we make decisions motivated by celebrity endorsements, we might literally be buying into a personal choice fantasy—no one is getting something they really want, but everyone is getting something for it. In the case of celebrities, it's money. In the case of companies, it's exposure. In the case of us, it's the illusion that we're just like our favorite stars.

Rejection of counterargument: writer cites source to support idea that flaunting togetherness is not sincere and leads us into false beliefs and emulation

4

Pro argument: we learn about ourselves from celebrity worship

This puts the responsibility on us to be mindful of our celebrity habits, but it doesn't discredit celebrity itself. Salon .com advice columnist Cary Tennis insists that our hunger for more is valuable: "It is natural for us to be transfixed by these characters because we are thirsty for magic. We are not satisfied with our earthly existence, nor should we be." (2) Furthermore, admiring celebrities gives us an opportunity to learn more about ourselves: "What do your likes and dislikes of various celebrities say about you as a person, your aspirations, your secret hopes, your values?" (2) he asks. If we think critically about the celebrity stories that appeal to us, we learn a lot about our fears and ambitions.

Writer cites source to support point about the value of celebrity habits

Writer cites an academic writer on value of celebrity worship in developing moral views

Karen Sternheimer, author of *Celebrity Culture and the American Dream*, agrees that celebrity culture helps form our values in a positive way. A professor of sociology, Sternheimer writes that without the shared experiences stimulated by celebrity culture, we'd miss a key aspect of our moral development: "Talking about celebrities, whether we express admiration, sympathy, or condemnation for them, offers us a framework through which to construct our social selves." (5) For example, we might erringly rationalize our own behavior by pointing to celebrities who behave similarly. By contrast, outrage over a celebrity's illegal drug use signals that we won't tolerate that behavior. Or, by harshly criticizing a celebrity's cheating scandal, we might position our values above those in the situation. On a personal level, evaluating celebrity behavior encourages self-discovery about what we do and don't find acceptable; on a pop culture level, such judgments set up a moral framework for long-term social bonds.

Conclusion: writer presents thesis that we can use celebrity worship as a mirror to see ourselves better

Although celebrity news might at first seem trivial, it's clear that its effects can be lasting and serious. We must maintain a healthy balance between sharing our own stories and those of our idols, and we must be skeptical about what reporters and advertisements claim as facts about celebrities' lives. At the same time, we can and should take advantage of those shared stories as a way to learn more about ourselves and others. A bit of aspiration will motivate us to work harder in our own lives, and a bit of comparison can help us clarify what we really want out of them. In this way, we can use celebrities to see both ourselves and our communities just a bit clearer.

Works Cited

Gabler, Neal. "The Greatest Show on Earth." *The Daily Beast.* The Newsweek/Daily Beast Company LLC, 11 Dec. 2009. Web. 1 Nov. 2012.

Piazza, Jo. "Americans Have an Unhealthy Obsession with Celebrities." *The Huffington Post.* TheHuffingtonPost.com Inc., 28 March 2012. Web. 28 Oct. 2012.

Sternheimer, Karen. *Celebrity Culture and the American Dream: Stardom and Social Mobility.* New York: Routledge, 2011. Print.

Tennis, Cary. "Why Am I Obsessed with Celebrity Gossip?" *Salon.com.* Salon Media Group, Inc., 6 Jan. 2006. Web. 28 Oct. 2012.

Analyzing Kate Suarez's Argumentation Essay: Questions for Discussion

1. In paragraph 3, Suarez claims that when we talk about celebrities it "helps us tackle more serious social and political issues." Can you offer some ways in which this statement is true?

2. In paragraph 4, Suarez claims that in our purchases "we make decisions motivated by celebrity endorsements." Have you ever been so influenced? Did you feel you were somehow manipulated or did you regard your decisions as relatively harmless ones?

3. Is celebrity watching something only women do or do men have their own celebrity obsessions? Explain.

4. What observations and insights regarding celebrity obsessions can you add to Suarez's argument?

SUGGESTIONS FOR USING ARGUMENTATION AS A WRITING STRATEGY

As you plan, write, and revise your argumentation essay, be mindful of the writing process guidelines described in Chapter 2. Pay particular attention to the basic requirements and essential ingredients of this writing strategy.

▶ Planning Your Argumentation Essay

Writing an argument can be very rewarding. By its nature, an argument must be carefully reasoned and thoughtfully structured to have maximum effect. In other words, the *logos* of the argument must be carefully tended. Allow yourself, therefore, enough time to think about your thesis, to gather the evidence you need, and to draft, revise, edit, and proofread your essay. Sloppy thinking, confused expression, and poor organization will be immediately evident to your reader and will make for weaker arguments.

For example, you might be given an assignment in your history class to write a paper explaining what you think was the main cause of the Civil War. How would you approach this topic? First, it would help to assemble a number of possible interpretations of the causes of the Civil War and to examine them closely. Once you have determined what you consider to be the main cause, you will need to develop points that support your position. Then you will need to explain why you did not choose other possibilities, and you will have to assemble reasons that refute them. For instance, you might write an opening similar to this example.

The Fugitive Slave Act Forced the North to Go to War

While the start of the Civil War can be attributed to many factors — states' rights, slavery, a clash between antithetical economic systems, and westward expansion — the final straw for the North was the Fugitive Slave Act. This act, more than any other single element of disagreement between the North and the South, forced the North into a position in which the only option was to fight.

Certainly, slavery and the clash over open lands in the West contributed to the growing tensions between the two sides, as did the economically incompatible systems of production — plantation and manufacture — but the Fugitive Slave Act required the North either to actively support slavery or to run the risk of becoming a criminal in defiance of it. The North chose not to support the Fugitive Slave Act and was openly angered by the idea that it should be required to do so by law. This anger and open defiance led directly to the Civil War.

In these opening paragraphs, the author states the main argument for the cause of the Civil War and sets up, in addition, the possible alternatives to this view. The points outlined in the introduction would lead, one by one, to a logical argument asserting that the Fugitive Slave Act was responsible for the onset of the Civil War and refuting the other interpretations.

This introduction is mainly a logical argument. As was mentioned before, writers often use persuasive, or emotional, arguments along with logical ones. Persuasive arguments focus on issues that appeal to people's subconscious or emotional nature, along with their logical powers and intellectual understanding. Such arguments rely on powerful and charged language, and they appeal to the emotions. Persuasive arguments can be especially effective but should not be used without a strong logical backing. Indeed, this is the only way to use emotional persuasion ethically. Emotional persuasion, when not in support of a logical point, can be dangerous in that it can make an illogical point sound appealing to a listener or reader.

DETERMINE YOUR THESIS OR PROPOSITION. Begin by determining a topic that interests you and about which there is some significant difference of opinion or about which you have a number of questions. Find out what's in the news, what people are talking about, what authors and instructors are emphasizing as important intellectual arguments. As you pursue your research, consider what assertion you can make about the topic you chose. The more specific this thesis or proposition, the more directed your research can become and the more focused your ultimate argument will be. While researching your topic, however, be aware that the information may point you in new directions. Don't hesitate at any point to modify or even reject an initial or preliminary thesis as continued research warrants.

A thesis can be placed anywhere in an argument, but it is probably best while learning to write arguments to place the statement of your controlling idea somewhere near the beginning of your composition. Explain the importance of the thesis, and make clear to your reader that you share a common concern or interest in this issue. You may wish to state your central assertion directly in your first or second paragraph so that there is no possibility for your reader to be confused about your position. You may also wish to lead off with a particularly striking piece of evidence to capture your reader's interest.

CONSIDER YOUR AUDIENCE. It is well worth remembering that in no other type of writing is the question of audience more important than in argumentation. Here again, the *ethos* and *pathos* aspects of argumentation come into play. The tone you establish, the type of diction you choose, the kinds of evidence you select to buttress your assertions, and indeed the organizational pattern you design and follow will all influence your audience's perception of your trustworthiness and believability. If you make good judgments about the nature of your audience, respect its knowledge of the subject, and correctly envision whether it is likely to be hostile, neutral, complacent, or receptive, you will be able to tailor the various aspects of your argument appropriately.

GATHER SUPPORTING EVIDENCE.   For each point of your argument, be sure to provide appropriate and sufficient supporting evidence: verifiable facts and statistics, illustrative examples and narratives, or quotations from authorities. Don't overwhelm your reader with evidence, but don't skimp either; it is important to demonstrate your command of the topic and your control of the thesis by choosing carefully from all the evidence at your disposal. If there are strong arguments on both sides of the issue, you will need to take this into account while making your choices. (See the Consider Refutations to Your Argument section below.)

▶ Organizing and Writing Your Argumentation Essay

CHOOSE AN ORGANIZATIONAL PATTERN.   Once you think that you have sufficient evidence to make your assertion convincing, consider how best to organize your argument. To some extent, your organization will depend on your method of reasoning: inductive, deductive, or a combination of the two. For example, is it necessary to establish a major premise before moving on to discuss a minor premise? Should most of your evidence precede or follow your direct statement of an assertion? Will induction work better with the particular audience you have targeted?

As you present your primary points, you may find it effective to move from those that are least important to those that are most important or from those that are least familiar to those that are most familiar. A scratch outline can help, but it is often the case that a writer's most crucial revisions in an argument involve rearranging its components into a sharper, more coherent order. It is often difficult to tell what that order should be until the revision stage of the writing process.

CONSIDER REFUTATIONS TO YOUR ARGUMENT.   As you proceed with your argument, you may wish to take into account well-known and significant opposing arguments. To ignore them would be to suggest to your readers any one of the following: You don't know about them, you know about them and are obviously and unfairly weighting the argument in your favor, or you know about them and have no reasonable answers to them. Grant the validity of the opposing argument or refute it, but respect your readers' intelligence by addressing the problems. Your readers will in turn respect you for doing so.

To avoid weakening your thesis, you must be very clear in your thinking and presentation. It must remain apparent to your readers why your argument is superior to opposing points of view. If you feel that you cannot introduce opposing arguments because they will weaken rather than strengthen your thesis, you should probably reassess your thesis and the supporting evidence.

USE OTHER RHETORICAL STRATEGIES.   Although argument is one of the most powerful single rhetorical strategies, it is almost always strengthened by incorporating other strategies. In every professional selection in this chapter, you will find a number of rhetorical strategies at work.

Combining strategies is probably not something you want to think about when you first try to write an argument. Instead, let the strategies develop naturally as you organize, draft, and revise your essay. As you develop your argument essay, use the following chart as a reminder of what the eight strategies covered previously can do for you.

Strategies for Development	
Narration	Telling a story or giving an account of an event
Description	Presenting a picture in words
Illustration	Using examples to explain a point or an idea
Process Analysis	Explaining how something is done or happens
Comparison and Contrast	Demonstrating likenesses and differences
Division and Classification	Separating a subject into its parts and placing them in appropriate categories
Definition	Explaining what something is or means
Cause and Effect Analysis	Explaining why something happens or the ramifications of an action

As you draft your essay, look for places where you can use the above strategies to strengthen your argument. For example, do you need a more convincing example, a term defined, a process explained, or the likely effects of an action detailed?

CONCLUDE FORCEFULLY.   In the conclusion of your essay, be sure to restate your position in different language, at least briefly. Besides persuading your reader to accept your point of view, you may also want to encourage some specific course of action. Above all, your conclusion should not introduce new information that may surprise your reader; it should seem to follow naturally, almost seamlessly, from the series of points that have been carefully established in the body of the essay.

❱ Revising and Editing Your Argumentation Essay

AVOID FAULTY REASONING.   Have someone read your argument, checking sentences for errors in judgment and reasoning. Sometimes others can see easily what you can't because you are so intimately tied to your assertion. Review the following list of errors in reasoning, making sure that you have not committed any of them.

Oversimplification—a foolishly simple solution to what is clearly a complex problem. *The reason we have a balance-of-trade deficit is that foreigners make better products than we do.*

Hasty generalization—in inductive reasoning, a generalization that is based on too little evidence or on evidence that is not representative. *It was the best movie I saw this year, and so it should get an Academy Award.*

Post hoc, ergo propter hoc ("after this, therefore because of this")— confusing chance or coincidence with causation. The fact that one event comes after another does not necessarily mean that the first event caused the second. *Every time I wear my orange Syracuse sweater to a game, we win.*

Begging the question—assuming in a premise something that needs to be proven. *Parking fines work because they keep people from parking illegally.*

False analogy—making a misleading analogy between logically connected ideas. *Of course he'll make a fine coach. He was an all-star basketball player.*

Either/or thinking—seeing only two alternatives when there may in fact be other possibilities. *Either you love your job or you hate it.*

Non sequitur ("it does not follow")—an inference or conclusion that is not clearly related to the established premises or evidence. *She is very sincere; she must know what she is talking about.*

Name-Calling—linking a person to a negative idea or symbol. The hope is that by invoking the name the user will elicit a negative reaction without the necessary evidence. *Senator Jones is a bleeding heart.*

SHARE YOUR DRAFTS WITH OTHERS.   Try sharing the drafts of your essay with other students in your writing class to make sure that your argument works, that it makes its point. Ask them if there are any parts that they do not understand. Have them restate your thesis in their own words. Ask them if you have overlooked any opposing arguments that you should consider and if you have provided enough evidence for your side of the argument to be convincing. If their answers differ from what you intended, have them point to the troublesome parts of your essay and discuss what you can do to improve your argument. If you find their suggestions valid, revise your text accordingly. To maximize the effectiveness of conferences with your peers, use the guidelines presented on page 36. Feedback from these conferences often provides one or more places where you can start revising.

QUESTION YOUR OWN WORK WHILE REVISING AND EDITING. Revision is best done by asking yourself key questions about what you have written. Begin by reading, preferably aloud, what you have written. Reading aloud forces you to pay attention to every single word, and you are more likely to catch lapses in the logical flow of thought. After you have read your paper through, answer the following questions for revising and editing, and make the necessary changes.

For help with twelve common writing problems, see Chapter 16, "Editing for Grammar, Punctuation, and Sentence Style."

Questions for Revising and Editing: Argumentation

1. Is my thesis or proposition focused? Do I state my thesis well?

2. Assess the different kinds of arguments. Am I using the right technique to argue my thesis? Does my strategy fit my subject matter and audience?

3. Does my presentation include enough evidence to support my thesis? Do I acknowledge opposing points of view in a way that strengthens, rather than weakens, my argument?

4. Have I chosen an appropriate organizational pattern that makes it easy to support my thesis?

5. Have I avoided faulty reasoning within my essay? Have I had a friend read the essay to help me find problems in my logic?

6. Is my conclusion forceful and effective?

7. Have I thought about or attempted to combine rhetorical strategies to strengthen my argument? If so, is the combination of strategies effective? If not, what strategy or strategies would help my argument?

8. Have I used a variety of sentences to enliven my writing? Have I avoided wordiness?

9. Have I avoided errors in grammar, punctuation, and mechanics?

The Declaration of Independence

THOMAS JEFFERSON

President, governor, statesman, diplomat, lawyer, architect, philosopher, thinker, and writer, Thomas Jefferson (1743–1826) is one of the most important figures in U.S. history. He was born in Albemarle County, Virginia, and attended the College of William and Mary. After being admitted to law practice in 1767, he began a long and illustrious career of public service to the colonies and, later, the new republic.

Jefferson drafted the Declaration of Independence in 1776. Although it was revised by Benjamin Franklin and his colleagues in the Continental Congress, in its sound logic and forceful, direct style the document retains the unmistakable qualities of Jefferson's prose.

Preparing to Read

What, for you, is the meaning of democracy? Where do your ideas about democracy come from?

When in the course of human events, it becomes necessary for one people to dissolve the political bonds which have connected them with another, and to assume among the Powers of the earth, the separate and equal station to which the Laws of Nature and of Nature's God entitle them, a decent respect to the opinions of mankind requires that they should declare the causes which impel them to the separation. 1

We hold these truths to be self-evident, that all men are created equal, that they are endowed by their Creator with certain unalienable Rights, that among these are Life, Liberty and the pursuit of Happiness. — That to secure these rights, Governments are instituted among Men, deriving their just powers from the consent of the governed, — That whenever any Form of Government becomes destructive of these ends, it is the Right of the People to alter or to abolish it, and to institute new Government, laying its foundation on such principles and organizing its powers in such form, as to them shall seem most likely to effect their Safety and Happiness. Prudence, indeed, will dictate that Governments long established should not be changed for light and transient causes; and accordingly all experience hath shewn, that mankind are more disposed to suffer, while evils are 2 sufferable, than to right themselves by abolishing the forms to which they are accustomed. But when a long train of abuses and usurpations, pursuing invariably the same Object evinces a design to reduce them under absolute Despotism, it is their right, it is their duty, to throw off such Government, and to provide new Guards for their future security. —Such has been the patient sufferance of these Colonies; and such is now the necessity which constrains them to alter their former Systems of Government. The history of the present King of Great Britain is a history of repeated injuries and usurpations, all having in direct object the establishment of an absolute Tyranny over these States. To prove this, let Facts be submitted to a candid world.

He has refused his Assent to Laws, the most wholesome and necessary 3
for the public good.

We hold these truths to be self-evident, that all men are created equal, that they are endowed by their Creator with certain unalienable Rights, that among these are Life, Liberty and the pursuit of Happiness.

He has forbidden his Governors to pass 4
Laws of immediate and pressing importance, unless suspended in their operation till his Assent should be obtained; and when so suspended, he has utterly neglected to attend to them.

He has refused to pass other Laws for 5
the accommodation of large districts of people, unless those people would relinquish the right of Representation in the Legislature, a right inestimable to them and formidable to tyrants only.

He has called together legislative bodies 6
at places unusual, uncomfortable, and distant from the depository of their public Records, for the sole purpose of fatiguing them into compliance with his measures.

He has dissolved Representative Houses repeatedly, for opposing with 7
manly firmness his invasions on the rights of the people.

He has refused for a long time, after such dissolutions, to cause others 8
to be elected; whereby the Legislative powers, incapable of Annihilation, have returned to the People at large for their exercise; the State remaining in the mean time exposed to all the dangers of invasion from without, and convulsions within.

He has endeavoured to prevent the population of these States; for that 9
purpose obstructing the Laws of Naturalization of Foreigners; refusing to pass others to encourage their migration hither, and raising the conditions of new Appropriations of Lands.

He has obstructed the Administration of Justice, by refusing his Assent 10
to Laws for establishing Judiciary Powers.

He has made Judges dependent on his Will alone, for the tenure of 11
their offices, and the amount and payment of their salaries.

He has erected a multitude of New Offices, and sent hither swarms of 12
Officers to harass our People, and eat out their substance.

He has kept among us, in times of peace, Standing Armies without the 13
Consent of our legislatures.

He has affected to render the Military independent of and superior to 14
the Civil power.

He has combined with others to subject us to a jurisdiction foreign to 15
our constitution, and unacknowledged by our laws; giving his Assent to
their Acts of pretended Legislation:

For quartering large bodies of armed troops among us: 16

For protecting them, by a mock Trial, from punishment for any 17
Murders which they should commit on the Inhabitants of these States:

For cutting off our Trade with all parts of the world: 18

For imposing Taxes on us without our Consent: 19

For depriving us in many cases, of the benefits of Trial by Jury: 20

For transporting us beyond Seas to be tried for pretended offenses: 21

For abolishing the free System of English Laws in a neighbouring 22
Province, establishing therein an Arbitrary government, and enlarging its
Boundaries so as to render it at once an example and fit instrument for
introducing the same absolute rule into these Colonies:

For taking away our Charters, abolishing our most valuable Laws, and 23
altering fundamentally the Forms of our Governments:

For suspending our own Legislatures, and declaring themselves 24
invested with power to legislate for us in all cases whatsoever.

He has abdicated Government here, by declaring us out of his 25
Protection and waging War against us.

He has plundered our seas, ravaged our Coasts, burnt our towns, and 26
destroyed the lives of our people.

He is at this time transporting large Armies of foreign Mercenaries to 27
compleat works of death, desolation and tyranny already begun with circumstances of Cruelty & perfidy scarcely paralleled in the most barbarous
ages, and totally unworthy the Head of a civilized nation.

He has constrained our fellow Citizens taken Captive on the high Seas 28
to bear Arms against their Country, to become the executioners of their
friends and Brethren, or to fall themselves by their Hands.

He has excited domestic insurrections amongst us, and has endeav- 29
oured to bring on the inhabitants of our frontiers, the merciless Indian
Savages, whose known rule of warfare, is an undistinguished destruction of
all ages, sexes and conditions.

In every stage of these Oppressions We Have Petitioned for Redress in 30
the most humble terms: Our repeated Petitions have been answered only

by repeated injury. A Prince, whose character is thus marked by every act which may define a Tyrant, is unfit to be the ruler of a free people.

Nor have We been wanting in attention to our Brittish brethren. 31 We have warned them from time to time of attempts by their legislature to extend an unwarrantable jurisdiction over us. We have reminded them of the circumstances of our emigration and settlement here. We have appealed to their native justice and magnanimity, and we have conjured them by the ties of our common kindred to disavow these usurpations, which, would inevitably interrupt our connections and correspondence. They too have been deaf to the voice of justice and of consanguinity. We must, therefore, acquiesce in the necessity, which denounces our Separation, and hold them, as we hold the rest of mankind, Enemies in War, in Peace Friends.

We, therefore, the Representatives of the united States of America, in 32 General Congress, Assembled, appealing to the Supreme Judge of the world for the rectitude of our intentions, do, in the Name, and by Authority of the good People of these Colonies, solemnly publish and declare, That these United Colonies are, and of Right ought to be Free and Independent States; that they are Absolved from all Allegiance to the British Crown, and that all political connection between them and the State of Great Britain, is and ought to be totally dissolved; and that as Free and Independent States, they have full Power to levy War, conclude Peace, contract Alliances, establish Commerce, and to do all other Acts and Things which Independent States may of right do. And for the support of this Declaration, with a firm reliance on the protection of divine Providence, we mutually pledge to each other our Lives, our Fortunes and our sacred Honor.

Thinking Critically about the Text

Why do you think the Declaration of Independence is still such a powerful and important document more than two hundred years after it was written? Do any parts of it seem more memorable than others? Did any part surprise you in this reading?

Questions on Subject

1. Where, according to Jefferson, do rulers get their authority? What does Jefferson believe is the purpose of government?

2. What argument does the Declaration of Independence make for overthrowing any unacceptable government? What assumptions underlie this argument?

3. In paragraphs 3–29, Jefferson lists the many ways King George has wronged the colonists. Which of these "injuries and usurpations" (paragraph 2) do you feel are just cause for the colonists to declare their independence?

4. According to the Declaration of Independence, how did the colonists try to persuade the English king to rule more justly?

5. What are the specific declarations that Jefferson makes in his final paragraph?

Questions on Strategy

1. The Declaration of Independence is a deductive argument; it is therefore possible to present it in the form of a syllogism. What is the major premise, the minor premise, and the conclusion of Jefferson's argument? (Glossary: *Syllogism*)

2. In paragraph 2, Jefferson presents certain "self-evident" truths. What are these truths, and how are they related to the intent of his argument?

3. The list of charges against the king is given as evidence in support of Jefferson's minor premise. Does he offer any evidence in support of his major premise? Why, or why not? (Glossary: *Evidence*)

4. What organizational pattern do you see in the list of grievances in paragraphs 3–29? (Glossary: *Organization*) Describe the cumulative effect of this list on you as a reader.

5. Explain how Jefferson uses cause and effect thinking to justify the colonists' argument in declaring their independence. (Glossary: *Cause and Effect Analysis*)

Questions on Diction and Vocabulary

1. Who is Jefferson's audience, and in what tone does he address this audience? Discuss why this tone is or isn't appropriate for this document. (Glossary: *Audience*)

2. Is the language of the Declaration of Independence coolly reasonable or emotional, or does it change from one to the other? Give examples to support your answer.

3. Paraphrase the following excerpt, and comment on Jefferson's diction and syntax: "They too have been deaf to the voice of justice and of consanguinity. We must, therefore, acquiesce in the necessity, which denounces our Separation, and hold them, as we hold the rest of mankind, Enemies in War, in Peace Friends" (paragraph 31). Describe the author's tone in these two sentences. (Glossary: *Diction; Tone*)

Classroom Activity Using Argumentation

Use the following test, developed by William V. Haney, to determine your ability to analyze accurately evidence that is presented to you. After completing Haney's test, discuss your answers with other members of your class, and then compare them to the correct answers printed at the bottom of page 515.

THE UNCRITICAL INFERENCE TEST

Directions

1. You will read a brief story. Assume that all of the information presented in the story is definitely accurate and true. Read the story carefully. You may refer back to the story whenever you wish.

2. You will then read statements about the story. Answer them in numerical order. *Do not go back* to fill in answers or to change answers. This will only distort your test score.

3. After you read each statement carefully, determine whether the statement is:

   a. "T" — meaning: On the basis of the information presented in the story the statement is *definitely true.*

   b. "F" — meaning: On the basis of the information presented in the story the statement is *definitely false.*

   c. "?" — The statement *may* be true (or false) but on the basis of the information presented in the story you cannot be definitely certain. (If any part of the statement is doubtful, mark the statement "?".)

4. Indicate your answer by circling either "T" or "F" or "?" opposite the statement.

The Story

Babe Smith has been killed. Police have rounded up six suspects, all of whom are known gangsters. All of them are known to have been near the scene of the killing at the approximate time that it occurred. All had substantial motives for wanting Smith killed. However, one of these suspected gangsters, Slinky Sam, has positively been cleared of guilt.

Statements about the Story

1. Slinky Sam is known to have been near the scene of the killing of Babe Smith.   T F ?
2. All six of the rounded-up gangsters were known to have been near the scene of the murder.   T F ?
3. Only Slinky Sam has been cleared of guilt.   T F ?
4. All six of the rounded-up suspects were near the scene of Smith's killing at the approximate time that it took place.   T F ?
5. The police do not know who killed Smith.   T F ?
6. All six suspects are known to have been near the scene of the foul deed.   T F ?
7. Smith's murderer did not confess of his own free will.   T F ?
8. Slinky Sam was not cleared of guilt.   T F ?
9. It is known that the six suspects were in the vicinity of the cold-blooded assassination.   T F ?

Writing Suggestions

1. To some people, the Declaration of Independence still accurately reflects America's political philosophy and way of life; to others, it does not. What is your position on this issue? Discuss your analysis of the Declaration of Independence's contemporary relevance, and try to persuade others to accept your position.

2. **Writing with Sources.** How does a monarchy differ from American democracy? Write an essay in which you compare and contrast a particular monarchy and the presidency. How are they similar? You might also consider comparing the presidency with the British monarchy of 1776. Do some research online or in the library to support your analysis. For models of and advice on integrating sources in your essay, see Chapters 14 and 15.

The Case for Short Words

RICHARD LEDERER

Born in 1938, Richard Lederer has been a lifelong student of language. He holds degrees from Haverford College, Harvard University, and the University of New Hampshire. For twenty-seven years he taught English at St. Paul's School in Concord, New Hampshire. Anyone who has read one of his more than thirty books will understand why he has been referred to as "Conan the Grammarian" and "America's wittiest verbalist." Lederer loves language and enjoys writing about its richness and usage by Americans. His books include *Anguished English* (1987), *Crazy English* (1989), *Adventures of a Verbivore* (1994), *Nothing Risque, Nothing Gained* (1995), *A Man of My Words: Reflections on the English Language* (2003), and *Word Wizard: Super Bloopers, Rich Reflections, and Other Acts of Word Magic* (2006). In addition to writing books, Lederer pens a weekly syndicated column called "Lederer on Language" for the San Diego *Union-Tribune*, which appears both in print and online. He has been the "Grammar Grappler" for *Writer's Digest*, the language commentator for National Public Radio, and the founding cohost of *A Way with Words*, a weekly radio program out of San Diego, California.

In the following selection, a chapter from *The Miracle of Language* (1990), Lederer sings the praises of short words and reminds us that well-chosen monosyllabic words can be a writer's best friends because they are functional and often pack a powerful punch. Note the clever way in which he uses short words throughout the essay itself to support his argument.

Preparing to Read

Find a paragraph you like in a book that you enjoyed reading. What is it that appeals to you? What did the author do to make the writing so appealing? Do you like the vocabulary, the flow of the words, the imagery it presents, or something else?

When you speak and write, there is no law that says you   1
have to use big words. Short words are as good as long
ones, and short, old words—like *sun* and *grass* and
home—are best of all. A lot of small words, more than
you might think, can meet your needs with a strength, grace, and charm
that large words do not have.

Big words can make the way dark for those who read what you write   2
and hear what you say. Small words cast their clear light on big things—night
and day, love and hate, war and peace, and life and death. Big words at
times seem strange to the eye and the ear and the mind and the heart. Small

words are the ones we seem to have known from the time we were born, like the hearth fire that warms the home.

Short words are bright like sparks that glow in the night, prompt like the dawn that greets the day, sharp like the blade of a knife, hot like salt tears that scald the cheek, quick like moths that flit from flame to flame, and terse like the dart and sting of a bee.

> A lot of small words, more than you might think, can meet your needs with a strength, grace, and charm that large words do not have.

Here is a sound rule: Use small, old words where you can. If a long word says just what you want to say, do not fear to use it. But know that our tongue is rich in crisp, brisk, swift, short words. Make them the spine and the heart of what you speak and write. Short words are like fast friends. They will not let you down.

The title of this chapter and the four paragraphs that you have just read are wrought entirely of words of one syllable. In setting myself this task, I did not feel especially cabined, cribbed, or confined. In fact, the structure helped me to focus on the power of the message I was trying to put across.

One study shows that twenty words account for twenty-five percent of all spoken English words, and all twenty are monosyllabic. In order of frequency they are: *I, you, the, a, to, is, it, that, of, and, in, what, he, this, have, do, she, not, on,* and *they.* Other studies indicate that the fifty most common words in written English are each made of a single syllable.

For centuries our finest poets and orators have recognized and employed the power of small words to make a straight point between two minds. A great many of our proverbs punch home their points with pithy monosyllables: "Where there's a will, there's a way," "A stitch in time saves nine," "Spare the rod and spoil the child," "A bird in the hand is worth two in the bush."

Nobody used the short word more skillfully than William Shakespeare, whose dying King Lear laments:

> And my poor fool is hang'd! No, no, no life!
> Why should a dog, a horse, a rat have life,
> And thou no breath at all? . . .
> Do you see this? Look on her; look, her lips.
> Look there, look there!

Shakespeare's contemporaries made the King James Bible a center-piece of short words — "And God said, Let there be light: and there was light. And God saw the light, that it was good." The descendants of such mighty lines live on in the twentieth century. When asked to explain his policy to Parliament, Winston Churchill responded with these ringing monosyllables: "I will say: It is to wage war, by sea, land, and air, with all our might and with all the strength that God can give us." In his "Death of the Hired Man" Robert Frost observes that "Home is the place where, when you have to go there, / They have to take you in." And William H. Johnson uses ten two-letter words to explain his secret of success: "If it is to be, / It is up to me."

You don't have to be a great author, statesman, or philosopher to tap   10
the energy and eloquence of small words. Each winter I ask my ninth grad-ers at St. Paul's School to write a composition composed entirely of one-syllable words. My students greet my request with obligatory moans and groans, but, when they return to class with their essays, most feel that, with the pressure to produce high-sounding polysyllables relieved, they have created some of their most powerful and luminous prose. Here are submis-sions from two of my ninth graders:

> What can you say to a boy who has left home? You can say that he has done wrong, but he does not care. He has left home so that he will not have to deal with what you say. He wants to go as far as he can. He will do what he wants to do.
>
> This boy does not want to be forced to go to church, to comb his hair, or to be on time. A good time for this boy does not lie in your reach, for what you have he does not want. He dreams of ripped jeans, shorts with no starch, and old socks.
>
> So now this boy is on a bus to a place he dreams of, a place with no rules. This boy now walks a strange street, his long hair blown back by the wind. He wears no coat or tie, just jeans and an old shirt. He hates your world, and he has left it.
>
> — CHARLES SHAFFER

> For a long time we cruised by the coast and at last came to a wide bay past the curve of a hill, at the end of which lay a small town. Our long boat ride at an end, we all stretched and stood up to watch as the boat nosed its way in.
>
> The town climbed up the hill that rose from the shore, a space in front of it left bare for the port. Each house was a clean white with sky blue or grey trim; in front of each one was a small yard, edged by a white stone wall strewn with green vines.
>
> As the town basked in the heat of noon, not a thing stirred in the streets or by the shore. The sun beat down on the sea, the land, and the back of our necks, so that, in spite of the breeze that made the vines sway, we all wished we could hide from the glare in a cool, white house. But, as there was no one to help dock the boat, we had to stand and wait.

At last the head of the crew leaped from the side and strode to a large house on the right. He shoved the door wide, poked his head through the gloom, and roared with a fierce voice. Five or six men came out, and soon the port was loud with the clank of chains and creak of planks as the men caught ropes thrown by the crew, pulled them taut, and tied them to posts. Then they set up a rough plank so we could cross from the deck to the shore. We all made for the large house while the crew watched, glad to be rid of us.

— CELIA WREN

You, too, can tap into the vitality and vigor of compact expression. 11
Take a suggestion from the highway department. At the boundaries of your speech and prose place a sign that reads "Caution: Small Words at Work."

Thinking Critically about the Text

Reread a piece of writing you turned in earlier this year for any class. Analyze your choice of words, and describe your writing vocabulary. Did you follow Lederer's admonition to use short words whenever they are appropriate, or did you tend to use longer, more important-sounding words? Is Lederer's essay likely to change the way you write papers in the future? Why, or why not?

Questions on Subject

1. What rule does Lederer present for writing? What does he do to demonstrate the feasibility of this rule?

2. Lederer states that the twenty words that account for a quarter of all spoken English words are monosyllabic. So are the fifty most common written words. Why, then, do you think Lederer felt it was necessary to argue that people should use them? Who is his audience? (Glossary: *Audience*)

3. How do his students react to the assignment he gives them requiring short words? How do their essays turn out? What does the assignment teach them?

4. In paragraph 10, Lederer refers to the relief his students feel when released from "the pressure to produce high-sounding polysyllables." Where does this pressure come from? How does it relate to the central purpose of his essay?

5. Do you think Lederer's argument will change the way you write? Explain.

Questions on Strategy

1. As you read Lederer's essay for the first time, were you surprised by his announcement in paragraph 5 that the preceding four paragraphs contained only single-syllable words? If not, when were you first aware of what he was doing? What does Lederer's strategy tell you about small words?

2. Lederer starts using multisyllabic words when discussing the process of writing with single-syllable words. Why do you think he abandons his single-syllable presentation? Does it diminish the strength of his argument? Explain.

3. Lederer provides two long examples of writing by his own students. What does he accomplish by using these examples along with ones from famous authors? (Glossary: *Illustration*)

4. Lederer illustrates his argument with examples from several prominent authors as well as from students. (Glossary: *Illustration*) Which of these examples did you find the most effective? Why? Provide an example from your own reading that you think is effective in illustrating Lederer's argument.

5. How does Lederer's final paragraph serve to close the essay effectively? (Glossary: *Beginnings/Endings*)

Questions on Diction and Vocabulary

1. Lederer uses similes to help the reader form associations and images with short words. (Glossary: *Figures of Speech*) What are some of these similes? Do you find the similes effective in the context of Lederer's argument? Explain.

2. In paragraph 9, Lederer uses such terms as *mighty* and *ringing monosyllables* to describe the passages he gives as examples. Do you think such descriptions are appropriate? Why do you think he includes them?

3. Carefully analyze the two student essays that Lederer presents. In particular, circle all the main verbs that each student uses. (Glossary: *Verb*) What, if anything, do these verbs have in common? What conclusions can you draw about verbs and strong, powerful writing?

Classroom Activity Using Argumentation

One strategy in developing a strong argument that most people find convincing is illustration. As Lederer demonstrates, an array of examples, both brief and extended, has a remarkable ability to convince readers of the truth of a proposition. While it is possible to argue a case with one specific example that is both appropriate and representative, most writers find that a varied set of examples often makes a more convincing case. Therefore, it is important to identify your examples before starting to write.

As an exercise in argumentation, choose one of the following position statements:

a. More parking spaces should be provided on campus for students.

b. Children's television programs are marked by a high incidence of violence.

c. Capital punishment is a relatively ineffective deterrent to crime.

d. More computer stations should be provided on campus for students.

e. In-state residency requirements for tuition are unfair at my school.

Make a list of the examples — types of information and evidence — you would need to write an argumentative essay on the topic you choose. Indicate where and how you might obtain this information. Finally, share your list of examples with other students in your class who chose the same topic.

Writing Suggestions

1. People tend to avoid single-syllable words because they are afraid they will look inadequate and that their writing will lack sophistication. Are there situations in which demonstrating command of a large vocabulary is desirable? If you answer yes, present one situation, and argue that the overuse of short words in that situation is potentially detrimental. If you answer no, defend your reasoning. How can the use of short words convey the necessary style and sophistication in all situations?

2. Advertising is an industry that depends on efficient, high-impact words. Choose ten advertising slogans and three jingles that you find effective. Consider phrases that are widely recognized even after their advertising cycle, such as "Just Do It" and "Think Different." Analyze the ratio of short to long words in the slogans and jingles, and write an essay in which you present your findings. What is the percentage of short words? Argue that the percentage supports or contradicts Lederer's contention that short words are often best for high-impact communicating.

I Have a Dream

MARTIN LUTHER KING JR.

Civil rights leader Martin Luther King Jr. (1929–1968) was the son of a Baptist minister in Atlanta, Georgia. Ordained at the age of eighteen, King went on to earn academic degrees from Morehouse College, Crozer Theological Seminary, Boston University, and Chicago Theological Seminary. He came to prominence in 1955 in Montgomery, Alabama, when he led a successful boycott against the city's segregated bus system. The first president of the Southern Christian Leadership Conference, King became the leading spokesperson for the civil rights movement during the 1950s and 1960s, espousing a consistent philosophy of nonviolent resistance to racial injustice. He also championed women's rights and protested the Vietnam War. Named *Time* magazine's Man of the Year in 1963, King was awarded the Nobel Peace Prize in 1964. King was assassinated in April 1968 after speaking at a rally in Memphis, Tennessee.

"I Have a Dream," the keynote address for the March on Washington in 1963, has become one of the most renowned and recognized speeches of the past century. Delivered from the steps of the Lincoln Memorial to commemorate the centennial of the Emancipation Proclamation, King's speech resonates with hope even as it condemns racial oppression.

Preparing to Read

Most Americans have seen film clips of King delivering the "I Have a Dream" speech. What do you know of the speech? What do you know of the events and conditions under which King presented it?

Five score years ago, a great American, in whose symbolic shadow we stand, signed the Emancipation Proclamation. This momentous decree came as a great beacon light of hope to millions of Negro slaves who had been seared in the flames of withering injustice. It came as a joyous daybreak to end the long night of captivity.   1

But one hundred years later, we must face the tragic fact that the Negro   2
is still not free. One hundred years later, the life of the Negro is still sadly crippled by the manacles of segregation and the chains of discrimination. One hundred years later, the Negro lives on a lonely island of poverty in the midst of a vast ocean of material prosperity. One hundred years later, the Negro is still languishing in the corners of American society and finds himself an exile in his own land. So we have come here today to dramatize an appalling condition.

In a sense we have come to our nation's Capitol to cash a check. When 3
the architects of our republic wrote the magnificent words of the
Constitution and the Declaration of Independence, they were signing a
promissory note to which every American was to fall heir. This note was a
promise that all men would be guaranteed the unalienable rights of life,
liberty, and the pursuit of happiness.

It is obvious today that America has defaulted on this promissory note 4
insofar as her citizens of color are concerned. Instead of honoring this
sacred obligation, America has given the Negro people a bad check; a
check which has come back marked "insufficient funds." But we refuse
to believe that the bank of justice is bankrupt. We refuse to believe that
there are insufficient funds in the great vaults of opportunity of this nation.
So we have come to cash this check—a check that will give us upon
demand the riches of freedom and the security of justice. We have also
come to this hallowed spot to remind America of the fierce urgency of
now. This is no time to engage in the luxury of cooling off or to take the
tranquilizing drug of gradualism. *Now* is the time to make real the promises of Democracy. *Now* is the time to rise from the dark and desolate valley of segregation to the sunlit path of racial justice. *Now* is the time to
open the doors of opportunity to all of God's children. *Now* is the time to
lift our nation from the quicksands of racial injustice to the solid rock of
brotherhood.

It would be fatal for the nation to overlook the urgency of the moment 5
and to underestimate the determination of the Negro. This sweltering
summer of the Negro's legitimate discontent will not pass until there is an
invigorating autumn of freedom and equality. Nineteen sixty-three is not
an end, but a beginning. Those who hope that the Negro needed to blow
off steam and will now be content will have a rude awakening if the nation
returns to business as usual. There will be neither rest nor tranquility in
America until the Negro is granted his citizenship rights. The whirlwinds
of revolt will continue to shake the foundations of our nation until the
bright day of justice emerges.

But there is something I must say to my people who stand on the warm 6
threshold which leads into the palace of justice. In the process of gaining our
rightful place we must not be guilty of wrongful deeds. Let us not seek to
satisfy our thirst for freedom by drinking from the cup of bitterness and
hatred. We must forever conduct our struggle on the high plane of dignity
and discipline. We must not allow our creative protest to degenerate into
physical violence. Again and again we must rise to the majestic heights of
meeting physical force with soul force. The marvelous new militancy which
has engulfed the Negro community must not lead us to a distrust of all white
people, for many of our white brothers, as evidenced by their presence here

today, have come to realize that their destiny is tied up with our destiny and their freedom is inextricably bound to our freedom. We cannot walk alone.

And as we walk, we must make the pledge that we shall march ahead. We cannot turn back. There are those who are asking the devotees of civil rights, "When will you be satisfied?" We can never be satisfied as long as the Negro is the victim of the unspeakable horrors of police brutality. We can never be satisfied as long as our bodies, heavy with the fatigue of travel, cannot gain lodging in the motels of the highways and the hotels of the cities. We cannot be satisfied as long as the Negro's basic mobility is from a smaller ghetto to a larger one. We can never be satisfied as long as a Negro in Mississippi cannot vote and a Negro in New York believes he has nothing for which to vote. No, no, we are not satisfied, and we will not be satisfied until justice rolls down like waters and righteousness like a mighty stream. 7

I am not unmindful that some of you have come here out of great trials and tribulations. Some of you have come fresh from narrow jail cells. Some of you have come from areas where your quest for freedom left you battered by the storms of persecution and staggered by the winds of police brutality. You have been the veterans of creative suffering. Continue to work with the faith that unearned suffering is redemptive. 8

> I have a dream that my four little children will one day live in a nation where they will not be judged by the color of their skin but by the content of their character.

Go back to Mississippi, go back to Alabama, go back to South Carolina, go back to Georgia, go back to Louisiana, go back to the slums and ghettoes of our northern cities, knowing that somehow this situation can and will be changed. Let us not wallow in the valley of despair. 9

I say to you today, my friends, that in spite of the difficulties and frustrations of the moment I still have a dream. It is a dream deeply rooted in the American dream. 10

I have a dream that one day this nation will rise up and live out the true meaning of its creed: "We hold these truths to be self-evident; that all men are created equal." 11

I have a dream that one day on the red hills of Georgia the sons of former slaves and the sons of former slaveowners will be able to sit down together at the table of brotherhood. 12

I have a dream that the state of Mississippi, a desert state sweltering with the heat of injustice and oppression, will be transformed into an oasis of freedom and justice. 13

I have a dream that my four little children will one day live in a nation 14
where they will not be judged by the color of their skin but by the content
of their character.

I have a dream today. 15

I have a dream that the state of Alabama, whose governor's lips are 16
presently dripping with the words of interposition and nullification, will be
transformed into a situation where little black boys and black girls will be
able to join hands with little white boys and white girls and walk together
as sisters and brothers.

I have a dream today. 17

I have a dream that one day every valley shall be exalted, every hill and 18
mountain shall be made low, the rough places will be made plain, and the
crooked places will be made straight, and the glory of the Lord shall be
revealed, and all flesh shall see it together.

This is our hope. This is the faith with which I return to the South. 19
With this faith we will be able to hew out of the mountain of despair a
stone of hope. With this faith we will be able to transform the jangling
discords of our nation into a beautiful symphony of brotherhood. With
this faith we will be able to work together, to pray together, to struggle
together, to go to jail together, to stand up for freedom together, knowing
that we will be free one day.

This will be the day when all of God's children will be able to sing with 20
new meaning.

> My country, 'tis of thee
> Sweet land of liberty,
>   Of thee I sing:
> Land where my fathers died,
> Land of the pilgrims' pride,
> From every mountainside
>   Let freedom ring.

And if America is to be a great nation this must become true. So let 21
freedom ring from the prodigious hilltops of New Hampshire. Let freedom ring from the mighty mountains of New York. Let freedom ring from
the heightening Alleghenies of Pennsylvania!

Let freedom ring from the snowcapped Rockies of Colorado! 22

Let freedom ring from the curvaceous peaks of California! 23

But not only that; let freedom ring from Stone Mountain of Georgia! 24

Let freedom ring from Lookout Mountain of Tennessee! 25

Let freedom ring from every hill and molehill of Mississippi. From 26
every mountainside, let freedom ring.

When we let freedom ring, when we let it ring from every village and 27 every hamlet, from every state and every city, we will be able to speed up that day when all of God's children, black men and white men, Jews and Gentiles, Protestants and Catholics, will be able to join hands and sing in the words of the old Negro spiritual, "Free at last! free at last! thank God almighty, we are free at last!"

Thinking Critically about the Text

King portrayed an America in 1963 in which there was still systematic oppression of African Americans. What is oppression? Have you ever felt yourself — or have you known others — to be oppressed or part of a group that is oppressed? Who are the oppressors? How can oppression be overcome?

Questions on Subject

1. Why does King say that the Constitution and the Declaration of Independence act as a "promissory note" (paragraph 3) to the American people? In what way has America "defaulted" (4) on its promise?

2. What does King mean when he says that in gaining a rightful place in society "we must not be guilty of wrongful deeds" (paragraph 6)? Why is the issue so important to him?

3. When *will* King be satisfied in his quest for civil rights?

4. What, in a nutshell, is King's dream? What vision does he have for the future?

5. How do you personally respond to the argument King puts forth?

Questions on Strategy

1. King delivered his address to two audiences: the huge audience that listened to him in person, and another, even larger audience. (Glossary: *Audience*) What is that larger audience? What did King do in his speech to catch its attention and to deliver his point?

2. Explain King's choice of a title. (Glossary: *Title*) Why is the title particularly appropriate given the context in which the speech was delivered? What other titles might he have used?

3. Examine the speech, and determine how King organized his presentation. (Glossary: *Organization*) What are the main sections of the speech and what is the purpose of each? How does the organization serve King's overall purpose? (Glossary: *Purpose*)

4. Review King's opening paragraph. What happened "Five score years ago" and what purpose does King have in invoking its memory? (Glossary: *Beginnings/Endings*)

5. In his final paragraph, King claims that by freeing the Negro we will all be free. What exactly does he mean? Is King simply being hyperbolic or does his claim embody an undeniable truth? Explain.

Questions on Diction and Vocabulary

1. King uses parallel constructions and repetition throughout his speech. Identify the phrases and words that he emphasizes. Explain what these techniques add to the persuasiveness of his argument.

2. King makes liberal use of metaphor — and metaphorical imagery — in his speech. (Glossary: *Figures of Speech*) Choose a few examples, and examine what they add to the speech. How do they help King engage his listeners' feelings of injustice and give them hope for a better future?

3. Comment on King's diction. Choose a half dozen words as evidence that his diction is well-chosen and rich.

Classroom Activity Using Argumentation

As Martin Luther King Jr.'s speech well demonstrates, the effectiveness of a writer's argument depends in large part on the writer's awareness of audience. For example, if a writer wished to argue for the use of more technology to solve our pressing environmental problems, that argument to a group of environmentalists would need to convince them that the technology would not cause as many environmental problems as it solves, while an argument designed for a group of industrialists might argue that the economic opportunity in developing new technologies is as important as the environmental benefits.

Consider the following proposition:

> The university mascot should be changed to reflect the image of our school today.

How would you argue this proposition to the following audiences?

a. the student body

b. the faculty

c. the alumni

d. the administration

As a class, discuss how the consideration of audience influences the purpose and content of an argument.

Writing Suggestions

1. King's language is powerful and his imagery is vivid, but the effectiveness of any speech partially depends on its delivery. If read in monotone, King's use

of repetition and parallel language would sound almost redundant rather than inspiring. Keeping presentation in mind, write a short speech that argues a point of view about which you feel strongly. Use King's speech as a model, and incorporate imagery, repetition, and metaphor to communicate your point. Read your speech aloud to a friend to see how it flows and how effective your use of language is. Refine your presentation — both your text and how you deliver it — and then present your speech to your class.

2. King uses a variety of metaphors in his speech, but a single encompassing metaphor can be useful to establish the tone and purpose of an essay. Write a description based on a metaphor that conveys an overall impression from the beginning. Try to avoid clichés ("My dorm is a beehive," "My life is an empty glass"), but make your metaphor readily understandable. For example, you could say, "A police siren is a lullaby in my neighborhood," or "My town is a car that has gone 15,000 miles since its last oil change." Carry the metaphor through the entire description.

In Defense of Dangerous Ideas

STEVEN PINKER

Internationally recognized language and cognition scholar and researcher Steven Pinker was born in Montreal, Quebec, Canada, in 1954. He immigrated to the United States shortly after receiving his B.A. from McGill University in 1976. After earning a doctorate from Harvard University in 1979, Pinker taught psychology at Stanford University and the Massachusetts Institute of Technology, where he directed the Center for Cognitive Neuroscience. Currently, he is a professor of psychology at Harvard University. Pinker has written extensively on language development in children, starting with *Language Learnability and Language Development* (1984). He has what one critic writing in the *New York Times Book Review* calls "that facility, so rare among scientists, of making the most difficult material . . . accessible to the average reader." Pinker's books, which include *The Language Instinct* (1994), *How the Mind Works* (1997), *Words and Rules: The Ingredients of Language* (1999), *The Stuff of Thought: Language as a Window into Human Nature* (2007), and *Learning and Cognition: The Acquisition of Argument Structure* (2013) all attest to the public's interest in human language and the world of ideas.

The following article was first published as the preface to *What Is Your Dangerous Idea? Today's Leading Thinkers on the Unthinkable* (2006, edited by John Brockman) and later posted at *Edge* (www.edge.com). In this essay Steven Pinker explores what makes an idea "dangerous" and argues that "important ideas need to be aired," especially in academia, no matter how discomfiting people find them. Notice how Pinker uses a number of examples from a wide range of academic disciplines to illustrate his points about dangerous ideas and the need to discuss them.

Preparing to Read

What did you think when you first read the title to Pinker's essay? For you, what would make an idea dangerous? Do any issues or questions make you uncomfortable or unwilling to discuss them? Explain.

n every age, taboo questions raise our blood pressure and threaten moral panic. But we cannot be afraid to answer them. 1

Do women, on average, have a different profile of aptitudes and emotions than men? 2

Were the events in the Bible fictitious—not just the miracles, but those involving kings and empires? 3

Has the state of the environment improved in the last fifty years? 4

Do most victims of sexual abuse suffer no lifelong damage? 5

Did Native Americans engage in genocide and despoil the landscape? 6

Do men have an innate tendency to rape? 7

Did the crime rate go down in the 1990s because two decades earlier 8
poor women aborted children who would have been prone to violence?

Are suicide terrorists well-educated, mentally healthy, and morally 9
driven?

Would the incidence of rape go down if prostitution were legalized? 10

Do African American men have higher levels of testosterone, on aver- 11
age, than white men?

Is morality just a product of the evolution of our brains, with no inher- 12
ent reality?

Would society be better off if heroin and cocaine were legalized? 13

Is homosexuality the symptom of an infectious disease? 14

Would it be consistent with our moral principles to give parents the 15
option of euthanizing newborns with birth defects that would consign
them to a life of pain and disability?

Do parents have any effect on the character or intelligence of their 16
children?

Have religions killed a greater proportion of people than Nazism? 17

Would damage from terrorism be reduced if the police could torture 18
suspects in special circumstances?

Would Africa have a better chance of rising out of poverty if it hosted 19
more polluting industries or accepted Europe's nuclear waste?

Is the average intelligence of Western nations declining because duller 20
people are having more children than smarter people?

Would unwanted children be better off if there were a market in adop- 21
tion rights, with babies going to the highest bidder?

Would lives be saved if we instituted a free market in organs for trans- 22
plantation?

Should people have the right to clone themselves, or enhance the 23
genetic traits of their children?

Perhaps you can feel your blood pressure rise as you read these ques- 24
tions. Perhaps you are appalled that people can so much as think such
things. Perhaps you think less of me for bringing them up. These are dangerous ideas — ideas that are denounced not because they are self-evidently
false, nor because they advocate harmful action, but because they are
thought to corrode the prevailing moral order.

THINK ABOUT IT

By "dangerous ideas" I don't have in mind harmful technologies, like those 25
behind weapons of mass destruction, or evil ideologies, like those of racist,
fascist, or other fanatical cults. I have in mind statements of fact or policy

that are defended with evidence and argument by serious scientists and thinkers but which are felt to challenge the collective decency of an age. The ideas listed above, and the moral panic that each one of them has incited during the past quarter century, are examples. Writers who have raised ideas like these have been vilified, censored, fired, threatened, and in some cases physically assaulted.

> Dangerous ideas are likely to confront us at an increasing rate, and we are ill-equipped to deal with them.

Every era has its dangerous ideas. For 26 millennia, the monotheistic religions have persecuted countless heresies, together with nuisances from science such as geocentrism, biblical archeology, and the theory of evolution. We can be thankful that the punishments have changed from torture and mutilation to the canceling of grants and the writing of vituperative reviews. But intellectual intimidation, whether by sword or by pen, inevitably shapes the ideas that are taken seriously in a given era, and the rear-view mirror of history presents us with a warning.

Time and again, people have invested factual claims with ethical impli- 27 cations that today look ludicrous. The fear that the structure of our solar system has grave moral consequences is a venerable example, and the foisting of "intelligent design" on biology students is a contemporary one. These travesties should lead us to ask whether the contemporary intellectual mainstream might be entertaining similar moral delusions. Are we enraged by our own infidels and heretics whom history may some day vindicate?

UNSETTLING POSSIBILITIES

Dangerous ideas are likely to confront us at an increasing rate, and we 28 are ill-equipped to deal with them. When done right, science (together with other truth-seeking institutions, such as history and journalism) characterizes the world as it is, without regard to whose feelings get hurt. Science in particular has always been a source of heresy, and today the galloping advances in touchy areas like genetics, evolution, and the environment sciences are bound to throw unsettling possibilities at us. Moreover, the rise of globalization and the Internet are allowing heretics to find one another and work around the barriers of traditional media and academic journals. I also suspect that a change in generational sensibilities will hasten the process. The term "political correctness" captures the 1960s conception of moral rectitude that we baby boomers brought with us as we took over academia, journalism, and government. In my experience, today's students—black and white, male and female—are bewildered by the idea, common among their parents, that certain scientific opinions are immoral or certain questions too hot to handle.

What makes an idea "dangerous"? One factor is an imaginable train of events in which acceptance of the idea could lead to an outcome recognized as harmful. In religious societies, the fear is that if people ever stopped believing in the literal truth of the Bible they would also stop believing in the authority of its moral commandments. That is, if today people dismiss the part about God creating the earth in six days, tomorrow they'll dismiss the part about "Thou shalt not kill." In progressive circles, the fear is that if people ever were to acknowledge any differences between races, sexes, or individuals, they would feel justified in discrimination or oppression. Other dangerous ideas set off fears that people will neglect or abuse their children, become indifferent to the environment, devalue human life, accept violence, and prematurely resign themselves to social problems that could be solved with sufficient commitment and optimism.

All these outcomes, needless to say, would be deplorable. But none of them actually follows from the supposedly dangerous idea. Even if it turns out, for instance, that groups of people are different in their averages, the overlap is certainly so great that it would be irrational and unfair to discriminate against individuals on that basis. Likewise, even if it turns out that parents don't have the power to shape their children's personalities, it would be wrong on grounds of simple human decency to abuse or neglect one's children. And if currently popular ideas about how to improve the environment are shown to be ineffective, it only highlights the need to know what would be effective.

Another contributor to the perception of dangerousness is the intellectual blinkers that humans tend to don when they split into factions. People have a nasty habit of clustering in coalitions, professing certain beliefs as badges of their commitment to the coalition and treating rival coalitions as intellectually unfit and morally depraved. Debates between members of the coalitions can make things even worse, because when the other side fails to capitulate to one's devastating arguments, it only proves they are immune to reason. In this regard, it's disconcerting to see the two institutions that ought to have the greatest stake in ascertaining the truth—academia and government—often blinkered by morally tinged ideologies. One ideology is that humans are blank slates and that social problems can be handled only through government programs that especially redress the perfidy of European males. Its opposite number is that morality inheres in patriotism and Christian faith and that social problems may be handled only by government policies that punish the sins of individual evildoers. New ideas, nuanced ideas, hybrid ideas—and sometimes dangerous ideas—often have trouble getting a hearing against these group-bonding convictions.

The conviction that honest opinions can be dangerous may even arise 32
from a feature of human nature. Philip Tetlock and Alan Fiske have argued
that certain human relationships are constituted on a basis of unshakable
convictions. We love our children and parents, are faithful to our spouses,
stand by our friends, contribute to our communities, and are loyal to our
coalitions not because we continually question and evaluate the merits of
these commitments but because we feel them in our bones. A person who
spends too much time pondering whether logic and fact really justify a
commitment to one of these relationships is seen as just not "getting it."
Decent people don't carefully weigh the advantages and disadvantages of
selling their children or selling out their friends or their spouses or their
colleagues or their country. They reject these possibilities outright; they
"don't go there." So the taboo on questioning sacred values makes sense in
the context of personal relationships. It makes far less sense in the context
of discovering how the world works or running a country.

EXPLORE ALL RELEVANT IDEAS

Should we treat some ideas as dangerous? Let's exclude outright lies, 33
deceptive propaganda, incendiary conspiracy theories from malevolent
crackpots, and technological recipes for wanton destruction. Consider
only ideas about the truth of empirical claims or the effectiveness of policies that, if they turned out to be true, would require a significant rethinking of our moral sensibilities. And consider ideas that, if they turn out to be
false, could lead to harm if people believed them to be true. In either case,
we don't know whether they are true or false a priori, so only by examining
and debating them can we find out. Finally, let's assume that we're not talking about burning people at the stake or cutting out their tongues but
about discouraging their research and giving their ideas as little publicity
as possible. There is a good case for exploring all ideas relevant to our current concerns, no matter where they lead. The idea that ideas should be
discouraged a priori is inherently self-refuting. Indeed, it is the ultimate
arrogance, as it assumes that one can be so certain about the goodness and
truth of one's own ideas that one is entitled to discourage other people's
opinions from even being examined.

Also, it's hard to imagine any aspect of public life where ignorance or 34
delusion is better than an awareness of the truth, even an unpleasant one.
Only children and madmen engage in "magical thinking," the fallacy that
good things can come true by believing in them or bad things will disappear
by ignoring them or wishing them away. Rational adults want to know the
truth, because any action based on false premises will not have the effects
they desire. Worse, logicians tell us that a system of ideas containing a

contradiction can be used to deduce any statement whatsoever, no matter how absurd. Since ideas are connected to other ideas, sometimes in circuitous and unpredictable ways, choosing to believe something that may not be true, or even maintaining walls of ignorance around some topic, can corrupt all of intellectual life, proliferating error far and wide. In our everyday lives, would we want to be lied to, or kept in the dark by paternalistic "protectors," when it comes to our health or finances or even the weather? In public life, imagine someone saying that we should not do research into global warming or energy shortages because if it found that they were serious the consequences for the economy would be extremely unpleasant. Today's leaders who tacitly take this position are rightly condemned by intellectually responsible people. But why should other unpleasant ideas be treated differently?

There is another argument against treating ideas as dangerous. Many of our moral and political policies are designed to preempt what we know to be the worst features of human nature. The checks and balances in a democracy, for instance, were invented in explicit recognition of the fact that human leaders will always be tempted to arrogate power to themselves. Likewise, our sensitivity to racism comes from an awareness that groups of humans, left to their own devices, are apt to discriminate and oppress other groups, often in ugly ways. History also tells us that a desire to enforce dogma and suppress heretics is a recurring human weakness, one that has led to recurring waves of gruesome oppression and violence. A recognition that there is a bit of Torquemada[1] in everyone should make us wary of any attempt to enforce a consensus or demonize those who challenge it. 35

"Sunlight is the best disinfectant," according to Justice Louis Brandeis's famous case for freedom of thought and expression. If an idea really is false, only by examining it openly can we determine that it is false. At that point we will be in a better position to convince others that it is false than if we had let it fester in private, since our very avoidance of the issue serves as a tacit acknowledgment that it may be true. And if an idea is true, we had better accommodate our moral sensibilities to it, since no good can come from sanctifying a delusion. This might even be easier than the ideaphobes fear. The moral order did not collapse when the earth was shown not to be at the center of the solar system, and so it will survive other revisions of our understanding of how the world works. 36

DANGEROUS TO AIR DANGEROUS IDEAS?

In the best Talmudic tradition of arguing a position as forcefully as possible and then switching sides, let me now present the case for discouraging certain lines of intellectual inquiry. . . . [Alison] Gopnik and [W. Daniel] Hillis offer as their "dangerous idea" the exact opposite of [Daniel] 37

---

[1]*Torquemada:* Tomás de Torquemada (1420–1498), Spanish grand inquisitor.

Gilbert's: They say that it's a dangerous idea for thinkers to air their dangerous ideas. How might such an argument play out?

First, one can remind people that we are all responsible for the foreseeable consequences of our actions, and that includes the consequences of our public statements. Freedom of inquiry may be an important value, according to this argument, but it is not an absolute value, one that overrides all others. We know that the world is full of malevolent and callous people who will use any pretext to justify their bigotry or destructiveness. We must expect that they will seize on the broaching of a topic that seems in sympathy with their beliefs as a vindication of their agenda.

Not only can the imprimatur of scientific debate add legitimacy to toxic ideas, but the mere act of making an idea common knowledge can change its effects. Individuals, for instance, may harbor a private opinion on differences between genders or among ethnic groups but keep it to themselves because of its opprobrium. But once the opinion is aired in public, they may be emboldened to act on their prejudice—not just because it has been publicly ratified but because they must anticipate that everyone else will act on the information. Some people, for example, might discriminate against the members of an ethnic group despite having no pejorative opinion about them, in the expectation that their customers or colleagues will have such opinions and that defying them would be costly. And then there are the effects of these debates on the confidence of the members of the stigmatized groups themselves.

Of course, academics can warn against these abuses, but the qualifications and nitpicking they do for a living may not catch up with the simpler formulations that run on swifter legs. Even if they did, their qualifications might be lost on the masses. We shouldn't count on ordinary people to engage in the clear thinking—some would say the hair-splitting—that would be needed to accept a dangerous idea but not its terrible consequence. Our overriding precept, in intellectual life as in medicine, should be "First, do no harm."

We must be especially suspicious when the danger in a dangerous idea is to someone other than its advocate. Scientists, scholars, and writers are members of a privileged elite. They may have an interest in promulgating ideas that justify their privileges, that blame or make light of society's victims, or that earn them attention for cleverness and iconoclasm. Even if one has little sympathy for the cynical Marxist argument that ideas are always advanced to serve the interest of the ruling class, the ordinary skepticism of a tough-minded intellectual should make one wary of "dangerous" hypotheses that are no skin off the nose of their hypothesizers. (The mind-set that leads us to blind review, open debate, and statements of possible conflicts of interest.)

But don't the demands of rationality always compel us to seek the complete truth? Not necessarily. Rational agents often choose to be ignorant. They may decide not to be in a position where they can receive a threat or be exposed to a sensitive secret. They may choose to avoid being asked an incriminating question, where one answer is damaging, another is dishonest, and a failure to answer is grounds for the questioner to assume the worst (hence the Fifth Amendment protection against being forced to testify against oneself). Scientists test drugs in double-blind studies in which they keep themselves from knowing who got the drug and who got the placebo, and they referee manuscripts anonymously for the same reason. Many people rationally choose not to know the gender of their unborn child, or whether they carry a gene for Huntington's disease, or whether their nominal father is genetically related to them. Perhaps a similar logic would call for keeping socially harmful information out of the public sphere.

INTOLERANCE OF UNPOPULAR IDEAS

As for restrictions on inquiry, every scientist already lives with them. They accede, for example, to the decisions of committees for the protection of human subjects and to policies on the confidentiality of personal information. In 1975, biologists imposed a moratorium on research on recombinant DNA pending the development of safeguards against the release of dangerous microorganisms. The notion that intellectuals have carte blanche in conducting their inquiry is a myth.   43

Though I am more sympathetic to the argument that important ideas be aired than to the argument that they should sometimes be suppressed, I think it is a debate we need to have. Whether we like it or not, science has a habit of turning up discomfiting thoughts, and the Internet has a habit of blowing their cover.   44

Tragically, there are few signs that the debates will happen in the place where we might most expect it: academia. Though academics owe the extraordinary perquisite of tenure to the ideal of encouraging free inquiry and the evaluation of unpopular ideas, all too often academics are the first to try to quash them. The most famous recent example is the outburst of fury and disinformation that resulted when Harvard president Lawrence Summers gave a measured analysis of the multiple causes of women's underrepresentation in science and math departments in elite universities and tentatively broached the possibility that discrimination and hidden barriers were not the only cause.   45

But intolerance of unpopular ideas among academics is an old story. Books like Morton Hunt's *The New Know-Nothings* and Alan Kors and Harvey Silverglate's *The Shadow University* have depressingly shown that universities cannot be counted on to defend the rights of their own heretics and that it's often the court system or the press that has to drag them into   46 policies of tolerance. In government, the intolerance is even more frightening, because the ideas considered there are not just matters of intellectual sport but have immediate and sweeping consequences. Chris Mooney, in *The Republican War on Science*, joins Hunt in showing how corrupt and demagogic legislators are increasingly stifling research findings they find inconvenient to their interests.

Thinking Critically about the Text

What do you think is Pinker's purpose in defending dangerous ideas? What does he want his readers to do after reading this essay? Did he achieve his purpose, in your case? Explain.

Questions on Subject

1. Pinker starts his essay with a list of twenty-two questions, each an example of a "dangerous" idea. What were you thinking as you read Pinker's list? Which questions touched a sensitive nerve for you? Explain.

2. Reread paragraph 32. Pinker writes that "the taboo on questioning sacred values makes sense in the context of personal relationships." Do you agree? Why do you think that Pinker believes that "[i]t makes far less sense in the context of discovering how the world works or running a country"?

3. What does Pinker mean when he says in paragraph 33, "The idea that ideas should be discouraged a priori is inherently self-refuting"?

4. How does Pinker's discussion of rational thinking help to support the ideas presented in the introduction to this chapter on argumentation?

5. In paragraph 46, Pinker writes, "But intolerance of unpopular ideas among academics is an old story." Why is the situation he points to ironic? (Glossary: *Irony*)

Questions on Strategy

1. How does Pinker define "dangerous idea"? (Glossary: *Definition*) Do you agree with his definition?

2. According to Pinker, fear is one of the main factors that contribute to the perception of dangerousness. What examples of fears does Pinker use to illustrate his claim? What other factors contribute to the perception of dangerousness? (Glossary: *Illustration*)

3. According to Pinker, what is the "case for discouraging certain lines of intellectual inquiry" (paragraph 37)? What evidence does he present to support this side of the issue? (Glossary: *Evidence*)

4. How does Pinker support his claim that "intolerance of unpopular ideas among academics is an old story" (paragraph 46)?

5. Pinker concludes his essay in paragraph 46 with a reference to Chris Mooney's *The Republican War on Science*. Is this a partisan reference? If so, does it

damage Pinker's analysis and purpose in this essay? Would you have ended the essay in a different manner? (Glossary: *Beginnings/Endings*) Explain.

Questions on Diction and Vocabulary

1. In paragraph 36, Pinker uses the term *ideaphobes*. What does the term mean?

2. What is the "magical thinking" that Pinker discusses in paragraph 34? Can you think of any examples of magical thinking that have currency today?

Classroom Activity Using Argumentation

Consider the following paragraph from the rough draft of a student paper on Americans' obsession with losing weight. In order to support the claim made in the opening sentence, the student writer wanted to show the extreme actions that people sometimes take to improve their appearance.

> Americans have long been obsessed with thinness — even at the risk of dying. In the 1930s, people took dinitrophenol, an industrial poison, to lose weight. It boosted metabolism but caused blindness and some deaths. Since that time, dieters have experimented with any number of bizarre schemes that seem to work wonders in the short term but often end in disappointment or disaster in the long term. Some weight-loss strategies have even led to life-threatening eating disorders.

Try your hand at revising this paragraph, supplying specific examples of "bizarre schemes" or "weight-loss strategies" that you have tried, observed, or read about. Share your examples with others in your class. Do you think specific examples are more persuasive than generalizations? Which examples best illustrate and support the central argument contained in the writer's topic sentence?

Writing Suggestions

1. Reread the list of twenty-two questions at the beginning of Pinker's essay. After giving them some thought, select one to use as a central example in an essay about the need to debate important ideas no matter how uncomfortable those ideas might make us. Before you start writing, consider the following questions: What about the question I've chosen makes me or others uncomfortable? What are some of the idea's implications if we find it to be true? What if we find it false? What would happen if we simply ignore this question?

2. In a case involving freedom of thought and expression, Justice Louis Brandeis said, "Sunlight is the best disinfectant" (paragraph 36). What do you think he meant? How do you think Justice Brandeis would respond to the proposition that "it's a dangerous idea for thinkers to air their dangerous ideas"? How do you respond to this proposition? Write an essay in which you present your position, and support that position with clear examples from your own experiences or reading.

Two Cheers for Sweatshops

NICHOLAS D. KRISTOF AND SHERYL WUDUNN

Nicholas D. Kristof and Sheryl WuDunn are the first husband-and-wife team to win a Pulitzer Prize for journalism, an award that recognized their work on the democracy movement in Tiananmen Square, China. Together and on their own, they are dynamic, well-traveled professionals with an impressive list of achievements, published books, and awards.

Kristof is a journalist, columnist, and author. He was born in 1959 in Yamhill, Oregon, where he grew up before entering Harvard College. At Harvard he graduated Phi Beta Kappa and then continued his studies at Oxford University's Magdalen College as a Rhodes Scholar. He has been nominated as a Pulitzer Prize finalist six times, and in addition to his award with WuDunn, won a second Prize for his writings focused on the genocide in Darfur. The celebrated Bishop Desmond Tutu called Kristof an "honorary African" for focusing the world's attention on the serious concerns of that part of the world.

Sheryl WuDunn, a third-generation Chinese American, grew up in New York and graduated from Cornell University before earning her M.B.A. from Harvard University and her M.P.A. from Princeton University. In the business world, WuDunn is a double-bottom-line banker, meaning that she strives to be financially competitive while at the same time forward-thinking socially, especially as concerns world economies and societies.

Together Kristof and WuDunn have coauthored three best-sellers, including the 2009 title *Half the Sky: Turning Oppression into Opportunity for Women Worldwide* (2009). *Half the Sky* is now a global movement, bringing together Web sites, online games, blogs, a 2012 PBS television series, and more to further its mission.

In the following article, first published in the *New York Times* on September 24, 2000, Kristof and WuDunn take a rather surprising argumentative position in favor of sweatshops as the best alternative for workers to climb out of a desperate set of economic circumstances, especially in Southeast Asia.

Preparing to Read

Are you comfortable buying apparel that is produced under such labels as Nike, Reebok, and Gap knowing that the goods were produced in sweatshops that pay workers but a small fraction of what workers in other parts of the world might make? Explain.

I t was breakfast time, and the food stand in the village in northeastern 1
Thailand was crowded. Maesubin Sisoipha, the middle-aged woman
cooking the food, was friendly, her portions large, and the price right.
For the equivalent of about 5 cents, she offered a huge green mango
leaf filled with rice, fish paste, and fried beetles. It was a hearty breakfast,
if one didn't mind the odd antenna left sticking in one's teeth.

One of the half-dozen men and women sitting on a bench eating was a 2
sinewy, bare-chested laborer in his late 30s named Mongkol Latlakorn. It
was a hot, lazy day, and so we started chatting idly about the food and,
eventually, our families. Mongkol mentioned that his daughter, Darin, was
fifteen, and his voice softened as he spoke of her. She was beautiful and
smart, and her father's hopes rested on her.

"Is she in school?" we asked. 3

"Oh, no," Mongkol said, his eyes sparkling with amusement. "She's 4
working in a factory in Bangkok. She's making clothing for export to
America." He explained that she was paid $2 a day for a nine-hour shift,
six days a week.

"It's dangerous work," Mongkol added. "Twice the needles went right 5
through her hands. But the managers bandaged up her hands, and both
times she got better again and went back to work."

"How terrible," we murmured sympathetically. 6

Mongkol looked up, puzzled. "It's good pay," he said. "I hope she can 7
keep that job. There's all this talk about factories closing now, and she said
there are rumors that her factory might close. I hope that doesn't happen.
I don't know what she would do then."

He was not, of course, indifferent to his daughter's suffering; he simply 8
had a different perspective from ours — not only when it came to food but
also when it came to what constituted desirable work.

Nothing captures the difference in mind-set between East and West 9
more than attitudes toward sweatshops. Nike and other American companies have been hammered in the Western press over the last decade for
producing shoes, toys, and other products in grim little factories with dis-
mal conditions. Protests against sweatshops and the dark forces of globalization that they seem to represent have become common at meetings of the
World Bank and the World Trade Organization and, this month, at a
World Economic Forum in Australia, livening up the scene for Olympic
athletes arriving for the competition. Yet sweatshops that seem brutal from
the vantage point of an American sitting in his living room can appear
tantalizing to a Thai laborer getting by on beetles.

Fourteen years ago, we moved to Asia and began reporting there. Like 10
most Westerners, we arrived in the region outraged at sweatshops. In time,
though, we came to accept the view supported by most Asians: that the

campaign against sweatshops risks harming the very people it is intended to help. For beneath their grime, sweatshops are a clear sign of the industrial revolution that is beginning to reshape Asia.

This is not to praise sweatshops. Some managers are brutal in the way   11
they house workers in firetraps, expose children to dangerous chemicals, deny bathroom breaks, demand sexual favors, force people to work double shifts, or dismiss anyone who tries to organize a union. Agitation for improved safety conditions can be helpful, just as it was in ninteenth-century Europe. But Asian workers would be aghast at the idea of American consumers boycotting certain toys or clothing in protest. The simplest way to help the poorest Asians would be to buy more from sweatshops, not less.

> The campaign against sweatshops risks harming the very people it is intended to help.

On our first extended trip to China, in 1987, we traveled to the Pearl   12
River delta in the south of the country. There we visited several factories, including one in the boomtown of Dongguan, where about one hundred female workers sat at workbenches stitching together bits of leather to make purses for a Hong Kong company. We chatted with several women as their fingers flew over their work and asked about their hours.

"I start at about 6:30, after breakfast, and go until about 7 p.m.,"   13
explained one shy teenage girl. "We break for lunch, and I take half an hour off then."

"You do this six days a week?"   14

"Oh, no. Every day."   15

"Seven days a week?"   16

"Yes." She laughed at our surprise. "But then I take a week or two off   17
at Chinese New Year to go back to my village."

The others we talked to all seemed to regard it as a plus that the factory   18
allowed them to work long hours. Indeed, some had sought out this factory precisely because it offered them the chance to earn more.

"It's actually pretty annoying how hard they want to work," said the   19
factory manager, a Hong Kong man. "It means we have to worry about security and have a supervisor around almost constantly."

It sounded pretty dreadful, and it was. We and other journalists wrote   20
about the problems of child labor and oppressive conditions in both China and South Korea. But, looking back, our worries were excessive. Those sweatshops tended to generate the wealth to solve the problems they created. If Americans had reacted to the horror stories in the 1980s by curbing imports of those sweatshop products, then neither southern China nor South Korea would have registered as much progress as they have today.

The truth is, those grim factories in Dongguan and the rest of southern   21
China contributed to a remarkable explosion of wealth. In the years since
our first conversations there, we've returned many times to Dongguan and
the surrounding towns and seen the transformation. Wages have risen
from about $50 a month to $250 a month or more today. Factory conditions have improved as businesses have scrambled to attract and keep the
best laborers. A private housing market has emerged, and video arcades
and computer schools have opened to cater to workers with rising incomes.
A hint of a middle class has appeared — as has China's closest thing to a
Western-style independent newspaper, *Southern Weekend.*

Partly because of these tens of thousands of sweatshops, China's econ-   22
omy has become one of the hottest in the world. Indeed, if China's thirty
provinces were counted as individual countries, then the twenty fastest-
growing countries in the world between 1978 and 1995 would all have
been Chinese. When Britain launched the Industrial Revolution in the late
eighteenth century, it took fifty-eight years for per capita output to double.
In China, per capita output has been doubling every ten years.

In fact, the most vibrant parts of Asia are nearly all in what might   23
be called the Sweatshop Belt, from China and South Korea to Malaysia,
Indonesia, and even Bangladesh and India. Today these sweatshop countries control about one-quarter of the global economy. As the industrial revolution spreads through China and India, there are good reasons
to think that Asia will continue to pick up speed. Some World Bank fore-
casts show Asia's share of global gross domestic product rising to 55 to
60 percent by about 2025 — roughly the West's share at its peak half
a century ago. The sweatshops have helped lay the groundwork for a
historic economic realignment that is putting Asia back on its feet.
Countries are rebounding from the economic crisis of 1997–98 and the
sweatshops — seen by Westerners as evidence of moribund economies —
actually reflect an industrial revolution that is raising living standards in
the East.

Of course, it may sound silly to say that sweatshops offer a route to   24
prosperity, when wages in the poorest countries are sometimes less than $1
a day. Still, for an impoverished Indonesian or Bangladeshi woman with a
handful of kids who would otherwise drop out of school and risk dying of
mundane diseases like diarrhea, $1 or $2 a day can be a life-transforming
wage.

This was made abundantly clear in Cambodia, when we met a forty-   25
year-old woman named Nhem Yen, who told us why she moved to an area
with particularly lethal malaria. "We needed to eat," she said. "And here
there is wood, so we thought we could cut it and sell it."

But then Nhem Yen's daughter and son-in-law both died of malaria,   26
leaving her with two grandchildren and five children of her own. With just
one mosquito net, she had to choose which children would sleep protected
and which would sleep exposed.

In Cambodia, a large mosquito net costs $5. If there had been a sweat-   27
shop in the area, however harsh or dangerous, Nhem Yen would have leapt
at the chance to work in it, to earn enough to buy a net big enough to cover
all her children.

For all the misery they can engender, sweatshops at least offer a pre-   28
carious escape from the poverty that is the developing world's greatest
problem. Over the past fifty years, countries like India resisted foreign
exploitation, while countries that started at a similar economic level — like
Taiwan and South Korea — accepted sweatshops as the price of development. Today there can be no doubt about which approach worked better.
Taiwan and South Korea are modern countries with low rates of infant
mortality and high levels of education; in contrast, every year 3.1 million
Indian children die before the age of five, mostly from diseases of poverty
like diarrhea.

The effect of American pressure on sweatshops is complicated.   29
While it clearly improves conditions at factories that produce branded
merchandise for companies like Nike, it also raises labor costs across
the board. That encourages less well established companies to mecha-
nize and to reduce the number of employees needed. The upshot is to
help people who currently have jobs in Nike plants but to risk jobs for
others. The only thing a country like Cambodia has to offer is terribly
cheap wages; if companies are scolded for paying those wages, they will
shift their manufacturing to marginally richer areas like Malaysia or
Mexico.

Sweatshop monitors do have a useful role. They can compel factories   30
to improve safety. They can also call attention to the impact of sweatshops
on the environment. The greatest downside of industrialization is not
exploitation of workers but toxic air and water. In Asia each year, three
million people die from the effects of pollution. The factories springing up
throughout the region are far more likely to kill people through the chemicals they expel than through terrible working conditions.

By focusing on these issues, by working closely with organizations and   31
news media in foreign countries, sweatshops can be improved. But refusing to buy sweatshop products risks making Americans feel good while
harming those we are trying to help. As a Chinese proverb goes, "First
comes the bitterness, then there is sweetness and wealth and honor for
10,000 years."

Thinking Critically about the Text

Does the claim made by Kristof and WuDunn that they do not want to praise sweatshops weaken their argument, or does it serve to strengthen it? Explain.

Questions on Subject

1. How would you describe the two different mind-sets that Westerners and Easterners bring to the question of the value of sweatshops?

2. What is so bad about sweatshops, according to the authors?

3. What environmental hazards are caused by sweatshops? Why are these hazards more harmful than poor working conditions?

4. Why do the authors say "The effect of American pressure on sweatshops is complicated"?

5. What is the meaning of the Chinese proverb that Kristof and WuDunn use to end their essay?

Questions on Strategy

1. What is Kristof and WuDunn's thesis? (Glossary: *Thesis*) Where in the essay do they offer their thesis?

2. Are Kristof and WuDunn authorities on their subject? Why, or why not?

3. Why do you suppose that, in paragraph 2, Kristof and WuDunn begin their essay with an up-close-and-personal look at Mongkol Latlakorn?

4. What evidence do the authors cite to bolster their argument that without sweatshops little economic progress would be made for Asian workers? (Glossary: *Evidence*)

5. Review Kristof and WuDunn's use of dialogue. How has it enabled them to show rather than tell? (Glossary: *Dialogue*)

Questions on Diction and Vocabulary

1. Use your dictionary or the Web to dig into the definition of the term *sweatshop*. What is the history of the term?

2. What is the "Sweatshop Belt" (paragraph 23)? What countries does it include, according to the authors?

Classroom Activity for Argumentation

An excellent way to gain some experience in formulating an argumentative position on an issue, and perhaps to establish a thesis, is to engage in a debate with someone who is on the other side of the question. When we listen to arguments and think of refutations and counterarguments, we have a chance to make a rehearsal and revision of our position before it is put in written form.

To try this out, use Kristof and WuDunn's exploration of sweatshops in Asia. Divide the class into pro and con sides — those for keeping sweatshops open and those in favor of eliminating them. Each side should elect a spokesperson to present its arguments before the class. Finally, have the class make some estimate of the success of each side in (1) articulating its position, (2) presenting ideas and evidence to support that position, and (3) convincing the audience of its position. The exercise should give you a good idea of the kind of work that's involved in preparing a written argument.

Writing Suggestions

1. **Writing with Sources.** Research the issue of environmental hazards as they exist in sweatshops around the world. What chemicals and types of pollution have been documented and what solutions have been sought to reduce these hazards, if any? Write an argument in favor of any solutions you discover in your research or for what must still be done. For models of and advice on integrating sources in your essay, see Chapters 14 and 15.

2. **Writing with Sources.** Kristof and WuDunn write that sweatshop operators are reluctant to invest in labor-saving equipment and modern manufacturing systems because such measures will force the operators to increase what they charge for manufactured goods, thus sending corporations elsewhere in search of cheaper labor. Investigate the merits of this argument through research in your library and on the Internet, and argue for or against the author's position. For models of and advice on integrating sources in your essay, see Chapters 14 and 15.

---

 e-Pages

How Many Slaves Work for You?
SLAVERY FOOTPRINT

Go to bedfordstmartins.com/subjectandstrategy for a companion video and study questions about the global economic supply chain.

ARGUMENT CLUSTER

Sports and Doping:
Is There a Solution?

In June of 2012, the United States Anti-Doping Agency (USADA) accused seven-time Tour de France cycling legend Lance Armstrong of using illegal drugs. Within months, they stripped him of his seven medals and his Olympic bronze medal. He was banned from the sport, generating a scandal centered on both the ambiguity of his guilt (he had repeatedly denied doping) and the integrity of the sport. After years of being lauded as an icon for both his racing accomplishments and his support for cancer patients through his Livestrong foundation, it was troubling to think he had violated the law, perhaps even repeatedly. In January of 2013, he put rumors to rest when he admitted in a televised interview that he had doped throughout his career. The public outcry was a mix of shock, resignation, confusion, and questions about where his situation should fall in the space between "right" and "wrong," if there's ever such a middle ground.

Unfortunately, the high-profile case is just one of many in a long line of doping controversies in the sports world. It will undoubtedly not be the last. The use of performance-enhancing drugs (PEDs) is ever on the rise, and arguments over how to control their use is the hottest topic in sports today. The causes and effects of doping are not confined to the sports world alone, however. They spill over into the world beyond the athletic arena.

The articles in this cluster on sports and doping raise important questions about the human condition, what it means to be "normal," and the limitations of the human body. They delve into the meaning and nature of sports, what the public wants from sports, what athletes are trying to achieve, and how far athletes are willing to go to win. They try to analyze why winning is so important and the role money plays in sports. At their core, they all try to navigate the dangers of PEDs and pinpoint whether and to what extent we must be cautious about using them. Of more recent interest is the provocative argument that because doping has become so prevalent in sports, we have already lost the battle against it. We should admit defeat, legalize the use of PEDs, and move on to more meaningful and practical discussions of governance and control. Doing so would have a number of benefits, not the least among them the health and welfare of all those who engage in sports.

We begin this cluster of arguments with journalist Ian Steadman's essay "How Sports Would Be Better with Doping," in which he contextualizes the controversy and presents the argument for legalizing the use of PEDs. We turn next to sports writer Reid Forgrave's poignant essay "No Easy Answers for PEDs, Youth" on the tragic case of high school football player Taylor Hooton, whose use of steroids led to his suicide at the age of sixteen and to the questions and answers that might have saved his life. In the third selection, "How to Get Doping Out of Sports," former professional cyclist Jonathan Vaughters argues that cyclists must choose to compete "clean" by refusing to buy into the argument that they need to dope to compete on a level playing field.

e-Pages

The e-Pages selection for this cluster is "Is Doping Wrong?" by the noted bioethicist Peter Singer, who takes issue with fellow philosopher Julian Savulescu's argument for dropping the ban on performance-enhancing drugs. Go to **bedfordstmartins.com/subjectandstrategy** to read Singer's argument and explore his perspective with study questions.

Preparing to Read

Do you think you and your friends — and especially those who played sports in high school and may be playing sports in college — have an adequate understanding of the issues involved in the use of PEDs? Are you fully aware of the inherent dangers of drugging? Do you know what drives people to use PEDs? Do you think coaches, schools, and athletic administrators are doing a good job of educating athletes in how to avoid PEDs, and how to get athletes off of them if they are already users?

How Sports Would Be Better with Doping

IAN STEADMAN

Ian Steadman is a staff journalist based in *Wired* magazine's London office. He was born in Berkeley, California, in 1987 and spent his childhood on the outskirts of San Francisco before moving with his family to the United Kingdom. He earned his B.A. with honors in philosophy at Nottingham University and then his M.A. with honors in magazine journalism at City University London. He has written extensively on science, technology, art, music, sports, and politics for a variety of small publications in London and around the United Kingdom. As a British American he divides his time between the two countries, though he spends a majority of his time in London.

Steadman's article "How Sports Would Be Better with Doping" was first published on Wired.com on September 10, 2012. He tells us that his article drew some interesting responses: "Some people have pointed out that the article rests upon the assumption that sports are only worthwhile as long as they're a spectacle, or at the very least that the spectacle is the most important consideration. It ignores that many people would train for sports even if nobody was watching — and the most important thing for them is that they remain true to the spirit of the sport and to their inner integrity rather than them performing for the benefit of audiences. The doping argument also doesn't really apply to team sports like soccer or basketball, where the benefits of doping and augmentation aren't so clear-cut. They don't contribute specifically either to team spirit or individual moments of flair, which aren't factors in track and field sports."

P oor Lance Armstrong. The seven-time Tour de France winner 1 has been stripped of his famous victories by the United States Anti-Doping Agency, which claims he used illicit performance-enhancing drugs. Armstrong never tested positive for anything, but his decision to quit fighting the charges has been seen by some as tantamount to a confession. So why shouldn't he be punished? Doping is, after all, widely considered the ultimate sin of professional athletes.

Dwain Chambers, the UK's fastest sprinter in the 100 meters, was 2 banned from competing in the Olympic Games after testing positive for the anabolic steroid tetrahydrogestrinone. He claimed in his autobiography that at least half of the U.S. racing team at the 2008 Summer Games used illegal substances. The battle to control drug use never, ever seems to end. Why don't we accept doping will always happen and legalize it?

More than 1,000 people, including 150 doctors, collected and analyzed some 6,250 blood and urine samples during the 2012 Summer Olympics. It was the most aggressive anti-doping campaign the Olympics had ever seen.

That may seem crazy, but a pro-doping culture might be the inevitable future of sport. It gets to the heart of what it is we want when we compete in and watch sports, and what we consider to be "normal" humanity. An athlete who takes a performance-enhancing drug is relying on something he doesn't actually have to improve performance—whether that drug is naturally occurring or designed by scientists, whether that extra help skews their genetics to alter their humanity. 3

Performance-enhancing drugs are that great leveler, that tool for athletes to bridge the unfair natural gap.

As training, coaching, nutrition, and equipment has been perfected, the best times of the best athletes have been increasing at a slower and slower rate. There are numerous estimates of what the fastest possible 100-meter time will be, based on extrapolating current trends. The most recent study found that 9.48 seconds was the predicted "fastest" time. 4

Eventually, athletes will reach a wall, and then we face the question of how to keep sport interesting. We could start measuring to the thousandth of a second, say, but how interesting would it be if every race were decided by margins undetectable to the naked eye? There's no narrative of success there, nothing as iconic as Usain Bolt strolling across the line with the swagger of a man who knows he has utterly destroyed his competition. Such accuracy is 5 also difficult to pull off in places like swimming pools, for instance, where distances of a couple of millimeters may be needed to decide a race.

That's where doping comes in. After all, it's not like it's going to go away, argues ethics professor Julian Savulescu of the Oxford Centre of Neuroethics. 6

"The war on doping has failed," he says. "Lance Armstrong never failed a doping test, despite being subjected to thousands. Nearly every recent winner of the Tour de France has been implicated in doping. About 80 percent of 100-meter finalists are or will be implicated in doping. The fact is that blood doping and use of growth hormone have not been possible to detect, and because doping mimics normal physiological process it will always be possible to beat the test." Thus, we should embrace the inevitable, and control doping as best we can. 7

This is a view echoed by bioethicist professor Andy Miah of the University of the West of Scotland. He argues that we should have a "World Pro-Doping Agency" to complement the World Anti-Doping Agency [WADA]. "At the moment athletes look to find dangerous substances with significant health risks, but with the correct framework in place athletes can know the risks involved," he says. 8

It makes sense to make sure that athletes know what they are ingesting, as opposed to the current free-for-all which can lead to awful side effects for athletes. Anabolic steroids, for instance, have adverse side effects which range from acne, infertility, and impotence, to hypertension, psychosis, and cardiovascular disease. A regulatory body that lets athletes know what they're ingesting would improve athletic health. 9

However, this doesn't address the issue of authenticity and integrity that professional sport is built upon. After all, cyclist Bradley Wiggins could easily get up a mountain faster if he was using a motorbike. Our societal conception of sport as competition between opponents rests on a certain sense of human nature—what will decide the battle is determination, effort, grit, and sweat. We can help the honest athlete compete with the doper by allowing both to use drugs, but that seems to start picking apart why we value sport. 10

Savulescu doesn't see this as a problem. 11

"Steroids augment the effects of training," he says. "They are like more effective training, which has been achieved in other ways. That does not corrupt the nature of sport. Caffeine is a performance enhancer which was banned but is now allowed. The relaxation has done nothing to affect the spectacle, nature, or definition of sport. It has just meant we don't have to waste time working out how much Coca-Cola an athlete has drunk." 12

People still need to train to make the most of their drugs, then. It doesn't help to look at sport as being a battle of wills if, as we've already 13 seen, the natural limits of the human body are increasingly the reason for success. I could try all I want, but I will never make it as a professional gymnast because I'm just too tall and awkward. The same applies to many athletes now who are never going to be able to beat Jessica Ennis, no matter how much they try.

We as spectators push athletes to be the absolute best, and in the process create the culture where doping is needed to reach those heights. It increasingly feels difficult to reconcile the purity of asking athletes to do whatever it takes to win as long as that isn't going beyond an arbitrary definition of "natural." Performance-enhancing drugs are that great leveler, that tool for athletes to bridge the unfair natural gap. 14

"Doping is not against the spirit of sport," Savulescu says. "It has always [been] part of the human spirit to use knowledge to make oneself better and doping has been a part of sport since its beginning. Doping should only be banned when it is significantly harmful relative to the inherent risks of sport, or against the spirit of a particular sport. For example, drugs to reduce tremor like beta blockers in archery or shooting are against the spirit of that sport as it is inherently a test of ability to control nerves. Drugs which removed fear in boxing would be against the spirit of boxing. But blood doping up to a haematocrit [percentage of red blood cells in blood] of 50 percent is safe and not against the spirit of cycling." 15

Miah also points out that there is a lot of legal doping going on already, such as altitude chambers, which recreate the experience of training in thinner air to give athletes a bigger oxygen capacity. WADA approved such chambers in 2006 because they were felt to recreate a natural phenomenon. But then what's the difference between that and injecting someone with natural growth hormones, for instance? 16

This points toward the fundamental problem many have with doping: its implications for what it is to be human. Athletics is at the forefront of that debate. Just look at Oscar Pistorius. 17

"He symbolizes the coming together of the two Olympic movements," says Miah. "If Pierre de Cobourtin founded the Olympic movement today, seeing how the gap between [the Olympic and Paralympic Games] is closing, there would be only one Games." 18

Pistorius represents a future where our ability to transcend what a "normal" human being is will also herald the end of a distinction between the able-bodied and paralympians — and drugs are a big part of that. 19

That's because, as Miah points out, human enhancement will become more and more common in everyday life. "The current problems will become less apparent because the athletes of the future will be enhanced before they even begin training for an event," he says. "Look at the human genome, for instance. Twenty years ago it took thousands of dollars to 20 sequence just one man, now it costs $5,000. That process will only get cheaper. The continual pursuit of enhanced life will lead to these things becoming normalized."

We can see, from the use of drugs by students to improve studying to the medication of children to keep them calm, that personal enhancement through drugs is more and more common. As genetic profiling becomes more common, too, that will also herald huge changes as people are screened for diseases at birth that they may only have come to discover in later life. You can already see this as an issue when it comes to so-called gene doping, where techniques used in gene therapy may be used to switch on or off certain genes associated with, for instance, improved muscle mass, or faster acceleration. 21

Doping, then, becomes part of the grand question that humanity is beginning to ask itself as nature is increasingly improved upon with technology. Just as innovations in Formula 1 cars eventually filter down to your humble hatchback, those pills and serums that athletes take to shave another 0.01 second off a personal best may well herald a common life-enhancing drug later down the line. 22

"What is a normal human?" asks Miah. "Athletes in the NFL have 20/15 vision, which is better than normal. People are concerned about genetic identification, that the use of genetic tests will be normal. People may recoil from that, thinking that it may compromise what it means to be human, but I don't think it changes any kind of internal human essence." 23

That may be the crux. If there were to be an Olympiad in, let's say . . . thirty years' time, then will there be a Paralympiad alongside? Or will there in fact be three, with a new Olympiad for those who choose to enhance their bodies beyond what they were born with? Whatever happens, it will be a reflection of wider society's attitudes toward human enhancement beyond what is natural, or normal. 24

Thinking Critically about the Text

What kinds of legal doping are already a part of some athletes' training? How does one make the distinction between legal and illegal doping?

Examining the Issue

1. What is Steadman's thesis in this essay and where does he state it? (Glossary: *Thesis*) Why do you think Steadman says his thesis "may seem crazy"?

2. Why does what we consider "normal" figure into issues concerning doping?

3. If Julian Savulescu and Andy Miah are some of the earliest scientists who favor doping, what role does Steadman play in the argument as a writer?

4. If the use of drugs in sports is made legal, will the role of training be diminished?

5. In paragraph 15, Steadman quotes Savulescu's statement that "Doping is not against the spirit of sport." How does Savulescu support this statement?

6. Who is Oscar Pistorius, and how does he figure into Steadman's argument?

7. What examples does Steadman give that suggest that we may already be on the way to using drugs for human enhancement?

No Easy Answers for PEDs, Youth

REID FORGRAVE

Reid Forgrave is a national sports writer for FOXSports .com. He was born in 1979 in Pittsburgh, Pennsylvania, and he grew up in Pennsylvania and in Columbus, Ohio. Forgrave is a 2001 graduate of the University of Missouri with a B.A. in journalism with an emphasis in magazine writing. He was formerly a writer for several daily newspapers. Asked to comment on his article, he wrote the following: "The subject of steroid abuse in professional sports is among the most over-examined questions in sports today. The most frequent position is one of moralizing on the evils of steroids and the ruining of the sanctity of the game without examining why, exactly, steroids are bad for sports. That was the point of this essay: To talk with a parent whose son tragically killed himself after delving into the performance-enhancing drug culture. I believe in putting faces on social issues instead of just discussing them in abstract, moralizing tones. This is what makes Don Hooton's story a powerful one."

Forgrave's "No Easy Answer for PEDs, Youth" first appeared on FOXSports. com on August 30, 2012. The article allowed readers to comment, creating an online discussion space for complicated questions about the moral, legal, and policy implications of PED use.

Perhaps we should not base the future of American professional sport on one family's private tragedy. Perhaps we should write off Taylor Hooton as an anomaly. Perhaps we shouldn't be swayed by the emotional testimony of one grieving father and should instead put our faith in researchers who use the fact-based world of science to make humanity bigger, faster, stronger, smarter. 1

Perhaps we should just listen to the reasons some angry people have given Don Hooton for his teenage son's 2003 suicide—that Hooton was a bad father, that his son was suffering from a mental disorder, that the sixteen-year-old should have had liver tests done and tracked his performance-enhancing drug use better—instead of putting the blame squarely on the shoulders of the steroids the tall, lanky pitcher was using to put on muscle and make the varsity team. 2

It would be easier if this were the case of just one boy who went too far. Wouldn't it? 3

But perhaps we should listen to the tragic story of Don Hooton's youngest son. And perhaps we should listen carefully, very carefully, as 4

Hooton talks about his boy in honest, frank tones. Because this family's private tragedy might just tell us more than we'd ever comfortably want to know about how performance-enhancing drug use at the elite level of sport trickles down to our youth.

A parent whose child has died loves to remember the best parts, and 5 this is the case with Don Hooton. Hooton remembers how Taylor had a 3.8 GPA at Plano West Senior High School in Texas. He remembers how he'd be the only kid to walk up to the group of adults, offer up a firm hand-shake, and look them in the eye. He remembers how, not long before Taylor's suicide, the boy took a bus to Florida for a Southern Baptist church camp, strode into the ocean, and got baptized in the surf.

But it is also the case with Don Hooton that he remembers Taylor's 6 worst parts, the steroid-fueled tailspin that ended in his suicide, and these are the parts that are difficult to hear.

It was his junior year when Taylor's coach told the 6-foot-2, 180-pound 7 kid that he needed to put on 20 pounds to make varsity. Taylor knew half his team was already juicing, so why shouldn't he? Hooton remembers his son's rapid weight gain, which saw him put on 30 pounds in the spring. He remembers the puffy face and the acne on his back. He remembers the bad breath. He remembers the violent outbursts. He remembers finally adding all these symptoms of steroid use together, taking Taylor to a therapist, and the therapist recommending Taylor quit cold turkey.

And he remembers those final weeks of Taylor's life, where his body 8 went from an overload of testosterone to none at all, and when he fell into a deep depression that ended in his death.

What does Taylor Hooton's ill-advised (and, it must be noted, unsu- 9 pervised) performance-enhancing drug use have to do with the multi-billion-dollar business of American professional sport in 2012?

Nothing. 10

And everything. We have Lance Armstrong pleading no contest to the 11 doping prosecutors and having his seven Tour de France titles stripped away. We have the top hitter in the National League, Melky Cabrera, ban-ished for the rest of the season for failing a PED test, coming after last year's National League MVP, Ryan Braun, escaped suspension on a technicality. We have a sport-obsessed public which either cynically assumes every pro-fessional or Olympic sport is dirty, or which just as cynically doesn't care.

And we have a discussion that centers on things like PED's effect on 12 an athlete's legacy and avoids the bigger issue.

Which is this: How does a tacit acceptance of performance-enhancing 13 drug use in elite sport seep into the rest of society?

On a recent afternoon I posed this question to Hooton, who has testi- 14 fied before Congress on the ills of PEDs and who runs a foundation in his son's memory. I also asked him this: What if researchers came up with an entirely safe drug that enhanced human performance? What if that super-drug, in the style of soma in "Brave New World," became legalized and accepted?

"I can't imagine what it would look like if there was not just tacit approval but also legal and medical approval of this," Hooton told FOXSports.com. "At the very core here, the 'Brave New World' kind of stuff takes us beyond what we're here to do as humans, as human souls. Sport is about fair play. It's honor. It's integrity. It's hard work. It's you and me going up against each other and competing. Not seeing who can get [the] next best drug that's undetectable. Whatever drugs are legalized, the next drug will be a step beyond and a step more risky. Then you get into genetic engineering. Where do you stop?"

I have no clear answer here. I cannot tell the ethical difference between Lasik surgery that helps a hitter's vision, and supplements at a health-food store that help a hitter's power. I do not know where to draw the line between a drug and a supplement. I do not know the proper way to punish professional athletes who cross that line. I do not know whether legalizing some performance-enhancing drugs would put the drugs into the safer realm of medical supervision — or whether it would ingrain the problem even deeper.

It is one of the most confounding questions in sports today.

I cannot tell you why I am against performance-enhancing drug use in professional sports, only that I am. I hate that elite sports can become a competition between which team has the better chemist instead of which team has the most talent and works hardest. I wonder if our win-at-all-costs society will have us injecting our kids with "safe" drugs that can make them perfect little humans, or genetically designing our kids to be tall, left-handed pitchers. I worry if the energy drinks I happily consume are just one step on our society's slippery slope to the belief that better performance can be found in a bottle, not inside the human soul.

> I wonder if our win-at-all-costs society will have us injecting our kids with "safe" drugs that can make them perfect little humans.

And I'm terrified when I hear statistics like this: More than half a million U.S. high school students are believed to have used illegal anabolic steroids.

The foundation of NFL legend Dick Butkus runs a program, Play Clean, that discourages youth from succumbing to performance-enhancing drug pressures.

"You want the stigma of being a cheater? I guess it doesn't bother 21 some people," Butkus told FOXSports.com. "Everyone feels they're entitled to everything they can get by hook or crook. But that means there's so much pressure on these kids, with their parents and their coaches."

Science that improves the human condition always looks great on 22 paper, and it always comes with unknown, far-flung consequences. The combustion engine led to human mobility but also to climate change. Atomic energy was the energy of the future until it became a weapon of mass destruction. Prescription medications were our way to lead happier, healthier lives until we began to abuse them en masse.

"If I have a pill, and you can take the pill once a day and it gives you 23 the effect of 1½ hours of exercise, picks up your heart rate and you get the benefit of exercise, would you take it?" asked Jeffrey Tanji, a sports medicine physician at the University of California-Davis. "But there's something about the process. You want to believe that when people exercise, the process of exercise, you think that while doing it it's good for [the] brain and does something. You don't want to shortcut. It's a means to an end."

Yet often the end is, simply, money. 24

"This is a very financially endowed phenomenon," said Dr. Gary 25 Wadler, an expert on drug use in sports and former chair of the World Anti-Doping Agency banned substances committee. "The marketing gurus have recognized that there's an opportunity to make money. When you get down to it, with doping and supplements, it's all about money. Money made by baseball contracts and football contracts. . . . That's a very seductive message out there."

It's one thing if the message seduces professional athletes, ruins the 26 supposed sanctity of professional sports, and lands a few of the ones who get caught on the suspension list.

But it's quite another if that message trickles down to a young athlete 27 like Taylor Hooton. Which, in this society that worships our sports heroes, is inevitable.

"Across society we are sending signals to our children that these drugs 28 are OK," Don Hooton said. "I just don't accept the hypothetical that this stuff can ever be made safe."

Thinking Critically about the Text

Discuss Forgrave's use of a powerful example as his argumentative technique in this essay. How well has it worked for you as a reader? How well do you think it might work for others?

Examining the Issue

1. What is Forgrave's thesis in this essay? Where does he state it?

2. What argumentative strategy does Forgrave use in the first four paragraphs of his essay? How effective did you find his approach? Explain.

3. Why do you suppose Forgrave thinks that the story of Taylor Hooton needs to be told? (Glossary: *Narration*)

4. In your own words, what happened to Taylor Hooton? Do you know of similar situations? Explain.

5. Does it help or hurt his argument for Forgrave to say the following: "I cannot tell you why I am against performance-enhancing drug use in professional sports, only that I am"? Is his statement true in the light of what he says elsewhere in his essay?

6. For Forgrave, what role does money play in PED use?

7. What does Forgrave fear will happen if PEDs are legalized in professional sports? Do you share his view? Explain.

How to Get Doping Out of Sports

JONATHAN VAUGHTERS

Jonathan Vaughters, a former professional cyclist, was born in 1973 in suburban Denver, Colorado. He now manages the Garmin-Sharp professional cycling team, which employs former dopers who have chosen to adhere to a no-doping policy. He began his career in the 1980s, and in 1993 he came in second in the Tour of Venezuela. Choosing not to go to college, he left for Spain hoping to get noticed in European racing circles. In 1997, back in the United States after gaining recognition abroad, he became U.S. National Time Trial Champion and came in third in the National Road Race. Subsequently, Vaughters has been a part of many teams and has had many cycling achievements, none more recognizable than being on the team of Lance Armstrong's first Tour de France victory.

In the following essay, first published in the New York Times on August 11, 2012, Vaughters argues that the dream he had when he was in middle school to become an elite cyclist was ultimately taken from him by a lack of choices, and that we must find a better way to once again allow such dreams to live.

1 Why does an athlete dope? I know why, because I faced that choice.

2 My life on a bike started in middle school. When the buzzer on my Goofy clock snapped on at 5:30 a.m., I popped out of bed with excitement and purpose. Rushing down the stairs, I stretched twenty some odd layers of still baggy spandex onto my 90-pound skeleton and flew out of the garage. Into the dark, freezing Colorado morning I rode. For the next 30 miles, I pushed my heart rate as high as it would go and the pedals as fast as they would go, giving various extremities frostbite and giving my parents cause to question my sanity.

3 These early rides make up many of my memories from my teenage years: the crashes, the adrenaline, and the discipline of training every day. But the most vivid memory from those rides was how I dreamed.

4 As I sped through the neighborhoods of suburban Denver, my mind was anywhere but. I was climbing the great alpine passes of the Tour de France. Erased from my mind were the bullies at school, the money troubles at home, and the sad fact that no one wanted to go to homecoming with me. I found escape in this dream, and when I returned to reality,

This graphic accompanied Vaughters's original article. How does it illustrate his thesis?

I decided there was no amount of hard work, suffering, discipline, and sacrifice that would keep me from achieving this dream. Determination didn't begin to describe what I felt inside. I felt destined.

Achieving childhood dreams is a hard road. I found that to be only truer as the years and miles passed. First, there is the physical effort of riding 20,000 miles a year for ten straight years to even get within spitting distance of ever riding the Tour de France. Then comes the strain on your family as they try to support, or at least understand, such a singular focus. Next, the loss of friends and social contact. While most of my friends were at prom, I was in bed early for a race the next day. During graduation, I drove my mom's '78 Oldsmobile across the country to a race where I might get "noticed." And while most kids went on to college, I went to a cold-water apartment in Spain, hoping to make it big.

People who end up living their dreams are not those who are lucky and gifted, but those who are stubborn, resolute, and willing to sacrifice. Now, imagine you've paid the dues, you've done the work, you've got the talent, and your resolve is solid as concrete. At that point, the dream is 98 percent complete but there is that last little bit you need to become great.

Then, just short of finally living your childhood dream, you are told, either straight out or implicitly, by some coaches, mentors, even the boss, that you aren't going to make it, unless you cheat. Unless you choose to dope. Doping can be that last 2 percent. It would keep your dream alive, at least in the eyes of those who couldn't see your heart. However, you'd have to lie. Lie to your mother, your friends, your fans. Lie to the world. This has been the harsh reality laid out before many of the most talented, hardest working, and biggest dreaming athletes.

How much does that last 2 percent really matter? In elite athletics, 2 percent of time or power or strength is an eternity. It is the difference in time between running 100 meters in 9.8 seconds and 10 seconds. In swimming it's between first and ninth place in the 100-meter breaststroke. And in the Tour de France, 2 percent is the difference between first and 100th place in overall time.

To be clear, running a 9.8 (or faster), winning the 100-meter breaststroke, or winning the Tour de France are all very possible and have been done without doping. But it is also clear that winning isn't possible if antidoping regulations aren't enforced. If you just said no when the antidoping regulations weren't enforced, then you were deciding to end your dream, because you could not be competitive. It's the hard fact of doping. The answer is not to teach young athletes that giving up lifelong dreams is better than giving in to cheating. The answer is to never give them the option. The only way to eliminate this choice is to put our greatest efforts into antidoping enforcement. The choice to kiss your childhood dream goodbye or live with a dishonest heart is horrid and tearing. I've been there, and I know. I chose to lie over killing my dream. I chose to dope. I am sorry for that decision, and I deeply regret it. The guilt I felt led me to retire from racing and start a professional cycling team where that choice was taken out of the equation through rigorous testing and a cultural shift that emphasized racing clean above winning. The choice for my athletes was eliminated.

> I chose to lie over killing my dream. I chose to dope.

I wasn't hellbent on cheating; I hated it, but I was ambitious, a trait we, as a society, generally admire. I had worked for more than half my life for one thing. But when you're ambitious in a world where rules aren't enforced, it's like fudging your income taxes in a world where the government doesn't audit. Think of what you would do if there were no Internal Revenue Service.

And think about the talented athletes who did make the right choice and walked away. They were punished for following their moral compass and being left behind. How do they reconcile the loss of their dream? It was stolen from them. When I was racing in the 1990s and early 2000s, the rules were easily circumvented by any and all—and if you wanted to be competitive, you first had to keep up. This environment is what we must continuously work to prevent from ever surfacing again. It destroys dreams. It destroys people. It destroys our finest athletes.

As I watched the Olympics these past two weeks, I was a bit envious, as I know that huge strides have been made by many since my time to rid sports of doping. Athletes have the knowledge and confidence that nowadays, the race can be won clean.

If the message I was given had been different, but more important, if the reality of sport then had been different, perhaps I could have lived my dream without killing my soul. Without cheating. I was fifteen years younger then, fifteen years less wise. I made the wrong decision, but I know that making that right decision for future generations must begin by making the right choice realistic. They want to make the right choice. This is the lesson I have learned from young athletes and why I have made it my life's work to help make the right choice real. 13

They must know, without doubt, that they will have a fair chance by racing clean. And for them to do that, the rules must be enforced, and the painful effort to make that happen must be unending and ruthless. Antidoping enforcement is 1,000 percent better than in my era of competition, and that brings me great satisfaction. But we must support these efforts even more. 14

Almost every athlete I've met who has doped will say they did it only because they wanted a level playing field. That says something: Everyone wants a fair chance, not more. So, let's give our young athletes a level playing field, without doping. Let's put our effort and resources into making sport fair, so that no athlete faces this decision ever again. We put so much emotion into marketing and idolizing athletes, let's put that same zeal into giving them what they really want: the ability to live their dreams without compromising their morals. 15

Thinking Critically about the Text

Is it a valid option for those in sports who are against doping to say, "Let's run clean"? Is it realistic to think that such an approach can gradually change the elite sports doping environment from the inside? Explain.

Examining the Issue

1. What is Vaughters's thesis? (Glossary: *Thesis*)

2. On the basis of what authority does Vaughters write? Is he a voice worth hearing in the argument over anti-doping enforcement?

3. Does Vaughters present his argument inductively, deductively, or as a combination of both methods? Explain.

4. Vaughters put a lot of emphasis on dreams. What points does he make about dreams in the world of elite sports?

5. Why does Vaughters see the doping dilemma as centering on the availability of appropriate choices and making the right ones? Explain.

6. What point does Vaughters make in his last paragraph about athletes' desire for a level playing field?

7. What is Vaughters's tone in this essay? (Glossary: *Tone*) Does he sound upbeat, regretful, sad, hopeful, self-righteous, or does he convey some other impression to you?

---

e-Pages

Is Doping Wrong?

PETER SINGER

Go to bedfordstmartins.com/subjectandstrategy for the final reading in this cluster. In "Is Doping Wrong?" Peter Singer takes issue with Julian Savulescu's argument for dropping the ban on performance-enhancing drugs.

MAKING CONNECTIONS

Writing and Discussion Suggestions
on Sports and Doping

1. **Writing with Sources.** Write a letter to the United States Anti-Doping Association (USADA) arguing that it must begin to think about legalizing the use of PEDs for athletes at the college and professional levels. Use information and arguments from Steadman's essay, other articles in this argument cluster, and articles and books that you find on the Internet and in your school library to help build your case. For models of and advice on integrating sources in your essay, see Chapters 14 and 15.

2. Assume that you are your college's soccer coach and that you have the information and experience to know that the war on sports doping is not working. You decide to write a report to your college athletic director arguing that your college should take a bold step and advocate for legalizing PEDs. What kinds of information should you include in the report? How will you organize and present that information for maximum impact? What opposing arguments will you bring to bear and how will you integrate them into your own argument?

3. Let's assume that you, like Don Hooton, had lost a child through the use of steroids and were called upon to testify before the U.S. Senate or House of Representatives about the dangers of performance-enhancing drugs. What arguments would you make against their use by professional athletes who were the role models for your son or daughter? Use the information and arguments found in the four arguments in this cluster as a starting point for building your own case, but also augment the material presented here.

4. Forgrave reports that Taylor Hooton suffered weight gain, puffiness, acne, bad breath, and a violent temper as a result of his steroid use. One of the best ways to argue against PEDs is to describe in some detail what these drugs do to a person. Research the subject in depth so that you can write an authoritative argument about the adverse effects specific drugs have, the symptoms they create, and the problems they cause.

5. One argument about doping in cycling is that things will never get better until the big money stops flowing into the sport. Large investments of money allow teams to get the best athletes; the best nutrition; the best, and often the most expensive, drugs; and the best doctors who know how to dope so participants will not get caught. Argue for or against the approach that Jonathan Vaughters has taken with his Garmin-Sharp team's no-tolerance philosophy.

6. Argue for or against the "level playing field" philosophy that advocates the legalization of doping in sports. What problems would such an approach create? What problems would be solved? Make sure to take into account major objections to your argument and answer them in ways that will convince your readers that your approach is the best for sports (either in sports generally or in a particular sport) and for the athletes who are involved.

ARGUMENT CLUSTER

Technology and Privacy: Are You Worried?

How much information is collected about you, and who has it? As Massimo Calabresi tells us later in this argument cluster, the government is interested: "In response to a request from Representative Ed Markey, major cell carriers revealed in July [2012] that they had received more than 1.3 million requests for cell-phone tracking data from federal, state, and local law-enforcement officials in 2011." Calabresi then points out that in 2010, there were only "3,000 wiretap warrants issued nationwide." These are astounding numbers, not least because authorities must obtain a court order to tap someone's *phone*, but no such order is required when obtaining information from *phone companies*. What these statistics also reveal is that we, as users of digital devices, are not only willing to share personal information about ourselves but also have it taken from us without our knowledge or even consent.

What no one really suspected when Representative Markey made his request was that our government itself was secretly spying on Americans' use of cell phones and the Internet. The stated objective of our National Security Agency (NSA) was to protect the nation from terrorist attacks. The thinking was, and still is, that if the authorities can learn who known terrorists are conspiring with via cell phones and the Internet, they can enhance their chances of warding off future attacks on Americans. The 2013 revelations about the NSA's activities naturally shocked the world as Americans were faced with trading their privacy for their safety. In Orwellian terms, Big Brother had arrived. Rather than examine both government and private invasions of our privacy, however, the following argument cluster narrows the focus to the efficacy of commercial entities that collect our personal data.

On the one hand, our new world offers us, free of ostensible charge, endless information from news, financial, educational, and countless other sources; the ability to connect to relatives, friends, and strangers through social media; and a myriad of services that affect our security and well-being. On the other hand, our privacy is at stake. It's ironic that while we seek to become connected to digital databases and leave our privacy behind, we also worry about revealing too much about ourselves. No one wants to share information that could be used against his or her best interests. How to strike a balance—to be of this world and yet maintain a degree of privacy—is the challenge of our age. It's an especially difficult task because many of the tools that businesses and data miners use are not known to the public. When we all-too-hastily submit to the privacy policies of Facebook, Foursquare, Twitter, or Instagram, we know what we want from them, but often don't know what they take from us.

We begin this cluster of arguments with Joel Stein's "Data Mining: How Companies Now Know Everything about You." Stein set out to see what kinds of personal information companies could discover about him from data-mining sources and his overall online activity, including purchases, Facebook photos, music habits, and subscriptions. While the accurate data alone could be troubling, its inaccuracy turns out to be utterly dismaying. Next, in "The Phone Knows All," Massimo Calabresi tells us about the kinds of information that can be mined from our cell phones, explores how law enforcement can use such data to both pursue criminals and yet also breech our privacy, and informs us of legislation trying to keep up with the pace of technology and protect our personal data. In the third selection, "Man versus Machine," Rafi Ron addresses airport security, a matter that concerns all of us flying in the post–9/11 era, a time of humiliating loss of our privacy at the hands of TSA agents and a system that relies too mindlessly on technology and not nearly enough on personal contact.

e-Pages

The e-Pages selection for this cluster is by information policy expert Jim Harper. In "It's Modern Trade: Web Users Get as Much as They Give," he explains that while we have some sense of how consumers fit into our data-mining economy, we pay for information and services with loss of privacy, and no one can predict how this arrangement will evolve. Go to **bedfordstmartins.com/subjectandstrategy** to read Harper's argument and explore his perspective with study questions.

Preparing to Read

You may take issue with the individual positions of the writers in this cluster, but you will not find it easy to ignore how technology and privacy have become entangled in our time. Do you care about protecting your privacy? What's at risk? Do you worry that corporations and the government may be accessing your personal information through data-mining programs and open access to your cell phone activities? How much of your privacy are you willing to give up for convenience and personal security?

Data Mining
How Companies Now Know Everything about You

JOEL STEIN

Joel Stein is a journalist who writes regularly for *Time*. He was born in 1971 in Edison, New Jersey, but now makes his home in Los Angeles, California. Stein graduated from Stanford University in 1993 with a B.A. and an M.A. in English. He first began working for *Martha Stewart Living* and then became a writer for *Time Out New York* before moving on to *Time* in 1997. Stein has on several occasions drawn serious fire for his writing. In the most publicized instance, he wrote a column in 2010 for *Time* in which he expressed his concern over the way his hometown of Edison had undergone significant changes because a large number of Indian immigrants had settled there. The column caused a huge furor, and Stein publicly apologized for whatever hurt he might have caused by criticizing the changes in the community.

In the following essay, first published in *Time* on March 21, 2011, with contributing reporting by Eben Harrell, Stein uses his own personal experiences as well as extensive research to argue that we pay for information online, rather than getting it for free as most people assume, by allowing browsers and search engines to mine our personal information in order to sell it to advertisers.

T hree hours after I gave my name and e-mail address to Michael   1
Fertik, the CEO of Reputation.com, he called me back and read my Social Security number to me. "We had it a couple of hours ago," he said. "I was just too busy to call."

In the past few months, I have been told many more-interesting facts   2
about myself than my Social Security number. I've gathered a bit of the vast amount of data that's being collected both online and off by companies in stealth — taken from the Web sites I look at, the stuff I buy, my Facebook photos, my warranty cards, my customer-reward cards, the songs I listen to online, surveys I was guilted into filling out, and magazines I subscribe to.

Google's Ads Preferences believes I'm a guy interested in politics, Asian   3
food, perfume, celebrity gossip, animated movies, and crime but who doesn't care about "books & literature" or "people & society." (So not true.) Yahoo! has me down as a 36-to-45-year-old male who uses a Mac computer and

likes hockey, rap, rock, parenting, recipes, clothes, and beauty products; it also thinks I live in New York, even though I moved to Los Angeles more than six years ago. Alliance Data, an enormous data-marketing firm in Texas, knows that I'm a 39-year-old college-educated Jewish male who takes in at least $125,000 a year, makes most of his purchases online, and spends an average of only $25 per item. Specifically, it knows that on January 24, 2004, I spent $46 on "low-ticket gifts and merchandise" and that on October 10, 2010, I spent $180 on intimate apparel. It knows about more than 100 purchases in between. Alliance also knows I owe $854,000 on a house built in 1939 that — get this — it thinks has stucco walls. They're mostly wood siding with a little stucco on the bottom! Idiots.

EXelate, a Manhattan company that acts as an exchange for the buying 4 and selling of people's data, thinks I have a high net worth and dig green living and travel within the United States. BlueKai, one of eXelate's competitors in Bellevue, Washington, believes I'm a "collegiate-minded" senior executive with a high net worth who rents sports cars (note to Time Inc. accounting: it's wrong unless the Toyota Yaris is a sports car). At one point BlueKai also believed, probably based on my $180 splurge for my wife Cassandra on HerRoom.com, that I was an 18-to-19-year-old woman.

RapLeaf, a data-mining company that was recently banned by Face- 5 book because it mined people's user IDs, has me down as a 35-to-44-year-old married male with a graduate degree living in L.A. But RapLeaf thinks I have no kids, work as a medical professional, and drive a truck. RapLeaf clearly does not read my column in *Time*.

Intellidyn, a company that buys and sells data, searched its file on me, 6 which says I'm a writer at Time Inc. and a "highly assimilated" Jew. It knows that Cassandra and I like gardening, fashion, home decorating, and exercise, though in my case the word *like* means "am forced to be involved in." We are pretty unlikely to buy car insurance by mail but extremely likely to go on a European river cruise, despite the fact that we are totally not going to go on a European river cruise. There are tons of other companies I could have called to learn more about myself, but in a result no one could have predicted, I got bored.

Each of these pieces of information (and misinformation) about me is 7 sold for about two-fifths of a cent to advertisers, which then deliver me an Internet ad, send me a catalog, or mail me a credit-card offer. This data is collected in lots of ways, such as tracking devices (like cookies) on Web sites that allow a company to identify you as you travel around the Web and apps you download on your cell that look at your contact list and location. You know how everything has seemed free for the past few years? It wasn't. It's just that no one told you that instead of using money, you were paying with your personal information.

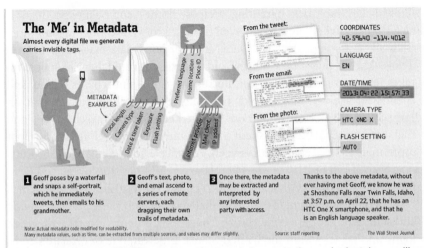

The 'Me' in Metadata
Almost every digital file we generate carries invisible tags.

METADATA EXAMPLES

Focal length
Camera type
Date & time taken
Exposure
Flash setting

Preferred language
Home location
Place ID

Internet provider
Mail client
IP address

From the tweet:

COORDINATES
42.59640 -114.4012

LANGUAGE
EN

From the email:

DATE/TIME
2013:04:22 15:57:33

From the photo:

CAMERA TYPE
HTC ONE X

FLASH SETTING
AUTO

1 Geoff poses by a waterfall and snaps a self-portrait, which he immediately tweets, then emails to his grandmother.

2 Geoff's text, photo, and email ascend to a series of remote servers, each dragging their own trails of metadata.

3 Once there, the metadata may be extracted and interpreted by any interested party with access.

Thanks to the above metadata, without ever having met Geoff, we know he was at Shoshone Falls near Twin Falls, Idaho, at 3:57 p.m. on April 22, that he has an HTC One X smartphone, and that he is an English language speaker.

Note: Actual metadata code modified for readability. Many metadata values, such as time, can be extracted from multiple sources, and values may differ slightly.   Source: staff reporting   The Wall Street Journal

This graphic from the *Wall Street Journal* suggests how tweeting and privately e-mailing a photo can reveal a great deal of personal information.

THE CREEP FACTOR

There is now an enormous multibillion-dollar industry based on the collection and sale of this personal and behavioral data, an industry that Senator John Kerry,[1] chair of the Subcommittee on Communications, Technology, and the Internet, is hoping to rein in. Kerry is about to introduce a bill that would require companies to make sure all the stuff they know about you is secured from hackers and to let you inspect everything they have on you, correct any mistakes, and opt out of being tracked. He is doing this because, he argues, "There's no code of conduct. There's no standard. There's nothing that safeguards privacy and establishes rules of the road."

At Senate hearings on privacy beginning March 16, the Federal Trade Commission (FTC) will be weighing in on how to protect consumers. It has already issued a report that calls upon the major browsers to come up with a do-not-track mechanism that allows people to choose not to have their information collected by companies they aren't directly doing business with. Under any such plan, it would likely still be OK for Amazon to remember your past orders and make purchase suggestions or for American Express to figure your card was stolen because a recent purchase doesn't fit your precise buying patterns. But it wouldn't be cool if they gave another company that information without your permission.

Taking your information without asking and then profiting from it isn't new: It's the idea behind the phone book, junk mail, and telemarketing. Worrying about it is just as old: In 1890, Louis Brandeis argued that printing a photograph without the subject's permission inflicts "mental

8

9

10

[1]John Kerry (b. 1943), longtime senator from Massachusetts, appointed U.S. Secretary of State in 2013.

pain and distress, far greater than could be inflicted by mere bodily harm."
Once again, new technology is making us weigh what we're sacrificing
in privacy against what we're gaining in instant access to information.
Some facts about you were always public—the price of your home, some
divorce papers, your criminal records, your political donations—but they
were held in different buildings, accessible only by those who filled out
annoying forms; now they can be clicked on. Other information was not
possible to compile pre-Internet because it would have required sending
a person to follow each of us around the
mall, listen to our conversations, and watch
what we read in the newspaper. Now all of
those activities happen online—and can be
tracked instantaneously.

> You know how everything seemed free the past few years? It wasn't. It's just that no one told you that instead of using money, you were paying with your personal information.

Part of the problem people have with 11
data mining is that it seems so creepy. Right
after I e-mailed a friend in Texas that I might
be coming to town, a suggestion for a restaurant in Houston popped up as a one-line
all-text ad above my Gmail inbox. But it's
not a barbecue-pit master stalking me,
which would indeed be creepy; it's an algorithm designed to give me more useful, specific ads. And while that doesn't sound like
all that good a deal in exchange for my pri-
vate data, if it means that I get to learn when the next Paul Thomas
Anderson movie is coming out, when Wilco is playing near my house, and
when Tom Colicchio is opening a restaurant close by, maybe that's not
such a bad return.

Since targeted ads are so much more effective than nontargeted ones, 12
Web sites can charge much more for them. This is why—compared with
the old banners and pop-ups—online ads have become smaller and less
invasive, and why Web sites have been able to provide better content and
still be free. Besides, the fact that I'm going to Houston is bundled with the
information that 999 other people are Houston-bound and is auctioned by
a computer; no actual person looks at my name or my Houston-boundness.
Advertisers are interested only in tiny chunks of information about my
behavior, not my whole profile, which is one of the reasons M. Ryan Calo,
a Stanford Law School professor who is director of the school's Consumer
Privacy Project, argues that data mining does no actual damage.

"We have this feeling of being dogged that's uncomfortable," Calo 13
says, "but the risk of privacy harm isn't necessarily harmful. Let's get serious and talk about what harm really is." The real problem with data mining, Calo and others believe, arises when the data is wrong. "It's one thing

to see bad ads because of bad information about you. It's another thing if you're not getting a credit card or a job because of bad information," says Justin Brookman, the former chief of the Internet bureau of the New York attorney general's office, who is now the director of the Center for Democracy and Technology, a nonprofit group in Washington.

Russell Glass, the CEO of Bizo—which mines the fact that people are 14 business executives and sells that info to hundreds of advertisers such as American Express, Monster.com, Citibank, Sprint, and Google—says the newness of his industry is what scares people. "It's the monster-under-the-bed syndrome," Glass says. "People are afraid of what they really don't understand. They don't understand that companies like us have no idea who they are. And we really don't give a s——. I just want a little information that will help me sell you an ad." Not many people, he notes, seem to be creeped out by all the junk mail they still get from direct-marketing campaigns, which buy the same information from data-mining companies. "I have a 2-year-old daughter who is getting mail at my home address," he says. "That freaks me out."

WHY THAT AD IS FOLLOWING YOU

Junk mail is a familiar evil that's barely changed over the decades. Data 15 mining and the advertising it supports get more refined every month. The latest trick to freak people out is retargeting—when you look at an item in an online store and then an ad for that item follows you around to other sites.

Last year, Zappos was the most prominent company in the United 16 States to go all out in behavioral retargeting. And people got pissed off. One of the company's mistakes was running ads too frequently and coming off as an annoying, persistent salesman. "We took that brick-and-mortar pet peeve and implied it online," says Darrin Shamo, Zappos' director of direct marketing. Shamo learned, the hard way, that people get upset when their computer shows lingerie ads, even if they had been recently shopping for G-strings, since people share computers and use them in front of their kids. He also learned that ads that reveal potential Christmas gifts are bad for business.

Since then, Zappos has been experimenting with new ads that people 17 will see no more than five times and for no longer than eight days. Zappos has also dumbed the ads down, showing items that aren't the ones you considered buying but are sort of close, which people greatly prefer. And much like Amazon's "Customers who bought *1984* also bought *Brave New World*"–style recommendation engine, the new ads tell people what Zappos knows about them and how they got that information ("a company called

Criteo helps Zappos to create these kinds of personalized ads"). It also tells them how they can opt out of seeing them ("Some people prefer rainbows. And others prefer unicorns. If you prefer not to see personalized ads, we totally get it").

If that calms the angry 15 percent of the people who saw these ads, 18 Zappos will stick with them. Otherwise, it plans on quitting the retargeting business. Shamo thinks he'll just need to wait until the newness wears off and people are used to ads tailored for them. "Sometimes things don't move as fast as you think," he says.

They're not even moving that much faster with the generation that 19 grew up with the Internet. While young people expect more of their data to be mined and used, that doesn't mean they don't care about privacy. "In my research, I found that teenagers live with this underlying anxiety of not knowing the rules of who can look at their information on the Internet. They think schools look at it, they think the government looks at it, they think colleges can look at it, they think employers can look at it, they think Facebook can see everything," says Sherry Turkle, a professor at MIT who is the director of the Initiative on Technology and Self and the author of *Alone Together: Why We Expect More from Technology and Less from Each Other.* "It's the opposite of the mental state I grew up in. My grandmother took me down to the mailbox in Brooklyn every morning, and she would say, 'It's a federal offense for anyone to look at your mail. That's what makes this country great.' In the old country they'd open your mail, and that's how they knew about you."

Data mining, Turkle argues, is a panopticon: the circular prison 20 invented by eighteenth-century philosopher Jeremy Bentham where you can't tell if you're being observed, so you assume that you always are. "The practical concern is loss of control and loss of identity," says Marc Rotenberg, executive director of the Electronic Privacy Information Center. "It's a little abstract, but that's part of what's taking place."

THE FACEBOOK AND GOOGLE TROVES

Our identities, however, were never completely within our control: Our 21 friends keep letters we've forgotten writing, our enemies tell stories about us we remember differently, our yearbook photos are in way too many people's houses. Opting out of all those interactions is opting out of society. Which is why Facebook is such a confusing privacy hub point. Many data-mining companies made this argument to me: How can I complain about having my Houston trip data-mined when I'm posting photos of myself with a giant mullet and a gold chain on Facebook and writing columns about how I want a second kid and my wife doesn't? Because, unlike when my data is secretly mined, I get to control what I share. Even narcissists want privacy. "It's the difference between sharing and tracking," says Bret Taylor, Facebook's chief technology officer.

To get into the Facebook office in Palo Alto, California, I have to sign   22
a piece of physical paper: a Single-Party Non-Disclosure Agreement, which legally prevents me from writing the last paragraph. But your privacy on Facebook—that's up to you. You choose what to share and what circle of friends gets to see it, and you can untag yourself from any photos of you that other people put up. However, from a miner's point of view, Facebook has the most valuable trove of data ever assembled: Not only have you told it everything you like but it also knows what your friends like, which is an amazing predictor of what you'll like.

Facebook doesn't sell any of your data, partly because it doesn't have   23
to—23.1 percent of all online ads not on search engines, video, or e-mail run on Facebook. But data-mining companies are "scraping" all your personal data that's not set to private and selling it to any outside party that's interested. So that information is being bought and sold unless you squeeze your Facebook privacy settings tight, which keeps you from a lot of the social interaction that drew you to the site in the first place.

The only company that might have an even better dossier on you than   24
Facebook is Google. In a conference room on the Google campus, I sit through a long privacy-policy PowerPoint presentation. Summary: Google cares! Specifically, Google keeps the data it has about you from various parts of its company separate. One category is the personally identifiable account data it can attach to your name, age, gender, e-mail address, and ZIP code when you signed up for services like Gmail, YouTube, Blogger, Picasa, iGoogle, Google Voice, or Calendar. The other is log data associated with your computer, which it "anonymizes" after nine months: your search history, Chrome browser data, Google Maps requests, and all the info its myriad data trackers and ad agencies (DoubleClick, AdSense, AdMob) collect when you're on other sites and Android phone apps. You can change your settings on the former at Google Dashboard and the latter at Google Ads Preferences—where you can opt out of having your data mined or change the company's guesses about what you're into.

Nicole Wong, deputy general counsel at Google, says the company   25
created these tools to try to reassure people who have no idea how all this information is being collected and used. "When I go to Time.com as a user, I think only Time.com is collecting my data. What I don't realize is that for every ad on that page, a company is also dropping a code and collecting my data. It's a black box—and we've tried to open up the box. Sometimes you're not even sure who the advertisers are. It's just a bunch of jumping monkeys or something." Google really does want to protect your privacy,

but it's got issues. First, it's profit-driven and it's huge. But those aren't the main reasons privacy advocates get so upset about Google. They get upset because the company's guiding philosophy conflicts with the notion of privacy. As the PowerPoint says right up top: "Google's mission: to organize the world's information and make it universally accessible and useful." Which is awesome, except for the fact that my information is part of the world's information.

TRACKING THE TRACKERS

To see just what information is being gathered about me, I downloaded Ghostery, a browser extension that lets you watch the watchers watching you. Each time you go to a new Web site, up pops a little bubble that lists all the data trackers checking you out. This is what I discovered: The very few companies that actually charge you for services tend not to data mine much. When you visit Time.com, several dozen tracking companies, with names such as Eyeblaster, Bluestreak, DoubleClick, and Factor TG, could be collecting data at any given time.   26

If you're reading this in print as a subscriber, *Time* has probably "rented" your name and address many times to various companies for a one-time use. This is also true if you subscribe to *Vanity Fair, Cosmopolitan,* or just about any other publication.   27

This being America, I don't have to wait for the government to give me an opt-out option; I can pay for one right now. Michael Fertik, the CEO and founder of Reputation.com, who nabbed my Social Security number, will do it for me for just $8.25 a month. His company will also, for a lot more money, make Google searches of your name come up with more flattering results—because when everyone is famous, everyone needs a public relations department. Fertik, who clerked for the chief judge of the Sixth Circuit after graduating from Harvard Law School, believes that if data mining isn't regulated, everyone will soon be assigned scores for attractiveness and a social-prowess index and a complainer index, so companies can avoid serving you—just as you now have a credit score that they can easily check before deciding to do business with you. "What happens when those data sets are used for life transactions: health insurance, employment, dating, and education? It's inevitable that all of these decisions will be made based on machine conclusions. Your FICO score is already an all-but-decisional fact about you. ABD, dude! All but decisional," says Fertik.   28

Even if I were to use the services of Reputation.com, there's still all the public information about me that I can't suppress. Last year, thousands of people sent their friends a Facebook message telling them to opt out of being listed on Spokeo.com, which they described as the creepiest   29 paparazzo of all, giving out your age, profession, address, and a photo of your house. Spokeo, a tiny company in Pasadena, California, is run by 28-year-old Stanford grad Harrison Tang. He was surprised at the outcry. "Some people don't know what Google Street View is, so they think this is magic," Tang says of the photos of people's homes that his site shows. The info on Spokeo isn't even all that revealing—he purposely leaves off criminal records and previous marriages—but Tang thinks society is still learning about data mining and will soon become inured to it. "Back in the 1990s, if you said, 'I'm going to put pictures on the Internet for everyone to see,' it would have been hard to believe. Now everyone does it. The Internet is becoming more and more open. This world will become more connected, and the distance between you and me will be a lot closer. If everybody is a walled garden, there won't be an Internet."

I deeply believe that, but it's still too easy to find our gardens. Your political donations, home value, and address have always been public, but you used to have to actually go to all these different places—courthouses, libraries, property-tax assessors' offices—and request documents. "You were private by default and public by effort. Nowadays, you're public by default and private by effort," says Lee Tien, a senior staff attorney for the Electronic Frontier Foundation, an advocacy group for digital rights. "There are all sorts of inferences that can be made about you from the Web sites you visit, what you buy, who you talk to. What if your employer had access to information about you that shows you have a particular kind of health condition or a woman is pregnant or thinking about it?" Tien worries that political dissidents in other countries, battered women, and other groups that need anonymity are vulnerable to data mining. At the very least, he argues, we're responsible to protect special groups, just as Google Street View allows users to request that a particular location, like an abused-women's shelter, not be photographed.

Other democratic countries have taken much stronger stands than the United States has on regulating data mining. Google Street View has been banned by the Czech Republic. Germany—after protests and much debate—decided at the end of last year to allow it but to let people request that their houses not be shown, which nearly 250,000 people had done as of last November. E.U. Justice Commissioner Viviane Reding is about to present a proposal to allow people to correct and erase information about themselves on the Web. "Everyone should have the right to be forgotten," she says. "Due to their painful history in the twentieth century, Europeans are naturally more sensitive to the collection and use of their data by public authorities."

After 9/11, not many Americans protested when concerns about security seemed to trump privacy. Now that privacy issues are being pushed in

Congress, companies are making last-ditch efforts to become more transparent. New tools released in February for Firefox and Google Chrome browsers let users block data collecting, though Firefox and Chrome depend on the data miners to respect the users' request, which won't stop unscrupulous companies. In addition to the new browser options, an increasing number of ads have a little *i* (an Advertising Option Icon), which you can click on to find out exactly which companies are tracking you and what they do. The technology behind the icon is managed by Evidon, the company that provides the Ghostery download. Evidon has gotten more than 500 data-collecting companies to provide their info.

It takes a lot of work to find out about this tiny little *i* and even more to   33
click on it and read the information. But it also took people a while to learn what the recycling symbol meant. And reading the info behind the *i* icon isn't necessarily the point, says Evidon CEO Scott Meyer, who used to be CEO of About.com and managed the *New York Times'* Web site. "Do I look at nutritional labeling? No. But would I buy a food product that didn't have one? Absolutely not. I would be really concerned. It's accountability."

FTC chairman Jon Leibowitz has been pleased by how effective he's   34
been at using the threat of legislation to scare companies into taking action and dropping their excuse that they don't know anything about you personally, just data associated with your computer. "We used to have a distinction ten years ago between personally identifiable information and non-PII. Now those distinctions have broken down." In November, Leibowitz hired Edward Felten, the Princeton computer-science professor famous for uncovering weaknesses in electronic-voting machines and digital-music protection, to serve as the FTC's chief technologist for the next year. Felten has found that the online-advertising industry is as eager as the government is for improved privacy protections. "There's a lot of fear that holds people back from doing things they would otherwise do online. This is part of the cost of privacy uncertainty. People are a little wary of trying out some new site or service if they're worried about giving their information," Felten says.

He's right: Oddly, the more I learned about data mining, the less con-   35
cerned I was. Sure, I was surprised that all these companies are actually keeping permanent files on me. But I don't think they will do anything with them that does me any harm. There should be protections for vulnerable groups, and a government-enforced opt-out mechanism would be great for accountability. But I'm pretty sure that, like me, most people won't use that option. Of the people who actually find the Ads Preferences page—and these must be people pretty into privacy—only 1 in 8 asks to opt out of being tracked. The rest, apparently, just like to read privacy rules.

We're quickly figuring out how to navigate our trail of data—don't say 36 anything private on a Facebook wall, keep your secrets out of e-mail, use cash for illicit purchases. The vast majority of it, though, is worthless to us and a pretty good exchange for frequent-flier miles, better search results, a fast system to qualify for credit, finding out if our babysitter has a criminal record, and ads we find more useful than annoying. Especially because no human being ever reads your files. As I learned by trying to find out all my data, we're not all that interesting.

Thinking Critically about the Text

Stein writes of us in his final sentence, "we're not all that interesting." When we contemplate the matter of our privacy in a data-mining environment, does it matter how interesting we are, or is there a larger principle at risk? Explain.

Examining the Issue

1. What is Stein's thesis? Where does he state it?

2. How comprehensive has Stein been in describing the ways in which data mining is occurring in the online and off-line digital world? How has he used illustration to build his case that the use of search engines is not, in fact, free of charge?

3. If our personal information was always available to those who tried to search for it, what's different now?

4. What use has Stein made of authority and citation? Cite some examples.

5. In paragraph 12, Stein says M. Ryan Calo "argues that data mining does no actual damage." If that's true, then what does Stein see as a major concern?

6. What is retargeting and what's so bad about it?

7. What particularly concerns young people about data mining?

8. In paragraph 30, Stein quotes Lee Tien as saying "You were private by default and public by effort. Nowadays, you're public by default and private by effort." What are the implications of the change, as Tien sees it?

9. Stein writes in paragraph 35, "The more I learned about data mining, the less concerned I was." Do you agree with him about data mining?

The Phone Knows All

MASSIMO CALABRESI

Massimo Calabresi is a writer for *Time*, where he has covered stories on a wide variety of subjects, including lobbying scandals; the terrorist attacks of September 11, 2001; how the Food and Drug Administration can be gamed; Barack Obama's counterterrorism policies; and ethnic cleansing in Kosovo. He began his career in journalism in 1991 as a freelance writer with the *National Review*, reporting from Moscow on the fall of the Soviet Union. He became bureau chief for Central Europe and the Balkans. He reported on the wars in Bosnia, Croatia, and Kosovo before being named White House correspondent in 2007, giving him the opportunity to cover the 2008 presidential election. Currently, Calabresi serves as a Washington correspondent for *Time*. He graduated from Yale University in 1989 with a B.A. in philosophy.

In the following article, first published in *Time* on August 27, 2012, Calabresi (with reporting and research by Alex Rogers and Angela Thornton) writes about how companies and criminal investigators enter into your digital life without your ever realizing they are doing so.

I f someone wanted to create a global system for tracking human beings and collecting information about them, it would look a lot like the digital mobile-device network. It knows where you are, and—the more you text, tweet, shop, take pictures, and navigate your surroundings using a smart phone—it knows an awful lot about what you're doing.

Which is one reason federal officials turned to Sprint, Verizon, AT&T, and T-Mobile in early 2009 when they needed to solve the robbery of a Berlin, Connecticut, branch of Webster Bank. Using a loophole in a 1986 law that allows warrantless searches of stored communications, the feds ordered the carriers to provide records of phones that used a nearby cell tower on the day of the crime. The carriers turned over to the prosecutors the identities, call records, and other personal information of 169 cell-phone users—including two men who were eventually sentenced to prison for the robbery. With a simple request, the feds cracked a case that might have otherwise taken years to solve. In the process, they collected information on 167 people who they had no reason to believe had committed a crime, including details like numbers dialed and times of calls that would have been protected as private on a landline.

Such cases are common. In response to a request from Representative   3
Ed Markey, major cell carriers revealed in July that they had received more
than 1.3 million requests for cell-phone tracking data from federal, state,
and local law-enforcement officials in 2011. By comparison, there were
3,000 wiretap warrants issued nationwide in 2010. That revelation has
added to a growing debate over how to balance the convenience and security consumers now expect from their smart phones with the privacy they
traditionally have wanted to protect. Every second we enjoy their convenience, smart phones are collecting information, recording literally millions
of data points every day.

> Every second we enjoy
> their convenience, smart
> phones are collecting
> information, recording
> literally millions of data
> points every day.

The potential for good is undeniable. In   4
recent years, the average time it takes the
U.S. Marshals Service to find a fugitive has
dropped from forty-two days to two, according to congressional testimony from Susan
Landau, a Guggenheim fellow. Cell phones
have changed criminal investigation from
the ground up. "There is a mobile device
connected to every crime scene," says Peter
Modafferi, the chief of detectives in
Rockland County, New York.

But as smart phones' tracking abilities have become more sophisti-   5
cated, law enforcement, phonemakers, cell carriers, and software makers
have come under fire for exploiting personal data without the knowledge
of the average user. Much of the law protecting mobile privacy in the
United States was written at the dawn of the cell-phone era in the 1980s,
and it can vary from state to state. Companies have widely differing privacy
policies. Now conservatives and liberals on Capitol Hill are pushing legislation that would set new privacy standards, limiting law-enforcement
searches and restricting what kinds of information companies can collect.

Government snooping is part of the worry. But market demand is driv-   6
ing some of the biggest collectors of data. Mobile advertising is now a $6
billion industry, and identifying potential customers based on their personal
information is the new frontier. Last year, reports showed that free and
cheap apps were capable of everything from collecting location information
to images a phone is seeing. One app with image-collection capabilities,
Tiny Flashlight, uses a phone's camera as a flashlight and has been installed
at least 50 million times on phones around the world. Tiny Flashlight's
author, Bulgarian programmer Nikolay Ananiyev, tells *Time* that his program does not collect the images or send them to third parties.

In November, news broke that a company named Carrier IQ had   7
installed software on as many as 150 million phones that accesses users'

texts, call histories, Web usage, and location histories without users' know-ing consent. Carrier IQ says it does not record, store, or transmit the data but uses it to measure performance. In February, Facebook, Yelp, Four-square, and Instagram apps, among others, were reported to be upload-ing contact information from iPhones and iPads. The software makers told the blog VentureBeat that they only use the contact information when prompted by users. "No app is free," says one senior executive at a phone carrier. "You pay for them with your privacy."

Many consumers are happy to do so, and so far there hasn't been much 8 actual damage, at least not that privacy advocates can point to. The ques-tion is where to draw the line. For instance, half of smart-phone users make banking transactions via their mobile device. The Federal Trade Commission has brought forty enforcement cases in recent years against companies for improperly storing customers' private information.

Law enforcement is subject to some oversight. Absent an emergency, 9 prosecutors and police must convince a judge that the cell information they are seeking from wireless companies is material to a criminal case under investigation. An unusual alliance between liberals and conserva-tives is pushing a bill to impose the same requirements for getting cell tracking data as those that are in place when cops want to get a warrant to search a house. Another bill would increase restrictions on what app writ-ers can do with personal information. Cases moving through the courts may limit what law enforcement can do with GPS tracking.

Tech companies are trying to get a handle on the issue. Apple has a 10 single customer-privacy policy. Google posts the permissions that consum-ers give each app to operate their phones' hardware and software, including authorization to access camera and audio feeds, and pass on locations or contact info. The rush to keep up with technology will only get harder: The next surge in surveillance is text messaging, industry experts say, as compa-nies and cops look for new ways to tap technology for their own purposes.

Thinking Critically about the Text

The police are sometimes able to apprehend suspected criminals within hours or several days with the aid of cell-phone companies, even though they may be vio-lating your privacy. Is the loss of your privacy a small price to pay for your greater safety? Explain.

Examining the Issue

1. How are criminal investigators able to invade our cell-phone privacy? Who is trying to rein in the investigators' access to our personal records?

2. Calabresi refers to "data points." What are they?

3. What's the problem with companies such as Tiny Flashlight and Carrier IQ?

4. What does Calabresi identify as the concern over cell-phone apps with millions of users, such as those of Facebook, Yelp, Foursquare, and Instagram?

5. If most users of cell phones seem not to be worried about the loss of their privacy, what's Calabresi's argument? Where does he see potential danger ahead?

6. What will happen when companies "look for new ways to tap technology for their own purposes"?

Man versus Machine

RAFI RON

Rafi Ron is an internationally recognized expert on transportation security and the head of New Age Security Solutions, a consulting company. From company headquarters in Dulles, Virginia, Ron directs air, marine, and land-based security programs both in the United States and abroad. Formerly the head of the Ben Gurion International Airport and the Israeli Airport Authority from 1997–2001, Ron began his career as a paratrooper in the Israeli Defense Forces before helping to form the El Al sky marshals program, in which he himself served as a marshal. Ron has shared his expertise by testifying before Congress on transportation security issues, lecturing on college campuses, and making numerous appearances in the media.

In the following essay, which first appeared on December 6, 2010, as a *Newsweek* "My Turn" column, Ron argues that the TSA and its agents rely too much on technology in their efforts to secure airports and planes from terrorist attacks.

O n September 11, 2001, I was sitting in my office at Tel Aviv's Ben Gurion airport, where I was director of security, and watched in horror as the world changed. During the next few months, I saw America quickly identify screenings as the source of all evil and the reason for the attacks — despite, illogically, the fact that Mohamed Atta and his terrorist teams didn't carry any weapons that were supposed to be detected at the checkpoints.

I've since moved to the United States to consult on airport security. Time after time, I've watched the country react retroactively — making us take off our footwear after Richard Reid's attempted shoe bombing, deciding not to let us bring water or shampoo on flights after a failed plot to blow up planes with liquid explosives, and, now, subjecting passengers to full-body scans or invasive searches after last December's thwarted underwear bombing. It's time to accept that terrorist attacks are not carried out by *things* but by *people*. A security strategy based on detection technology alone is a failed one. Our great love of gadgetry — and the belief that it can solve all our problems, without a personal touch — has only led to one failure after another.

Looking for better solutions takes me back to Ben Gurion. Israeli aviation security manages to create a reasonable balance between detection technology and human interaction. While at American airports we deploy people to support technology, in Tel Aviv technology is deployed to support people. Does it work? Ask Anne Marie Murphy, a young Irishwoman who, in 1986, nearly boarded a plane while carrying an explosive device without her knowledge. Her terrorist boyfriend, who was supposed to be on a separate flight, had given her a bag with a concealed bomb. When a profiler began to ask her a standard set of questions, it became clear that she was an anomaly (she had no accommodations lined up, among other issues). The device, which was cleverly hidden, would not have been detected during a pat-down, or even by an X-ray scanner. But the profiler, who was not distracted by her ethnicity, religion, gender, or her obvious pregnancy, saved Murphy and hundreds of other passengers—simply by taking her aside and talking to her.

> Our great love of gadgetry — and the belief that it can solve all our problems, without a personal touch — has only led to one failure after another.

The Murphy case illustrates the limitations of ethnic and racial profiling. Not only does the P word contradict values so dear to us, it's just not the smartest tactic. Analyzing someone's behavior through observation and conversation—in real time and cumulatively—makes more sense. Screeners should be able to comb through a more comprehensive database of government and law-enforcement data as well as information from the airlines about, say, who has paid cash for a ticket and who is flying one way. These "tells" are unusual and would cause screeners to pay closer attention when it matters. (They're also the behaviors that Atta, Reid, and the "underpants bomber" displayed.) Which is what's needed: By relying on a one-size-fits-all approach to security, we spend too much time searching harmless travelers—and too little time rooting out legitimate threats.

4

Thinking Critically about the Text

Discuss Ron's statement that "Our great love of gadgetry — and the belief that it can solve all our problems, without a personal touch — has only led to one failure after another" (paragraph 2).

Examining the Issue

1. What is Ron's thesis? (Glossary: *Thesis*) Where does he state his thesis?

2. In paragraph 2, what does Ron mean when he claims with respect to security that "Time after time, I've watched the country react retroactively"?

3. Is Ron against using technology in airport security? What role, if any, does he think technology should play in airport security? Explain.

4. What is profiling and what do you think are the pros and cons of using it as one part of an airport passenger security-screening program?

5. Is the act of interrogating passengers a violation of their rights? Why, or why not?

6. How much of our privacy do you think we must forego if we want to travel safely today?

7. Do you think Ron would be in favor of using full-body scanners in our airports? Why, or why not?

8. Does Ron's argument make sense to you? Why, or why not?

---

 e-Pages

It's Modern Trade
Web Users Get as Much as They Give

JIM HARPER

Go to bedfordstmartins.com/subjectandstrategy for the final reading in this cluster. In "It's Modern Trade: Web Users Get as Much as They Give," information policy expert Jim Harper explores the trade-off between loss of privacy and receiving information that's tailored to our personal interests.

MAKING CONNECTIONS

Writing and Discussion Suggestions
on Technology and Privacy

1. Do you regard data mining as dangerous, benign, or both at the same time? Consider: What is the nature of privacy? How has it evolved over the years, if at all? Is it possible to be a completely private person? If so, is it advisable to do so? Is it ethical for one company to sell your personal information to another company? What's wrong with public information being more easily accessible? When forming your answer, you might consult additional scholarly articles in your library or on the Web.

2. Is data mining helpful in fighting terrorism and other crimes? Is it useful for public health officials, as when they track epidemics, drug use, influenza outbreaks, or the way colds are being treated by the public? In what ways can data-mining strategies that were originally developed for commercial gain be used to better our lives?

3. Stein says that a percentage of data-mined information is inevitably incorrect and hurts people by affecting their reputations, relationships, families, and jobs. Assuming that what Lee Tien says is true — "Nowadays, you're public by default and private by effort," as quoted by Stein in paragraph 29 — write an essay in which you argue that it is necessary to be proactive in protecting your identity. Explain the various ways that you can protect information about yourself and your reputation.

4. Assume you are the parents of children who want to sign up for Facebook. You agree they can do so, but only if you have their passwords, hoping your surveillance will discourage them from disclosing immature, inadvisable, or risky information. Suppose you then learn that your children surreptitiously signed up for additional Facebook accounts with secret passwords. Write a well-thought-out letter to your children arguing that what they did is not only against your wishes but also represents a real danger. Include examples of what can go wrong when one's privacy is violated or carelessly shared with others. Pay particular attention to the tone of your letter, which should be forceful and convincing, but also caring and supportive. You may find it helpful to explore Facebook's online help section to learn what topics often concern parents and educators.

5. **Writing with Sources.** The ever-changing nature of modern technology means that companies and individuals are always reaching out to us in new ways, hoping to intrigue us. When it works, we may be amused, but

those advances may also invade our privacy without regard for our consent or awareness. Research a few popular software or mobile apps that have been discussed in the media, and then think about their potential uses, implications, or effects. Explain how those apps illustrate the double-edged nature of a technology, working both for and against our interests. For models of and advice on integrating sources in your essay, see Chapters 14 and 15.

6. **Writing with Sources.** When we buy smartphones and sign up for applications such as Facebook, Yelp, Foursquare, and Twitter, we are asked to read and agree to the terms of service and privacy policies that they offer. Do you agree to such policies without reading them, as do many others? If you read them, do you read carefully enough to make an informed decision? Do you agree to such policies because you assume that others before you have done so? Do you think such polices are important? Write an essay in which you examine the detailed language of several of these privacy policies, perhaps even comparing and contrasting their language on various issues, and then argue for or against signing them. For models of and advice on integrating sources in your essay, see Chapters 14 and 15.

7. As Calabresi writes, Representative Ed Markey of Massachusetts introduced legislation to restrict government or law enforcement access to your cell-phone records. Research the details of Markey's proposed legislation. Make sure you understand the issues fully. What exactly is the loophole that presently permits access, and what changes is Markey proposing? Write a letter to Markey in which you exhibit a detailed understanding of his legislation and offer support for or against it.

8. We're accustomed to thinking of leaving behind material items such as letters, contracts, or journals in a will. We now live in a world that allows us to have digital lives as well as material ones. In fact, such digital records may be larger than traditional kinds. What should we do to have control of this new personal dimension? For example, should something happen to you, what will become of your Facebook page, your medical records, your financial data, the thousands of photographs you have taken and stored in the cloud and on your computer and smartphone, the text messages and e-mails you filed away, or the blog you kept for years? Research the ramifications of having a robust digital presence, and write an argument proposing that your digital life is an important aspect of who you are and needs to be managed.

9. Write an essay in which you argue for the importance of one's identity and reputation. Include the steps that should be taken to protect them. What happens when your identity is stolen or your reputation is challenged online by others? What are the consequences, and what recourses do you have to re-establish who you are?

10. Personal branding is a popular concept today. Research the term and argue that the way an individual uses digital devices and social media applications is a critical enabler of personal branding. What does your personal brand communicate to others? For example, how do your community-related charitable activities, as promoted through your tweets and Facebook posts, enhance your attractiveness when applying for a job? Do you take steps to present yourself as a caring and forward-looking person? How do your exercise and sports activities round out your personality profile? Do your activities indicate that you have expertise in particular areas? If you choose to brand yourself through social media, how attractively or unattractively do you present yourself?

ARGUMENT CLUSTER

The Value of College:
Is It Worth the Cost?

The cost of a college education has never been far from the minds of students and parents, but at no time has the spotlight shone more brightly on college costs than in our stressful economic times. In recent years, students have increasingly taken out loans to help with expenses, chosen to attend community and junior colleges to minimize the cost of tuition, and even decided to forgo higher education altogether. More than ever before, troubled by economic and media reports about college graduates struggling to find jobs, prospective students and their parents are asking hard questions about the value of a college degree. Even students and parents who are able to pay for college now wonder if they should use that money for something else, such as starting a business. One way to approach these questions is to arm oneself with solid statistical information comparing the lifetime earnings of high school dropouts and graduates to those of college attendees and graduates. It's also reasonable to ask how money spent on college compares with other investments.

Beyond finance, there are valid concerns about the value of the education you'll likely receive at a given college or university. What does a student receive for each dollar spent? Although it's fairly easy to determine the financial metrics, it's much harder to quantify the intangible or experiential benefits of a degree. In what ways can we — and should we — measure the value of an education? Does value depend on the type of institution one attends? Does it depend solely on what one learns in the classroom, in the lab, onstage, and on the athletic field? Are there other advantages the institution provides beyond direct instruction? Should these advantages be merely a personal and subjective consideration, or are there estimates of value that reach beyond to a profession, the community, the state, and the nation?

We begin this cluster of arguments with public policy experts Michael Greenstone and Adam Looney asking, "Where Is the Best Place to Invest $102,000 — In Stocks, Bonds, or a College Degree?" Their thorough discussion of incomes and alternative investment strategies provides a necessary foundation and context for the financial considerations of attending college. Next, Teresa Sullivan's "Four Kinds of Value in Higher Education" brings the question of value into focus. As the president of the University of

Virginia, she is well positioned to argue for the various kinds of an institution's value as well as why and how those values must be cultivated in an atmosphere geared toward excellence. Third, we offer a rather specific but nonetheless hugely important argument: "The Student Loan Crisis That Can't Be Gotten Rid Of," by journalist Maureen Tkacik. One way that students seek to pay for their college educations is through student loans largely guaranteed by the federal government. By her calculations, between one-quarter and one-third of a billion dollars of existing student loans have not been repaid — a shocking statistic. Her analysis of how student loans were designated by federal law as nondischargeable (that is, not capable of being dismissed in bankruptcy court), forms the basis of her argument that a massive fraud has been perpetrated by the federal government, banks, and Wall Street. For Tkacik, the time has come to restore students' financial rights.

e e-Pages

The e-Pages selection for this cluster is "The Three-Year Solution" by U.S. Senator Lamar Alexander, in which he argues that we could reduce costs for both students and their institutions by offering students the option of graduating in three (rather than four) years. Go to **bedfordstmartins.com/ subjectandstrategy** to read Alexander's argument and explore his perspective with study questions.

Preparing to Read

In the end, understanding the arguments for the financial rewards of attending college, for maximizing the value of that education, for consumer awareness of student loan risks, and for trying alternative formats are just that — prerequisites for making informed decisions. In large measure, the readings in this cluster focus on averages and normal expectations, on educational ideals and values, and on a broad perspective of risk, all of which leaves us to each chart the best course for our own future. How much have you thought about these issues? Do you have a clear purpose for going to college? Do you feel confident in your understanding of the costs associated with that decision? What are your expectations, and how will you achieve them?

Where Is the Best Place to Invest $102,000 — In Stocks, Bonds, or a College Degree?

MICHAEL GREENSTONE AND ADAM LOONEY

Michael Greenstone and Adam Looney are both part of the Hamilton Project at the Brookings Institution, a Washington-based nonprofit public policy organization that does independent research. Greenstone, the Director of the Hamilton Project, is also 3M Professor of Environmental Economics at the Massachusetts Institute of Technology. He earned his B.A. with honors from Swarthmore College in 1991 and his Ph.D. in economics from Princeton University. His fields of interest include public finance, regulation of financial markets, and the economics of global warming and air quality. Adam Looney, the Policy Director of the Hamilton Project, earned his B.A. in 1999 from Dartmouth College before going on to Harvard University for his M.A. in 2001 and his Ph.D. in 2004. His fields of interest are taxes, labor policy, U.S. economic performance, inequality, and fiscal policy.

Greenstone and Looney's "Where Is the Best Place to Invest $102,000 — In Stocks, Bonds, or a College Degree?" was first published as a paper of the Brookings Institution on June 25, 2011. They determine that a college education costs $102,000 and then ask an increasingly common question: Is investing in a college education the best place to put that money? They base their argument on evidence derived from statistical data and comparative analyses. To explore how these authors hyperlinked footnotes and in-text citations in the original paper, go to www.brookings.edu and search for the article by its title.

A s the college class of 2011 graduates in the aftermath of the Great Recession, some graduates are struggling to find a good job — or any job at all. As a result, many are questioning whether the time and expense of college was worth it. We try to answer this question by comparing the economic benefits of a college degree to its costs, as one would for any other investment. When compared to other types of investments, how does a college degree really stack up? 1

The answer is clear: Higher education is a much better investment than almost any other alternative, even for the "Class of the Great Recession" (young adults ages 23–24). In today's tough labor market, a college degree dramatically boosts the odds of finding a job and making more money.

In today's tough labor market, a college degree dramatically boosts the odds of finding a job and making more money.

On average, the benefits of a four-year college degree are equivalent to an investment that returns 15.2 percent per year. This is more than double the average return to stock market investments since 1950, and more than five times the returns to corporate bonds, gold, long-term government bonds, or home ownership. From any investment perspective, college is a great deal.

THE VALUE OF A COLLEGE DEGREE

As we are all aware, a college degree is a significant investment involving up-front costs of money and time. First, there are the financial outlays: the cost of tuition and fees (but not room and board—you need to eat and sleep whether or not you go to college). The total average cost of a four-year college degree (public and private) is roughly $48,000, and a two-year associate's degree costs about $5,200.[1]

An additional cost of college is the foregone earnings or "opportunity cost" of not working. On average, 18 and 19 year olds right out of high school earn about $11,600 per year, while 20 and 21 year olds with a high school degree average about $15,400 per year (this average reflects the fact that high school workers are less likely to find a full-time job and more likely to be unemployed).

When you add up the various costs of college, the total investment for a four-year college degree is about $102,000; for a two-year associate's degree, it's about $28,000.

These significant costs lead to the question, "Is college worth it?" Put another way, would an 18 year old be better served by investing in college or putting that money into the stock market or with some other type of investment?

To answer this question, imagine that you sit down your 18-year-old daughter and offer her $102,000 to either pay for college or to invest elsewhere. If she chooses to invest in college, she will have the job

[1]Source: NCES.

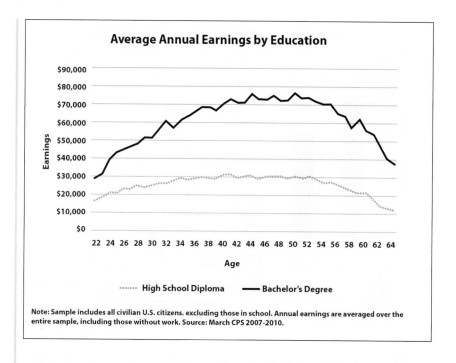

Average Annual Earnings by Education

Note: Sample includes all civilian U.S. citizens. excluding those in school. Annual earnings are averaged over the entire sample, including those without work. Source: March CPS 2007-2010.

opportunities and earnings of a college graduate for the remainder of her working years (until she is 65). If she chooses the latter, she'll face the job prospects and earning power of a high school graduate.

These two paths are starkly different, as shown in the chart above. At age 22, the average college graduate earns about 70 percent more than the average person with a high school degree only. But that is only the beginning. For instance, in 2010, a college graduate at age 50 (the peak of her career) earns approximately $46,500 more than someone with only a high school diploma.

Further, at the peak of her earning power, the average worker with only a high school degree earns only about as much as a college graduate one year out of school. In other words, the average college graduate will surpass the highest earnings of the average high school graduate soon after graduating.

THE $102,000 INVESTMENT —
WHERE TO FIND THE BEST DEAL

It's clear that college graduates fare better than their peers with a high school degree only. But from an investment perspective are these higher earnings worth the up-front cost of $102,000?

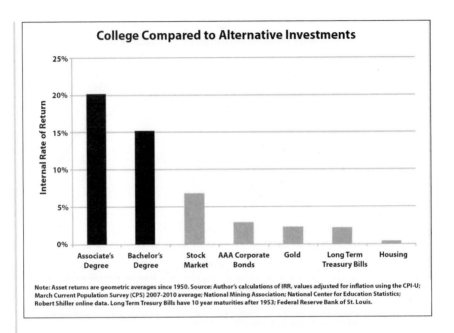

College Compared to Alternative Investments

Note: Asset returns are geometric averages since 1950. Source: Author's calculations of IRR, values adjusted for inflation using the CPI-U; March Current Population Survey (CPS) 2007-2010 average; National Mining Association; National Center for Education Statistics; Robert Shiller online data. Long Term Tresury Bills have 10 year maturities after 1953; Federal Reserve Bank of St. Louis.

We answer this question by calculating the rate of return to college 12 compared to other investments, shown in the figure above. The $102,000 investment in a four-year college yields a rate of return of 15.2 percent per year — more than double the average return over the last 60 years experienced in the stock market (6.8 percent), and more than five times the return to investments in corporate bonds (2.9 percent), gold (2.3 percent), long-term government bonds (2.2 percent), or housing (0.4 percent).[2]

At first blush, the value of the associate's degree really stands out 13 because it provides a higher percentage return of over 20 percent. However, this impressive return mostly reflects the much lower cost of an associate's degree relative to a four-year degree rather than a boost to long-run earnings. When compared to the lifetime earnings of four-year college graduates, workers with an associate's degree still earn a good deal less. Thus, the rate of return does not tell the full story.

Another way to view the total dollar benefit of a four-year college 14 degree is to compare the cumulative lifetime earnings of workers based on their educational attainment — as shown in the graph at right. Through this lens, a bachelor's degree clearly provides the largest boost to earnings.

[2]The rate of return is estimated as an "internal rate of return or IRR." Estimates by Heckman, Lochner, and Todd based on 2000 census data found the IRR to a college degree to be 14 percent for whites and even higher (18 percent) for blacks. See James Heckman, Lance Lochner, and Petra Todd, "Earnings Functions and Rates of Return," NBER Working Paper #13780, 2008.

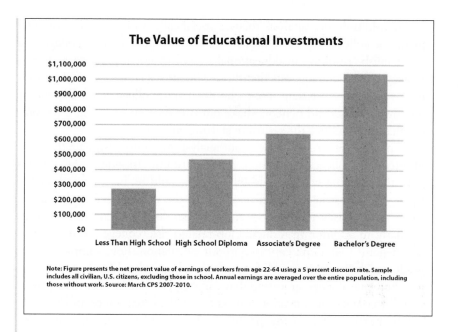

The Value of Educational Investments

Note: Figure presents the net present value of earnings of workers from age 22-64 using a 5 percent discount rate. Sample includes all civilian, U.S. citizens, excluding those in school. Annual earnings are averaged over the entire population, including those without work. Source: March CPS 2007-2010.

Over a lifetime, the average college graduate earns roughly $570,000   15
more than the average person with a high school diploma only—a tremendous return to the average upfront investment of $102,000.[3] An associate's degree is worth approximately $170,000 more than a high school diploma.

ABOUT THE ANALYSIS

There are many factors that play a role in a worker's lifetime earnings. This   16
analysis focuses on the average earnings of a college graduate compared to the average person with only a high-school diploma. But we all know that each person is different, and it's possible (and even likely) that individual college graduates have different aptitudes and ambitions, and might even have access to different levels of family resources. All of these factors can impact earnings. However, the evidence suggests that these factors don't drive the impressive return to college; instead the increased earning power of college graduates appears to be caused by their educational investments (Kane and Rouse 1995; Card 1995, 2001).

[3]Similar analysis by Barrow and Rouse using 2003 data found the earnings boost from a college degree to be between $412,984 to $469,835 in 2009 dollars, depending on assumptions. The benefit to a college degree appears to have increased since then, in part because of the differential impact of the recession on high school educated workers. See Lisa Barrow and Cecilia Rouse, "Does College Still Pay?," Volume 2, Issue 4, 2005.

In addition, our analysis focuses specifically on the benefits of completing a college degree. Unfortunately, many people start college and don't finish, resulting in educational costs but not leading to a degree. However, evidence suggests that those who attend college, even if it's only for a year, earn more than those who don't start college at all. Depending on how the costs and benefits shake out (the data on this is hard to come by) this could reduce the return to starting college.

There are other reasons why our analysis may underestimate the value of attending college. First, these returns are not risk-adjusted—there is both the risk that wages could fall or jobs could be hard to find, just as those who invest in the stock market face the risk of declines in market value. These risks tend to be much higher for less-educated workers. Similarly, in addition to reducing job-related risk, college has many indirect benefits that aren't captured in our calculation. For example, college graduates are healthier and live longer than high school graduates; studies also find that college graduates have higher job satisfaction than people with lower levels of education (Grossman 2006; Oreopoulos and Salvanes 2009). Furthermore, many people find college an enjoyable and life-changing experience.

CONCLUSION

Much of the debate over the value of a college degree focuses on the here and now—what opportunities are available to recent graduates during our nation's economic recovery. It's worth taking a step back, however, and focusing on the long-term impacts of a college investment.

Indeed, the recession has not fundamentally changed the math: Although a college degree has upfront costs, it is important to remember that it is an investment that pays off over time. The evidence clearly shows more education improves your chances in the labor market, in both good times and bad. Yet over the last forty years, increases in college attainment have slowed considerably, especially for men. Given these results, the real mystery may be why more people aren't going to college or getting a two-year degree.

Warren Buffett recently told Columbia Business School students, "Right now, I would pay $100,000 for 10 percent of the future earnings of any of you" (Tucker 2009). He is not a legendary value investor for nothing: When compared to other investment options, a college degree stands out as one of the best investments one can make.

Thinking Critically about the Text

Greenstone and Looney present useful information based on statistical averages, comparisons, and graphics, but should this be the only data used in making decisions about one's future? What questions still need to be asked? What problems might be overlooked in their statistics? What counterarguments can you present?

Examining the Issue

1. What approach do the authors take in estimating the value of a college education?

2. What is the authors' thesis? (Glossary: *Thesis*)

3. Do the authors position their thesis in the best place in their essay? Why, or why not?

4. How much does a college degree cost, according to Greenstone and Looney?

5. What do the authors mean by "opportunity cost"?

6. Do the graphs Greenstone and Looney provide help your understanding of the points they are trying to make? Why, or why not?

7. What does the graph on page 593 demonstrate about the comparative earning power of a high school graduate versus a college graduate?

8. Is it a waste of money if one doesn't finish college? Why, or why not?

9. How effective is Greenstone and Looney's conclusion? Explain.

Four Kinds of Value in Higher Education

TERESA SULLIVAN

Teresa Sullivan became the eighth president of the University of Virginia in 2010. She was born in 1949 in Kewanee, Illinois, and received her undergraduate degree from James Madison College of Michigan State University before continuing on for her Ph.D. at the University of Chicago. After she earned her doctorate, Sullivan began her academic career as a sociology instructor at the University of Texas and then began to rise through the academic ranks, eventually becoming chair of her department, vice provost, vice president for academic affairs, and dean of graduate studies. She was also a member of the law school faculty. Her professional focus is in the areas of consumer debt, economic marginality, and questions regarding who files for bankruptcy and why. A past secretary of the American Sociological Society, she is the author or coauthor of six books and over fifty articles.

"Four Kinds of Value in Higher Education" was first published in the *Daily Progress*, the leading newspaper in Charlottesville, Virginia. Sullivan argues that there are four senses of the word *value* when we use the phrase "value of a college education," and colleges need more than ever to demonstrate their excellence in delivering each type of value.

1 In our national conversation about higher education—in Congress, in state legislatures, and in living rooms across the country—the buzzword is "value." Everyone seems to be talking and writing about the value of a college degree. If you type the words "value of college education" into Google's search box, you will get 20 million results.

2 When we talk about the "value of a college education," we are typically using the word *value* to mean the worth, or the importance, of getting a degree. As tuition rates in colleges and universities across the country continue to rise faster than the rate of inflation, parents and politicians want to know if the money that families are spending on their sons' and daughters' college degrees will justify the investment. Will it be worth it in the long run?

3 The quick answer is: Yes. A college degree has become the standard prerequisite for a financially secure middle-class life. Here's proof: A college graduate with a bachelor's degree typically earns about 66 percent more than a high school graduate during a forty-year career. The unem-

ployment rate for college graduates remains about half that of high school graduates, and a quarter of the rate of high school dropouts. And beyond the financial benefits of getting a college degree, a liberal education teaches us to be critical thinkers; to write clearly and persuasively; to appreciate different cultures and beliefs; and to integrate multiple perspectives before arriving at decisions. These skills hold lifelong value.

Retention rates and graduation rates are two metrics of value. At the University of Virginia, we have a 97 percent retention rate for our students, and a 94 percent six-year graduation rate. This means that almost all of the students who come here stay here, and almost all of the students who stay here also graduate. In addition, we have the highest graduation rate for African American students among all public universities in the country, at about 85 percent. 4

> A liberal education teaches us to be critical thinkers; to write clearly and persuasively; to appreciate different cultures and beliefs; and to integrate multiple perspectives before arriving at decisions.

UVa and other colleges and universities that offer rigorous academic programs and retain and graduate most of their students on time are offering a valuable education. That's one way we use the word *value* when we talk about higher education. 5

Accepting the idea that a college degree is worth the expense generally, one could still argue that it's not worth any level of expense—not worth some astronomical cost. For students, it might not be worth taking on a mountain of debt they will carry around for years. Recent reports show that national student loan debt now stands at $870 billion, surpassing the outstanding balances on car loans ($730 billion) and credit cards ($693 billion). Someday soon, the national total for student loan debt will reach the $1 trillion mark. 6

Facing those kinds of numbers, we use the word *value* in a second sense—to mean a good deal, or a bargain. Students and their families want a college education that will be valuable for the long term, and they want it at a value price. 7

In this country, we have more than 4,000 colleges and universities. Many of them offer an academically rigorous education that will hold value for students for their entire lives. And many others offer a college education at a reasonable price—although some of these schools offer programs of questionable educational value. 8

But there is a sweet spot occupied by universities that offer both kinds of value: a valuable education at a value price. Each year, Kiplinger's magazine ranks the "100 Best Values in Public Colleges." This year, UVa held 9 the No. 3 ranking for the sixth time in seven years. The University of North Carolina–Chapel Hill was No. 1; the University of Florida was No. 2; and the College of William & Mary was No. 4. It's great that we have so many universities offering strong academic programs at reasonable prices in Virginia and across the country.

But there is also a third kind of value to consider. Many universities, especially research universities, create value by contributing to the economic strength of their home regions and the nation. A study estimated that university-based inventions contributed $450 billion to U.S. gross industrial output and created 280,000 new high-tech jobs between 1999 and 2007. That's a lot of economic value coming from universities.   10

Universities are in the business of creating the future. Innovation is always risky, because no one has a crystal ball. Innovation often depends on making new discoveries at the frontiers of knowledge, and then linking those new discoveries with markets and social needs. One way we create value is through "proof of concept" research — research so risky that private-sector companies and investors are frequently unwilling to perform this work.   11

In one proof-of-concept research program, UVa's Coulter Program in biomedical technology, we have invested $7 million over seven years, with an independently audited 7–1 return on investment in follow-on funding to these projects. The projects include new ways to detect pancreatic cancer, and a diagnostic instrument to help surgeons treat blood-clotting problems so they can make surgeries faster. The return on investment yielded about $50 million in follow-on funding, and, at the leveraging rate of 4–1 for state or other outside funding, this means the program brought $200 million in overall funds into Virginia, based on an initial $7 million investment.   12

Just a few universities in this country are creating economic value for the nation while also offering a valuable education at a best-value price. At UVa, we add a fourth kind of value — a value system grounded in the university's Honor Code. The core values of honor, integrity, ethics, and accountability are engrained in every aspect of academic and social life, and students carry these values with them when they leave Charlottesville.   13

At a time when the value of college education is under such intense scrutiny, colleges and universities need to demonstrate their value in every sense of the word.   14

Thinking Critically about the Text

Sullivan is the president of the University of Virginia. Can she be considered an expert on her subject? Can she also be considered unbiased about her subject? Explain.

Examining the Issue

1. Sullivan uses information about the University of Virginia to make her argument that it delivers value in four key senses of the term. Does that help or hinder her argument about the value of a college degree in general? Explain.

2. Even though Sullivan's statistics about the higher earning power of college graduates as compared to high school graduates and high school dropouts are impressive, they represent effects that will take place over many years. Can all students wait for the benefits to really pay off, especially if jobs are difficult to find and college loans need to be repaid? Explain.

3. What other senses of the word *value*, if any, might Sullivan have mentioned and measured?

4. What argument does Sullivan make about retention rates and graduation rates? Wouldn't those two metrics seem to be more the responsibility of the student than the institution per se? Explain.

5. What point does Sullivan make in paragraph 9 about the "sweet spot" achieved by institutions that offer both "a valuable education" and a "value price"?

6. What, in your own words, is "proof-of-concept research"? Do you think the institution you are attending engages in that kind of research? Why, or why not?

7. How is proof-of-concept research important to you as an undergraduate? Is it a function of a university that your tuition should support? Explain.

The Student Loan Crisis That Can't Be Gotten Rid Of

MAUREEN TKACIK

Maureen Tkacik is a Brooklyn-based journalist writing on a wide range of topics, from economics and Wall Street to feminism and personal narratives. She often writes using her nickname "Moe." She was born in Washington, D.C., in 1978 and briefly studied at the University of Pennsylvania. She began her journalism career as an intern with *Philadelphia* magazine before moving on to cover youth culture in the *Wall Street Journal*'s Los Angeles bureau for just over two years. She then moved to Hong Kong for two years to work for *Time*'s international editions. Tkacik was named to The Journalist & Financial Reporter Group's "30 Under 30" list of young business journalists in 2002 and 2003. With Anna Holmes, in 2007 she founded *Jezebel*, an editorial Web site that takes on celebrity, fashion, and sex from a feminist perspective. Tkacik currently runs her own Web site, DasKrap.com, an independent take on politics, the media, and major news. She has been published in the *Nation*, *New York Magazine*, *Gawker*, the *Baffler*, *Business Week*, and the *New York Times*.

In "The Student Loan Crisis That Can't Be Gotten Rid Of," which first appeared as a Reuters.com column on August 15, 2012, Tkacik chronicles the evolution of the student loan industry and argues just who (and what) is to blame for a system in which powerful lobbies and loan corporations often profit at the expense of young and eager college graduates.

You have probably mentally cataloged the student loan crisis 1 alongside all the other looming trillion-dollar crises busy imperiling civilization but also enriching the already rich.

But it is different from those crises in a few significant 2 ways, starting with the fact that the entire loan business is arguably unconstitutional. You don't have to take it from me: A preeminent bankruptcy scholar made precisely this argument under oath before Congress. In December 1975, when Congress was debating the first law that made student loans nondischargeable in bankruptcy, University of Connecticut law professor Philip Shuchman testified that students:

> should not be singled out for special and discriminatory treatment. I have the further very literal feeling that this is almost a denial of their right to equal protection of the laws . . . Nor do I think has any evidence been presented that these people, these young people just beginning their years on the whole should be singled out for special and as I view it discriminatory

treatment. I suggest to you that this may at least in spirit be a denial of their right to equal protection with the virtual pole star of our constitutional ambit.

The thing is, though, discrimination was kind of the whole idea. Stagflation was sending an unprecedented number of Silent Majority members into bankruptcy, and the bank lobby was fighting back with a propaganda assault that scapegoated counterculture student delinquents who were allegedly taking loans with no goal of paying them. As Shuchman and others explained in hearings, only about 4 percent of people who filed for bankruptcy protection in 1975 had student loans on their balance sheets, and of those, fewer than one-fifth did not have substantial other debts motivating them to file.

> The Internet is a rich trove of surreal personal accounts of being penalized for overpaying student loan bills. But no one notices, because student borrowers are so utterly powerless.

But try telling that to anyone who'd been reading the papers! A typical syndicated dispatch on the surge in student deadbeats was the August 27, 1972, exposé by *Los Angeles Times* reporter Linda Mathews, which began with the personal anecdote of an anonymous "Washington banker" who purported to have once "handed a $1,500 check" for the year's tuition to a nameless "18-year-old college freshman" only to be insouciantly told, "Oh, I never intend to repay this loan." The anonymous banker—who had since joined "the staff of the American Banking [sic] Association"—helpfully explained to Mathews that the kid was, "acting on advice in underground newspapers urging students to use bankruptcy to avoid paying loans."

"Elitist cheaters" and "professional deadbeats" had driven default rates "as high as 40 percent in some cases," the *Chicago Tribune* claimed. "Sometimes when I see someone come out before me with a job and no other debt but a college loan—and not even a big one at that—I feel like saying, 'Why you little stinker,'" a judge told the *New York Times*. A *Wall Street Journal* editorial on "the educational subculture" blamed the "crisis" on "an attitude of unconcern" apparently widespread throughout the entire education establishment—"that default really isn't like ripping off anybody, just the large, impersonal government that wastes plenty of money on other things."

But to the credit of Congress in that era, the majority of its members were still capable of distinguishing between PR and reality. It concluded its round of hearings in February 1976 by postponing the vote on the non-dischargeability amendment pending a formal Government Accounting

Office study on the matter, which in turn confirmed earlier findings that deliberate student deadbeats accounted for a virtually infinitesimal proportion of bankruptcies. In the meantime, mainstream journalists who spent more time in reality than their trend-setting contemporaries uncovered some troubling (and real) trends while scouring bankruptcy filings. Of the small population of twentysomethings who did seek to use bankruptcy protection primarily to discharge student loans, many had been defrauded by fly-by-night "correspondence schools" that had forged the students' signatures and saddled them with staggering loans. They hadn't even known about them until they started getting hounded by collection agencies.

By 1977 even the American Bankers Association had joined the conference of bankruptcy judges in lobbying—formally, anyway—against the cruel and unusual punishment of making student debt nondischargeable. As James O'Harra, the congressman who had commissioned the GAO study, pointed out in his testimony, to enact such a law would be tantamount to "treating students, all students, as though they were suspected frauds and felons" while according arbitrary second-class creditor status to "the grocery store, the tailor, or the doctor to whom the same student may also owe money." In 1978 the House of Representatives voted to pass a bankruptcy reform bill that specifically restored student loans to their original status as equivalent to any other form of unsecured debt. 7

BUT LIKE A (BABY) BOOMERANG . . .

But then, in 1978, the bill went to conference committee with the Senate, and the clause came back. Like the loans themselves, it could not be gotten rid of. 8

At first this provision applied only during the first five years of the life of the loan; then it was seven, then eternity. Until 2005 it only applied to federally guaranteed loans; now, thanks to the Bankruptcy Abuse Prevention and Consumer Protection Act, it applies to all. 9

And as the loans became more steadily impervious to the usual laws of credit and debt, they became bigger and more profitable. In the years since the Bankruptcy Reform Act passed in 1978, the nominal price of college tuition has risen more than 900 percent. Over the same period the median male income—again, nominally—has risen 165 percent. And since the percentage of the workforce boasting a bachelor's degree has expanded from less than 20 percent to nearly a third, I don't have to convince you that the median de facto return on investment on those diplomas has diminished greatly over the same years. Which brings us to the second way in which the student debt bubble differs from all the others you've seen: It is legally impossible to pop. By law it can only grow very fast. The profits 10 in this racket are downright hallucinogenic: A military veteran sharing his story with Occupy Student Debt has paid $18,000 on a $2,500 loan, and Sallie Mae claims he still owes $5,000; the husband of a social worker bankrupt and bedridden after a botched surgery tells Student Loan Justice of a $13,000 college loan balance from the 1980s that ballooned to $70,000. A grandmother subsisting on Social Security has her payments garnished to pay off a $20,000 loan balance resulting from a $3,500 loan she took out ten years ago, before she underwent brain surgery.

The human toll exacted by this immortal, justice-resistant debt fills Web   11 sites and Student Loan Justice founder Alan Collinge's horrifying book *Student Loan Scam: The Most Oppressive Debt in U.S. History—And How We Can Fight Back.* And yet I didn't even really know about it—not the brutality and scope of it—until I volunteered to research "fighting back" possibilities for an Occupy Wall Street–affiliated group. Neither did any of the other predatory lending buffs I polled; we'd been preoccupied by mortgages, and the government's alarming indifference to the foreclosure epidemic.

We weren't ultimately aware of the student loan crisis because there is no   12 legitimate way of fighting back. Under the current regime, the most effective means of sticking it to the proverbial man would in theory be for all students to simply pay off all their debts at once. But even if they could scrounge together a trillion dollars out of their collective couches just like that, there is little doubt in my mind that Sallie Mae and its student-loan-sharking brethren would simply see it as an opportunity to levy a massive prepayment penalty. The Internet is a rich trove of surreal personal accounts of being penalized for overpaying student loan bills. But no one notices, because student borrowers are so utterly powerless. They can borrow a trillion dollars and still pose no threat to the immediate solvency of the financial system.

SHARK-TANK SALLIE

Naturally, this story has its brighter side, with enterprising corporate lead-   13 ership generating shareholder value. The finances of Sallie Mae, the former government-sponsored enterprise formally called SLM Corp, are a bit difficult to divine, but the operating profit margin is over 50 percent. It will surely surge higher if CEO Albert Lord executes on his current strategy of turning the $700 million "sweet spot" that is its "fee income" division into a billion-dollar business. "Fee income" means collections, but student loan collectors "do things that no other industry could get away with," a veteran debt collector named Joseph Leal told Student Loan Justice. They stalk, threaten family members, and jack up loan balances by thousands of dollars at whim, and they do it all with impunity, because they are legally entitled to garnish your wages.

Fee income is not just a sweet spot for Sallie. The fee collections sub- 14
sidiary of its fiercest rival, Nelnet, is so flush it keeps a 3,800-gallon saltwa-
ter shark tank in its main lobby. The margins on college-loan-sharking are
so grotesquely fat that the government even rakes in a juicy cut: In 2010 the
Department of Education reported collecting $1.22 for every dollar in
defaulted student loans it had guaranteed—and that's after the sharks and
their shareholders and the obligatory outright fraud had taken their first
round of cuts. Between a quarter and a third of about $850 billion worth
of federally guaranteed loans are already in default, so this is real money we
are talking about. Given the $23 trillion worth of other securities the fed-
eral government has pledged to guarantee over the past few years, we can
only expect the default rate to surge higher.

Leveraged buyout titan J. C. Flowers made a $25 billion bid to pur- 15
chase Sallie Mae in 2007, only to back out of the deal in the wake of a
confluence of negative headlines: Rating agencies threatened to downgrade
the company's debt to junk status if it went through; Sallie's dealings with
the Department of Education and the financial aid authorities at various
universities were the subject of an assortment of investigations; and the
SEC was sniffing around an $18.3 million stock sale Lord had made in
anticipation of the takeover announcement. (Lord sued Flowers for $900
million for walking away from the deal, but dropped the suit as a condition
of obtaining the aforementioned 4.5 percent credit line.)

Maybe the student-loan-shark hustle was too fishy even for Wall Street, 16
even in 2007, to want to get too close to the action. And if Lord has been
spreading the no-risk wealth around Wall Street in the aftermath of the
credit crisis, it is not apparent from securitization volume, which has
slowed to a trickle even as student borrowing keeps setting new records. In
2010 students borrowed $100 billion, but Student Loan Asset Backed
Securities (SLABS) issuance was a meager $13.6 billion, down from a peak
of $78.7 billion in 2006.

Perhaps this lack of Wall Street skin in the game is partially responsi- 17
ble for the fact that such reliable business lobby organs as Forbes have
demonstrated refreshing equanimity to the cause of restoring students'
financial rights. The student loan shark bubble will, after all, ultimately
prove far worse for business than the subprime mortgage bubble. But it
also demonstrates that the shadowy ruling elite's overwhelming contempt
toward its citizenry runs deeper and dates back farther than full-time
chroniclers of American decline ever believed.

Thinking Critically about the Text

Tkacik refers to the student loan crisis as "loan sharking" with students as the
victims. What is loan sharking? Do you think she is correct in her use of the term?
Why, or why not?

Examining the Issue

1. What is Tkacik's thesis and where does she state it? (Glossary: *Thesis*)

2. What does the term *nondischargeability* mean? How important is the term for Tkacik's argument?

3. Tkacik quotes University of Connecticut law school professor Philip Shuchman as saying that the law in question "is almost a denial of their [students'] right to equal protection of the laws." Why do you think he says "almost"? In the same quotation, Shuchman uses the phrase "pole star of our constitutional ambit." What does it mean? (Glossary: *Figures of Speech*)

4. What does Tkacik mean when she writes that "discrimination was kind of the whole idea" of the nondischargeability law? What evidence does she use to back up her claim?

5. In paragraph 7, Tkacik calls the nondischargeability of student loans a "cruel and unusual punishment." Do you think that is a fair statement to make? Why, or why not?

6. Tkacik's approach to the student loan crisis is cynical at best. Cite some examples of the language she uses that support that impression. Is she, in your opinion, justified in her cynicism? Explain.

7. Tkacik goes into some detail in her evidence of how the lucrative nature of the student loan business was not only bad for students and their parents but was also highly profitable for the government. In your own words, explain what has happened since J. C. Flowers made a bid to purchase Sallie Mae. Why does Tkacik think that when Wall Street backed away from the student loan business, sentiment began to change about efforts to restore students' rights?

8. How effective is Tkacik's conclusion, particularly her last sentence, in pointing to a larger problem within American society? Explain.

---

 e-Pages

The Three-Year Solution

LAMAR ALEXANDER

Go to bedfordstmartins.com/subjectandstrategy for the final reading in this cluster. In "The Three-Year Solution," U.S. Senator Lamar Alexander argues that we could reduce costs for both students and their institutions by offering students the option of graduating in three (rather than four) years.

MAKING CONNECTIONS

Writing and Discussion Suggestions on the Value of College

1. Do you agree or disagree with the argument that a college education is worth the cost and is the best investment one can make with $102,000, as Greenstone and Looney have written? If you agree, what new information, ideas, and insights on the question can you bring to your argument? If you disagree, what new and convincing evidence do you have to controvert their findings? Have they left out any counterarguments that might undermine their conclusion?

2. It's often pointed out that a liberal arts education was never designed to train students for jobs in any specific sense. Instead, the purpose of a liberal arts curriculum is to expose students to a wide array of disciplines, the focus and purpose of each one, and the way that scholars and researchers go about their work in their chosen specialties. Even when jobs were more plentiful, students were advised that it was not the responsibility of their institutions to help them find employment. Write an argument in favor or against this point of view. How much of a responsibility do higher education institutions have in helping to place their students in jobs when they graduate, especially when college costs have risen dramatically and jobs are harder to find?

3. What's your take on the question of student loans? Do you side with Tkacik and her evidence that suggests students have been discriminated against and are not being accorded equal treatment under the Constitution? Or, would you argue that students knew the laws that applied to student loans when they arranged for those loans and that they should accept their responsibility to pay down their debts?

4. Teresa Sullivan argues that there are four senses of the word *value* when we use the phrase "the value of a college education." As she is the president of a prestigious university, some might find her comments encompassing and philosophic, while others might argue that her views are self-serving. From your perspective as a student, what senses of the word *value* do you find most convincing? Do you think your tuition should go to support research, especially "proof of concept research" as she puts it, and to contribute to the economic strength of your area and region? Do you believe that this supports our national strength? Write an essay in which you argue for a set of non-financial-related priorities we should use for determining value.

5. Assume you have graduated college and are burdened by a sizeable student loan debt. Write a letter to your senator or congressional representative arguing that the nondischargeability of student loans is unfair and that it is crippling you and many others as they attempt to find jobs and begin their careers. Explain the situation, demonstrating your thorough knowledge of the issue and marshaling both anecdotal and objective information as well as statistical evidence to support your claims. Try to make the case that some relief has to be found for the debt amassed by you and others in the form of a federal paydown of those debts or by the forbearance of those loan obligations.

6. All statements regarding the benefits of a college education are based on the law of averages. But, as the advertisements warn, your gas mileage may differ. People differ and any given person may not measure up to the averages. What are the factors that need to be considered when thinking about whether or not a person may be a good candidate for college and whether they'll achieve success both as a student and as a graduate? Here is a prompt you may want to use for your argument: A college education offers many rewards, but what does it ask of you? You might want to consider a younger sibling or friend who is considering going to college as your audience for this argument.

7. **Writing with Sources.** Write an argument in which you support the view that student loans are a good idea if they are "sold" properly by loan officers and agents, both of whom should make all the provisions of the law clear to loan applicants and their cosigners. Argue that student loans are an excellent way to get an education and pay for it over the working life of the borrower. Before you begin writing, research the language of typical college loan contracts. What provisions do the loan contracts contain, and what do those provisions mean? What kinds of information should be made clear, what liabilities should be explained, and what risks must applicants know before signing for loans? Is it generally thought that such explanations are always proffered by loan officers? If not, why not? For models of and advice on integrating sources in your essay, see Chapters 14 and 15.

WRITING SUGGESTIONS FOR ARGUMENTATION

1. Think of a product that you like and want to use even though it has an annoying feature. Write a letter of complaint in which you attempt to persuade the manufacturer to improve the product. Your letter should include the following points:
   a. A statement concerning the nature of the problem
   b. Evidence supporting or explaining your complaint
   c. Suggestions for improving the product

2. Select one of the position statements that follow, and write an argumentative essay in which you defend that statement.
   a. Living in a dormitory is (or is not) as desirable as living off campus.
   b. Student government shows (or does not show) that the democratic process is effective.
   c. America should (or should not) be a refuge for the oppressed.
   d. School spirit is (or is not) as important as it ever was.
   e. Interest in religion is (or is not) increasing in the United States.
   f. We have (or have not) brought air pollution under control in the United States.
   g. The need to develop alternative energy sources is (or is not) serious.
   h. America's great cities are (or are not) thriving.
   i. Fraternities and sororities do (or do not) build character.
   j. We have (or have not) found effective means to dispose of nuclear or chemical wastes.
   k. Fair play is (or is not) a thing of the past.
   l. Human life is (or is not) valued in a technological society.
   m. The consumer does (or does not) need to be protected.
   n. The family farm in America is (or is not) in danger of extinction.
   o. Grades do (or do not) encourage learning.
   p. America is (or is not) a violent society.
   q. Television is (or is not) a positive cultural force in America.
   r. America should (or should not) feel a commitment to the starving peoples of the world.
   s. The federal government should (or should not) regulate all utilities.
   t. Money is (or is not) the path to happiness.
   u. Animals do (or do not) have rights.
   v. Competition is (or is not) killing us.
   w. America is (or is not) becoming a society with deteriorating values.

3. Think of something on your campus or in your community that you would like to see changed. Write a persuasive argument that explains what is wrong and how you think it ought to be changed. Make sure you incorporate other writing strategies into your essay — for example, description, narration, or illustration — to increase the effectiveness of your persuasive argument. (Glossary: *Description; Illustration; Narration*)

4. Read some articles in the editorial section of today's paper (in print or online), and pick one with which you agree or disagree. Write a letter to the editor that presents your point of view. Use a logical argument to support or refute the editorial's assertions. Depending on the editorial, you might choose to use different rhetorical strategies to reach your audience. (Glossary: *Audience*) You might use cause and effect, for example, to show the correct (or incorrect) connections made by the editorial. (Glossary: *Cause and Effect Analysis*)

5. **Writing with Sources.** Working with a partner, choose a controversial topic like the legalization of medical marijuana or any of the topics in writing suggestion 2. Each partner should argue one side of the issue. Decide who is going to write on which side of the issue, and keep in mind that there are often more than two sides to an issue. Then each of you should write an essay trying to convince your partner that your position is the most logical and correct.

   You'll both need to do research online or in the library to find support for your position. For models of and advice on integrating sources in your essay, see Chapters 14 and 15.

6 **Working with Sources.** Visit the World Wildlife Foundation online to learn more about the wildlife protection campaign that prompted this chapter's opening image (see worldwildlife.org/pages/stop-wildlife-crime). Once you have a good understanding of the site's message and goals, write an essay in which you analyze whether this chapter's opening image works, carefully explaining your reasoning in the context of the campaign's audience and mission. What argument is at the core of the campaign? How did the campaign use visuals — both in print and online — to give its message impact? What other types of images might they have used, and would those have been effective? Online, the foundation encourages visitors to share the ads via social media. Is this something you would e-mail to your friends or post on Facebook or Twitter? Why, or why not? For models of and advice on integrating sources in your essay, see Chapters 14 and 15.

7. Read or reread Michael Jonas's essay "The Downside of Diversity" on page 476 and discuss its relationship to the issues Steven Pinker raises in his essay "In Defense of Dangerous Ideas" on page 529. Write an argument in which you make the case that Jonas supports Pinker's thesis that dangerous ideas need to be brought out into the open and discussed.

8. Take a close look at the public service advertisement at the top of this page. What kind of an argument does it represent? Is it effective, in your opinion? Why, or why not? If you were going to create an ad responding to this one — or an ad similarly warning against violence — what would it look like?

9. **Writing in the Workplace.** You're a summer intern at a midsized news Web site. A freelance journalist sends you the final draft of his commissioned article so that you can correct any grammar mistakes before it's read by your boss. As you read it, you realize that a few sentences stand out for their distinct, different style. You run those sentences through a search engine and, sure enough, the freelancer plagiarized them from an independent, personally run blog. Write a thorough, professional e-mail to your boss explaining the

situation and why the plagiarism is a concern. Can you run the piece? How does this affect the credibility and reputation of the journalist? To what extent must freelancers produce original content? How might the freelancer defend his actions? Would that defense matter? Since you're on a deadline, propose a solution to your boss. What next steps can your organization take in order to accurately and ethically report on the story?

 e-Pages

See how argument works on the Web. Go to bedfordstmartins.com/subjectand strategy for a variety of readings, video, and study questions that connect to the themes and strategies in this chapter.

I was raised to believe that milk was part of a healthy diet. Then I discovered that to increase production, many dairy companies inject cows with hormones and antibiotics that we end up drinking. And that cows are kept "artificially" pregnant so they'll produce milk all year long. So I scrapped my milk mustache for a soy one. It's healthier for me AND the cows.

WHY MILK?
Try soy instead.

CHAPTER 13

Combining Strategies

WHAT DOES IT MEAN TO COMBINE STRATEGIES?

Each of the preceding chapters of *Subject & Strategy* emphasizes a particular writing strategy: narration, description, illustration, process analysis, and so forth. The essays and selections within each of these
chapters use the given strategy as the dominant method of development.
It is important to remember, however, that the *dominant* strategy is rarely
the *only* one used to develop a piece of writing. To fully explore their topics, writers often use other strategies in combination with the dominant
strategy.

To highlight and reinforce this point, we focus on the use of multiple
strategies in the Questions on Strategy section following each professional
selection. In this chapter on combining strategies, we offer a collection of
essays that make notable use of several different strategies. You will encounter such combinations of strategies in the reading and writing you do in
other college courses. Beyond the classroom, you might write a business
proposal using both description and cause and effect to make an argument
for a new marketing plan, or you might use narration, description, and illustration to write a news story for a company blog or a letter to the editor
of your local newspaper.

For an example of a visual text that combines strategies, see the advertisement on the opposite page. Few ad campaigns have been more successful than the California Milk Processor Board's "Got Milk?" promotion
initiated in 1993. That campaign's use of celebrities, serial format, striking
visuals, and pared-down, direct language made it instantly recognizable,
and, inevitably, widely imitated. Among its many imitators is this Adbusters
parody ad, "Why Milk?," which seeks to promote soy milk as a healthier
alternative to cow's milk. While the Adbusters ad is primarily an argument
for drinking soy milk and avoiding cow's milk, the ad copy and image of the
soy-milk lover also implicitly rely for their impact on the strategies of narration, illustration, comparison and contrast, and cause and effect analysis.

COMBINING STRATEGIES IN WRITTEN TEXTS

The following essay by Sydney Harris reveals how several strategies can be used effectively, even in a brief piece of writing. Although primarily a work of definition, notice how "A Jerk" also uses illustration and personal narrative to engage the reader and achieve Harris's purpose.

A JERK

I don't know whether history repeats itself, but biography certainly does. The other day, Michael came in and asked me what a "jerk" was — the same question Carolyn put to me a dozen years ago.

At that time, I fluffed her off with some inane answer, such as "A jerk isn't a very nice person," but both of us knew it was an unsatisfactory reply. When she went to bed, I began trying to work up a suitable definition.

It is a marvelously apt word, of course. Until it was coined, not more than twenty-five years ago, there was really no single word in English to describe the kind of person who is a jerk — "boob" and "simp" were too old hat, and besides they really didn't fit, for they could be lovable, and a jerk never is.

Thinking it over, I decided that a jerk is basically a person without insight. He is not necessarily a fool or a dope, because some extremely clever persons can be jerks. In fact, it has little to do with intelligence as we commonly think of it; it is, rather, a kind of subtle but persuasive aroma emanating from the inner part of the personality.

I know a college president who can be described only as a jerk. He is not an unintelligent man, nor unlearned, nor even unschooled in the social amenities. Yet he is a jerk *cum laude*, because of a fatal flaw in his nature — he is totally incapable of looking into the mirror of his soul and shuddering at what he sees there.

A jerk, then, is a man (or woman) who is utterly unable to see himself as he appears to others. He has no grace, he is tactless without meaning to be, he is a bore even to his best friends, he is an egotist without charm. All of us are egotists to some extent, but most of us — unlike the jerk — are perfectly and horribly aware of it when we make asses of ourselves. The jerk never knows.

Essays that employ thoughtful combinations of rhetorical strategies have some obvious advantages for the writer and the reader. By reading the work of professional writers, you can learn how multiple strategies can be used to your advantage—how a paragraph of narration, a vivid description, a clarifying instance of comparison and contrast, or a clear definition can help convey your purpose and thesis.

For example, let's suppose you wanted to write an essay on the slang you hear on campus. You might find it helpful to use a variety of strategies.

Definition—to explain what slang is

Illustration—to give examples of slang

Comparison and contrast—to differentiate slang from other types of speech, such as idioms or technical language

Division and classification—to categorize different types of slang or different topics that slang terms are used for, such as courses, students, food, grades

Or let's say you wanted to write a paper on the Japanese Americans who were sent to internment camps during World War II while the United States was at war with Japan. The following strategies would be available to you.

Illustration—to illustrate several particular cases of families that were sent to internment camps

Narration—to tell the stories of former camp residents, including their first reaction to their internment and their actual experiences in the camps

Cause and effect—to examine the reasons why the United States government interned Japanese Americans and the long-term effects of this policy

When you rely on a single mode or approach to an essay, you lose the opportunity to come at your subject from a number of different angles, all of which complete the picture and any one of which might be the most insightful or engaging and, therefore, the most memorable for the reader. This is particularly the case with essays that attempt to persuade or argue. The task of changing readers' beliefs and thoughts is so difficult that writers look for any combination of strategies that will make their arguments more convincing.

SAMPLE STUDENT ESSAY USING A COMBINATION OF STRATEGIES

While a senior at the University of Vermont, English major Tara E. Ketch took a course in children's literature and was asked to write a term paper on some aspect of the literature she was studying. She knew that she would soon be looking for a teaching position and realized that any teaching job she accepted would bring her face-to-face with the difficult task of selecting appropriate reading materials. Ketch understood, as well, that she would have to confront criticism of her choices, so she decided to delve a little deeper into the subject of censorship, particularly of literature for children and adolescents. She was interested in learning more about why people want to censor certain books so that she could consider an appropriate response to their efforts. In a way, she wanted to begin to develop her own teaching philosophy with respect to text selection. Her essay naturally incorporated several rhetorical modes working in combination. As you read Ketch's essay, notice how naturally she has used the supporting strategies of definition, cause and effect, and illustration to enhance the dominant strategy of argumentation.

Kids, You Can't Read That Book!
Tara E. Ketch

Defines censorship and suggests cause and effect

Censorship is the restriction or suppression of speech or writing. In schools, debates about censorship arise when school officials, librarians, parents, or other adults in the community attempt to keep students from gaining access to particular books. Such attempts present serious questions for educators. How should educators decide what materials are fit for American schoolchildren? On what basis should they decide? A review of the reasons for challenges to books suggests that educators might forestall outright bans on books by paying more attention to age-appropriateness and to the kinds of guidance given to students who are reading challenging material. [1]

Argument: educators need to take steps to forestall outright censorship

Illustration: Supreme Court decision

The federal government has not set clear limits on censorship in the schools. In the 1968 case of *Epperson v. Arkansas*, the Supreme Court stated, "Public education in our Nation is committed to the control of state and local authorities. Courts do not and cannot intervene in the resolution of conflicts which arise in the daily operation of school systems and which do not directly and sharply implicate basic constitutional values" (Reichman 3). Yet in 1982, the Supreme Court ruled that "local school boards may not remove books from school library shelves simply because they dislike the ideas contained in those books and seek by their removal to prescribe what shall be orthodox in politics, nationalism, religion, or other matters of opinion" (Reichman 4). Different interpretations of rulings such as these have led to frequent efforts to ban children's books in school systems for a wide variety of reasons. Generally speaking, most attempts to ban books from school systems stem from the perception that the books offend community, family, or religious values. [2]

Cause and effect: consequences of decisions

Challenges based on "offensive" or profane language are especially common in the area of adolescent literature. In the American Library Association's Office for Intellectual [3]

Cause and effect: first ground for bans

Freedom's (OIF) list of the most frequently challenged books from 1990-2000, J. D. Salinger's 1951 novel *Catcher in the Rye*, a perennial target of would-be censors, took the number thirteen slot, largely because of objections to its language, includ-

Examples of challenges based on language

ing the "F-word" (Office for Intellectual Freedom). In a debate about Katherine Paterson's 1977 novel *Bridge to Terabithia* (number nine on the OIF's list), one Lincoln, Nebraska, parent protested the use of the words *snotty* and *shut up* along with *Lord* and *damn*, saying, "Freedom of speech was not intended to guarantee schools the right to intrude on traditional family values without warning and regardless of the availability of nonoffensive alternatives" (Reichman 47-48). The school board in this case decided that the book had a value that transcended the use of offensive language.

Cause and effect: second ground for bans

Other challenges come from adults' idea that children   4
should be protected from sexual content. Maya Angelou's 1969 autobiographical novel *I Know Why the Caged Bird Sings* (number three on the OIF's list) portrays rape, among other frankly sexual topics, and has since publication been banned from many school libraries and curricula. On what some would con-

Examples of challenges based on sexual content

sider the opposite end of the spectrum, Maurice Sendak's 1970 illustrated book *In the Night Kitchen* (number twenty-five on the OIF list) shows a naked little boy, and although there is no explicit sexual content, many people have found the book offensive. According to an online exhibit at the site of the University of Virginia Libraries, "[i]n Springfield, Missouri, the book was expurgated by drawing shorts on the nude boy" ("Through the Eyes"). In New York, in 1990, parents tried to have the book removed from an elementary school, and in Maine, a parent wanted the book removed because she felt it encouraged child molestation (Foerstel 201).

Additional examples

Many of Judy Blume's books have likewise come under fire   5
for their portrayal of sexual themes: In fact, Blume has authored a total of five of the books on the OIF's top 100 list. *Are You There, God? It's Me, Margaret* (number sixty-two) has been banned for its frank discussion of menstruation and adoles-

Cause and effect: clarifies reasoning of bans based on sexual content

cent development. *Forever*, which discusses intercourse and abortion, comes in at number eight. These topics are clearly disturbing to many adults who grew up in environments where sex was not openly discussed and who may worry that these books will encourage sexual activity.

Cause and effect: third ground for bans

A related source of debate is gay and lesbian content.   6
(The OIF categorizes challenges based on homosexual content

separately from those based on sexual explicitness.) Two children's books designed to explain gay lifestyles to children, Michael Willhoite's *Daddy's Roommate* and Leslea Newman's *Heather Has Two Mommies*, rank as number two and number eleven, respectively, on the OIF list. Henry Reichman writes that in 1990, Frank Mosca's *All-American Boys* (1983) and Nancy Garden's *Annie on My Mind* (1982), two books with gay themes, were donated to high schools in Contra Costa, California; at three of these high schools, the books were seized by administrators and then "lost" (53).

Examples of challenges based on gay/lesbian content

Religion, not surprisingly, has been the focus of many challenges to literature in the schools. The Bible's presence in the classroom has generated criticism from both religious and nonreligious groups: Those arguing from a religious perspective have objected when the Bible has been taught as literature, rather than as a sacred text, and those arguing from a secular perspective have objected to its being taught on any basis (Burress 219). Some critics speaking from a religious perspective object to portrayals of the occult in books. The Harry Potter series (collectively number seven on the OIF list) is perhaps the most famous recent target of such objections, the latest of which was leveled by a Gwinnett County, Georgia, parent in 2005, whose lawsuit to have the books removed from county schools was dismissed in 2007 ("Harry Potter"). 7

Cause and effect: fourth ground for bans

Examples of books banned on religious grounds

Another frequently cited reason for challenges to books is their portrayal of content considered to be racist or sexist. Mark Twain's *Adventures of Huckleberry Finn* (number five on the OIF list), the source of perhaps the most heated controversy of this type, has often been challenged and banned outright because of its use of racist language. Defenders of the text point out that such criticism ignores context and intent—Twain was writing specifically to draw negative attention to the South's racist attitudes and practices. Nevertheless, some critics claim that *any* use of such offensive terms, particularly in a text presented as a classic, can do more harm than good. 8

Cause and effect: fifth ground for bans

Example of challenge based on racism

Presentation of counterargument

This brief review of some of the reasons used to ban children's books leaves us with the questions "How should educators decide what materials are fit for American schoolchildren?" and "On what basis should they decide?" It might be that the issue of age-appropriateness—the third most frequent reason given for challenges to books over the last decade and a half, according to the OIF—requires more attention than it gets from educators. A relatively large number of 9

Argument: age-appropriateness needs more attention from educators concerned adults seem interested not in banning books, necessarily, but in ensuring that the right books reach the right audiences in our schools.

Most educators likely agree that it is possible to identify age-appropriate (and age-inappropriate) themes in many of the books under discussion. Most would probably agree that elementary school children should not be exposed to the issues of rape and abortion present in some young-adult fiction. Many would rightly question whether young adults should be exposed to extremely violent novels such as Anthony Burgess's *A Clockwork Orange*, given that they are still too young to put what they read into proper context. Does this mean, however, that such books should be removed altogether from school libraries? Perhaps not.

Libraries and classrooms should be resources for children to broaden their horizons. Students need to learn about the range of human experience in order to make judgments about it; leaving them guessing, or gleaning what information they can from schoolyard conversations, will lead to misunderstood, or perhaps worse, half-understood "facts" of life. As Natalie Goldberg writes, "When we know the name of something . . . [i]t takes the blur out of our mind" (5)—and isn't that the purpose of an education?

While outright censorship defeats the purpose of an education, educators must guide children in choosing age-appropriate material and then aid them in understanding material that might prove challenging. As Diane Ravitch writes, "Teachers have a responsibility to choose readings for their students based on their professional judgment of what students are likely to understand and what they need to learn" (506). If a child independently seeks out a controversial novel, educators should oversee the process, in order to give context to what might otherwise be a bewildering experience. In the case of a novel like *Catcher in the Rye*, which most critics agree has literary merit, but whose message is couched in profanity, it is the job of school educators to teach students how to read such literature critically and to understand the distance between the world of the novel and the student's own reality.

Similarly, novels like Maya Angelou's *I Know Why the Caged Bird Sings*, which have strong sexual content, need to be introduced to students old enough to understand something about mature sexual behavior, and discussion needs to focus on the

---

Argument: appeals to common ground

Argument (assumption): censorship is contrary to aims of education

Argument: educators need to guide children in selecting and understanding material

Support (expert opinion)

Examples of appropriate introduction of controversial literature

10

11

12

13

meaning of the content within the world of the novel. Books with content deemed racist or sexist should likewise not automatically be banned: Provided they have intrinsic merit, such books can be useful tools for increasing understanding in our society. Finally, while volatile religious topics are possibly best left outside of classroom discussion, children should have access to religious materials in school libraries in order to allow them to explore various systems of belief.

Conclusion   The efforts to censor what children read can generate potentially explosive conflicts within schools and communities. Understanding the reasons that people seek to censor what children are reading in school will better prepare educators to respond to those efforts in a sensitive and reasonable manner. More importantly, educators will be able to provide the best learning environment for children, one that neither overly restricts the range of their reading nor exposes them, unaided, to material they have neither the experience nor the intellectual maturity to understand.   14

Works Cited

Burress, Lee. *Battle of the Books: Literary Censorship in the Public Schools, 1950-1985.* Metuchen: Scarecrow, 1989. Print.

Foerstel, Herbert N. *Banned in the USA: A Reference Guide to Book Censorship in Schools and Public Libraries.* Revised and expanded edition. London: Greenwood, 2002. Print.

Goldberg, Natalie. "Be Specific." *Language Awareness.* Ed. Paul Eschholz, Alfred Rosa, and Virginia Clark. 10th ed. Boston: Bedford, 2009. 4-5. Print.

"Harry Potter to Remain on Gwinnett County School Library Shelves." *School Library Journal* 31 May 2007: n. pag. Web. 23 Apr. 2008.

Office for Intellectual Freedom. "The 100 Most Frequently Challenged Books of 1990-2000 and Challenges by Initiator, Institution, Type, and Year." *ALA.* American Library Association, 2008. Web. 23 Apr. 2008.

Ravitch, Diane. "The Language Police." *Language Awareness.* Ed. Paul Eschholz, Alfred Rosa, and Virginia Clark. 10th ed. Boston: Bedford, 2009. 506-17. Print.

Reichman, Henry. *Censorship and Selection: Issues and Answers for Schools.* 3rd ed. Chicago: American Library Association, 2001. Print.

"Through the Eyes of a Child." *Censorship: Wielding the Red Pen.* The University of Virginia Libraries, 2000. Web. 23 Apr. 2008.

> ### Analyzing Tara E. Ketch's Essay:
> ### Questions for Discussion
>
> 1. What is Ketch's thesis?
>
> 2. How do the two rulings of the U.S. Supreme Court on educational decisions within communities conflict with each other?
>
> 3. What reasons does Ketch give for the banning of children's and adolescents' books in schools?
>
> 4. How does Ketch answer the question "Should we censor children's books?" Do you agree with her?

SUGGESTIONS FOR USING A COMBINATION OF STRATEGIES IN AN ESSAY

As you plan, write, and revise your essay using a combination of strategies, be mindful of the writing process guidelines described in Chapter 2. Pay particular attention to the basic requirements and essential ingredients of this writing strategy.

❯ Planning Your Combined Strategies Essay

Planning is an essential part of writing any good essay. You can save yourself a great deal of trouble by taking the time to think about the key building blocks of your essay before you actually begin to write. Before you can start combining strategies in your writing, it's essential that you have a firm understanding of the purposes and workings of each strategy. Once you become familiar with how the strategies work, you should be able to recognize ways to use and combine them in your writing.

Sometimes you will find yourself using a particular strategy almost intuitively. When you encounter a difficult or abstract term or concept—*liberal*, for example—you will define it almost as a matter of course. If you become perplexed because you are having trouble getting your readers to appreciate the severity of a problem, a quick review of the strategies will remind you that you could also use description and illustration.

Knowledge of the individual strategies is crucial because there are no formulas or prescriptions for combining strategies. The more you write and the more aware you are of the options available to you, the more skillful you will become at thinking critically about your topic, developing your ideas, and conveying your thoughts to your readers.

DETERMINE YOUR PURPOSE. The most common purposes in nonfiction writing are (1) to express your thoughts and feelings about a life experience, (2) to inform your readers by explaining something about the world around them, and (3) to persuade readers to embrace some belief or action. Your purpose will determine the dominant strategy you use in your essay.

If your major purpose is to tell a story of a river-rafting trip, you will primarily use narration. If you wish to re-create the experience of a famous landmark for the first time, you may find description most helpful. If you wish to inform your readers, you may find definition, cause and effect, process analysis, comparison and contrast, and/or division and classification to be best suited to your needs. If you wish to convince your readers of a certain belief or course of action, argumentation is an obvious choice.

FORMULATE A THESIS STATEMENT. Regardless of the purpose you have set for yourself in writing an essay, it is essential that you commit to a thesis statement, usually a one- or two-sentence statement giving the main point of your essay.

> Party primaries are an indispensable part of the American political process.

> Antibiotic use must be curtailed. Antibiotics have been overprescribed and are not nearly as effective as they once were at combating infections among humans.

A question is not a thesis statement. If you find yourself writing a thesis statement that asks a question, answer the question first and then turn your answer into a thesis statement. A thesis statement can be presented anywhere in an essay, but usually it is presented at the beginning of a composition, sometimes after a few introductory sentences that set a context for it.

▶ Organizing Your Combined Strategies Essay

DETERMINE YOUR DOMINANT STRATEGY. Depending on your purpose for writing, your thesis statement, and the kinds of information you have gathered in preparing to write your essay, you may use any of the following strategies as the dominant strategy for your essay: narration, description, illustration, process analysis, comparison and contrast, division and classification, definition, cause and effect analysis, or argumentation.

DETERMINE YOUR SUPPORTING STRATEGIES. The questions listed below — organized by rhetorical strategy — will help you decide which strategies will be most helpful to you in the service of the dominant strategy you have chosen for your essay and in achieving your overall purpose.

Narration. Are you trying to report or recount an anecdote, an experience, or an event? Does any part of your essay include the telling of a story (something that happened to you or to a person you include in your essay)?

Description. Does a person, a place, or an object play a prominent role in your essay? Would the tone, pacing, or overall purpose of your essay benefit from sensory details?

Illustration. Are there examples—facts, statistics, cases in point, personal experiences, interview quotations—that you could add to help you achieve the purpose of your essay?

Process analysis. Would any part of your essay be clearer if you included concrete directions about a certain process? Are there processes that readers would like to understand better? Are you evaluating any processes?

Comparison and contrast. Does your essay contain two or more related subjects? Are you evaluating or analyzing two or more people, places, processes, events, or things? Do you need to establish the similarities and differences between two or more elements?

Division and classification. Are you trying to explain a broad and complicated subject? Would it benefit your essay to reduce this subject to more manageable parts to focus your discussion?

Definition. Who is your audience? Does your essay focus on any abstract, specialized, or new terms that need further explanation so readers understand your point? Does any important word in your essay have many meanings and need to be clarified?

Cause and effect analysis. Are you examining past events or their outcomes? Is your purpose to inform, speculate, or argue about why an identifiable fact happens the way it does?

Argumentation. Are you trying to explain aspects of a particular subject, and are you trying to advocate a specific opinion on this subject or issue in your essay?

▸ Revising and Editing Your Combined Strategies Essay

LISTEN TO WHAT YOUR CLASSMATES HAVE TO SAY. The importance of student peer conferences cannot be stressed enough, particularly as you revise and edit your essay. Others in your class will often see, for example, that the basis for your classification needs adjustment or that there are inconsistencies in your division categories that can easily be corrected— problems that you can't see yourself because you are too close to your essay. To maximize the effectiveness of work with your classmates, use the guidelines on page 36. Take advantage of suggestions when you know them to be valid, and make revisions accordingly.

QUESTION YOUR OWN WORK WHILE REVISING AND EDITING. Revision is best done by asking yourself key questions about what you have written. Begin by reading, preferably aloud, what you have written. Reading aloud forces you to pay attention to every single word, and you are more likely to catch lapses in the logical flow of thought. After you have read your paper through, answer the following questions for revising and editing and make the necessary changes.

For help with twelve common writing problems, see Chapter 16, "Editing for Grammar, Punctuation, and Sentence Style."

Questions for Revising and Editing: Combining Strategies

1. Do I have a purpose for my essay?

2. Is my thesis statement clear?

3. Does my dominant strategy reflect my purpose and my thesis statement?

4. Do my subordinate strategies effectively support the dominant strategy of my essay?

5. Are my subordinate strategies woven into my essay in a natural manner?

6. Have I revised and edited my essay to avoid wordiness?

7. Have I used a variety of sentences to enliven my writing?

8. Have I avoided errors in grammar, punctuation, and mechanics?

On Dumpster Diving

LARS EIGHNER

Born in Corpus Christi, Texas, in 1948, Lars Eighner grew up in Houston and attended the University of Texas–Austin. After graduation, he wrote essays and fiction, and several of his articles were published in magazines like *Threepenny Review*, the *Guide*, and *Inches*. A volume of short stories, *Bayou Boy and Other Stories*, was published in 1985. Eighner became homeless in 1988 when he left his job as an attendant at a mental hospital. The following piece, which appeared in the *Utne Reader*, is an abridged version of an essay that first appeared in *Threepenny Review*. The piece eventually became part of Eighner's startling account of the three years he spent with his dog as a homeless person, *Travels with Lizbeth* (1993). His publications include the novel *Pawn to Queen Four* (1995), the short-story collection *Whispered in the Dark* (1996), and the nonfiction book of essays *Gay Cosmos* (1995).

Eighner uses a number of rhetorical strategies in "On Dumpster Diving," but pay particular attention to how his process analysis of the "stages that a person goes through in learning to scavenge" contributes to the success of the essay as a whole.

Preparing to Read

Are you a pack rat, or do you get rid of what is not immediately useful to you? Outside of the usual kitchen garbage and empty toothpaste tubes, how do you make the decision to throw something away?

began Dumpster diving about a year before I became homeless. 1

I prefer the term *scavenging.* I have heard people, evidently meaning to be polite, use the word *foraging,* but I prefer to reserve that word for gathering nuts and berries and such, which I also do, according to the season and opportunity. 2

I like the frankness of the word *scavenging.* I live from the refuse of others. I am a scavenger. I think it a sound and honorable niche, although if I could I would naturally prefer to live the comfortable consumer life, perhaps—and only perhaps—as a slightly less wasteful consumer owing to what I have learned as a scavenger. 3

Except for jeans, all my clothes come from Dumpsters. Boom boxes, candles, bedding, toilet paper, medicine, books, a typewriter, a virgin male love doll, coins sometimes amounting to many dollars: All came from Dumpsters. And, yes, I eat from Dumpsters, too. 4

There is a predictable series of stages that a person goes through in learning to scavenge. At first the new scavenger is filled with disgust and self-loathing. He is ashamed of being seen. 5

This stage passes with experience. The scavenger finds a pair of running shoes that fit and look and smell brand-new. He finds a pocket calculator in perfect working order. He finds pristine ice cream, still frozen, more than he can eat or keep. He begins to understand: People do throw away perfectly good stuff, a lot of perfectly good stuff.

At this stage he may become lost and never recover: All the Dumpster divers I have known come to the point of trying to acquire everything they touch. Why not take it, they reason, it is all free. This is, of course, hopeless, and most divers come to realize that they must restrict themselves to items of relatively immediate utility.

The finding of objects is becoming something of an urban art. Even respectable, employed people will sometimes find something tempting sticking out of a Dumpster or standing beside one. Quite a number of people, not all of them of the bohemian type, are willing to brag that they found this or that piece in the trash.

> I live from the refuse of others. I am a scavenger.

But eating from Dumpsters is the thing that separates the dilettanti from the professionals. Eating safely involves three principles: using the senses and common sense to evaluate the condition of the found materials; knowing the Dumpsters of a given area and checking them regularly; and seeking always to answer the question "Why was this discarded?"

Yet perfectly good food can be found in Dumpsters. Canned goods, for example, turn up fairly often in the Dumpsters I frequent. I also have few qualms about dry foods such as crackers, cookies, cereal, chips, and pasta if they are free of visible contaminants and still dry and crisp. Raw fruits and vegetables with intact skins seem perfectly safe to me, excluding, of course, the obviously rotten. Many are discarded for minor imperfections that can be pared away.

A typical discard is a half jar of peanut butter—though nonorganic peanut butter does not require refrigeration and is unlikely to spoil in any reasonable time. One of my favorite finds is yogurt—often discarded, still sealed, when the expiration date has passed—because it will keep for several days, even in warm weather.

No matter how careful I am I still get dysentery at least once a month, oftener in warm weather. I do not want to paint too romantic a picture. Dumpster diving has serious drawbacks as a way of life.

I find from the experience of scavenging two rather deep lessons. The first is to take what I can use and let the rest go. I have come to think that there is no value in the abstract. A thing I cannot use or make useful, perhaps by trading, has no value, however fine or rare it may be.

The second lesson is the transience of material being. I do not suppose 14
that ideas are immortal, but certainly they are longer-lived than material
objects.

The things I find in Dumpsters, the love letters and rag dolls of so 15
many lives, remind me of this lesson. Now I hardly pick up a thing without
envisioning the time I will cast it away. This, I think, is a healthy state of
mind. Almost everything I have now has already been cast out at least
once, proving that what I own is valueless to someone.

I find that my desire to grab for the gaudy bauble has been largely sated. 16
I think this is an attitude I share with the very wealthy—we both know there
is plenty more where whatever we have came from. Between us are the rat-
race millions who have confounded their selves with the objects they grasp
and who nightly scavenge the cable channels for they know not what.

I am sorry for them. 17

Thinking Critically about the Text

In paragraph 15, Eighner writes, "I hardly pick up a thing without envisioning the time I will cast it away. This, I think, is a healthy state of mind." React to this
statement. Do you think such an attitude is healthy or defeatist? If many people
thought this way, what impact would it have on our consumer society?

Questions on Subject

1. What stages do beginning Dumpster divers go through before they become
   what Eighner terms "professionals" (paragraph 9)? What examples does
   Eighner use to illustrate the passage through these stages? (Glossary:
   Illustration)

2. What three principles does one need to follow in order to eat safely from
   Dumpsters? What foods are best to eat from Dumpsters? What are the risks?

3. What two lessons has Eighner learned from his Dumpster diving experiences?
   Why are they significant to him?

4. Dumpster diving has had a profound effect on Eighner and the way he lives.
   How do his explanations of choices he makes, such as deciding which items
   to keep, enhance his presentation of the practical art of Dumpster diving?

5. How do you respond to Eighner's Dumpster-diving practices? Are you
   shocked? Bemused? Accepting? Challenged?

Questions on Strategy

1. Eighner's essay deals with both the immediate, physical aspects of Dumpster
   diving, such as what can be found in a typical Dumpster and the physical
   price one pays for eating out of them, and the larger, abstract issues that

Dumpster diving raises, such as materialism and the transience of material objects. (Glossary: *Concrete/Abstract*) Why does he describe the concrete things before he discusses the abstract issues raised by their presence in Dumpsters? What does he achieve by using both types of elements?

2. Eighner's account of Dumpster diving focuses primarily on the odd appeal and interest inherent in the activity. Paragraph 12 is his one disclaimer, in which he states, "I do not want to paint too romantic a picture." Why does Eighner include this disclaimer? How does it add to the effectiveness of his piece? Why do you think it is so brief and abrupt?

3. Eighner uses many rhetorical techniques in his essay, but its core is a fairly complete process analysis of how to Dumpster dive. (Glossary: *Process Analysis*) Summarize this process analysis. Why do you think Eighner did not title the essay "How to Dumpster Dive"?

4. Discuss how Eighner uses illustration to bring the world of Dumpster diving to life. (Glossary: *Illustration*) What characterizes the examples he uses?

5. Writers often use process analysis in conjunction with other strategies, especially argument, to try to improve the way a process is carried out. (Glossary: *Argument; Process Analysis*) In this essay, Eighner uses a full process analysis to lay out his views on American values and materialism. How is this an effective way to combine strategies? Think of other arguments that could be strengthened if they included elements of process analysis.

Questions on Diction and Vocabulary

1. Eighner says he prefers the word *scavenging* to *Dumpster diving* or *foraging*. What do those three terms mean to him? Why do you think he finds the discussion of the terms important enough to include it at the beginning of his essay? (Glossary: *Diction*)

2. According to Eighner, "eating from Dumpsters is the thing that separates the dilettanti from the professionals" (paragraph 9). What do the words *dilettante* and *professional* connote to you? (Glossary: *Connotation/Denotation*) Why does Eighner choose to use them instead of the more straightforward *casual* and *serious*?

3. Eighner says, "The finding of objects is becoming something of an urban art" (paragraph 8). What does this sentence mean to you? Based on the essay, do you find his use of the word *art* appropriate when discussing any aspect of Dumpster diving? Why, or why not?

Classroom Activity for Combining Strategies

As a class, discuss the strategies that Eighner uses in his essay: narration, process analysis, cause and effect, illustration, and definition, for example. Where in the essay has he used each strategy and to what end? Has he used any other strategies not mentioned above? Explain.

Writing Suggestions

1. Write a process analysis in which you relate how you acquire a consumer item of some importance or expense to you. (Glossary: *Process Analysis*) Do you compare brands, store prices, and so on? (Glossary: *Comparison and Contrast*) What are your priorities — must the item be stylish or durable, offer good overall value, give high performance? How do you decide to spend your money? In other words, what determines which items are worth the sacrifice?

2. In paragraph 3, Eighner states that he "live[s] from the refuse of others." How does his confession affect you? Do you think that we have become a throwaway society? If so, how? How do Eighner's accounts of homelessness and Dumpster diving make you feel about your own consumerism and trash habits? Write an essay in which you examine the things you throw away in a single day. What items did you get rid of? Why? Could those items be used by someone else? Have you ever felt guilty about throwing something away? If so, what was it and why?

3. One person's treasure is another person's trash. In the photograph below, young adults in their early twenties explore what's available inside a Dumpster near a supermarket in Charlotte, North Carolina. Stephanie Braun, in plaid, hands a fruit to Kaitlyn Tokay, pictured in front. Choose a theme derived from the photograph and Eighner's essay — for example, the treasure/trash statement above or whether this sort of Dumpster diving is the purest form of recycling — and write an essay developed by using at least three different strategies in combination.

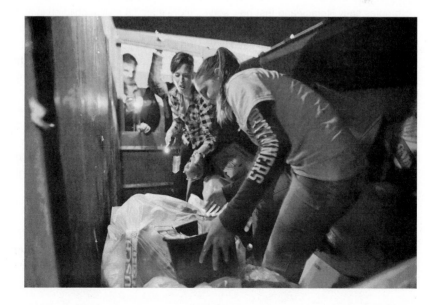

How Babies Sort Out Language

PERRI KLASS

Perri Klass was born in Trinidad in 1958. The daughter of two academics — her father an anthropologist and her mother a novelist and English professor — Klass grew up in New York City and Leonia, New Jersey, and in 1979 graduated from Harvard University with a B.A. in biology. In 1986 she earned her M.D. from Harvard Medical School, and she followed her residency in pediatrics at Children's Hospital, Boston, with a fellowship in pediatric infectious diseases at Boston City Hospital. Klass loved writing even as a child. Throughout her school years, she wrote fiction and nonfiction, contributing stories and articles to *Mademoiselle* and the *New York Times*. Her first book, *A Not Entirely Benign Procedure* (1987) chronicles her pursuit of medicine and introduction to motherhood. A prolific author, Klass continues to write about medicine, children, parenting, literacy, and knitting. Her many books include the memoir *Quirky Kids: Understanding and Helping Your Child Who Doesn't Fit In* (2003), coauthored with Dr. Eileen Costello; several novels; two short-story collections; and such nonfiction books as *Treatment Kind and Fair: Letters to a Young Doctor* (2007) and *The Real Life of a Pediatrician* (2009). Her most recent book is *Second Impact: Making the Hardest Call of All* (2013), coauthored with brother David Klass.

As a pediatrician and writer, Klass knew the importance of books in a young person's life and early on joined forces with Reach Out and Read, a nonprofit that promotes early literacy and that now serves more than 3.8 million children in all fifty states. She writes, "When I think about children growing up in homes without books, I have the same visceral reaction as I have when I think of children in homes without milk or food or heat: It cannot be, it must not be. It stunts them and deprives them before they've had a fair chance." In 2007, Klass received the American Academy of Pediatrics Education Award for her work with the organization.

In "How Babies Sort Out Language," first published in the *New York Times* on October 11, 2011, Klass reports on current research with monolingual and bilingual infants, using four studies to illustrate "the earliest differences between brains exposed to one language and brains exposed to two." Notice in particular how comparison and contrast and cause and effect analysis are used as supporting strategies.

Preparing to Read

Although the ability to use language is perhaps the most distinguishing characteristic of human beings, most people don't give the language they speak a second thought. Linguist Richard Lederer has written a book called *The Miracle of Language*. In what sense can language be deemed a "miracle"? Consider: How do children growing up anywhere on earth learn to speak the language they hear in their speech community? What are your earliest memories of learning to talk? How do you think you learned to speak the language that you do?

Once, experts feared that young children exposed to more than one language would suffer "language confusion," which might delay their speech development. Today, parents often are urged to capitalize on that early knack for acquiring language. Upscale schools market themselves with promises of deep immersion in Spanish—or Mandarin—for everyone, starting in kindergarten or even before.

Yet while many parents recognize the utility of a second language, families bringing up children in non-English-speaking households, or trying to juggle two languages at home, are often desperate for information. And while the study of bilingual development has refuted those early fears about confusion and delay, there aren't many research-based guidelines about the very early years and the best strategies for producing a happily bilingual child.

But there is more and more research to draw on, reaching back to infancy and even to the womb. As the relatively new science of bilingualism pushes back to the origins of speech and language, scientists are teasing out the earliest differences between brains exposed to one language and brains exposed to two.

Researchers have found ways to analyze infant behavior—where babies turn their gazes, how long they pay attention—to help figure out infant perceptions of sounds and words and languages, of what is familiar and what is unfamiliar to them. Now, analyzing the neurologic activity of babies' brains as they hear language, and then comparing those early responses with the words that those children learn as they get older, is helping explain not just how the early brain listens to language, but how listening shapes the early brain.

Recently, researchers at the University of Washington used measures of electrical brain responses to compare so-called monolingual infants, from homes in which one language was spoken, to bilingual infants exposed to two languages. Of course, since the subjects of the study, adorable in their infant-size EEG caps, ranged from 6 months to 12 months of age, they weren't producing many words in any language.

Still, the researchers found that at 6 months, the monolingual infants could discriminate between phonetic sounds, whether they were uttered in the language they were used to hearing or in another language not spoken in their homes. By 10 to 12 months, however, monolingual babies were no longer detecting sounds in the second language, only in the language they usually heard.

The researchers suggested that this represents a process of "neural commitment," in which the infant brain wires itself to understand one language and its sounds. 7

In contrast, the bilingual infants followed a different developmental trajectory. At 6 to 9 months, they did not detect differences in phonetic sounds in either language, but when they were older—10 to 12 months—they were able to discriminate sounds in both. 8

"What the study demonstrates is that the variability in bilingual babies' experience keeps them open," said Dr. Patricia Kuhl, co-director of the Institute for Learning and Brain Sciences at the University of Washington and one of the authors of the study. "They do not show the perceptual narrowing as soon as monolingual babies do. It's another piece of evidence that what you experience shapes the brain." 9

The learning of language — and the effects on the brain of the language we hear — may begin even earlier than 6 months of age.

The learning of language—and the effects on the brain of the language we hear—may begin even earlier than 6 months of age. 10

Janet Werker, a professor of psychology at the University of British Columbia, studies how babies perceive language and how that shapes their learning. Even in the womb, she said, babies are exposed to the rhythms and sounds of language, and newborns have been shown to prefer languages rhythmically similar to the one they've heard during fetal development. 11

In one recent study, Dr. Werker and her collaborators showed that babies born to bilingual mothers not only prefer both of those languages over others—but are also able to register that the two languages are different. 12

In addition to this ability to use rhythmic sound to discriminate between languages, Dr. Werker has studied other strategies that infants use as they grow, showing how their brains use different kinds of perception to learn languages, and also to keep them separate. 13

In a study of older infants shown silent videotapes of adults speaking, 4-month-olds could distinguish different languages visually by watching mouth and facial motions and responded with interest when the language changed. By 8 months, though, the monolingual infants were no longer responding to the difference in languages in these silent movies, while the bilingual infants continued to be engaged. 14

"For a baby who's growing up bilingual, it's like, 'Hey, this is impor- 15
tant information,'" Dr. Werker said.

Over the past decade, Ellen Bialystok, a distinguished research profes- 16
sor of psychology at York University in Toronto, has shown that bilingual
children develop crucial skills in addition to their double vocabularies, learning different ways to solve logic problems or to handle multitasking, skills
that are often considered part of the brain's so-called executive function.

These higher-level cognitive abilities are localized to the frontal and 17
prefrontal cortex in the brain. "Overwhelmingly, children who are bilingual from early on have precocious development of executive function,"
Dr. Bialystok said.

Dr. Kuhl calls bilingual babies "more cognitively flexible" than mono- 18
lingual infants. Her research group is examining infant brains with an even
newer imaging device, magnetoencephalography, or MEG, which combines an MRI scan with a recording of magnetic field changes as the brain
transmits information.

Dr. Kuhl describes the device as looking like a "hair dryer from Mars," 19
and she hopes that it will help explore the question of why babies learn
language from people, but not from screens.

Previous research by her group showed that exposing English- 20
language infants in Seattle to someone speaking to them in Mandarin
helped those babies preserve the ability to discriminate Chinese language
sounds, but when the same "dose" of Mandarin was delivered by a television program or an audiotape, the babies learned nothing.

"This special mapping that babies seem to do with language happens 21
in a social setting," Dr. Kuhl said. "They need to be face-to-face, interacting with other people. The brain is turned on in a unique way."

Thinking Critically about the Text

Why do you think there has been more research in bilingual development in recent
years? In the past, why was it so difficult to study children before they were producing words? What new technologies are helping researchers study monolingual
and bilingual infants?

Questions on Subject

1. According to Klass, why were parents once reluctant to expose their young children to more than one language? How has recent research with infants quieted
   parents' fears? What do you see as the advantages of raising a bilingual child?

2. What has research with monolingual infants and bilingual infants aged six to
   twelve months demonstrated about their abilities to listen to language in their
   environments?

3. What do researchers mean when they say monolingual infants exhibit "neural commitment" (paragraph 7)? What evidence does Klass offer to support the idea that "experience shapes the brain" (9)?

4. What did Dr. Janet Werker and her collaborators learn when they showed both four- and eight-month-old infants silent movies of adults speaking? How does this information relate to the research conducted at the University of Washington, reported in paragraphs 5 through 9?

5. How did researchers discover that babies needed face-to-face interaction with other human beings in order to discriminate language sounds?

Questions on Strategy

1. What is Klass's purpose in this essay — to report information, to argue a point, or to show what research still needs to be done? (Glossary: *Purpose*) What authority does Klass have to write about language acquisition in young children?

2. How does Klass use the strategies of illustration, comparison and contrast, and cause and effect analysis to develop her thesis and purpose?

3. Klass cites a study done at the University of Washington, one carried out at the University of British Columbia, and a third conducted at York University in Toronto. What similarities and differences do these three studies have? What does each add to Klass's essay? Explain.

4. Klass directly quotes the chief researcher in each of the three studies she utilizes. What does each quotation add to her essay? What would have been lost had Klass chosen to present the same information in her own words?

5. How does paragraph 10 function in the context of Klass's essay?

6. How does Klass organize her essay? (Glossary: *Organization*) Why do you think she ordered the three studies the way that she did?

Questions on Diction and Vocabulary

1. In paragraph 19, researcher Kuhl uses a simile to describe the new imaging device. (Glossary: *Figures of Speech*) What verbal picture does this simile create for you? Is it effective?

2. How would you describe Klass's diction? Identify several instances where Klass carefully explains what might be linguistic terms or concepts so that her readers can readily understand them. Did you find her brief explanations necessary or helpful? Explain.

3. Refer to your dictionary to determine the meanings of the following words as Klass uses them in this selection: *knack* (paragraph 1), *discriminate* (6), *phonetic* (6), *trajectory* (8), *cognitive* (17), *precocious* (17).

Classroom Activity for Combining Strategies

Examine the following conversation (documented by Ursula Bellugi in 1970) between Eve, a twenty-four-month-old child, and her mother:

Eve: Have that?

Mother: No, you may not have it.

Eve: Mom, where my tapioca?

Mother: It's getting cool. You'll have it in just a minute.

Eve: Let me have it.

Mother: Would you like to have your lunch right now?

Eve: Yeah. My tapioca cool?

Mother: Yes, it's cool.

Eve: You gonna watch me eat my lunch?

Mother: Yeah, I'm gonna watch you eat your lunch.

Eve: I eating it.

Mother: I know you are.

Eve: It time Sarah take a nap.

Mother: It's time for Sarah to have some milk, yeah. And then she's gonna take a nap and you're gonna take a nap.

Eve: And you?

Mother: And me too, yeah.

Compare the grammar of Eve's speech with that of her mother. What grammatical features are systematically missing from Eve's speech? Now look at a conversation between Eve and her mother recorded only three months later:

Mother: Come and sit over here.

Eve: You can sit down by me. That will make me happy. Ready to turn it.

Mother: We're not quite ready to turn the page.

Eve: Yep, we are.

Mother: Shut the door, we won't hear her then.

Eve: Then Fraser won't hear her too. Where he's going? Did you make a great big hole there?

Mother: Yes, we made a great big hole in here; we have to get a new one.

Eve: Could I get some other piece of paper?

Mother: You ask Fraser.

Eve: Could I use this one?

Mother: I suppose so.

Eve: Is Fraser goin take his pencil home when he goes?

Mother: Yes he is.

When you compare Eve's speech at twenty-four months to her speech at twenty-seven months, what changes do you notice? Try to describe the grammatical understanding or rules Eve seems to have acquired. What parts of her speech provide evidence for the grammar she has learned? Using these conversations and your comparisons of Eve's grammatical constructions, discuss Eve's language learning process.

Writing Suggestions

1. As a native speaker of a language, you have several basic language competencies. For example, you can determine whether or not an utterance is a grammatical sentence. Other competencies include the ability to tell when two or more sentences are synonymous, recognize ambiguity in a sentence, and interpret completely novel utterances. Discuss these competencies, suggesting examples from your own speech to illustrate each one of the skills.

2. Write an essay in which you explore your experiences learning a second language. Did you grow up in a household in which two or more languages were spoken? If so, were you encouraged to be bilingual or monolingual? At what grade level was a second language introduced in school? For you, what were the greatest stumbling blocks in learning a second language, and what did you do to overcome them? Based on your own experiences with languages, what are the advantages and disadvantages of being bilingual?

Shooting an Elephant

GEORGE ORWELL

George Orwell (1903–1950) was capable of capturing the reader's imagination as few writers have ever done. Born in Bengal, India, but raised and educated in England, he chose to work as a civil servant in the British colonies after his schooling and was sent to Burma at nineteen as an assistant superintendent of police. Disillusioned by his firsthand experiences of public life under British colonial rule, he resigned in 1929 and returned to England to begin a career in writing. He captured the exotic mystery of life in the colonies, along with its many injustices and ironies, in such works as *Down and Out in Paris and London* (1933) and *The Road to Wigan Pier* (1937). His most famous books are *Animal Farm* (1945), a satire on the Russian Revolution, and *1984* (1949), a chilling novel set in an imagined totalitarian state of the future. Orwell maintained a lifelong interest in international social and political issues.

"Shooting an Elephant" was published in the British magazine *New Writing* in 1936. Adolf Hitler, Benito Mussolini, and Joseph Stalin were in power, building the "younger empires" that Orwell refers to in the second paragraph, and the old British Empire was soon to decline, as Orwell predicted. In this essay, Orwell tells of a time when, in a position of authority, he found himself compelled to act against his convictions.

Preparing to Read

Have you ever acted against your better judgment to save face with your friends or relatives? What motivated you to take the action that you did, and what did you learn from the experience?

I n Moulmein, in Lower Burma, I was hated by large numbers of people — the only time in my life that I have been important enough for this to happen to me. I was subdivisional police officer of the town, and in an aimless, petty kind of way anti-European feeling was very bitter. No one had the guts to raise a riot, but if a European woman went through the bazaars alone somebody would probably spit betel juice[1] over her dress. As a police officer I was an obvious target and was baited whenever it seemed safe to do so. When a nimble Burman tripped me up on the football field and the referee (another Burman) looked the other way, the crowd yelled with hideous laughter. This happened more than once. In the end the sneering yellow faces of young men that met me everywhere,

[1]The juice of an Asiatic plant whose leaves are chewed to induce narcotic effects. — ED.

the insults hooted after me when I was at a safe distance, got badly on my nerves. The young Buddhist priests were the worst of all. There were several thousands of them in the town and none of them seemed to have anything to do except stand on street corners and jeer at Europeans.

All this was perplexing and upsetting. For at that time I had already made up my mind that imperialism was an evil thing and the sooner I chucked up my job and got out of it the better. Theoretically—and secretly, of course—I was all for the Burmese and all against the oppressors, the British. As for the job I was doing, I hated it more bitterly than I can perhaps make clear. In a job like that you see the dirty work of Empire at close quarters. The wretched prisoners huddling in the stinking cages of the lockups, the grey, cowed faces of the long-term convicts, the scarred buttocks of the men who had been flogged with bamboos—all these oppressed me with an intolerable sense of guilt. But I could get nothing into perspective. I was young and ill-educated and I had had to think out my problems in the utter silence that is imposed on every Englishman in the East. I did not even know that the British Empire is dying, still less did I know that it is a great deal better than the younger empires that are going to supplant it. All I knew was that I was stuck between my hatred of the empire I served and my rage against the evil-spirited little beasts who tried to make my job impossible. With one part of my mind I thought of the British Raj[2] as an unbreakable tyranny, as something clamped down, in *saecula saeculorum*,[3] upon the will of prostrate peoples; with another part I thought that the greatest joy in the world would be to drive a bayonet into a Buddhist priest's guts. Feelings like these are the normal byproducts of imperialism; ask any Anglo-Indian official, if you can catch him off duty.

> When I pulled the trigger I did not hear the bang or feel the kick — one never does when a shot goes home — but I heard the devilish roar of glee that went up from the crowd.

One day something happened which in a roundabout way was enlightening. It was a tiny incident in itself, but it gave me a better glimpse than I had had before of the real nature of imperialism—the real motives for which despotic governments act. Early one morning the subinspector at a police station the other end of town rang me up on the phone and said that an elephant was ravaging the bazaar. Would I please come and do something about it? I did not know what I could do, but I wanted to see what

---

[2]British rule, especially in India—ED.
[3]From time immemorial.—ED.

was happening and I got on to a pony and started out. I took my rifle, an old .44 Winchester and much too small to kill an elephant, but I thought the noise might be useful *in terrorem*. Various Burmans stopped me on the way and told me about the elephant's doings. It was not, of course, a wild elephant, but a tame one which had gone "must."[4] It had been chained up, as tame elephants always are when their attack of "must" is due, but on the previous night it had broken its chain and escaped. Its mahout,[5] the only person who could manage it when it was in that state, had set out in pursuit, but had taken the wrong direction and was now twelve hours' journey away, and in the morning the elephant had suddenly reappeared in the town. The Burmese population had no weapons and were quite helpless against it. It had already destroyed somebody's bamboo hut, killed a cow and raided some fruit stalls and devoured the stock; also it had met the municipal rubbish van and, when the driver jumped out and took to his heels, had turned the van over and inflicted violences upon it.

The Burmese subinspector and some Indian constables were waiting 4 for me in the quarter where the elephant had been seen. It was a very poor quarter, a labyrinth of squalid bamboo huts, thatched with palmleaf, winding all over a steep hillside. I remember that it was a cloudy, stuffy morning at the beginning of the rains. We began questioning the people as to where the elephant had gone and, as usual, failed to get any definite information. That is invariably the case in the East; a story always sounds clear enough at a distance, but the nearer you get to the scene of events the vaguer it becomes. Some of the people said that the elephant had gone in one direction, some said that he had gone in another, some professed not even to have heard of any elephant. I had almost made up my mind that the whole story was a pack of lies, when we heard yells a little distance away. There was a loud, scandalized cry of "Go away, child! Go away this instant!" and an old woman with a switch in her hand came round the corner of a hut, violently shooing away a crowd of naked children. Some more women followed, clicking their tongues and exclaiming; evidently there was something that the children ought not to have seen. I rounded the hut and saw a man's dead body sprawling in the mud. He was an Indian, a black Dravidian coolie,[6] almost naked, and he could not have been dead many minutes. The people said that the elephant had come suddenly upon him round the corner of the hut, caught him with its trunk, put its foot on his back and ground him into the earth. This was the rainy season and the ground was soft, and his face had scored a trench a foot deep and a couple of yards long. He was lying on his belly with arms crucified and head

[4]That is, gone into an uncontrollable frenzy. — ED.
[5]The keeper and driver of an elephant. — ED.
[6]An unskilled laborer. — ED.

sharply twisted to one side. His face was coated with mud, the eyes wide open, the teeth bared and grinning with an expression of unendurable agony. (Never tell me, by the way, that the dead look peaceful. Most of the corpses I have seen looked devilish.) The friction of the great beast's foot had stripped the skin from his back as neatly as one skins a rabbit. As soon as I saw the dead man I sent an orderly to a friend's house nearby to borrow an elephant rifle. I had already sent back the pony, not wanting it to go mad with fright and throw me if it smelled the elephant.

The orderly came back in a few minutes with a rifle and five cartridges, and meanwhile some Burmans had arrived and told us that the elephant was in the paddy fields below, only a few hundred yards away. As I started forward practically the whole population of the quarter flocked out of the houses and followed me. They had seen the rifle and were all shouting excitedly that I was going to shoot the elephant. They had not shown much interest in the elephant when he was merely ravaging their homes, but it was different now that he was going to be shot. It was a bit of fun to them, as it would be to an English crowd; besides they wanted the meat. It made me vaguely uneasy. I had no intention of shooting the elephant—I had merely sent for the rifle to defend myself if necessary—and it is always unnerving to have a crowd following you. I marched down the hill, looking and feeling a fool, with the rifle over my shoulder and an ever-growing army of people jostling at my heels. At the bottom, when you got away from the huts, there was a metalled road[7] and beyond that a miry waste of paddy fields a thousand yards across, not yet ploughed but soggy from the first rains and dotted with coarse grass. The elephant was standing eight yards from the road, his left side towards us. He took not the slightest notice of the crowd's approach. He was tearing up bunches of grass, beating them against his knees to clean them and stuffing them into his mouth.

I had halted on the road. As soon as I saw the elephant I knew with perfect certainty that I ought not to shoot him. It is a serious matter to shoot a working elephant—it is comparable to destroying a huge and costly piece of machinery—and obviously one ought not to do it if it can possibly be avoided. And at that distance, peacefully eating, the elephant looked no more dangerous than a cow. I thought then and I think now that his attack of "must" was already passing off; in which case he would merely wander harmlessly about until the mahout came back and caught him. Moreover, I did not in the least want to shoot him. I decided that I would watch him for a little while to make sure that he did not turn savage again, and then go home.

---

[7]A road made of broken or crushed stone. —ED.

But at that moment, I glanced round at the crowd that had followed 7
me. It was an immense crowd, two thousand at the least and growing every
minute. It blocked the road for a long distance on either side. I looked at
the sea of yellow faces above the garish clothes—faces all happy and
excited over this bit of fun, all certain that the elephant was going to be
shot. They were watching me as they would watch a conjuror about to
perform a trick. They did not like me, but with the magical rifle in my
hands I was momentarily worth watching. And suddenly I realized that I
should have to shoot the elephant after all. The people expected it of me
and I had got to do it; I could feel their two thousand wills pressing me
forward, irresistibly. And it was at this moment, as I stood there with the
rifle in my hands, that I first grasped the hollowness, the futility of the
white man's dominion in the East. Here was I, the white man with his gun,
standing in front of the unarmed native crowd—seemingly the leading
actor of the piece; but in reality I was only an absurd puppet pushed to and
fro by the will of those yellow faces behind. I perceived in this moment that
when the white man turns tyrant it is his own freedom that he destroys. He
becomes a sort of hollow, posing dummy, the conventionalized figure of a
sahib.[8] For it is the condition of his rule that he shall spend his life in trying
to impress the "natives," and so in every crisis he has got to do what the
"natives" expect of him. He wears a mask, and his face grows to fit it. I had
got to shoot the elephant. I had committed myself to doing it when I sent
for the rifle. A sahib has got to act like a sahib; he has got to appear resolute, to know his own mind and do definite things. To come all that way,
rifle in hand, with two thousand people marching at my heels, and then to
trail feebly away, having done nothing—no, that was impossible. The
crowd would laugh at me. And my whole life, every white man's life in the
East, was one long struggle not to be laughed at.

But I did not want to shoot the elephant. I watched him beating his 8
bunch of grass against his knees, with that preoccupied grandmotherly air
that elephants have. It seemed to me that it would be murder to shoot him.
At that age I was not squeamish about killing animals, but I had never shot
an elephant and never wanted to. (Somehow it always seems worse to kill
a *large* animal.) Besides, there was the beast's owner to be considered.
Alive, the elephant was worth at least a hundred pounds; dead, he would
only be worth the value of his tusks, five pounds, possibly. But I had got to
act quickly. I turned to some experienced-looking Burmans who had been
there when we arrived, and asked them how the elephant had been behaving. They all said the same thing: He took no notice of you if you left him
alone, but he might charge if you went too close to him.

---

[8]A title of respect when addressing Europeans in colonial India.—ED.

It was perfectly clear to me what I ought to do. I ought to walk up to 9 within, say, twenty-five yards of the elephant and test his behavior. If he charged, I could shoot; if he took no notice of me, it would be safe to leave him until the mahout came back. But also I knew that I was going to do no such thing. I was a poor shot with a rifle and the ground was soft mud into which one would sink at every step. If the elephant charged and I missed him, I should have about as much chance as a toad under a steamroller. But even then I was not thinking particularly of my own skin, only of the watchful yellow faces behind. For at that moment, with the crowd watching me, I was not afraid in the ordinary sense, as I would have been if I had been alone. A white man mustn't be frightened in front of "natives"; and so, in general, he isn't frightened. The sole thought in my mind was that if anything went wrong those two thousand Burmans would see me pursued, caught, trampled on, and reduced to a grinning corpse like that Indian up the hill. And if that happened it was quite probable that some of them would laugh. That would never do. There was only one alternative. I shoved the cartridges into the magazine and lay down on the road to get a better aim.

The crowd grew very still, and a deep, low, happy sigh, as of people 10 who see the theater curtain go up at last, breathed from innumerable throats. They were going to have their bit of fun after all. The rifle was a beautiful German thing with cross-hair sights. I did not then know that in shooting an elephant one would shoot to cut an imaginary bar running from ear-hole to ear-hole. I ought, therefore, as the elephant was sideways on, to have aimed straight at his ear-hole; actually I aimed several inches in front of this, thinking the brain would be further forward.

When I pulled the trigger I did not hear the bang or feel the kick — one 11 never does when a shot goes home — but I heard the devilish roar of glee that went up from the crowd. In that instant, in too short a time, one would have thought, even for the bullet to get there, a mysterious, terrible change had come over the elephant. He neither stirred nor fell, but every line of his body had altered. He looked suddenly stricken, shrunken, immensely old, as though the frightful impact of the bullet had paralyzed him without knocking him down. At last, after what seemed a long time — it might have been five seconds, I dare say — he sagged flabbily to his knees. His mouth slobbered. An enormous senility seemed to have settled upon him. One could have imagined him thousands of years old. I fired again into the same spot. At the second shot he did not collapse but climbed with desperate slowness to his feet and stood weakly upright, with legs sagging and head drooping. I fired a third time. That was the shot that did for him. You could see the agony of it jolt his whole body and knock the last remnant of strength from his legs. But in falling he seemed for a moment to rise, for as his hind legs collapsed beneath him he seemed to tower upward like a huge rock toppling, his trunk reaching skywards like a tree. He trumpeted, for the first and only time. And then down he came, his belly towards me, with a crash that seemed to shake the ground even where I lay.

I got up. The Burmans were already racing past me across the mud. It was obvious that the elephant would never rise again, but he was not dead. He was breathing very rhythmically with long rattling gasps, his great mound of a side painfully rising and falling. His mouth was wide open. I could see far down into caverns of pale pink throat. I waited a long time for him to die, but his breathing did not weaken. Finally I fired my two remaining shots into the spot where I thought his heart must be. The thick blood welled out of him like red velvet, but still he did not die. His body did not even jerk when the shots hit him, the tortured breathing continued without a pause. He was dying, very slowly and in great agony, but in some world remote from me where not even a bullet could damage him further. I felt I had got to put an end to that dreadful noise. It seemed dreadful to see the great beast lying there, powerless to move and yet powerless to die, and not even to be able to finish him. I sent back for my small rifle and poured shot after shot into his heart and down his throat. They seemed to make no impression. The tortured gasps continued as steadily as the ticking of a clock.

In the end I could not stand it any longer and went away. I heard later that it took him half an hour to die. Burmans were bringing dahs[9] and baskets even before I left, and I was told they had stripped his body almost to the bones by the afternoon.

Afterwards, of course, there were endless discussions about the shooting of the elephant. The owner was furious, but he was only an Indian and could do nothing. Besides, legally I had done the right thing, for a mad elephant has to be killed, like a mad dog, if its owner fails to control it. Among the Europeans opinion was divided. The older men said I was right, the younger men said it was a damn shame to shoot an elephant for killing a coolie, because the elephant was worth more than any damn Coringhee coolie. And afterwards I was very glad that the coolie had been killed; it put me legally in the right and it gave me sufficient pretext for shooting the elephant. I often wondered whether any of the others grasped that I had done it solely to avoid looking a fool.

[9]Heavy knives. — ED.

Thinking Critically about the Text

Even though Orwell does not want to shoot the elephant, he does. How does he rationalize his behavior? On what grounds was Orwell legally in the right? What alternatives did he have? What do you think Orwell learned from this incident?

Questions on Subject

1. What do you suppose would have happened had Orwell not sent for an elephant rifle?

2. What is imperialism, and what discovery about imperialism does Orwell make during the course of the event he narrates?

3. What does Orwell mean when he says, "I was very glad that the coolie had been killed" (paragraph 14)?

4. What is the point of Orwell's final paragraph? How does that paragraph affect your response to the whole essay?

5. Orwell wrote "Shooting an Elephant" some years after the event occurred. What does his account of the event gain with the passage of time? Explain.

Questions on Strategy

1. Why do you think Orwell is so meticulous in establishing the setting for his essay in paragraphs 1 and 2?

2. What do you think was Orwell's purpose in telling this story? (Glossary: *Purpose*) Cite evidence from the text that indicates to you that purpose. Does he accomplish his purpose?

3. Orwell is quick to capitalize on the ironies of the circumstances surrounding the events he narrates. (Glossary: *Irony*) Identify any circumstances you found ironic, and explain what this irony contributes to Orwell's overall purpose.

4. What part of the essay struck you most strongly? The shooting itself? Orwell's feelings? The descriptions of the Burmese and their behavior? What is it about Orwell's prose that enhances the impact of that passage for you? Explain.

5. "Shooting an Elephant" is, first of all, a narrative; Orwell has a story to tell. (Glossary: *Narration*) But Orwell uses other strategies in support of narration to help develop and give meaning to his story. Identify passages in which Orwell uses description, illustration, and cause and effect analysis, and explain how each enhances the incident he narrates. (Glossary: *Cause and Effect Analysis; Description; Illustration*)

Questions on Diction and Vocabulary

1. A British citizen, Orwell uses British English. Cite several examples of this British diction. How might an American say the same thing?

2. Identify several of the metaphors and similes that Orwell uses, and explain what each adds to his descriptions in this essay. (Glossary: *Figures of Speech*)

3. As a writer, Orwell always advocated using strong action verbs because they are vivid and eliminate unnecessary modification. (Glossary: *Verb*) For example, in paragraph 1 he uses the verb *jeer* instead of the verb *yell* plus the adverb

derisively. Identify other strong verbs that you found particularly striking. What do these strong verbs add to Orwell's prose style?

Classroom Activity for Combining Strategies

Orwell's argument is couched in a very moving and affecting narrative replete with powerful descriptions. Think about how you might use narration to enhance an argument you have already written or are planning to write. How might your case, in effect, be made by telling a story — by showing rather than telling? Think about whether it would be more effective in your case to present your argument in one long narrative or to use several episodes to make your point. Discuss your approach with other members of your class to get their responses to your plans.

Writing Suggestions

1. Write an essay recounting a situation in which you felt compelled to act against your convictions. (Glossary: *Narration*) Before you start writing, you may find it helpful to consider one or more of the following questions and to review your Preparing to Read response for this essay. How can you justify your action? How much freedom of choice did you actually have, and what were the limits on your freedom? On what basis can you refuse to subordinate your convictions to others' or to society's?

2. Consider situations in which you have been a leader, like Orwell, or a follower. As a leader, what was your attitude toward your followers? As a follower, what did you feel toward your leader? Using Orwell's essay and your own experiences, what conclusions can you draw about leaders and followers? Write an essay in which you explore the relationship between leaders and followers.

A Modest Proposal

JONATHAN SWIFT

One of the world's great satirists, Jonathan Swift was born in 1667 to English parents in Dublin, Ireland, and was educated at Trinity College. When his early efforts at a literary career in England met no success, he returned to Ireland in 1694 and was ordained an Anglican clergyman. From 1713 until his death in 1745, he was dean of Dublin's St. Patrick's Cathedral. A prolific chronicler of human folly, Swift is best known as the author of *Gulliver's Travels* and of the work included here, "A Modest Proposal."

In the 1720s Ireland had suffered several famines, but the English gentry, who owned most of the land, did nothing to alleviate the suffering of tenant farmers and their families; nor would the English government intervene. A number of pamphlets were circulated proposing solutions to the Irish problem.

"A Modest Proposal," published anonymously in 1729, was Swift's ironic contribution to the discussion.

Preparing to Read

Satire is a literary and dramatic art form wherein the shortcomings, foibles, abuses, and idiocies of both people and institutions are accented and held up for ridicule in order to shame their perpetrators into reforming themselves. Perhaps the very easiest way to see satire around us today is in the work of our political cartoonists. Think of individuals and institutions both here and abroad who today might make good subjects for satire.

For Preventing the Children of Poor People in Ireland from Being a Burden to Their Parents or Country, and for Making Them Beneficial to the Public

I t is a melancholy object to those who walk through this great town[1] or travel in the country, when they see the streets, the roads, and cabin doors, crowded with beggars of the female sex, followed by three, four, or six children, all in rags and importuning every passenger for an alms. These mothers, instead of being able to work for their honest livelihood, are forced to employ all their time in strolling to beg sustenance for their helpless infants, who, as they grow up, either turn thieves for want of work,

1

[1]Dublin. —Ed.

or leave their dear native country to fight for the Pretender in Spain, or sell themselves to the Barbadoes.[2]

I think it is agreed by all parties that this prodigious number of children in the arms, or on the backs, or at the heels of their mothers, and frequently of their fathers, is in the present deplorable state of the kingdom a very great additional grievance; and therefore whoever could find out a fair, cheap, and easy method of making these children sound, useful members of the commonwealth would deserve so well of the public as to have his statue set up for a preserver of the nation.

But my intention is very far from being confined to provide only for the children of professed beggars; it is of a much greater extent, and shall take in the whole number of infants at a certain age who are born of parents in effect as little able to support them as those who demand our charity in the streets.

As to my own part, having turned my thoughts for many years upon this important subject, and maturely weighed the several schemes of other projectors,[3] I have always found them grossly mistaken in their computation. It is true, a child just dropped from its dam may be supported by her milk for a solar year, with little other nourishment; at most not above the value of two shillings, which the mother may certainly get, or the value in scraps, by her lawful occupation of begging; and it is exactly at one year old that I propose to provide for them in such a manner as instead of being a charge upon their parents or the parish, or wanting food and raiment for the rest of their lives, they shall on the contrary contribute to the feeding, and partly to the clothing, of many thousands.

There is likewise another great advantage in my scheme, that it will prevent those voluntary abortions, and that horrid practice of women murdering their bastard children, alas, too frequent among us, sacrificing the poor innocent babes, I doubt, more to avoid the expense than the shame, which would move tears and pity in the most savage and inhuman breast.

The number of souls in this kingdom[4] being usually reckoned one million and a half, of these I calculate there may be about two hundred thousand couples whose wives are breeders; from which number I subtract thirty thousand couples who are able to maintain their own children, although I apprehend there cannot be so many under the present distresses of the kingdom; but this being granted, there will remain an hundred and seventy thousand breeders. I again subtract fifty thousand for those women

---

[2]Many Irish Catholics were loyal to James Stuart, a claimant (or "pretender") to the English crown, and followed him into exile. Others, stricken by poverty, sold themselves into virtual slavery in order to escape to British colonies (like Barbados) in the New World. —ED.

[3]Proposers of solutions. —ED.

[4]Ireland. —ED.

who miscarry, or whose children die by accident or disease within the year. There only remain an hundred and twenty thousand children of poor parents annually born. The question therefore is, how this number shall be reared and provided for, which, as I have already said, under the present situation of affairs, is utterly impossible by all the methods hitherto proposed. For we can neither employ them in handicraft or agriculture; we neither build houses (I mean in the country) nor cultivate land. They can very seldom pick up a livelihood by stealing till they arrive at six years old, except where they are of towardly parts;[5] although I confess they learn the rudiments much earlier, during which time they can however be looked upon only as probationers, as I have been informed by a principal gentleman in the county of Cavan, who protested to me that he never knew above one or two instances under the age of six, even in a part of the kingdom so renowned for the quickest proficiency in that art.

A young healthy child well nursed is at a year old a most delicious, nourishing, and wholesome food, whether stewed, roasted, baked, or boiled. . . .

I am assured by our merchants that a boy or a girl before twelve years old is no salable commodity; and even when they come to this age they will not yield above three pounds, or three pounds and half a crown at most on the Exchange; which cannot turn to account either to the parents or the kingdom, the charge of nutriment and rags having been at least four times that value.

I shall now therefore humbly propose my own thoughts, which I hope will not be liable to the least objection.

I have been assured by a very knowing American of my acquaintance in London, that a young healthy child well nursed is at a year old a most delicious, nourishing, and wholesome food, whether stewed, roasted, baked, or boiled; and I make no doubt that it will equally serve in a fricassee or a ragout.[6]

I do therefore humbly offer it to public consideration that of the hundred and twenty thousand children, already computed, twenty thousand may be reserved for breed, whereof only one fourth part to be males, which is more than we allow to sheep, black cattle, or swine; and my reason is that these children are seldom the fruits of marriage, a circumstance not much regarded by our savages, therefore one male will be sufficient to serve four females. That the remaining hundred thousand may at a year old be offered

---

[5]Or "advanced for their age." —ED.
[6]Types of stews. —ED.

in sale to the persons of quality and fortune through the kingdom, always advising the mother to let them suck plentifully in the last month, so as to render them plump and fat for a good table. A child will make two dishes at an entertainment for friends; and when the family dines alone, the fore or hind quarter will make a reasonable dish, and seasoned with a little pepper or salt will be very good boiled on the fourth day, especially in winter.

11 I have reckoned upon a medium that a child just born will weigh twelve pounds, and in a solar year if tolerably nursed increaseth to twenty-eight pounds.

12 I grant this food will be somewhat dear, and therefore very proper for landlords, who, as they have already devoured most of the parents, seem to have the best title to the children.

13 Infant's flesh will be in season throughout the year, but more plentiful in March, and a little before and after. For we are told by a grave author, an eminent French physician,[7] that fish being a prolific diet, there are more children born in Roman Catholic countries about nine months after Lent than at any other season; therefore, reckoning a year after Lent, the markets will be more glutted than usual, because the number of popish infants is at least three to one in this kingdom; and therefore it will have one other collateral advantage, by lessening the number of papists among us.

14 I have already computed the charge of nursing a beggar's child (in which list I reckon all cottagers, laborers, and four fifths of the farmers) to be about two shillings per annum, rags included; and I believe no gentleman would repine to give ten shillings for the carcass of a good fat child, which, as I have said, will make four dishes of excellent nutritive meat, when he hath only some particular friend or his own family to dine with him. Thus the squire will learn to be a good landlord, and grow popular among the tenants; the mother will have eight shillings net profit, and be fit for work till she produces another child.

15 Those who are more thrifty (as I must confess the times require) may flay the carcass; the skin of which artificially[8] dressed will make admirable gloves for ladies, and summer boots for fine gentlemen.

16 As to our city of Dublin, shambles[9] may be appointed for this purpose in the most convenient parts of it, and butchers we may be assured will not be wanting; although I rather recommend buying the children alive, and dressing them hot from the knife as we do roasting pigs.

17 A very worthy person, a true lover of his country, and whose virtues I highly esteem, was lately pleased in discoursing on this matter to offer

---

[7]François Rabelais (c. 1494–1553), a French satirist—not at all "grave"—whom Swift admired for his broad humor and sharp wit.—ED.

[8] Skillfully, artfully.—ED.

[9]Slaughterhouses.—ED.

a refinement upon my scheme. He said that many gentlemen of this kingdom, having of late destroyed their deer, he conceived that the want of venison might be well supplied by the bodies of young lads and maidens, not exceeding fourteen years of age nor under twelve, so great a number of both sexes in every county being now ready to starve for want of work and service; and these to be disposed of by their parents, if alive, or otherwise by their nearest relations. But with due deference to so excellent a friend and so deserving a patriot, I cannot be altogether in his sentiments; for as to the males, my American acquaintance assured me from frequent experience that their flesh was generally tough and lean, like that of our schoolboys, by continual exercise, and their taste disagreeable; and to fatten them would not answer the charge. Then as to the females, it would, I think with humble submission, be a loss to the public, because they soon would become breeders themselves: and besides, it is not improbable that some scrupulous people might be apt to censure such a practice (although indeed very unjustly) as a little bordering upon cruelty; which, I confess, hath always been with me the strongest objection against any project, how well soever intended.

But in order to justify my friend, he confessed that this expedient was 18 put into his head by the famous Psalmanazar,[10] a native of the island Formosa, who came from thence to London above twenty years ago, and in conversation told my friend that in his country when any young person happened to be put to death, the executioner sold the carcass to persons of quality as a prime dainty; and that in his time the body of a plump girl of fifteen, who was crucified for an attempt to poison the emperor, was sold to his Imperial Majesty's prime minister of state, and other great mandarins of the court, in joints from the gibbet, at four hundred crowns. Neither indeed can I deny that if the same use were made of several plump young girls in this town, who without one single groat to their fortunes cannot stir abroad without a chair, and appear at the playhouse and assemblies in foreign fineries which they never will pay for, the kingdom would not be the worse.

Some persons of a desponding spirit are in great concern about that 19 vast number of poor people who are aged, diseased, or maimed, and I have been desired to employ my thoughts what course may be taken to ease the nation of so grievous an encumbrance. But I am not in the least pain upon that matter, because it is very well known that they are every day dying and rotting by cold and famine, and filth and vermin, as fast as can be reasonably expected. And as to the younger laborers, they are now in almost as hopeful a condition. They cannot get work, and consequently pine away

[10]George Psalmanazar (c. 1679–1763), a French imposter who fooled London society with his tales of human sacrifice and cannibalism on Formosa. — ED.

for want of nourishment to a degree that if at any time they are accidentally hired to common labor, they have not strength to perform it; and thus the country and themselves are happily delivered from the evils to come.

I have too long digressed, and therefore shall return to my subject. I [20] think the advantages by the proposal which I have made are obvious and many, as well as of the highest importance.

For first, as I have already observed, it would greatly lessen the num- [21] ber of Papists, with whom we are yearly overrun, being the principal breeders of the nation as well as our most dangerous enemies; and who stay at home on purpose to deliver the kingdom to the Pretender, hoping to take their advantage by the absence of so many good Protestants, who have chosen rather to leave their country than stay at home and pay tithes against their conscience to an Episcopal curate.

Secondly, the poorer tenants will have something valuable of their [22] own, which by law may be made liable to distress,[11] and help to pay their landlord's rent, their corn and cattle being already seized and money a thing unknown.

Thirdly, whereas the maintenance of an hundred thousand children, [23] from two years old and upwards, cannot be computed at less than ten shillings a piece per annum, the nation's stock will be thereby increased fifty thousand pounds per annum, besides the profit of a new dish introduced to the tables of all gentlemen of fortune in the kingdom who have any refinement in taste. And the money will circulate among ourselves, the goods being entirely of our own growth and manufacture.

Fourthly, the constant breeders, besides the gain of eight shillings ster- [24] ling per annum by the sale of their children, will be rid of the charge of maintaining them after the first year.

Fifthly, this food would likewise bring great custom to taverns, where [25] the vintners will certainly be so prudent as to procure the best receipts for dressing it to perfection, and consequently have their houses frequented by all the fine gentlemen, who justly value themselves upon their knowledge in good eating; and a skillful cook, who understands how to oblige his guests, will contrive to make it as expensive as they please.

Sixthly, this would be a great inducement to marriage, which all wise [26] nations have either encouraged by rewards or enforced by laws and penalties. It would increase the care and tenderness of mothers toward their children, when they were sure of a settlement for life to the poor babes, provided in some sort by the public, to their annual profit instead of expense. We should see an honest emulation among the married women, which of them could bring the fattest child to the market. Men would

---

[11]Subject to seizure by creditors. —ED.

become as fond of their wives during the time of their pregnancy as they are now of their mares in foal, their cows in calf, or sows when they are ready to farrow; nor offer to beat or kick them (as is too frequent a practice) for fear of a miscarriage.

Many other advantages might be enumerated. For instance, the addition of some thousand carcasses in our exportation of barreled beef, the propagation of swine's flesh, and improvement in the art of making good bacon, so much wanted among us by the great destruction of pigs, too frequent at our tables, which are no way comparable in taste or magnificence to a well-grown, fat, yearling child, which roasted whole will make a considerable figure at a lord mayor's feast or any other public entertainment. But this and many others I omit, being studious of brevity. 27

Supposing that one thousand families in this city would be constant customers for infants' flesh, besides others who might have it at merry meetings, particularly weddings and christenings, I compute that Dublin would take off annually about twenty thousand carcasses, and the rest of the kingdom (where probably they will be sold somewhat cheaper) the remaining eighty thousand. 28

I can think of no one objection that will possibly be raised against this proposal, unless it should be urged that the number of people will be thereby much lessened in the kingdom. This I freely own, and it was indeed one principal design in offering it to the world. I desire the reader will observe, that I calculate my remedy for this one individual kingdom of Ireland and for no other that ever was, is, or I think ever can be upon earth. Therefore let no man talk to me of other expedients: of taxing our absentees at five shillings a pound: of using neither clothes nor household furniture except what is of our own growth and manufacture: of utterly rejecting the materials and instruments that promote foreign luxury: of curing the expensiveness of pride, vanity, idleness, and gaming in our women: of introducing a vein of parsimony, prudence, and temperance: of learning to love our country, in the want of which we differ even from Laplanders and the inhabitants of Topinamhoo:[12] of quitting our animosities and factions, nor acting any longer like the Jews, who were murdering one another at the very moment their city was taken:[13] of being a little cautious not to sell our country and conscience for nothing: of teaching landlords to have at least one degree of mercy toward their tenants: lastly, of putting a spirit of honesty, industry, and skill into our shopkeepers; who, if a resolution could now be taken to buy only our native goods, would immediately unite to 29

---

[12]In other words, even from Laplanders who love their icy tundra and primitive Brazilian tribes who love their jungle. —ED.

[13]Swift refers to the Roman siege of Jerusalem in A.D. 70; the inhabitants lost the city because they dissolved into violent factions. —ED.

cheat and exact upon us in the price, the measure, and the goodness, nor could ever yet be brought to make one fair proposal of just dealing, though often and earnestly invited to it.

Therefore I repeat, let no man talk to me of these and the like expedi- 30 ents, till he hath at least some glimpse of hope that there will ever be some hearty and sincere attempt to put them in practice.

But as to myself, having been wearied out for many years with offering 31 vain, idle, visionary thoughts, and at length utterly despairing of success, I fortunately fell upon this proposal, which, as it is wholly new, so it hath something solid and real, of no expense and little trouble, full in our own power, and whereby we can incur no danger in disobliging England. For this kind of commodity will not bear exportation, the flesh being of too tender a consistence to admit a long continuance in salt, although perhaps I could name a country which would be glad to eat up our whole nation without it.

After all, I am not so violently bent upon my own opinion as to reject 32 any offer proposed by wise men, which shall be found equally innocent, cheap, easy, and effectual. But before something of that kind shall be advanced in contradiction to my scheme, and offering a better, I desire the author or authors will be pleased maturely to consider two points. First, as things now stand, how they will be able to find food and raiment for an hundred thousand useless mouths and backs. And secondly, there being a round million of creatures in human figure throughout this kingdom, whose sole subsistence put into a common stock would leave them in debt two millions of pounds sterling, adding those who are beggars by profession to the bulk of farmers, cottagers, and laborers, with their wives and children who are beggars in effect; I desire those politicians who dislike my overture, and may perhaps be so bold to attempt an answer, that they will first ask the parents of these mortals whether they would not at this day think it a great happiness to have been sold for food at a year old in the manner I prescribe, and thereby have avoided such a perpetual scene of misfortunes as they have since gone through by the oppression of land-lords, the impossibility of paying rent without money or trade, the want of common sustenance, with neither house nor clothes to cover them from the inclemencies of the weather, and the most inevitable prospect of entail-ing the like or greater miseries upon their breed forever.

I profess, in the sincerity of my heart, that I have not the least personal 33 interest in endeavoring to promote this necessary work, having no other motive than the public good of my country, by advancing our trade, pro-viding for infants, relieving the poor, and giving some pleasure to the rich. I have no children by which I can propose to get a single penny; the young-est being nine years old, and my wife past childbearing.

Thinking Critically about the Text

Satire often has a "stealth quality" about it; that is, the audience for it often does not realize at first that the author of the satire is not being serious. At some point in the satire the audience usually catches on and then begins to see the larger issue at the center of the satire. At what point in your reading did you begin to catch on to Swift's technique and larger, more important, message?

Questions on Subject

1. What problem is being addressed in this essay? Describe the specific solution being proposed. What are the proposal's "advantages" (paragraph 20)?

2. What "other expedients" (paragraph 29) are dismissed as "vain, idle, visionary thoughts" (31)? What do paragraphs 29 through 31 tell you about Swift's purpose? (Glossary: *Purpose*)

3. Describe the "author" of the proposal. Why does Swift choose such a character to present this plan? When can you detect Swift's own voice coming through?

4. What is the meaning and the significance of the title? (Glossary: *Title*)

5. In paragraph 2, Swift talks of making Ireland's "children sound, useful members of the commonwealth." In what way is this statement ironic? Cite several other examples of Swift's irony. (Glossary: *Irony*)

Questions on Strategy

1. Toward what belief and/or action is Swift attempting to persuade his readers? How does he go about doing so? For example, did you feel a sense of outrage at any point in the essay? Did you feel that the essay was humorous at any point? If so, where and why?

2. What is the effect of the first paragraph of the essay? How does it serve to introduce the proposal? (Glossary: *Beginnings/Endings*)

3. What strategies does Swift use in this essay to make his proposer sound like an authority? Explain how this sense of authority relates to Swift's real purpose.

4. In what ways can the argument presented in this essay be seen as logical? What is the effect, for example, of the complicated calculations in paragraph 6?

5. What strategies, in addition to argumentation, does Swift use to develop his satire? Cite examples to support your answer. (Glossary: *Argument*)

Questions on Diction and Vocabulary

1. It is not easy to summarize Swift's tone in a single word, but how would you describe the overall tone he establishes? Point to specific passages in the essay where you find his language particularly effective.

2. What is Swift's intent in using the term *modest*? (Glossary: *Purpose*)

3. In paragraph 6, Swift refers to women as "breeders." In terms of his proposal, why is the diction appropriate? (Glossary: *Diction*) Cite other examples of such diction used to describe the poor people of Ireland.

Classroom Activity for Combining Strategies

Imagine that you will write a satire based on the model of Swift's "A Modest Proposal." Think in terms of attacking the foolish thinking or absurdity of a situation you find on the national, state, or local level and how your satire will get people to think about that issue in productive ways. What additional strategies might you employ to accomplish your satire? Discuss your possible approaches to this assignment with other members of your class.

Writing Suggestions

1. **Writing with Sources.** Write a modest proposal of your own to solve a difficult social or political problem of the present day or, on a smaller scale, a problem you see facing your school or community. Do some research on your topic in the library or online. For models of and advice on integrating sources in your essay, see Chapters 14 and 15.

2. **Writing with Sources.** What is the most effective way to bring about social change and to influence societal attitudes? Would Swift's methods work today, or would they have to be significantly modified? Concentrating on the sorts of changes you have witnessed over the last ten years, write an essay in which you describe how best to influence public opinion. Do some research on your topic in the library or online. For models of and advice on integrating sources in your essay, see Chapters 14 and 15.

WRITING SUGGESTIONS FOR COMBINING STRATEGIES

1. Select a piece you have written for this class in which you used one primary writing strategy, and rewrite it using another. For example, choose a description you wrote and redraft it as a process analysis. Remember that the choice of a writing strategy influences the writer's "voice" — a descriptive piece might be lyrical, while a process analysis might be straightforward. How does your voice change along with the strategy? Does your assumed audience change as well? (Glossary: *Audience*)

   If time allows, exchange a piece of writing with a partner, and rewrite it using a different strategy. Discuss the choices you each made.

2. Select an essay you have written this semester, either for this class or another class. What was the primary writing strategy you used? Build on this essay by integrating another strategy. For example, if you wrote an argument paper for a political science class, you might try using narrative to give some historical background to the paper. (Glossary: *Argument; Narration*) For a paper in the natural sciences, you could use subjective description to open the paper up to nonscientists. (Glossary: *Objective/Subjective*) When you're finished, ask yourself: How did use of the new strategy affect your paper?

3. The choice of a writing strategy reflects an author's voice — the persona he or she assumes in relation to the reader. Read back through any personal writing you've done this semester — a journal, letters to friends, e-mail. Can you identify the strategies you use outside of formal academic writing, as part of your natural writing voice? Write a few pages analyzing these strategies and your writing voice, using one of the rhetorical strategies studied this term. For example, you could compare and contrast your e-mail postings to your letters home. (Glossary: *Comparison and Contrast*) Or you could do a cause and effect analysis of how being at college has changed the tone or style of your journal writing. (Glossary: *Cause and Effect Analysis*)

4. **Writing with Sources.** Review the "Why Milk?" ad that opens this chapter (page 614). Write an essay in which you discuss the ad and the issues that underlie it. As you work, consider these questions: What are the potentially harmful effects of producing milk by using hormones and antibiotics? Of drinking such milk? If you agree that change is needed, explain what you would change and how. If you disagree with the ad, respond to the implicit claims of those who *do* call for change. Consider placing your argument in the context of economic, social, scientific, ethical, or ideological discussions of

modern agriculture, the environment, health, diet, capitalism, advertising, political correctness, or another related topic that interests you.

You will need to do some research to bolster your claims. For models of and advice on integrating sources in your essay, see Chapters 14 and 15.

5. **Writing in the Workplace.** Find a local newspaper editorial dealing with a controversial social or educational problem. Outline the issues involved and the strategies that the editorial writer used to present his or her argument. Then, assume that you — a concerned citizen — are given equal space in the newspaper to present an opposing viewpoint. Make notes for a rebuttal argument and for the development strategies you might use to support your argument, considering, for example, narration, process analysis, comparison and contrast, and/or illustration. Finally, write your response to the editorial, and submit a copy to the newspaper that published the original piece.

 e-Pages

Why Is the Sky Blue?

HALFTONE

See how combining strategies works on the Web. Go to bedfordstmartins.com/subjectandstrategy for a video and study questions about how particles affect the way we see the color of the sky.

CHAPTER 14

Writing with Sources

WHAT DOES IT MEAN TO WRITE WITH SOURCES?

MANY OF YOUR COLLEGE ASSIGNMENTS WILL CALL UPON YOU TO DO research and write using information from sources. To do this effectively, you will have to learn some basic research practices—locating and evaluating print and online sources, taking notes from those sources, and documenting those sources. (For help with research and documentation, see Chapter 15, pages 710–33.) Even more fundamental than this, however, is to understand what it *means* to do research and to write with sources.

Your purpose in writing with sources is not to present a collection of quotations that report what others have said about your topic. Rather, your goal is to *analyze, evaluate,* and *synthesize* the materials you have researched so that you become a full-fledged participant in the conversation about your topic. To enter into this conversation with authority, you will have to learn how to use sources ethically and effectively. To help you on your way, this chapter provides advice on summarizing, paraphrasing, and quoting sources; integrating sources; and avoiding plagiarism. In addition, two student papers and two professional essays model different ways of engaging meaningfully with sources and of reflecting that engagement in writing.

On the opposite page, note how Joel Robison's surreal photograph plays with the idea of writing with sources. Using books and other sources as his literal foundation, his writing transforms from mere words on a page into elegant, butterfly-like origami structures with an identity of their own.

WRITING WITH SOURCES

Outside sources can be used to:

- Support your thesis and points with statements from noted authorities
- Offer memorable wording of key terms or ideas
- Extend your ideas by introducing new information
- Articulate opposing positions for you to argue against

Consider Sharon Begley's use of an outside source in the following paragraph from her *Newsweek* essay "Praise the Humble Dung Beetle":

> Of all creatures great and small, it is the charismatic megafauna — tigers and rhinos and gorillas and pandas and other soulful-eyed, warm, and fuzzy animals — that personify endangered species. That's both a shame and a dangerous bias. "Plants and invertebrates are the silent majority which feed the entire planet, stabilize the soil, and make all life possible," says Kiernan Suckling, cofounder of the Center for Biological Diversity. They pollinate crops and decompose carcasses, filter water and, lacking weapons like teeth and claws, brew up molecules to defend themselves that turn out to be remarkably potent medicines: The breast-cancer compound taxol comes from a yew tree, and a leukemia drug from the rosy periwinkle. Those are tricks that, Suckling dryly notes, "polar bears and blue whales haven't mastered yet."

Here Begley quotes Kiernan Suckling, a biologist specializing in biodiversity, to support her contention that it's "both a shame and a dangerous bias" to have tigers, polar bears, and other photogenic mammals be the headliners for all endangered species.

Sometimes source material is too long and detailed to be quoted directly in its entirety. In such cases, a writer will choose to summarize or paraphrase the material in his or her own words before introducing it in an essay. For example, notice how Judith Newman summarizes two lengthy sleep studies for use in her essay "What's Really Going On Inside Your Teen's Head," which appeared in the November 28, 2010, issue of *Parade* magazine.

> In a pair of related studies published in 1993 and 1997 by Mary Carskadon, a professor of psychiatry at Brown University and director of the Sleep Research program at Bradley Hospital in Rhode Island, Carskadon and colleagues found that more physically mature girls preferred activities later in the day than did less-mature girls and that the sleep-promoting hormone melatonin rises later in teenagers than in children and adults. Translation: Teenagers are physically programmed to stay up later and sleep later.

Here, Newman introduces her summary with an extensive signal phrase highlighting Mary Carskadon's academic credentials, and she concludes with a pointed statement of the researchers' conclusion, information that is needed to broaden her discussion.

In the following passage from "Blaming the Family for Economic Decline," Stephanie Coontz uses outside sources to present the position that she will argue against.

> The fallback position for those in denial about the socioeconomic transformation we are experiencing is to admit that many families are in economic stress but to blame their plight on divorce and unwed motherhood.

Lawrence Mead of New York University argues that economic inequalities stemming from differences in wages and employment patterns "are now trivial in comparison to those stemming from family structure." David Blankenhorn claims that the "primary fault line" dividing privileged and nonprivileged Americans is no longer "race, religion, class, education, or gender" but family structure. Every major newspaper in the country has published editorials and opinion pieces along these lines. This "new consensus" produces a delightfully simple, inexpensive solution to the economic ills of America's families. From Republican Dan Quayle to the Democratic Party's Progressive Policy Institute, we hear the same words: "Marriage is the best antipoverty program for children."

Now I am as horrified as anyone by irresponsible parents who yield to the temptations of our winner-take-all society and abandon their family obligations. But we are kidding ourselves if we think the solution to the economic difficulties of America's children lies in getting their parents back together. Single-parent families, it is true, are five to six times more likely to be poor than two-parent ones. But correlations are not the same as causes. The association between poverty and single parenthood has several different sources, suggesting that the battle to end child poverty needs to be fought on a number of different fronts.

By letting the opposition articulate their own position, Coontz reduces the possibility of being criticized for misrepresenting her opponents; at the same time, she sets herself up to give strong voice to her thesis.

LEARNING TO SUMMARIZE, PARAPHRASE, AND QUOTE FROM YOUR SOURCES

When taking notes from your sources, you must decide whether to summarize, paraphrase, or quote directly. The approach you take is largely determined by the content of the source passage and the way you envision using it in your paper. Be aware, however, that making use of all three of these techniques—rather than relying on only one or two—will keep your text varied and interesting.

Learning to summarize, paraphrase, and quote effectively and correctly is essential for the writing you'll do in school, at work, and in everyday life. The following sections will help you understand how the three techniques differ, when to use these techniques, and how to make them work within the context of your writing.

▶ Summarizing

When you *summarize* material from one of your sources, you use your own words to capture in condensed form the essential idea of a passage, article, or entire chapter. Summaries are particularly useful when you are working with lengthy, detailed arguments or long passages of narrative or descriptive background information not germane to the overall thrust of your paper. You simply want to capture the essence of the passage while dispensing with the details because you are confident that your readers will readily understand the point being made or will not need to be convinced about the validity of the point. Because you are distilling information, a summary is always shorter than the original; often a chapter or more can be reduced to a paragraph, or several paragraphs to a sentence or two. Remember, in writing a summary you should use your own words.

Consider the following paragraphs in which Richard Lederer compares big words with small words.

> When you speak and write, there is no law that says you have to use big words. Short words are as good as long ones, and short, old words—like *sun* and *grass* and *home*—are best of all. A lot of small words, more than you might think, can meet your needs with a strength, grace, and charm that large words do not have.
>
> Big words can make the way dark for those who read what you write and hear what you say. Small words cast their clear light on big things—night and day, love and hate, war and peace, and life and death. Big words at times seem strange to the eye and the ear and the mind and the heart. Small words are the ones we seem to have known from the time we were born, like the hearth fire that warms the home.
>
> —RICHARD LEDERER,
> "The Case for Short Words," pages 516–17

A student wishing to capture the gist of Lederer's point without repeating his detail wrote the following summary.

Lederer favors short words for their clarity, familiarity, durability, and overall usefulness (516–17).

▶ Paraphrasing

When you *paraphrase* a source, you restate the information in your own words instead of quoting directly. Unlike a summary, which gives a brief overview of the essential information in the original, a paraphrase seeks to maintain the same level of detail as the original to aid readers in understanding or believing the information presented. A summary, then, condenses the original material, while a paraphrase presents the original information in approximately the same number of words as the original.

Paraphrase can be thought of as a sort of middle ground between summary and quotation, but beware: While a paraphrase should closely parallel the presentation of ideas in the original it should not use the same words or sentence structure as the original. Even though you are using your own words in a paraphrase, it's important to remember that you are borrowing ideas and therefore must acknowledge the source of these ideas with a citation.

How would you paraphrase the following passage from a speech by Martin Luther King Jr.?

> But one hundred years later [after the Emancipation Proclamation], we must face the tragic fact that the Negro is still not free. One hundred years later, the life of the Negro is still sadly crippled by the manacles of segregation and the chains of discrimination. One hundred years later, the Negro lives on a lonely island of poverty in the midst of a vast ocean of material prosperity. One hundred years later, the Negro is still languishing in the corners of American society and finds himself an exile in his own land.
>
> —MARTIN LUTHER KING JR.,
> "I Have a Dream," page 522

The following illustrates how one student paraphrased the passage from King's speech.

Speaking on the one hundredth anniversary of the Emancipation Proclamation, King observed that African Americans still found themselves a marginalized people. He contended that African Americans did not experience the freedom that other Americans did—in a land of opportunity and plenty, racism and poverty affected the way they lived their lives, separating them from mainstream society (522).

In most cases, it is better to summarize or paraphrase materials—which by definition means using your own words—instead of quoting verbatim (word for word). Capturing an idea in your own words ensures that you have thought about and understood what your source is saying.

▶ Using Direct Quotation

You should reserve direct quotation for important ideas stated memorably, for especially clear explanations by authorities, and for arguments by proponents of a particular position. Consider the following direct quotation that one student chose. The student quotes a passage from Malcolm Jones's article "Who Was More Important: Lincoln or Darwin?" that appeared in *Newsweek* on July 14, 2008. Notice how Jones captures Charles Darwin's mixed emotions upon realizing the impact his theory of evolution would have on the world.

> "As delighted as he was with his discovery, Darwin was equally horrified, because he understood the consequences of his theory. Mankind was no longer the culmination of life but merely part of it; creation was mechanistic and purposeless. In a letter to a fellow scientist, Darwin wrote that confiding his theory was 'like confessing a murder.' Small wonder that instead of rushing to publish his theory, he sat on it—for twenty years."

The skillful prose Jones uses to describe Darwin's state of mind makes this passage well worth quoting in full, rather than summarizing or paraphrasing it.

▶ Using Direct Quotation with Summary or Paraphrase

On occasion, you'll find a useful passage with some memorable phrases in it. Avoid the temptation to quote the whole passage; instead you can combine summary or paraphrase with direct quotation. Consider, for example, the following paragraph from Rosalind Wiseman's essay on schoolgirls' roles in cliques.

> Information about each other is currency in Girl World. The Banker creates chaos everywhere she goes by banking information about girls in her social sphere and dispensing it at strategic intervals for her own benefit. For instance, if a girl has said something negative about another girl, the Banker will casually mention it to someone in conversation because she knows it's going to cause a conflict and strengthen her status as someone "in the know." She can get girls to trust her because when she pumps them for information it doesn't seem like gossip; instead, she does it in an innocent, I'm-trying-to-be-your-friend way.
>
> — ROSALIND WISEMAN,
> "The Queen Bee and Her Court," page 353

Note how one student cited this passage using paraphrase *and* quotation.

> In Wiseman's schema, the most dangerous character in the clique is the Banker, who "creates chaos everywhere she goes by banking information about girls in her social sphere and dispensing it at strategic intervals for her own benefit" (353). The Banker spreads gossip freely in order to cement her position as someone " 'in the know' " (353).

Be sure that when you directly quote a source, you copy the words *exactly* and put quotation marks around them. Check and double-check your copy for accuracy, whether it's handwritten, transcribed, or cut-and-pasted from the original source.

▶ Integrating Borrowed Material into Your Text

Whenever you use borrowed material, be it a quotation, paraphrase, or summary, your goal is to integrate it smoothly and logically so as not to disrupt the flow of your paper or to confuse your readers. It is best to introduce such material with a *signal phrase*, which alerts readers that borrowed information is about to be presented. A signal phrase minimally consists of the author's name and a verb (e.g., *Michael Pollan contends*).

How well you integrate a quote, paraphrase, or summary into your paper depends partly on varying your signal phrases and, in particular, choosing verbs for these signal phrases that accurately convey the tone and intent of the writers you are citing. Signal phrases help readers better follow your train of thought. If a writer is arguing, use the verb *argues* (or *asserts*, *claims*, or *contends*); if the writer is contesting a particular position or fact, use the verb *contests* (or *denies*, *disputes*, *refutes*, or *rejects*). In using verbs that are specific to the situation in your paper, you bring your readers into the intellectual debate as well as avoid the monotony of repeating such all-purpose verbs as *says* or *writes*.

The following are just a few examples of how you can vary signal phrases to add interest to your paper.

> Malcolm X confesses that . . .
>
> As professor of linguistics at Georgetown University Deborah Tannen has observed . . .
>
> Bruce Catton, noted Civil War historian, emphasizes . . .
>
> Rosalind Wiseman rejects the widely held belief that . . .
>
> Robert Ramírez enriches our understanding of . . .
>
> Jane Shaw, formerly a senior fellow at the Property and Environment Research Center, contends . . .

Here are other verbs that you might use when constructing signal phrases:

acknowledges	declares	points out
adds	endorses	reasons
admits	grants	reports
believes	implies	responds
compares	insists	suggests
confirms		

Signal phrases also let your reader know exactly where your ideas end and someone else's begin. Never confuse your reader by inserting a quotation that appears suddenly without introduction in your paper. Unannounced quotations leave your reader wondering how the quoted material relates to the point you are trying to make.

Unannounced Quotation

> It's no secret that digital technology is having profound effects on American society, often shaping our very attitudes about the world. We're living at a time when this technology makes it not only possible, but also surprisingly easy for us to copy and share software, music, and video. Is this a good situation? Software and music companies see such copying as theft or a violation of copyright law. "[M]any of my students see matters differently. They freely copy and share music. And they copy and share software, even though such copying is often illegal" (413).

In the following revision, the student integrated the quotation from Gorry's essay "Steal This MP3 File: What Is Theft?" by giving the name of the writer being quoted, referring to his authority on the subject, noting that the writer is speaking from experience, and using the verb *counters*.

Integrated Quotation

> It's no secret that digital technology is having profound effects on American society, often shaping our very attitudes about the world. We're living at a time when this technology makes it not only possible, but also surprisingly easy for us to copy and share software, music, and video. Is this a good situation? Software and music companies see such copying as theft or a violation of copyright law. "[M]any of my students see matters differently," counters information technology specialist and Rice University professor G. Anthony Gorry. "They freely copy and share music. And they copy and share software, even though such copying is often illegal" (413).

▶ Synthesizing Several Sources to Deepen Your Discussion

Synthesis enables you to weave your ideas with the ideas of others in a single paragraph, deepening your discussion and often helping you arrive at a new interpretation or conclusion. By learning how to synthesize the results of your research from your own perspective, you can arrive at an informed opinion of your topic.

When you synthesize several sources in your writing, you get your sources to "talk" with one another. You literally create a conversation in which you take an active role. Sometimes you will find yourself discussing two or three sources together to show a range of views regarding a particular topic or issue—this is called *informational* or *explanatory synthesis*. At other times, you will have opportunities to play your sources off against one another so as to delineate the opposing positions—this is called *persuasive* or *argument synthesis*.

In the following example from her essay "The Qualities of Good Teachers," student Marah Britto uses informational synthesis to combine her own thoughts about good teachers with the thoughts of three other writers. In doing so, she explains the range of attributes that distinguish good teachers from their peers.

We have all experienced a teacher who in some way stands out from all the others we have had, a teacher who has made an important difference in each of our lives. While most of us can agree on some of the character traits—dedication, love for students, patience, passion for his/her subject—that such teachers have in common, we cannot agree on that special something that sets them apart, the something that distinguishes them from the crowd. For me, it was my sixth-grade teacher Mrs. Engstrom, a teacher who motivated with her example. She never asked me to do anything that she was not willing to do herself. How many teachers show their love of ornithology by taking a student out for a bird walk at 5:30 in the morning, on a school day no less? For Thomas L. Friedman, it was his high school journalism teacher Hattie M. Steinberg. In "My Favorite Teacher," he relates how her insistence upon the importance of "fundamentals" made a lifelong impression on him, so much so that he never had to take another journalism course (12). For Carl Rowan, it was his high school English, history, and civics teacher Miss Bessie Taylor Gwynn, whose influence he captures in "Unforgettable Miss Bessie." Miss Bessie taught Rowan to hold himself to high standards, to refuse "to lower [his] standards to those of the crowd" (87). And for Joanne Lipman, it was Mr. Jerry Kupchynsky, her childhood music teacher. She remembers how tough and demanding he was on his students, how he made his students "better than we had any right to be." Ironically, Lipman muses, "I doubt any of us realized how much we loved him for it." Interestingly, isn't it mutual respect and love that is at the heart of any memorable student-teacher bond?

Sources

Friedman, Thomas L. "My Favorite Teacher." *Subject & Strategy.* Ed. Paul Eschholz and Alfred Rosa. 13th ed. Boston: Bedford, 2014. 12-14. Print.

Lipman, Joanne. "And the Orchestra Played On." *New York Times*. New York Times, 28 Feb. 2010. Web. 14 Feb. 2013.

Rowan, Carl T. "Unforgettable Miss Bessie." *Reader's Digest* Mar. 1985: 87-91. Print.

The second example is taken from student Bonnie Sherman's essay "Should Shame Be Used as Punishment?" Here she uses argument synthesis deftly to combine Hawthorne's use of shame in *The Scarlet Letter* with two opposing essays about shame as punishment, both of which appeared together in the *Boston Globe*. Notice how Sherman uses her own reading of *The Scarlet Letter* as evidence to ultimately side with Professor Kahan's position.

Shame has long been used as an alternative punishment to more traditional sentences of corporeal punishment, jail time, or community service. American colonists used the stocks to publically humiliate citizens for their transgressions. In *The Scarlet Letter*, author Nathaniel Hawthorne recounts the story of how the community of Boston punished Hester Prynne for her adulterous affair by having her wear a scarlet letter "A" on her breast as a badge of shame. Such punishments were controversial then and continue to spark heated debate in today's world of criminal justice. Like June Tangney, psychology professor at George Mason University, many believe that shaming punishments—those designed to humiliate offenders—are unusually cruel and should be abandoned. In her article "Condemn the Crime, Not the Person," she argues that "shame serves to escalate the very destructive patterns of behavior we aim to curb" (34). Interestingly, Hester Prynne's post-punishment life of community service and charitable work does not seem to bear out Tangney's claim. In contrast, Yale Law School professor Dan M. Kahan believes that Tangney's "anxieties about shame . . . seem overstated," and he persuasively supports this position in his essay "Shame Is Worth a Try" by citing a study showing that the threat of public humiliation generates more compliance than does the threat of jail time (34).

Sources

Hawthorne, Nathaniel. *The Scarlet Letter*. New York: Bantam Books, 1981. Print.

Kahan, Dan M. "Shame Is Worth a Try." *Boston Globe* 5 Aug. 2001: A34. Print.

Tangney, June. "Condemn the Crime, Not the Person." *Boston Globe* 5 Aug. 2001: A34. Print.

In your essay, instead of simply presenting your sources with a quotation here and a summary there, look for opportunities to use synthesis, to go beyond an individual source by relating several of your sources to one another and to your own thesis. Use the following checklist to help you with synthesis in your writing.

Checklist for Writing a Synthesis

1. Start by writing a brief summary of each source that you will refer to in your synthesis.

2. Explain in your own words how your sources are related to one another and to your own ideas. For example, what assumptions do your sources share? Do your sources present opposing views? Do your sources illustrate a range or diversity of opinions? Do your sources support or challenge your ideas?

3. Have a clear idea or topic sentence for your paragraph before starting to write.

4. Combine information from two or more sources with your own ideas to support or illustrate your main idea.

5. Use signal phrases and parenthetical citations to show your readers the source of your borrowed materials.

6. Have fresh interpretations or conclusions as a goal each time you synthesize sources.

AVOIDING PLAGIARISM

The importance of honesty and accuracy in doing library research can't be stressed enough. Any material borrowed word for word must be placed within quotation marks and properly cited; any idea, explanation, or argument you have paraphrased or summarized must be documented, and it must be clear where the paraphrased material begins and ends. In short, to use someone else's ideas, whether in their original form or in an altered form, without proper acknowledgment is to be guilty of plagiarism.

You must acknowledge and document the source of your information whenever you do any of the following:

- Quote a source word for word
- Refer to information and ideas from another source that you present in your own words, as either a paraphrase or a summary
- Cite statistics, tables, charts, graphs, or other visuals

You do not need to document the following types of information:

- Your own observations, experiences, ideas, and opinions
- Factual information available in a number of sources (information known as "common knowledge")
- Proverbs, sayings, or familiar quotations

For a discussion of MLA-style in-text documentation, see pages 722–24.

The Council of Writing Program Administrators offers the following helpful definition of *plagiarism* in academic settings for administrators, faculty, and students: "In an instructional setting, plagiarism occurs when a writer deliberately uses someone else's language, ideas, or other (not common knowledge) material without acknowledging its source." Note, however, that accusations of plagiarism can be substantiated even if plagiarism is accidental. A little attention and effort at the note-taking stage can go a long way toward eliminating the possibility of such inadvertent plagiarism. While taking notes, check all direct quotations against the wording of the original, and double-check your paraphrases to be sure that you have not used the writer's wording or sentence structure. It is easy to forget to put quotation marks around material taken verbatim or to use the same sentence structure and most of the same words — substituting a synonym here and there — and record it as a paraphrase. In working closely with the ideas and words of others, intellectual honesty demands that you distinguish between what you borrow — and therefore acknowledge in a citation — and what is your own.

While writing your paper, be careful whenever you incorporate one of your notes into your paper: Make sure that you put quotation marks around material taken verbatim, and double-check your text against your notes — or, better yet, against the original if you have it on hand — to make sure that your quotations are accurate and that all paraphrases and summaries are really in your own words.

▶ Using Quotation Marks for Language Borrowed Directly

Whenever you use another person's exact words or sentences, you must enclose the borrowed language in quotation marks. Without quotation marks you give your reader the impression that the wording is your own. Even if you cite the source, you are guilty of plagiarism if you fail to use quotation marks. The following example demonstrates both plagiarism and a correct citation for a direct quotation.

Original Source

On my father's side, I figured, high cheekbones and almond eyes probably showed evidence of native-Andean blood. The aquiline profiles and curly hair on my mother's side, on the other hand, are common on Mediterranean shores. My best guess: I was mostly European, a bit of native South American, and perhaps a dash of Middle Eastern.

—CAROLINA A. MIRANDA,
"Diving into the Gene Pool,"
Time magazine, 20 Aug. 2006, page 64

Plagiarism

On my father's side, I figured, high cheekbones and almond eyes probably showed evidence of native-Andean blood, confesses Carolina A. Miranda. The aquiline profiles and curly hair on my mother's side, on the other hand, are common on Mediterranean shores. My best guess: I was mostly European, a bit of native South American, and perhaps a dash of Middle Eastern (64).

Correct Citation of Borrowed Words in Quotation Marks

"On my father's side, I figured, high cheekbones and almond eyes probably showed evidence of native-Andean blood," confesses Carolina A. Miranda. "The aquiline profiles and curly hair on my mother's side, on the other hand, are common on Mediterranean shores. My best guess: I was mostly European, a bit of native South American, and perhaps a dash of Middle Eastern" (64).

▶ Using Your Own Words and Word Order When Summarizing and Paraphrasing

When summarizing or paraphrasing a source, you need to use your own language. Pay particular attention to word choice and word order, especially if you are paraphrasing. Remember, it is not enough simply to use a synonym here or there and think you have paraphrased the source; you *must* restate the idea from the original in your own words, using your own style and sentence structure. In the following example, notice how plagiarism can occur when care is not taken in the wording or sentence structure of a paraphrase. Notice that in the acceptable paraphrase, the student writer uses her own language and sentence structure.

Original Source

Stereotypes are a kind of gossip about the world, a gossip that makes us prejudge people before we ever lay eyes on them. Hence it is not surprising that stereotypes have something to do with the dark world of prejudice. Explore most prejudices (note that the word means prejudgment) and you will find a cruel stereotype at the core of each one.

—ROBERT L. HEILBRONER,
"Don't Let Stereotypes Warp Your Judgments,"
Think magazine, June 1961, page 43

Unacceptably Close Wording

According to Heilbroner, we prejudge other people even before we have seen them when we think in stereotypes. That stereotypes are related to the ugly world of prejudice should not surprise anyone. If you explore the heart of most prejudices, beliefs that literally prejudge, you will discover a mean stereotype lurking (43).

Unacceptably Close Sentence Structure

Heilbroner believes that stereotypes are images of people, images that enable people to prejudge other people before they have seen them. Therefore, no one should find it surprising that stereotypes are somehow related to the ugly world of prejudice. Examine most prejudices (the word literally means prejudgment) and you will uncover a vicious stereotype at the center of each (43).

Acceptable Paraphrase

Heilbroner believes that there is a link between stereotypes and the hurtful practice of prejudice. Stereotypes make for easy conversation, a kind of shorthand that enables us to find fault with people before ever meeting them. If you were to dissect most human prejudices, you would likely discover an ugly stereotype lurking somewhere inside it (43).

Preventing Plagiarism

Questions to Ask about Direct Quotations

- Do quotation marks clearly indicate the language that I borrowed verbatim?
- Is the language of the quotation accurate, with no missing or misquoted words or phrases?
- Do brackets or ellipsis marks clearly indicate any changes or omissions I have introduced?
- Does a signal phrase naming the author introduce each quotation? Does the verb in the signal phrase help establish a context for each quotation?
- Does a parenthetical page citation follow each quotation?

Questions to Ask about Summaries and Paraphrases

- Is each summary and paraphrase written in my own words and style?
- Does each summary and paraphrase accurately represent the opinion, position, or reasoning of the original writer?
- Does each summary and paraphrase start with a signal phrase so that readers know where my borrowed material begins?
- Does each summary and paraphrase conclude with a parenthetical page citation?

> **Questions to Ask about Facts and Statistics**
>
> • Do I use a signal phrase or some other marker to introduce each fact or statistic that is not common knowledge so that readers know where the borrowed material begins?
>
> • Is each fact or statistic that is not common knowledge clearly documented with a parenthetical page citation?

Finally, as you proofread your final draft, check all your citations one last time. If at any time while you are taking notes or writing your paper you have a question about plagiarism, consult your instructor for clarification and guidance before proceeding.

SAMPLE STUDENT ESSAY USING LIBRARY AND INTERNET SOURCES

Courtney Sypher wrote the following essay following a unit on the uses and abuses of social media in one of her psychology courses. At about the same time, the news was full of sordid stories about how students were using social media and the Internet to bully their peers. Sypher decided to explore the world of cyberbullying, especially as it manifested itself on college campuses.

Sypher began by brainstorming about her topic, listing recent news stories that had received a great deal of attention. She then went to her college library and searched the Internet, where she located additional information about these stories and about current research on cyberbullying from a number of credible sources. After carefully reading her sources and taking notes, she decided to organize her essay around two central examples of cyberbullying on college campuses.

Sypher's essay is annotated so that you can readily see how she has effectively integrated sources into her paper and has used them to establish, explore, and support her key points. Sypher uses MLA-style documentation.

From Computer Cruelty to Campus Crime:
Cyberbullying at College
Courtney Sypher

Does anyone really believe that "sticks and stones may
break your bones, but names will never hurt you?" Words hurt,
especially now that they come in through every laptop, tablet,
and phone we own. And today, this *cyberbullying* doesn't just
stop with words, but can also include compromising images or
videos that are stolen or coerced. Cyberbullying has only been
possible in the past decade, and yet it's everywhere, affecting
students from grade school through college. Distressingly, not
everyone sees it as a true cultural problem. Some people believe that bullying is a natural part of growing up, and the
Facebook page "Cyberbullying is a Joke" has more than five
hundred "likes." Rightly, many more people disagree, as evidenced by a more popular page titled "Stop Cyberbullying,"
which has tens of thousands of fans. Such numbers suggest
that, on the whole, awareness and prevention movements are
popular, but the newness of cyberbullying means that we understand very little about it. This is especially troubling when
we look at college campuses, where students' independence
and lack of parental supervision (and protection) have led to
deadly consequences.

Ongoing research in the fields of psychology, sociology, and
education is working not only to define what cyberbullying is,
but also to understand its effects. In some ways cyberbullying is
simply a new type of bully behavior. In their book *Cyber Bullying:
Bullying in the Digital Age*, psychologists Robin M. Kowalski, Susan
P. Limber, and Patricia W. Agatston call the phenomenon a "recent variant of the traditional bullying process, in which individuals use electronic communication as a medium to harass,
degrade, embarrass, and deliberately hurt others" (23). Other
research studies identify several distinguishing features that
make cyberbullying seem more dangerous than what had been
seen with traditional bullying. In their 2006 study entitled
"Bullies Move Beyond the Schoolyard," criminal justice professors Justin W. Patchin and Sameer Hinduja suggest that cyberbullying's "perceived anonymity" and ability to "exten[d] into
the home environment via personal computers or cell phones"
can make it seem "more volatile" and more invasive than typical afterschool banter (qtd. in Dempsey et al. 963). And in a 2012

1

2

Introductory
paragraph
establishes
context for
discussion,
grabs readers'
attention, and
involves them
in the issue of
cyberbullying at
college

In-text citation
begins with
authors' names
given in signal
phrase; the page
number is given
in parentheses

Parenthetical
citation shows
that the borrowed
material is an
indirect source,
first quoted on
page 963 of the
article written by
Dempsey and her
colleagues

study, Allison G. Dempsey and her colleagues noted that because of the far-reaching, always-on nature of our devices, "cyber aggressors have the opportunity to victimize a greater number of people and in front of a larger audience than in traditional peer victimization" (963). Ultimately, cyberbullying means *non-stop* harassment by *more bullies* against *more victims*.

> *Sypher synthesizes sources to arrive at a definition of cyberbullying*

At least one college campus recently documented a sort of hybrid case: a traditional bullying tactic possibly emboldened by the perceived anonymity of cyberbullying. ABC News reported that on October 8, 2012, at Miami University of Ohio (MU), a typed flier titled "Top Ten Ways to Get Away with Rape" was found hanging in the men's bathroom of a coed dormitory. The flier included tips "encouraging men to have sex with unconscious women because it 'doesn't count,' drugging women with 'roofies,' and slitting women's throats if they recognized their attackers" (Curry). While some may dismiss the flier as a vague example of traditional harassment, the anonymity of its typed print and its display in a busy public space are similar to—and perhaps even inspired by—a public Facebook post. In fact, social media enabled news of the flier to spread rapidly, with a mix of consequences. As more students found out about it, more students (especially women) felt threatened and victimized. Yet, that attention also helped the MU campus to alert the national press, which put pressure on the university to conduct a stronger investigation. Technology's ability to instantaneously spread information both exacerbated and helped to resolve the situation.

> *Sypher introduces a "hybrid" case of cyberbullying with a signal phrase and marks the end with a parenthetical citation of author's name*

> *Sypher then analyzes and interprets the meaning of the MU Ohio example*

3

More typically, when we talk about cyberbullying, we refer to behavior that's exclusively in the digital realm. For some, cyberbullying may be personal, harassing name calling via text messages, while for others that name calling may occur in a social media forum that encourages others to participate, resulting in a wall full of slams. For others still, cyberbullying may be even more invasive, involving private, often revealing, videos or photos that bullies repost to public sites. This broad range of possible activities could be a driving force in the large number of college students who report being victims of cyberbullying tactics. Research by to Indiana State University counseling and school psychology professors Bridget Roberts-Pittman and Christine MacDonald reported that "almost 22 percent of college students reported being cyberbullied," an appalling statistic that

> *Sypher transitions to discussion of cyberbullying in the digital realm; she uses a quote to support her point about the large number of incidents on college campuses*

4

suggests as many as 1 in 5 college students has been a victim (Sicking).

5

Rutgers University student Tyler Clementi's cyber victimization and resultant suicide in 2010 is perhaps the most notorious case of cyberbullying on a college campus. As reported by PCMag.com, on September 19, 2010, Clementi's roommate and bully, Dharun Ravi, used his computer to film Clementi having an "intimate encounter with another man." Ravi streamed the live video to another computer and then tweeted about it, ultimately "outing the 18-year-old Clementi as gay" (Poeter). Clementi, who only recently came out to his parents, committed suicide three days later in the wake of Ravi's very public invasion of his privacy. Mainstream media coverage of the case led to bullying-awareness and prevention campaigns that focused on exposing and ending the harassment faced by LGTBQ teens and young adults, but it also raised a number of questions about the responsibilities of the community at large.

Sypher introduces an example at Rutgers University and cites an outside source to provide essential details of the case

Sypher comments on Ravi's bullying of Clementi

6

Ravi's behavior raises important questions about how to appropriately punish adult perpetrators of cyberbullying. ABC News reported that Ravi and another student were charged with "invasion of privacy" and fined. Ravi was also "convicted of a hate crime for using a webcam to spy on Clementi" and served twenty days of a thirty-day jail sentence. For many people—including the prosecution who sought a more substantial prison term—this punishment seemed insufficient (Koenigs et al.). Even the MU Ohio rape flier creators could face serious charges (Curry). As many researchers, including the U.S. Department of Education, are noting, college bullying occurs among adults, which makes "the legal framework very, very different." In college, the consequences for bullying are often much more stringent, which may be a reason behaviors most would consider "bullying" elsewhere are swept instead into the broader, more lenient category of campus "hazing" (U.S. Dept. of Ed. Higher Ed. Center). A link between bullying and hazing and between hazing and sorority/fraternity life—or simply among freshman students—is unsurprising. According to one developmental psychologist, making friends is often a primary student goal, and bullies often have, or are at least perceived to have, more friends and power (Marshall).

Signal phrase introduces a passage in which Sypher both paraphrases and quotes from her U.S. Department of Education source

Sypher begins her conclusion by referring to the MU Ohio flier and bullying at Rutgers

The rocky transition from the support systems of high school to the often radical aloneness of college may explain the appeal of bullying and of the more anonymous practice of cyberbullying in particular. For largely friendless first-year students, new media may help maintain old support systems, but it may also become a space for asserting themselves to new "friends." Classmates often become cyber friends first, using social media to bond over common interests and antagonisms. It is not difficult, then, to imagine that the two young men believed responsible for the MU Ohio rape flier may have built a friendship over the flier's creation, or that Ravi bonded with the others involved in his bullying of Clementi.

7

Sypher calls for action: increase awareness by holding more public educational events and discussions on college campuses

Perhaps our loosely defined attention to college hazing allows us to skip over a serious conversation about the prevalence and harm of bullying, a conversation that maybe we're scared to have. Incidents like those at MU and Rutgers, however, reinforce the importance of having these conversations on campus, of increasing cyberbullying awareness, and of focusing discussion not on the ills of hazing, but on the crime of being an adult aggressor, both in person and online.

8

Works Cited

MLA style used for list of works cited: entries are presented in alphabetical order by authors' last names; first line of each entry begins at the left margin and subsequent lines are indented

Curry, Colleen. "'Top Ten Ways to Get Away With Rape' Flier Posted at Miami University in Ohio." *ABC News*. ABC News Network, 15 Oct. 2012. Web. 30 Oct. 2012.

Dempsey, Allison G., Michael L. Sulkowski, Rebecca Nichols, and Eric A. Storch. "Differences Between Peer Victimization in Cyber and Physical Settings and Associated Psychosocial Adjustment in Early Adolescence." *Psychology in the Schools* 46.10 (2009): 962-72. Web. 30 Oct. 2012.

Koenigs, Michael, Candace Smith, and Christina Ng. "Rutgers Trial: Dharun Ravi Sentenced to 30 Days in Jail." *ABC News*. ABC News Network, 21 May 2012. Web. 30 Oct. 2012.

Kowalski, Robin M., Susan P. Limber, and Patricia W. Agatston. *Cyber Bullying: Bullying in the Digital Age*. Oxford, Eng.: Blackwell, 2007.

The correct MLA forms for other kinds of publications are given on pages 724-33

Marshall, Jessica. "Why Do People Bully?" *Discovery News*. Discovery Communications, 1 Apr. 2010. Web. 30 Oct. 2012.

Poeter, Damon. "Mystery Witness Testifies in Rutgers Cyberbullying Trial." *PC Magazine*. Ziff Davis, 2 Mar. 2012. Web. 30 Oct. 2012.

Sicking, Jennifer. "ISU Study: Nearly 40 Percent of College Students Report Being Bullied." *Indiana Statesman*. Indiana Statesman, 24 Oct. 2011. Web. 30 Oct. 2012.

U.S. Department of Education's Higher Education Center. "Bullying and Cyberbullying at Colleges and Universities." GPO, Jan. 2012. Web. 30 Oct. 2012.

Analyzing Courtney Sypher's Source-Based Essay

1. What is Sypher's thesis? Does she support it adequately? Are there any places where you think she needs additional evidence to support her claims?

2. What is Sypher's purpose in writing this essay? Is she more interested in persuading us to adopt a certain position or in informing us about cyberbullying?

3. What kinds of sources does Sypher use? Are they credible? Are they appropriately current? Do they represent a wide enough range of sources?

4. Do you agree with Sypher's conclusion? Why, or why not?

5. Generally speaking, how could Sypher make her essay even stronger? If you had the opportunity to talk with her, what questions would you ask her? What recommendations for revision would you make?

The Case of the Disappearing Rabbit

LILY HUANG

Born in Beijing, China, in 1984, Lily Huang immigrated with her parents to the United States, landing first in Columbia, Missouri, and later in South Pasadena, California, the place she now calls home. She graduated from Harvard University in 2006 and traveled in France and Switzerland on a fellowship before accepting a publishing internship at Farrar, Straus and Giroux, where she wrote jacket copy for children's books. Later she took a three-month internship at *Newsweek* in Cambridge, Massachusetts. This internship evolved into a staff writing position, which she held for nearly a year and a half. During her time at *Newsweek*, Huang wrote a series of articles focusing on environmental issues. When not writing, she worked at CYCLE Kids, a nonprofit organization that teaches children how to have active lifestyles, how to ride bikes, and how not to become overweight. Currently Huang is completing a doctorate in the history of science at the University of Chicago where she focuses on the study of Darwin, natural history, and ideas about consciousness.

"The Case of the Disappearing Rabbit" first appeared in the August 3, 2009, issue of *Newsweek*. For this story Huang spent ten days in and around the Crown of the Continent in Montana, interviewing local climate experts and U.S. Forest Service biologists and experiencing the wilderness area up close. She remembers riding "on the back of John Squire's snowmobile, flying across a frozen Seeley Lake toward his trapline high above the valley. Here I saw three golden eagles rise up from the carcass of an elk, and in the surrounding snow there were patches of pink and the tracks of a mountain lion. I had a sense, in that distant place, of being in the real world for the first time, and of how much of this world would always be unobserved, kept secret — would reveal itself only as tracks in the snow. I tried to capture this about the Crown in the story."

As you read this essay, notice how Huang uses her interviews to tell the story of the snowshoe rabbit and the lynx and to support and explain her central ideas about environmental change.

Preparing to Read

Where do you stand on the issue of climate change? What kinds of evidence about climate change have impressed you the most? The least? Explain why.

n the roadless, snow-muffled back-country of northwestern Montana   1
lies your best chance of ever seeing a wild Canada lynx. An improbable
creature, it is small on the spectrum of wildcats — about three times the
size of a house cat — and stands on disproportionately long legs, on

which it is uncommonly fast. Its great head seems larger and wiser for its tuft of beard and the birdish plumes at the tips of its ears, but its feet spoil its air of gravitas. They are enormous. They act like snowshoes, and they are part of what makes the lynx supremely adapted to this part of the Rocky Mountains. Another inhabitant, the snowshoe hare, is adapted to life here, too. A lynx, if it could, would eat nothing but snowshoe hares its whole life, and pretty much does.

An animal so specialized that it only eats one kind of food has a tenuous place in the world. But this stretch of Montana — what the nineteenth-century naturalist George Grinnell named the Crown of the Continent — is unlike most places, or even most wildernesses. In an age of daily extinctions, the Crown has not lost any of the vertebrate species present when the first Europeans ventured this far west — creatures seen, heard, and feared by Lewis and Clark. If the Crown is a window into the past, it is also a particularly privileged window: No other intact ecosystem on the continent affords a view this grand. Only here do you find the full suite of North America's big predators — wolves, cougars, coyotes, and black and grizzly bears. Then there are the stranger beings: cutthroat trout, bull trout, and Arctic grayling in the glacial waters; river otter, bobcats, fishers, martens, lynxes, and wolverines. Between Glacier National Park and the Bob Marshall Wilderness Complex, the Crown is 10 million acres of the West as it once was and as it would have been. 2

Yet it is not a time capsule. Being free from development by people hasn't made it a static place: The Crown rearranges itself, in a constant flux between the living and the dying, as the planet rolls on. Historically, this has happened on a time scale largely beyond our power of perception — "glacial pace" is not far from the mark. The problem is that glacial pace is not what it used to be. It is speeding up, as the glaciers melt into the Rockies, retreating up to 90 feet each year. For the first time in geological history, you can watch glacial ice move, and by the current projection, twenty years from now there will be nothing to see. Altogether, climate change is a phenomenon more keenly felt in a place like the Crown — a mountainous landscape with reservoirs of ice and snow — than anywhere else. This makes it the best possible natural laboratory, a window into the large-scale ecological change that global warming will bring. The effects of warming are magnified two to three times in the Crown, says Dan Fagre, climate ecologist in Glacier National Park, though the 3

> For the first time in geological history, you can watch glacial ice move, and by the current projection, 20 years from now there will be nothing to see.

Crown's persistent biodiversity suggests that the ecosystem is weathering the difference so far. But Fagre thinks this persistence has a limit: At some point, the pressure of the changes will be too great, and beyond this unmarked boundary the present system will come apart. An ecosystem doesn't die, but as species depart or spread, it will change the way it operates, take a different form. Potentially, the Crown has innumerable thresholds—the last of the glaciers, the first animal extinction—beyond which it could rapidly become a fundamentally altered place: different trees, different cycles, different lives. Whatever will trip that invisible wire, a look now at the Crown is a look at final moments—the last of a storied American West, of the natural wealth that once enabled this extravagant diversity of life. What awaits, in a climate-changed world, is a new era of uniformity.

What sets the Crown apart from every other ecosystem on earth is its   4
ecological schizophrenia. Straddling the Continental Divide, it is besieged by disparate climates from the fertile west, the open prairie to the east, and the cold north; even its rivers, issuing from Triple Divide Peak, flow in all four compass directions into the Pacific, the Atlantic, and the Arctic oceans. In all this, the mountains are the agents of volatility: They toss wind and snow to different sides of the Divide and wildly apportion sunlight to different slopes; historically, their dramatic nightly cooling has produced some of the coldest temperatures ever recorded below the Arctic. The convergence of these forces is what packs into the Crown the widest range of life on the continent, a diversity as distinctive as the tight profusion of Madagascar or the sweeping wealth of the Serengeti. "We have this incredible mix of microclimates," says University of Montana climate expert Steve Running, who shared the Nobel Peace Prize in 2007 with the Intergovernmental Panel on Climate Change, "which then allows an incredible mix of microhabitats for animals."

To a certain extent, this patchwork of habitats is its own refuge against   5
ecological disturbance, which is why, though records of a warming trend go back to the nineteenth century, no population has yet abandoned the ecosystem. "The animals can make use of those gradients," Running explains. "They can go from the Pacific side over toward the continental side, they can walk from the southern end of the Rockies farther north, and then they walk up in elevation. When their habitat goes off the top of the mountain, then it's all over." Global warming has a leveling effect on mountains: Under an atmosphere thick with carbon, mountains cool less, allowing lower-elevation plants and animals to push into the upper reaches. We get more of one kind of habitable world, but we lose the planet's extremes, along with their wholly unique strata of life—lynxes, for instance, and snow-colored hares.

On paper, the lynx population in the Crown goes back to the 1810s, in 6
the records of the old Hudson Bay Company fur trade. In 2000, when the
species was pronounced "threatened" under the Endangered Species Act,
trapping became illegal. This February the amount of lynx habitat singled
out for protection dramatically increased, and of the nearly 43,000 square
miles of new critical habitat spread across a handful of northern states, just
under half is in one ecosystem: the Crown. Rarity, for a species, is a biological Catch-22: The animals are so well adapted to their particular ecological
niche that they are unable to spread indiscriminately in larger numbers,
but specialization is what makes their lives possible at all—by allowing
them to survive in places where most others cannot. Lynxes, says Forest
Service biologist John Squires, are "long, thin, and light"; with those over-
sized paws, they have "everything for flying through snow, trying to catch
snowshoe hares." But while these animals are untouchable on their territory, they are the most vulnerable in the larger scheme of ecosystem change:
As the Crown teeters toward a new balance of species and habitats, their
niches will be among the first to wink out.

For the last ten years, Squires has tracked lynxes in the Crown using 7
radio telemetry and, more recently, data-streaming GPS collars. Between
one study site in the Seeley-Swan Valley, near the southern limits of the
Crown, and a second in the Purcell Mountains, near Glacier National
Park, he typically has about 60 cats "on air" every year. He does not know
in what proportion the collared cats stand to the whole population, but
from their movements he has come to understand their narrow world.
"Clearly, there are places where this animal goes and places where it
doesn't," he says, with GPS points plotted in clusters on a map. Unfailingly,
lynx territories are boreal forests, congregations of subalpine fir, larch, and
Engelmann spruce trees whose wide-reaching boughs come so low to the
ground, they touch the snow. Snowshoe hares, a default prey species for
nearly all predators in the Crown, cling to this protected setting, and where
the hares are, so are the lynxes.

Trapping a lynx is like trapping a ghost. Even its thick coat is the color 8
of ashes. In the winter, its distinctive tracks show up in the snow. When
one is caught, the invisibility cloak falls away, and it's as though the cat has
been momentarily plucked from the whole mysterious whirl, a piece of the
shifting wilderness held in an uncommon state of arrest. The trap Squires
uses to catch and collar lynxes is his own design: a wire-mesh cage the size
of a doghouse with a suspended door tautly held to an angled floor piece.
The cat walks over the floor piece to reach the mounted bait and triggers
the door. This year, Squires has caught fewer new cats and almost no
females. In March, two weeks before the bears would emerge from their
dens—at which point all bait becomes bear bait—he has collared only

one female in Seeley and says, "I think something's going on." His mind goes briefly to the new surge of mountain lions in the Crown, a cat that kills lynxes on sight to eliminate competition, but reasons that lions stay out of snow-thick lynx territory in winter. But the one thing Squires can count on to affect the population of lynx is the population of hares, which has always, in this lowest fringe of the North American boreal forest, been on the brink. In fact, the fragile footing of this frontier population of hares is precisely what makes them valuable, because the moment the ecosystem falls out of balance, the hares will tell. If hare and lynx habitat ranges farther north as temperatures warm across the map, Squires's southern outpost is the best "early-warning system"—the animals will stop showing up.

Unseasonable warmth is a problem for hares for a not-immediately- 9 obvious reason: It isn't the heat itself but what it does to the single most important constant in the Crown—the snow. As the largest perennial food prize in the ecosystem, snowshoe hares have just one good trick—turning white in winter, brown the rest of the year—cued by the changing length of days. Now winter snow melts nearly a month earlier in the Crown than it did just a century ago, causing, says Dan Fagre, a "decoupling" between two cycles that used to be synchronized: light and temperature. This means that a snow-white hare will end up sitting on brown earth—and have no idea. Researcher Scott Mills at the University of Montana, with his own set of radio-collar signals, has found more and more compromised hares in recent years and believes that they are dying for it, in increasingly large numbers, every spring and fall. Given enough time, hares may genetically sort themselves out, along with all the other species that have evolved, over millennia, a certain exquisite timing for their migrations, for giving birth, or for coming out of the ground. But in a fast-decoupling world, expecting snowshoe hares to survive by adaptation is like trying to engineer a genetic jackpot. Statistically, it could happen, but every spring and fall, you lose a lot of chances.

Biodiversity happens when an ecosystem brings competing species to 10 a stalemate: All have their niche, all get by, none can completely suppress another. Global warming doesn't so much tip this finely wrought balance in the Crown one way or another as knock it all down: No niche wins out; the real winners are the species that don't have a niche. These are the ones who don't have to change their genes. Grizzly bears may be the world's least choosy eaters, omnivores par excellence that can live on anything and learn what they need to survive. Wolves, mountain lions, and coyotes are also versatile generalists. Populations of these animals have become more and more robust in the Crown, and so long as they avoid getting shot by people, they will live just as well in an ecosystem restructured by climate change. So across the current range of species in the Crown "there's going to be a shakeout," says Fagre, "because some will be able to adapt better than others. The ability to change your behavior will be really important." Species that are "hard-wired" to live a certain way—hares who change color for winter, or bull trout that only spawn in clean, icy waters—will be hard pressed to do things differently in their lifetime. And the world that leaves them behind is not necessarily one we would recognize. For all life in the Crown is checked by the available water, and mountains unable to hold onto snow and glaciers trickling to nothing can no longer provide a steady supply. That leaves the species that can make do with least, and an ecosystem determined not by the resources it has but by what it lacks. In place of a lively mosaic of habitats, Fagre has a vision of Glacier National Park as a single landscape of "wall-to-wall lodgepole pine," a tree that needs little water and is always the first to leap up after a forest fire, like a weed. In this impoverished place, the lynx—built for one niche, one prey—is an impossible biological flourish, a dream.

In a last effort to find cats, John Squires sent Dustin Ranglack, a member of his Seeley Lake crew, to scout out the slopes of Fawn Peak, which had been consumed by a forest fire in 2003. It was the only place he hadn't trapped, and now he thought he might as well try. Ranglack returned to report that there was no sign of life there—no tracks of deer, or mountain lions, or hares. "When there're no hares, there's nothing," said Squires. "There's no place else to go." He loaded his truck, and with two snow machines in tow, drove north.

Thinking Critically about the Text

Why is it important that scientists find answers to the case of the disappearing rabbit? What do you see as the big-picture implications of the drama being played out at the Crown of the Continent?

Questions on Subject

1. According to Huang, what makes the area called "the Crown of the Continent" unique? What sets it apart from other ecosystems?

2. According to Huang, the mountains are an important feature of the Crown. In what sense are the mountains "agents of volatility" (paragraph 4)?

3. What do you think Huang means when she says, "Rarity, for a species, is a biological Catch-22" (paragraph 6)? How does this apply to the lynx?

4. Why is unseasonable warmth a problem for snowshoe hares? How does the population of hares affect the population of lynx?

5. Who will be the winners and the losers in the Crown as a result of global warming?

Questions on Strategy

1. Huang opens her essay with a description of a Canada lynx. Which specific details best help create a mental picture of this animal for you? (Glossary: *Description*) Why is it important for Huang's readers to understand what a lynx is and how it looks?

2. Identify the signal phrases that Huang uses to introduce her sources. How do these signal phrases help you as a reader? Besides giving the name of each source, what other information does Huang provide?

3. In paragraph 4, Huang quotes University of Montana climate expert Steve Running. How does Huang use this quotation in the context of the paragraph? What would have been lost had she not used the quotation?

4. Where does Huang use cause and effect analysis to explain how global warming affects mountains? Briefly describe the causal chain of events that occurs when there is warming. (Glossary: *Cause and Effect Analysis*)

Questions on Diction and Vocabulary

1. In paragraph 3, Huang introduces the term "glacial pace." What did this term mean in past years? Is "glacial pace" still a useful measure of time? Why, or why not? How else could you express the same idea?

2. Huang uses a number of interesting strong verbs—*affords, apportion, toss, teeters,* and *wink out,* for example. Identify six other strong verbs. What do these verbs add to Huang's writing? (Glossary: *Verbs*)

3. Refer to your dictionary to determine the meanings of the following words as Huang uses them in this selection: *gravitas* (paragraph 1), *tenuous* (2), *suite* (2), *flux* (3), *convergence* (4), *decoupling* (9), *stalemate* (10), *mosaic* (10).

Classroom Activity for Writing with Sources

Using the examples of signal phrases and parenthetical citations on pages 667–68 as models, rewrite the following paragraphs in order to correctly and smoothly integrate the embedded quotations.

The quotation in the first example comes from Ruth Russell's "The Wounds That Can't Be Stitched Up," a firsthand account of how her family life was tragically shattered by a drunk driver. Russell's essay appeared on page 17 of the December 20, 1999, issue of *Newsweek*.

America has a problem with drinking and driving. In 2008 drunk drivers killed almost 14,000 people and injured 500,000 others. While many are quick to condemn drinking and driving, they are also quick to defend or offer excuses for such behavior, especially when the offender is a friend. "Many local people who know the driver are surprised when they hear about the accident, and they are quick to defend him. They tell me he was a war hero. His parents aren't well. He's an alcoholic. Or my favorite: 'He's a good guy when he doesn't drink.'" When are we going to get tough on drunk drivers?

The quotation in the second example comes from page 100 of William L. Rathje's article entitled "Rubbish!" in the Atlantic Monthly in December 1989. Rathje teaches at the University of Arizona, where he directs the Garbage Project.

> Most Americans think that we are producing more trash per person than ever, that plastic is a huge problem, and that paper biodegrades quickly in landfills. "The biggest challenge we will face is to recognize that the conventional wisdom about garbage is often wrong."

Compare your signal phrases with those of your classmates, and discuss how smoothly each integrates the quotation into the passage.

Writing Suggestions

1. **Writing with Sources.** Visit the Earth's Endangered Creatures Web site (earthsendangered.com) to learn about endangered species around the world. Locate the organization's list of North American endangered species, including vertebrate and invertebrate animals and flowering and nonflowering plants. Using these lists, adopt an endangered species from your region, and write a report about it. In your report be sure to include a description of your plant or "critter," an explanation of where it is found and what it does, and an argument for why it should be protected. For models of and advice on integrating sources in your essay, see this chapter and Chapter 15.

2. **Writing with Sources.** Consider the following cartoon by Joel Pett about climate change:

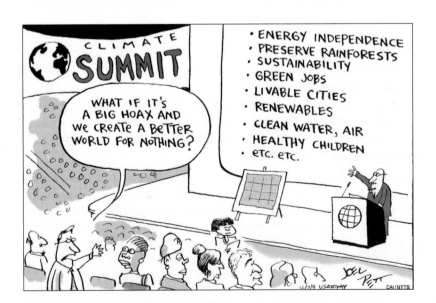

What do you think Pett is saying about the climate-change debate? Where do you stand on this issue? How did you react to the man's question in Pett's cartoon? How do you think Huang would react to this question?

Do some research online and write an essay proposing measures that could be taken on your college campus to make it more climate friendly. What energy-saving measures are already being taken? What can be done to control carbon dioxide emissions? What measures do you think would have the greatest impact? If possible, interview students and/or school officials for their reactions to your proposed solution, and integrate their perspectives into your essay. You may find it helpful to review your response to the Preparing to Read prompt for this selection before you start writing. For models of and advice on integrating sources in your essay, see this chapter and Chapter 15.

Nature in the Suburbs

JANE S. SHAW

Born in 1944, Jane S. Shaw graduated from Wellesley College in 1965 with a degree in English.

She started her professional career as a journalist at the *Jamaica Plain Citizen* in Boston, Massachusetts, later becoming an associate economics editor at *Business Week* in New York City. In 1984 she moved to Montana, where she spent twenty-two years with the Property and Environment Research Center (PERC) as a senior fellow, writing articles on improving the environment without government intervention or regulation. While at PERC, Shaw coauthored *Facts, Not Fear: Teaching Children about the Environment* (1999), a book designed to help students more fully understand pressing environmental issues, from acid rain to global warming. She followed this book by editing a series of books for high school readers called "Critical Thinking about Environmental Issues." Shaw also coedited *A Guide to Smart Growth: Shattering Myths and Providing Solutions* (2000) with Ronald D. Utt. Her articles have appeared in newspapers and journals including the *Wall Street Journal*, *USA Today*, *Liberty*, and the *Cato Journal*. In 2006 she joined the John W. Pope Center for Higher Education Policy, a Raleigh-based nonprofit organization dedicated to improving higher education in North Carolina and the nation. Currently, Shaw serves as the Center's president.

The following essay first appeared in *A Guide to Smart Growth*, and it was later adapted and published separately by the Heritage Foundation in 2004. Here Shaw uses a variety of sources to draw into question the traditional thinking about the negative effects that suburban development has on our wildlife populations. She is able to take the complex, often sophisticated work of environmental researchers and write about it in language that a general audience can understand. As you read, notice how she deftly uses her sources to argue that "there is no reason to be pessimistic about the ability of wildlife to survive and thrive in the suburbs." Shaw uses footnotes to document her sources.

Preparing to Read

What kinds of birds and animals do you remember seeing in your neighborhood while growing up? Did you ever have a memorable encounter with birds or animals? Did your hometown have any special initiatives or projects to help preserve and protect the natural beauty and wildlife in the community? Do you recall there being any restrictions on developers building subdivisions in your hometown? If so, what were they?

A decade ago, who would have thought that New Jersey would host a black bear hunt—the first in 33 years? Or that Virginia, whose population of bald eagles was once down to 32 breeding pairs, would have 329 known active bald eagle nests? Who would have expected *Metropolitan Home* magazine to be advising its readers about ornamental grasses to keep away white-tailed deer, now found in the millions around the country?

Such incidents illustrate a transformed America. This nation, often condemned for being crowded, paved over, and studded with nature-strangling shopping malls, is proving to be a haven for wild animals.

It is difficult to ignore this upsurge of wildlife, because stories about bears raiding trashcans and mountain lions sighted in subdivisions frequently turn up in the press or on television. Featured in these stories are animals as large as moose, as well as once-threatened birds such as eagles and falcons and smaller animals like wolverines and coyotes.

> This nation, often condemned for being crowded, paved over, and studded with nature-strangling shopping malls, is proving to be a haven for wild animals.

One interpretation of these events is that people are moving closer to wilderness and invading the territory of wild animals. But this is only a small part of the story. As this essay will show, wild animals increasingly find suburban life in the United States to be attractive.

The stories, while fascinating, are not all upbeat. Americans are grappling with new problems—the growing hazard of automobile collisions with deer, debates over the role of hunting, the disappearance of fragile wild plants gobbled up by hungry ruminants, and even occasional human deaths caused by these animals.

At the same time, the proliferation of wildlife should assure Americans that the claim that urban sprawl is wiping out wildlife is simply poppycock. Human settlement in the early twenty-first century may be sprawling and suburban—about half the people in this country live in suburbs—but it is more compatible with wildlife than most people think. There may be reasons to decry urban sprawl or the suburbanization of America, but the loss of wildlife is not one of them.

WHY SO MANY WILD ANIMALS?

Two phenomena are fueling this increase in wild animals. One is natural reforestation, especially in the eastern United States. This is largely a result of the steady decline in farming, including cotton farming, a decline that allows forests to retake territory they lost centuries ago. The other is suburbanization, the expansion of low-density development outside cities, which provides a variety of landscapes and vegetation that attract animals. Both trends undermine the claim that wild open spaces are being strangled and that habitat for wild animals is shrinking.

The trend toward regrowth of forest has been well-documented. The percent of forested land in New Hampshire increased from 50 percent in the 1880s to 86 percent 100 years later. Forested land in Connecticut, Massachusetts, and Rhode Island increased from 35 percent to 59 percent over that same period. "The same story has been repeated in other places in the East, the South, and the Lake States," writes forestry expert Roger Sedjo.[1]

8

Environmentalist Bill McKibben exulted in this "unintentional and mostly unnoticed renewal of the rural and mountainous East" in a 1995 article in the *Atlantic Monthly.* Calling the change "the great environmental story of the United States, and in some ways of the whole world," he added, "Here, where 'suburb' and 'megalopolis' were added to the world's vocabulary, an explosion of green is under way."[2] Along with the reforestation come the animals; McKibben cites a moose "ten miles from Boston," as well as an eastern United States full of black bears, deer, alligators, and perhaps even mountain lions.

9

This re-greening of the eastern United States explains why some large wild animals are thriving, but much of the wildlife Americans are seeing today is a direct result of the suburbs. Clearly, suburban habitat is not sterile.

10

HABITAT FOR WILDLIFE

When people move onto what once was rural land, they modify the landscape. Yes, they build more streets, more parking lots, and more buildings. Wetlands may be drained, hayfields may disappear, trees may be cut down, and pets may proliferate. At the same time, however, the new residents will create habitat for wildlife. They will create ponds, establish gardens, plant trees, and set up bird nesting-boxes. Ornamental nurseries and truck farms may replace cropland, and parks may replace hedgerows.

11

This new ecology is different, but it is often friendly to animals, especially those that University of Florida biologist Larry Harris calls "mesomammals," or mammals of medium size.[3] They do not need broad territory

12

---

[1]Roger A. Sedjo, "Forest Resources," in Kenneth D. Frederick and Roger A. Sedjo, eds., *America's Renewable Resources: Historical Trends and Current Challenges* (Washington, D.C.: Resources for the Future, 1991), p. 109.
[2]Bill McKibben, "An Explosion of Green," *Atlantic Monthly*, April 1995, p. 64.
[3]Larry D. Harris, in e-mail communication with the author, January 16, 2000.

for roaming to find food, as moose and grizzly bears do. They can find places in the suburbs to feed, nest, and thrive, especially where gardens flourish.

One example of the positive impact of growth is the rebound of the [13] endangered Key deer, a small white-tailed deer found only in Florida and named for the Florida Keys. According to *Audubon* magazine, the Key deer is experiencing a "remarkable recovery."[4] The news report continues: "Paradoxically, part of the reason for the deer's comeback may lie in the increasing development of the area." Paraphrasing the remarks of a university researcher, the reporter says that human development "tends to open up overgrown forested areas and provide vegetation at deer level—the same factors fueling deer population booms in suburbs all over the country."

Indeed, white-tailed deer of normal size are the most prominent species [14] proliferating in the suburbs. In the *New York Times*, reporter Andrew C. Revkin has commented that "suburbanization created a browser's paradise: a vast patchwork of well-watered, fertilizer-fattened plantings to feed on and vest-pocket forests to hide in, with hunters banished to more distant woods."[5]

The increase in the number of deer in the United States is so great that [15] many people, especially wildlife professionals, are trying to figure out what to do about them. In 1997, the Wildlife Society, a professional association of wildlife biologists, devoted a special 600-page issue of its *Bulletin* to "deer overabundance." The lead article noted, "We hear more each year about the high costs of crop and tree-seedling damage, deer-vehicle collisions, and nuisance deer in suburban locales."[6] Insurance companies are worried about the increase in damage from automobile collisions with deer and similar-sized animals. And there are fears that the increase in deer in populated areas means that the deer tick could be causing the increased number of reported cases of Lyme disease.

Yes, the proliferation of deer poses problems, as do geese, whose [16] flocks can foul ponds and lawns and are notorious nuisances on golf courses, and beaver, which can cut down groves of trees. Yet the proliferation of deer is also a wildlife success story. At least that is the view of Robert J. Warren, editor of the *Bulletin*, who calls the resurgence of deer "one of the premier examples of successful wildlife management."[7] Today's

---

[4]Nancy Klingener, "Doe, Re, Key Deer," *Audubon*, January–February 2000, p. 17.
[5]Andrew C. Revkin, "Out of Control: Deer Send Ecosystem into Chaos," *New York Times*, November 12, 2002.
[6]Donald M. Waller and William S. Alverson, "The White-Tailed Deer: A Keystone Herbivore," *Wildlife Society Bulletin*, Vol. 25, No. 2 (Summer 1997), p. 217.
[7]Robert J. Warren, "The Challenge of Deer Overabundance in the Twenty-first Century," *Wildlife Society Bulletin*, Vol. 25, No. 2 (Summer 1997), p. 213.

deer population in the United States may be as high as 25 million, says Richard Nelson, writing in *Sports Afield*.[8]

People have mixed feelings about deer. In the *Wildlife Society Bulletin*, Dale R. McCullough and his colleagues reported on a survey of households in El Cerrito and Kensington, two communities near Berkeley, California. Twenty-eight percent of those who responded reported severe damage to vegetation by the deer, and 25 percent reported moderate damage. Forty-two percent liked having the deer around, while 35 percent disliked them and 24 percent were indifferent. The authors summarized the findings by saying: "As expected, some residents loved deer, whereas others considered them 'hoofed rats.'"[9] [17]

James Dunn, a geologist who has studied wildlife in New York State, believes that suburban habitat fosters deer more than forests do. Dunn cites statistics on the harvest of buck deer reported by the New York State government. Since 1970 the deer population has multiplied 7.1 times in suburban areas (an increase of 610 percent), but only 3.4 times (an increase of 240 percent) in the state overall.[10] [18]

Dunn explains that the forests have been allowed to regrow without logging or burning, so they lack the "edge" that allows sunlight in and encourages vegetation suitable for deer. In his view, that explains why counties with big cities (and therefore with suburbs) have seen a greater increase in deer populations than have the isolated, forested rural counties. Supporting this point, Andrew Revkin quotes a wildlife biologist at the National Zoo in Washington, D.C. "Deer are an edge species," he says, "and the world is one big edge now."[11] [19]

Deer are not the only wild animals that turn up on lawns and doorsteps, however. James Dunn lists species in the Albany, New York, suburbs in addition to deer: birds such as robins, woodpeckers, chickadees, grouse, finches, hawks, crows, and nuthatches, as well as squirrels, chipmunks, opossums, raccoons, foxes, and rabbits.[12] Deer attract coyotes too. According to a 1999 article in *Audubon*, biologists estimate that the coyote population (observed in all states except Hawaii) is about double what it was in 1850.[13] [20]

---

[8]Richard Nelson, "Deer Nation," *Sports Afield*, September 1998, p. 40.
[9]Dale R. McCullough, Kathleen W. Jennings, Natalie B. Gates, Bruce G. Elliott, and Joseph E. DiDonato, "Overabundant Deer Populations in California," *Wildlife Society Bulletin*, Vol. 25, No. 2 (1997), p. 481.
[10]James R. Dunn, "Wildlife in the Suburbs," Political Economy Research Center, PERC Reports, September 1999, pp. 3–5. See also James R. Dunn and John E. Kinney, *Conservative Environmentalism: Reassessing the Means, Redefining the Ends* (Westport, Conn.: Quorum Books, 1996).
[11]Revkin, "Out of Control."
[12]Dunn, "Wildlife in the Suburbs," p. 3.
[13]Mike Finkel, "The Ultimate Survivor," *Audubon*, May–June 1999, p. 58.

Joel Garreau, author of *Edge City*, includes black bears, red-tailed   21
hawks, peregrine falcons, and beaver on his list of animals that find suburban niches. Garreau still considers these distant "edge city" towns a "far
less diverse ecology than what was there before." However, he writes, "if
you measure it by the standard of city, it is a far more diverse ecology than
anything humans have built in centuries, if not millennia."[14]

For one reason or another, some environmental activists tend to dis-   22
miss the resurgence of deer and other wildlife. In an article criticizing suburban sprawl, Carl Pope, executive director of the Sierra Club, says that
the suburbs are "very good for the most adaptable and common creatures — raccoons, deer, sparrows, starlings, and sea gulls" but "devastating
for wildlife that is more dependent upon privacy, seclusion, and protection
from such predators as dogs and cats."[15]

Yet the suburbs attract animals larger than meso-mammals, and the   23
suburban habitat may be richer than what they replace. In many regions,
suburban growth comes at the expense of agricultural land that was cultivated for decades, even centuries. Cropland doesn't necessarily provide
abundant habitat. Environmental essayist Donald Worster, for example,
has little favorable to say about land cultivated for crops or used for live-
stock grazing. In Worster's view, there was a time when agriculture was
diversified, with small patches of different crops and a variety of animals affecting the landscape. Not now. "[T]he trend over the past two
hundred years or so," he writes, "has been toward the establishment of
monocultures on every continent."[16] In contrast, suburbs are not
monocultures.

Even large animals can be found at the edges of metropolitan areas.   24
Early in 2004, a mountain lion attacked a woman riding a bicycle in the
Whiting Ranch Wilderness Park in the foothills above populous Orange
County, and the same animal may have killed a man who was found dead
nearby. According to the *Los Angeles Times*, if the man's death is confirmed as caused by the mountain lion, it would be the first death by a
mountain lion in Orange County. The *Times* added, however, that "[m]oun-
tain lions are no strangers in Orange County's canyons and wilderness
parks."[17] Indeed, in 1994, mountain lions killed two women in state parks

[14]Joel Garreau, *Edge City: Life on the New Frontier* (New York: Random House, 1991), p. 57.
[15]Carl Pope, "Americans Are Saying No to Sprawl," Political Economy Research Center, PERC Reports, February 1999, p. 6.
[16]Donald Worster, *The Wealth of Nature: Environmental History and the Ecological Imagination.* (New York: Oxford University Press, 1993), p. 59.
[17]Kimi Yoshino, David Haldane, and Daniel Yi, "Lion Attacks O.C. Biker; Man Found Dead Nearby," *Los Angeles Times*, January 9, 2004.

near San Diego and Sacramento. Deer may be attracting the cats, suggests Paul Beier, a professor at the University of California at Berkeley.[18]...

SHARING OUR TURF

The fact that wildlife finds a home in suburban settings does not mean that all wildlife will do so. The greening of the suburbs is no substitute for big stretches of land—both public and private—that allow large mammals such as grizzly bears, elk, antelope, and caribou to roam. The point of this essay is that the suburbs offer an environment that is appealing to many wild animal species.

If the United States continues to prosper, the twenty-first century is likely to be an environmental century. Affluent people will seek to maintain or, in some cases, restore an environment that is attractive to wildlife, and more parks will likely be nestled within suburban developments, along with gardens, arboreta, and environmentally compatible golf courses. As wildlife proliferates, Americans will learn to live harmoniously with more birds and meso-mammals. New organizations and entrepreneurs will help integrate nature into the human landscape. There is no reason to be pessimistic about the ability of wildlife to survive and thrive in the suburbs.

[18]McCullough et al., "Overabundant Deer Populations in California," p. 479.

Thinking Critically about the Text

How would you characterize Shaw's presentation: Is she pro-environment or pro-development? Is there a clear answer, or does she present a balanced picture of what's happening in America's suburbs? Point to passages in her essay that support your position.

Questions on Subject

1. What does Shaw see as the downside of living alongside growing populations of wildlife in suburbia? Did you think that it was important for her to include this information in her essay?

2. What two phenomena does Shaw give for causing the increasing numbers of wild animals in suburban America? Did you find each of these causal explanations plausible?

3. In what ways can the "proliferation of deer" in the United States be called a "wildlife success story" (paragraph 16)?

4. Shaw states that "cropland doesn't necessarily provide abundant habitat" (paragraph 23) for many animals. What about agricultural practices in the United States has changed over the last two hundred years to cause this?

5. In paragraph 4, Shaw promises that, contrary to the popular belief that humans are "invading the territory of wild animals," her essay will show that "wild animals increasingly find suburban life in the United States to be attractive." How convincing did you find her presentation? Which pieces of evidence did you find most persuasive? Explain.

Questions on Strategy

1. Shaw begins this essay with a series of three questions. What do you suppose was her purpose in starting this way? Did you find it effective? How else could she have introduced her essay? (Glossary: *Beginnings/Endings*)

2. What is Shaw's thesis, and where does she present it? (Glossary: *Thesis*)

3. Identify several of the signal phrases that Shaw uses to introduce borrowed source material. How do these signal phrases help you as a reader, particularly in the case of paraphrase and summary? Besides giving the name of the author or researcher for each source, what other information does Shaw provide?

4. In paragraphs 13–19, Shaw uses a number of sources to document deer as "one example of the positive impact of growth" (13). What does each source add to the conversation about deer? How does synthesis help Shaw show the complexity of the deer example? (Glossary: *Synthesis*)

5. Shaw's dominant strategy in this essay is cause and effect analysis. Does she focus more on causes, effects, or both causes and effects? (Glossary: *Cause and Effect Analysis*) How does she use examples to support her analysis? (Glossary: *Illustration*) Which examples did you find most helpful? Explain.

Questions on Diction and Vocabulary

1. Shaw is known for her ability to write about environmental issues in language that people without any training in these matters can understand. How well does she live up to that reputation in this essay? Did you find any of her explanations of scientific terms difficult to follow? How would you describe Shaw's diction in this essay? (Glossary: *Diction*)

2. In paragraph 17, Shaw quotes from the conclusion of a study that appeared in the *Wildlife Society Bulletin*: "As expected, some residents loved deer, whereas others considered them 'hoofed rats.'" What do you think the residents meant by the metaphor "hoofed rats"? (Glossary: *Figures of Speech*)

3. Refer to your dictionary to determine the meanings of the following words as Shaw uses them in this selection: *haven* (paragraph 2), *ruminants* (5), *proliferation* (6), *poppycock* (6), *wetlands* (11), *ecology* (12), *paradoxically* (13), *fosters* (18), *niches* (21), *monocultures* (23).

Classroom Activity for Writing with Sources

Using the examples on pages 665 and 673–74 as a model, write a *paraphrase* for each of the following paragraphs — that is, restate the original ideas in your own words, using your own sentence structure.

> The history of life on earth has been a history of interaction between living things and their surroundings. To a large extent, the physical form and the habits of the earth's vegetation and its animal life have been molded by the environment. Considering the whole span of earthly time, the opposite effect, in which life actually modifies its surroundings, has been relatively slight. Only within the moment of time represented by the present century has one species — man — acquired significant power to alter the nature of his world.   — RACHEL CARSON, "The Obligation to Endure," *Silent Spring*

> Extroverts are energized by people, and wilt or fade when alone. They often seem bored by themselves, in both senses of the expression. Leave an extrovert alone for two minutes and he will reach for his cell phone. In contrast, after an hour or two of being socially "on," we introverts need to turn off and recharge. My own formula is roughly two hours alone for every hour of socializing. This isn't antisocial. It isn't a sign of depression. It does not call for medication. For introverts, to be alone with our thoughts is as restorative as sleeping, as nourishing as eating. Our motto: "I'm okay, you're okay — in small doses."   — JONATHAN RAUCH, "Caring for Your Introvert"

> Most of the people I've talked with say that they find social lying acceptable and necessary. They think it's the civilized way for folks to behave. Without these little white lies, they say, our relationships would be short and brutish and nasty. It's arrogant, they say, to insist on being so incorruptible and so brave that you cause other people unnecessary embarrassment or pain by compulsively assailing with your honesty. I basically agree. What about you?   — JUDITH VIORST, "The Truth about Lying"

> No, the romance and beauty were all gone from the river. All the value any feature of it had for me now was the amount of usefulness it could furnish toward compassing the safe piloting of a steamboat. Since those days, I have pitied doctors from my heart. What does the lovely flush in a beauty's cheek mean to a doctor but a "break" that ripples above some deadly disease? Are not all her visible charms sown thick with what are to him the signs and symbols of hidden decay? Does he ever see her beauty at all, or doesn't he simply view her professionally and comment upon her unwholesome condition all to himself? And doesn't he sometimes wonder whether he has gained most or lost most by learning his trade?   — MARK TWAIN, *Life on the Mississippi*

Writing Suggestions

1. **Writing with Sources.** Shaw claims that "There may be reasons to decry urban sprawl or the suburbanization of America, but the loss of wildlife is not one of them" (paragraph 6). What are some of the negative aspects of suburban developments? Has the impact of such development been as positive as Shaw seems to suggest? After doing some research of your own on the impact of urban sprawl on wildlife, write an essay in which you either agree or disagree with Shaw's conclusions. For models of and advice on integrating sources in your essay, see this chapter and Chapter 15.

2. **Writing with Sources.** The Nature Conservancy (www.nature.org) and the American Land Conservancy (www.alcnet.org) are two of many organizations committed to protecting land and water resources for the benefit of people and wildlife. They seek to conserve critical habitat areas, protect threatened land and rivers, clean up polluted land and waterways, and preserve working farms. Research what's being done in your state to conserve and protect land and water resources. How do you think Jane Shaw would react to such conservation efforts? Write a report about one important conservation project currently underway in your state. You may find it helpful to interview project staff or volunteers about their work to supplement your online and library research. For models of and advice on integrating sources in your essay, see this chapter and Chapter 15.

3. **Writing with Sources.** Some people argue that America is being homogenized as our cities continue to expand into the surrounding countryside so that everywhere is beginning to look like everywhere else. They claim that cities and towns throughout America are beginning to look alike because of an influx of malls and chain stores with similar appearance and cookie-cutter-like parks and open spaces. Do we want to live in a country that is dotted with large cities surrounded by suburbs and towns that are interchangeable? Write an essay in which you argue against such homogenization as a threat not only to our regional and cultural identities but also to our native wildlife. You may find it helpful to review your response to the Preparing to Read prompt for this selection before researching this topic or writing your essay. For models of and advice on integrating sources in your essay, see this chapter and Chapter 15.

The English-Only Movement
Can America Proscribe
Language with a
Clear Conscience?

JAKE JAMIESON

An eighth-generation Vermonter, Jake Jamieson was born in the town of Berlin and grew up in nearby Waterbury, home of Ben & Jerry's Ice Cream. He graduated from the University of Vermont with a degree in elementary education and a focus in English. After graduation Jamieson "bounced around" California and Colorado before landing in the Boston area, where he directs the product innovation and training department for iProspect, a search-engine marketing company.

Jamieson wrote the following essay while he was a college student and has updated it for inclusion in this book. As one who believes in the old axiom "If it isn't broken, don't fix it," Jamieson is intrigued by the official-English movement, which advocates fixing a system that seems to be working just fine. In this essay he tackles the issue of legislating English as the official language for the United States. As you read, notice how he uses outside sources to set out the various pieces of the English-only position and then uses his own thinking and examples, as well as experts who support his side, to undercut that position. Throughout his essay, Jamieson uses MLA-style in-text citations together with a list of works cited.

Preparing to Read

It is now possible to go many places in the world and get along pretty well using English, no matter what other languages are spoken in the host country. If you were to emigrate, how hard would you work to learn the predominant language of your chosen country? What advantages would there be in learning that language, even if you could get by with English? How would you feel if the country had a law that forced you to learn and use its language as quickly as possible? Write down your thoughts about these questions.

Jamieson 1

Jake Jamieson

Professor Rosa

Composition 101

May 10, 2010

The English-Only Movement:

Can America Proscribe Language with a

Clear Conscience?

Many people think of the United States as a giant cultural "melting pot" where people from other countries come together and bathe
in the warm waters of assimilation. In this scenario the newly arrived
immigrants readily adopt American cultural ways and learn to speak
English. For others, however, this serene picture of the melting pot
does not ring true. These people see the melting pot as a giant cauldron into which immigrants are tossed; here their cultures, values,
and backgrounds are boiled away in the scalding waters of discrimination. At the center of the discussion about immigrants and assimilation is language: Should immigrants be required to learn English or
should accommodations be made so they can continue to use their
native languages?

Those who argue that the melting-pot analogy is valid believe that
immigrants who come to America do so willingly and should be expected to become a part of its culture instead of hanging on to their
past. For them, the expectation that immigrants will celebrate this
country's holidays, dress as Americans dress, embrace American values, and most importantly, speak English is not unreasonable. They
believe that assimilation offers the only way for everyone in this
country to live together in harmony and the only way to dissipate the
tensions that inevitably arise when cultures clash.

A major problem with this argument, however, is that there is no
agreement on what exactly constitutes the "American way" of doing
things. Not everyone in America is of the same religious persuasion or
has the same set of values, and different people affect vastly different
styles of dress. There are so many sets of variables that it would be
hard to defend the argument that there is only one culture in the
United States.

Currently, the one common denominator in America is that the
majority of us speak English, and because of this a major movement
is being staged in favor of making English the country's "official"

language while it is still the country's national and common language. Making English America's official language would change the
ground rules and expectations surrounding immigrant assimilation.
According to the columnist and social commentator Charles
Krauthammer, making English the official language has important
implications:

> "Official" means the language of the government and its
> institutions. "Official" makes clear our expectations of
> acculturation. "Official" means that every citizen, upon
> entering America's most sacred political space, the voting
> booth, should minimally be able to identify the words
> president and vice president and county commissioner
> and judge. The immigrant, of course, has the right to speak
> whatever he wants. But he must understand that when he
> comes to the United States, swears allegiance, and accepts
> its bounty, he undertakes to join its civic culture. In
> English. (521)

Many reasons are given to support the notion that making English   5
the official language of the land is a good idea and that it is exactly
what this country needs, especially in the face of the growing diversity of languages in metropolitan areas. Indeed, the National Center
for Education Statistics reports that in 2008, 21 percent of children
ages 5-17 spoke a language other than English at home (Sec. 1).

Supporters of English-only contend that all government commu-   6
nication must be in English. Because communication is absolutely
necessary for democracy to survive, they believe that the only way to
ensure the existence of our nation is to make sure a common language exists. Making English official would ensure that all government
business, from ballots to official forms to judicial hearings, would
have to be conducted in English. According to former senator and
presidential candidate Bob Dole, "Promoting English as our national
language is not an act of hostility but a welcoming act of inclusion."
He goes on to state that while immigrants are encouraged to continue
speaking their native languages, "thousands of children [are] failing to
learn the language, English, that is the ticket to the 'American Dream'"
(qtd. in Donegan 51). Political and cultural commentator Greg Lewis
echoes Dole's sentiments when he boldly states, "to succeed in
America . . . it's important to speak, read, and understand English as

most Americans speak it. There's nothing cruel or unfair in that; it's just the way it is" (par. 5).

For those who do not subscribe to this way of thinking, however, this type of legislation is anything but the "welcoming act of inclusion" that it is described to be. Many of them, like Myriam Marquez, readily acknowledge the importance of English but fear that "talking in Spanish—or any other language, for that matter—is some sort of litmus test used to gauge American patriotism" ("Why and When" A12). Others suggest that anyone attempting to regulate language is treading dangerously close to the First Amendment and must have a hidden agenda of some type. Why, it is asked, make a language official when it is already firmly entrenched and widely used in this country without legislation to mandate it?

According to language diversity advocate James Crawford, the answer is plain and simple: "discrimination." He states that "it is certainly more respectable to discriminate by language than by race" or ethnicity. He points out that "most people are not sensitive to language discrimination in this nation, so it is easy to argue that you're doing someone a favor by making them speak English" (qtd. in Donegan 51). English-only legislation has been criticized as bigoted, anti-immigrant, mean-spirited, and steeped in nativism by those who oppose it, and some go so far as to say that this type of legislation will not foster better communication, as is the claim, but will instead encourage a "fear of being subsumed by a growing 'foreignness' in our midst" (Underwood 65).

For example, when a judge in Texas ruled that a mother was abusing her five-year-old girl by speaking to her only in Spanish, an uproar ensued. This ruling was accompanied by the statement that by talking to her daughter in a language other than English, the mother was "abusing that child and . . . relegating her to the position of housemaid." The National Association for Bilingual Education (NABE) condemned this statement for "labeling the Spanish language as abuse." The judge, Samuel C. Kiser, subsequently apologized to the housekeepers of the country, adding that he held them "in the highest esteem," but stood firm on his ruling (qtd. in Donegan 51). One might notice that he went out of his way to apologize to the housekeepers he might have offended but saw no need to apologize to the millions of Spanish speakers whose language had just been belittled in a nationally publicized case.

Jamieson 4

This tendency of official-English proponents to put down other languages is one that shows up again and again, even though they maintain that they have nothing against other languages or the people who speak them. If there is no malice intended toward other languages, why is the use of any language other than English so often portrayed by them as tantamount to lunacy? In a listing of the "New Year's Resolutions" of various conservative organizations, a group called U.S. English, Inc., stated that the U.S. government was not doing its job of convincing immigrants that they "must learn English to succeed in this country." Instead, according to Stephen Moore and his associates, "in a bewildering display of irrationality, the U.S. government makes it possible to vote, file a tax return, get married, obtain a driver's license, and become a U.S. citizen in many languages" (46). 10

Now, according to this mind-set, speaking any language other than English is "abusive," "irrational," and "bewildering." What is this world coming to when people want to speak and make transactions in their native language? Why do they refuse to change and become more like us? Why can't immigrants see that speaking English is quite simply the right way to go? These and many other questions like them are implied by official-English proponents when they discuss the issue. 11

Conservative attorney David Price argues that official-English legislation is a good idea because most English-speaking Americans prefer "out of pride and convenience to speak their native language on the job" (A13). Not only does this statement imply that the pride and convenience of non-English-speaking Americans is unimportant but also that their native tongues are not as important as English. The scariest prospect of all is that this opinion is quickly gaining popularity all around the country. It appears to be most prevalent in areas with high concentrations of Spanish-speaking residents. 12

To date a number of official-English bills and one amendment to the Constitution have been proposed in the House and Senate. There are more than twenty-seven states—including Missouri, North Dakota, Florida, Massachusetts, California, Virginia, and New Hampshire—that have made English their official language, and more are debating the issue every day. An especially disturbing fact about this debate—and it was front and center in 2007 during the discussions and protests about what to do with America's 12.5 million illegal immigrants—is 13 that official-English laws always seem to be linked to anti-immigration legislation, such as proposals to limit immigration or to restrict government benefits to immigrants.

Although official-English proponents maintain that their bid for language legislation is in the best interest of immigrants, the facts tend to show otherwise. University of Texas professor Robert D. King strongly believes that "language does not threaten American unity." He recommends that "we relax and luxuriate in our linguistic richness and our traditional tolerance of language differences" (531). A decision has to be made in this country about what kind of message we will send to the rest of the world. Do we plan to allow everyone in this country the freedom of speech that we profess to cherish, or will we decide to reserve it only for those who speak English? Will we hold firm to our belief that everyone is deserving of life, liberty, and the pursuit of happiness in this country? Or will we show the world that we believe in these things only when they pertain to us and people like us? "The irony," as columnist Myriam Marquez observes, "is that English-only laws directed at government have done little to change the inevitable multicultural flavor of America" ("English-Only Laws").

14

Jamieson 6

Works Cited

Donegan, Craig. "Debate over Bilingualism: Should English Be the Nation's Official Language?" *CQ Researcher* 19 Jan. 1996: 51-71. Print.

King, Robert D. "Should English Be the Law?" *Subject & Strategy*. Ed. Alfred Rosa and Paul Eschholz. 11th ed. Boston: Bedford, 2008. 522-31. Print.

Krauthammer, Charles. "In Plain English: Let's Make It Official." *Subject & Strategy*. Ed. Alfred Rosa and Paul Eschholz. 11th ed. Boston: Bedford, 2008. 519-21. Print.

Lewis, Greg. "An Open Letter to Diversity's Victims." *Washington Dispatch.com*. Washington Dispatch, 12 Aug. 2003. Web. 11 Mar. 2010.

Marquez, Myriam. "English-Only Laws Serve to Appease Those Who Fear the Inevitable." *Orlando Sentinel* 10 July 2000: A10. Print.

---. "Why and When We Speak Spanish Among Ourselves in Public." *Orlando Sentinel* 28 June 1998: A12. Print.

Moore, Stephen, et al. "New Year's Resolutions." *National Review* 29 Jan. 1996: 46-48. Print.

Price, David. "English-Only Rules: EEOC Has Gone Too Far." *USA Today* 28 Mar. 1996, Final ed.: A13. Print.

Underwood, Robert L. "At Issue: Should English Be the Official Language of the United States?" *CQ Researcher* 19 Jan. 1996: 65. Print.

United States. Dept. of Educ. Inst. of Educ. Sciences. Natl. Center for Educ. Statistics. *The Condition of Education 2010*. NCES, 2010. Web. 13 Mar. 2010.

Thinking Critically about the Text

Jamieson claims that "[t]here are so many sets of variables that it would be hard to defend the argument that there is only one culture in the United States" (paragraph 3). Do you agree with him, or do you see a dominant "American culture" with many regional variations? Explain.

Questions on Subject

1. What question does Jamieson seek to answer in his paper? How does he answer that question?

2. How does Jamieson counter the argument that the melting-pot analogy is valid? Do you agree with his counterargument?

3. Former senator Bob Dole believes that English "is the ticket to the 'American Dream'" (paragraph 6). In what ways can it be considered a "ticket"?

4. James Crawford believes that official-English legislation is motivated by "discrimination" (paragraph 8). What exactly do you think he means? Do you think Crawford would consider Bob Dole's remarks in paragraph 6 discriminatory? Explain.

5. In his concluding paragraph, Jamieson leaves his readers with three important questions. How do you think he would answer each one? How would you answer them?

Questions on Strategy

1. What is Jamieson's thesis, and where does he present it? (Glossary: *Thesis*)

2. How has Jamieson organized his argument? (Glossary: *Organization*)

3. Jamieson is careful to use signal phrases to introduce each of his quotations and paraphrases. How do these signal phrases help readers follow the flow of the argument in his essay? (Glossary: *Signal Phrases*)

4. For what purpose does Jamieson quote Greg Lewis in paragraph 6? What would have been lost had he dropped the Lewis quotation? Explain.

5. In paragraph 9, Jamieson presents the example of the Texas judge who ruled that speaking to a child only in Spanish constituted abuse. What point does this example help Jamieson make?

Questions on Diction and Vocabulary

1. What for you constitutes the "'American way' of doing things" (paragraph 3)? Do you think the meaning of "American way" has changed in the last decade or two? Explain.

2. What are the connotations of the words *official* and *English-only*? In your opinion, do these connotations help or hinder the English-only position? What

are the connotations of the word *immigrant*? What insights into America's language debate do these connotations give you? (Glossary: *Connotation/Denotation*)

3. Consult your dictionary to determine the meanings of the following words as Jamieson uses them in this selection: *assimilation* (paragraph 1), *dissipate* (2), *implications* (4), *nativism* (8), *malice* (10).

Classroom Activity for Writing with Sources

For each of the following quotations, write an acceptable paraphrase and then a paraphrase including a partial quotation that avoids plagiarism (see pages 664–66 and 671–75). Pay particular attention to the word choice and the sentence structure of the original.

> The sperm whale is the largest of the toothed whales. Moby-Dick was a sperm whale. Generally, male toothed whales are larger than the females. Female sperm whales may grow 35 to 40 feet in length, while the males may reach 60 feet.
> — RICHARD HENDRICK,
> *The Voyage of the Mimi*

> A truly equal world would be one where women ran half of our countries and companies and men ran half of our homes. The laws of economics and many studies of diversity tell us that if we tapped the entire pool of human resources and talent, our performance would improve.
> — SHERYL SANDBERG,
> *Lean In*

> Astronauts from over twenty nations have gone into space and they all come back, amazingly enough, saying the very same thing: The earth is a small, blue place of profound beauty that we must take care of. For each, the journey into space, whatever its original intents and purposes, became above all a spiritual one.
> — AL REINHERT,
> *For All Mankind*

> One of the usual things about education in mathematics in the United States is its relatively impoverished vocabulary. Whereas the student completing elementary school will already have a vocabulary for most disciplines of many hundreds, even thousands of words, the typical student will have a mathematics vocabulary of only a couple of dozen words.
> — MARVIN MINSKY,
> *The Society of Mind*

Writing Suggestions

1. **Writing with Sources.** While it's no secret that English is the common language of the United States, few of us know that our country has been extremely cautious about promoting a government-mandated "official language." Why do you suppose the federal government has chosen to take a hands-off position on the language issue? If it has not been necessary to

mandate it in the past, why do you think that people now feel a need to declare English the "official language" of the United States? Do you think that this need is real? Write an essay articulating your position on the English-only issue. Support your position with your own experiences and observations as well as several outside sources. For models of and advice on integrating sources in your essay, see this chapter and Chapter 15.

2. **Writing with Sources.** In preparation for writing an essay about assimilating non-English-speaking immigrants into American society, consider the following three statements:

   a. At this time, it is highly unlikely that Congress will legislate that English is the official language of the United States.

   b. Immigrants should learn English as quickly as possible after arriving in the United States.

   c. The cultures and languages of immigrants should be respected and valued so that bitterness and resentment will not be fostered, even as immigrants are assimilated into American society.

In your opinion, what is the best way to assimilate non-English-speaking immigrants into our society? After doing some research on the issue, write an essay in which you propose how the United States, as a nation, can make the two latter statements a reality without resorting to an English-only solution. How can we effectively transition immigrants to speaking English without provoking ill will? For models of and advice on integrating sources in your essay, see this chapter and Chapter 15.

3. **Writing with Sources.** Is the English-only debate a political issue, a social issue, an economic issue, or some combination of the three? In this context, what do you see as the relationship between language and power? After doing some research on the topic, write an essay in which you explore the relationship between language and power as it pertains to the non-English-speaking immigrants trying to live and function within the dominant English-speaking culture. For models of and advice on integrating sources in your essay, see this chapter and Chapter 15.

---

 e-Pages

The Curator's Guide to the Galaxy

MEGAN GARBER

See how writing with sources works on the Web. Go to bedfordstmartins.com/subjectandstrategy for a reading with hyperlinks and study questions that explore the importance of acknowledging sources online.

CHAPTER 15

A Brief Guide to Researching and Documenting Essays

IN THIS CHAPTER, YOU WILL LEARN SOME VALUABLE RESEARCH techniques:

- How to establish a realistic schedule for your research project
- How to conduct research online using directory and keyword searches
- How to evaluate sources
- How to analyze sources
- How to develop a working bibliography
- How to take useful notes
- How to acknowledge your sources using Modern Language Association (MLA) style in-text citations and a list of works cited

ESTABLISHING A REALISTIC SCHEDULE

A research project easily spans several weeks. So as not to lose track of time and find yourself facing an impossible deadline at the last moment, establish a realistic schedule for completing key tasks. By thinking of the research paper as a multistaged process, you avoid becoming overwhelmed by the size of the whole undertaking.

Your schedule should allow at least a few days to accommodate unforeseen needs and delays. Use the following template, which lists the essential steps in writing a research paper, to plan your own research schedule:

Research Paper Schedule

Task	Completion Date
1. Choose a research topic and pose a worthwhile question.	____/____/____
2. Locate print and electronic sources.	____/____/____
3. Develop a working bibliography.	____/____/____
4. Evaluate your sources.	____/____/____
5. Read your sources, taking complete and accurate notes.	____/____/____
6. Develop a preliminary thesis and make a working outline.	____/____/____
7. Write a draft of your paper, integrating sources you have summarized, paraphrased, and quoted.	____/____/____
8. Visit your college writing center for help with your revision.	____/____/____
9. Decide on a final thesis and modify your outline.	____/____/____
10. Revise your paper and properly cite all borrowed materials.	____/____/____
11. Prepare a list of works cited.	____/____/____
12. Prepare the final manuscript and proofread.	____/____/____
13. Submit your research paper.	____/____/____

FINDING AND USING SOURCES

You should use materials found through a search of your school library's holdings—including books, newspapers, journals, magazines, encyclopedias, pamphlets, brochures, and government documents—as your primary tools for research. These sources, unlike many open-Internet sources,* are reviewed by experts in the field before they are published, generally overseen by a reputable publishing company or organization, and examined by editors and fact checkers for accuracy and reliability.

---

*By "open Internet," we mean the vast array of resources, ranging from Library of Congress holdings to pictures of a stranger's summer vacation, available to anyone using a search engine. Because anyone with a computer and Internet access can post information online, sources found on the open Internet should be scrutinized more carefully for relevance and reliability than those found through a search of academic databases or library holdings.

The best place to start your search, in most cases, is your college library's home page (see figure below). Here you will find links to the library's computerized catalog of hard-copy holdings, online reference works, periodical databases, electronic journals, and a list of full-text databases. Most libraries also provide links to other helpful materials, including subject study guides and guides to research.

To get started, decide on some likely search terms and try them out. You might have to try a number of different terms related to your topic in order to generate the best results. (For tips on refining your searches, see pages 714–16.) Your goal is to create a preliminary listing of books, magazine and newspaper articles, public documents and reports, and other sources that may be helpful in exploring your topic. At this early stage, it is better to err on the side of listing too many sources. Then, later on, you will not have to backtrack to find sources you discarded too hastily.

You will likely find some open-Internet sources to be informative and valuable additions to your research. The Internet is especially useful in providing recent data, stories, and reports. For example, you might find a

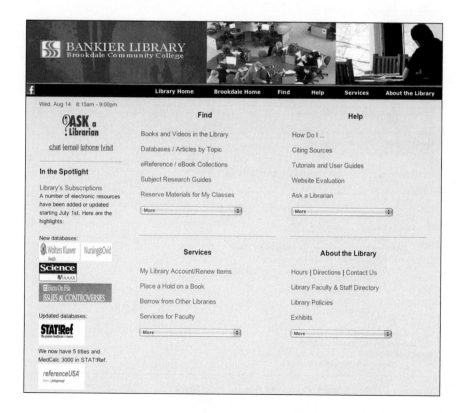

just-published article from a university laboratory or a news story in your local newspaper's online archives. Generally, however, open-Internet sources should be used alongside other sources and not as a replacement for them. The Internet offers a vast number of useful and carefully maintained resources, but it also contains much unreliable information. It is your responsibility to determine whether a given Internet source should be trusted. (For advice on evaluating sources, see pages 716–18.)

❱ Conducting Keyword Searches

When searching for sources about your topic in an electronic database, in the library's computerized catalog, or on the Internet, you should start with a keyword search. To make the most efficient use of your time, you will want to know how to conduct a keyword search that is likely to yield solid sources and leads for your research project. As obvious or simple as it may sound, the key to a successful keyword search is the quality of the keywords you generate about your topic. You might find it helpful to start a list of potential keywords as you begin your research and add to it as your work proceeds. Often you will discover combinations of keywords that will lead you right to the sources you need.

Databases and library catalogs index sources by author, title, and year of publication, as well as by subject headings assigned by a cataloger who has

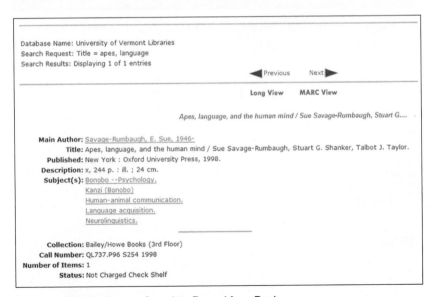

Computer Catalog Screen: Complete Record for a Book

previewed the source. In order to generate results, the keywords you use will have to match words found in one or more of these categories. Once you begin to locate sources that are on your topic, be sure to note the subject headings listed for each source. You can use these subject headings as keywords to lead you to additional book sources or, later, to articles in periodicals cataloged by full-text databases like *InfoTrac*, *LexisNexis*, *Expanded Academic ASAP*, or *JSTOR* to which your library subscribes. The figure on page 714 shows a typical book entry in a computer catalog. Notice the subject headings, all of which can be used as possible keywords.

The keyword search process is somewhat different—more wide open—when you are searching on the Web. It is always a good idea to look for search tips on the help screens or advanced search instructions for the search engine you are using before initiating a keyword search. When you type in a keyword in the "Search" box on a search engine's home page, the search engine electronically scans Web sites looking for matches to your keywords. On the Web, the quality of the keywords used determines the relevance of the hits on the first page or two that comes up. While it is not uncommon for a search on the Internet to yield between 500,000 and 1,000,000 hits, the search engine's algorithm puts the best sources up front. If after scanning the first couple of pages of results you determine that these sites seem off topic, you will need to refine your search terms to either narrow or broaden your search.

Refining Keyword Searches on the Web

While some variation in command terms and characters exists among databases and popular search engines, the following functions are almost universally accepted. If you have a particular question about refining your keyword search, seek assistance by clicking on "Help" or "Advanced Search."

- Use quotation marks or parentheses to indicate that you are searching for words in exact sequence — e.g., "whooping cough"; (Supreme Court).

- Use AND or a plus sign (+) between words to narrow your search by specifying that all words need to appear in a document — e.g., tobacco AND cancer; Shakespeare + sonnet.

- Use NOT or a minus sign (–) between words to narrow your search by eliminating unwanted words — e.g., monopoly NOT game, cowboys–Dallas.

- Use OR to broaden your search by requiring that only one of the words need appear — e.g., buffalo OR bison.

- Use an asterisk (*) to indicate that you will accept variations of a term — e.g., "food label*" for food labels, food labeling, and so forth.

◗ Using Subject Directories to Define and Develop Your Research Topic

If you are undecided as to your exact topic, general search engines might not yield the credible depth of information you need for initial research and brainstorming. Instead, explore subject directories—collections of sites and online resources organized and edited by human experts. Search *subject directories* online, or try popular options like *INFOMINE: Scholarly Internet Resource Collections* and the Best of the Web Directory. Subject directories can also help if you simply want to see if there is enough material to supplement your print-source research. Once you choose a directory's subject area, you can select more specialized subcategories, eventually arriving at a list of sites closely related to your topic.

The most common question students have at this stage of a Web search is, "How can I tell if I'm looking in the right place?" There is no straight answer; if more than one subject area sounds plausible, you will have to dig more deeply into each of their subcategories, using logic and the process of elimination to determine which one is likely to produce the best leads for your topic. In most cases, it doesn't take long—usually just one or two clicks—to figure out whether you're searching in the right subject area. If you click on a subject area and none of the topics listed in its subcategories seems to pertain even remotely to your research topic, try a different subject area. As you browse through various subject directories, keep a running list of keywords associated with your topic that you can use in subsequent keyword searches.

EVALUATING YOUR SOURCES

You do not have to spend much time in the library to realize that you do not have time to read every print and online source that appears relevant. Given the abundance of print and Internet sources, the key to successful research is identifying those books, articles, Web sites, and other online sources that will help you most. You must evaluate your potential sources to determine which materials you will read, which you will skim, and which you will simply eliminate. Here are some evaluation strategies and questions to assist you in identifying your most promising sources.

Strategies for Evaluating Print and Online Sources

Evaluating a Book

- Read the back or inside cover copy for insights into the book's coverage and currency as well as the author's expertise.
- Scan the table of contents and identify any promising chapters.
- Read the author's preface, looking for his or her thesis and purpose.

- Check the index for key words or key phrases related to your research topic.
- Read the opening and concluding paragraphs of any promising chapter; if you are unsure about its usefulness, skim the whole chapter.
- Ask yourself: Does the author have a discernible bias? If so, you must be aware that this bias will color his or her claims and evidence. (See Analyzing Your Sources, pages 718–19.)

Evaluating an Article

- Ask yourself what you know about the journal or magazine publishing the article:
  - Is the publication scholarly or popular? Scholarly journals (*American Economic Review, Journal of Marriage and Family*, the *Wilson Quarterly*) publish articles representing original research written by authorities in the field. Such articles always cite their sources in footnotes or bibliographies, which means you can check their accuracy and delve deeper into the topic by locating these sources. Popular news and general interest magazines (*National Geographic, Smithsonian, Time, Ebony*), on the other hand, publish informative, entertaining, and easy-to-read articles written by editorial staff or freelance writers. Popular essays sometimes cite sources but often do not, making them somewhat less authoritative and less helpful in terms of extending your own research.
  - What is the reputation of the journal or magazine? Determine the publisher or sponsor. Is it an academic institution or a commercial enterprise or individual? Does the publisher or publication have a reputation for accuracy and objectivity?
  - Who are the readers of this journal or magazine?
- Try to determine the author's credentials. Is he or she an expert?
- Consider the title or headline of the article as well as the opening paragraph or two and the conclusion. Does the source appear to be too general or too technical for your needs and audience?
- For articles in journals, read the abstract (a summary of the main points) if there is one. Examine any photographs, charts, graphs, or other illustrations that accompany the article and determine how useful they might be for your research purposes.

Evaluating a Web Site or Document Found on the Open Internet

- Consider the original location of the document or site. Often the URL, especially the top-level domain name, can give you a clue about the kinds of information provided and the type of organization behind the site. Common suffixes include:

.com — business/commercial/personal

.edu — educational institution

(continued on next page)

(continued from previous page)

.gov — government sponsored

.net — various types of networks

.org — nonprofit organization, but also some commercial or personal

(Be advised that *.org* is not regulated like *.edu* and *.gov*, for example. Most nonprofits use *.org*, but many commercial and personal sites do as well.)

- Examine the home page of the site:

  - Does the content appear to be related to your research topic?

  - Is the home page well maintained and professional in appearance?

  - Is there an *About* link on the home page that takes you to background information on the site's sponsor? Is there a mission statement, history, or statement of philosophy? Can you verify whether the site is official — actually sanctioned by the organization or company?

- Identify the author of the document or site. What are the author's qualifications for writing on this subject?

- Determine whether a print equivalent is available. If so, is the Web version identical to the print version, or is it altered in some way?

- Determine when the site was last updated. Is the content current enough for your purposes?

You can also find sources on the Internet itself that offer useful guidelines for evaluating electronic sources. One excellent example was created by reference librarians at the Wolfgram Memorial Library of Widener University. Type *Wolfgram evaluate web pages* into a search engine to access that site.

On the basis of your evaluation, select the most promising books, articles, and Web sites to pursue in depth for your research project.

ANALYZING YOUR SOURCES

Before you begin to take notes, it is essential that you read critically and carefully analyze your sources for their theses, overall arguments, amount and credibility of evidence, bias, and reliability in helping you explore your research topic. Look for the writers' main ideas, key examples, strongest arguments, and conclusions. While it is easy to become absorbed in sources that support your own beliefs, always seek out several sources with opposing viewpoints, if only to test your own position. Look for information about the authors themselves — information that will help you determine their authority and where they position themselves in the broader conversation on the issue. You should also know the reputation and special interests of book publishers and magazines, because you are likely to get different views—conservative, liberal, international, feminist—on the same topic depending on the publication you read. Use the following checklist to assist you in analyzing your print and online sources.

Checklist for Analyzing Print and Online Sources

- What is the writer's thesis or claim?
- How does the writer support this thesis? Does the evidence seem fact-based, or is it mainly anecdotal?
- Does the writer consider opposing viewpoints?
- Does the writer have any obvious political or religious biases? Is the writer associated with any special-interest groups such as Planned Parenthood, Greenpeace, Amnesty International, or the National Rifle Association?
- Is the writer an expert on the subject? Do other writers mention this author in their work?
- Is important information documented through footnotes or links so that it can be verified or corroborated in other sources?
- What is the author's purpose—to inform; to argue for a particular position or action; something else?
- Do the writer's thesis and purpose clearly relate to your research topic?
- Does the source reflect current thinking and research in the field?

DEVELOPING A WORKING BIBLIOGRAPHY FOR YOUR SOURCES

As you discover books, journal and magazine articles, newspaper stories, and Web sites that you think might be helpful, you need to start maintaining a record of important information about each source. This record, called a working bibliography, will enable you to know where sources are located as well as what they are when it comes time to consult them or acknowledge them in your list of works cited or final bibliography. In all likelihood, your working bibliography will contain more sources than you actually consult and include in your list of works cited.

Some people make separate bibliography cards, using a 3- by 5-inch index card, for each work that might be helpful to their research. By using a separate card for each book, article, or Web site, they can continually edit their working bibliography, dropping sources that did not prove helpful for one reason or another and adding new ones.

With the digitization of most library resources, you now have the option to copy and paste bibliographic information from the library computer catalog and periodical indexes or from the Internet into a document on your computer that you can edit throughout the research process. You can also track your project online with a citation manager like Zotero, Mendeley, or EndNote. One advantage of the copy/paste option over the index card method is accuracy, especially in punctuation, spelling, and capitalization — details that are essential in accessing Internet sites.

Checklist for a Working Bibliography of Print and Online Sources

For Books

- Library call number
- Names of all authors, editors, and translators
- Title and subtitle
- Publication data:
    - Place of publication (city and state)
    - Publisher's name
    - Date of publication
- Edition (if not the first) and volume number (if applicable)

For Periodical Articles

- Names of all authors
- Name and subtitle of article
- Title of journal, magazine, or newspaper
- Publication data:
    - Volume number and issue number
    - Date of issue
    - Page numbers

For Internet Sources

- Names of all authors and/or editors
- Title and subtitle of the document
- Title of the longer work to which the document belongs (if applicable)
- Title of the site or discussion list
- Name of company or organization that owns the Web site
- Date of release, online posting, or latest revision
- Format of online source (Web page, .pdf, podcast, etc.)
- Date you accessed the site
- Electronic address (URL)

For Other Sources

- Name of author, government agency, organization, company, recording artist, personality, etc.
- Title of the work
- Format (pamphlet, unpublished diary, interview, television broadcast, etc.)
- Publication or production data:

    Name of publisher or producer

    Date of publication, production, or release

    Identifying codes or numbers (if applicable)

TAKING NOTES

As you read, take notes. You're looking for ideas, facts, opinions, statistics, examples, and evidence that you think will be useful in writing your paper. As you work through the articles, look for recurring themes, and mark the places where the writers are in agreement and where they differ in their views. Try to remember that the effectiveness of your paper is largely determined by the quality—not necessarily the quantity—of your notes. The purpose of a research paper is not to present a collection of quotes that show you've read all the material and can report what others have said about your topic. Your goal is to analyze, evaluate, and synthesize the information you collect—in other words, to enter into the discussion of the issues and thereby take ownership of your topic. You want to view the results of your research from your own perspective and arrive at an informed opinion of your topic. (For more on Writing with Sources, see Chapter 14.)

Now for some practical advice on taking notes: First, be systematic. If you use note cards, write one note on a card, and use cards of uniform size, preferably 4- by 6-inch cards because they are large enough to accommodate even a long note on a single card and yet small enough to be easily handled and carried. If you keep notes electronically, consider creating a separate file for each topic or source, or use a digital research application like those mentioned previously (Zotero, Mendeley, or EndNote). If you keep your notes organized, when you get to the planning and writing stage, you will be able to sequence your notes according to the plan you have envisioned for your paper. Furthermore, should you decide to alter your organizational plan, you can easily reorder your notes to reflect those revisions.

Second, try not to take too many notes. One good way to help decide whether to take a note is to ask yourself, "How exactly does this material help prove or disprove my thesis?" You might even try envisioning where in your paper you could use the information. If it does not seem relevant to your thesis, don't bother to take a note.

Once you decide to take a note, you must decide whether to summarize, paraphrase, or quote directly. The approach that you take is largely determined by the content of the passage and the way you envision using it in your paper. For detailed advice on summary, paraphrase, and quotation, see Chapter 14, pages 663–66.

DOCUMENTING SOURCES

When you summarize, paraphrase, or quote a person's thoughts and ideas, and when you use facts or statistics that are not commonly known or believed, you must properly acknowledge the source of your information. You must document the source of your information when you

- Quote a source word for word
- Refer to information and ideas from another source that you present in your own words as either a paraphrase or a summary
- Cite statistics, tables, charts, or graphs

You do not need to document

- Your own observations, experiences, and ideas
- Factual information available in a number of reference works (known as "common knowledge")
- Proverbs, sayings, and familiar quotations

A reference to the source of your borrowed information is called a *citation*. There are many systems for making citations, and your citations must consistently follow one of these systems. The documentation style recommended by the Modern Language Association (MLA) is commonly used in English and the humanities and is the style used for student papers throughout this book. Another common system is American Psychological Association (APA) style, which is used in the social sciences. In general, your instructor will tell you which system to use. For more information on documentation styles, consult the appropriate manual or handbook. For MLA style, consult the *MLA Handbook for Writers of Research Papers*, 7th ed. (New York: MLA, 2009).

There are two components of documentation in a research paper: the *in-text citation*, placed in the body of your paper, and the *list of works cited*, which provides complete publication data on your sources and is placed at the end of your paper.

❱ In-Text Citations

Most in-text citations, also known as parenthetical citations, consist of only the author's last name and a page reference. Usually, the author's name is given in an introductory or signal phrase (see pages 667–68) at the beginning of the borrowed material, and the page reference is given in parentheses at the end. If the author's name is not given at the beginning, it belongs in the parentheses along with the page reference. The parenthetical reference signals the end of the borrowed material and directs your readers to the list of works cited should they want to pursue a source.

Consider the following examples of in-text citations from a student paper on the debate over whether to make English America's official language.

In-Text Citations (MLA Style)

Diaz 4

Many people are surprised to discover that English is not the official language of the United States. Today, even as English literacy becomes a necessity for people in many parts of the world, some people in the United States believe its primacy is being threatened right at home. Much of the current controversy focuses on Hispanic communities with large Spanish-speaking populations who may feel little or no pressure to learn English. Columnist and cultural critic Charles Krauthammer believes English should be America's official language. He notes that this country has been

Citation with author's name in the signal phrase

"blessed . . . with a linguistic unity that brings a critically needed cohesion to a nation as diverse, multiracial and multi-ethnic as America" and that communities such as these threaten the bond created by a common language (112). There are others, however, who think that "language does not threaten American unity. Benign neglect is a good policy for

Citation with author's name in parentheses

any country when it comes to language, and it's a good policy for America" (King 64).

Diaz 5

Works Cited

King, Robert D. "Should English Be the Law?" *Atlantic Monthly* Apr. 1997: 55-64. Print.

Krauthammer, Charles. "In Plain English: Let's Make It Official." *Time* 12 June 2006: 112. Print.

In the preceding example, the student followed MLA guidelines for documentation. The following sections provide MLA guidelines for documenting periodical print publications, nonperiodical print publications, Web publications, and other common sources. For advice on documenting additional, less frequently cited sources, consult the *MLA Handbook for Writers of Research Papers,* 7th ed. (New York: MLA, 2009).

LIST OF WORKS CITED

In this section, you will find general guidelines for creating a list of works cited, followed by sample entries designed to cover the citations you will use most often.

Guidelines for Constructing Your Works Cited Page

1. Begin the list on a new page following the last page of text.

2. Center the title *Works Cited* at the top of the page.

3. Double-space both within and between entries on your list.

4. Alphabetize your sources by the authors' last names. If you have two or more authors with the same last name, alphabetize by first names.

5. If you have two or more works by the same author, alphabetize by the first word of the titles, not counting *A, An,* or *The.* Use the author's name in the first entry and three unspaced hyphens followed by a period in subsequent entries:

   > Twitchell, James B. *Branded Nation: The Marketing of Megachurch, College Inc., and Museumworld.* New York: Simon, 2005. Print.
   >
   > ---. "The Branding of Higher Ed." *Forbes* 25 Nov. 2002: 50. Print.
   >
   > ---. *Look Away, Dixieland: A Carpetbagger's Great-Grandson Travels Highway 84.* Baton Rouge: Louisiana State UP, 2011. Print.

6. If no author is known, alphabetize by title.

7. Begin each entry at the left margin. If the entry is longer than one line, indent the second and subsequent lines one-half inch.

8. Italicize the titles of books, journals, magazines, and newspapers. Use quotation marks for titles of periodical articles, chapters and essays within books, short stories, and poems.

9. Provide the medium of the source (i.e., *Print, Web, Film, Television, Performance*).

▶ Periodical Print Publications:
  Journals, Magazines, and Newspapers

Standard Information for Periodical Print Publications

1. Name of the author of the work; for anonymous works, begin entry with the title of the work

2. Title of the work, in quotation marks

3. Name of the periodical, italicized

4. Series number or name, if relevant

5. Volume number (for scholarly journals that use volume numbers)

6. Issue number (if available, for scholarly journals)

7. Date of publication (for scholarly journals, year; for other periodicals, day, month, and year, as available)

8. Page numbers

9. Medium of publication (for print sources, use *Print*)

Scholarly Journal Article

For all scholarly journals—whether paginated continuously throughout a given year or not—provide the volume number (if one is given), the issue number, the year, the page numbers, and the medium. Separate the volume number and the issue number with a period.

> Ercolino, Stefano. "The Maximalist Novel." *Comparative Literature* 64.3 (2012): 241-56. Print.

Magazine Article

When citing a weekly or biweekly magazine, give the complete date (day, month, year).

> Perry, Alex. "Africa Rising." *Time* 3 Dec. 2012: 48-52. Print.

When citing a magazine published every month or every two months, provide the month or months and year. If an article in a magazine is not printed on consecutive pages—for example, an article might begin on page 45, then skip to 48—include only the first page followed by a plus sign.

> Mascarelli, Amanda Leigh. "Fall Guys." *Audubon* Nov.-Dec. 2009: 44+. Print.

Newspaper Article

> Bellafante, Ginia. "When the Law Says a Parent Isn't a Parent." *New York Times* 3 Feb. 2013, natl. ed.: 27. Print.

Review (Book or Film)

Stott, Rebecca. "Under the Microscope." Rev. of *Louis Agassiz: Creator of American Science*, by Christoph Irmscher. *New York Times Book Review* 3 Feb. 2013: 13. Print.

Denby, David. "Dead Reckoning." Rev. of *Zero Dark Thirty*, dir. Kathryn Bigelow. *New Yorker* 24 Dec. 2012: 130-32. Print.

If the review has no title, simply begin with *Rev.* after the author's name. If there is neither a title nor an author, begin with *Rev.* and alphabetize by the title of the book or film being reviewed.

Anonymous Article

When no author's name is given, begin the entry with the title.

"Pompeii: Will the City Go from Dust to Dust?" *Newsweek* 1 Sept. 1997: 8. Print.

Editorial (Signed/Unsigned)

Stengel, Richard. "In Drones We Trust." Editorial. *Time* 11 Feb. 2013: 2. Print.

"A Real Schedule for Ground Zero." Editorial. *New York Times* 18 June 2008, natl. ed.: A22. Print.

Letter to the Editor

Lyon, Ruth Henriquez. Letter. *Audubon* Jan.-Feb. 2013: 10. Print.

❱ Nonperiodical Print Publications: Books, Brochures, and Pamphlets

Standard Information for Nonperiodical Print Publications

1. Name of the author, editor, compiler, or translator of the work; for anonymous works, begin entry with the title
2. Title of the work, italicized
3. Edition
4. Volume number
5. City of publication, name of the publisher, and year of publication
6. Medium of publication (for print sources, use *Print*)

Book by a Single Author

Al-Maria, Sophia. *The Girl Who Fell to Earth*. New York: Harper, 2012. Print.

Use a shortened version of the publisher's name—for example, *Houghton* for "Houghton Mifflin" or *Cambridge UP* for "Cambridge University Press."

Anthology

Rosa, Alfred, and Paul Eschholz, eds. *Models for Writers*. 11th ed. Boston: Bedford, 2012. Print.

Book by Two or More Authors

For a book by two or three authors, list the authors in the order in which they appear on the title page.

O'Reilly, Bill, and Martin Dugard. *Killing Kennedy*. New York: Holt, 2012. Print.

For a book by four or more authors, list the first author in the same way as for a single-author book, followed by a comma and the abbreviation *et al.* ("and others").

Beardsley, John, et al. *Gee's Bend: The Women and Their Quilts*. Atlanta: Tinwood, 2002. Print.

Book by Corporate Author

Carnegie Foundation for the Advancement of Teaching. *Campus Life: In Search of Community*. Princeton: Princeton UP, 1990. Print.

Work in Anthology

Include the page numbers of the selection after the anthology's year of publication.

Ackerman, Diane. "Why Leaves Turn Color in the Fall." *Models for Writers*. Ed. Alfred Rosa and Paul Eschholz. 11th ed. Boston: Bedford, 2012. 438-43. Print.

Note that *Ed.* here stands for "Edited by," so no plural is necessary.

Article in Reference Book

Anagnost, George T. "Sandra Day O'Connor." *The Oxford Companion to the Supreme Court of the United States*. 2nd ed. 2005. Print.

If an article is unsigned, begin with the title.

"Evers, Medgar Wiley." *The Encyclopedia Americana*. 2006 ed. Print.

Note that widely used reference works such as these do not require a publisher's name. Also note that page numbers are not necessary if entries in a reference work are arranged alphabetically.

Introduction, Preface, Foreword, or Afterword to Book

Wirzba, Norman. Introduction. *The Art of the Commonplace: The Agrarian Essays of Wendell Berry*. By Wendell Berry. Washington: Shoemaker, 2002. vii-xx. Print.

Anonymous Book

Children of the Dragon: The Story of Tiananmen Square. New York: Collier-Macmillan, 1990. Print.

Translation

> Yan, Mo. *Sandalwood Death: A Novel.* Trans. Howard Goldblatt. Norman: U of Oklahoma P, 2013. Print.

Illustrated Book or Graphic Novel

> Clemens, Samuel L. *The Adventures of Huckleberry Finn.* Illus. Norman Rockwell. New York: Heritage, 1940. Print.

> Byrne, Eugene, writer. *Darwin: A Graphic Biography.* Illus. Simon Gurr. Washington: Smithsonian, 2013. Print.

Book Published in Second or Subsequent Edition

> Hassan, Ihab. *The Dismemberment of Orpheus: Toward a Postmodern Literature.* 2nd ed. Madison: U of Wisconsin P, 1982. Print.

> Modern Language Association of America. *MLA Handbook for Writers of Research Papers.* 7th ed. New York: MLA, 2009. Print.

Brochure or Pamphlet

> Thomas Edison and Henry Ford Winter Estates. *Historic Winter Estates of Edison and Ford.* Fort Myers, FL: Edison & Ford, 2012. Print.

Government Publication

> United States. Dept. of Transportation. *Emergency Response Guidebook.* Washington: GPO, 2012. Print.

Give the government, the agency, and the title with a period and a space after each. For most federal publications, the publisher is the Government Printing Office (GPO).

▌ Web Publications

The following guidelines and models for citing information retrieved from the World Wide Web have been adapted from the most recent advice of the MLA — as detailed in the *MLA Handbook for Writers of Research Papers*, 7th ed. (2009) — and from the "MLA Style" section on MLA's Web site (www.mla.org). You will notice that citations of Web publications have some features in common with both print publications and reprinted works, broadcasts, and live performances.

Standard Information for Web Publications

1. Name of the author, editor, or compiler of the work

   (For works with more than one author, a corporate author, or an unnamed author, apply the guidelines for print sources; for anonymous works, begin entry with the title.)

2. Title of the work, italicized, unless it is part of a larger work, in which case put it in quotation marks

3. Title of the overall Web site, italicized (if distinct from item 2 above)

4. Version or edition of the site, if relevant

5. Publisher or sponsor of the site; if this information is not available, use *n.p.* ("no publisher")

6. Date of publication (day, month, and year); if no date is given, use *n.d.*

7. Medium of publication (for online sources use *Web*)

8. Date of access (day, month, and year)

MLA style does not require URLs in works cited entries. However, if your instructor wants you to include URLs in your citations or if you believe readers will not be able to locate the source without the URL, insert it as the last item in an entry, immediately after the date of access. Enclose the URL in angle brackets, followed by a period. The following example illustrates an entry with the URL included:

> Pounder, Diana. "School Leadership Preparation and Practice Survey Instruments and Their Uses." *Journal of Research on Leadership Education* 7.2 (2012): 254-74. Web. 20 Jan. 2013. <http://jrl.sagepub.content/7/2/254.full.pdf+html>.

MLA style requires that you break URLs extending over more than one line only after a slash. Do *not* add spaces, hyphens, or any other punctuation to indicate the break.

ONLINE SCHOLARLY JOURNALS. To cite an article, review, editorial, or letter to the editor in a scholarly journal existing only in electronic form on the Web, provide the author, the title of the article, the title of the journal, the volume and issue, and the date of issue, followed by the page numbers (if available), the medium, and the date of access.

Article in Online Scholarly Journal

> Blamires, Adrian. "Homoerotic Pleasure and Violence in the Drama of Thomas Middleton." *Early Modern Literary Studies* 16.2 (2012): n. pag. Web. 4 Feb. 2013.

Book Review in Online Scholarly Journal

> Law, Ian. Rev. of *Deconstructing Europe: Postcolonial Perspectives*, ed. Sandra Ponzanesi and Bolette B. Blaagaard. *Postcolonial Text* 7.3 (2012): n. pag. Web. 17 Apr. 2013.

Editorial in Online Scholarly Journal

> Goins, Elizabeth, and Frederick Coye Heard. "Diverse People, Diverse Approaches." Editorial. *Praxis: A Writing Center Journal* 10.1 (2012): n. pag. Web. 24 Jan. 2013.

PERIODICAL PUBLICATIONS IN ONLINE DATABASES

Journal Article from Online Database or Subscription Service

Greeson, Jennifer. "American Enlightenment: The New World and Modern Western Thought." *American Literary History* 25.1 (2013): 6-17. *Project Muse*. Web. 15 June 2013.

Magazine Article from Online Database or Subscription Service

Keizer, Garret. "Sound and Fury: The Politics of Noise in a Loud Society." *Harper's* Mar. 2001: 39-48. *Expanded Academic ASAP Plus*. Web. 14 Dec. 2012.

Newspaper Article from Online Database or Subscription Service

Sanders, Joshunda. "Think Race Doesn't Matter? Listen to Eminem." *San Francisco Chronicle* 20 July 2003: n. pag. *LexisNexis*. Web. 29 Dec. 2012.

McEachern, William Ross. "Teaching and Learning in Bilingual Countries: The Examples of Belgium and Canada." *Education* 123.1 (2002): 103. *Expanded Academic ASAP Plus*. Web. 17 Sept. 2012.

NONPERIODICAL WEB PUBLICATIONS. This category of Web publication includes all Web-delivered content that does not fit into one of the previous two categories (online scholarly journal publications and periodical publications from an online database).

Online Magazine Article

Gambino, Megan. "How Big Data Has Changed Dating." *Smithsonian.com*. Smithsonian Media, 29 Jan. 2013. Web. 10 Mar. 2013.

Winter, Jessica. "Kathryn Bigelow: The Art of Darkness." *Time*. Time, 4 Feb. 2013. Web. 22 Mar. 2013.

Online Newspaper Article

Sullivan, Jennifer. "Death-Penalty Ruling Goes to Supreme Court." *Seattletimes .com*. The Seattle Times Company, 5 Feb. 2013. Web. 20 Apr. 2013.

"To Kill an American." Editorial. *New York Times*. New York Times, 5 Feb. 2013. Web. 17 Mar. 2013.

Online Scholarly Project

Stolley, Karl, Allen Brizee, and Joshua M. Paiz. "Is It Plagiarism Yet?" *The OWL at Purdue*. Purdue U Online Writing Lab, 21 Apr. 2010. Web. 12 Feb. 2013.

Book or Part of Book Accessed Online

For a book available online, provide the author, the title, the editor (if any), original publication information, the name of the database or Web site, the medium (*Web*), and the date of access.

Hawthorne, Nathaniel. *The Blithedale Romance.* Boston: Ticknor, 1862. *Google Book Search.* Web. 28 Sept. 2012.

If you are citing only part of an online book, include the title or name of the part directly after the author's name.

Woolf, Virginia. "Kew Gardens." *Monday or Tuesday.* New York: Harcourt, 1921. *Bartleby.com: Great Books Online.* Web. 10 Oct. 2012.

Online Speech, Essay, Poem, or Short Story

Mandela, Nelson. "I Am Prepared to Die." 20 Apr. 1964. *The History Place: Great Speeches Collection.* Web. 12 May 2013.

Online News Services

Rizzo, Patrick. "Postal Service Bids Farewell to Mail Deliveries on Saturday." *NBCNewYork.com.* NBC, 6 Feb. 2013. Web. 7 Feb. 2013.

Basi, Moni. "Richard Blanco Becomes America's First Latino, Openly Gay Inaugural Poet." *CNN.com.* CNN Cable News Network, 9 Jan. 2013. Web. 10 Feb. 2013.

Online Encyclopedia or Other Reference Work

"Hillary Rodham Clinton." *Encyclopaedia Britannica Online.* Encyclopaedia Britannica, 2013. Web. 28 Feb. 2013.

"Discriminate." *Merriam-Webster Online Dictionary.* Merriam-Webster, 2013. Web. 27 Jan. 2013.

Online Artwork, Photographs, Maps, Charts, and Other Images

da Vinci, Leonardo. *Mona Lisa.* 1503-6. Musée du Louvre, Paris. *WebMuseum.* Web. 8 Dec. 2012.

"Houston, Texas." Map. *Google Maps.* Google, 2013. Web. 14 Jan. 2013.

Online Government Publication

United States. Dept. of Treasury. Internal Revenue Service. *Your Rights as a Taxpayer.* GPO, Sept. 2012. Web. 3 Mar. 2013.

Home Page for Academic Department

Dept. of English. Home page. Arizona State U, n.d. Web. 2 Dec. 2012.

Wiki Entry

"C. S. Lewis." *Wikipedia.* Wikimedia Foundation, 5 Feb. 2013. Web. 6 Feb. 2013.

No author is listed for a Wiki entry because the content is written collaboratively.

Blog Posting

Sullivan, Andrew. "The Pro-Life Movement and Gun Control." *The Dish*. 31 Jan. 2013. Web. 13 Feb. 2013.

Online Video Recording

Betbet27. "The Beauty of Mathematics!" *YouTube*. YouTube, 14 Sept. 2010. Web. 10 Mar. 2013.

▶ Additional Common Sources

Television or Radio Broadcast

"Revenge Play." *Enlightened*. Prod. Mike White. Perf. Laura Dern, Luke Wilson, Diane Ladd, Sarah Burns, Mike White, Timm Sharp, Dermot Mulroney, Amy Hill, and Charles Esten. HBO. 20 Jan. 2013. Television.

Sound Recording

Beethoven, Ludwig van. *The Complete Sonatas*. Perf. Richard Goode. Warner, 1993. CD.

Film or Video Recording

Argo. Dir. Ben Affleck. Perf. Affleck, Bryan Cranston, Alan Arkin, and Clea DuVall. 2012. Warner, 2013. DVD.

Work of Visual Art

Botticelli, Sandro. *Birth of Venus*. 1485-86[?] Tempera on panel. Uffizi Gallery, Florence.

If you use a reproduction of a piece of visual art, give the institution and city as well as the complete publication information for the source, omitting the medium of reproduction.

Parks, Gordon. *Muhammad Ali*. 1970. Capital Group Foundation, Atlanta. *Bare Witness: Photographs by Gordon Parks*. Milan: Skira, 2007. Print.

Interview

Spielberg, Steven. Interview. *Time* 5 Nov. 2012: 44. Print.

For interviews that you conduct, provide the name of the person interviewed, the type of interview (personal, telephone, e-mail), and the date.

Proulx, E. Annie. Telephone interview. 27 Jan. 2013.

Cartoon or Comic Strip

Koren, Edward. Cartoon. *New Yorker* 4 Feb. 2013. Print.

Advertisement

Panasonic Lumix G. Advertisement. *Audubon* Jan.-Feb. 2013: 5. Print.

Lecture, Speech, Address, or Reading

Lynch, Jonathan, and James Jennings. "Wind Power from Vermont to the World: Solving Economic, Political, and Technical Challenges." Coll. of Engineering and Mathematical Sciences. U of Vermont, Davis Center, Burlington. 5 Feb. 2013. Lecture.

Letter, Memo, or E-Mail Message

Indicate the medium, using *MS* (handwritten manuscript), *TS* (typescript), or *E-mail.*

Bohjalian, Chris. Letter to the author. 15 Jan. 2013. MS.

CD-Rom or DVD-Rom Publication

Cite CD-ROMs published as a single edition as you would a book, being careful to add *CD-ROM* as the medium.

Shakespeare, William. *Macbeth.* Ed. A. R. Branmuller. New York: Voyager, 1994. CD-ROM.

Some CD-ROMs and DVD-ROMs are updated on a regular basis because they cover publications such as journals, magazines, and newspapers that are themselves published periodically. Start your entry with the author's name, the publication information for the print source, followed by the medium of publication, the title of the database (italicized), the name of the vendor, and the electronic publication date.

James, Caryn. "An Army Family as Strong as Its Weakest Link." *New York Times* 16 Sept. 1994, late ed.: C8. CD-ROM. *New York Times OnDisc.* UMI-ProQuest, 1994.

Digital File

A number of different types of work—a book, typescript, photograph, or sound recording—can be available as a digital file. It is important that you record the format of the digital file in the space reserved for publication medium (*JPEG file, PDF file,* Microsoft Word *file, MP3 file,* to name a few).

Dengle, Isabella. *Eben Peck Cabin.* 1891. Wisconsin Hist. Soc., Madison. JPEG file.

Demirjian, Alyssa. "Re: Visuals for Chapter Openers." Message to the author. 5 Feb. 2013. E-mail.

Federman, Sarah. "International Relations and the Language of Conflict." 2013. *Microsoft Word* file.

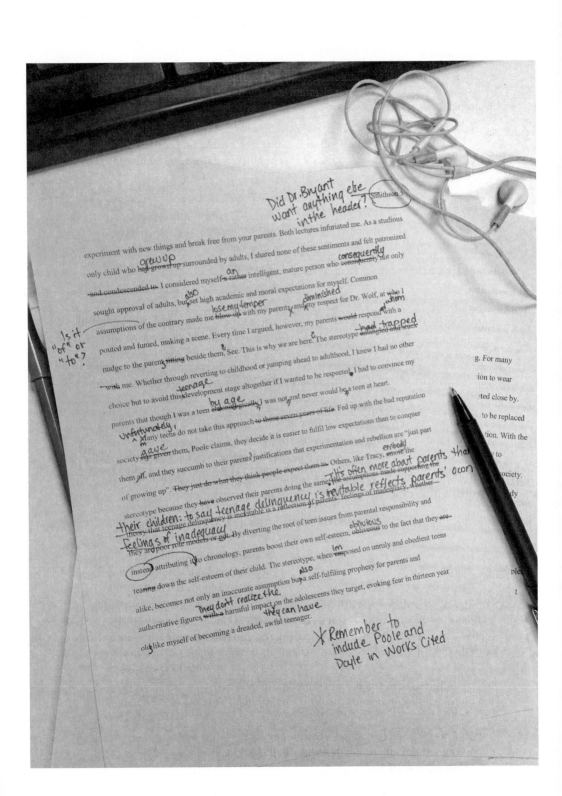

experiment with new things and break free from your parents. Both lectures infuriated me. As a studious

only child who ~~had grown up~~ [grew up] surrounded by adults, I shared none of these sentiments and felt patronized

~~and condescended to.~~ I considered myself ~~a rather~~ [an] intelligent, mature person who ~~consequently~~ [consequently] not only

sought approval of adults, but [also] set high academic and moral expectations for myself. Common

assumptions of the contrary made me ~~blow up~~ [lose my temper] with my parents and my respect for Dr. Wolf, at ~~who I~~ [whom] [diminished]

pouted and fumed, making a scene. Every time I argued, however, my parents ~~would~~ respond with a [had trapped] ~~entangled and stuck~~

nudge to the parent ~~sitting~~ beside them, See. This is why we are here. The stereotype ~~entangled and stuck~~

~~with me.~~ Whether through reverting to childhood or jumping ahead to adulthood, I knew I had no other

choice but to avoid this development stage altogether if I wanted to be respected. I had to convince my [teenage]

parents that though I was a teen ~~chronologically~~ [by age], I was not and never would be a teen at heart.

[Unfortunately,] ^Many teens do not take this approach ~~to those seven years of life.~~ Fed up with the bad reputation

society ~~has~~ [have] given them, Poole claims, they decide it is easier to fulfil low expectations than to conquer

them off, and they succumb to their parents' justifications that experimentation and rebellion are "just part [embody]

of growing up". ~~They just do what they think people expect them to.~~ Others, like Tracy, ~~emote the~~ [It's often more about parents that ~~the assumptions made supporting the~~] [inevitable reflects parents' own]

stereotype because they ~~have~~ observed their parents doing the same. ~~The assumptions made supporting the~~ feelings of inadequacy, whether

~~theory that teenage delinquency is inevitable is a reflection of parents'~~ [their children: to say teenage delinquency is inevitable is a reflection of parents'] [feelings of inadequacy]

~~They are poor role models or not.~~ By diverting the root of teen issues from parental responsibility and [oblivious]

(instead) attributing it to chronology, parents boost their own self-esteem, ~~oblivious~~ to the fact that they ~~are~~

tearing down the self-esteem of their child. The stereotype, when [im]posed on unruly and obedient teens

alike, becomes not only an inaccurate assumption but [also] a self-fulfiling prophesy for parents and

authoritative figures, ~~with a~~ harmful impact on the adolescents they target, evoking fear in thirteen year [They don't realize the] [they can have]

old like myself of becoming a dreaded, awful teenager.

✶ Remember to include Poole and Doyle in Works Cited

"Is it "of" or "to"?"

g. For many
ion to wear
ted close by.
to be replaced
tion. With the
... to
... society.
... dy
ple...
3

Editing for Grammar, Punctuation, and Sentence Style

Once you have revised your essay and you are confident that you have said what you wanted to say, you are ready to begin editing your essay. It's at the editing stage of the writing process that you identify and correct errors in grammar, punctuation, and sentence style. You don't want a series of small errors to detract from your paper: Such errors can cause confusion in some cases, and they can also cause readers to have second thoughts about your credibility as an author.

This chapter addresses twelve common writing problems that instructors from around the country told us trouble their students most. For more guidance with these or other editing concerns, be sure to refer to a writer's handbook or ask your instructor for help.

1 Run-ons: Fused Sentences and Comma Splices

Writers can become so absorbed in getting their ideas down on paper that they sometimes incorrectly combine two independent clauses — word groups that could stand on their own as complete sentences — incorrectly, creating a *run-on sentence*. A run-on sentence fails to show where one thought ends and another begins, and it can confuse readers. There are two types of run-on sentences: the fused sentence and the comma splice.

A *fused sentence* occurs when a writer joins two independent clauses with no punctuation and no coordinating conjunction.

> **fused** The delegates at the state political convention could not decide on a
> **sentence** leader they were beginning to show their frustration.

A *comma splice* occurs when a writer uses only a comma to join two or more independent clauses.

comma splice The delegates at the state political convention could not decide on a
leader, they were beginning to show their frustration.

There are five ways to fix run-on sentences.

1. **Create two separate sentences with a period.**

    edited The delegates at the state political convention could not decide on a
    . They
    leader ~~they~~ were beginning to show their frustration.

2. **Use a comma and a coordinating conjunction to join the two sentences.**

    edited The delegates at the state political convention could not decide on a
    , and
    leader they were beginning to show their frustration.

3. **Use a semicolon to separate the two clauses.**

    edited The delegates at the state political convention could not decide on a
    ;
    leader they were beginning to show their frustration.

4. **Use a semicolon followed by a transitional word or expression and a comma to join the two clauses.**

    edited The delegates at the state political convention could not decide on a
    ; consequently,
    leader they were beginning to show their frustration.

5. **Subordinate one clause to the other, using a subordinate conjunction or a relative pronoun.**

    When the
    edited ~~The~~ delegates at the state political convention could not decide on a
    leader, they were beginning to show their frustration.

    , who were beginning to show their frustration,
    edited The delegates at the state political convention could not decide on a
    leader. ~~they were beginning to show their frustration.~~

2 Sentence Fragments

A *sentence fragment* is a part of a sentence presented as if it were a complete sentence. Even if a word group begins with a capital letter and ends with a period, a question mark, or an exclamation point, it is not a sentence unless it has a subject (the person, place, or thing the sentence is about) and a verb (a word that tells what the subject does) and expresses a complete thought.

> **sentence fragment**   My music group decided to study the early works of Mozart. *The child prodigy from Austria.*

Word groups that do not express complete thoughts are often free-standing subordinate clauses beginning with a subordinating conjunction such as *although, because, since, so, that,* or *unless.*

> **sentence fragment**   The company president met with the management team every single week. *So that problems were rarely ignored.*

You can correct sentence fragments in one of two ways.

1. **Integrate the fragment into a nearby sentence.**

> **edited**   My music group decided to study the early works of Mozart, ~~The~~ the child prodigy from Austria.

> **edited**   The company president met with the management team every single week, ~~So~~ so that problems were rarely ignored.

2. **Develop the fragment into a complete sentence by adding a subject or a verb.**

> **edited**   My music group decided to study the early works of Mozart. The child prodigy was from Austria.

> **edited**   The company president met with the management team every single week. Problems ~~So that problems~~ were rarely ignored.

Sentence fragments are not always wrong. In fact, if used deliberately, a sentence fragment can add useful stylistic emphasis. In narratives, deliberate sentence fragments are most commonly used in dialogue and in descriptive passages that set a mood or tone. In the following passage taken from "Not Close Enough for Comfort" (pages 103–05), David P. Bardeen uses fragments to convey the awkwardness of the luncheon meeting he had with his brother Will:

> I asked him about his recent trip. He asked me about work. Short questions. One-word answers. Then an awkward pause.

3 Comma Faults

Commas help communicate meaning by eliminating possible misreadings. Consider this sentence:

> After visiting William Alan Lee went to French class.

Depending upon where you put the comma, it could be Lee, Alan Lee, or William Alan Lee who goes to French class.

> edited   After visiting William Alan, Lee went to French class.

> edited   After visiting William, Alan Lee went to French class.

> edited   After visiting, William Alan Lee went to French class.

The comma, of all the marks of punctuation, has the greatest variety of uses, which can make its proper use seem difficult. It might help to think of the comma's role this way: In every case the comma functions in one of two basic ways—to *separate* or to *enclose* elements in a sentence. By learning a few basic rules based on these two functions, you will be able to identify and correct common comma errors.

1. **Use a comma to separate two independent clauses joined by a coordinating conjunction.**

   > incorrect   Tolstoy wrote many popular short stories but he is perhaps best known for his novels.

   > edited   Tolstoy wrote many popular short stories, but he is perhaps best known for his novels.

2. **Use a comma to separate an introductory phrase or clause from the main clause of a sentence.**

   > incorrect   In his book *Life on the Mississippi* Mark Twain describes his days as a riverboat pilot.

   > edited   In his book *Life on the Mississippi*, Mark Twain describes his days as a riverboat pilot.

   > incorrect   When the former Soviet Union collapsed residents of Moscow had to struggle just to survive.

   > edited   When the former Soviet Union collapsed, residents of Moscow had to struggle just to survive.

3. **Use commas to enclose nonrestrictive elements.** When an adjective phrase or clause adds information that is essential to the meaning of a sentence, it is said to be *restrictive* and should not be set off with commas.

> The woman wearing the beige linen suit works with Homeland Security.

The adjective phrase "wearing the beige linen suit" is essential and thus should not be set off with commas; without this information, we have no way of identifying which woman works with Homeland Security.

When an adjective phrase or clause does not add information that is essential to the meaning of the sentence, it is said to be *nonrestrictive* and should be enclosed with commas.

> incorrect Utopian literature which was popular during the late nineteenth century seems to emerge at times of economic and political unrest.

> edited Utopian literature͵which was popular during the late nineteenth century͵seems to emerge at times of economic and political unrest.

4. **Use commas to separate items in a series.**

> incorrect The three staples of the diet in Thailand are rice fish and fruit.

> edited The three staples of the diet in Thailand are rice͵fish͵and fruit.

4 Subject-Verb Agreement

Subjects and verbs must agree in number — that is, a singular subject (one person, place, or thing) must take a singular verb, and a plural subject (more than one person, place, or thing) must take a plural verb. While most native speakers of English use proper subject-verb agreement in their writing without thinking about it, some sentence constructions can be troublesome to native and non-native speakers alike.

INTERVENING PREPOSITIONAL PHRASES

When the relationship between the subject and the verb in a sentence is not clear, the culprit is usually an intervening prepositional phrase (a phrase that begins with a preposition such as *on, of, in, at,* or *between*). To make sure the subject agrees with its verb in a sentence with an intervening prepositional phrase, mentally cross out the phrase (*of the term* in the following example) to isolate the subject and the verb and determine if they agree.

incorrect The first one hundred days of the term has passed quickly.

edited The first one hundred days of the term ~~has~~ passed quickly. *(have)*

COMPOUND SUBJECTS

Writers often have difficulty with subject-verb agreement in sentences with compound subjects (two or more subjects joined together with the word *and*). As a general rule, compound subjects take plural verbs.

incorrect My iPod, computer, and television was stolen.

edited My iPod, computer, and television ~~was~~ stolen. *(were)*

However, in sentences with subjects joined by *either . . . or, neither . . . nor,* or *not only . . . but also,* the verb must agree with the subject closest to it.

incorrect Neither the students nor the professor are satisfied with the lab equipment.

edited Neither the students nor the professor ~~are~~ satisfied with the lab *(is)*

equipment.

5 Unclear Pronoun References

The noun to which a pronoun refers is called its *antecedent* or *referent.* Be sure to place a pronoun as close to its antecedent as possible so that the relationship between them is clear. The more words that intervene between the antecedent and the pronoun, the more chance there is for confusion. When the relationship between a pronoun and its antecedent is unclear, the sentence becomes inaccurate or ambiguous. While editing your writing, look for and correct ambiguous, vague, or implied pronoun references.

AMBIGUOUS REFERENCES

Make sure all your pronouns clearly refer to specific antecedents. If a pronoun can refer to more than one antecedent, the sentence is ambiguous.

ambiguous Adler sought to convince the reader to mark up *his* book.

In this sentence, the antecedent of the pronoun *his* could be either *Adler* or *reader.* Does Adler want his particular book marked up, or does he want the reader to mark up his or her own book? To make an ambiguous antecedent clear, either repeat the correct antecedent or rewrite the sentence.

edited Adler sought to convince the reader to mark up ~~his~~ book.
Adler's

edited Adler sought to convince the reader to mark up ~~his~~ book.
his or her

VAGUE REFERENCES

Whenever you use *it*, *they*, *you*, *this*, *that*, or *which* to refer to a general idea in a preceding clause or sentence, be sure that the connection between the pronoun and the general idea is clear. When these pronouns lack a specific antecedent, you give readers an impression of vagueness and carelessness. To correct the problem, either substitute a noun for the pronoun or provide an antecedent to which the pronoun can clearly refer.

vague The tornadoes damaged many of the homes in the area, but it has not yet been determined.

edited The tornadoes damaged many of the homes in the area, but it has not
the extent of the damage

yet been determined.

vague In the book, they wrote that Samantha had an addictive personality.

edited In the book, ~~they wrote that~~ Samantha had an addictive personality.

Whenever the connection between the general idea and the pronoun is simple and clear, no confusion results. Consider the following example:

> The stock market rose for a third consecutive week, and this lifted most investors' spirits.

IMPLIED REFERENCES

Make every pronoun refer to a stated, not an implied, antecedent. Every time you use a pronoun in a sentence, you should be able to identify its noun equivalent. If you cannot, use a noun instead.

implied After all of the editing and formatting, it was finished.

edited After all of the editing and formatting, it was finished.
the research report

Sometimes a modifier or possessive that implies a noun is mistaken for an antecedent.

implied In G. Anthony Gorry's "Steal This MP3 File: What Is Theft?," he shows how technology might be shaping the attitudes of today's youth.

edited In ~~G. Anthony Gorry's~~ "Steal This MP3 File: What Is Theft?," he shows
G. Anthony Gorry

how technology might be shaping the attitudes of today's youth.

6 Pronoun-Antecedent Agreement

Personal pronouns must agree with their antecedents in *person*, *number*, and *gender*.

AGREEMENT IN PERSON

There are three types of personal pronouns: first person (*I* and *we*), second person (*you*), and third person (*he*, *she*, *it*, and *they*). To agree in person, first-person pronouns must refer to first-person antecedents, second-person pronouns to second-person antecedents, and third-person pronouns to third-person antecedents.

incorrect A scientist should consider all the data carefully before you draw a conclusion.

edited A scientist should consider all the data carefully before

he or she draws
~~you draw~~ a conclusion.

AGREEMENT IN NUMBER

To agree in number, a singular pronoun must refer to a singular antecedent, and a plural pronoun must refer to a plural antecedent. When two or more antecedents are joined by the word *and*, the pronoun must be plural.

incorrect Karen, Rachel, and Sofia took her electives in history.

their
edited Karen, Rachel, and Sofia took ~~her~~ electives in history.

When the subject of a sentence is an indefinite pronoun such as *everyone*, *each*, *everybody*, *anyone*, *anybody*, *everything*, *either*, *one*, *neither*, *someone*, or *something*, use a singular pronoun to refer to it, or recast the sentence to eliminate the agreement problem.

incorrect Each of the women submitted their résumé.

her
edited Each of the women submitted ~~their~~ résumé.

Both   **résumés**
edited ~~Each~~ of the women submitted their ~~résumé~~.

If a collective noun (*army, community, team, herd, committee, association*) is understood as a unit, it takes a singular pronoun; if it is understood in terms of its individual members, it takes a plural pronoun.

as a unit The class presented its annual spring musical.

as individual The class agreed to pay for their own art supplies.
members

AGREEMENT IN GENDER

Traditionally, a masculine, singular pronoun has been used for indefinite antecedents (such as *anyone, someone,* and *everyone*) and to refer to generic antecedents (such as *employee, student, athlete, secretary, doctor,* and *computer specialist*). But *anyone* can be female or male, and women are employees (or students, athletes, secretaries, doctors, and computer specialists), too. The use of masculine pronouns to refer to both females and males is considered sexist; that is, such usage leaves out women as a segment of society or diminishes their presence. Instead, use *he or she, his or her,* or, in an extended piece of writing, alternate in a balanced way the use of *he* and *she* throughout. Sometimes the best solution is to rewrite the sentence to put it in the plural or to avoid the problem altogether.

sexist If any student wants to attend the opening performance of *King Lear,* he will have to purchase a ticket by Wednesday.

edited If any student wants to attend the opening performance of *King Lear,*
       he or she
      ~~he~~ will have to purchase a ticket by Wednesday.

          students
edited If any ~~student~~ wants to attend the opening performance of *King Lear,*
      they   **tickets**
      ~~he~~ will have to purchase ~~a ticket~~ by Wednesday.

          All tickets for
edited ~~If any student wants to attend~~ the opening performance of *King Lear,*
      must be purchased
      ~~he will have to purchase a ticket~~ by Wednesday.

7 Dangling and Misplaced Modifiers

A *modifier* is a word or group of words that describes or gives additional information about other words in a sentence. The words, phrases, and clauses that function as modifiers in a sentence can usually be moved around freely, so place them carefully to avoid unintentionally confusing—or amusing—your reader. As a rule, place modifiers as close as possible to the words you want to modify. Two common problems arise with modifiers: the misplaced modifier and the dangling modifier.

MISPLACED MODIFIERS

A *misplaced modifier* unintentionally modifies the wrong word in a sentence because it is placed incorrectly.

misplaced The waiter brought a steak to the man covered with onions.

covered with onions
edited The waiter brought a steak to the man ~~covered with onions~~.

DANGLING MODIFIERS

A *dangling modifier* usually appears at the beginning of a sentence and does not logically relate to the main clause of the sentence. The dangling modifier wants to modify a word—often an unstated subject—that does not appear in the sentence. To eliminate a dangling modifier, give the dangling phrase a subject.

dangling Staring into the distance, large rain clouds form.

Jon saw
edited Staring into the distance, large rain clouds form.

dangling Walking on the ceiling, he noticed a beautiful luna moth.

He   *walking on the ceiling*
edited ~~Walking on the ceiling, he~~ noticed a beautiful luna moth.

8 Faulty Parallelism

Parallelism is the repetition of word order or grammatical form either within a single sentence or in several sentences that develop the same central idea. As a rhetorical device, parallel structure can aid coherence and add emphasis. Franklin Roosevelt's famous Depression-era statement "I see one-third of a nation *ill-housed, ill-clad*, and *ill-nourished*" illustrates effective parallelism. Use parallel grammatical structures to emphasize the similarities and differences between the items being compared. Look for opportunities to use parallel constructions with paired items or items in a series, paired items using correlative conjunctions, and comparisons using *than* or *as*.

PAIRED ITEMS OR ITEMS IN A SERIES

parallel structures can be used to balance a word with a word, a phrase with a phrase, or a clause with a clause whenever you use paired items or items in a series—as in the Roosevelt example above.

1. **Balance a word with a word.**

    faulty Like the hunter, the photographer has to understand the animal's patterns, characteristics, and where it lives.

    edited Like the hunter, the photographer has to understand the animal's

    habitat
    patterns, characteristics, and ~~where it lives~~.

2. Balance a phrase with a phrase.

faulty   The hunter carries a handgun and two rifles, different kinds of
ammunition, and a variety of sights and telescopes to increase his
chances of success.

several types of guns

edited   The hunter carries ~~a handgun and two rifles~~, different kinds of

ammunition, and a variety of sights and telescopes to increase his

chances of success.

3. Balance a clause with a clause.

faulty   Shooting is highly aggressive, photography is passive; shooting
eliminates forever, photography preserves.

edited   Shooting is ~~highly~~ aggressive, photography is passive; shooting

eliminates ~~forever~~, photography preserves.

PAIRED ITEMS USING CORRELATIVE CONJUNCTIONS

When linking paired items with a correlative conjunction (*either/or,
neither/nor, not only/but also, both/and, whether/or*) in a sentence, make
sure that the elements being connected are parallel in form. Delete any unnecessary or repeated words.

incorrect   The lecture was both enjoyable and it was a form of education.

educational

edited   The lecture was both enjoyable and ~~it was a form of education~~.

COMPARISONS USING *THAN* OR *AS*

make sure that the elements of the comparison are parallel in form. Delete
any unnecessary or repeated words.

incorrect   It would be better to study now than waiting until the night before
the exam.

to wait

edited   It would be better to study now than ~~waiting~~ until the night before

the exam.

9 Weak Nouns and Verbs

The essence of a sentence is its subject and its verb. The subject—usually a
noun or pronoun—identifies who or what the sentence is about, and the
verb captures the subject's action or state of being. Sentences often lose their

vitality and liveliness when the subject and the verb are lost in weak language or buried.

WEAK NOUNS

Always opt for specific nouns when you can; they make your writing more visual. While general words like *people, animal,* or *dessert* name groups or classes of objects, qualities, or actions, specific words like *Samantha, camel,* and *pecan pie* appeal to readers more because they name individual objects, qualities, or actions within a group. Think about it—don't you prefer reading about specifics rather than generalities?

> weak noun   The flowers stretched toward the bright light of the sun.
>
> edited   The ~~flowers~~ tulips stretched toward the bright light of the sun.

STRONG VERBS

Strong verbs energize your writing by giving it a sense of action. Verbs like *gallop, scramble, snicker, tweak, fling, exhaust, smash, tear, smear, wrangle,* and *flog* provide readers with a vivid picture of specific actions. As you reread what you have written, be on the lookout for weak verbs like *is, are, have, deal with, make, give, do, use, get, add, become, go, appear,* and *seem.* When you encounter one of these verbs or others like them, seize the opportunity to substitute a strong action verb for a weak one.

> weak verb   Local Boys and Girls Clubs in America assist in the promotion of self-esteem, individual achievement, and teamwork.
>
> edited   Local Boys and Girls Clubs in America ~~assist in the promotion of~~ promote self-esteem, individual achievement, and teamwork.

While editing your essay, look for opportunities to replace weak nouns and verbs with strong nouns and action verbs. The more specific and strong you make your nouns and verbs, the more lively, descriptive, and concise your writing will be.

When you have difficulty thinking of strong, specific nouns and verbs, reach for a dictionary or a thesaurus—but only if you are sure you can discern the best word for your purpose. Thesauruses are available free online and in inexpensive paperback editions; most word processing programs include a thesaurus as well.

10 Shifts in Verb Tense, Mood, and Voice

SHIFTS IN TENSE

A verb's tense indicates when an action takes place—sometime in the past, right now, or in the future. Using verb tense correctly helps your readers understand time changes in your writing. Shifts in tense—using different verb tenses within a sentence without a logical reason—confuse readers. Unnecessary shifts in verb tense are especially noticeable in narration and process analysis writing, which are sequence and time oriented. Generally, you should write in the present or past tense and maintain that tense throughout your sentence.

> incorrect   The painter studied the scene and pulls a fan brush decisively from
>   her cup.
>
>   *pulled*
> edited   The painter studied the scene and ~~pulls~~ a fan brush decisively from
>
>   her cup.

SHIFTS IN MOOD

Verbs in English have three moods: *indicative*, *imperative*, and *subjunctive*. Problems with inconsistency usually occur with the imperative mood.

> incorrect   In learning a second language, arm yourself with basic vocabulary,
>   and it is also important to practice speaking aloud daily.
>
> edited   In learning a second language, arm yourself with basic vocabulary,
>
>   and ~~it is also important to~~ practice speaking aloud daily.

SHIFTS IN VOICE

Shifts in voice—from active voice to passive voice—usually go hand in hand with inconsistencies in the subject of a sentence.

> incorrect   The archeologists could see the effects of vandalism as the Mayan
>   tomb was entered.
>
>   *they entered*
> edited   The archeologists could see the effects of vandalism as the Mayan
>
>   tomb ~~was entered~~.

11 Wordiness

Wordiness occurs in a sentence that contains words that do not contribute to the sentence's meaning. Wordiness can be eliminated by (1) using the active voice, (2) avoiding "there is" and "it is," (3) eliminating redundancies, (4) deleting empty words and phrases, and (5) simplifying inflated expressions.

1. **Use the active voice rather than the passive voice.** The active voice emphasizes the doer of an action rather than the receiver of an action. Not only is the active voice more concise than the passive voice, it is a much more vigorous form of expression.

    passive *The inhabitants of Londonderry were overwhelmed* by the burgeoning rodent population.

    active *The burgeoning rodent population overwhelmed* the inhabitants of Londonderry.

In the active sentence, *The burgeoning rodent population* is made the subject of the sentence and is moved to the beginning of the sentence—a position of importance—while the verb *overwhelmed* is made an active verb.

2. **Avoid "There is" and "It is."** "There is" and "It is" are expletives—words or phrases that do not contribute any meaning but are added only to fill out a sentence. They may be necessary with references to time and weather, but they should be avoided in other circumstances.

    wordy There were many acts of heroism following the earthquake.

              Many   followed
    edited ~~There were many~~ acts of heroism ~~following~~ the earthquake.

Notice how the edited sentence eliminates the expletive and reveals a specific subject—*acts*—and an action verb—*followed*.

3. **Eliminate redundancies.** Unnecessary repetition often creeps into our writing and should be eliminated. For example, how often have you written expressions such as *large in size, completely filled, academic scholar,* or *I thought in my mind*? Edit such expressions by deleting the unnecessary words or using synonyms.

Sometimes our intent is to add emphasis, but the net effect is extra words that contribute little or nothing to a sentence's meaning.

    redundant A big huge cloud was advancing on the crowded stadium.

    edited A ~~big~~ huge cloud was advancing on the crowded stadium.

    redundant After studying all night, he knew the basic and fundamental principles of geometry.

    edited After studying all night, he knew the basic ~~and fundamental~~ principles of geometry.

4. **Delete empty words and phrases.** Look for words and phrases we use every day that carry no meaning—words that should be eliminated from your writing during the editing process.

> **empty** One commentator believes that America is for all intents and purposes a materialistic society.

> **edited** One commentator believes that America is ~~for all intents and purposes~~ a materialistic society.

Following are examples of some other words and expressions that most often can be eliminated.

basically	surely	it seems to me	extremely
essentially	truly	kind of/sort of	severely
generally	really	tend to	
very	I think/I feel/I believe	quite	

5. **Simplify inflated expressions.** Sometimes we use expressions we think sound authoritative in hopes of seeming knowledgable. We write *at this point in time* (instead of *now*) or *in the event that* (instead of *if*). However, it is best to write directly and forcefully and to use clear language. Edit inflated or pompous language to its core meaning.

> **inflated** The law office hired two people who have a complete knowledge of environmental policy.

> **edited** The law office hired two people who ~~have a complete knowledge of~~ ^are^ environmental policy. ^experts.^

> **inflated** The president was late on account of the fact that her helicopter would not start.

> **edited** The president was late ~~on account of the fact that~~ ^because^ her helicopter would not start.

12 Sentence Variety

While editing your essays, you can add interest and readability to your writing with more sentence variety. You should, however, seek variety in sentence structure not as an end in itself but as a more accurate means of reflecting your thoughts and giving emphasis where emphasis is needed. Look for opportunities to achieve sentence variety by combining short choppy sentences, varying sentence openings, and reducing the number of compound sentences.

SHORT CHOPPY SENTENCES

To make your writing more interesting, use one of the following five methods to combine short choppy sentences into one longer sentence.

1. **Use subordinating and coordinating conjunctions to relate and connect ideas.** The coordinating conjunctions *and*, *but*, *or*, *nor*, *for*, *so*, and *yet* can be used to connect two or more simple sentences. A subordinating conjunction, on the other hand, introduces a subordinate clause and connects it to a main clause. Common subordinating conjunctions include:

after	before	so	when
although	even if	than	where
as	if	that	whereas
as if	in order that	though	wherever
as though	rather than	unless	whether
because	since	until	while

short and choppy Short words are as good as long ones. Short old words—like *sun* and *grass* and *home*—are best of all.

                                             , and short

combined Short words are as good as long ones ~~short~~ old words—like *sun* and grass and *home*—are best of all.

— RICHARD LEDERER,
"The Case for Short Words," page 516

2. **Use modifiers effectively.** Instead of writing a separate descriptive sentence, combine an adjective modifier to convey a more graphic picture in a single sentence.

short and choppy The people who breed German shepherds in Appleton, Wisconsin, are also farmers. And they are wonderful farmers.

combined The people who breed German shepherds in Appleton, Wisconsin,
            wonderful
are also farmers. ~~And they are wonderful farmers.~~

3. **Use a semicolon or colon to link closely related ideas.**

short and choppy Pollution from carbon emissions remains a serious environmental problem. In some respects it is the most serious problem.

combined Pollution from carbon emissions remains a serious environmental
           ; in
problem.~~In~~ some respects it is the most serious problem.

4. **Use parallel constructions.** Parallel constructions use repeated word order or repeated grammatical form to highlight and develop a central idea. As a rhetorical device, parallelism can aid coherence and add emphasis.

short and choppy
The school busing issue is not about comfort. It concerns fairness.

combined
but about
The school busing issue is not about comfort. ~~It concerns~~ fairness.

SENTENCE OPENINGS

More than half of all sentences in English begin with the subject of the sentence followed by the verb and any objects. The following sentences all illustrate this basic pattern:

Martha plays the saxophone.

The president vetoed the tax bill before leaving Washington for the holidays.

The upcoming lecture series will formally launch the fund-raising campaign for a new civic center.

If all the sentences in a particular passage in your essay begin this way, the effect on your readers is monotony. With a little practice, you will discover just how flexible the English language is. Consider the different ways in which one sentence can be rewritten so as to vary its beginning and add interest.

original
Candidates debated the issue of military service for women in the auditorium and did not know that a demonstration was going on outside.

varied openings
Debating the issue of military service for women, the candidates in the auditorium did not know that a demonstration was going on outside.

In the auditorium, the candidates debated the issue of military service for women, not knowing that a demonstration was going on outside.

As they debated the issue of military service for women, the candidates in the auditorium did not know that a demonstration was going on outside.

Another way of changing the usual subject-verb-object order of sentences is to invert—or reverse—the normal order. Do not, however, sacrifice proper emphasis to gain variety.

USUAL ORDER	**INVERTED ORDER**
The crowd stormed out.	Out stormed the crowd.
The enemy would never accept that.	That the enemy would never accept.
They could be friendly and civil.	Friendly and civil they could be.

COMPOUND SENTENCES

Like a series of short, simple sentences, too many compound sentences — two or more sentences joined by coordinating conjunctions — give the impression of haste and thoughtlessness. As you edit your paper, watch for the word *and* used as a coordinating conjunction. If you discover that you have overused *and*, try one of the following four methods to remedy the situation, giving important ideas more emphasis and making it easier for your reader to follow your thought.

1. **Change a compound sentence into a simple sentence with a modifier or an appositive.**

   compound   Richard Lederer is a linguist, and he is humorous, and he has a weekly

   radio program about language.

   ␣␣␣␣␣␣␣␣␣␣␣␣␣␣␣␣␣␣␣␣␣␣␣␣ , a humorous

   appositive   Richard Lederer ~~is a~~ linguist, ~~and he is humorous, and he~~ has a

   weekly radio program about language.

2. **Change a compound sentence into a simple sentence with a compound predicate.**

   compound   Martin Luther King Jr. chastises America for not honoring its
   obligations to people of color, and he dreams of a day when
   racism will no longer exist.

   compound
   predicate   Martin Luther King Jr. chastises America for not honoring its

   obligations to people of color, and ~~he~~ dreams of a day when

   racism will no longer exist.

3. **Change a compound sentence into a simple sentence with a phrase or phrases.**

compound   Women have a number of options in the military, and the responsibilities are significant.

with significant responsibilities

with a phrase   Women have a number of options in the military, ~~and the responsibilities are significant~~.

4. **Change a compound sentence into a complex sentence.**

compound   Farmers are using new technologies, and agriculture is becoming completely industrialized.

Because farmers

complex   ~~Farmers~~ are using new technologies, ~~and~~ agriculture is becoming completely industrialized.

Thematic Writing Assignments

GREAT WRITING BEGINS WITH THE IDEAS WE FORM AS WE READ.
When we read, we follow the logic of people with different backgrounds and beliefs. We reach conclusions that challenge us to reflect on the world and our experiences in new ways. We spend time wandering through someone else's mind, discovering insights we love and outlooks that strike us as odd — sometimes at the same time. Just as visiting a new place forms lasting memories, reading shapes our perception. When we sit back down to write, we discover that we have important things to say. Things that we *must* say.

This appendix helps you practice the leap from reading to writing using visuals, readings, and media that are already part of the book. Each cross-chapter cluster reveals multiple aspects of engaging topics and shows how different writing strategies and a range of ideas work together to bring a single subject to life. Specific assignments help you articulate your reaction and enter into the conversation.

Whether your instructor uses these thematic writing assignments in class discussion, for weekly assignments, or as a reference for your final paper, this appendix is your concrete guide for practicing reading as a writer.

Note: For a complete, alternative thematic table of contents, see pages xxxv–xlviii.

Diversity and the Immigration Experience

e bedfordstmartins.com/subjectandstrategy

Why might an essay on immigration focus on individuals instead of a whole society? What are the pros and cons of the micro and the macro perspectives? Are they mutually exclusive? Write a brief reflection detailing the ways in which each author used his or her scope to further their message. Conclude with how they'd likely respond to one another. How might Lee and Mukherjee react to Jonas and Jamieson? If all four were presented with the infographic on the changing American dream, what might they say?

Education

Maya Angelou, *Sister Flowers* 164

Russell Baker, *Discovering the Power of My Words* 50

Thomas L. Friedman, *My Favorite Teacher* 11

Megan Garber, *The Curator's Guide to the Galaxy* e

Tara E. Ketch, *Kids, You Can't Read That Book!* (student essay) 618

Teresa Sullivan, *Four Kinds of Value in Higher Education* 598

Write a brief essay identifying and defining three to five principles that you believe are the foundation of a strong education system. Consider: What environments were most conducive to your personal learning? What other factors contributed to the success of those experiences? Did you have an instructor or mentor, or did you teach yourself? Should students always have complete access to information, or are there advantages to limiting content? How important is it for students to enjoy what they learn? How does Garber's discussion of how to explore information on the Web suggest ways that students might learn in the future?

Gender Stereotypes

David P. Bardeen, *Not Close Enough for Comfort* 103

Lt. Dan Choi, *Don't Tell, Martha!* e

Jon Katz, *How Boys Become Men* 451

Deborah M. Roffman, *What Does "Boys Will Be Boys" Really Mean?* 416

Rosalind Wiseman, *The Queen Bee and Her Court* 349

Write an essay on your experience with the gendered, cultural expectations discussed by Katz, Roffman, and Wiseman. Do such expectations help people find themselves, or are they too quick to gloss over our human vulnerabilities? Is it harder for men or for women? Do you feel pressure to conform to gender stereotypes, or have you ever pressured others to do so? How might these stereotypes have contributed to Bardeen and Choi's hesitations?

Humans and Nature

Write a journal entry in which you explore how technology, urbanization, and modern life shape the way that humans experience nature. Compare White's inspired time in rural Maine with the suburbia described by Shaw. What has happened to our wild spaces as depicted by Huang and Snider? What will it be like in fifty years? In what ways are you inspired or disillusioned knowing that the scientific community still grapples with great natural mysteries, like the genetic makeup of butterflies? Other topics are much better understood, such as why the sky is blue. What drives scientists to learn more about nature? What should be our relationship to nature?

Industrial Food, Our Eating Habits, and Health

Describe how Kersch, Pollan, Bittman, or Eighner might react to your consumption habits. To what extent do health or production ethics affect your choices? Do Kersch and Bittman agree with one another about what should motivate our eating behavior? How might Pollan respond? Both Eighner and the process analysis image prioritize reuse. To what extent do you recycle or compost? What other strategies reduce food waste?

Inequality, Economics, and Society

Slavery Footprint, *How Many Slaves Work for You?* 🄴

Vocativ, *Tower of David* 🄴

Jeannette Walls, *A Woman on the Street* 138

Poverty is part of a chain of consumption, habits, and economic forces often outside of an individual's control. Write an essay in which you define poverty and economic inequality. To what extent are your answers influenced by the country in which you were born? Have you ever participated in philanthropy or volunteered to assist the disadvantaged? Do you feel any responsibility to do so? In what ways do these selections prompt you to rethink your purchasing habits?

Innovation and Ideas

Jonathan Beer, *Writing Process Animation* 🄴

Walter Isaacson, *The Genius of Jobs* 427

Anne Lamott, *Shitty First Drafts* 55

Steven Pinker, *In Defense of Dangerous Ideas* 529

Kal Raustiala and Chris Sprigman, *In Praise of Copycats* 195

Write a reflection comparing each author's thoughts about how we develop new ideas. How might Isaacson respond to Raustiala and Sprigman's thesis? If Pinker, Lamott, and Beer worked together to develop concrete writing-process advice, what might the process look like? Conclude with how you might apply their approaches to your own writing. Which parts of their advice match the way you like to work? Are there new approaches you'd like to try?

Justice, Ethics, and Crime

Shoshanna Lew, *How (Not) to Be Selected for Jury Duty* (student essay) 233

Elisa Mala, *Crime Family* 98

Ian Steadman, *How Sports Would Be Better with Doping* 548

Andrew Vachss, *The Difference between "Sick" and "Evil"* 312

Barry Winston, *Stranger Than True* 109

World Wildlife Foundation, *I Am Not a Souvenir* (advertisement) 488

Write an editorial on why it is difficult to form absolute judgments about criminal situations. Consider the following: What complexities must we address in a thoughtful discussion of a crime? How do we reconcile the systematic process described by Lew with the emotional aspects described by Mala or Winston? What might Vachss or Winston—both lawyers—say about the importance of the law? The WWF ad suggests that there are larger economic forces that contribute to criminal activity, and Steadman raises questions of legal authority and legal blame. To what extent do you believe that the current legal system is fair and just?

Power of Language

Lokesh Dhakar, *Types of Coffee Drinks* (infographic)   386

Jake Jamieson, *The English-Only Movement: Can America Proscribe Langugae with a Clear Conscience?*   700

Maria Konnikova, *"Beam Us Up, Mr. Scott!": Why Misquotations Catch On*   375

Malcolm X, *Coming to an Awareness of Language*   92

Deborah Tannen, *How to Give Orders Like a Man*   214

What affects how we construct our sentences, our tone, and our message? Are the factors psychological, sociological, biological, or a combination of those types? Write a reflection comparing how Malcolm X, Konnikova, or Tannen might respond. What advice might Tannen or Konnikova share with Malcolm X about motivating his readers? To what extent is precision important in our word choice, even when discussing a simple thing like coffee? How important is such precision when discussing more abstract ideas?

Privacy in the Information Age

Flowtown, *Social Media Demographics: Who's Using Which Sites?*   :e

Jim Harper, *It's Modern Trade: Web Users Get as Much as They Give*   :e

Joel Stein, *Data Mining: How Companies Now Know Everything about You*   568

Courtney Sypher, *From Computer Cruelty to Campus Game: Cyberbullying at College* (student essay)   676

Wall Street Journal, *Doing Their Homework* (infographic)   18

XPLANE, *Did You Know?*   :e

When every app, network, and site asks for a profile and personal status, is oversharing online inevitable? Brainstorm a list of things a casual browser might learn about you on the Internet, and then write a journal entry speculating three to five ways they might use that information. Reflect on how you'd feel if those scenarios were true. Should companies profit from information that you post publicly? Should they have access to demographic data and to your online habits? How important is it to maintain a private life online? Is that even possible in today's media landscape?

Reading Critically

Mortimer Adler, *How to Mark a Book*   241

Carl M. Cannon, *The Real Computer Virus*   467

Tara E. Ketch, *Kids, You Can't Read That Book!* (student essay)   618

Stephen King, *Reading to Write*   72

Joel Robison, *Air Mail* (photograph)   660

Write an encouraging essay on the importance of reading, aimed at an audience of infrequent readers. Include advice on how to develop reading skills. What are common *reader* mistakes, and what are the best strategies to avoid them? What sorts of *writer* mistakes will a smart, alert reader likely encounter? What are good ways to find new reading material? Are there any benefits to limiting reading materials, or is it important to read everything that's available? How does Joel Robison's photograph illustrate the connection between critical reading and writing?

Technology in Modern Life

Gerald Dromos, *NYM's Talk* (student essay)   336

Casey Neistat, *Texting While Walking*   🅴

Grant Snider, *Life in the Woods* (cartoon)   78

Andrew Sullivan, *iPod World: The End of Society?*   462

XPLANE, *Did You Know?*   🅴

Technology fosters social connections, but it also disconnects us from real-life surroundings. Write an essay about what we gain—and perhaps lose—when we focus on our devices instead of what's around us. How has technology affected the ways you interact with family, friends, and acquaintances? Why are we obsessed with our screens? How has your perspective evolved over time?

Urbanization and Sense of Place

Kevin Cunningham, *Gentrification* (student essay)   443

Nigel Homes, *Rebuilding Process in New Orleans* (infographic)   280

Robert Ramírez, *The Barrio*   149

Jane S. Shaw, *Nature in the Suburbs*   690

Vocativ, *Tower of David*   🅴

How does place affect who we are? Write an editorial for your local or college newspaper about how the geography of your community contributes to its identity. Imitate the ways in which Ramírez and Cunningham describe their emotional, nostalgic connections to specific elements of their hometowns. Consider your community historically, particularly keeping in mind the community values discussed in "Tower of David" and the changes discussed in "Nature in the Suburbs" and "Rebuilding Progress in New Orleans." Address how large-scale trends like increased population, demographic shifts, and urbanization could affect your community in thirty or fifty years.

Glossary of Rhetorical Terms

Abstract See *Concrete/Abstract*.

Allusion An allusion is a passing reference to a familiar person, place, or thing drawn from history, the Bible, mythology, or literature. An allusion is an economical way for a writer to capture the essence of an idea, atmosphere, emotion, or historical era, as in "The scandal was his Watergate," or "He saw himself as a modern Job," or "Everyone there held those truths to be self-evident." An allusion should be familiar to the reader; if it is not, it will add nothing to the meaning.

Analogy Analogy is a special form of comparison in which the writer explains something unfamiliar by comparing it to something familiar: "A transmission line is simply a pipeline for electricity. In the case of a water pipeline, more water will flow through the pipe as water pressure increases. The same is true of a transmission line for electricity." See also the discussion of analogy on pages 283–84.

Analytical Reading Reading analytically means reading actively, paying close attention to both the content and the structure of the text. Analytical reading often involves answering several basic questions about the piece of writing under consideration:

1. What does the author want to say? What is his or her main point?
2. Why does the author want to say it? What is his or her purpose?
3. What strategy or strategies does the author use?
4. Why and how does the author's writing strategy suit both the subject and the purpose?
5. What is special about the way the author uses the strategy?
6. How effective is the essay? Why?

For a detailed example of analytical reading, see Chapter 1.

Appropriateness See *Diction*.

Argument Argument is one of the four basic types of prose. (Narration, description, and exposition are the other three.) To argue is to attempt to convince the reader to agree with a point of view, to make a given decision, or to pursue a particular course of action. Logical argument is based on reasonable explanations and appeals to the reader's intelligence. See Chapter 12 for further discussion of argumentation. See also *Logical Fallacies; Persuasion*.

Assertion The thesis or proposition that a writer puts forward in an argument.

Assumption A belief or principle, stated or implied, that is taken for granted.

Attitude A writer's attitude reflects his or her opinion on a subject. For example, a writer can think very positively or very negatively about a subject. In most cases, the writer's attitude falls somewhere between these two extremes. See also *Tone*.

Audience An audience is the intended readership for a piece of writing. For example, the readers of a national weekly newsmagazine come from all walks of life and have diverse opinions, attitudes, and educational experiences. In contrast, the readership for an organic chemistry journal is made up of people whose interests and educational backgrounds are quite similar. The essays in this book are intended for general readers—intelligent people who may lack specific information about the subject being discussed.

Beginnings/Endings A *beginning* is the sentence, group of sentences, or section that introduces an essay. Good beginnings usually identify the thesis or controlling idea, attempt to interest the reader, and establish a tone. Some effective ways in which writers begin essays include (1) telling an anecdote that illustrates the thesis, (2) providing a controversial statement or opinion that engages the reader's interest, (3) presenting startling statistics or facts, (4) defining a term that is central to the discussion that follows, (5) asking thought-provoking questions, (6) providing a quotation that illustrates the thesis, (7) referring to a current event that helps establish the thesis, or (8) showing the significance of the subject or stressing its importance to the reader.

   An *ending* is the sentence or group of sentences that brings an essay to closure. Good endings are purposeful and well planned. Endings satisfy readers when they are the natural outgrowths of the essays themselves and convey a sense of finality or completion. Good essays do not simply stop; they conclude.

Cause and Effect Analysis Cause and effect analysis is one of the types of exposition. (Process analysis, definition, division and classification, illustration, and comparison and contrast are the others.) Cause and effect analysis answers the question *why?* It explains the reasons for an occurrence or the consequences of an action. See Chapter 11 for a detailed discussion of cause and effect analysis. See also *Exposition*.

Claim The thesis or proposition put forth in an argument.

Classification Classification, along with division, is one of the types of exposition. (Process analysis, definition, comparison and contrast, illustration, and cause and effect analysis are the others.) When classifying, the writer arranges and sorts people, places, or things into categories according to their differing characteristics, thus making them more manageable for the writer and more understandable for the reader. See Chapter 9 for a detailed discussion of classification. See also *Division; Exposition*.

Cliché A cliché is an expression that has become ineffective through overuse. Expressions such as *quick as a flash*, *dry as dust*, *jump for joy*, and *slow as molasses* are all clichés. Good writers normally avoid such trite expressions and seek instead to express themselves in fresh and forceful language.

Coherence Coherence is a quality of good writing that results when all sentences, paragraphs, and longer divisions of an essay are naturally connected. Coherent writing is achieved through (1) a logical sequence of ideas (arranged in chronological order, spatial order, order of importance, or some other appropriate order), (2) the thoughtful repetition of key words and ideas, (3) a pace suitable for your topic and reader, and (4) the use of transitional words and expressions. Coherence should not be confused with unity. See *Unity*. See also *Transitions*.

Colloquial Expressions A colloquial expression is characteristic of or appropriate to spoken language, or to writing that seeks its effect. Colloquial expressions are informal, as *chem, gym, come up with, be at loose ends, won't*, and *photo* illustrate. Thus, colloquial expressions are acceptable in formal writing only if they are used purposefully.

Comparison and Contrast Comparison and contrast is one of the types of exposition. (Process analysis, definition, division and classification, illustration, and cause and effect analysis are the others.) In comparison and contrast, the writer points out the similarities and differences between two or more subjects in the same class or category. The function of any comparison and contrast is to clarify—to reach some conclusion about the items being compared and contrasted. See Chapter 8 for a detailed discussion of comparison and contrast. See also *Exposition*.

Conclusions See *Beginnings/Endings*.

Concrete/Abstract A *concrete* word names a specific object, person, place, or action that can be directly perceived by the senses: *car, bread, building, book, Abraham Lincoln, Chicago*, or *hiking*. An *abstract* word, in contrast, refers to general qualities, conditions, ideas, actions, or relationships that cannot be directly perceived by the senses: *bravery, dedication, excellence, anxiety, stress, thinking*, or *hatred*.

Although writers must use both concrete and abstract language, good writers avoid using too many abstract words. Instead, they rely on concrete words to define and illustrate abstractions. Because concrete words affect the senses, they are easily comprehended by the reader.

Connotation/Denotation Both connotation and denotation refer to the meanings of words. *Denotation* is the dictionary meaning of a word, the literal meaning. *Connotation*, on the other hand, is the implied or suggested meaning of a word. For example, the denotation of *lamb* is "a young sheep." The connotations of *lamb* are numerous: *gentle, docile, weak, peaceful, blessed, sacrificial, blood, spring, frisky, pure, innocent,* and so on. Good writers are sensitive to both the denotations and the connotations of words, and they use these meanings to their advantage in their writing. See also *Slanting*.

Controlling Idea See *Thesis*.

Deduction Deduction is the process of reasoning from a stated premise to a necessary conclusion. This form of reasoning moves from the general to the specific. See Chapter 12 for a discussion of deductive reasoning and its relation to argumentative writing. See also *Induction; Syllogism*.

Definition Definition is one of the types of exposition. (Process analysis, division and classification, comparison and contrast, illustration, and cause and effect analysis are the others.) Definition is a statement of the meaning of a word. A definition may be either brief or extended, part of an essay or an entire essay itself. See Chapter 10 for a detailed discussion of definition. See also *Exposition*.

Denotation See *Connotation/Denotation*.

Description Description is one of the four basic types of prose. (Narration, exposition, and argument are the other three.) Description tells how a person, place, or thing is perceived by the five senses. Objective description reports these sensory qualities factually, whereas subjective description gives the writer's interpretation of them. See Chapter 5 for a detailed discussion of description.

Dialogue Dialogue is conversation that is recorded in a piece of writing. Through dialogue writers reveal important aspects of characters' personalities as well as events in the narrative.

Diction Diction refers to a writer's choice and use of words. Good diction is precise and appropriate—the words mean exactly what the writer intends, and the words are well suited to the writer's subject, intended audience, and purpose in writing. The word-conscious writer knows that there are differences among *aged*, *old*, and *elderly*; *blue*, *navy*, and *azure*; and *disturbed*, *angry*, and *irritated*. Furthermore, this writer knows in which situation to use each word. See also *Connotation/Denotation*.

Division Like comparison and contrast, division and classification are separate yet closely related mental operations. Division involves breaking down a single large unit into smaller subunits or breaking down a large group of items into discrete categories. For example, the student body at your college or university can be divided into categories according to different criteria (by class, by home state or country, by sex, and so on). See also *Classification*.

Dominant Impression A dominant impression is the single mood, atmosphere, or quality a writer emphasizes in a piece of descriptive writing. The dominant impression is created through the careful selection of details and is, of course, influenced by the writer's subject, audience, and purpose. See also the discussion on pages 127–37 in Chapter 5.

Draft A draft is a version of a piece of writing at a particular stage in the writing process. The first version produced is usually called the *rough draft* or *first draft* and is a writer's beginning attempt to give overall shape to his or her ideas. Subsequent versions are called *revised drafts*. The copy presented for publication is the *final draft*.

Editing During the editing stage of the writing process, the writer makes his or her prose conform to the conventions of the language. This includes making final improvements in sentence structure and diction, and proofreading for wordiness and errors in grammar, usage, spelling, and punctuation. After editing, the writer is ready to prepare a final copy.

Emphasis Emphasis is the placement of important ideas and words within sentences and longer units of writing so that they have the greatest impact. In general, the end has the most impact, and the beginning nearly as much; the middle has the least. See also *Organization*.

Endings See *Beginnings/Endings*.

Essay An essay is a relatively short piece of nonfiction in which the writer attempts to make one or more closely related points. A good essay is purposeful, informative, and well organized.

Ethos A type of argumentative proof having to do with the ethics of the arguer: honesty, trustworthiness, and even morals.

Evaluation An evaluation of a piece of writing is an assessment of its effectiveness or merit. In evaluating a piece of writing, you should ask the following questions: What is the writer's purpose? Is it a worthwhile purpose? Does the writer achieve the purpose? Is the writer's information sufficient and accurate? What are the strengths of the essay? What are its weaknesses? Depending on the type of writing and the purpose, more specific questions can also be asked. For example, with an argument you could ask: Does the writer follow the principles of logical thinking? Is the writer's evidence convincing?

Evidence Evidence is the data on which a judgment or an argument is based or by which proof or probability is established. Evidence usually takes the form of statistics, facts, names, examples or illustrations, and opinions of authorities.

Examples Examples illustrate a larger idea or represent something of which they are a part. An example is a basic means of developing or clarifying an idea. Furthermore, examples enable writers to show and not simply tell readers what they mean. The terms *example* and *illustration* are sometimes used interchangeably. See also the discussion of illustration on pages 177–90 in Chapter 6.

Exposition Exposition is one of the four basic types of prose. (Narration, description, and argument are the other three.) The purpose of exposition is to clarify, explain, and inform. The methods of exposition presented in this text are process analysis, definition, division and classification, comparison and contrast, illustration, and cause and effect analysis. For a detailed discussion of each of these methods of exposition, see the appropriate chapter.

Fact A piece of information presented as having a verifiable certainty or reality.

Fallacy See *Logical Fallacies.*

Figures of Speech Figures of speech are brief, imaginative comparisons that highlight the similarities between things that are basically dissimilar. They make writing vivid and interesting and therefore more memorable. The most common figures of speech are these:

Simile—An implicit comparison introduced by *like* or *as*: "The fighter's hands were *like* stone."

Metaphor—An implied comparison that uses one thing as the equivalent of another: "All the world's a stage."

Personification—A special kind of simile or metaphor in which human traits are assigned to an inanimate object: "The engine coughed and then stopped."

Focus Focus is the limitation that a writer gives his or her subject. The writer's task is to select a manageable topic given the constraints of time, space, and purpose. For example, within the general subject of sports, a writer could focus on government support of amateur athletes or narrow the focus further to government support of Olympic athletes.

General See *Specific/General.*

Idiom An idiom is a word or phrase that is used habitually with a particular meaning in a language. The meaning of an idiom is not always readily apparent to nonnative speakers of that language. For example, *catch cold, hold a job, make up your mind,* and *give them a hand* are all idioms in English.

Illustration Illustration is a type of exposition. (Definition, division and classification, comparison and contrast, cause and effect analysis, and process analysis are the others.) With illustration the writer uses examples—specific facts, opinions, samples, and anecdotes or stories—to support a generalization and to make it more vivid, understandable, and persuasive. See Chapter 6 for a detailed discussion of illustration. See also *Examples.*

Induction Induction is the process of reasoning to a conclusion about all members of a class through an examination of only a few members of the class. This form of reasoning moves from the particular to the general. See Chapter 12 for a discussion of inductive reasoning and its relation to argumentative writing. Also see *Deduction.*

Introductions See *Beginnings/Endings.*

Irony Irony is the use of words to suggest something different from their literal meaning. For example, when Jonathan Swift proposes in "A Modest Proposal" that Ireland's problems could be solved if the people of Ireland fattened their babies and sold them to the English landlords for food, he meant that almost any other solution would be preferable. A writer can use irony to establish a special relationship with the reader and to add an extra dimension or twist to the meaning of a word or phrase.

Jargon See *Technical Language.*

Logical Fallacies A logical fallacy is an error in reasoning that renders an argument invalid. Some of the more common logical fallacies are these:

> *Oversimplification*—The tendency to provide simple solutions to complex problems: "The reason we have inflation today is that OPEC has unreasonably raised the price of oil."
>
> *Non sequitur* ("it does not follow")—An inference or conclusion that does not follow from established premises or evidence: "It was the best movie I saw this year, and it should get an Academy Award."
>
> *Post hoc, ergo propter hoc* ("after this, therefore because of this")—Confusing chance or coincidence with causation. Because one event comes after another one, it does not necessarily mean that the first event caused the second: "I won't say I caught a cold at the hockey game, but I certainly didn't have it before I went there."
>
> *Begging the question*—Assuming in a premise that which needs to be proven: "If American autoworkers built a better product, foreign auto sales would not be so high."
>
> *False analogy*—Making a misleading analogy between logically unconnected ideas: "He was a brilliant basketball player; therefore, there's no question in my mind that he will be a fine coach."

Either/or thinking—The tendency to see an issue as having only two sides: "Used car salespeople are either honest or crooked."

See also Chapter 12.

Logical Reasoning See *Deduction; Induction.*

Logos A type of argumentative proof having to do with the logical qualities of an argument: data, evidence, and factual information.

Metaphor See *Figures of Speech.*

Narration Narration is one of the four basic types of prose. (Description, exposition, and argument are the other three.) To narrate is to tell a story, to tell what happened. Although narration is most often used in fiction, it is also important in nonfiction, either by itself or in conjunction with other types of prose. See Chapter 4 for a detailed discussion of narration.

Objective/Subjective *Objective* writing is factual and impersonal, whereas *subjective* writing, sometimes called *impressionistic* writing, relies heavily on personal interpretation. For a discussion of objective description and subjective description, see Chapter 5.

Opinion An opinion is a belief or conclusion not substantiated by positive knowledge or proof. An opinion reveals personal feelings or attitudes or states a position. Opinion should not be confused with argument.

Organization In writing, organization is the thoughtful arrangement and presentation of one's points or ideas. Narration is often organized chronologically. Exposition may be organized from simplest to most complex or from most familiar to least familiar. Argument may be organized from least important to most important. There is no single correct pattern of organization for a given piece of writing, but good writers are careful to discover an order of presentation suitable for their audience and their purpose.

Paradox A paradox is a seemingly contradictory statement that may nonetheless be true. For example, "We little know what we have until we lose it" is a paradoxical statement.

Paragraph The paragraph, the single most important unit of thought in an essay, is a series of closely related sentences. These sentences adequately develop the central or controlling idea of the paragraph. This central or controlling idea, usually stated in a topic sentence, is necessarily related to the purpose of the whole composition. A well-written paragraph has several distinguishing characteristics: a clearly stated or implied topic sentence, adequate development, unity, coherence, and an appropriate organizational strategy.

Parallelism Parallel structure is the repetition of word order or form either within a single sentence or in several sentences that develop the same central idea. As a rhetorical device, parallelism can aid coherence and add emphasis. Roosevelt's statement, "I see one third of a nation ill-housed, ill-clad, ill-nourished," illustrates effective parallelism.

Pathos A type of argumentative proof having to do with audience: emotional language, connotative diction, and appeals to certain values.

Personification See *Figures of Speech*.

Persuasion Persuasion, or persuasive argument, is an attempt to convince readers to agree with a point of view, to make a given decision, or to pursue a particular course of action. Persuasion appeals heavily to the emotions, whereas logical argument does not. For the distinction between logical argument and persuasive argument, see Chapter 12.

Point of View Point of view refers to the grammatical person of the speaker in an essay. For example, a first-person point of view uses the pronoun *I* and is commonly found in autobiography and the personal essay; a third-person point of view uses the pronouns *he*, *she*, or *it* and is commonly found in objective writing. See Chapter 4 for a discussion of point of view in narration.

Prewriting Prewriting encompasses all the activities that take place before a writer actually starts a rough draft. During the prewriting stage of the writing process, the writer selects a subject area, focuses on a particular topic, collects information and makes notes, brainstorms for ideas, discovers connections between pieces of information, determines a thesis and purpose, rehearses portions of the writing in his or her mind or on paper, and makes a scratch outline. For some suggestions about prewriting, see Chapter 2, pages 28–31.

Process Analysis Process analysis is a type of exposition. (Definition, division and classification, comparison and contrast, illustration, and cause and effect analysis are the others.) Process analysis answers the question *how?* and explains how something works or gives step-by-step directions for doing something. See Chapter 7 for a detailed discussion of process analysis. See also *Exposition*.

Publication The publication stage of the writing process is when the writer shares his or her writing with the intended audience. Publication can take the form of a typed or an oral presentation, a photocopy, or a commercially printed rendition. What's important is that the writer's words are read in what amounts to their final form.

Purpose Purpose is what the writer wants to accomplish in a particular piece of writing. Purposeful writing seeks to *relate* (narration), to *describe* (description), to *explain* (process analysis, definition, division and classification, comparison and contrast, illustration, and cause and effect analysis), or to *convince* (argument).

Revision During the revision stage of the writing process, the writer determines what in the draft needs to be developed or clarified so that the essay says what the writer intends it to say. Often the writer needs to revise several times before the essay is "right." Comments from peer evaluators can be invaluable in helping writers determine what sorts of changes need to be made. Such changes can include adding material, deleting material, changing the order of presentation, and substituting new material for old.

Rhetorical Question A rhetorical question is a question that is asked but requires no answer from the reader. "When will nuclear proliferation end?" is such a question. Writers use rhetorical questions to introduce topics they plan to discuss or to emphasize important points.

Rough Draft See *Draft.*

Sequence Sequence refers to the order in which a writer presents information. Writers commonly select chronological order, spatial order, order of importance, or order of complexity to arrange their points. See also *Organization.*

Signal Phrase A signal phrase introduces borrowed material—a summary, paraphrase, or quotation—in a researched paper and usually consists of the author's name and a verb (*Daphna Oyserman contends*). Signal phrases let readers know who is speaking and, in the case of summaries and paraphrases, exactly where the writer's ideas end and the borrowed material begins. For suggestions on using signal phrases, see Chapter 14, pages 667–68.

Simile See *Figures of Speech.*

Slang Slang is the unconventional, very informal language of particular subgroups of a culture. Slang, such as *bummed, coke, split, hurt, dis, blow off,* and *cool,* is acceptable in formal writing only if it is used purposefully.

Slanting The use of certain words or information that results in a biased viewpoint.

Specific/General *General* words name groups or classes of objects, qualities, or actions. *Specific* words, in contrast, name individual objects, qualities, or actions within a class or group. To some extent, the terms *general* and *specific* are relative. For example, *dessert* is a class of things. *Pie,* however, is more specific than *dessert* but more general than *pecan pie* or *chocolate cream pie.*

   Good writing judiciously balances the general with the specific. Writing with too many general words is likely to be dull and lifeless. General words do not create vivid responses in the reader's mind as concrete, specific words can. However, writing that relies exclusively on specific words may lack focus and direction—the control that more general statements provide.

Strategy A strategy is a means by which a writer achieves his or her purpose. Strategy includes the many rhetorical decisions that the writer makes about organization, paragraph structure, syntax, and diction. In terms of the whole essay, strategy refers to the principal rhetorical mode that the writer uses. If, for example, a writer wishes to show how to make chocolate chip cookies, the most effective strategy would be process analysis. If it is the writer's purpose to show why sales of American cars have declined in recent years, the most effective strategy would be cause and effect analysis.

Style Style is the individual manner in which a writer expresses ideas. Style is created by the author's particular selection of words, construction of sentences, and arrangement of ideas.

Subject The subject of an essay is its content, what the essay is about. Depending on the author's purpose and the constraints of space, a subject may range from one that is broadly conceived to one that is narrowly defined.

Subjective See *Objective/Subjective.*

Supporting Evidence See *Evidence.*

Syllogism A syllogism is an argument that utilizes deductive reasoning and consists of a major premise, a minor premise, and a conclusion. For example:

All trees that lose leaves are deciduous. (*Major premise*)

Maple trees lose their leaves. (*Minor premise*)

Therefore, maple trees are deciduous. (*Conclusion*)

See also *Deduction*.

Symbol A symbol is a person, place, or thing that represents something beyond itself. For example, the eagle is a symbol of the United States, and the bear is a symbol of Russia.

Syntax Syntax refers to the way in which words are arranged to form phrases, clauses, and sentences as well as to the grammatical relationship among the words themselves.

Technical Language Technical language, or jargon, is the special vocabulary of a trade or profession. Writers who use technical language do so with an awareness of their audience. If the audience is a group of peers, technical language may be used freely. If the audience is a more general one, technical language should be used sparingly and carefully so as not to sacrifice clarity. See also *Diction*.

Thesis A thesis is a statement of the main idea of an essay. Also known as the *controlling idea*, a thesis may sometimes be implied rather than stated directly.

Title A title is a word or phrase set off at the beginning of an essay to identify the subject, to capture the main idea of the essay, or to attract the reader's attention. A title may be explicit or suggestive. A subtitle, when used, extends or restricts the meaning of the main title.

Tone Tone is the manner in which a writer relates to an audience—the "tone of voice" used to address readers. Tone may be described as friendly, serious, distant, angry, cheerful, bitter, cynical, enthusiastic, morbid, resentful, warm, playful, and so forth. A particular tone results from a writer's diction, sentence structure, purpose, and attitude toward the subject. See also *Attitude*.

Topic Sentence The topic sentence states the central idea of a paragraph and thus limits and controls the subject of the paragraph. Although the topic sentence most often appears at the beginning of the paragraph, it may appear at any other point, particularly if the writer is trying to create a special effect. Also see *Paragraph*.

Transitions Transitions are words or phrases that link sentences, paragraphs, and larger units of a composition to achieve coherence. These devices include parallelism, pronoun references, conjunctions, and the repetition of key ideas, as well as the many conventional transitional expressions, such as *moreover, on the other hand, in addition, in contrast*, and *therefore*. Also see *Coherence*.

Unity Unity is achieved in an essay when all the words, sentences, and paragraphs contribute to its thesis. The elements of a unified essay do not distract the reader. Instead, they all harmoniously support a single idea or purpose.

Verb Verbs can be classified as either strong verbs (*scream, pierce, gush, ravage,* and *amble*) or weak verbs (*be, has, get,* and *do*). Writers prefer to use strong verbs to make their writing more specific, more descriptive, and more action filled.

Voice Verbs can be classified as being in either the active or the passive voice. In the active voice, the doer of the action is the grammatical subject. In the passive voice, the receiver of the action is the subject:

Active: Glenda questioned all the children.

Passive: All the children were questioned by Glenda.

Also, voice refers to the way an author "talks" or "sounds" in a particular work as opposed to a style that characterizes an author's total output. Voice is generally considered to be made up of a combination of such elements as pacing or sense of timing, word choice, sentence and paragraph length, or the way characters sound in a written composition.

Writing Process The writing process consists of five major stages: prewriting, writing drafts, revision, editing, and publication. The process is not inflexible, but there is no mistaking the fact that most writers follow some version of it most of the time. Although orderly in its basic components and sequence of activities, the writing process is nonetheless continuous, creative, and unique to each individual writer. See Chapter 2 for a detailed discussion of the writing process. See also *Draft*; *Editing*; *Prewriting*; *Publication*; *Revision*.

Acknowledgments (continued from page ii)

Mortimer Adler, "How to Mark a Book." Originally published in *Saturday Review of Literature*, July 6, 1940. Reprinted by permission.

Mitch Albom, "If You Had One Day with Someone Who's Gone," originally appeared in the September 17, 2006, issue of *Parade*. Copyright © 2006 by Mitch Albom. Reprinted by permission.

Lamar Alexander, "The Three-Year Solution," *Newsweek*, October 16, 2009. Copyright © 2009 The Newsweek/Daily Beast Company LLC. All rights reserved. Reprinted by permission.

Maya Angelou, "Sister Flowers," from *I Know Why the Caged Bird Sings*. Copyright © 1969 and renewed 1997 by Maya Angelou. Reprinted by permission of Random House, Inc.

Carrie Arnold, "Is Anorexia a Cultural Disease?" from *Slate,* September 27, 2012. Copyright © 2012 The Slate Group. All rights reserved. Reprinted by permission.

Russell Baker, "Discovering the Power of My Words." Copyright © 1982 by Russell Baker. Reprinted by permission of Don Congdon Associates, Inc.

David P. Bardeen, "Not Close Enough for Comfort," *New York Times*, February 29, 2004. Reprinted by permission of David Bardeen.

Mark Bittman, "Which Diet Works?" *New York Times*, June 26, 2012. Copyright © 2012 The New York Times. All rights reserved. Reprinted by permission.

Suzanne Britt, "Neat People vs. Sloppy People." Reprinted by permission of the author.

Massimo Calabresi, "The Phone Knows All," *Time,* August 27, 2012. Copyright © TIME Inc. Reprinted by permission. TIME is a registered trademark of Time Inc. All rights reserved.

Carl M. Cannon, "The Real Computer Virus," from *American Journalism Review*, April 2001. Reprinted by permission of the American Journalism Review.

Bruce Catton, "Grant and Lee: A Study in Contrasts," originally published in *The American Story,* edited by Earl Schneck Miers, 1956. Copyright © 1956 U.S. Capitol Historical Society. Reprinted by permission. All rights reserved.

Firoozeh Dumas, "Hot Dogs and Wild Geese," from *Funny in Farsi: A Memoir of Growing Up Iranian in America.* Copyright © 2003 by Firoozeh Dumas. Reprinted by permission of Villard Books, a division of Random House, Inc.

Lars Eighner, "On Dumpster Diving," from *Travels with Lizbeth: Three Years on the Road and on the Streets*. Copyright © 1993 by Lars Eighner. Reprinted by permission of St. Martin's Press, LLC.

Linda S. Flower, "Writing for an Audience," from *Problem-Solving Strategies for Writing*, Fourth Edition. Copyright © 1993 Harcourt College Publishing. Reprinted by permission of the author.

Reid Forgrave, "No Easy Answers for PEDs, Youth," *FoxSports*, August 30, 2012. Reprinted by permission of Foxsports.com.

Thomas L. Friedman, "My Favorite Teacher," *New York Times*, January 9, 2001. Copyright © 2001 The New York Times. All Rights Reserved. Reprinted by permission.

Megan Garber, "The Curator's Guide to the Galaxy," *Atlantic*, March 11, 2012. Copyright © 2012 The Atlantic Media Co. All rights reserved. Distributed by Tribune Media Services. Reprinted by permission.

Nikki Giovanni, "Campus Racism 101," from *Racism 101*. Copyright © 1994 by Nikki Giovanni. Reprinted by permission of HarperCollins Publishers.

Natalie Goldberg, "Be Specific," from *Writing Down the Bones: Freeing the Writer Within*. Copyright © 1986 by Natalie Goldberg. Reprinted by arrangement with The Permissions Company, Inc., on behalf of Shambhala Publications, Inc., Boston, MA. www.shambhala.com.

G. Anthony Gorry, "Steal This MP3 File: What Is Theft?" Reprinted by permission of the author.

Michael Greenstone and Adam Looney, "Where Is the Best Place to Invest $102,000 — In Stocks, Bonds, or a College Degree?" June 25, 2011. Reprinted by permission of The Brookings Institution.

Jim Harper, "It's Modern Trade: Web Users Get as Much as They Give," *Wall Street Journal*, August 8, 2010 . Copyright © 2010 Dow Jones & Company, Inc. All Rights Reserved Worldwide. Reprinted by permission.

Lily Huang, "The Case of the Disappearing Rabbit," *Newsweek,* July 25, 2009. Copyright © 2009 Newsweek, Inc. All rights reserved. Reprinted by permission.

Walter Isaacson, "The Genius of Jobs," *New York Times*, October 30, 2011. Copyright © 2011 The New York Times. All rights reserved. Reprinted by permission.

Michael Jonas, "The Downside of Diversity," *New York Times*, August 5, 2007. Copyright © 2007 The New York Times. All rights reserved. Reprinted by permission.

Jon Katz, "How Boys Become Men," from *Glamour* Magazine. Copyright © 1993 by Jon Katz. Reprinted with permission of International Creative Management, Inc.

Martin Luther King Jr. "I Have a Dream." Reprinted by arrangement with The Heirs to the Estate of Martin Luther King Jr., c/o Writers House as agent for the proprietor, New York, NY. Copyright © 1958, 1963 Martin Luther King Jr. Copyright © renewed 1991 Coretta Scott King.

Martin Luther King Jr., "The Ways of Meeting Oppression." Reprinted by arrangement with The Heirs to the Estate of Martin Luther King Jr., c/o Writers House as agent for the proprietor, New York, NY. Copyright © 1958, 1963 Martin Luther King Jr. Copyright © renewed 1991 Coretta Scott King.

Stephen King, "Reading and Writing," from *On Writing: A Memoir of the Craft*. Copyright © 2000 by Stephen King. Reprinted by permission of Scribner, a division of Simon & Schuster, Inc.

Perri Klass, "Hearing Bilingual: How Babies Sort Out Language," *New York Times*, October 11, 2011. Copyright © 2011 The New York Times. All Rights Reserved. Reprinted by permission.

Maria Konnikova, "'Beam Us Up, Mr. Scott!': Why Misquotations Catch On," *Atlantic*, August 15, 2012. Copyright © 2012 Maria Konnikova. Reprinted by permission.

Nicholas D. Kristof and Sheryl WuDunn, "Two Cheers for Sweatshops," *New York Times*, September 4, 2000. Copyright © 2000 The New York Times. All rights reserved. Reprinted by permission.

Robert Krulwich, "Are Butterflies Two Different Animals in One? The Death and Resurrection Theory," from Krulwich Wonders on NPR. Copyright © 2012 National Public Radio, Inc. NPR news commentary titled "Are Butterflies Two Different Animals in One? The Death and Resurrection Theory" by Robert Krulwich was originally published on NPR.org and is used with the permission of NPR. Any unauthorized duplication is strictly prohibited.

Anne Lamott, "Shitty First Drafts," from *Bird by Bird*. Copyright © 1994 by Anne Lamott. Reprinted by permission of Pantheon Books, a division of Random House, Inc.

Richard Lederer, "The Case for Short Words," from *The Miracle of Language*. Copyright © 1991 by Richard Lederer. All rights reserved. Reprinted by permission of Atria Publishing Group.

Jennifer 8. Lee, "For Immigrant Family, No Easy Journeys," *New York Times*, January 4, 2003. Copyright © 2003 The New York Times. All rights reserved. Reprinted by permission.

Dahlia Lithwick, "Chaos Theory: A Unified Theory of Muppet Types," from *Slate,* June 8, 2012. Copyright © 2012 The Slate Group. All rights reserved. Reprinted by permission.

Elisa Mala, "Crime Family," from *New York Times,* November 11, 2012. Copyright © 2012 The New York Times. All rights reserved. Reprinted by permission.

Cherokee Paul McDonald, "A View from the Bridge," originally published in the *Sun Sentinel, Sunshine* Magazine (Fort Lauderdale, FL). Copyright © 1989 by Cherokee Paul McDonald. All rights reserved. Reprinted by permission.

Pat Mora, "Remembering Lobo," currently published in *Nepantla: Essays from the Land in the Middle*, published by University of New Mexico Press. Copyright © 1993 by Pat Mora. Reprinted by permission of Curtis Brown, Ltd.

Bharati Mukherjee, "Two Ways to Belong in America," originally published in *New York Times*, September 22, 1996. Copyright © 1996 by Bharati Mukherjee. Reprinted by permission of the author.

Tiffany O'Callaghan, "Young Love," *Time* Magazine, January 17, 2008. Copyright © TIME Inc. Reprinted by permission. TIME is a registered trademark of Time Inc. All rights reserved.

Susan Orlean, "On Voice," from *Telling True Stories*, ed. by Mark Kramer and Wendy Cal, Plume, 2007. Reprinted by permission of Susan Orlean.

George Orwell, "Shooting an Elephant" from *Shooting an Elephant and Other Essays*. Copyright © 1946 George Orwell. Copyright © 1950 by Sonia Brownell Orwell. Copyright © renewed 1978 by Sonia Pitt-Rivers. Reprinted by permission of Houghton Mifflin Harcourt Publishing Com-

Barry Winston, "Stranger Than True," *Harper's* Magazine, December 1986. Copyright © 1986 by Harper's Magazine. All rights reserved. Reprinted by special permission of Harper's Magazine.

Rosalind Wiseman, "The Queen Bee and Her Court," from *Queen Bees & Wannabes*. Copyright © 2002 by Rosalind Wiseman. Reprinted by permission of Crown Publishers, a division of Random House, Inc.

Malcolm X, "Coming to an Awareness of Language," from *The Autobiography of Malcolm X* by Malcolm X and Alex Haley. Copyright © 1946 by Alex Haley and Malcolm X. Copyright © 1965 by Alex Haley and Betty Shabazz. Reprinted by permission of Random House, Inc.

William Zinsser, "Simplicity." Copyright © 1976, 1980, 1985, 1988, 1990, 1994, 1998, 2001, 2006 by William K. Zinsser. Reprinted by permission of the author.

Photo/Art Credits

2, Joel Robison; **5**, Cherokee Paul McDonald; **12**, Nancy Ostertag/Getty Images; **17**, Mark Henley/Panos Pictures; **18**, Reprinted with permission of The Wall Street Journal, Copyright © 2012 Dow Jones & Company, Inc. All Rights Reserved Worldwide.; **22**, Copyright © 2011 Condé Nast. From The New Yorker Magazine. All rights reserved. Illustration by Alison Bechdel. Reprinted by permission.; **48**, © Alison Jones/DanitaDelimont.com; **50**, Yvonne Hemsey/Getty Images; **53**, © Matthew Henry Hall; **55**, Sam Lamott; **60**, Tim Flower; **64**, William Zinsser/Getty Images; **68**, Mark Parisi, Permission granted for use, www.offthemark.com; **69**, Amanda Edwards/FilmMagic/Getty Images; **72**, AFP/Getty Images; **77**, Matthew Diffee/The New Yorker Collection; **78**, Grant Snider; **92**, Library of Contress, Prints & Photographs Division, U.S. News & World Report Magazine Collection, LC-DIG-ppmsc-01274/LC-U9-11695-5; **98**, Elisa Mala; **103**, Courtesy of David Bardeen; **108**, © Bob Daemmrich/The Image Works; **115**, Courtesy of Jenny8Lee; **126**, Library of Congress, Prints & Photographs Division, FSA/OWI Collection, LC-DIG-fsa-8b14845 (digital file from original neg.) LC-DIG-ppmsc-00237 (digital file from print) LC-USF34-T01-013407-C (b&w film dup. neg.) LC-USZ62-80024 (b&w film copy neg. from print); **138**, © Todd Selby/Corbis Outline; **143**, Cheron Bayna; **149**, Courtesy Robert Ramirez; **154**, Tim Sloan/AFP/Getty Images; **156**, Photo by New York Times Co./Getty Images; **164**, © Syracuse Newspapers/The Image Works; **174**, CALVIN AND HOBBES © 1986 Watterson. Reprinted with permission of Universal Uclick. All rights reserved.; **176**, Levni Yilmaz, www.ingredientx.com; **191**, Photo by Ritch Davidson; **195**, Courtesy of Kal Raustiala; **195**, Courtesy of Christopher John Sprigman; **201**, © Katy Winn/Corbis; **207**, Aicha Nystrom; **212**, Courtesy of Borders Perrin Nerander; **213**, Courtesy of Borders Perrin Nerander; **214**, Stephen Voss; **228**, Heather Jones; **241**, Alfred Eisenstaedt/Pix Inc./Time Life Pictures/Getty Images; **248**, Tiffany O'Callaghan/Image by: David Stock; **255**, Photo © Ken Light; **262**, Alan Klein; **264**, Jim Zipp/Science Source; **268**, By permission of Nikki Giovanni; **274**, © Flip Schulke/Corbis; **277**, Tom Cheney/The New Yorker Collection/www.cartoonbank.com; **280**, Graphic by Nigel Holems for the New York Times, 2009; **295**, By permission of Suzanne Britt; **300**, Dan Herrick/ZUMAPRESS/Newscom; **306**, Reagan Louie; **311**, Michael Maslin/www.cartoonbank.com; **312**, AP Photo/ Mark Lennihan; **318**, www.cartoonstock.com; **319**, Hank Walker//Time Life Pictures/Getty Images; **320**, National Archives and Records Administration; **322**, National Archives and Records Administration; **330**, Courtesy the Smithsonian's National Musuem of Natural History; designed by Jennifer Renteria; 2013; **344**, Jordan Strauss/WireImage/Getty Images; **349**, Rosalind Wiseman; **362**, © Stephanie Felix; **363**, Brendan Smialowski /The New York Times/Redux; **370**, © Flip Schulke/Corbis; **375**, Margaret Singer and Max Freeman; **383**, Bernard Schoenbaum/The New Yorker Collection/www.cartoonbank.com; **386**, Lokesh Dhakar http://lokeshdhakar.com; **410**, Courtesy of G. Anthony Gorry; **416**, Joe Rubino; **421**, GRAND AVENUE © 2009 Reprint with permission of Universal Uclick for UFS. All rights reserved.; **423**, Gladstone Collection of African American Photographs/Library of Congress; **426**, © A. Inden/Corbis; **427**, David Paul Morris/Bloomberg via Getty Images; **436**, Emilia Klimiuk; **451**, Photo by James Lattanzio; **456**, Photo courtesy Carrie Arnold; **462**, Peter Kramer/Getty Images; **466**, Staci Schwartz/stacipop.com; **467**, Liz Lynch; **476**, Mary Beth Meehan; **488**, World Wildlife Fund 2012 Public Service Announcement; **509**, Library of Congress, Prints & Photographs Division, Theodor Horydczak Collection, [reproduction number, e.g., LC-H824-0224]; **516**, Richard Lederer; **522**, Flip

Schulke/Corbis; **529**, David Levenson/Getty Images; **539**, Joshua Lutz/Redux; **548**, Courtesy Ian Steadman; **549**, Philippe Lopez/AFP/Getty Images; **554**, Courtesy Reid Forgrave; **559**, Doug Pensinger/Getty Images; **560**, Jacob Thomas Illustrator; **568**, John Beebe/Aurora Photos; **570**, The Wall Street Journal by Dow Jones & Company, Inc.(Chicago). Reproduced with permission of Dow Jones & Company, Inc. (Chicago) in the format Republish in a book via Copyright Clearance Center; **579**, Sipa via AP Images; **583**, © Rick Friedman/Corbis; **591**, Courtesy MIT News; **591**, Courtesy of The Brookings Institution; **593**, The Hamilton Project; **594**, The Hamilton Project; **595**, The Hamilton Project; **598**, The Washington Post/Getty Images; **602**, Michael Nagle; **612**, Copyright © Bill Aron / PhotoEdit—All rights reserved.; **614**, Courtesy of Adbusters Media Foundation; **627**, Courtesy of Lars Eighner; **631**, Gary O'Brien/Charlotte Observer/MCT via Getty Images; **632**, Frances M. Roberts/Newscom; **639**, AP Photo; **648**, Beinecke Rare Book and Manuscript Library; **660**, Joel Robison; **681**, Thomas Gibaud; **688**, PETT, Lexington Herald-Leader/Cartoon Arts International/The New York Times Syndicate; **690**, Courtesy of Jane S. Shaw; **700**, Courtesy of Jake Jamieson; **710**, © AfriPics.com/Alamy; **713**, Homepage of Bankier Library, Brookdale Community College; **714**, Courtesy of University of Vermont Libraries; **734**, Courtesy of Bedford/St. Martin's

e-Pages Credits

[**Chapter 3**] *Video:* Created by Jonathan Beer, artwork by Lauren Ellis (http://www.laurenellis .ca); [**Chapter 4**] *Video:* The Moth; [**Chapter 5**] *Video:* Courtesy of Vocativ; [**Chapter 6**] *Video:* XPLANATIONS by XPLANE; [**Chapter 7**] *Infographic:* Sustainable America; [**Chapter 8**] *Video:* Courtesy *BU Today*, Boston University; [**Chapter 9**] *Infographic:* Flowtown, a Demandforce company; [**Chapter 10**] *Infographic:* Originally appeared on www.GOOD.is on January 26, 2012. Reprinted with permission from GOOD Worldwide Inc.; [**Chapter 11**] *Video:* Casey Neistat for The New York Times; [**Chapter 12**] *Video:* Created by Made in a Free World; [**Chapter 12**] *Article:* Lamar Alexander, "The Three-Year Solution," *Newsweek*, October 16, 2009. Copyright © 2009 The Newsweek/Daily Beast Company LLC. All rights reserved. Reprinted by permission. *Photo:* Senate Photographic Service; [**Chapter 12**] *Article:* Jim Harper, "It's Modern Trade: Web Users Get as Much as They Give," *Wall Street Journal*, August 8, 2010. Copyright © 2010 Dow Jones & Company, Inc. All Rights Reserved Worldwide. Reprinted by permission. *Photo:* Andrew Harrer/ Bloomberg via Getty Images; [**Chapter 12**] *Article:* Peter Singer, "Is Doping Wrong?" from *Project Syndicate*, August 2007. Reprinted by permission of Project Syndicate. *Photo:* AP Photo/Brian Branch-Price; [**Chapter 13**] *Video:* Halftone.co; [**Chapter 14**] *Article:* Megan Garber, "The Curator's Guide to the Galaxy," *Atlantic*, March 11, 2012. Copyright © 2012 The Atlantic Media Co. All rights reserved. Distributed by Tribune Media Services. Reprinted by permission. *Web site:* Concept and copy by Maria Popova. Design by Kelli Anderson. www.curatorscode.org. *Photo:* Rogelio Bernal Andreo (DeepSkyColors.com)

Index

🔵e bedfordstmartins.com/subjectandstrategy

Missing something? To access the online material that accompanies this text, visit **bedfordstmartins.com /subjectandstrategy**. Students who do not buy a new book can purchase access at this site.

Inside the Bedford Integrated Media for
Subject & Strategy

e-Pages	Strategy
Jonathan Beer *Writing Process Animation* [VIDEO]	Chapter 3, Writers on Writing
Lt. Dan Choi *Don't Tell, Martha!* [VIDEO]	Chapter 4, Narration
Vocativ *Tower of David* [VIDEO]	Chapter 5, Description
XPLANE *Did You Know?* [VIDEO]	Chapter 6, Illustration
Sustainable America *How to Compost in Your Apartment* [INFOGRAPHIC]	Chapter 7, Process Analysis
Devin Hahn *One Small Step for Man* [VIDEO]	Chapter 8, Comparison and Contrast
Flowtown *Social Media Demographics* [INFOGRAPHIC]	Chapter 9, Division and Classification
GOOD *Not Your Parents' American Dream* [INFOGRAPHIC]	Chapter 10, Definition
Casey Neistat *Texting While Walking* [VIDEO]	Chapter 11, Cause and Effect Analysis
Slavery Footprint *How Many Slaves Work for You?* [VIDEO]	Chapter 12, Argumentation
Peter Singer *Is Doping Wrong?* [ARTICLE]	Chapter 12, Argumentation
Jim Harper *It's Modern Trade* [ARTICLE]	Chapter 12, Argumentation
Lamar Alexander *The Three-Year Solution* [ARTICLE]	Chapter 12, Argumentation
Halftone *Why Is the Sky Blue?* [VIDEO]	Chapter 13, Combining Strategies
Megan Garber *The Curator's Guide to the Galaxy* [ARTICLE]	Chapter 14, Writing with Sources